P9-AGT-328

Queer Theory/Sociology

Twentieth-Century Social Theory

Series Editor: Charles C. Lemert

Twentieth-Century Social Theory invites authors respected for their contributions in the prominent traditions of social theory to reflect on past and present in order to propose what comes next. Books in the series will consider critical theory, race, symbolic interactionism, functionalism, feminism, world systems theory, psychoanalysis, and Weberian social theory, among current topics. Each will be plain to read, yet provocative to ponder. Each will gather up what has come to pass in the twentieth century in order to define the terms of social theoretical imagination in the twenty-first.

Titles in the series include:

Queer Theory/Sociology

Edited by

Steven Seidman

Copyright © Blackwell Publishers Ltd, 1996

First published 1996

Reprinted 1997

Blackwell Publishers Inc
350 Main Street
Malden, Massachusetts 02148, USA

Blackwell Publishers Ltd
108 Cowley Road
Oxford OX4 1JF, UK

All rights reserved. Except for the quotation of short passages for the purposes of criticism and review, no part of this publication may be reproduced, stored in a retrieval system, or transmitted, in any form or by any means, electronic, mechanical, photocopying, recording or otherwise, without the prior permission of the publisher.

Except in the United States of America, this book is sold subject to the condition that it shall not, by way of trade or otherwise, be lent, re-sold, hired out, or otherwise circulated without the publisher's prior consent in any form of binding or cover other than that in which it is published and without a similar condition including this condition being imposed on the subsequent purchaser.

Library of Congress Cataloging in Publication Data
Queer theory/sociology/edited by Steven Seidman.
p. cm. — (Twentieth-century social theory)
Includes bibliographical references and index.
ISBN 1-55786-739-9 — ISBN 1-55786-740-2 (pbk)
1. Homosexuality—Philosophy. 2. Sociology—Methodology.
3. Gays—Identity. 4. Lesbians—Identity. I. Seidman, Steven. II. Series.
HQ76.25.S65   1996   95-48247
306.76'6'01—dc20   CIP

British Library Cataloguing in Publication Data
A CIP catalogue record for this book is available from the British Library

Typeset in Sabon 10/12pt
by Pure Tech India Ltd., Pondicherry, India
Printed and bound in Great Britain
by T. J. International Limited, Padstow, Cornwall

This book is printed on acid-free paper

Contents

Series Editor's Preface

It may well surprise some to learn that there is such a vital subfield of work in sociology as that represented by the authors of this collection. There was a time when members of an academic discipline were so few in number that they could annually meet all in one modest-sized room to learn what everyone else is doing. Those days are long gone of course. Many regret their disappearance.

One of a few benefits of the profligate size of today's academic disciplines is the pleasure of discovering exciting work being done very often right in one's own intellectual neighborhood. *Queer Theory/-Sociology* will delight its readers in just this way. By bringing together the work of the leading sociological writers in gay and lesbian studies. Steven Seidman has given sociologists and other readers a lovely gift. This book offers many pleasures, most significantly that of an opportunity to think about sociology and social theory in exciting new ways.

As Seidman explains in his introduction, sociology had formerly ignored sex and sexuality altogether or, in more recent years, treated it as one of any number of social problems subject to the investigations of a sociology of deviance. Though not all those who write sociologies of gay and lesbian social lives would accept the name, it is common practice today to consider their subject under the more inclusive and intentionally provocative name of queer theory. Whether the name is used or not, the sociological study of other-than-hetero-sexual social experience, once it is freed of the stigma of being a "social problem," calls forth a new understanding of social life itself. When it demonstrates the historical and sociological conditions by which the "homosexual" is constructed, work of this sort brings into vision the foundational desire of "heterosexual" culture to use the homosexual as one of the defining, pathological limits of its pretense of establishing the good and liberal society. This is the point made in Mary

McIntosh's now classic 1968 article on "The Homosexual Role" – the lead essay in the collection. One need only tune in talk radio to see how deep and ugly this pretense remains today.

Queer theory is one of the most important developments in social theory today precisely because it has so devastatingly completed the process of queering the naïve assumptions of our most cherished traditions. Earlier developments in race, feminist, and postcolonial theories have disabused the social and human sciences (as well as sturdier souls in the general public) of the naïve modernist notion that "all men are created equal" – that humans are, thereby, of one ideal, universal kind. Queer theory, in effect, completes the process which, as Seidman reminds, Weber called the disenchantment of social life. Once gay and lesbian social experience is disenchanted of its negative status as a form of deviant behavior, we who have neither enjoyed nor suffered the experience itself begin to see just what we have denied for so long. We can see that desire and sexuality are very much more than mere, even minor, features of social life. They are, in fact, constitutive elements every bit as central as race, gender, or class. If sexual desire is a social, not a natural, thing, then clearly the deep feelings with which the heterosexual norm is enforced must be symptomatic of a basic social and cultural process. The hatred and violence that heterosexuals direct at those who openly defy their norms is now known to be every bit as frequent and ugly as racial, gender, and class hatreds. This fact can only mean that heterosexual norms are jealously considered important to a way of life of which its proponents are themselves unsure. Social hatred we know very well is founded in social insecurity.

The study of all the various other-than-hetero-sexualities thereby queers both the traditional moral values of the society and the social sciences which, in their misplaced quest for value-freedom, served to advance that traditional morality. The work collected in *Queer Theory/Sociology* does just this, and it does it in a way that is at once provocative and serious. Considered together, these essays remind us just to what extent sociology and the social sciences have resisted and denied one of the most central, if repressed, features of their own natures – desire!

Sociology, in particular among the social sciences, began in the nineteenth century as a loosely organized variety of attempts to account for a strange, new, and persistent desire. "How did it happen, and what does it mean, that men and women in so many parts of Europe and North America have come so decisively to desire such an intangible object as a rationally acquired improvement of their capital worth?" Roughly put, this is Max Weber's version of a question all the social thinkers of his day were asking. The rationally disciplined Protestant puritans Weber made so famous are commonly pictured as entrepreneurs utterly lacking in desires of the more earthy kind. Yet, even Weber was well aware that the new capitalist entrepreneurs had their desires. In his well-known meditation on the iron cage of rationality at the end of *The Protestant Ethic and the Spirit of Capitalism* Weber complained that they were, among other things, "sensualists without heart" – that is, their desires were, in his view, real but unprincipled. In this ethical prejudice, Weber encouraged the widespread illusion that true human desire required a reining-in that only a stern moral regulation could provide. This, of course, was precisely the ethical attitude of Durkheim who considered the modern man subject to anomie because he (he, most decidedly) required the social order of domestic and other societies to control his animal passions. Nor should we let whatever sympathies we might have for Marx's politics blind us to the fact that, among much else, *Capital* was a moralistic denunciation of the capitalist's greedy, fetishized desire for profit in favor of the ideal working man's more ethically reliable universal values.

Queer sociologies remind us most concretely just to what extent modern social science was founded in the duplicitous rejection of desire itself in the name of a scientific reasonableness that was, of course, a desire of its own kind. Weber, the rational social scientist, was himself a spiritual descendent of the very rationalizing puritan spirit he wrote about. Until the last generation or so, not very much social science – whether liberal, positivist, humanistic, Marxist, or even feminist – has been an exception to this rule. *Queer Theory/Sociology* is, thus, as good a guide as there is to the ways in which social theory might return itself to a more balanced understanding not just of its own desires but of the place of desire itself in social life. For too long we have collectively avoided, or at least played with, this fact of our disciplinary nature, without facing it straight away.

Hence, among the pleasures to be found in this book, is that of facing up to ourselves and our traditions – not to reject them, but to open them to a more realistic range of social experience. Who would say that the societies in which we live today are not products of manufactured, commodified, and advertised desires of various kinds? Who, specifically, would deny that sexual desire in all its many forms is not one of the most constant and unavoidable sources of the commercial images by which we are seduced into falsifying our public presentations in order to gain whatever we desire in a world which, in reality, offers less and less of what we need? How can social science hope to explain or critique such a world if it does not allow a full recognition of the centrality of desire to its own work? The debt we owe to queer theories like those here collected is that of inviting us to accept the importance of desire, not excluding sexual desire, to our beings, our social arrangements, our civilization.

When it was first conceived, *Twentieth-Century Social Theory* was planned as a series of single-authored works. This volume departs from the original plan in order to comply with another of the rules of the series. All the books in the series are intended to summarize the subject and point it in a new direction. In the cases of subjects with already lengthy histories this is a rule readily obeyed by a single author. But, in the case of gay and lesbian studies in sociology, there is no history of any great moment. As in other disciplines, the subject is new in the last generation or so. Thus it is a subject well presented by a group of writers, and especially well presented when the writers are, as they are in this case, the leading figures in the field.

Steven Seidman is surely at the top of a list of those who could have, had he so chosen, summarized on his own accord the history and future of queer theory in sociology. It is typical of his uncommon ability to work creatively with others that he chose instead to edit such a book. In so doing he invites into a larger public awareness not just those like Jeffrey Weeks, Ken Plummer, Mary McIntosh, David Greenberg, and Barry Adam who are already well known, but new (in many cases, younger) scholars whose work, by its relative newness, is not yet well known. Some of the names may, therefore, be unfamiliar to the general reader. But this is how it should and must be.

The authors of this book are, in effect, creating a field before our very eyes. Just a few years ago such a collection would not have been possible. Today it is a reality because of the work being done to bring ideas from other fields into sociology while, at the same time, returning the favor of offering sociology's strengths to extra-sociological queer theories. The slash in the book's title, *Queer Theory/Sociology*, is one of the rare instances where such an odd editorial mark is required – here to signify that two distinct traditions of study are being brought into a still indefinite relationship. We have only to read and watch to see how this new relationship develops and how those of us not primary parties to it respond to the gracious challenges it presents. The phrase is over-used I know, but this is truly a "state of the art" work as few others, thus advertised, are.

Charles Lemert

Acknowledgements

The editor and publisher gratefully acknowledge the following for kind permission to reprint:

The University of California Press for excerpts from Mary McIntosh, "The Homosexual Role," © by the Society of Social Problems, reprinted from *Social Problems*, 16/2 (1968), 182–92; and for Joshua Gamson, "Must Identity Movements Self-Destruct? A Queer Dilemma," © by the Society of Social Problems, reprinted from *Social Problems*, 42/3 (1995).

The Longman Group for excerpts from chapter 6 of Jeffrey Weeks, *Sex, Politics and Society: The Regulation of Sexuality since 1800* (London, 1981).

Ken Plummer for excerpts from *Sexual Stigma* (London: Routledge, 1975).

Elsevier Science B.V., Amsterdam, The Netherlands, for David F. Greenberg and Marcia H. Bystryn, "Capitalism, Bureaucracy, and Male Homosexuality," *Contemporary Crimes: Crime, Law and Social Policy*, 8 (1984), 33–56.

Cambridge University Press and Barry D. Adam, for Adam, "Structural Foundations of the Gay World," © Society for Comparative Study of Society and History, *Comparative Studies in Society and History*, 27 (1985), 658–71.

The American Sociological Association for five essays which appeared in *Sociological Theory*, 12 (July, 1994), edited by Steven Seidman: Arlene Stein and Ken Plummer, "I Can't Even Think Straight"; Steven Epstein, "A Queer Encounter"; Chrys Ingraham, "The Heterosexual Imaginary"; Ki Namaste, "The Politics of Inside/Out," and Janice Irvine, "A Place in the Rainbow."

The Asian American Studies Center, University of California, Los Angeles, and Dana Y. Takagi, Takagi, "Maiden Voyage: Excursion into Sexuality and Identity Politics in Asian America," *Amerasia*, 20/1.

Every effort has been made to trace all copyright holders, but if any have been inadvertently overlooked the publishers will be pleased to make the necessary arrangement at the first opportunity.

Introduction

Max Weber thought that one of the defining features of Western modernization was a process of "disenchantment." In a secular or disenchanted culture individuals would no longer look to spiritual or sacred forces – Gods, divine beings, or metaphysical principles such as Karma – to explain events or make sense of their lives. The world would be viewed as an order of natural and human forces – a universe of impulse, instinct, desire, evolution, mechanical laws of gravity and motion, etc. Sociology has not only sought to study this secularizing dynamic but has itself been a "disenchanting" discipline. Whereas the social thinkers of the eighteenth century revealed religion as a human artifice, sociologists exposed the new God of many secular moderns as equally a human creation: nature.

Sociology has been a de-naturalizing force. Sociologists aim to explain human behaviors as social and historical, not natural, occurrences. The idea of the "natural" functions for sociologists like that of "religion" for the figures of the Enlightenment – as an ideology concealing social processes and inequalities. Thus, while some classical economists described capitalism as rooted in a human instinct towards greed, competition, or survival, Karl Marx argued that capitalism is a social and historical phenomenon. Similarly, W. E. B. Du Bois de-naturalized race when he explained racial inequality as a legacy of slavery and racism rather than assume a natural hierarchy of the races. Sociologists have de-naturalized religion, economic behavior, race, gender, social class, the division of social labor, bureaucracy, and so on.

However, there is one aspect of human life that has resisted disenchantment: sexuality. Until recently, sociologists have viewed sexuality as a part of nature. They have shared with popular opinion the view that sexuality is biologically structured into the human species and obeys natural laws. Moreover, where sexuality was not defined as natural, it was approached as strictly a matter of individual feelings and behavior. To the extent that sexuality was framed as a sphere of nature or a merely individual matter, there could be no sociology of sexuality.

Sexuality is perhaps the last human dimension that many of us refuse to grant is socially created, historically variable, and therefore deeply political. However, this is changing. And while psychoanalysis, feminism, and poststructural literary approaches have been important in de-naturalizing sex, so too has sociology. Sociologists in the last few decades have fashioned varied frameworks for analyzing sexuality. This volume presents a range of current sociological perspectives on issues relating to homosexuality, identity, and power.

This Introduction has two aims. First, I provide an overview of the history of sociology and sex studies. I detail the neglect of sexuality and homosexuality in early classical European and American sociology. I sketch the rise of a sociology of homosexuality and its complex interconnections to a history of political activism and the development of a robust lesbian and gay studies outside sociology and often outside the academy. Second, I provide a summary of the four parts of this book which might be useful as a guide to the volume and to the key debates around the question of homosexual desire and lesbian, gay, and bisexual identity.

Sociology and the Study of Homosexual Desire: An Historical and Conceptual Perspective

We are familiar with the standard accounts of the rise of sociology. For example, sociology is described as born in the great transformation from a traditional, agrarian, corporatist, hierarchical order to a modern, industrial, class-based, but formally democratic system. The so-called classic sociologists are "classics" precisely because they have presumably provided the core perspectives and themes in terms of which contemporary social scientists analyze the great problems of modernity. These perspectives include Marx's understanding of capitalism as a class-divided system, Weber's thesis of the bureaucratization of modern institutions, and Durkheim's theory of social evolution as a process of social differentiation. If our view of modernity derived exclusively from the sociological classics, we would not know that a central part of the great transformation consisted of efforts to organize bodies, pleasures, and desires as they relate to personal and public life, and that this entailed constructing sexual (and gender) identities. In short, the making of sexual selves and codes has been interlaced with the making of the cultural and institutional life of Western societies.

The standard histories link the rise of the modern social sciences to social modernization (e.g. industrialism, class conflict, and bureaucracy), but are silent about sexual (and gender) conflicts. At the very time in which the social sciences emerged proposing a social understanding of the human condition, they never questioned a natural order linking sex, gender, and sexuality. Such silences cannot be excused on the grounds that "sexuality" had not become a site of public conflict and knowledges. From the eighteenth through the nineteenth centuries, there were social conflicts focused on the body, desire, pleasure, intimate acts and their public expression – struggles in the family, church, law, and in the realm of knowledges and the state. The women's movement flourished in Europe in the 1780s and 1790s, the 1840s to 1860s and between the 1880s and 1920 – key junctures in the development of modern sociology. Struggles over the "women's question" were connected to public conflicts around "sexuality." Sexual conflicts escalated in intensity and gained public attention between the 1880s and World War I – the breakthrough period of classical sociology. In Europe and the United States, the body and sexuality were sites of moral and political struggle through such issues as divorce, free love, abortion, masturbation, homosexuality, prostitution, obscenity, and sex education. This period experienced the rise of sexology, psychoanalysis, and psychiatry (Irvine 1990; Birken 1988; Weeks 1985). Magnus Hirshfeld created the Scientific Humanitarian Committee and Institute for Sex Research in Germany. Homosexuality became an object of knowledge. For example, Karl Heinrich Ulrichs published twelve volumes on homosexuality between 1864 and 1879. One historian estimates that over 1,000 publications on homosexuality appeared in Europe between 1898 and 1908 (Weeks 1985: 67).

What is striking is the silence in classical sociological texts regarding these sexual conflicts and knowledges. Despite their aim to view the human condition as socially constructed, and to sketch a social history of the contours of modernity, the classical sociologists offered no accounts of the social making of modern bodies and sexualities. Marx analyzed the social reproduction and organization of labor but not the process by which laborers are materially reproduced. Weber sketched what he took to be the historical uniqueness of the modern West. He traced the rise of modern capitalism, the modern state, formal law, modern cities, a culture of risk-taking individualism, but had little to say about the making of the modern regime of sexuality. The core premises and conceptual strategies of classical sociology defined the important social facts as the economy, church, military, formal organizations, social classes, and collective representations.

Perhaps the silence of the classical sociologists on "sexuality" is related to their privileged gender and sexual social position. They took for granted the naturalness and validity of their own gender and sexual status the way, as we sociologists believe, any individual unconsciously assumes as natural those aspects of one's life that confer privilege and power. Thus, just as the bourgeoisie asserts the naturalness of class inequality and their rule, individuals whose social identity is that of male and heterosexual do not question the naturalness of a male-dominated, normatively heterosexual social order. It is then hardly surprising that the classics never examined the social formation of modern regimes of bodies and sexualities. Moreover, their own science of society contributed to the making of this regime whose center is the hetero/homo binary and the heterosexualization of society.

Sociology's silence on "sexuality" was broken as the volume level of public sexual conflicts was turned up so high that even sociologist's trained incapacity to hear such sounds was pierced. Confining my remarks to early American sociology, isolated and still faint voices speaking to the issue of sexuality can be heard through the first half of the twentieth century. Indeed, sociologists could not entirely avoid addressing this theme in the first few decades of this century.

Issues such as municipal reform, unionization, economic concentration, the commercialization of everyday life, race relations, and the internationalization of politics were important topics of public debate. At the same time, Americans were gripped by conflicts that placed the body at the center of contention. The women's movement, which in the first two decades of this century was often closely aligned to socialist and cultural radical politics, emerged as a national movement. Although the struggle for the right to vote was pivotal, no less important were feminist struggles to eliminate the double standard that permitted men sexual pleasure while pressuring women to conform to Victorian purity norms or suffer degradation if their erotic desires were acted upon. As women were demanding erotic equality, there were public struggles to liberalize divorce, abortion, and pornography; battles over obscenity, prostitution, and marriage were in the public eye (e.g., Peiss 1986; D'Emilio and Freedman 1988; Seidman 1991; Smith-Rosenberg 1990). Sex was being talked about in magazines, newspapers, journals, books, the theater, and in the courts. For example, in the literally millions of volumes of sex-advice literature published in the early decades of this century there existed a process of the sexualization of love and marriage (Seidman 1991). Books such as Theodore Van de

Velde's *Ideal Marriage* ([1930] 1950), which constructed an eroticized body and intimacy, sold in the hundreds of thousands. Americans were in the first stages of a romance with Freud and psychoanalysis; social radicals such as Max Eastman, Emma Goldman, Edward Bourne, and Margaret Sanger, connected institutional change to an agenda of sexual and gender change (Marriner 1972; Simmons 1982; Trimberger 1983). Despite the vigorous efforts of vice squads and purity movements, pornography flourished and obscenity laws were gradually liberalized.

In the first half of this century, sex entered the public culture of American society in a manner that sociology could not ignore. And yet sociologists managed to do just that to a considerable degree. Through the mid-century, sociologists had surprisingly little to say about sexuality. For example, the Chicago School of sociology studied cab drivers, immigrants, factory workers, and youth but had little to say about the domain of sexuality. Sociologists such as Park, Cooley, Thomas, Parsons, and Ogburn, had much to say about urban patterns, the development of the self, political organization, the structure of social action, and technological development, but little or nothing to say on the making of sexualized selves and patterns. Finally, while sociologists were surveying every conceivable topic, and while a proliferation of sex surveys were stirring public debate (e.g., Dickinson and Beam 1932; Davis 1929; Kinsey 1948 and 1953), sociologists did not deploy their empirical techniques to study human sexuality.[1]

It took the changes of the 1950s and the public turmoil of the 1960s for sociologists to begin to take sex seriously. The immediate postwar years are sometimes perceived as conservative. However, the war and patterns of mobility, prosperity, and social liberalization relaxed sexual constraints. Indicative of changes in the American culture of the body and sexuality, the fifties witnessed Rock music, the beginnings of the women's movement, the appearance of homophile organizations, and the figures of the beatnik and the rebel for whom social and sexual transgression went hand in hand. The sixties made sexual rebellion into a national public drama. The women's movement, gay liberation, lesbian feminism, the counterculture, magazines such as *Playboy*, sex manuals such as *The Joy of Sex*, and cultural radicals like Herbert Marcuse and Norman O. Brown, made sexual rebellion central to social change.

A sociology of sexuality emerged in postwar America (e.g., Henslin 1971; Reiss 1967). Sociologists approached sex as a specialty area like crime or demography. Sex was imagined as a property of the individual whose personal expression was shaped by social norms and attitudes.

Sex and society were viewed as antithetical; society took on importance as either an obstacle or tolerant space for sexual release. The idea
of a "sexual system" or a field of sexual meanings, discourses, and
practices that are interlaced with social institutions, was absent from
sociological perspectives. Moreover, although sociologists studied patterns of conventional sexuality, most conspicuously, premarital, marital, and extramarital sex, much of this literature was preoccupied with
"deviant" sexualities, for example, prostitution, pornography, and
most impressively, homosexuality.

A sociology of homosexuality emerged as part of the emerging field
of the sociology of sex (e.g., Reiss Jr. 1964; Gagnon and Simon 1967a,
1967b; Sagarin 1969). Sociologists turned to the study of homosexuality in the context of the heightened public visibility and politicization of homosexuality.

Between the early decades of this century and the mid-1970s, homoerotic desire was defined by scientific-medical knowledges as indicative of a distinctive sexual and personal identity: the homosexual. In
other words, individuals for whom homosexual desire was important
in their emotional and sexual desires now saw themselves as a unique
type of person. Ironically, the framing of homosexuality as a social
identity contributed to the rise of homosexual subcultures. To simplify
a very complicated story, homosexual subcultures evolved from the
largely informal networks of pre-World War II, to the marginal, clan-
destine homophile organizations of the fifties, to the public cultures
and movements of affirmation and public contestation of lesbian feminism and gay liberation in the seventies (Adam 1987; D'Emilio 1983;
Faderman 1981). Integral to the redefinition of homosexual desire into
a homosexual/lesbian and gay identity were the changing meanings of
homosexuality in scientific-medical discourses. From the early 1900s
through the 1950s, a psychiatric discourse that figured the homosexual
as a perverse, abnormal human type dominated public discussion.
Kinsey (1948, 1953) challenged this psychiatric model by viewing
sexuality as a continuum. Instead of assuming that individuals are
either exclusively heterosexual or homosexual, Kinsey proposed that
human sexuality is ambiguous with respect to sexual orientation; most
individuals were said to experience both hetero- and homosexual
feelings and behaviors. Kinsey's critique of the psychiatric model was
met with a hardline defense of the medical model (e.g., Bergler 1956;
Bieber 1962; Socarides 1968). At the same time, new social models of
homosexuality appeared which suggested an alternative to both the
biological and psychological models of psychiatry and Kinsey. These
social approaches viewed the homosexual as an oppressed minority, a

victim of unwarranted social prejudice and discrimination (e.g., Cory 1951; Hoffman 1968; Hooker 1965; Martin and Lyon 1972). By the early seventies, the women's and gay liberation movements fashioned sophisticated social understandings of homosexuality. These movements proposed images of homosexual desire and identity as normal and natural; moreover, they criticized the institutions of heterosexuality, marriage and the family, and conventional gender roles for not only oppressing homosexuals but for oppressing women (e.g., Altman 1971; Atkinson 1974; Bunch 1975; Rich 1976).

The growing national public awareness of homosexuality and the rise of new social concepts of homosexuality prompted sociologists to study homosexuality. Through the early 1970s, sociologists viewed homosexuality as a social stigma to be managed; they analyzed the ways homosexuals adapted to a hostile society. Sociologists studied the homosexual (mostly the male homosexual) as part of a deviant sexual underworld of hustlers, prostitutes, prisons, tearooms, baths, and bars (e.g., Reiss 1967; Humphreys 1970; Weinberg and Williams 1975; Kirkham 1971). My impression is that much of this sociology aimed to figure the homosexual as a victim of unjust discrimination. Nevertheless, sociologists contributed to the public perception of the homosexual as a strange, exotic human type in contrast to the normal, respectable heterosexual.

Sociological perspectives on sexuality in the sixties and early seventies proved influential in shaping knowledges of sexuality and homosexuality, in particular, the labeling theory of Howard Becker (1963), Goffman (1963), and Schur (1971) and the "sexual script" perspective of John Gagnon and William Simon (1973). However, in the late seventies and early eighties a new sociology of homosexuality was fashioned primarily by lesbian and gay identified and often feminist sociologists. This new cadre of sociologists took over the conceptual tools of sociology as well as drew heavily from feminism and critical social approaches circulating in the lesbian and gay movements (e.g., Plummer 1975, 1981; Troiden 1988; Warren 1974; Levine 1979a, 1979b; Murray 1979; Harry and Devall 1978). This work underscored the social meaning of homosexuality. It contributed to recent gay theory which has largely neglected sociological research as a distinctive social tradition of sex studies. The sociology of homosexuality from the early 1970s through the 1980s has not played a major role in recent lesbian and gay theory debates, in part because sociologists did not critically investigate the categories of sexuality, heterosexuality, and homosexuality. They did not question the social functioning of the hetero/homosexual binary as the master category of a modern regime of sexuality. Moreover, many sociologists lacked an historical perspective while perpetuating an approach that isolated the question of homosexuality from dynamics of social modernization and politics.

As sociologists were beginning to approach sex as a social fact, there were, as I alluded to previously, social perspectives on sexuality that were developed by the women's and gay movements. With the formation of homophile groups in the 1950s (e.g., the Mattachine Society and the Daughters of Bilitis), homosexuality was alternatively theorized as a property of all individuals or as a property of a segment of the human population. Viewing homosexuality as natural was intended to legitimate it. Moreover, despite the radicalization of gay theory in lesbian feminism and gay liberation in the seventies, few challenged the view of homosexuality as a basis of individual and social identity. A good deal of lesbian-feminist and gay liberationist theory aimed to reverse dominant sexual views by asserting the naturalness and normality of homosexuality. The notion of homosexuality as a universal category of the self and sexual identity was rarely questioned in the homophile, lesbian-feminist, and gay liberationist discourses (exceptions include Altman 1971; MacIntosh 1968).

As the initial wave of a gay affirmative politics, roughly from 1968–73, passed into a period of community building, personal empowerment, and local struggles, we can speak of a new period in lesbian and gay theory – the age of "social constructionism." Drawing from labeling and phenomenological theory, and influenced heavily by Marxism and feminism, social constructionists had roots in both academia and political activism. Social-constructionist perspectives challenge the antithesis of sex and society. Sex is viewed as fundamentally social; the modern categories of sexuality, most importantly, those of heterosexuality and homosexuality, are understood as social and historical creations. Social constructionist perspectives suggested that "homosexuality" was not a uniform, identical phenomenon but that its meaning and social role varied historically. In particular, constructionists argued that instead of assuming that "the homosexual" is a transhistorical identity or a universal human type, the idea that homosexual desire reveals a distinctive human type or social identity is said to be unique to modern Western societies. Michel Foucault (1980) provided the classic statement. "As defined by ancient civil or canonical codes, sodomy was a category of forbidden acts; their perpetrator was nothing more than the juridical subject of them. The nineteenth-century homosexual became a personage, a past, a case history, a life form . . . Nothing that went into total composition was unaffected by his sexuality. It was everywhere present in him: at the root of all his actions ... because it was a secret that always gave itself away" (p. 43). Foucault's thesis of the social construction of "the homosexual" found support in the concurrent work of Jeffrey Weeks (1977), Jonathan Katz (1976), Carroll Smith-Rosenberg (1975), and Randolph Trumbach (1977).

Social constructionism emerged in the context of prodigious efforts at lesbian and gay community building in the seventies. Constructionist studies sought to explain the origin, social meaning, and changing forms of the modern homosexual (e.g., D'Emilio 1983; Plummer 1981; Faderman 1981). As much as these perspectives challenged essentialist or universalistic understandings of homosexuality, they contributed to a politics of the making of a homosexual minority. Instead of asserting the homosexual as a natural fact made into a political minority by social prejudice, constructionists traced the social factors that produced a homosexual identity which functioned as the foundation for homosexuals as a new ethnic minority (e.g. D'Emilio 1983; Faderman 1981). Social-constructionist studies legitimated a model of lesbian and gay subcultures as ethnic-like minorities (Epstein 1987; Seidman 1993).[2]

Social-constructionist perspectives dominated analyses of homosexuality through the eighties and have been institutionalized in lesbian and gay studies programs in the nineties. Debates about essentialism (Stein 1992) and the rise, meaning, and changing social forms of homosexual identities and communities, are at the core of lesbian and gay studies. However, since the late eighties aspects of this constructionist perspective have been contested. In particular, discourses that sometimes circulate under the rubric of Queer theory, though often impossible to differentiate from constructionist texts, have sought to shift the debate somewhat away from explaining the modern homosexual to questions of the operation of the hetero/homosexual binary, from an exclusive preoccupation with homosexuality to a focus on heterosexuality as a social and political organizing principle, and from a politics of minority interest to a politics of knowledge and difference (Seidman 1995).

What is the social context of the rise of Queer theory?

By the end of the seventies, the gay and lesbian movement had achieved such a level of subcultural elaboration and general social tolerance, at least in the US, that a gay politics focused on social assimilation far overshadowed the liberationist politics of the previous decade. Thus, Dennis Altman (1982), a keen observer of the gay movement in the seventies, could speak of the homosexualization of

America. And yet at this very historical moment events were conspiring to put lesbian and gay life into crisis.

A backlash against homosexuality, spearheaded by the New Right but widely supported by neoconservatives and mainstream Republicans, punctured illusions of a coming era of tolerance and sexual pluralism (Adam 1987; Seidman 1992). The AIDS epidemic energized an anti-gay backlash and put lesbians and gay men on the defensive as religious and medicalized models which discredited homosexuality were rehabilitated. While the AIDS crisis also demonstrated the strength of established gay institutions, for many lesbians and gay men it underscored the limits of a politics of minority rights and inclusion. Both the backlash and the AIDS crisis prompted a renewal of radical activism, of a politics of confrontation, coalition building, and the need for a critical theory that links gay affirmation to broad institutional change.

Internal developments within gay and lesbian subcultures also prompted a shift in gay theory and politics. Social differences within the gay and lesbian communities erupted into public conflict around the issues of race and sex. By the early eighties, a public culture fashioned by lesbian and gay people of color registered sharp criticisms of mainstream gay culture for its devaluation and exclusion of their experiences, interests, values, and unique forms of life – e.g., their writing, political perspectives, relationships, and particular modes of oppression. The concept of a lesbian and gay identity that served as the foundation for building a community and organizing politically was criticized as reflecting a white, middle-class experience (Anzaldua and Moraga 1983; Lorde 1984; Beam 1986; Moraga 1983). The categories of "lesbian" and "gay" were criticized for functioning as disciplining political forces. Simultaneously, lesbian feminism was further put into crisis by challenges to its foundational concept of sexuality and sexual ethics. At the heart of lesbian feminism, especially in the late seventies, was an understanding of the difference between men and women anchored in a spiritualized concept of female sexuality and an eroticization of the male that imagined male desire as revealing a logic of misogyny and domination. Being a woman and a lesbian meant exhibiting in one's desires and behaviors a lesbian-feminist sexual and social identity. Many lesbians, and feminists in general, criticized lesbian feminism for stigmatizing their own erotic and intimate lives as deviant or male-identified (e.g. Rubin 1984; Allison 1981; Bright 1984; Califia 1979, 1981). In the course of the feminist "sex wars," a virtual parade of female and lesbian sexualities entered the public life of lesbian culture, e.g., butch-fems, sadomasochists, sexualities of all kinds mocking the idea of a unified lesbian sexual identity (Phelan 1989; Ferguson 1989; Seidman 1992). If the intent of people of color and sex rebels was to encourage social differences to surface in gay and lesbian life, one consequence was to raise questions about the very idea of a lesbian or gay identity as the foundations of gay culture and politics.

Some in the lesbian and gay communities reacted to the "crisis" by reasserting a natural foundation for homosexuality (e.g., the gay brain) in order to unify homosexuals in the face of a political backlash, to defend themselves against attacks prompted by the plague, and to overcome growing internal discord. However, many activists and intellectuals moved in the opposite direction, affirming a stronger thesis of the social construction of homosexuality that took the form of a radical politics of difference. Although people of color and sex rebels pressured gay culture in this direction, there appeared a new cadre of "Queer" theorists. Influenced profoundly by French poststructuralism and Lacanian psychoanalysis, they have altered the terrain of gay theory and politics (e.g. Sedgwick 1991; Butler 1991; Fuss 1991; de Lauretis 1991; Warner 1993; Doty 1993).

Queer theory has accrued multiple meanings, from a merely useful shorthand way to speak of all gay, lesbian, bisexual, and transgendered experiences to a theoretical sensibility that pivots on transgression or permanent rebellion. I take as central to Queer theory its challenge to what has been the dominant foundational concept of both homophobic and affirmative homosexual theory: the assumption of a unified homosexual identity. I interpret Queer theory as contesting this foundation and therefore the very telos of Western homosexual politics.

Modern Western homophobic and gay-affirmative theory has assumed a homosexual subject. Dispute revolved around its origin (natural or social), changing social forms and roles, its moral meaning, and political strategies of repression and resistance. There has been little serious disagreement regarding the assumption that homosexual theory and politics has as its object "the homosexual" as a stable, unified, and identifiable human type. Drawing from the critique of unitary identity politics by people of color and sex rebels, and from the poststructural critique of "representational" models of language, Queer theorists argue that identities are always multiple or at best composites with literally an infinite number of ways in which "identity-components" (e.g., sexual orientation, race, class, nationality, gender, age, able-ness) can intersect or combine. Any specific identity construction, moreover, is arbitrary, unstable, and exclusionary. Identity constructions necessarily entail the silencing or exclusion of some experiences or forms of life. For example, asserting a black, middle-class, American lesbian identity silences differences that relate to religion, regional location, subcultural identification, relation to feminism, age, or education. Identity constructs are necessarily unstable since they elicit opposition or resistance by people whose experiences or interests are submerged by a particular assertion of identity. Finally, rather than viewing the affirmation of identity as necessarily liberating, Queer theorists view them as, in part, disciplinary and regulatory structures. Identity constructions function as templates defining selves and behaviors and therefore excluding a range of possible ways to frame the self, body, desires, actions, and social relations.

Approaching identities as multiple, unstable, and regulatory may suggest to critics the undermining of gay theory and politics, but, for Queer theorists, it presents new and productive possibilities. Although I detect a strain of anti-identity politics in some Queer theory, the aim is not to abandon identity as a category of knowledge and politics but to render it permanently open and contestable as to its meaning and political role. In other words, decisions about identity categories become pragmatic, related to concerns of situational advantage, political gain, and conceptual utility. The gain, say Queer theorists, of figuring identity as permanently open as to its meaning and political use is that it encourages the public surfacing of differences or a culture where multiple voices and interests are heard and shape gay life and politics.

Queer theory articulates a related objection to a homosexual theory and politics organized on the foundation of the homosexual subject: This project reproduces the hetero/homosexual binary, a code that perpetuates the heterosexualization of society. Modern Western affirmative homosexual theory may naturalize or normalize the gay subject or even register it as an agent of social liberation, but it has the effect of consolidating heterosexuality and homosexuality as master categories of sexual and social identity; it reinforces the modern regime of sexuality. Queer theory wishes to challenge the regime of sexuality itself, that is, the knowledges that construct the self as sexual and that assume heterosexuality and homosexuality as categories marking the truth of sexual selves. The modern system of sexuality organized around the heterosexual or homosexual self is approached as a system of knowledge, one that structures the institutional and cultural life of Western societies. In other words, Queer theorists view heterosexuality and homosexuality not simply as identities or social statuses but as categories of knowledge, a language that frames what we know as bodies, desires, sexualities, identities. This is a normative language as it shapes moral boundaries and political hierarchies. Queer theorists shift their focus from an exclusive preoccupation with the oppression and liberation of the homosexual subject to an analysis of the institutional practices and discourses producing sexual knowledges and the ways they organize social life, attending in particular to the way these knowledges and social practices repress differences. In this regard, Queer theory is suggesting that the study of homosexuality should not be a study of a minority – the making of the lesbian/gay/bisexual subject – but a study of those knowledges and social practices that organize "society" as a whole by sexualizing – heterosexualizing or homosexualizing – bodies, desires, acts, identities, social relations, knowledges, culture, and social institutions. Queer theory aspires to transform homosexual theory into a general social theory or one standpoint from which to analyze social dynamics.

Queer theory and sociology have barely acknowledged one another. Queer theory has largely been the creation of academics, mostly feminists and mostly humanities professors. Sociologists have been almost invisible in these discussions. This is somewhat ironic in light of the gesturing of Queer theory towards a general social analysis. Moreover, the silence of sociologists is most unfortunate since Queer theory has been criticized for its textualism or "underdeveloped" concept of the social (e.g., Seidman 1993, 1995; Warner 1993). Sociologists have both much to learn from Queer theory and the opportunity to make a serious contribution.

This volume has several aims: I hope to show that sociology has its own traditions of thinking about homosexual desire that have shaped much current political and intellectual debate about homosexuality and should continue to do so. I wish to showcase some important perspectives and social research by sociologists. At the same time, it is also clear that some of the most innovative work in lesbian and gay studies has occurred in the humanities. Queer theory has been dominated by literary theorists. I think sociologists have much to learn from this work. Hence, in part, this volume is an effort to carry on a dialogue between Queer theory and sociology. A fruitful exchange means both subjecting sociological perspectives to critique and criticizing Queer theory from the vantage point of sociology. Finally, the value of such a dialogue is, in the end, to be evaluated by the kinds of social and political analyses and opportunities it makes possible. Thus, this volume intends to showcase some recent sociological work that has attempted to conceptually and empirically bring together sociology and Queer theory.

Overview of *Queer Theory/Sociology*

This book begins with what are perhaps the core questions in the sociology of homosexuality: Is homosexuality based in nature or human biology, or is it a psychological or social phenomenon? What role do social factors play in shaping sexuality and homosexuality? Is homosexuality to be approached as a condition, identity, or a social minority? What factors influence the organization of homosexuality in society? How to account for anti-homosexual attitudes and practices? Part I presents some of the most important general perspectives on homosexuality developed by sociologists.

For much of this century, homosexuality was seen as a natural, biologically rooted, psychological condition. It was said to define an individual's biological, psychological, and even social nature. It was often assumed that some people were simply born homosexual or become homosexual at a very early age. The role of social factors was limited to controlling the expression of homosexuality through social norms, laws, and customs. Although sociologists and others had begun to analyze the social life of homosexuals by the 1960s (for example, there were studies of the social life of hustlers or bar life), it was still assumed that homosexuality is natural and that "the homosexual" is a unique type of person.

The British sociologist Mary McIntosh (Chapter 1 in this volume) was one of the first thinkers to challenge this perspective. Instead of viewing society as merely an environment, sometimes positive but mostly negative for homosexuals, she approached homosexuality as a social role. Rather than ask why some people become homosexuals, she asked what social conditions gave rise to the idea that homosexuality is a distinctive human identity. Drawing from functionalist sociology, McIntosh proposed that societies establish a homosexual role or identity in order to distinguish acceptable from non-acceptable behavior. Specifically, by defining homosexuality as impure or polluted, heterosexuality is defined as pure and desirable. The homosexual role functions to both segregate "sexual deviants" and "normalize" heterosexuality.

McIntosh suggested that while homosexual desire may be present in all societies, only some societies create a homosexual identity. But where and when did such homosexual identities emerge? McIntosh's breakthrough work was taken seriously by her British colleague, Jeffrey Weeks. Weeks (1977; also chapter 2 in this volume) argued that it was only in late nineteenth-century Europe that homosexual desire was taken as a sign of a distinctive human type, "the homosexual."

Weeks emphasized the role of medical and scientific discourses in the making of a homosexual identity. He recognized that there were individuals engaging in homoerotic behavior prior to the appearance of these discourses, but these new knowledges created a framework for society to interpret same-sex desires and behaviors as indicative of a homosexual identity. Moreover, these new constructions of homosexuality gained wide popularity through the role of public scandals or famous court trials such as that of Oscar Wilde toward the end of the nineteenth century.

The work of McIntosh and Weeks was important for sociologists. They shifted the focus from the study of the social repression or tolerance of a universal homosexual desire towards an historical analysis of the rise of homosexual identities and subcultures. This work made possible the recovery of a "hidden history" of homosexuality (Duberman et al. 1989).

While McIntosh drew on functionalism to frame the idea of a homosexual role, and Weeks absorbed various currents of Marxism, historical sociology, and feminism, other social analysts were drawing on different sociological perspectives. In particular, the sociological work of Howard Becker (1963), Erving Goffman (1963), Edwin Schur (1971), and Peter Berger and Thomas Luckmann (1967) pointed to an alternative social-constructionist approach to homosexuality. Broadly speaking, symbolic interactionist or phenomenological approaches emphasized that the meaning of desires and actions are socially constructed and vary historically and within societies. This perspective was applied to sexuality by the British sociologist Ken Plummer (1975; see also chapter 3 in this volume). Plummer argued that individuals are not born, but become, homosexuals. Same-sex desires may be innate but it is only in social interaction that people learn that such desires indicate a homosexual identity. Like McIntosh and Weeks, Plummer insists that a homosexual identity is not natural or psychologically necessary but is socially formed. However, instead of analyzing the socio-historical conditions that give rise to a homosexual identity, Plummer studies the "micro-interactionist" processes through which individuals "come out," acquire a homosexual identity, and sometimes become part of a homosexual subculture. Plummer's interactionist approach stresses that individuals are not simply victimized by a homosexual label, but resist by rejecting the negative identification or building subcultures that are based on affirmative constructions of a homosexual identity.

The work of McIntosh and especially Weeks generated a new historical scholarship that analyzed the rise of unique homosexual identities and subcultures (e.g., Chauncey Jr. 1982; Faderman 1981; Halperin 1990; Trumbach 1977). Similarly, the interactionist approach influenced a wide range of work on identity formation, coming out, and the making of a homosexual community (e.g., Troiden 1988; Warren 1974). Yet this work mostly neglected the broader social-structural context of homosexuality. The social role of discourses or labels is attended to but "structural" factors are not. Moreover, there was little effort to explain the development of anti-homosexual attitudes and practices.

Greenberg and Bystryn (Chapter 4, in this volume) propose precisely a social-structural theory of homosexuality. Criticizing explanations of modern anti-homosexual attitudes that appeal to a Judeo-Christian legacy, they emphasize a culture of "sexual asceticism" promoted by competitive capitalism and the dynamics of bureaucratization. For example, they argue that capitalism encourages competition between men, a culture of self-restraint and an ideology of family that reinforces repressive attitudes towards homosexuality. Similarly, Barry Adam (chapter 5) insists on the importance of social-structural analysis. He notes that while there has been a great deal of research charting the rise of homosexual identities and subcultures, there are very few structural explanations of the conditions that made this possible. For example, most accounts view homosexual subcultures as responses to social oppression. Adam examines the role of structural conditions such as the separation of the household and the economy, the role of the state, and the growing "autonomy" of sexual desires. The work of Greenberg and Bystryn and Adam points to the importance of a social-structural analysis of homosexuality.

Social-structural approaches have been virtually absent in recent lesbian and gay or queer studies which has been dominated by the more "cultural" approaches of the humanities and literary studies. In this regard, with their tradition of social-institutional analysis, sociologists have a contribution to make to a social analysis of queer life. At the same time, recent queer studies is quite imaginative and innovative but has been until recently ignored by sociologists.

Part II chronicles the efforts of some sociologists to engage the latest conceptual developments in lesbian and gay studies, in particular Queer theory. The aim of this section is to foster dialogue, not with the intention of dismissing either sociology or Queer theory, but with the hope that bringing these two "traditions" into communication might be productive.

Stein and Plummer (chapter 6) suggest that these two general approaches to sexual desire may not be as different as is often assumed.

Much that is claimed to be new in Queer theory was already developed by sociologists. For example, the symbolic interactionism of Becker and the social constructionism of Berger and Luckmann analyzed the social construction of social categories. Nevertheless, Queer theory has opened up fresh avenues of thinking that sociologists should consider. For example, Queer theorists approach identities as thoroughly social and pluralistic; they encourage analyses of the ways sexual categories operate in a wide range of social institutions and cultural forms that are not explicitly sexual. Stein and Plummer propose a "more queer sociology." Such a sociology would be more critical of its categories, would consider the way knowledges, including sociology, shape sexual and social orders, and would take seriously the texts of mass culture. A queer sociology would analyze the social construction and dynamics of heterosexuality. At the same time, a "more queer sociology" would be decidedly sociological as it would integrate the emphasis on discourse in queer studies with a sociological focus on social institutions.

Like Stein and Plummer, Epstein (chapter 7) is somewhat critical of the shift of the center of lesbian, gay, and bisexual studies from the human sciences to the humanities. He also insists that many of the key positions of Queer theory have their roots in sociology. Sociologists such as Gagnon and Simon (1973), McIntosh (1968), and Plummer (1975) developed social-constructionist analyses of sexual identities and meanings. Nevertheless, Epstein believes that Queer theory points to a potentially productive shift in social and political analysis – in particular, its decentering of sexual identities, its greater appreciation of sexual fluidity, its emphasis on knowledge as a social force, and its claim that the categories of hetero/homosexuality shape the broader culture and institutional order of societies. Queer theory suggests to sociologists a more reflexive analysis of sexual categories and the ways these sexual meanings intersect with institutions to shape dynamics of order and oppression. Sociologists, in turn, have something crucial to offer: a rich tradition of social-structural and cultural analysis that can give empirical richness to the often literary or abstract conceptual analyses of Queer theory.

The idea that Queer theory prompts sociology to reexamine its foundational assumptions is pivotal to the contribution of Chrys Ingraham (chapter 8). She argues that the heterosexist assumptions of feminist sociology have been one of its major failures. While feminist sociologists have analyzed the social process of becoming men and women in a way that maintains male dominance, they have not examined the link between gender and sexuality. Specifically, feminist sociologists have not traced the ways a binary gender system is connected to a system of compulsive heterosexuality, producing what Ingraham calls a "heterogender" system. While Ingraham draws from Queer theory to expose the ways feminist sociology unintentionally perpetuates a system of normative heterosexuality, she is critical of Queer theory to the extent that it neglects the "material" conditions of life. She favors a queer materialist-feminist theory that links sexuality and gender to the material conditions of a patriarchal, capitalist system.

The Canadian sociologist Ki Namaste (chapter 9) offers perhaps the strongest defense of Queer theory. Namaste does not deny that sociology has studied the social construction of homosexuality. Yet he underscores the point that the study of heterosexuality has been seriously neglected in sociology, even in social-constructionist approaches. Namaste defends a poststructuralist Queer theory that would analyze the social production of all sexual categories, meanings, and identities, tracing their mutual interrelation and dependency. Thus, the study of the origin, formation, and operation of heterosexuality would move to the forefront of queer studies. Moreover, queer studies would analyze the formation of a range of different sexualities, such as bisexuality, transgendered desires, and S/M. A poststructural Queer theory would be connected less to a narrow gay or lesbian liberationism than to a politics affirming a democratic culture of sexual difference.

Whereas Namaste makes a general case for a queer social theory, the American sociologist Janice Irvine (chapter 10) argues for the opportunities recent gay and lesbian studies have created for sociology. Current social and political conflicts around educational canons and curriculum – for example, the conflicts over the Rainbow Curriculum in New York City – underscore the centrality today of issues of sexuality, identity, culture, and social difference. Recent lesbian and gay studies, moreover, have fashioned sophisticated socio-historical understandings of identities, subcultures, and group conflict. Queer analysts have put questions of identity and difference, knowledge and power, and the intersection of identities and politics, at the center of social analysis. Queer studies can be a major intellectual resource for sociology. Unfortunately, sociologists have neglected not only the study of sexual identities and cultures but, until recently, have marginalized the study of cultural meanings. Irvine encourages a sustained dialogue where sociologists are exposed to new areas of research and discover new approaches to old questions, while queer studies locates in sociology a rich legacy of social analysis.

The dialogue between sociology and Queer theory has begun to yield some intellectual gems. Parts III and IV showcase a range of innovative essays which aim to both queer the sociology of homosexuality and make queer studies more sociological.

The question of identity has been and remains at the center of modern Western homosexual studies and politics. Analyzing the historical formation of identities, their social construction or acquisition, and processes of coming out is pivotal to the sociology of homosexual desire. However, under the influence of Queer theory, recent sociological work has begun to alter its approach to identity. Instead of viewing identity as something an individual learns or accomplishes or fashions as a positive basis for self-evaluation and politics, new sociological queer perspectives emphasize the unstable, multiple character of identities, the performative aspects of identity, and identity as a mode of social control. Part III consists of highly original essays written by a new generation of sociologists which aim to create a queer sociology of homosexual desire.

A key assumption of the sociology of homosexuality and gay politics has been the notion that there is a common or more or less identical experience of being homosexual. For example, some sociologists argue that because all homosexuals experience the "closet" and "coming out," they share certain core experiences that form the basis of their identity. This notion of a common sexual identity has been understood as the basis for community building and politics. The new queer sociology has challenged this core assumption.

Dana Takagi (chapter 11) underscores how an Asian-American ethnic identity shapes homosexual experiences in ways not shared by white European Americans. Racial or ethnic difference does not amount to merely an additional dimension of gay experience or a minor variation of a common homoerotic experience but produces a homosexual desire that is unique in certain important ways. For example, homosexuality is often viewed in Asian-American cultures as a "white European" experience and therefore the very idea of a gay Asian-American identity would be viewed as contradictory. Addressing questions of identity in general terms, Takagi argues that homosexual identity never exists apart from differences of race, class, gender, age, or religion. Sexual identity should be analyzed in relation to these various social differences in order to avoid suppressing the multiple ways of experiencing homosexual desire. This view of homosexual identity suggests a view of sexual and social identities as non-unitary, unstable, pluralistic, and an ongoing site of social and political conflict.

Whereas Takagi highlights identity as pluralistic and protean in order to criticize unitary or essentialist notions of identity which conceal a multiplicity of differences, Kristin Esterberg (chapter 12) takes for granted the decentered character of identity. She explores the ways identities are produced through everyday performances. Rather than seeing homosexual identity as something an individual discovers about herself or himself, Esterberg – having absorbed Queer theory – researches identity as theatrically or dramatically produced through behaviors and gestures that project to oneself and others a particular sexual identity. From this perspective, a homosexual identity is not simply socially learned or accomplished but is re-enacted daily through innumerable actions and always exists as a field of shifting, multiple meanings and practices.

Lesbian and gay politics have often assumed that adopting an affirmative sexual identity is a emancipatory personal and political act. Indeed, the process of coming out or publicly declaring a lesbian, gay, or bisexual identity has been considered the most authentic sexual political act. While none of the authors in Parts III or IV are against coming out or affirming a queer sexual identity, some new approaches have suggested that identities, including affirmative sexual identities, function, in part, as modes of social control in that they mark off normal from deviant populations, are repressive of difference, and impose normalizing judgments on desires. At a minimum, identity is now seen as a major site of social and political conflict, both within and beyond the lesbian, gay, and bisexual communities.

Of course much of the work in lesbian, gay, and bisexual studies has exposed the ways a norm of heterosexuality has created and controlled populations of "deviant" sexual identities. For example, Cheryl Cole (chapter 13) focuses on the ways the popular media shapes and legitimates an ideal of a white, middle-class, heterosexual, nuclear-family pattern. Cole's essay underscores the importance of the politics of identity in the Age of AIDS. If constructing positive identities was pivotal to lesbian and gay movements, the reconstruction of these now public sexual identities has been central to movements aimed at marginalizing or victimizing "homosexuals." AIDS has been used by anti-gay movements to, once again, define homosexual desire as deviant, abnormal, and socially dangerous. Sexual identity now functions as a fulcrum of social control through the association of homosexual desire with disease and death. Using the case of the media construction of Magic Johnson and AIDS, Cole explores the ways sexuality and race are implicated in strategies of power and social control. She shows how popular media narratives of Magic Johnson operated as a normalizing social logic, reinforcing a norm of a heteronormative and white privileged society.

Whereas Cole's essay emphasizes the ways a dominant norm of

heterosexuality creates and perpetuates deviant identities (e.g., lesbian and gay), Amber Ault (Chapter 14) shows how oppressed sexual identities (e.g., lesbian or gay) themselves help to create categories of deviant sexual identities (e.g., bisexual). Specifically, Ault documents that some lesbians define bisexual women as "deviant." Bisexuality may be viewed as potentially a challenge to a sexual system that defines all sexual desires and identities in terms of a hetero/homosexual dichotomy. Bisexual individuals point to a sexual order that, in principle, permits a wider latitude of sexual choice – either by expanding the range of legitimate sexual identities (to include same-sex identities and bisexual ones) or by weakening the authority of gender preference as a basis of sexual identity. We would expect then that lesbians would be friendly towards bisexuality. However, in her interviews Ault found that many lesbians reject bisexuality and stigmatize bisexual women. Moreover, many bisexual women fashion discursive strategies that allow them to continue to maintain a lesbian sexual identity. In this way, Ault reveals the various ways socially "deviant" or oppressed sexual groups reinforce a binary heterosexual/homosexual social order.

Queer-informed social analysis has challenged perspectives that assume that coming out is a process of self-revelation and that adopting a positive lesbian or gay identity has only a liberating effect. Queer perspectives approach coming out less as a process of revealing one's true nature than a process of constructing or performatively enacting a sexual identity. Moreover, positive sexual identities have been exposed as socially constraining and exclusionary. Yet, as much as identities operate as modes of social control, queer perspectives do not deny their enabling or positive personal and political roles. It is only by asserting lesbian, gay, or bisexual identities that community building and movements of social change are possible. Part IV deals with some of the dilemmas around identity and movement politics.

Scott Bravmann's essay (chapter 15) poses the issue of identity, politics, and knowledge in a provocative way. He argues that historical narratives produced by gay men and lesbians with the aim of recovering their hidden histories and promoting their political agenda, unintentionally functioned to constrain their personal lives and political movements. With the formation of gay and lesbian subcultures in this century new narratives were fashioned detailing the making of the homosexual. These were often heroic tales of homosexuals struggling against a reign of intolerance or stories of the making of gay counter-cultures. These narratives were part of the making of affirmative homosexual identities and subcultures. Although these historical knowledges were empowering in many ways, Bravmann suggests that they have been tied to "modern" notions of a unitary homosexual identity or to an ethnic identity politics, both of which have been repressive of difference and hostile to coalitional politics. Bravmann's essay aims to trouble this "modernist" linkage of identity, politics, and knowledge. He alludes to new "postmodern" historical narratives that build difference and multiplicity into their stories.

Cathy Cohen (chapter 16) similarly underscores the dangers of a community and politics organized on the basis of a unitary or essentialist identity. To the extent that the African-American community has been based on a unitary concept of racial identity that does not include being gay or lesbian, African-American leaders and politics have not recognized black gay men or lesbians as part of their community. One consequence has been the failure of African-American communities to respond effectively to AIDS among black gay men and lesbians. AIDS has often been defined as a white or European social problem to the extent that it is associated with homosexuality. This de-homosexualized construction of African-American identity has also created serious internal divisions and hierarchies within these racialized communities.

But what happens to a movement when multiple identities are admitted? Does not conceding difference greatly weaken social movements? This then is the dilemma: social movements seem strong when they pivot around a unitary (racial, gender, or sexual) identity but this same heightened solidarity is purchased at the cost of increased internal repression as well as potential social and political isolation. Admitting multiplicity within a movement, however, seems to threaten its stability and political effectiveness.

Joshua Gamson (chapter 17) argues that there is no escape from both essentializing and destabilizing social identities. Social movements, at least in the United States today, gain credibility and effectiveness when their political demands appeal to some notion of a unitary (racial, class, gender, or sexual) identity. Simultaneously, such identities must be, and have been, deconstructed in order to promote tolerance of internal differences and coalition building. The problem with the queer "deconstructive" position is not that it makes political mobilization impossible but that its focus on destabilizing identities lacks an institutional emphasis. Queer theory and politics is preoccupied with disturbing popular ideas about sexuality but has failed to understand the complex ways representations are anchored in social institutions. In this regard, Queer theory should draw on the social-structural perspectives of sociologists. While sociology has a strong tradition of social-institutional analysis, sociologists can learn much from queer studies with regard to rethinking the dynamics of collective identity formation which involves both stabilization and destablization. In this regard, Gamson suggests a "pragmatic" approach to collective identity in which we understand emphases on the stability or multiplicity of collective identities as more situational and political than as a matter to be settled by strictly theoretical arguments.

These dilemmas regarding identity-based social movements are serious, but Jan Willem Duyvendak's essay (chapter 18) suggests that, in part, they are more pertinent to the American or British rather than the broadly west-European context. In many, if not most, European nations there have developed lesbian and gay subcultures but not necessarily sharply defined sexual identities or political movements. Specifically, Duyvendak shows that, even in the face of the AIDS crisis, a queer movement has not developed in Holland. In part, this was because ethnic models of lesbian and gay identity, which have been a chief impetus for the rise of queer politics in the United States, never materialized in Holland. In place of politicized subcultures and identities driving a political movement, Holland witnessed the separation of gay subcultures from politics. This nation saw the rise of a depoliticized subculture combined with gay elites who negotiated as part of the government. This national configuration reflects Dutch traditions of tolerance and a political culture organized around elite cooperation and accommodation. Duyvendak's paper is a sharp reminder that questions of identity and politics take different forms in various national contexts.

The present time in the United States and in many parts of Europe seems favorable for sociologists and social scientists in general to reconsider the social importance of dynamics of sexual desire, meanings, and identity. Social movements and ideas associated with feminism, gay liberationism, and cultural studies have pushed issues centered on the body and sexual meanings to the center of social analysis and politics. In this regard, a sociology of homosexual desire might have implications for sociology beyond rethinking sex studies as general social dynamics concerned with social control, power, social movements, and social change may be rethought.

Sociologists will need to listen to what feminists, queer theorists, or poststructuralists are saying. These intellectual movements have suggested new ways of framing and analyzing social realities (Bauman 1992; Clough 1994; Denzin 1991; Lemert 1995; Seidman 1994). For example, as this volume suggests, queer studies proposes distinctive ways of thinking about the body, sexual desire and meanings, social identities, collective life and social movements, the intersection of gender and sexuality and desire and knowledge. Sociologists have much to learn from these perspectives and must not be constrained by narrow disciplinary-boundary concerns. As sociologists or social scientists we must learn new languages of the social – the languages of feminism, Queer theory, poststructuralism, postcolonial theory, cultural studies. At the same time, sociologists should not renounce their own disciplinary history. Sociology has a vital tradition of social-structural, cultural, and historical analysis that offers, in my view, powerful ways to analyze social processes and critique social inequalities and injustice.

Sociologists have much to teach Queer theory regarding, for example, the institutional formation of desire and identity, the interrelation of knowledges, discourses and social structure, the cultural dynamics of purity and pollution, the shaping of movements and civil society. Developing hybrid knowledges or social knowledges that are interdisciplinary and, at times, "postdisciplinary" (i.e. more public-centered than academic-centered) is perhaps urgent today in a world of multiculturalism, hybrid identities, and globalization. This volume points forward – towards a continued dialogue between sociologists and queer studies and towards a world proud of its queers, in all their many, many forms/personas.

Notes

1 The index of the *American Journal of Sociology* indicates that between 1895 and 1965 there was 1 article printed on homosexuality and 13 articles listed under the heading of "Sex," most of which addressed issues of gender, marriage, or lifestyle. The index of the *American Sociological Review* indicates that between 1936 and 1960 there were 14 articles published under the heading of "Sexual Behavior," most of which did not address issues of sexuality. One journal article commented on the absence of a sociology of sexuality. "The sociology of sex is quite undeveloped, although sex is a social force of the first magnitude. Sociologists have investigated the changing roles of men and women . . . [and] the sexual aspects of marriage. . . .. Occasionally a good study on illegitimacy or prostitution appears. However, when it is stated that a sociology of sex does not exist, I mean that our discipline has not investigated, in any substantial manner, the social causes, conditions and consequences of heterosexual and homosexual activities of all types" (Bowman 1949). Another sociologist, one who later became President of the American Sociological Association, also studied sexuality, Kingsley Davis (1937, 1939). Some twenty years after Bowman lamented the absence of a sociology of sexuality, Edward Sagarin (1971) reiterated this

lament. "Here and there an investigation, a minor paper, a little data, particularly in the literature of criminology . . . and what at the time was called social disorganization . . . marked the totality of sex literature in sociology" (p. 384).

2 Placing all innovative homosexual studies in the 1970s and 1980s under the rubric of social constructionism and the project of minority theory simplifies matters. In particular, it marginalizes a powerful current of lesbian-feminist inspired theorizing (e.g., Rich [1980] 1983; MacKinnon 1989; Ferguson 1989). Much of this work was less concerned with issues of essentialism and constructionism or the rise of homosexual identities than analyzing the social forces creating, maintaining, and resisting the institution of heterosexuality. Departing from a tendency in constructionist studies to approach lesbian and gay theory as separate from feminism, this literature insists on tracing the link between a system of compulsive heterosexuality and patterns of male dominance.

References

Adam, Barry. 1987. *The Rise of a Gay and Lesbian Movement*. Boston: G. K. Hall and Co.

Allison, Dorothy. 1981. "Lesbian Politics in the '80s." *New York Native*, Dec. 7–20.

Altman, Dennis. 1971. *Homosexual Liberation and Oppression*. New York: Avon.

—— 1982. *The Homosexualization of America*. Boston: Beacon.

Anzaldua, Gloria and Moraga, Cherrie (eds). 1983. *This Bridge Called My Back*. New York: Kitchen Table Press.

Atkinson, Ti-Grace. 1974. *Amazon Odyssey*. New York: Links Books.

Bauman, Zygmunt. 1992. *Intimations of Postmodernity*. New York: Routledge.

Beam, Joseph (ed.). 1986. *In the Life*. Boston: Alyson.

Becker, Howard. 1963. *Outsiders*. New York: Free Press.

Berger, Peter and Luckmann, Thomas. 1967. *The Social Construction of Reality*. New York: Anchor.

Bergler, Edmund. 1956. *Homosexuality: Disease or Way of Life*. New York: Hill & Wang.

Bieber, Irving et al. 1962. *Homosexuality*. New York: Basic Books.

Birken, Lawrence. 1988. *Consuming Desire*. Ithaca, NY: Cornell University Press.

Bowman, Claude. 1949. "Cultural Ideology and Heterosexual Reality: A Preface to Sociological Research." *American Sociological Review*, 14: 624–33.

Bright, Susie. 1984. "The Year of the Lustful Lesbian." *New York Native*, July 30–Aug. 12.

Bunch, Charlotte. 1975. "Lesbians in Revolt." In Bunch and N. Myron (eds), *Lesbianism and the Women's Movement*. Baltimore: Diana Press.

Bunch, Charlotte. 1976. "Learning from Lesbian Separatism." *Ms*, Nov.

Butler, Judith. 1991. *Gender Trouble*. New York: Routledge.

Califia, Pat. 1981. "What is Gay Liberation?" *The Advocate*, June 25.

—— 1979. "A Secret Side of Lesbian Sexuality." *The Advocate*, Dec. 27.

Chauncey, George, Jr. 1982. "From Sexual Inversion to Homosexuality: Medicine and the Changing Conceptualization of Female Deviance." *Salmagundi*, 58/59: 114–46.

Clough, Patricia. 1994. *Feminist Social Thought*. Oxford: Blackwell.

Cory, Daniel Webster (psuedonym Edward Sagarin). 1951. *The Homosexual in America*. New York: Peter Nevill.

Culler, Jonathan. 1982. *On Deconstruction*. Ithaca, NY: Cornell University Press.

Davis, Katherine Benet. 1929. *Factors in the Sex Life of Twenty-Two Hundred Women*. New York: Harper and Brothers.

Davis, Kingsley, 1937. "The Sociology of Prostitution." *American Sociological Review*, 2: 744–55.

—— 1939. "Illegitimacy and the Social Structure." *American Journal of Sociology*, 45: 215–33.

D'Emilio, John. 1983. *Sexual Politics, Sexual Communities*. Chicago: University of Chicago Press.

—— and Freedman, Estelle. 1988. *Intimate Matters*. New York: Harper & Row.

de Lauretis, Teresa. 1991. "Queer Theory: Lesbian and Gay Sexualities." *Differences*, 3: iii–xviii.

Denzin, Norman. 1991. *Images of Postmodernism*. London: Sage.

Dickinson, Robert and Beam, Laura. 1932. *A Thousand Marriages*. Baltimore: Williams and Wilkins Co.

Doty, Alexander. 1993. *Making Things Perfectly Queer*. Minneapolis: University of Minnesota Press.

Duberman, Martin, Vicinus, Martha, and Chauncy, George, Jr. (eds). 1989. *Hidden From History*. New York: Meridian.

Epstein, Steven. 1987. "Gay Politics, Ethnic Identity: The Limits of Social Constructionism." *Socialist Review*, 93/94 (May–Aug.): 9–54.

Faderman, Lillian. 1981. *Surpassing the Love of Men*. New York: Morrow.

Ferguson, Ann. 1989. *Blood at the Root*. Boston: Pandora Press.

Foucault, Michel. 1980. *The History of Sexuality, Volume 1*. New York: Vintage.

Fuss, Diana (ed). 1991. *Inside/Out*. New York: Routledge.

Gagnon, John and Simon, William. 1967a. "Homosexuality: The Formulation of a Sociological Perspective." *Journal of Health and Social Behavior* 8: 177–85.

—— and——. 1967b. "The Lesbians: A Preliminary Overview." In Gagnon and Simon (eds), *Sexual Deviance*. New York: Harper & Row.

—— and——. 1973. *Sexual Conduct*. Chicago: Aldine.

Goffman, Erving. 1963. *Stigma*. Englewood Cliffs, NJ: Prentice-Hall.

Halperin, David. 1990. *One Hundred Years of Homosexuality*. New York: Routledge.

Harry, Joseph and Devall, William. 1978. *The Social Organization of Gay Males*. New York: Praeger.

Hemphill, Essex (ed.). 1991. *Brother to Brother*. Boston: Alyson.

Hennessy, Rosemary. 1995. "Queer Theory: A Review of the Differences Special Issue and Wittig's *The Straight Mind*." *Signs*, 18: 964–73.

Henslin, James (ed.). 1971. *Studies in the Sociology of Sex*. New York: Appleton-Century-Crofts.

Hoffman, Martin. 1968. *The Gay World*. New York: Basic Books.

Hooker, Evelyn. 1965. "Male Homosexuals and Their Worlds." In J. Marmor (ed.), *Sexual Inversion*, New York: Basic Books.

Humphreys, Laud. 1970. *Tearoom Trade*. Chicago: Aldine.

Irvine, Janice. 1990. *Disorders of Desire*. Philadelphia: Temple University Press.

Johnston, Jill. 1973. *Lesbian Nation*. New York: Harper & Row.

Katz, Jonathan. 1976. *Gay American History*. New York: Thomas Y. Crowell.

—— 1983. *Gay/Lesbian Almanac*. New York: Harper & Row.

Kinsey, Alfred et al. 1948. *Sexual Behavior in the Human Male*. Philadelphia: W. B. Saunders.

—— .1953. *Sexual Behavior in the Human Female*. Philadelphia, Penn.: W. B. Saunders.

Kirkham, George. 1971. "Homosexuality in Prison." In J. Henslin (ed.), *Studies in the Sociology of Sex*. New York: Appleton-Century-Crofts, pp. 325–49.

Lemert, Charles. 1995. *After the Crisis*. Boulder, Colo: Westview.

Levine, Martin. 1979a. "Gay Ghetto." *Journal of Homosexuality*, 4: 363–77.

—— (ed). 1979b. *The Sociology of Male Homosexuality*. New York: Harper & Row.

Lorde, Audre. 1984. *Sister Outsider*. Freedom, Calif: The Crossing Press.

McIntosh, Mary. 1968. "The Homosexual Role." See chapter 1 in this volume.

MacKinnon, Catherine. 1989. *Toward a Feminist Theory of the State*. Cambridge, Mass.: Harvard University Press.

Marriner, Gerald. 1972. "The Estrangement of the Intellectuals in America: The Search for New Life Styles in the Early Twentieth Century." Ph.D. dissertation, Dept. of History, University of Colorado.

Martin, Dell and Lyon, Phyllis. 1972. *Lesbian/Woman*. San Francisco: Glide.

Moraga, Cherrie. 1983. *Loving in the War Years*. Boston: South End Press.

Murray, Stephen. 1979. "The Institutional Elaboration of a Quasi-Ethnic Community." *International Review of Modern Sociology*, 9: 165–78.

Peiss, Kathy. 1986. *Cheap Amusements*. Philadelphia: Temple University Press.

Phelan, Shane. 1989. *Identity Politics*. Philadelphia: Temple University Press.

Plummer, Ken. 1975. *Stigma*. London: Routledge.

—— (ed). 1981. *The Making of the Modern Homosexual*. London: Hutchinson.

Reiss, Albert, Jr. 1964. "The Social Integration of Queers and Peers." *Social Problems*, 9: 102–20.

Reiss, Ira. 1967. *The Social Context of Premarital Sexual Permissiveness*. New York: Holt, Rinehart and Winston.

Rich, Adrienne. 1976. *Of Woman Born*. New York: W. W. Norton.

—— [1980] 1983. "Compulsory Heterosexuality and the Lesbian Existence" In A. Snitow et al. (eds), *Powers of Desire*. New York: Monthly Review Press pp. 177–205.

Rubin, Gayle, 1984. "Thinking Sex." C. Vance (ed.), *Pleasure and Danger*. Boston: Routledge, pp. 267–319.

Sagarin, Edward. 1969. *Odd Man In*. Chicago: Quadrangle Books.

—— 1971. "Sex Research and Sociology: Retrospective and Prospective." In J. Henslin (ed.), *Studies in the Sociology of Sex*. New York: Appleton-Century-Crofts, pp. 377–408.

Schur, Edwin. 1971. *Labeling Deviant Behavior*. New York: Harper & Row.

Sedgwick, Eve. 1991. *The Epistemology of the Closet*. Berkeley: University of California Press.

Seidman, Steven. 1991. *Romantic Longings*. New York: Routledge.

—— 1992. *Embattled Eros*. New York: Routledge.

—— .1993. "Identity and Politics in a Postmodern Gay Culture: Some Conceptual and Historial Notes." In M. Warner (ed.), *Fear of a Queer Planet*. Minneapolis: University of Minnesota Press.

—— .1994. *Contested Knowledge*. Oxford: Blackwell.

—— .1995. "Deconstructing Queer Theory or the Under-Theorizing of the Social and the Ethical." In L. Nicholson and S. Seidman (eds), *Social Postmodernism*. Cambridge: Cambridge University Press.

Simmons, Christina. 1982. "Marriage in the Modern Manner: Sexual Radicalism and Reform in America, 1914–1941." Ph.D. dissertation, Dept. of Brown University.

Smith-Rosenberg, Carroll. 1975. "The Female World of Love and Ritual: Relations Between Women in Nineteenth-Century America." *Signs*, 9: 1–29.

—— 1990. "Discourses of Sexuality and Subjectivity: The New Woman, 1870–1936." In M. Duberman et al. (eds), *Hidden from History*. New York: Penguin, pp. 264–80.

Socarides, Charles. 1968. *The Overt Homosexual*. New York: Grune and Stratton.

Stein, Edward (ed.). 1992. *Forms of Desire*. New York: Routledge.

Trimberger, Ellen Kay. 1983. "Feminism, Men, and Modern Love: Greenwich Village, 1900–1925." In A. Snitow et al. (eds), *Powers of Desire*. New York: Monthly Review Press, pp. 131–52.

Troiden, Richard. 1988. *Gay and Lesbian Identity*. New York: General Hall.

Trumbach, Randolph. 1977. "London's Sodomites: Homosexual Behavior and Western Culture in the Eighteenth Century." *Journal of Social History*, 11: 1–33.

Van de. Velde, Theodore [1930] 1950. *Ideal Marriage*. Westport, Conn.: Greenwood.

Warner, Michael (ed.). 1993. *Fear of a Queer Planet*. Minneapolis: University of Minnesota Press.

Warren, Carol. 1974. *Identity and Community in the Gay World.* New York: Wiley.

Weeks, Jeffrey. 1977. *Coming Out.* London: Quartet.

——.1985. *Sexuality and Its Discontents.* London: Routledge.

Weinberg, Martin and Williams, Colin. 1975. "Gay Baths and the Social Organization of Impersonal Sex." *Social Problems,* 23: 124–36.

Part I

Sociological Perspectives on Homosexual Desire

The Homosexual Role
Mary McIntosh

The Construction of Homosexuality
Jeffrey Weeks

Symbolic Interactionism and the Forms of Homosexuality
Ken Plummer

Capitalism, Bureaucracy, and Male Homosexuality
David F. Greenberg and Marcia H. Bystryn

Structural Foundations of the Gay World
Barry D. Adam

1

The Homosexual Role

Mary McIntosh

Recent advances in the sociology of deviant behavior have not yet affected the study of homosexuality, which is still commonly seen as a condition characterizing certain persons in the way that birthplace or deformity might characterize them. The limitations of this view can best be understood if we examine some of its implications. In the first place, if homosexuality is a condition, then people either have it or do not have it. Many scientists and ordinary people assume that there are two kinds of people in the world: homosexuals and heterosexuals. Some of them recognize that homosexual feelings and behavior are not confined to the persons they would like to call "homosexuals" and that some of these persons do not actually engage in homosexual behavior. This should pose a crucial problem, but they evade the crux by retaining their assumption and puzzling over the question of how to tell whether someone is "really" homosexual or not. Lay people too will discuss whether a certain person is "queer" in much the same way as they might question whether a certain pain indicated cancer. And in much the same way they will often turn to scientists or to medical men for a surer diagnosis. The scientists, for their part, feel it incumbent on them to seek criteria for diagnosis.

Thus one psychiatrist, discussing the definition of homosexuality, has written:

> I do not diagnose patients as homosexual unless they have engaged in overt homosexual behaviour. Those who also engage in heterosexual activity are diagnosed as bisexual. An isolated experience may not warrant the diagnosis, but repetitive homosexual behaviour in adulthood, whether sporadic or continuous, designates a homosexual. (Bieber 1965: 248)

Along with many other writers, he introduces the notion of a third type of person, the "bisexual," to handle the fact that behavior patterns cannot be conveniently dichotomized into heterosexual and homosexual. But this does not solve the conceptual problem, since bisexuality too is seen as a condition (unless as a passing response to unusual situations such as confinement in a one-sex prison). In any case there is no extended discussion of bisexuality; the topic is usually given a brief mention in order to clear the ground for the consideration of "true homosexuality."

To cover the cases where the symptoms of behavior or of felt attractions do not match the diagnosis, other writers have referred to an adolescent homosexual phase or have used such terms as "latent homosexual" or "pseudo homosexual." Indeed one of the earliest studies of the subject, by Krafft-Ebing (1965), was concerned with making a distinction between the "invert" who is congenitally homosexual and others who, although they behave in the same way, are not true inverts.

A second result of the conceptualization of homosexuality as a condition is that the major research task has been seen as the study of its etiology. There has been much debate as to whether the condition is innate or acquired. The first step in such research has commonly been to find a sample of "homosexuals" in the same way that a medical researcher might find a sample of diabetics if he wanted to study that disease. Yet after a long history of such studies, the results are sadly inconclusive, and the answer is still as much a matter of opinion as it was when Havelock Ellis's *Sexual Inversion* was published seventy years ago. The failure of research to answer the question has not been due to lack of scientific rigor or to any inadequacy of the available evidence; it results rather from the fact that the wrong question has been asked. One might as well try to trace the etiology of "committee chairmanship" or "Seventh Day Adventism" as of "homosexuality."

The vantage point of comparative sociology enables us to see that the conception of homosexuality as a condition is, in itself, a possible object of study. This conception and the behavior it supports operate as a form of social control in a society in which homosexuality is condemned. Furthermore the uncritical acceptance of the conception by social scientists can be traced to their concern with homosexuality as a social problem. They have tended to accept the popular definition of what the problem is, and they have been implicated in the process of social control.

The practice of the social labeling of persons as deviant operates in two ways as a mechanism of social control. In the first place it helps to provide a clear-cut, publicized, and recognizable threshold between permissible and impermissible behavior. This means that people cannot so easily drift into deviant behavior. Their first moves in a deviant direction immediately raise the question of a total move into a deviant role with all the sanctions that this is likely to elicit. Second, the labeling serves to segregate the deviants from others, and this means that their deviant practices and their self-justifications for these practices are contained within a relatively narrow group. The creation of a specialized, despised, and punished role of homosexual keeps the bulk of society pure in rather the same way that the similar treatment of some kinds of criminals helps keep the rest of society law-abiding.

However, the disadvantage of this practice as a technique of social control is that there may be a tendency for people to become fixed in their deviance once they have become labeled. This too is a process that has become well-recognized in discussion of other forms of deviant behavior, such as juvenile delinquency and drug taking, and indeed of other kinds of social labeling, such as streaming in schools and racial distinctions. One might expect social categorizations of this sort to be to some extent self-fulfilling prophecies: if the culture defines people as falling into distinct types – black and white, criminal and non-criminal, homosexual and normal – then these types will tend to become polarized, highly differentiated from each other. Later in this paper I shall discuss whether this is so in the case of homosexuals and "normals" in the United States today.

It is interesting to notice that homosexuals themselves welcome and support the notion that homosexuality is a condition. For just as the rigid categorization deters people from drifting into deviancy, so it appears to foreclose on the possibility of drifting back into normality and thus removes the element of anxious choice. It appears to justify the deviant behavior of the homosexual as being appropriate for him as a member of the homosexual category. The deviancy can thus be seen as legitimate for him and he can continue in it without rejecting the norms of the society.

The way in which people become labeled as homosexual can now be seen as an important social process connected with mechanisms of social control. It is important therefore that sociologists should examine this process objectively and not lend themselves to participation in it, particularly since, as we have seen, psychologists and psychiatrists on the whole have not retained their objectivity but have become involved as diagnostic agents in the process of social labeling.

It is proposed that the homosexual should be seen as playing a social role rather than as having a condition. The role of "homosexual," however, does not simply describe a sexual behavior pattern. If it did, the idea of a role would be no more useful than that of a condition. For the purpose of introducing the term "role" is to enable us to handle the fact that behavior in this sphere does not match popular beliefs: that sexual behavior patterns cannot be dichotomized in the way that the social roles of homosexual and heterosexual can.

It may seem rather odd to distinguish in this way between role and behavior, but if we accept a definition of role in terms of expectations (which may or may not be fulfilled), then the distinction is both legitimate and useful. In modern societies where a separate homosexual role is recognized, the expectation, on behalf of those who play the role and of others, is that a homosexual will be exclusively or very predominantly homosexual in his feelings and behavior. In addition there are other expectations that frequently exist, especially on the part of non-homosexuals, but affecting the self-conception of anyone who sees himself as homosexual. These are the expectation that he will be effeminate in manner, personality, or preferred sexual activity, the expectation that sexuality will play a part of some kind in all his relations with other men, and the expectation that he will be attracted to boys and very young men and probably willing to seduce them. The existence of a social expectation, of course, commonly helps to produce its own fulfillment. But the question of how far it is fulfilled is a matter for empirical investigation rather than *a priori* pronouncement.

In order to clarify the nature of the role and demonstrate that it exists only in certain societies, we shall present the cross-cultural and historical evidence available. This raises awkward problems of method because the material has hitherto usually been collected and analysed in terms of culturally specific modern Western conceptions.

The Homosexual Role in Various Societies

To study homosexuality in the past or in other societies we usually have to rely on secondary evidence rather than on direct observation. The reliability and the validity of such evidence is open to question because what the original observers reported may have been distorted by their disapproval of homosexuality and by their definition of it, which may be different from the one we wish to adopt. . . .

Allowing for such weaknesses, the Human Relations Area Files are the best single source of comparative information. Their evidence on homosexuality has been summarized by Ford and Beach (1952), who identify two broad types of accepted patterns: the institutionalized homosexual role and the liaison between men and boys who are otherwise heterosexual.

The recognition of a distinct role of *berdache* or transvestite is, they say, "the commonest form of institutionalized homosexuality." This form shows a marked similarity to that in our own society, though in some ways it is even more extreme. The Mojave Indians of California and Arizona, for example, recognized both an *alyhā*, a male transvestite who took the role of the woman in sexual intercourse, and a *hwamē*, a female homosexual who took the role of the male. People were believed to be born as *alyhā* or *hwamē*, hints of their future proclivities occurring in their mothers' dreams during pregnancy. If a young boy began to behave like a girl and take an interest in women's things instead of men's, there was an initiation ceremony in which he would become an *alyhā*. After that he would dress and act like a woman, would be referred to as "she" and could take "husbands."

But the Mojave pattern differs from ours in that although the *alyhā* was considered regretable and amusing, he was not condemned and was given public recognition. The attitude was that "he was an *alyhā*, he could not help it." But the "husband" of an *alyhā* was an ordinary man who happened to have chosen an *alyhā*, perhaps because they were good housekeepers or because they were believed to be "lucky in love," and he would be the butt of endless teasing and joking.

This radical distinction between the feminine, passive homosexual and his masculine, active partner is one which is not made very much in our own society, but which is very important in the Middle East. There, however, neither is thought of as being a "born" homosexual, although the passive partner, who demeans himself by his feminine submission, is despised and ridiculed while the active one is not. In most of the ancient Middle East, including among the Jews until the return from the Babylonian exile, there were male temple prostitutes. Thus even cultures that recognize a separate homosexual role may not define it in the same way as our culture does.

Many other societies accept or approve of homosexual liaisons as part of a variegated sexual pattern. Usually these are confined to a particular stage in the individual's life. Among the Aranda of Central Australia, for instance, there are long-standing relationships of several years' duration between unmarried men and young boys, starting at the age of 10 to 12 years (Ford and Beach 1952: 132). This is rather similar to the well-known situation in classical Greece, but there, of course, the older man could have a wife as well. Sometimes, however, as among the Siwans of North Africa (Ford and Beach 1952: 131–2), all men and boys can and are expected to engage in homosexual activities, apparently at every stage of life. In all of these societies there may be much homosexual behaviour, but there are no "homosexuals."

The Development of the Homosexual Role in England

The problem of method is even more acute in dealing with historical material than with anthropological, for history is usually concerned with "great events" rather than with recurrent patterns. There are some records of attempts to curb sodomy among minor churchmen during the medieval period (May 1938: 65, 101), which seem to indicate that it was common. At least they suggest that laymen feared on behalf of their sons that it was common. The term "catamite," meaning "boy kept for immoral purposes," was first used in 1593, again suggesting that this practice was common then. But most of the historical references to homosexuality relate either to great men or to great scandals. However, over the last seventy years or so various scholars have tried to trace the history of sex, and it is possible to glean a good deal from what they have found and also from what they have failed to establish.

Their studies of English history before the seventeenth century consist usually of inconclusive speculation as to whether certain men, such as Edward II, Christopher Marlowe, William Shakespeare, were or were not homosexual. Yet the disputes are inconclusive not because of lack of evidence but because none of these men fits the modern stereotype of the homosexual.

It is not until the end of the seventeenth century that other kinds of information become available, and it is possible to move from speculations about individuals to descriptions of homosexual life. At this period references to homosexuals as a type and to a rudimentary homosexual subculture, mainly in London, begin to appear. But the earliest descriptions of homosexuals do not coincide exactly with the modern conception. There is much more stress on effeminacy and in particular on transvestism, to such an extent that there seems to be no distinction at first between transvestism and homosexuality. The terms emerging at this period to describe homosexuals – Molly, Nancy-boy, Madge-cull – emphasize effeminacy. In contrast the modern terms – like fag, queer, gay, bent – do not have this implication.

By the end of the seventeenth century, homosexual transvestites were a distinct enough group to be able to form their own clubs in London. Edward Ward's *History of the London Clubs*, first published in 1709, describes one called "The Mollie's Club" which met "in a certain tavern in the City" for "parties and regular gatherings." The members "adopt[ed] all the small vanities natural to the feminine sex to such an extent that they try to speak, walk, chatter, shriek and scold as women do, aping them as well in other respects." The other respects apparently included the enactment of marriages and childbirth. The club was discovered and broken up by agents of the Reform Society. There were a number of similar scandals during the course of the eighteenth century as various homosexual coteries were exposed.

A writer in 1729 describes the widespread homosexual life of the period:

> They also have their Walks and Appointments, to meet and pick up one another, and their particular Houses of Resort to go to, because they dare not trust themselves in an open Tavern. About twenty of these sort of Houses have been discovered, besides the Nocturnal Assemblies of great numbers of the like vile Persons, what they call the Markets, which are the Royal Exchange, Lincoln's Inn, Bog Houses, the south side of St James's Park, the Piazzas in Covent Garden, St Clement's Churchyard, etc.
>
> It would be a pretty scene to behold them in their clubs and cabals, how they assume the air and affect the name of Madam or Miss, Betty or Molly, with a chuck under the chin, and "Oh you bold pullet, I'll break your eggs," and then frisk and walk away. [Taylor 1965: 142]

The notion of exclusive homosexuality became well established during this period:

> two Englishmen, Leith and Drew, were accused of paederasty. . . . The evidence given by the plaintiffs was, as was generally the case in these trials, very imperfect. On the other hand the defendants denied the accusation, and produced witnesses to prove their predeliction for women. They were in consequence acquitted. [Bloch 1938: 334]

This could only have been an effective argument in a society that perceived homosexual behaviour as incompatible with heterosexual tastes.

During the nineteenth century there are further reports of raided clubs and homosexual brothels. However, by this time the element of transvestism had diminished in importance. Even the male prostitutes are described as being of masculine build, and there is more stress upon sexual licence and less upon dressing up and play-acting. . . .

Conclusion

This paper has dealt with only one small aspect of the sociology of homosexuality. It is, nevertheless, a fundamental one. For it is not until he sees homosexuals as a social category, rather than a medical or psychiatric one, that the sociologist can begin to ask the right questions about the specific content of the homosexual role and about the organization and functions of homosexual groups. All that has been done here is to indicate that the role does not exist in many societies, that it only emerged in England towards the end of the seventeenth century, and that, although the existence of the role in modern America appears to have some effect on the distribution of homosexual behaviour, such behaviour is far from being monopolized by persons who play the role of homosexual.

References

Bieber, I. 1965. *Homosexuality*. New York: Basic Books.
Bloch, I. 1938. *Sexual Life in England, Past and Present*. London: Francis Alder.
Ford, C. S. and Beach, F. 1952. *Patterns of Sexual Behavior*. London: Metheun.
Krafft-Ebing, R. Von 1965. *Psychopathia Sexualis*. New York: G. P. Putnam's & Sons.
May, G. 1938. *Social Control of Sex*. London: Allen & Unwin.

2

The Construction of Homosexuality

Jeffrey Weeks

Homosexuality: Concepts and Consequences

Most works on the history of sex tend to concentrate on the major forms of sexual experience to the exclusion of the minority forms. This is not surprising given the centrality in our society of the great rituals of birth, maturation, pair-bonding, and reproduction. But to ignore extra-marital, non-reproductive, non- monogamous, or even non-heterosexual forms is to stifle an important aspect of our social history. Nor indeed are they independent aspects. The regulation of extra-marital sex has been a major concern for the forces of moral order throughout the history of the West, whether through the canonical controls of the church over adultery and sodomy in the medieval period, or the state's ordering of prostitution and homosexuality in the modern.

Of all the "variations" of sexual behaviour, homosexuality has had the most vivid social pressure, and has evoked the most lively (if usually grossly misleading) historical accounts. It is, as many sexologists from Havelock Ellis to Alfred Kinsey have noted, the form closest to the heterosexual norm in our culture, and partly because of that it has often been the target of sustained social oppression. It has also, as an inevitable effect of the hostility it has evoked, produced the most substantial forms of resistance to hostile categorization and has, consequently, a long cultural and subcultural history. A study of homosexuality is therefore essential, both because of its own intrinsic interest and because of the light it throws on the wider regulation of sexuality, the development of sexual categorization, and the range of possible sexual identities.

In recent years it has become increasingly clear, first to sociologists, and belatedly to historians, that it is essential to distinguish between on the one hand, homosexual behavior, and on the other homosexual roles, categorizations, and identities.[1] It has been apparent to anthropologists and sexologists since at least the nineteenth century that homosexual behaviour has existed in a variety of different cultures, and that it is an ineradicable part of human sexual possibilities. But what has been equally apparent are the range of different responses towards homosexuality. Attitudes towards homosexual behavior are, that is to say, culturally specific and have varied enormously across different cultures and through various historical periods. What is less obvious, but is now central to any historical work, is the realization not only that *attitudes* towards same sex activity have varied but that the social and subjective meanings given to homosexuality have similarly been culturally specific. Bearing this in mind it is no longer possible to talk of the possibility of a universalistic history of homosexuality; it is only possible to understand the social significance of homosexual behavior, both in terms of social response and in terms of individual identity, in its exact historical context. To put it another way, the various possibilities of same sex behavior are variously constructed in different cultures as an aspect of wider gender and sexual regulation. The physical acts might be similar, but their social implications are often profoundly different. In our culture homosexuality has become an excoriated experience, severely socially condemned at various periods, and even today seen as a largely unfortunate, minority form by a large percentage of the population. It is this that demands explanation.

The general tendency is still to assume that "deviance," and especially sexual unorthodoxy, is somehow a quality inherent in the individuals, to which the social then has to respond. Over the past twenty years, however, it has been increasingly recognized that the social not only defines, but actually in part constructs the deviance. The classic statement of the impact of social labeling was made by Edwin Lemert, who drew a distinction between what he termed "primary" and "secondary" deviance, the first being intrinsic, for whatever reason, to the individual, the second the result of social definition.[2] This suggests that there are two levels of analysis, one of which is more susceptible to historical understanding than the other. First of all there is the question of the actual creation of gendered and sexed individuals, whether as heterosexual or homosexual. Recent advances in social psychology and in neo-Freudian thought have suggested that the development of heterosexual or homosexual propensities at the level of the young human are not a product of inherent biological imperatives but are the effect of historically conditioned familial and other social influences channeling the sexual possibilities which exist in the young child.[3] It is quite possible, that is to say, that changing family forms, changing notions of childhood, of the role of parents and so on actually have profound effects in the construction of individual heterosexuals, homosexuals, or other sexual categorizations. Emotions are differentially structured according to different social forms and pressures. But even if primary differences were biologically formed, this would not fundamentally alter the argument. For secondly, what makes this *historically* important are the social reactions to the sexed individuals that emerge in any particular form of society, and the ways in which these shape individual meanings. For to feel or experience something is not the same thing as to adopt a specific social identity, with all its often problematical effects. The historical problem therefore is to explain the various sources of the social stigmatization of homosexuality, and the individual and collective response to this broadly hostile regulation. But the way to do this is not to seek out a single causative factor. The crucial question must be: what are the conditions for the emergence of this particular form of regulation of sexual behaviour in this particular society? In our own history this must involve an exploration of what Mary McIntosh pinpointed as the significant problem: the emergence of the notion that homosexuality is a psychological or emotional condition peculiar to some people and not others, and the social implications of this conceptualization.

Mary McIntosh herself has theorized this, in a highly suggestive essay, in terms of the emergence of what she describes as a "homosexual role."[4] That is to say, under specific historical circumstances, which McIntosh traces to the late seventeenth century, there emerges a specific male (and it has usually been a male) role, a specialized, despised and punished role which "keeps the bulk of society pure in rather the same way that the similar treatment of some kinds of criminal helps keep the rest of society law abiding."[5] Such a role has two effects: it helps to provide a clear-cut threshold between permissible and impermissible behavior; and secondly, it helps to segregate those labeled as deviant from others, and thus contains and limits their behavior patterns. In the same way, a homosexual subculture, which is the correlative of the development of a specialized role, provides both access to the socially outlawed need (sex) and contains the deviant.

This insight has been enormously influential but, as in all exploratory essays, it has left many questions unanswered. More recent work has attempted to challenge it both in terms of its relationship to role theory and functionalism generally, and because of its apparent denial of any pre-given sexual orientation.[6] This however is to misconstrue its real importance. The essay itself suffers from the usual defects of a

structuralist-functionalist approach, particularly in the purposive
effort at social control that it implies. But what it points to is an
approach that can bear much historical fruit, indicating the necessity
of studying homosexuality (as with other forms of sexual behavior)
both in terms of the social categorization that shapes the experience,
and in terms of the response itself, which in relationship to homosexuality has, over a long historical development, given rise to complex
cultural and subcultural forms, and a distinctive series of sexual identities. These identities must, however, be understood in all their specificities, historical, class, and gender. This last point is particularly
important because though social scientists and historians have, by and
large, sought to explain male and female homosexualities in terms of
the same etiologies and characteristics, their social histories, though
obviously related, are distinctive. For both male and female homosexualities are social and historical divisions of the range of sexual possibilities and as such have to be understood in terms of their social
implications.[7]

Moral, Legal, and Medical Regulation

There is a long tradition in the Christian West of hostility towards
homosexuality, although this usually took the form of the formal
regulation of male homosexual activity rather than of lesbian. The
West during the Christian era was in fact unique in its taboo against
all forms of homosexuality. Cross-cultural evidence demonstrates very
clearly that other cultures have successfully integrated some forms at
least of homosexual behavior into its sexual *mores*, whether in the
form of the socially accepted pedagogic relations common to ancient
Greece, or in the development of the transvestite (berdache) roles in
certain tribal societies.[8] But though persistent, the Christian taboos
against homosexuality have varied in strength throughout time and
have had differential effects on male and female homosexual behavior.
In England before 1885 the only legislation which *directly* affected
homosexual behavior was in fact that referring to sodomy. This "sin
against nature," the crime not to be named amongst Christians, evoked
acute horrors. The classic position was summed up by the jurist, Sir
William Blackstone, in the late eighteenth century, who felt that its
very mention was "a disgrace to human nature." But this defiance of
nature's will was not a solely homosexual offence. The 1533 Act of
Henry VIII which first brought buggery within the scope of statute
law, superseding ecclesiastical law, adopted the same criterion as the

church: all acts of buggery were equally condemned as being "against nature," whether between man and woman, man and beast, or man and man. The penalty for "the abominable vice of buggery" was death, and the death penalty continued on the statute books, formally at least, until 1861. This enactment was the basis for all homosexual convictions up to 1885 in England and Wales. Other forms of homosexual activity were subsumed under the major form either as assault or as attempts at the major crime. The central point we must grasp was that the law was directed against a series of sexual acts, not a particular type of *person*, although in practice most people prosecuted under the buggery laws were probably prosecuted for homosexual behavior (sodomy). It seems likely that homosexuality was regarded not as a particular attribute of a certain type of person but as a potential in all sensual creatures. The prime task seems to have been protection of reproductive sex in marriage. The law against sodomy was a central aspect of the regulation of all non-procreative sex and it was directed at men. Though lesbian behavior was variously condemned its threat was less explicitly recognized in legal regulation, in Anglo-Saxon cultures at least.[9]

The "sin against nature" seems to have evoked a peculiar hostility. One of the sailors court-martialed for buggery on HMS *Africaine* in 1815 spoke of "a crime which would to God t'were never more seen on earth from those shades of hellish darkness whence to the misery of Man its propensity has been vomited forth."[10] The epithet "sodomite" was certainly one to be feared throughout the nineteenth century. In the early part of the century there is some evidence of great public antipathy towards convicted sodomites, while in 1895 Oscar Wilde was stirred into his disastrous libel case against the Marquis of Queensberry after being accused of posing, in his inimitable misspelling, as a "somdomite." As Lord Sumner put it in 1918, setting the stamp of an admired judge on social stigmatization, sodomites were stamped with "the hallmark of a specialised and extraordinary class as much as if they had carried on their bodies some physical peculiarities."[11]

Despite this evidence it is difficult to trace in any detail the actual enforcement of the sodomy law or to understand the sorts of sexual identities that those prosecuted under it developed. Its enforcement varied throughout time and between different social classes. There seems to have been a spate of convictions at the end of the seventeenth century and in the 1720s, coinciding significantly enough with morality crusades and the emergence of a distinctive male homosexual subculture in some of the larger cities. And there appears to have been an increase in prosecutions in the first third of the nineteenth century when more than 50 men were hanged for sodomy in England. In one year, 1806, there were more executions for sodomy than for murder, while in 1810 four out of five convicted sodomists were hanged.[12] The law appears to have been particularly severe on members of the armed forces, where it was often employed with particularly dramatic and exemplary results. In 1811 Ensign John Hepburn and Drummer Thomas White were "launched into eternity" before a "vast concourse of spectators" including many notables and members of the Royal Family. And in February 1816, four members of the crew of the *Africaine* were hanged for buggery after a major naval scandal. Buggery has been mentioned in the articles of war since the seventeenth century and was treated as seriously as desertion, mutiny, or murder.[13]

There does seem to be a pattern, certainly in the early nineteenth century, of an increase in the prosecution of buggery related to whether or not Britain was at war or in a state of social turmoil; as in later periods, homosexual behavior was often a funnel for wider social anxieties. Efforts to remove the death penalty for sodomy were generally unsuccessful. Sir Robert Peel reaffirmed it in his reforms, in 1826; and when Lord John Russell attempted to remove "unnatural offences" from the list of capital crimes in 1841 he was forced to withdraw through lack of parliamentary support. In practice, however, the death penalty was not applied after the 1830s, and was finally removed in 1861 (to be replaced by sentences of between ten years and life imprisonment).

Severe as the law was in theory, it was a catch-all rather than a refined legal weapon, reflecting a generalized legal control rather than detailed individual surveillance. As late as 1817 a man was sentenced to death under the sodomy laws for oral sex with a boy (he was later pardoned), and the term "unnatural crimes" often covered a multitude of meanings, from bestiality to birth control. The uncertain status of sodomy was underlined in the notorious prosecution of the two transvestites, Ernest Boulton and Frederick William Park, who with others were tried for conspiracy to commit sodomite acts in the early 1870s. Police, legal, and medical attitudes were manifestly confused. When Boulton and Park were arrested in 1870 for indecent behavior (constituted by their public cross-dressing), they were immediately examined, without authorization, for evidence of sodomy. It becomes clear from the transcripts of the trial (itself a major public event, held before the Lord Chief Justice in Westminster Hall and producing saturation press coverage) that neither the police nor the court were familiar with the patterns of male homosexuality. The opening remarks of the

Attorney General hinted that it was their transvestism, their soliciting men as *women* which was the core of their crime. A Dr. Paul, who examined them for sodomy on their arrest, had never encountered a similar case in his whole career. His only knowledge came from a half-remembered case history in Alfred Swaine Taylor's *Medical Jurisprudence*. But even Dr. Taylor himself, who gave evidence in the case, had had no previous experience apart from this case, and the other doctors called in could not agree on what the signs of sodomitical activity were. The Attorney General observed that: "It must be a matter of rare occurrence in this country at least for any person to be discovered who has any propensity for the practices which are imputed to them.[14] Their only recourse to the "scientific" literature that was by then appearing was to the French, and then reluctantly. Dr. Paul had never heard of the work of Tardieu, who had investigated over 200 cases of sodomy for purposes of legal proof, until an anonymous letter informed him of its existence. The Attorney General suggested that it was fortunate that there was "very little learning or knowledge upon this subject in this country." One of the defense counsel was more bitter, attacking Dr. Paul for relying on "the newfound treasures of French literature upon the subject – which thank God is still foreign to the libraries of British surgeons."[15]

What is striking in all this is that as late as 1871, concepts of homosexuality were extremely undeveloped both in the Metropolitan Police and in high medical and legal circles, suggesting the absence of any clear notion of a homosexual category or of any social awareness of what a homosexual identity might consist of. Certainly from the early seventeenth century, if not earlier, there was a widespread appreciation of the existence of a sort of transvestite and male prostitution subculture, and by the early nineteenth century it was often assumed in court cases that a married man was less likely to be guilty of buggery offences with another man.[16] But even this issue was a matter of debate in the Boulton and Park case in 1871. Such popular notions as did exist invariably associated male homosexual behavior with effeminacy and probably transvestism as well. The counter-evidence that was present always produced surprise. The author of *The Phoenix of Sodom*, published in 1813, was amazed to discover that males who prostituted themselves were often not effeminate men, but coalmerchants, police runners, drummers, waiters, servants, and a grocer.[17] There was no awareness of homosexuality constituting the center of a life "career." Even Jeremy Bentham, the utilitarian philosopher, who had produced extraordinarily advanced views at the turn of the eighteenth and nineteenth centuries, almost always conceived of sodomites as "bisexual," capable of marriage, and attracted to adolescent boys, rather than as adult men who love other adult men.[18]

The latter part of the nineteenth century, however, saw the clear emergence of new conceptualizations of homosexuality although the elements of the new definitions and practices can be traced to earlier periods. The sodomite, as Foucault has put it, was a temporary aberration. The "homosexual," on the other hand, belonged to a species, and it is this new concern with the homosexual person, both in legal practice and in psychological and medical categorization, that marks the crucial change, both because it provided a new subject of social observation and speculation, and because it opened up the possibility of new modes of self-articulation. It is precisely at this period that we see the development of new terms to describe those interested in the same sex. The adoption in the last decades of the nineteenth century of words like "homosexual" or "invert," both by sexologists and by the homosexuals themselves, marked as crucial a change in consciousness as did the widespread adoption of the term "gay" in the 1970s. Changing legal and medical attitudes were important elements in this development. The 1861 Offences Against the Person Act represented a formal move towards civilization and removed the death penalty for buggery (replacing it by sentences of between ten years and life). In the next twenty years there is clear evidence in the Home Office files of attempts to distinguish the various forms of buggery, which in practice meant a separation of bestiality from homosexual activity, which was being more closely defined as an individual trait.[19] This in turn was being more directly controlled. By the famous Labouchère Amendment to the Criminal Law Amendment Act of 1885, acts of gross indecency between men were as "misdemeanors" made punishable by up to two years' hard labor, and this in effect brought within the scope of the law all forms of male homosexual activity. In 1898 the Vagrancy Act tightened up the law relating to importuning for "immoral purposes" and this was effectively applied exclusively against homosexual men. By a further Criminal Law Amendment Act in 1912, the sentence for this offence was set at six months' imprisonment with flogging for a second offense, on summary jurisdiction.[20]

Henry Labouchère stated that his stimulus to introduce this amendment was a report on male prostitution sent to him by W. T. Stead, and he argued that its introduction was essentially to facilitate proof.[21] The new laws were of course formally less repressive than the sodomy law, which still carried for a while a maximum of life imprisonment. Moreover the application of the laws varied throughout time and between different places at different times, with juries still reluctant to convict. There was even some opposition at governmental level to the fact that the Labouchère Amendment applied to private as well as public behavior. The Director of Public Prosecutions noted in 1889 "the expediency of not giving unnecessary publicity" to cases of gross indecency; and at the same time he felt that much could be said for allowing "private persons – being full grown men – to indulge their unnatural tastes in private." Often it seems juries were reluctant to convict, while the police directed a blind eye to private activity before the First World War, as long as "public decency" was not too offended.[22] When the law was applied however, as it was for instance in the case of Oscar Wilde in 1895, it was applied with rigor, with the maximum penalty of two years' hard labor under the 1885 Act often being enforced. Similarly, the clauses against importuning were vigorously applied. Compared to the shillings fine imposed on female prostitutes under the Vagrancy Act, the maximum sentence of six months' imprisonment for men under the same provision ground particularly hard on male homosexuals, particularly as a prosecution was usually associated with social obloquy and moral revulsion. As a libertarian writer observed in the 1930s, speaking of private enforcements by the Public Morality Council, "It is gratifying to note that in respect of female soliciting action is only taken where actual annoyance or disorderly conduct are apparent. All cases of importuning by male persons are however reported."[23] The law did not *create* hostility, but as part of a wider restructuring of the social regulation of sex, it helped shape a new mood, particularly in its operation. Perhaps even more important than the individual prosecutions were the outbursts of moral panic that often accompanied some of the more sensational cases. This was particularly exemplified in the furore surrounding the "Three Trials" of Oscar Wilde in 1895. The downfall of Oscar Wilde was a most significant event for it created a public image for the "homosexual," a term by now coming into use, and a terrifying moral tale of the dangers that trailed closely behind deviant behavior. The Wilde trials were in effect labeling processes of a most explicit kind drawing a clear border between acceptable and abhorrent behavior. But they also of course had paradoxical effects. As Havelock Ellis said of the Oscar Wilde trials, they appeared "to have generally contributed to give definiteness and self-consciousness to the manifestations of homosexuality, and to have aroused inverts to take up a definite stand."[24] It seems likely that the new forms of legal regulation, whatever their vagaries in application, had the effect of forcing home to many the fact of their difference and thus creating a new community of knowledge, if not of life and feeling, amongst many men with homosexual leanings. There was clear evidence in the later decades of the nineteenth century of the development of a new sense of identity amongst many homosexual individuals, and a crucial element in this would undoubtedly have been the new public salience of homosexuality, dramatised by the legal situation.

The changing legal situation was intricately associated with the emergence of a "medical model" of homosexuality which helped provide theoretical explanation for the individualizing of the crime. The most commonly quoted European writers on homosexuality in the mid-1870s were Casper and Tardieu, the leading medical and legal experts of Germany and France respectively, and both seemed to have been primarily concerned with the need to define the new type of "degenerates" who were coming before the courts, and to test whether they could be held legally responsible for their acts.[25] The same problem was apparent in Britain. Most of the works on homosexuality that appeared up to the First World War were directed, in part at least, at the legal profession. Even J. A. Symonds's privately printed pamphlet *A Problem in Modern Ethics* declared itself to be addressed "especially to medical psychologists and jurists," while Havelock Ellis's *Sexual Inversion* (1897) was attacked for its opposite policy, for not being published by the medical press and being too popular in tone. The medicalization of homosexuality – a transition from notions of sin to concepts of sickness or mental illness – was a vitally significant move, even though, like the new legal model, its application was uneven. Around it the poles of scientific discourse raged for decades: was homosexuality congenital or acquired, ineradicable or susceptible to cure, to be quietly if unenthusiastically accepted as unavoidable (even the liberal Havelock Ellis in his pioneering study of homosexuality found it necessary to warn his invert reader not to "set himself in violent opposition" to his society), or to be resisted with all the force of one's Christian will?[26] Older notions of the immorality or sinfulness of homosexual behavior did not of course die in the nineteenth century. But from the nineteenth century they were inextricably entangled with would-be scientific theory which formed the boundaries against and within which homosexuals had to define themselves.

What in effect many of the pioneering sexologists of the late nineteenth and early twentieth centuries were doing was to develop the notion that homosexuality was the characteristic of a particular type of person. Karl Westphal, for instance, in the 1860s described a "contrary sexual feeling" and argued that homosexuality was a product of moral insanity resulting from "congenital reversal of sexual feeling." Karl Ulrichs, a German lawyer and writer and himself homosexually inclined, who pioneered congenital theories in Germany from the 1860s, argued that the "urning" was the product of the anomalous development of the originally undifferentiated human embryo, resulting in a female mind in a male body or vice versa. The theories of an intermediate sex popularized by Edward Carpenter in the early twentieth century were logical extensions of Ulrichs' ideas. On a more scientific level, the great German sexologist Magnus Hirschfeld was able to develop notions of a third sex and to integrate into this notion discoveries of the significance of hormones in the development of sexual differentiation. Hormonal explanations also supplement Ellis's congenital theories. Many of these ideas in turn were taken up by homosexual apologists to form the basis for an explanation of homosexuality which was free of the pejorative implications of the sin or moral-weakness theories.

Alongside these congenital theories, environmentalist notions of corruption of "degeneration" continued to flourish. And discussion continued as to whether, as liberals like Havelock Ellis agreed, homosexuality was a congenital and relatively harmless "anomaly," or whether it was evidence of moral insanity or mental sickness. The sickness theory of homosexuality was to have profound social reasonance from the 1930s onwards, but even earlier many homosexuals themselves had a deeply rooted belief that they were sick. Oscar Wilde complained in prison that he had been led astray by "erotomania" and extravagant sexual appetite which indicated temporary mental collapse.[27] Sir Roger Casement, the Irish patriot, thought his homosexuality was a terrible disease which ought to be cured, while Goldsworthy Lowes Dickinson, a liberal humanist famed for his rationalism, believed his homosexuality to be a misfortune: "I am like a man born crippled."[28] With such a deeply rooted self-conception often went a willingness to accept a hegemony of (often dubious) medical knowledge and that in turn encouraged would-be cures, from hypnotism through to chemical experimentation and in the 1960s to aversion therapy.[29] But in the early decades of the twentieth century the medical model still to a large extent stayed at the level of theory and most doctors seemed to have been indifferent to or ignorant of the phenomena, reflecting as usual all the prejudices of the wider society. The old morality rather than the new psychology retained its influence until at least the inter-war years. Nevertheless, the existence of a medical model was profoundly to shape the individualization of homosexuality, and contribute to the construction of the notion of a distinct homosexual person.

Although the theorizing of homosexuality applied indifferently to males and females, it is striking that it was male homosexuality that was chiefly subject to new regulation. Lesbianism continued to be ignored by the criminal codes. An attempt in 1921 to introduce provisions against lesbianism similar to those of the Labouchère Amendment ultimately failed to get through Parliament, and the reasons were instructive. Lord Desart, who had been Director of Public Prosecutions when Wilde was indicated, opposed the provision with the comment: "You are going to tell the whole world that there is such an offence, to bring it to the notice of women who have never heard of it, never thought of it, never dreamt of it. I think that is a very great mischief." Lord Birkenhead, the Lord Chancellor made the same point: "I would be bold enough to say that of every thousand women, taken as a whole, 999 have never even heard a whisper of these practices. Among all these, in the homes of this country . . . the taint of this noxious and horrible suspicion is to be imparted."[30] It is clear in such comments that there was both an awareness of the contradictory effect of severe laws against homosexual behavior, and a belief that the control of male homosexuality was of greater social salience than of female. It was not that lesbian behavior was approved – but it did not enter the same domain of debate as male homosexuality.

It is this preoccupation with male sexuality that allows us to indicate at least some of the concerns which acted as preconditions for the refinement of social regulations in the latter part of the nineteenth century. These cannot be understood by trying to locate a simple programme of social control. On the contrary, it seems likely that the changes in attitudes towards homosexuality were often unintended consequences of other major changes. What was happening was that the ensemble of traditional assumptions was meeting new categorization and together being transformed by a series of intersecting influences.

An important factor here was the renewed emphasis in the social-purity campaigns of the latter part of the nineteenth century on the dangers of male lust, and on the necessity for public decency. It is striking that the social-purity campaigners of the 1880s saw both prostitution and male homosexuality as products of undifferentiated male desire and it is significant in this respect that the major enactments affecting male homosexuality from the 1880s (the Labouchère Amendment, the 1898 Vagrancy Act, the 1912 Criminal Law Amendment Act) were aspects of the general moral restructuring, and were primarily concerned with female prostitution. Indeed, as late as the 1950s it was still seen as logical to set up a single government committee – the Wolfenden Committee – to study both prostitution and male homosexuality. In the debates before the 1885 Criminal Law Amendment Act was rushed through Parliament, male homosexual behavior was quite clearly linked with the activities of those who corrupted young girls. What was at stake was on the one hand the uncontrolled lusts of certain types of men, and on the other the necessary sanctity of the sexual bond within marriage.[31]

At this point several apparently extraneous themes intervene, which in particular demonstrate the influence of the new attitudes towards childhood and adolescence. The progress of civilization, the headmaster of Clifton College, Bristol, the Reverend J. M. Wilson, intoned in the 1880s, was in the direction of purity. This was threatened by sins of the flesh which undermined both the self and the nation. He advised his students to "strengthen your will by practice: subdue your flesh by hard work and hard living; by temperance; by avoiding all luxury and effeminacy, and all temptation."[32] Such beliefs and adjurations constantly invade the discussion of and responses to homosexuality.

In the scandals around the Cleveland Street brothel in 1889/90 and in the Oscar Wilde scandal, the corruption of youth was again a central issue. The Director of Public Prosecutions, reflecting on the Cleveland Street scandal, observed that there was a duty "to enforce the law and protect the children of respectable parents taken into the service of the public . . . from being made the victims of the unnatural lusts of full grown men."[33] The efforts through the raising of the age of consent for girls to 16 to prevent the seduction of minors was therefore paralleled by the regulation of male homosexual behavior. In the mythology of the twentieth century the homosexual, as the archetypal sexed being, a person whose sexuality pervaded him in his very existence, threatened to corrupt all around him and particularly the young. The most pervasive stereotype of the male homosexual was as a "corrupter of youth."

Another vital complex of attitudes, those associated with imperialist sentiment, also entered the development of attitudes towards homosexuality. Here there was a complex pattern related not only to the notion of corruption and degeneration but also to the vital importance of the family to imperial security. Attitudes to homosexuality have of course long been linked to fears of imperial decline, from Gibbon's description of the decline and fall of the roman empire, through to those who opposed homosexual law reform in the 1960s. These had no more relevance in the 1880s than at other times. But to the social-purity advocate it was lust which threatened both the family and national decay. "Rome fell; other nations have fallen; and if England falls it will be this sin, and her unbelief in God, that will have been her ruin."[34] The puritan emphasis on the family, and on sexual life as being necessarily confined to the marital bed, offered an antidote to social crisis and a counter to the fear of decline.

But there is an even wider factor that needs to be emphasised. Homosexuality only becomes a matter for social concern when sexuality as a general category becomes of major public importance. The debates on "natural" sexuality in the nineteenth century, and particularly the focusing on the sanctity of the marital bond in social-purity discourse, by a necessary rebound demands the more refined control of extra-marital sexuality, however trivial. Sodomy was a catch-all which marked the distinction between non-reproductive and reproductive sexuality, but whose character, as description and as legal category, remained vague. Homosexuality and the other categories that were so intricately described by Krafft-Ebing and others in the late nineteenth century spoke of the pleasures and dangers of sex in general, in all its forms, pleasures, and dangers that not only addressed reproductive sexuality but also the privileged role of sex in cementing the marriage alliance. As sex was ideologically privatized, in the privileged domain of the sacramental marriage, as its discretion and "control" became *the* mark of respectability, so its variant forms needed ever more refined definitions and control – and ever more discussion and debate and analysis. But inevitably, simultaneously, they also provided the space for new sexual localizations: for, indeed, sharper sexual identities. The inevitable contradictory effect was that a growing awareness of homosexuality, an ever-expanding explosion of works about it, accompanied its more detailed organization and control; and this in turn created the elements of resistance and self-definition that led to the growth of distinctive homosexual identities. . . .

Homosexuality has existed in various types of societies, but it is only in some cultures that it becomes organized into distinctive subcultures, and only in contemporary cultures that these became public. Homosexual behavior in the Middle Ages and after was no doubt recurrent, but only in certain closed communities was it ever probably institutionalized: in some monasteries and nunneries, as many of the medieval penitentiaries suggest; in some of the chivalric orders; in the courts of certain monarchs, such as James I and William III; and in and around the theatrical profession, and such like fringe cultural activities. Other homosexual contacts are likely to have been casual, fleeting, and undefined. The development of wider, more open subcultures was probably of a comparatively recent origin. Though in Italy and France there is evidence for some sort of male homosexual subculture in the towns in the fourteenth and fifteenth centuries, in Britain there was no obvious public subculture, bringing together various social strata, until the late seventeenth century. Certainly by the early 1700s there were signs of a distinctive network of overlapping homosexual subcultures in London associated with open spaces, pederastic brothels, and latrines. From the eighteenth century these were known as "markets," reflecting in part the current heterosexual usage, as in the term "marriage market." But it does underline what seems to have been characteristic of these subcultural formations well into the twentieth century: their organization around forms of prostitution, the exchange of money and services between unequals, rather than peer partnerships. It seems quite likely that the only frequent or regular participants in these subcultures were the relatively few "professionals." The evidence of the trials from the eighteenth century suggest that a wide variety of men from all sorts of social classes participated in the subculture, but very few organized their lives around them . . .

By the latter decades of the nineteenth century we can see the emergence of groups of people with a much more clearly defined sense of a homosexual identity. From the 1860s the poet and critic John Addington Symonds was attempting to grapple with the new theories on inversion which were appearing in Europe. His essay *A Problem in Greek Ethics*, privately printed in 1883, examined homosexuality as a valid lifestyle in Ancient Greece and this emphasis on the Greek ideal, despite its transparent anachronisms, was a very important one for self-identified homosexuals into the twentieth century. His essay *A Problem in Modern Ethics*, privately published in 1891, was a synthesis of recent views and a plea for law reform. With Havelock Ellis he began the preparation for the first comprehensive British study of the subject, *Sexual Inversion*, which appeared after his death, and after his family had withdrawn their consent, under Ellis's name alone. Although married, with children, there is no doubt that J. A. Symonds was striving to articulate a way of life quite distinct from those which had gone before. Edward Carpenter and his circle of socialists and libertarians provide another example of the development of a distinctive homosexual identity, in his case associated with politico-social commitment. From the 1890s he lived a relatively open homosexual life with his partner, George Merrill. Oscar Wilde and his circle also constitute an example of a social network where a sense of a homosexual way of life was developing. Individuals from these interlocking circles, such as George Cecil Ives, later became important in the small-scale homosexual reform movements which began to develop in the early years of the twentieth century, and saw themselves very much as fighting for "the Cause" against legal and moral repression. . . .

The keynote of the homosexual world was ambivalence and ambiguity. It *was* possible to lead a successful homosexual life within the interstices of the wider society. Nor was the life entirely shaped by legal repression. Jack Saul in his deposition in 1889 was asked:

> "Were you hunted out by the police?"
> "No, they have never interfered. They have always been kind to me."
> "Do you mean they have deliberately shut their eyes to your infamous practices?"
> "They have to shut their eyes to more than me."[35]

Probably more important than the legal situation was the social stigma that attached to homosexual behavior and that seems to have increased in the late nineteenth and early twentieth centuries. It is this which gives social significance to the development of the small-scale and secretive homosexual reform movement. One circle associated with the criminologist George Cecil Ives, the Order of Chaeronea, appears, on the evidence of his three-million-word diary, to have been active from the early 1890s in succoring homosexuals in trouble with the law. It developed an almost Masonic style and ritual, insisting on secrecy and loyalty, and developed international "chapters." Many of the participants in this Order, men like Ives and Laurence Housman, were active in the British Society for the Study of Sex Psychology, founded on the eve of the First World War to campaign for general changes in attitudes towards sexuality. One of the major planks of the society was reform of the law relating to homosexuality, and in the 1920s this too became part of an international movement for sex reform. It is characteristic of these movements that although they were generally founded and operated by homosexuals they were not ostensibly homosexual organizations. On the contrary, their ability to remain publicly respectable was an important part of what success they gained.

Despite the ambiguities, it is clear that by the end of the nineteenth century a recognizably "modern" male homosexual identity was beginning to emerge, but it would be another generation before female homosexuality reached a corresponding level of articulacy. The lesbian identity was much less clearly defined, and the lesbian subculture was minimal in comparison with the male, and even more overwhelmingly upper class or literary. Berlin and Paris might have had their meeting places by the turn of the nineteenth century and there is clear evidence of coteries of literary lesbians such as those associated with the Paris salon of Natalie Clifford Barney. A chronicler of homosexual life in the early part of this century mentions various lesbian meeting places, including the London Vapour Bath on ladies" day, and by the 1920s the better-off lesbians could meet in some of the new nightclubs. But it is striking that the best-recorded examples of a lesbian presence referred to the defiantly "masculine appearance and manner" of the participant. The novelist, Radclyffe Hall, for instance, became notorious for her masculine appearance. Only by asserting one's identity so vehemently, as Radclyffe Hall recognized, could you begin to be noticed and taken seriously. But the numbers who could dress this way and could afford to defy conventional opinion were tiny and the lives of the vast majority of women with lesbian feelings were unknown, perhaps unknowable. Even the enthusiastic categorizers of early twentieth-century sexology stopped short of female homosexuality. In 1901 Krafft-Ebing noted that there were only 50 known case histories of lesbianism, and even in the early 1970s, two modern writers on homosexuality could note that "the scientific literature on the lesbian is exceedingly sparse." Writers like Magnus Hirschfeld and Havelock Ellis whose scientific and polemical interest in the subject was genuine seem to have found it difficult to discover much information, or many lesbians whose case histories they could record.

No doubt the absence of any legal regulation of lesbian behavior and a consequent absence of public pillorying and scandal was an influence in shaping the low social profile of female homosexuality, but the basic reason for the indifference towards lesbianism is probably more fundamental. It relates precisely to different social assumptions about the sexuality of men and women and in particular to dominant notions of female sexuality. Havelock Ellis, whose wife was lesbian, felt the need to stress that female homosexuals were often particularly masculine, and in Radclyffe Hall's *The Well of Loneliness*, a major novel of lesbian love published in 1928, it is the "masculine" woman in the story who is the true invert. Stephen, masculine in name and behavior, is forced to endure the agonies of her nature, the biologically given essence, while the feminine Mary in the story is in the end able to opt for a heterosexual married life.

This concern with the masculinity of lesbians can only be explained in terms of the overwhelming weight of assumptions concerning female sexuality. As J. H. Gagnon and William Simon have put it, "the patterns of overt sexual behaviour on the part of homosexual females tends to resemble those of heterosexual females and to differ radically from the sexual patterns of both heterosexual and homosexual males."[36] Several intertwined elements determined attitudes to lesbianism, and the consequent possibilities for lesbian identity: the roles that society assigned women; the ideology which articulated, organized, and regulated this; the dominant notions of female sexuality in the ideology; and the actual possibilities for the development by women of an autonomous sexuality. The prevailing definitions of female sexuality in terms of the "maternal instinct," or as necessarily responsive to the stimulation of the male, were overwhelming barriers in attempts to conceptualize the subject. Ideology limited the possibility for even an attempt at scientific definition of lesbianism. But even more important, the social position of most women militated against the easy emergence of a distinctive lesbian identity. It remained very difficult for respectable young ladies to be "independent." So it is likely that most women with lesbian inclinations fitted inconspicuously into the general world of women. There is as we have seen abundant evidence in eighteenth- and nineteenth-century diaries and letters that women as a matter of routine formed long-lived emotional ties with other women. Such relationships ranged from a close supportive love of sisters, through adolescent enthusiasms, to mature avowals of eternal affection. Many of the early writers on lesbianism spoke of the greater emphasis on cuddling, on physical warmth and comforting, of kissing and holding hands between female homosexuals, at the expense of exclusively sexual activity. This was precisely the line of continuity between all women whatever their sexual orientation. Deep and passionate declarations of love recur without any obvious signs of sexual expression.[37] The conditions for a polarity between "normal" female sexuality and "abnormal" were almost non-existent and it is this which makes it presumptuous to attempt to explore female homosexuality in terms of categories derived from male experiences.

It is striking that it is amongst the new professional women of the 1920s that the articulation of any sort of recognizable lesbian identity became possible for the first time, and it was indeed in the 1920s that lesbianism became in any way an issue of public concern, following a series of sensational scandals. Towards the end of the First World War the criminal libel prosecution brought by the dancer Maude Allan against the right-wing Member of Parliament, Noel Pemberton Billing, who had accused her of being on a German list of sexual perverts, was a *cause célèbre* which brought lesbianism to the headlines. In 1921 there were attempts, as we have seen, to bring lesbianism into the scope of the Criminal Law. During the 1910s and 1920s a series of novels, and even a film, portrayed lesbian experiences; and in 1928 came the most famous event of all, the banning and prosecution of Radclyffe Hall's lesbian novel, *The Well of Loneliness*. As Lord Birkett, who appeared for the publishers, later pointed out, the Chief

Metropolitan Magistrate, Sir Chartres Biron, found against the novel largely because Radclyffe Hall "had not stigmatised this relationship as being in any way blameworthy". Nevertheless, paradoxically, and in line with the impact of the Oscar Wilde trial, the prosecution gave unprecedented publicity to homosexuality. This perhaps is the outstanding feature of the case: the publicity it aroused did more than anything to negate the hopes of reticence expressed by Lords Desart and Birkenhead in 1921. Thousands of lesbian- inclined women wrote to Radclyffe Hall. She more than anyone else during this period gave lesbianism a name and an image. As a lesbian of a later generation put it, "When . . . I read *The Well of Loneliness* it fell upon me like a revelation. I identified with every line. I wept floods of tears over it, and it confirmed my belief in my homosexuality."[38]

In any study of homosexuality the important point to observe is that there is no automatic relationship between social categorization and individual sense of self or identity. The meanings given to homosexual activities can vary enormously. They depend on a variety of factors: social class, geographical location, gender differentiation. But it is vital to keep in mind when exploring homosexuality, which has always been defined in our culture as a deviant form, that what matters is not the inherent nature of the act but the social construction of meanings around that activity, and the individual response to that. The striking feature of the "history of homosexuality" over the past hundred years or so is that the oppressive definition and the defensive identities and structures have marched together. Control of sexual variations has inevitably reinforced and reshaped rather than repressed homosexual behavior. In terms of individual anxiety, induced guilt, and suffering, the cost of moral regulation has often been high. But the result has been a complex and socially significant history of resistance and self-definition which historians have hitherto all too easily ignored.

Notes

1 Or as the French theorist Guy Hocquenghem puts it, between "desire," and homosexuality as a psychological category: See his *Homosexual Desire*, London, Allison and Busby, 1978. A Preface by Jeffrey Weeks discusses the general placing of his theories. For a major discussion of the distinctions drawn here see the essays in Kenneth Plummer (ed.), *The Making of the Modern Homosexual*, London, Hutchinson, 1981. A longer theoretical exploration of the issues referred to in this chapter can be found in Jeffrey Weeks, "Discourses, Desire and Sexual Deviance: Problems in a History of Homosexuality," in that volume. See also Kenneth Plummer, *Sexual*

Stigma: An Interactionist Account, London, Routledge & Kegan Paul, 1975, which is the most important British work of sociology on these themes.

2   Edwin M. Lemert, *Human Deviance, Social Problems and Social Control*, Englewood Cliffs, Prentice-Hall, NJ, 1967, p. 40.

3   These are themes discussed in Hocquenghem, op. cit. and in Deleuze and Guattari, *Anti-Oedipus: Capitalism and Schizophrenia*, New York, Viking Press, 1977.

4   Mary McIntosh, "The Homosexual Role," *Social Problems*, 16, no. 2 (1968). Partly reproduced as ch. 1 above.

5   McIntosh, op. cit., p. 184.

6   Compare Frederick L. Whitam, "The Homosexual Role: A Reconsideration," *Journal of Sex Research*, 13, no. 1, (Feb. 1977); and Randolph Trumbach, "London's Sodomites: Homosexual Behaviour and Western Culture in the 18th Century," *Journal of Social History* (fall 1977).

7   This point is forcefully argued by Annabel Faraday, "Liberating Lesbian Research" in Plummer (ed.), *The Making*.

8   The anthropological and cross-cultural data is summarized in McIntosh, "The Homosexual Role," and in Trumbach, "London's Sodomites." The most comprehensive discussion of ancient Greek attitudes is in K. G. Dover, *Greek Homosexuality*, London, Duckworth, 1978. On the berdache see Donald G. Forgey, "The Institution of Berdache Among the North American Plains Indians," *Journal of Sex Research*, 11, no. 1, (Feb. 1975). On a different form of cross-dressing see Martin Baumi Duberman, Fred Eggan, and Richard Clemmer (eds), "Documents in Hopi Indian Sexuality: Imperialism, Culture, and Resistance," *Radical History Review*, 20 (spring/summer 1979).

9   For a general discussion of the legal situation, see Jeffrey Weeks, *Coming Out: Homosexual Politics in Britain from the Nineteenth Century to the Present*, London, Quartet, 1977, chs 1–3. (This present chapter is a development of themes discussed in that book.) For a further discussion of the legal situation, see D. J. West, *Homosexuality Revisited*, London, Duckworth, 1977, ch. 10. On the general taboo on sodomy, see Michael Goodich, *The Unmentionable Vice*, Oxford, Clio, 1978; and John Boswell, *Christianity, Social Tolerance and Homosexuality*, Chicago and London, University of Chicago Press, 1980; and on the confusion in the use of the term in another, though related culture, see Robert F. Oaks, "'Things Fearful to Name': Sodomy and Buggery in Seventeenth Century New England," *Journal of Social History*, 12 (1978). On reasons for the absence of legislation relating to lesbian behavior, see the statement of the British government, quoted in *Gay News*, 144 (June 1–14, 1978), p. 3 "the question of homosexual acts by females has never – so far as the government of the United Kingdom are aware – been generally considered to raise social problems of the kind raised by masculine homosexuality."

10 Quoted in A. N. Gilbert, "The Africaine Court Martial," *Journal of Homosexuality*, 1, no. 1 (fall 1974).

11 Quoted in Sir L. Radzinowicz, *A History of the English Criminal Law*, 4, *Grappling for Control*, London, Stevens and Son, 1968, p. 432.

12 On the eighteenth century, see Trumbach, "London's Sodomites"; on the early nineteenth century, see A. D. Harvey, "Prosecutions for Sodomy in England at the Beginning of the Nineteenth Century," *Historical Journal*, 2, no. 4 (1978); see also Radzinowicz, *Grappling for Control*; and the review article by Louis Crompton, *Victorian Studies* (winter 1979), pp. 211–13. Crompton makes the point that in no other Western country was the law so severe. No executions elsewhere have been documented after 1784. And the policy of *sentencing* to death continued to the eve of repeal. In the years 1856–9, 54 men were sentenced to death for sodomy, though the capital punishment was not carried through.

13 See Gilbert, op. cit.; "Buggery and the British Navy 1700–1861," *Journal of Social History*, 10, no. 1 (Fall 1976); "Social Deviance and Disaster during the Napoleonic Wars," *Albion*, 9 (1977).

14 Public Record Office: DPP4/6. Transcript of the trial, Day 1, p. 21. This account is based on the manuscript transcript.

15 Ibid.: Day 2, p. 276; Day 1, p. 82; Day 3, p. 299.

16 McIntosh, "The Homosexual Role"; Trumbach, "London's Sodomites," p. 18.

17 *The Phoenix of Sodom or the Vere Street Coterie*, London, Robert Holloway, ca. 1813, p. 13.

18 Louis Crompton, "Jeremy Bentham: Essay on 'Paederasty': An Introduction," *Journal of Homosexuality*, 3, no. 4 (summer 1978), p. 386.

19 See for example "Opinions of certain judges on Unnatural Offences Cases," Public Record Office: HO 144/216/A 49134/2. Mr. Justice Hawkins suggested with regard to bestiality that "for the most part that crime is committed by young persons, agricultural labourers etc. out of pure ignorance. The crime of sodomy with mankind stands upon a different footing . . ." See also HO 144/216/A 49134/4, a memorandum from the Under Secretary. I am grateful to the Departmental Record Officer at the Home Office who gave me access to the hitherto closed files in the HO 144 series.

20 See Weeks, *Coming Out*, ch. 1; D. J. West, op. cit.; and G. C. Ives, *The Continued Extension of the Criminal Law*, London, 1922.

21 On Labouchère's motive see his Parliamentary statement, *The Times*, March 1, 1890, and his comments in *Truth*, May 30, 1895; and the discussion in F. B. Smith, "Labouchère's Amendment to the Criminal Law Amendment Act," *Historical Studies*, 17, no. 67 (1976).

22 For the DPP's comments, see Public Record Office: DPP 1/95/1: July 20, 1889, and Sept. 14, 1889. On the reluctance of juries to convict (sometimes because they could not believe respectable people could commit such deeds), see H. Montgomery Hyde, *The Other Love: An Historical and Contemporary Survey of Homosexuality in Britain*, London, Mayflower Books, 1972, p. 19. On police attitudes in the early twentieth century, see

Havelock Ellis, *The Task of Social Hygiene*, London, Constable, 1912, p. 272.

23 Alec Craig, *The Banned Books of England*, London, George Allen & Unwin, 1937, p. 86. *The Report of the Royal Commission upon the Duties of the Metropolitan Police*, Cd 4156, London, HMSO 1908, vol. 1, p. 119, makes clear that there is nothing in the 1898 Act which would have inhibited prosecuting of men soliciting women; in practice it was never used for this purpose. It was effectively directed against homosexual offenses. For the flogging provision of the 1912 Act, see Bristow, *Vice and Vigilance*, p. 193; Ian Gibson, *The English Vice: Beating, Sex and Shame in Victorian England and After*, London, Duckworth, 1978, p. 161; Hermann Mannheim, *Social Aspects of Crime in England between the Wars*, London, George Allen & Unwin, 1939, table V, p. 51.

24 Havelock Ellis, *Studies in the Psychology of Sex* (4 vols), vol. 2, *Sexual Inversion*, New York, Random House, 1936, p. 352.

25 Arno Karlen, *Sexuality and Homosexuality*, London, Macdonald, 1971, p. 185.

26 For a fuller discussion see Weeks, *Coming Out*, ch. 2.

27 See Wilde's petition for reducing his sentence, July 2, 1896, HO 144/A 56887/19. The eloquence of his petition, as the prison staff did not fail to point out, contradicted his supposed mental weakness.

28 Dennis Proctor (ed.), *The Autobiography of G. Lowes Dickinson*, London, Duckworth, 1973, pp. 10–11; Brian Inglis, *Roger Casement*, London, Coronet, 1973, pp. 67–8; Public Record Office: Casement Diaries, entry for April 17, 1903.

29 For an excellent summary of theories of intersexuality, the incorporation of hormonal theories, and the debate over "cures," see Max Hodann, *History of Modern Morals*, London, William Heinemann, 1937.

30 See Hyde, *The Other Love*, pp. 200 ff.

31 For a fuller discussion of these ideas see Weeks, *Coming Out*, ch. 1.

32 Rev J. M. Wilson, *Social Purity*, London, Social Purity Alliance, 1884; *Sins of the Flesh*, London, Social Purity Alliance, 1885, p. 7.

33 Quoted in L. Chester, D. Leitch, and C. Simpson, *The Cleveland Street Affair*, London, Weidenfeld & Nicolson, 1976, p. 73.

34 Wilson, *Sins of the Flesh*, p. 7. "This sin" in fact referred to masturbation, but masturbation (not surprisingly, given the public-school tradition) was intimately linked to homosexuality. Cf. V. L. Bullough and M. Voght, "Homosexuality and its Confusion with the 'Secret Sin' in pre-Freudian America," *Journal of the History of Medicine*, 27 no. 2 (April 1973).

35 Public Record Office: DPP 1/95/4, File 2: Saul's deposition.

36 Gagnon and Simon, *Sexual Conduct*, p. 180.

37 Carroll Smith-Rosenberg, "The Female World of Love and Ritual: Relations between Women in Nineteenth Century America," *Signs: Journal of Women in Culture and Society*, 1, no. 1 (autumn 1975). See also Blanche Wiesen Cook, "Female Support Networks and Political Activism: Lillian

Wald, Crystal Eastman and Emma Goldman," *Chrysalis*, 3, (autumn 1977); reprinted as a pamphlet by Out and Out books 1979. For similar British references see Weeks, *Coming Out*, ch. 7.

38 Quoted in Charlotte Wolff, *Love Between Women*, London, Duckworth, 1971.

3

Symbolic Interactionism and the Forms of Homosexuality

Ken Plummer

Homosexuality and the Assumptions of Interactionism

One prevalent way of looking at homosexuality is to view it as an abnormality of the personality. At the very least it is seen as a "condition", but in its more extreme forms it is seen as a sickness, a neurosis, or even a psychosis. Accompanying such notions frequently are assumptions about the nature of science: that it is possible to apply the methods of the physical sciences to social phenomena. At the very least it is possible to divorce the researched homosexual from the researcher; it is possible to exclude "values" from the research; it is possible to isolate the deviant from the meaningful world in which he is enmeshed. Homosexuality, in sum, is a condition of individuals which can be studied objectively. Such a position is not objectivity: rather it is objectivation. In other words, through the procedures of positivistic science, homosexuality is simultaneously explained as and rendered as a condition; it is simultaneously explained as and rendered as a sickness. Clearly, homosexuality may be constituted as both a condition and a sickness in this society; but the point remains that it need not be.

I have expressed in a few words a complex argument . . . Three general observations need adding here.

First, I am *not* denying that homosexuality is either a condition or a sickness in *this* society. Clearly, in a society where homosexuals go to psychiatrists for cures and treatments, and where many people see it as a sickness, it is effectively constituted as a sickness. It serves as the "objectified reality" which is regarded as natural.

Second, however, I am suggesting that the meanings of homosexuality need to be seen in the context of the preconstituted social world, and that things need not be the way they are currently constituted. Clearly, and importantly, the homosexual experience has been organized socially in many ways other than that of the medical model. Thus, though much of the homosexual experience may be a "sickness" now, it was not in the past and need not be in the future. Indeed, the ongoing debate between various schools of scientific thought and between the homophile movements and the public concerning the nature of homosexuality suggests that it might be reconceptualized in the immediate future as either a relationship or a political phenomenon.

Third, and as I have commented throughout, the debate as to the ultimate validity of these conceptualizations is not part of this book.

The interactionist, then, in trying to remain sensitive to the preconstituted and emergent meanings of the social world, works from a different series of underlying assumptions about the nature of homosexuality. Homosexuality may ultimately become solidified into a "sick condition" of individuals in this culture: but the interactional concern is with viewing homosexuality as a process emerging through interactive encounters (part of which will include a potentially hostile reaction) in an intersubjective world. His concern rests with processes, reactions, and subjective realities. I will look at each briefly in turn.

Reactions

A key assumption of the interactionist approach is that homosexuality cannot be understood in isolation from the reactions of a society which potentially stigmatizes it. It is true that if homosexuality were commonplace, accepted everyday behavior in society, the major area of analysis could perhaps be satisfacttorily confined to the isolated actor. But much of what is distinctive about homosexuality as it exists in England is a direct consequence of the fact that it has been bedeviled by ban, has been rendered deviant. The features of homosexuality as it is found in this society do not simply emerge from same-sex experiences: rather they flow from the social contexts in which they are located. Thus, it may be true that homosexuals exhibit pathology, are promiscuous, are exaggeratedly effeminate, and so forth. But if this is the case (and I suspect that it is not generally true), the explanation for this may not reside in the homosexual experience *per se*, but rather in the hostile reactions surrounding it – which lead for example to self- devaluation and despair, and inhibit stable relationships.

Homosexuality cannot be understood as an individualistic phenomenon: rather it needs to be seen as an interactive phenomenon, and constantly linked to the reactions of society's members. As Schur (1969) comments:

> In the broadest sense, then, the main "cause" of deviance is the societal reaction to it. This does not primarily mean, of course, that the *behaviour* itself is *created* by the reaction to it (although there is some element of truth in that too . . .) but rather that the *meaning* of the behaviour (including its characterisation as deviance) and its place in the social order is produced through this process of reaction.

[In the following,] the homosexual experience and the reaction towards it will be seen as constantly interrelated. One cannot be comprehended without the other.

Homosexuality as a process

Most recent researchers depict homosexuality as a condition, which people either have or do not have. The world thus conceived is populated by two "kinds" of people – homosexuals and heterosexuals, although to account for ambiguity in such a picture, a spectrum of subtypes may be introduced. The portrait given tends to emphasize the fashion in which homosexuals differ from heterosexuals; and to provide static snap-shots of the experience rather than ongoing sequences. The interactionist, while he would not deny that homosexuality becomes stabilized and polarized in this society, starts from an assumption that homosexuality is best viewed as a process. Thus in trying to comprehend homosexuality at a moment in time, he sees it as part of an ongoing accomplishment and not a finished product, and in trying to comprehend the causal factors involved in homosexuality, he sees it as part of a sequential process and not simply as an abrupt leap from one state to another.

A useful concept in this task is that of *role*, which sensitizes the interactionist not only to the patterned expectations surrounding homosexuality (and which vary from culture to culture, as well as perhaps group to group), but also to the dynamics of taking and making roles in everyday situations. While a condition is something which one either has or does not have, a role is something which one can adopt and drop, embrace, or become distant from, and as a metaphor it raises more subtle problems than that of a condition. Under what situations are homosexual roles adopted? How are they built up, modified, sustained? How might individuals become committed to them, and stabilized within them? Howmight homosexual roles be related to other roles an individual takes?

Homosexuality within a subjective reality

The interactionist does not take the socially constructed world for granted but renders it problematic. Thus, while most researchers into homosexuality can assume that homosexuality constitutes some form of "oddity" – an evil, a sin, a sickness, a miserable situation to be in – the interactionist throws such assumptions into disarray, showing their socially constructed nature and the processes by which they become objectified into the "truth." What was once part of an "objective" truth becomes visible as a subjective value stance; what was once taken to be absolute becomes highly relativized. My central concern will be with analysing the nature and emergence of this broader subjective reality.

In sum, in the pages that follow homosexuality will be conceptualized as a form of role-playing, juxtaposed constantly with the reactions of society's members, and located in a subjective world where meanings are problematic. . . .

Some Elements of Adult Socialization

At least five elements need to be considered in any "dense" analysis of adult socialization: the underlying processes, the content, the agents involved, the stages, and the properties of the status passage.

First, it is clear that the selection of a theoretical paradigm will affect the task of analyzing *processes*. In looking at the emergence of homosexuality in the past, two main paradigms have been used – one drawn from Freudianism, the other from behaviorism. The former has focused upon the emotional preconditions for sexual development and highlighted the processes of introjection and identification. The latter has focused upon stimulus-response learning and highlighted the process of conditioning. In both cases, scant attention is paid to the role of meanings, symbols, and significant others which are the hallmark of the interactionist approach. Further, both perspectives essentially seem to be very heavily rooted in what Allport has called the Lockean tradition in psychology (Allport 1955: chs 2 and 3). Man is seen here as essentially a receptor, rather than a self-conscious reactor. This is not my approach. Instead, the underlying process that guides human action is assumed to be an ongoing interaction between selves and significant others, in which life is constantly built, altered, but never completed. The concept of stable personalities is not consistent with others advanced here. Rather, I prefer to talk of "personality drift"; of individuals constantly striving but never arriving; of change, flux, and modifications; in short, of becoming. While, therefore, there may be emerging commitments and perspectives that maintain a person within the homosexual role, even this role will constantly be changing and modified through interaction with others. It is with this never-ending interaction as a source for understanding socialization that I will be concerned in what follows.

Second, in analyzing the *content* of the homosexual socialization process, the interactionist perspective is at odds with much that has been written in the past. For the central concern of most earlier studies has been with depicting the contents of homosexual socialization almost exclusively in terms of homosexual orientation and sexuality. The sole concern has been with how an individual comes to be attracted towards his or her own sex. But it should be clear that there is much more to homosexuality in our culture than sexuality. Indeed, some of the primary attributes of homosexuality are derived from its stigmatizing properties. Homosexuality is always only one small part of an individual's total life experience, and it is dangerous to rip it entirely "from its broader context".

Third, previous studies have looked at only a limited range of *agents* – notably the mother and father. But in the analysis that follows, these are widened to include all those significant others – real or imaginary – with whom one has contact over one's life span. At different phases, groups will play lesser or greater parts, the family being particularly influential in the early stages, and others playing more significant parts later. Thus access to other homosexuals may be of considerable importance in providing a series of socially learnt "accounts" which validate homosexuality, as well as providing a series of socially learned strategies for homosexual encounters. Again, access to a control agency may provide a guiding series of expectations as to how homosexuals behave and what they are like, while the constant exposure to stereotypes of homosexuality presented in the media are another important source for learning the homosexual role. Only a narrow understanding of the process of becoming a homosexual can come from looking solely at the influences of the family.

One important agent of socialization – often overlooked – is that of the self, and the self-initiating process. In line with my earlier argument, socialization cannot be viewed merely as a pouring process, by which external agents of socialization pour into the individual the social roles he is supposed to enact. Rather, the individual has considerable say at a large number of "turning-points" as to which path or direction he will take.

The most obvious example of a self-initiated learning process for many homosexuals occurs when they actively decide to seek out other homosexuals. As I shall argue later, few homosexuals "stumble" accidentally upon the existence of other homosexuals; discovery of their whereabouts often depends upon a quite painful experience of searching.

Fourth, *properties* of status passages need to be considered. Key properties for understanding the status passage to homosexuality as a way of life are that it is usually seen as an *undesirable* passage; one which, once embarked upon, is generally *irreversible* (although it may stop dead in its tracks): one which for the most part (and certainly in its earlier stages) is conducted in relative *isolation*; one which is marked by a lack of *clarity* of signs, and which finally can become a *central* passage for an individual undergoing it.

In the analysis that follows, I have emphasized the stages through which some homosexuals pass in adopting homosexuality as a way of life. In summary, these are depicted as sensitization, signification, "coming out," and stabilization; and together they may be taken as an "ideal type" of career route for that homosexual who lives his life primarily as a homosexual in contact with other homosexuals. Such a trajectory is obviously less applicable in the later stages to those homosexuals who do not enter the subculture or who "fight their tendencies all life long." For them, only the early stages are applicable. There are several important things to notice about the career type of analysis. First, attention is drawn to the continuity of experiences, how one experience builds upon the other, and how "an identity once gained is never lost." At any stage of analysis, an individual can be seen to lie at the mid-point between his past experiences (latent culture) and his future one (anticipatory culture), and it is not possible to divorce him from these wider experiences. Second, the socialization process is seen as essentially a problem-solving mechanism; individuals in their daily round are constantly facing problems and having to resolve them as best they can. Often the solutions are highly unsatisfactory, but it is through this cumulative problem-solving that socialization takes place. Third, the concern is placed upon the "turning-points" at which crucial decisions are taken. Man, of course, is not invariably "rational," does not possess full knowledge, and is not always clear even about his immediate goals; and he thus acts at these "turning-points" in an unreflexive mood. The sociologist, with his desire for clarity and precision, armed with his analytic and conceptual baggage, often loses sight of this important characteristic of "turning-points" and, although, in what follows, it may appear at times as though the homosexual is acting very self-consciously, in fact he is doing this in a semi-slumbering mood.

With these cautions in mind, I can move on to consider the four problem stages in becoming a homosexual mentioned above.

Career Stages and the Homosexual Role

Sensitization

From an interactionist viewpoint, the most appropriate take-off stage in understanding the process of "becoming homosexual" rests neither with the unconscious psychodynamics of an individual, nor with the myriad other biological, psychological, and structural factors. Rather, the initial concern rests with those first conscious and semi-conscious moments in which an individual comes to perceive of himself potentially as a homosexual: with the general process of constructing sexual meanings, modifying them, and in many instances neutralizing them. One cannot see the individual "automatically" and "intrinsically" "knowing" that he is a homosexual – as the simple interpretation of prior elements. Rather, one must analyze the social situations and interaction styles that lead to an individual building up a particular series of sexual meanings, a particular sexual identity. It is with those factors that create a potentiality for "homosexual identification" that an interactionist analysis most suitably starts.

A number of potential sources for homosexual identification are readily discernible because they lie in the spheres of genitality and emotionality which are so closely identified with sexuality in this culture. Thus, for example, any actor who commits a genital act (e.g. masturbation) with a member of the same sex, who develops a strong emotional attachment to a member of the same sex, or who spends time daydreaming of his own sex in fictional erotic encounters, develops an apparent source for subsequent ponderings over potential homosexuality. Less apparent may be those situations in which there arises a "spillover effect" – the linkage of one series of meanings in which there may be no clear sexual connotation with others where the sexual meaning is clearer. An individual may become attached to, interested in, or fascinated by a number of "objects" – penises, bottoms, football boots, and other male-orientated objects – which may subsequently come to symbolize his whole being as homosexual.

Less obviously, a series of explicitly social events may be interpreted as "homosexual." For example, some actors may well find a base created for subsequent homosexual interpretation through gender confusions – a child coming to see his bodily self as in some ways inappropriate to the cultural definitions of his gender: a small, frail, fragile boy may come to perceive himself as "not like other men," and go on from this belief to build up a definition of being a homosexual. Others may develop a sense of "differentness" – only later to be translated into sexual differentness – which cuts them off from everybody else: the boy who prefers to be alone, or the boy whose interest is in the arts and literature finds himself distinguished markedly from his "football crazy" peers. This sense of "differentness" is a fairly common experience in homosexual case histories. As a simple example, four working-class homosexuals interviewed revealed a highly sensitive childhood – playing violins, visiting art museums, developing taste in the arts, literature, and music, taking an interest in fashion and clothes, to an extent that seems strangely at odds with the traditional working-class male culture in which they were brought up. They were all incidentally characterized by very slender and frail physical frames. I am *not* saying here that "homosexuality" gives rise to these interests or physiques. Quite the contrary: the interests and physique may well provide a subsequent base for interpreting oneself as a homosexual. They provide clues for retrospective interpretation.

In each of these early *social* experiences, a potential base is created for a subsequent *sexual* interpretation. Gender confusion, feelings of apartness, partialism, or even genital acts are not "intrinsically sexual," but can later be defined as such. Each of the above examples is similar in that a source is provided for subsequent homosexual self-indication. Some sources, however, may not be derived reflexively from the self; they may be thrust upon one. Consider the following interview response, relating a homosexual incident at school (Hauser 1962: 147):

> I was told, when I got myself into trouble, that I was a dirty, filthy, queer. I did not even know what this was so I was told that this meant that I would never be able to love a girl, that I could never have kids, that I had "had" it, and would most likely end up my life in prisons for having been caught interfering with small children. These were the crimes of Sodom and Gomorrah, for which they were destroyed by God, and for the rest of my life I would have to expiate this filth and wickedness. I was half hysterical and I simply could not understand what they meant, as all that

had happened had been weeks ago, I had forgotten it all by then, but
somebody was made to blab by the Coppers and the Head had been
brought in.

Thus labeling by parents, teachers, and even peers may have manifest
consequences for an individual's self-conception. A child who is constantly being told that he is "not like other children," a boy who is
caught *in flagrante delicto* with another boy, or a boy accused of being
a "cissy" or "mother's boy" may subsequently incorporate these hostile reactions into his own self-conception. Not only may he be given a
notion of being "queer" – he may also be provided with a full-blown
stereotyped imagery, as in the case cited above.

In sum, then, the sources for interpreting oneself as possibly homosexual are many and varied. They can arise at many points in an
individual's life history. While I have spoken above of sexual labeling
arising at adolescence – that most critical period of sexual identification – it may also take place at other times. From a small initial
sensitization the experience may become heightened and signified, and
it is this process which I wish to examine [next] . . .

Signification and disorientation

Signification begins where sensitization ends. It entails all those processes which lead to a heightened homosexual identity: subjectively,
from the nagging inner feeling that one may be "different" through to
a developed homosexual identity, and objectively, from minor homosexual involvements through to the stage known as "coming out." For
some these changes are passed quickly; for others they groan through
the life span. For some, the awakening sense of homosexual identity
comes as a positive relief; for others it is an issue to be constantly
debated, challenged, and surrounded with ambiguity. This process of
high anxiety and confusion in coping with one's life situation may be
termed "disorientation"; the process of heightened self-awareness and
meaning about the experience of homosexuality may be termed "signification" (Matza, 1969: ch. 7).

Disorientation and signification arise not simply because of personality factors, but rather because of the structural properties of the
wider society in which the neophyte finds himself. Both the positive
and negative elements of the societal reaction to homosexuality give
rise to particular sets of problems and the consequential signification
of the homosexual experience. On the negative side, the devaluation of
homosexuality may lead to problems of secrecy, guilt, and access; on

the positive side, the importance attached to gender roles and the general privatization surrounding sexuality may lead to problems of identity and solitariness respectively. Through these various problems, an actor's random and fortuitous homosexuality may become crystalized and signified. A minor sensitivity may be rendered all important, and the path towards secondary deviance, pivotal deviance, or role engulfment may be seriously embarked upon.

I wish now to look briefly at a few elements of the societal reaction, and suggest ways in which problems may emerge and signification ensue.

First, the homosexual experience is, in Matza's fine phrase: "bedevilled by ban." As a homosexual spokesman commented (Cory, 1953: 12):

> A person cannot live in an atmosphere of universal rejection, of widespread pretence, of a society that outlaws and banishes his activities and desires, or a social world that jokes and sneers at every turn, without a fundamental influence on his personality.

It is not surprising that such influences begin from the earliest moment of sensitivity for many actors. The condemnation and degradation of the homosexual experience by society renders the individual "worried" and "guilty." Confronted with stereotypes of sin, sickness, and sadness when not veiled in silence, the neophyte comes to perceive his initial experience with increasing anxiety and possible guilt. In *Giovanni's Room*, James Baldwin (1963: 11) vividly recounts the first childhood experiences of his homosexual hero, David:

> I awoke whilst Joey was still sleeping. . . . I was suddenly afraid. It was borne in on me: *But Joey is a Boy*. . . . The power and the promise and the mystery of that body made me suddenly afraid. That body suddenly seemed the black opening of a cavern in which I would be tortured till madness came, in which I would lose my manhood. . . . The sweat on my back grew cold. I was ashamed. The very bed in its sweet disorder testified to vileness. I wondered what Joey's mother would say when she saw the sheets. Then I thought of my father who had no one in the world but me. . . . A cavern opened in my mind, black, full of rumour, suggestion, of half heard, half forgotten, half understood stories, full of dirty words. I thought I saw my future in that cavern. I was afraid. I could have cried, cried for shame and terror, cried for not understanding how this could have happened to me, how this could have happened *in* me. And I made my decision. I got out of bed and took a shower and was dressed.

Such sensitivity will increase the potential homosexual's attentiveness to the negative imagery of homosexuality in society at large, an imagery which he may only remotely have been aware of formerly. At school, at home, in the media, what others may ignore he will find increasingly important. And, at each point, the message will be the same: homosexuality is, at the very least, odd.

An important part of the process of becoming sexual is sex education, and for the sensitized homosexual, this is invariably negative. Each source reinforces the "abnormality" of homosexuality and the normality of heterosexuality. By evasion or by devaluation, the homosexual experience is always shown to be inferior. For the peer group, homosexuality is possibly only mentioned at the level of the "queer joke," and for the teacher it will be limited to that part of the lesson that deals with "perversions, abnormality, and deviation," if it is discussed at all. In sex-education books it is often not mentioned: only 11 out of the 42 books discussed by Hill and Lloyd-Jones (1970: 20) dealt with the topic. When it is raised, however, it is couched in the language of abnormality. Barnes (1962: 166–7), by no means atypical, defines homosexual acts as "abnormal sexual acts between two persons of the same, not opposite, sex . . . usually thought of as immortal," and comments in a well-known Penguin handbook (his capitals, my italics):

> It is *normal* for people to pass through a STAGE in growing up that can broadly be termed as homosexual. *Ordinarily* they *grow through* this homosexual stage and out of it, later falling in love and marrying *normally* . . . at present it is a fact that an adult who is *deeply* homosexual, either because of his *bodily make up* or because of *wrong treatment in his early life*, is very difficult to *help*. He *cannot deliberately* change himself by turning his attention towards girls.

Likewise, Dawkins (1967: 76), in a textbook designed for "club leaders, teachers, clergy . . . all who have to face the problem of sex education with the young," advises:

> Homosexuals must be regarded *compassionately*. Many of them are *suffering from a psychological disturbance*, and none of them can ever find the *happiness* of raising their own family. There is evidence that homosexuals have not, *from a very early age*, been *able to accept their own sexuality*: consequently they *cannot love* a member of the opposite sex my italics.

Here again homosexuality is located in almost entirely negative terms.

In the main, then, wherever the sensitized homosexual turns, he is likely to find his potentiality devalued and denounced in various guises. Clearly, under these conditions there is a firm basis for casting guilt, shame, and even hatred on to the self.

Yet another important consequence flows from the act of ban: the transformation of homosexuality into a secret. Homosexuality, perhaps more than other sexuality, is a furtive exercise. Neither spoken about openly, nor immediately visible, it is something that can be kept to oneself, debated inwardly, and defended from public gaze. And like most secrets, "what is private becomes even more private," an inward spiraling takes place. As Simmel (in Wolff 1950: 333) observes:

> From secrecy . . . grows the typical error according to which everything mysterious is something important and essential. Before the unknown, man's natural impulse to idealise and his natural fearfulness co-operate toward the goal: to intensify the unknown through imagination, and to pay attention to it with an emphasis that is not usually accorded to patent reality.

In other words, secrecy once again leads to signification. In part the problem that emerges at this stage is one of not being recognized, of not becoming transparent, of keeping the secret (Matza 1969: 150). There are several structural features in society that render this task relatively easy. The point, however, for the neophyte, is that he will increasingly feel that others suspect, that they "must have guessed by now," even when the "objective situation" has not changed and nobody is actually aware. As Matza says: "Conscious of ban, and conscious that he has flaunted it, the subject becomes self conscious. Little else need be assumed to raise the possibility of human transparency" (Matza 1969: 150). And with such transparency comes further signification.

Keeping a secret raises a further and very serious problem for the neophyte homosexual: the problem of access. For as long as he guards his secret well, people will probably not know he is "one of them." But as long as he does this the chance of ever meeting somebody else who experiences the world in the same way remains slight. Flowing from this then, and closely linked to the more general process of the privatization of sexuality, a third factor which contributes greatly to signification arises: that of solitude.

Partly because homosexuality is perceived as deviant and partly because it is a secret, the neophyte will typically confront his initial sensitization experiences alone. When he has access to supportive reference-group structures, as I have earlier depicted, the experience may be considerably less stressful and less significant. But where he is confronted with these worrying doubts about his sexuality in isolation from helpful others, signification proceeds apace. Hours, days, even years may be spent wondering and worrying about it. Sometimes the secret and the solitude are carried with the "homosexual" to the grave.

There are two sides to this isolation process. One comes from a lack of contact with other homosexuals, the other from a lack of support from heterosexual companions. The first source of isolation may mean that the neophyte comes to perceive himself as "the only one in the world," or as one respondent said to me "it was me and a lot of dirty old men." If one is confronted naïvely with a societal reaction that says homosexuality is odd and that nobody should be engaged in it, it is difficult for the neophyte to actually believe that many people are so engaged. But to this feeling of "uniqueness" must be added the related feeling of pain for, after all, the base of the homosexual experience is a longing for homosexual contact – emotional or physical contact with the same sex. And the devaluation of homosexuality and the privatization of sexuality make it extremely difficult for the neophyte to find legitimate sexual expressions. Elements of frustration may thus add to the signification experience.

The second source of isolation comes from a (justified) unwillingness to broach the subject with family, peers, or "officials." As Westwood's respondents commented: "I was much too scared to tell anyone about it"; "I daren't mention it to anyone. It was very difficult in those days" (aged 58); "Until quite recently I wouldn't talk to anyone about it" (aged 23).

Not only are peers and families generally inaccessible on the subject, official agencies have not developed any well-defined and "well-known" paths to offer "help." Recently, of course, there has been an increase in organizations developed to help homosexuals and to provide forums for discussion; but in the past such bodies were nonexistent.

In addition to the unavailability of others with whom one can talk about homosexual experiences, there may also arise over time a gradual exclusion from heterosexual contacts: "As his friends start to go out with girls and eventually marry, he finds other interests and gradually drifts away from their company" (Westwood 1960: 183). Not only then is he cut off from homosexual experience and contact, he is slowly pushed away from heterosexual ones.

One of Westwood's (1960: 38) respondents illustrates much of the above discussion, and anticipated what is to follow, when he remarked:

Round about my early twenties I went through an agonising period. I thought I was the only one in the universe – struck down by some terrible fate, I watched others getting married, settling down and I hadn't the slightest interest in any girl. By then I knew it wasn't a passing phase; it had been there from the beginning. I got a book on psychology out of the library, but it was not much help. It was only when I met others, after a long period of struggle, that I became first resigned, then adjusted, and now happy with my situation.

A final factor which contributes to signification may be briefly mentioned. Homosexual sensitivity touches upon a core identity. In our society, the positive elements of the societal reaction stress the importance of gender distinctions, of appropriate male-behavior and female-behavior, and such gender identities become (in Everett Hughes's oft-quoted phrase) "master-determining status traits." Now, deviant traits are often likely to become "pivotal" to an individual's lifestyle; but, when they are, not only is there an issue of deviant identity, there is also a problem of gender identity. The sensitivity to being a potential homosexual thus goes right to the very heart of the matter of identity. "Who am I?" becomes a key problem that leads to signification.

In summary, then, the homosexual experience is likely to become highly significant for the individual through its linkages with guilt, secrecy, solitariness, and central identities. And such features of the early homosexual experience are derived very largely from the broader structure of society: from the hostile imagery of homosexuality, the privatization of sexuality, and the emphasis placed upon appropriate gender behavior. The homosexual experience becomes significant because society largely renders it so.

From such matters as ban, secrecy, and solitariness flow particular problems which every homosexual neophyte must face, and resolve more or less satisfactorily. Three problems can be identified as crucial:

(a) The problem of access: how to remove the solitariness of the earlier experiences, find both social and sexual partners, and companions willing to talk about homosexuality.
(b) The problem of guilt: how to cope with the doubts and anxieties, guilts and fears that one experiences as a consequence of knowing homosexuality to be "deviant."
(c) The problem of identity: how to evolve a satisfactory self-image and sense of identity.

Such problems as these, if unresolved, serve to heighten disorientation and amplify the significance of the experience; and for many homosexuals such problems may well linger on for long periods, if not the entire life span. These homosexuals may well appear before a psychiatrist, a social worker, or a priest as disturbed and maladjusted. But, equally, large numbers of individuals confronted with such problems attempt to evolve resolutions in a number of different ways. I wish now to turn to one particular way that is fairly common and seems fairly successful: the path of taking on homosexuality as "a way of life."

"Coming out"

At least three different meanings have been given to the phrase "coming out" in a homosexual context. Most social scientists favor the one given by Simon and Gagnon as "the point in time when there is self-recognition as a homosexual, and the first major exploration of the homosexual community" (Simon and Gagnon 1967: 181). In other words, two elements are seen as central: an identity, and contact with other homosexuals. Alternatively Dank (1971), in the only systematic study of homosexual "coming out" to date, suggests that this is not how the term is used by homosexuals themselves. Rather, for the homosexual (and concomitantly for Dank), "coming out" refers to the process of "identifying oneself as a homosexual," whether or not such identification occurs within a homosexual context. Dank's definition would be helpful if it were true that most homosexuals used the term exclusively in this way. But I suspect that this is not the case; and it is not possible to use members' definitions without problems of ambiguity. A third meaning – quite different to the two given above – is the one used by members of the Gay Liberation Front, for whom it means "going public" – letting oneself be seen in the "straight" world as homosexual. In the homosexual world, then, there are at least two meanings for this phrase, and probably more.

I shall use the term "coming out" for the process by which individuals pass out of the moratorium just described, and are "reborn" into the organized aspects of the homosexual community – a process during which they come to identify themselves as "homosexuals." It is neither an inevitable nor a necessary stage in becoming a homosexual – one may develop self-conceptions as homosexual without contact with this world (as Dank rightly points out) – but it is crucial in taking on homosexuality as a "way of life," the kind of homosexual experience that is the concern here. Thus, at this point in the homosexual career, the individual defines himself as homosexual and through interaction with other self-defined homosexuals begins to resolve the previously mentioned objective and subjective problems that emerge through signification. Thus, an identity is rebuilt and involvement with others may lead to an enhanced self-image and self-valuation. Through such interaction patterns, access is found to socially constructed "accounts" which may serve to legitimate the homosexual experience and neutralize feelings of guilt. Further, one gains access to partners – both sexual and social. The individual moves from a world characterized by secrecy, solitude, ambiguity, and guilt to a subworld where homosexual role models are available, where homosexuality may be temporarily rendered public, where "coaches" are willing to guide him into homosexual roles (Strauss 1959) and where a belief system is on hand to legitimize the experience. A highly diffuse, unstructured experience, somewhat akin to anomie, becomes translated into one that is more clearly socially organized and ultimately stabilized. The first experience of "going social" can have an enormous impact (Dank 1971: 187):

> The time I really caught myself coming out is the time I walked into this bar and saw a whole crowd of groovy, groovy guys. And I said to myself . . . that not all gay men are dirty old men or idiots, silly queens, but there are some just normal looking and acting people, as far as I could see. I saw gay society and I said "Wow, I'm home."

Not all experiences are as sudden as this, and some may take place in other contexts. Respondents have related how their first homosexual contacts arose in work situations, in public places, through pen-pal magazines, through homophile movements, at public meetings, etc., as well as the gay-bar system. Surprisingly, Dank's study – which provides an empirical analysis of the coming-out contexts of 180 homosexuals – suggests that the gay bar was not as frequent a context as some other researchers have thought. Dank's findings, however, may reflect his different definition of "coming out." Following that definition, it is possible for 15 percent of his sample to "come out" simply by "reading about homosexuality for the first time." There is little doubt that an individual can become aware of his homosexuality before gaining access to other homosexuals (one respondent of mine spent nearly 20 years in this state), but such self-awareness is hardly "coming out."

Sometimes the experience of coming out is a relatively simple one – a chance contact on a railway platform turns out to be a homosexual who is willing to introduce the neophyte to the "scene"; more typically the experience is a prolonged and often stressful one. For, even assuming that the neophyte is aware of the existence of other homosexuals and has decided to locate them, they may not be readily available for him. As Cloward and Ohlin have noted in the broader context of subcultural theory, access to illegitimate cultures cannot be assumed but must itself be seen as problematic (Cloward and Ohlin 1960). Further, even assuming that there is access to this illegitimate opportunity structure, an individual may be unable to avail himself of it.

Thus, in "coming out," the neophyte has to have both the *knowledge* and the *ability* to mix with other homosexuals. Neither of these factors may be present. In the past, knowledge of where to meet other homosexuals was particularly difficult for many individuals, but there is evidence that it may be becoming slightly easier for today's younger homosexuals with their widely advertised meeting places and organizations. Once one has entered the subculture, a snowballing process enables one to discover many other places where homosexuals have contact with each other. But in the first instance the problem is one of locating such a source – a problem that may be particularly acute for those with restrictive (geographical and social) home backgrounds.

Knowledge, however, is not enough. Also crucial is the ability of the neophyte to mix with other homosexuals in these social settings. Much may depend here upon the previous cultural and socialization experiences that the neophyte has undergone. Sometimes, far from the initial contact with other homosexuals being a satisfactory experience for coming to terms with oneself, it can be an experience in which guilt and worry are accentuated. One homosexual for example related how much difficulty he had experienced in buying a homosexual handbook:

> I was just looking in some window around Piccadilly and saw this homosexual guide, and I thought this is it – that'll tell me where to meet them. But I just couldn't get up courage to go in and buy it straightway. Do you know I went back to that shop five or six times before I finally plucked up courage enough to go in. And when I finally did, the man [behind the counter] didn't think anything of it at all. (author's research notes, 18.10.70)

Another young homosexual commented that although he had been to a club once it was raided by the police and that he just couldn't go back to them: "I can't relax in clubs. I keep thinking I might see someone from work, or that the police might raid." Earlier he had commented: "It's my problem and I've had to live with it for the past seven years, I think of it all the time – every day. I just can't see where it's all going to lead – I wish I was dead" (author's research notes, 27.9.70).

This homosexual seemed permanently lodged in the signification and disorientation stage, even though he had been to a club on one occasion. Many other homosexuals have related their difficulties in going to homosexual meeting-grounds of all kinds. Many fears exist – fears of being recognized, fears of shame, fears of the unknown, of possibly becoming involved in the criminal underworld, of being "bashed up," of getting into trouble with the police. And even if these general fears do not exist, the neophyte may find himself quite simply unprepared and unable to cope with the norms and values of the homosexual world. The requirements of sociability, youthfulness, and attractiveness in the bar setting, for example, may disqualify a shy, unattractive old man and simply render him a double failure: a failure in the heterosexual world and a failure in the homosexual world.

"Coming out," then, is by no means a simple, automatic, or immediate process. Nevertheless, for a sizeable group of people who confront the homosexual experience, its occurrence marks a significant change in lifestyle . . .

Conclusion

. . . My intention in this chapter has been to show the role that the social context plays in shaping homosexual socialization. Especially in the early stages of sensitivity and signification, the societal reaction of hostility plays a crucial role in bringing about an exaggerated concern with matters of homosexuality, and a strong potential for polarization. But a concluding caution is in order. The recent signs of change in our sexual mores may well mean that in the distant future, the process of becoming a homosexual will be a less significant one and a less painful one. This may result in a decrease of polarization so that individuals come to see themselves as simultaneously occupying homosexual and heterosexual roles, with an accompanying decrease in rigid, exclusive forms of sexuality. This remains conjecture.

References

Allport, G. 1955. *Becoming: Basic Considerations for a Psychology of Personality*. New Haven: Yale University Press.
Baldwin, J. 1963. *Giovanni's Room*. London: Corgi.
Barnes, K. C. 1962. *He and She*. New York: Penguin.

Cloward, R. and Ohlin, L. 1960. *Delinquency and Opportunity*. Chicago: Free Press.

Cory, D. 1953. *The Homosexual Outlook*. London: Nevill.

Dank, B. 1971. "Coming Out in the Gay World." *Psychiatry*, 34: 180–97.

Dawkins, J. 1967. *A Textbook for Sex Education*. Oxford: Blackwell.

Simon, W. and Gagnon, J. (eds). 1967. *Sexual Deviance*. London: Harper & Row.

Hauser, R. 1962. *The Homosexual Society*. London: Mayflower-Dell.

Hill, M. and Lloyd-Jones, M. 1970. *Sex Education*. London: National Secular Society.

Matza, D. 1969. *Becoming Deviant*. London: Wiley & Sons.

Schur, E. 1969. *Sociological Factors in Homosexual Behavior*. Working paper of Hooker Report, unpublished.

Simmel, G. 1906. "Friendship, Love and Secrecy." *American Journal of Sociology*, 11: 457–66.

Strauss, A. 1959. *Mirrors and Masks*. Chicago: Free Press.

Westwood, G. 1960. *Society and the Homosexual*. London: Gollancz.

Wolff, K. 1950. *The Sociology of Georg Simmel*. Glencoe, Ill.: Free Press.

4

Capitalism, Bureaucracy, and Male Homosexuality

David F. Greenberg and Marcia H. Bystryn

The Early Modern Legacy

By the end of the thirteenth century, scholastic theologians had re-classified sodomy as an "unnatural" sin, far more serious than other sexual infractions such as fornication and adultery. The Central- and West-European monarchies had all made sodomy a capital offense, and many cities had enacted municipal legislation against it. These measures were fairly new, and made Europe far less tolerant of sexual diversity than it had been in the early Middle Ages. Although these enactments generally prohibited both heterosexual and homosexual sodomy, enforcement seems to have been directed more toward homosexual than to heterosexual violations.[1]

Enforcement of anti-sodomy legislation was episodic, and often less harsh in practice than statute-books might lead one to believe. Many death sentences are recorded for late fifteenth-century Spain, but most were commuted. In practice, only those with multiple convictions were executed.[2] In England, an Act of Henry VIII issued in 1533 specified that those convicted of "Buggery committed with mankind or beast" should be hanged. Yet eight years later, when the headmaster of Eton confessed to having had sexual relations with his male students and with a servant, he was not even prosecuted. He did lose his headmastership, but later held prominent positions in the Anglican Church, and was appointed headmaster at Westminster.[3] The first execution under the Act took place almost a century after it was promulgated, in 1631. It was not a simple case of consensual homosexuality, but involved group rape, and the defendant was a political adversary of the king. Convictions of common people are not recorded in England until the early eighteenth century,[4] suggesting that no attempt was made to enforce the statute vigorously. Most of those convicted in the seventeenth and eighteenth centuries were not sentenced to death, but to a few hours in the pillory, the least serious sentence permitted by law.[5] Given the prevalence of homosexual affairs in royal circles in the seventeenth century, it is understandable that the government did not want to pursue a policy of repression.

Homosexual affairs were also common among the French, German, and Russian aristocracy of the seventeenth and eighteenth centuries. Though not necessarily approved, they received little notice as long as the participants were circumspect. The libertine atmosphere of the courts was extremely tolerant of extra-marital sexual activity, whether heterosexual or homosexual, provided that no scandal broke out. Indeed, Philip, Duc d'Orleans' homosexual tastes and transvestism were deplored at the French court, but did not arouse the scandal that Louis XIV's illegitimate children did.[6] The French poet Theophile was sentenced to burn for sodomy in 1623, but the sentence was annulled. His partner, known as Des Barreaux, remained a magistrate and patron of letters, and became a Councillor to Parlement despite public knowledge of his homosexuality.[7] Although commoners did not enjoy such immunity, in the seventeenth century they were ordinarily prosecuted only in cases of flagrant scandal, political intrigue, or where violence was involved.

Popular literature of this period shows no horror of homosexuality. In England, Paul Bunyan's *Pilgrim's Progress*, an expression of seventeenth-century Puritan thought, pays it very little attention; and Restoration drama treats it with moral indifference.[8] French erotic literature of the eighteenth and early nineteenth centuries, sold primarily to the nobility, did not discriminate between heterosexual and homosexual activity.[9]

The situation in colonial America was similar. The death penalty was imposed on violators on several occasions under English law[10] but many incidents were ignored or punished quite leniently when they came to light.[11]

This conjuncture of extremely punitive legislation, erratic enforcement, and popular indifference was to change in the modern era. Here we sketch the nature of these changes, suggest an explanation for them, and present evidence bearing on the validity of our explanations. Most of this evidence concerns nineteenth- and twentieth-century England and the United States, but where information about other societies is available and relevant, we will make use of it. As the evidence currently available is fragmentary and inconclusive, we cannot regard our interpretation as anything more than speculative and provisional.

It is, however, generally consistent with what is presently known about social responses to homosexuality in this period.

We suggest that two developments were particularly important in shaping a distinctively modern response to homosexuality,[12] the development of competitive capitalism, and the spread of bureaucratic principles of social organization. The effects of these developments were contradictory, but their net effect was to strengthen anti-homosexual attitudes in the general population. The further development of capitalism in the post-World War II period has moderated these feelings, but only to a limited degree.

Competitive Capitalism and Homosexuality

Much of the statutory regulation of economic activity found in England and its colonies was repealed during the late eighteenth and early nineteenth centuries,[13] and small-scale, competitive business enterprises grew in number. Sodomy remained criminal in the US following Independence, but the death penalty was abolished as part of a broader movement to ameliorate the harshness of the English criminal code. In England the penalty was reduced only in 1861 – to life imprisonment. Prosecutions were uncommon in both countries,[14] both because the scope of the law was limited by judicial interpretation to anal intercourse alone, and because a defendant could not be convicted of a felony on the basis of the unsupported testimony of an accomplice. Minimal precautions to ensure privacy would ordinarily have sufficed to preclude prosecution.

One might have expected the rise of capitalism to bring about a greater tolerance of homosexual activity. The *laissez-faire* doctrines associated with the competitive stage of capitalism asserted the desirability of leaving private citizens free to negotiate their own contractual arrangements so long as no one else was injured, and this would seem to imply tolerance of non-coercive sexual diversity. In fact, a few figures (Voltaire, Bentham) did call for the repeal of laws against consensual homosexuality, arguing that it was harmless;[15] and the post-Revolutionary French Penal Code of 1791 decriminalized consensual homosexual acts involving adults.

Nevertheless, homosexuality was highly stigmatized in nineteenth-century France, as well as in England and the United States, where the law remained more rigorous. The new capitalist order contributed to this stigmatization by intensifying competition among men, by fostering an ethos of self-restraint antagonistic to sexual expression, by sharpening the sexual division of labor and strengthening the ideology of the family, and by giving rise to an ideology which reinterpreted deviance in medical terms.

Competition and character

To succeed in the face of vigorous competition, entrepreneurs had to be competitive, aggressive, and unswayed by affective ties to competitors or employees, for the market is concerned only with the balance sheet. In the US, the democratic ideology of the post-Independence period increased the intensity of competition and sharpened the symbolic meaning of failure by opening the competition to all (except slaves and women), and by making success appear to be a function of personal character alone.

Parents who cared about their children's future would have attempted to mold their children's character in directions they considered optimal for success. Parental ability to do this is always constrained in a variety of ways, and outcomes in individual cases are never entirely predictable. Nevertheless, we can reasonably assume that on the average, such attempts are at least moderately successful, and produce at least a rough correspondence between character types and anticipated occupational prospects.

On this assumption, early nineteenth-century middle-class parents would have begun raising their male children in ways that would foster self-assertion and competitiveness, while discouraging such traits as emotional expressiveness, emotional dependence, and nurturance – traits that would have been dysfunctional in the competition. The unusual degree of independence that de Tocqueville had noted in young boys during his visit to America in 1831 has been attributed to this sort of process.[16] If this is so, middle-class socialization patterns would have tended to discourage the acceptance of emotionally intimate or sexual relationships between men.

Capitalism and self-restraint

Where enterprises are labor-intensive, and personal savings constitute a major source of capital, employers must restrict their own consumption as much as possible. Those who do not do so will deplete their capital, and their businesses will fail. This possibility was especially acute in the early nineteenth century because the increasingly productive economies of England, the United States, and Western Europe were beginning to place comparatively inexpensive, mass-produced goods within reach of worker and capitalist, while the growth of cities led to a level of informal social control that was much weaker than it had been in small towns. Under these circumstances, the restriction of consumption required for capitalist expansion could come about only through internalized control. To meet this need, the petty bourgeoisie created a morality that placed a high premium on self-discipline and frugality.[17]

The temperance movement was one consequence of this bourgeois emphasis on austerity and self-restraint.[18] A similar emphasis appears in writings on sex. Men are viewed as having a fixed amount of bodily energy; excessive discharge of this energy through sexual release, it is asserted, would deplete the supply available for other purposes, and would thus lead to enervation and lethargy. Ejaculation was described as "spending" the semen,[19] a metaphor that would have made sense to those who had learned from *Poor Richard's Almanack* that "a penny saved is a penny earned." Masturbation, which one Elizabethan sex manual had recommended to men as a way of increasing penis size, was now subjected to vigorous suppression in juveniles, and adult men were strongly urged to refrain from "self-abuse".[20] Sexual intercourse between spouses was to occur as infrequently as possible, with some marriage manuals recommending a frequency of no more than once a month,[21] and then only for the purpose of procreation. Premarital chastity acquired greater importance. Toward the end of the century, campaigns against prostitution were waged throughout the United States, and laws were passed banning the sale or use of contraceptive devices.

To be sure, the Victorians were not completely unanimous in this rejection of sexual expression, and sexual practices did not invariably conform to the ideal standards expressed in purity manuals and in the medical literature.[22] But diaries, private correspondence, and the large market for popular literature urging sexual restraint indicate that this literature was influential. What is significant is not that middle-class audiences conformed to these norms of self-restraint, but rather that they thought they should, and tried to do so.

The ideological rejection of sexual pleasure as valuable for its own sake had as its corollary the condemnation of prostitution, masturbation, and the use of contraception – all "unproductive" forms of sexual expression. Homosexuality was excluded by the same logic. Thus, toward the end of the eighteenth century, just at the time that fear of masturbation became a prominent theme in medical writings about children, middle-class English parents began to show more concern with the prevention of homosexuality in their adolescent children; and the more expensive boarding schools began to make it possible for youths to have beds of their own, instead of sharing a bed Prior to the 1770s, this does not appear to have been of any concern.[23]

The ideology of the family

In England; the commercial revolution of the sixteenth and seventeenth centuries removed men's work from the household, transforming the sexual division of labor within the family. At about the same time, Puritanism reconceived marriage as a contractual union of individuals (not families) bound together by mutual love.[24]

Although Puritanism dominated the religious culture of colonial New England, the household remained the basis for most economic activity until the early nineteenth century. The growth of commercial capitalism in the Jacksonian era led to the confinement of women to the home, and transformed the family from a unit of production to what was, at least ideally, a "haven in a heartless world"[25] for men who came to rely on their wives to repair the psychic costs of alienated labor. To legitimate the exclusion of women from jobs, men drew on Puritan doctrine in elaborating a cult of domesticity – which some women subsequently embraced.

The resulting ideology of the family called for monogamy, linked sex inextricably with love and procreation, asserted the sexual innocence of children despite prolonged adolescence, and endorsed a sharp sexual division of labor. Although extra-marital sexuality need not be a threat to some types of family arrangements, it is arguably a threat to families held together primarily by emotional ties, which can be fragile.

Even though threat to the family is not a significant theme in nineteenth-century writings on male homosexuality,[26] the normative standards by which sexuality was judged were those derived from the ideology of the heterosexual, sexually exclusive family. By these standards, homosexuality was deviant. As we note below, the theme of homosexuality as a threat to the family was to become more explicit in the late twentieth century.

The medicalization of homosexuality

In the decades following 1879, most states amended their sodomy statutes or passed new legislation criminalizing oral sex for the first time. The medical profession played a particularly active role in campaigning for this legislation.[27] Between 1880 and 1890, the number of persons in prison for "unnatural crimes" increased by a factor of 3.5,[28] even though the population increase during this decade was just 25 percent. The scope of this legislation, like that of the Middle Ages, was extremely broad and not restricted to homosexual activity, but in practice enforcement was largely directed to homosexual violations.

In England, homosexuality was not a major public concern in 1885 when the Labouchère Amendment was adopted, extending the scope of the legal prohibition of sodomy to include "any male person who, in public or private, commits, or is a party to the commission of, or procures or attempts to procure the commission by any male person of, any act of gross indecency with another male person,"[29] but homosexuality scandals and prosecutions in the last few years of the century (the most well-known of these being the trial of Oscar Wilde) show evidence of mounting fear of homosexuality.[30]

As in the United States, English and Continental physicians of the late nineteenth century began to write of homosexuality as a form of medical pathology or abnormality. This development marked a secularization of the earlier Christian prohibition, and also implied a shift away from the overt behavior needed to obtain a criminal conviction, toward a focus on homosexual desire or attraction, whether or not it was acted upon. It is at this point that the notion of a homosexual *person*, as distinct from a homosexual act, first appears.[31]

Since nineteenth-century medicine was a particularly competitive profession in England and America,[32] it is hardly surprising that physicians shared anti-homosexual sentiments: they would have been subject to much the same social and psychological pressures as the larger middle class. On the other hand, their prominence is not explained. Why were they so deeply involved in reconceptualizing homosexuality, and in devising and implementing new methods for controlling it? And why did the new medical conception of homosexuality they introduced gain credence outside the medical profession?

Jeffrey Weeks[33] points out that several of the leading proponents of a medical conception of homosexuality were themselves homosexual or spouses of homosexuals. Their contention that much homosexual behavior was congenital and beyond control was a strategy for gaining immunity in the context of a legal system that viewed crime voluntaristically. "If they can't help what they do," the argument went, "they shouldn't be punished for it." The hope was to exploit established grounds for acquittal, such as the insanity defense, to end the legal persecution of homosexuality.

Although a handful of "medicalizers" may have hoped to erect a shield against persecution, this was clearly not the case for others. Thus the Italian physician and positivist criminologist Cesare Lombroso[34] thought that those whose homosexual infractions were circumstantial (soldiers or students deprived of heterosexual outlets) could be given a light punishment, since they were unlikely to relapse in a normal environment, but he also advocated long-term incarceration for "congenital" homosexuals to stop contagion at the source.[35] The surgical treatments of the period are unlikely to have been devised by anyone sympathetic to homosexuals. Moreover, reference to the motives of the medicalizers, whether benign or repressive, does not explain why a view of homosexuality as congenital developed at a particular historical moment, or why it gained some degree of acceptance.

Biological explanations of many forms of deviance (crime, insanity, mental retardation, pauperism, alcoholism) gained currency in late nineteenth-century Europe and America.[36] Starting in the 1860s, French psychiatrists attributed these diverse forms of deviance to progressive degeneracy, a hereditary condition that could be caused by bad habits (e.g., overindulgence in alcohol) or an unhealthy environment (overcrowded housing, improper working conditions). The French defeat at the hands of the German army in 1870–1 gave credibility to the notion that the French population was indeed deteriorating.[37] However, degeneracy theory quickly spread beyond France, perhaps because the unhygienic environment of the nineteenth-century city and factory gave the theory wider plausibility. By 1886, the German neurologist Krafft-Ebing was writing of homosexuality in the *Psychopathia Sexualis* in the context of degeneracy.

An alternative perspective drawing on Darwin's theory of evolution was introduced in the 1870s by Lombroso, who proposed that deviants were biological atavisms – throwbacks to an earlier stage of evolution – who were incapable of functioning adequately in the modern world. This perspective, too, colored the medical literature on homosexuality. Both perspectives situated sexual orientation in the biological makeup of the individual, and saw a homosexual orientation as medically abnormal.

These biological explanations of deviance enjoyed great popularity in the late nineteenth and early twentieth centuries because they provided a focus for middle-and upper-class anxieties over urbanization, class conflict, and immigration. The high demand for scarce labor drove wages up and attracted streams of immigrants from Europe and the Orient. Toward the end of the century, violent labor disputes and the participation of the immigrant population in the urban political machines threatened the political dominance of the native Protestant middle and upper classes.

Degeneracy theory and Darwinism appealed particularly to these classes because they legitimated the existing distribution of property and power. Earlier in the century, when business enterprises were still small in size, poverty and its associated "pathologies" such as crime could be attributed to moral inadequacies such as laziness and insufficient "will-power" with some degree of plausibility. But as occupations became specialized and required technical skills, as work increasingly involved employment in bureaucratic organizations, and as larger amounts of capital were required to open a business, *moral* deficiencies no longer provided a plausible explanation for failure. Increasingly, explanations were couched in terms of innate intellectual deficiencies.[38] The growing social distance between classes also made more plausible theories of poverty and deviance that posited innate differences between deviants and respectables, and between classes and races. Finally, Darwinian doctrine legitimated imperial expansion at the expense of "inferior" peoples, giving it an added appeal at the point when the United States was beginning to challenge the European powers for world dominance.

Although a strict Darwinian analysis might have suggested that "defectives" should be left alone to die out, reformers feared that *laissez-faire* policy toward natural selection and evolution would fail. Inspired by a Hegelian view of the positive state and an organic conception of society, they called on government to assist nature in weeding out the unfit. Reformers feared that continued immigration, declining native fertility rates, and the enfeebling effects of urban, industrial life would lead to a decline in Anglo-Saxon civilization unless drastic action were taken. According to Weeks,[39] a crisis in British imperialism in the late nineteenth century raised similar concerns in England about the vigor and manliness of English youth.

Since degeneracy and evolutionary theories provided an explanation for a very wide range of social problems, including poverty, insanity, crime, idiocy, labor strife, and sexual inversion, the scope of government intervention suggested by the theory was also wide. Public health and sanitation measures were advocated, and in many instances adopted, to eliminate the pernicious effects of an unhealthy environment. For cases at hand, eugenics and sterilization provided obvious solutions, since they would prevent propagation of hereditary defects to the next generation. These measures were adopted to control "the dependent and dangerous classes," among them homosexuals.

The corporatist ideology of the Progressive reformers provided the positive vision that gave added impetus to these efforts. Faced with class conflict, they sought to inhibit greediness, achieve recognition of the mutual dependence of classes, and imbue public life with greater spirituality and purity of motive. Male lust, as manifested in masturbation, homosexuality, and the patronizing of prostitutes, epitomized the selfishness that reformers hoped to stamp out.[40] Sexual restraint had become less a matter of self-control for a penny-pinching petit bourgeoisie than part of a broad strategy for transforming conflict between men and women, and between the bourgeoisie and the working class, into social harmony.

Beyond its general appeal to the middle and upper classes, the biological explanation of deviance had an immediate appeal to the medical profession. It was more consistent with physicians' occupational ideology than with the ideology of any other occupation (and ran contrary to the occupational ideologies of other controllers of deviance, notably lawyers and ministers of religion). Then, too, the medicalization of social problems offered physicians the prospect of enhancing their occupational prestige by broadening the scope of their traditional jurisdiction beyond what had previously been recognized as illness. For example, turn-of-the-century physicians called on legislators to consult the medical profession when drafting morals legislation. As noted earlier, physicians figured prominently in creating a new quasi-scientific ideology that legitimated the repression of homosexuality, and a practice for carrying out that repression.[41]

The aura of prestige conferred on the medical profession by advances in biology and medicine in the late nineteenth century, and the benevolence associated with traditional medical care no doubt helped to gain wider acceptance of the new ideas regarding the etiology and "therapeutic" practice associated with the medical response to homosexuality. The construction of sexual deviants as not responsible for their own actions on account of disease, and the recasting of compulsory surgical procedures such as sterilization and castration as helpful, made it possible to legitimate coercive intervention that traditional legal principles would otherwise have precluded.

Bureaucracy and Homosexuality

The spread of bureaucratic forms of social organization has been one of the most striking features of modern life. Bureaucracy, we argue, has been important in shaping social responses to homosexuality in three ways. Bureaucracies influence the way social norms are enforced; they potentially conflict with some forms of nonbureaucratic affiliation; and they influence childhood socialization.

The nature of bureaucracy

The early twentieth-century German sociologist Max Weber[42] delineated the features of an ideal bureaucracy. In his portrayal, an ideal bureaucracy operates on the basis of officially defined areas of jurisdiction "which are generally ordered by rules, that is, by laws or administrative regulations." Authority to give commands is likewise "strictly delimited by rules." The administration of the office is sharply distinguished from the private affairs of the office-holder: "bureaucracy segregates official activity from the sphere of private life." This administration is governed by general rules:

> The reduction of modern office management to rules is deeply embedded in its very nature. The theory of modern public administration, for instance, assumes that the authority to order certain matters by decree – which has been legally granted to public authorities – does not entitle the bureau to regulate the matter by commands given for each case, but only to regulate the matter abstractly. This stands in extreme contrast to the regulation of all relationships through individual privileges and bestowals of favor . . . (p. 198)

Administration on the basis of general rules that regulate the rights and duties of office-holders implies that cases are to be decided by impersonal criteria, rather than by whim, subjectively determined criteria, or personal favoritism. Loyalty is owed to the goals of the organization rather than to particular superordinate individuals, and recruitment and promotions are to be based on objective merit.[43]

These principles of bureaucratic administration contrast sharply with those of a kinship-structured society, in which loyalty is to a clan or lineage; or of a feudal society, which is structured on the basis of vertical ties of personal loyalty. The feudal vassal swears an oath of homage and fealty to his lord, not to his office. The administration of the patrimonial ruler of a feudal kingdom is staffed by members of the king's personal household, and is properly influenced by personal loyalty to his family and vassals. The distribution of land to followers is from the king's own patrimony, and is not subject to evaluation on the basis of universalistic criteria.

Bureaucratic social control

In general, social control is organized differently in a society whose structuring principle is bureaucratic than in societies where kinship or feudal bonds are the fundamental principles of social organization. Instead of being carried out by an injured party, rule enforcement lies in the hands of a salaried, full-time staff, which can be deployed in a sustained and organized campaign of repression, even though individual members have little personal commitment to the campaign. In addition, enforcement agencies typically have resources with which to finance surveillance and prosecution far in excess of those available to individuals.

The great prosecutions of homosexuality in the modern age have all been carried out by the bureaucracies of Church and State. Thus, when the Spanish Inquisition received jurisdiction over sodomy cases in 1451, persecution of homosexuals was stepped up. By contrast, in Italy, where the Inquisition did not receive this jurisdiction, travellers reported that homosexual relationships were carried on quite openly.[44] In France, the establishment of the Paris police force under Louis XIV, with its vast network of secret informers, greatly enhanced the capacity of the state to ferret out unreported homosexual activity. Police files of the period show that they made use of this capability, and kept records on hundreds of homosexuals.[45] The McDonald Report on the Canadian Royal Mounted Police, released in August, 1981, indicates that the Mounties have kept files on homosexuals on an even larger scale in recent years. The massive deportation of homosexuals to Nazi extermination camps could not have been carried out except by means of a bureaucratic organization. Police entrapment and arrests on charges related to homosexuality in public places – a pattern of enforcement that has prevailed in twentieth-century England and the United States – are also greatly facilitated by bureaucratic organization.

On the other hand, the staffs of bureaucracies do not necessarily have any personal interest in the enforcement of the orders their superiors give them. This lays the basis for an official policy of repression that in practice is mitigated by the indifference or corruption of the enforcement staff. This is a pattern seen often in the area of "victimless crime" legislation.[46]

Bureaucracy and impersonality

Unlike other forms of social organization, such as kinship, bureaucratic organizations are expected to be universalistic, or impartial, in the way they make decisions. This feature of bureaucracies requires a degree of impersonality in the way employees deal with outsiders, and with one another. Conversely, the universalistic quality of decision-making is potentially threatened when members of an organization are linked to one another or to outsiders by affective ties, for in that circumstance, an office-holder might be influenced by personal considerations involving someone whose case is being decided.

Even when decision-makers actually remain uninfluenced by personal considerations, the appearance of impartiality which a bureaucracy must maintain to preserve its legitimacy will be threatened if intimate personal relationships are publicized. Moreover, jealousy within an organization on the part of those excluded from a sexual relationship might tend to interfere with the harmonious cooperation that a bureaucracy requires from its staff.

Some modern bureaucracies that employ both men and women – notably universities and business corporations – promulgate nepotism rules to prevent heterosexual relationships among staff from interfering with the functioning of the organization. We might expect that a prohibition against male homosexuality would have been established (or preserved, if it already existed) for the same reason at a time when bureaucracies were staffed only by men.[47] Since women were excluded from public and private bureaucracies prior to the twentieth century, lesbian and heterosexual relationships would not have excited the same degree of public concern as male homosexuality – as indeed they did not.

Of course, this line of reasoning can be taken too far. Perhaps personal ties between bureaucratic office-holders interfere with rational decision-making and raise doubts about impartiality. Yet we are all familiar with organizations where ties of this sort develop. Decisions may or may not be influenced by these ties; observers may grumble at real or imagined favoritism, but the organization continues to function.[48]

Moreover, if office-holders segregate their work from their personal lives, restricting their affective and sexual involvements to organizational outsiders who have no dealings with the organization, the impartiality of decisions will not be threatened even in appearance. The large size of urban populations has made this sort of segregation relatively easy to maintain. Indeed, many homosexuals have kept their positions in just this way, effectively withholding information about their sexual orientation from possibly hostile organizational superiors.[49]

For these reasons, organizations would not necessarily need to discourage homosexual activity on the part of their members, as the argument suggested. We must anticipate, then, that organizational considerations would come into play *vis-à-vis* homosexuality most strongly where the "total" quality of the organization precludes significant outside relationships (that is, where people's entire lives are encompassed by the organization), and where the efficient and impersonal functioning of the organization is of particular concern.

One bureaucracy that clearly meets this criteria is the military, and it has shown an exceptional preoccupation with homosexuality. The

Articles of War for the British navy included buggery as a capital offense, and punished it with execution more consistently than mutiny or desertion; the British army, in which life would not have been quite as totalized as life on a ship, relied more heavily on whippings.[50] In 1967, when the legal prohibition against homosexuality was lifted in England, men in the armed forces were explicitly excluded. In the US, a Senate Subcommittee[51] investigating the employment of homosexuals in government noted that the armed services had been much more aggressive than the civilian branches in attempting to exclude homosexuals. Pearce[52] notes that the conviction of an American navy officer for fraternizing with an enlisted man was upheld on appeal because "Some acts are by their very nature palpably and directly prejudicial to the good order and discipline of the services." The judge was evidently concerned that the hierarchical line of command would be subverted by a personal relationship between an officer and an enlisted man. This difference in policy between the military and civilian branches of the US government persists to this day; each year hundreds of men and women are discharged from the armed services (mostly from the navy), while nothing comparable is done elsewhere in government.

Bureaucracy and personality

Apart from organizational considerations, there are reasons for thinking that bureaucratization would have consequences for attitudes toward homosexuality through its effect on the personality. Bureaucracies can ensure compliance with organizational rules by making symbolic and material rewards contingent on compliance. In so doing, they mold what has been called the "bureaucratic personality" – methodical, rational, prudent, disciplined, unemotional, and preoccupied with conformity to expectations.[53] By contrast, a social system in which legitimate authority is exercised on the basis of tradition or personal charisma would have no reason to reinforce these traits. A charismatic leader can throw a temper tantrum, but a modern bureaucrat is expected to exhibit emotional self-restraint.

Through internalization, the cold impersonality of the bureaucrat's "working personality" can come to comprise a set of behavioral responses that carry over from work to interpersonal interaction outside the work setting. Until quite recently, few women were employed in bureaucracies. Thus adult socialization of this sort would have affected men almost exclusively. It is thus hardly a coincidence that what we have described as the *bureaucratic* personality is essentially what writers on gender have portrayed as the *male* personality.[54]

Because the formation of the bureaucratic personality in men entails (among other things) the suppression of affective emotional responses toward other males, men will tend to experience anxiety in the presence of expressions of emotional intimacy or sexual contact between men – or even at the thought of intimacy. It is this anxiety, we suggest, that lies behind irrational anger toward male homosexuality. The violence that is directed toward gay men walking along city streets with their arms about one another's shoulders is not provoked by their sexual preference or conduct so much as by their exhibition of affection toward one another.

Patterns of evidence

Since people tend to be reticent about sexual matters, and are usually not fully aware of the social influences that shape their sexual preferences and attitudes, evidence for the sorts of processes theorized here must be sought indirectly. We do this by examining the patterns of response to homosexuality comparatively and historically, as well as the psychological correlates of hostility toward homosexuality in modern times.

If our reasoning is correct, attitudes toward homosexuality should be comparatively tolerant in societies where social relations are not bureaucratized. The anthropological literature is generally consistent with this picture.[55] Conversely, bureaucratized societies should be inhospitable to homosexuality.

The special features of the Ottoman bureaucracy make it especially suitable for examining the relationship between bureaucracy and acceptance of homosexuality. Prior to the nineteenth century, much of the Ottoman state administration was staffed by janissaries – children of Christian parents who were conscripted at an early age and trained collectively by palace eunuchs for military and political careers. Training lasted until age 25 or 30, during which time the janissaries were not permitted to marry. Advancement was on the basis of seniority and merit rather than birth; and in this respect, the Ottoman state resembled a modern bureaucracy. We should thus expect to find homosexual relationships prohibited, and they were. During the period of training, the youths were subjected to strict surveillance to prevent homosexual behavior, and were punished severely for violations of the prohibition.[56]

In one respect, the Ottoman state differed from a modern, rational bureaucracy: government officials were personal slaves of the Sultan, who ruled as an absolute monarch. In this respect, the administration was patrimonial, and loyalty was to the person of the Sultan, rather than to his office or to the law. Homosexual relationships between the Sultan and his high officials would have posed no structural problem, and indeed commonly occurred.[57] With the exception of state functionaries, the Turkish population was not bureaucratized and not trained for future employment in a bureaucracy. Travellers' reports suggest that male homosexuality was extremely widespread.[58]

The Chinese Empire was also a patrimonial bureaucracy. For long periods in its history, palace eunuchs played a major role in state administration. While not all eunuchs were involved in homosexual relations, it was not unusual for the Emperor to have homosexual relationships with some eunuchs, as well as with men who were not eunuchs.[59] Although Chinese criminal law did prohibit sexual relations between consenting men, homosexuality was treated in law as a form of fornication – not a very serious offense. Participation appears to have been extremely widespread throughout all ranks of society, and evoked no moral outrage whatsoever.[60] However, the criminal code specified that officials who engaged in fornication (whether heterosexual or homosexual) with inhabitants of their districts were to receive a penalty two degrees higher than that for civilians. This provision was evidently an attempt to preserve the impartiality of state administration in a society that with the exception of the state was not bureaucratized, and did not generally stigmatize homosexuality.

In the USSR, homosexuality, which had been decriminalized in the immediate aftermath of the Bolshevik Revolution, was recriminalized during the Stalin administration, a period during which major bureaucratization of the state and economy took place.[61] Official policy toward homosexuality in post-Revolutionary China and Cuba (whose states are both highly bureaucratized) has also been hostile.[62]

In Western Europe, bureaucratic forms of social organization were introduced slowly and unevenly. The bureaucratization of military combat began in the fourteenth century,[63] while major steps toward the bureaucratization of state administration, and the rationalization of law, were taken in sixteenth-century England under Henry VIII, and in seventeenth-century France during the reigns of Louix XIII and Louis XIV. Ariès[64] and Foucault[65] have noted the introduction of age-grading, rationalization of the curriculum, classification, individualized ranking, surveillance, and discipline into the French educational system, hospitals, and factories at this time.

Despite these important steps, the adoption of bureaucratic principles of administration was still quite limited during the Age of Absolutism. In France it did not include the court aristocracy (Louis XIV preferred to employ bourgeoisie who would be dependent on him for salaries). The purchase and inheritance of offices profoundly limited the rationalization of the state. And outside of government, bureaucracy was virtually unknown.

Only in the late nineteenth and early twentieth centuries was a large proportion of the male population employed in bureaucracies. The large manufacturing plant, for example, was highly atypical in American industry until quite late in the nineteenth century. The years from 1880 to 1920 saw not only an appreciable growth in the average number of employees per plant, but also a rationalization of work organization and the tightening of lines of hierarchical authority.[66] Thus it is only in the last century that most men would have been exposed as adults to workplace socialization of a sort that would inhibit emotional or physical involvement with other men.

Changes in the socialization of children were also taking place in this period. In both England and the United States, efforts were made to extend and make compulsory formal schooling for the entire juvenile population. Parents were compelled by law to send their children to school, and penalties were imposed on those who did not do so. In the US, public school enrollments more than doubled between 1890 and 1910. The proportion of the juvenile population attending school daily increased from 44 percent to 67 percent, and the school year was extended from 135 to 173 days over these two decades.[67] For the first time in history, everyone was being exposed at an early age to the reward contingencies of a bureaucracy.

In addition, as bureaucracies became major sources of employment for adults, parents and schools would have begun to socialize their children in ways that would help them meet the expectations of future employers. Personal traits that would be valuable in occupational settings in adulthood would have been encouraged by both parents and teachers. Since occupational careers in modern societies tend to be formally open to all, all children would have been exposed to similar socialization processes (with some variation on the basis of race and class made possible by tracking and by residential segregation) – even children whose future employment will not be in a bureaucracy.

The strengthening of anti-homosexual attitudes at the turn of the century in England and the United States, and their persistence in the twentieth century, can plausibly be attributed to these developments. The concentration of these attitudes in the middle class lends strength to our argument. We do not have survey data for earlier generations, but scattered evidence suggests that casual involvement in homosexuality, and a more comfortable acceptance of same-sex physical contact, was a distinctive feature of British male working-class life in the nineteenth century.[68] Boys from the working class, of course, had a much more limited exposure to formal education, and were not destined, as their middle-class counterparts would have been, for bureaucratic employment.

Our argument that socialization generates subconscious conflict to which hostility toward homosexuality is a psychological defense receives support from an experimental study of aggression toward homosexuals.[69] In the study, male heterosexual college students who had negative views of homosexuality were found to be more aggressive toward homosexual targets they believed to be similar to themselves than toward those they considered dissimilar. When the targets were heterosexual, subjects were more aggressive to those they believed to be dissimilar to themselves than to those they believed similar. This difference in patterns of aggressiveness suggests that aggressiveness toward homosexuals may be provoked by an irrational sense of personal threat aroused by unconscious homosexual impulses.

The Advent of Gay Liberation

Law and psychiatry have continued to share the social control of homosexuality in the twentieth century. Until quite recently, the criminal law in almost all states continued to classify homosexual acts as felonies. Men convicted in the Boise, Idaho scandal in the mid-1950s were sent to prison for long periods, in one case with a maximum sentence of life. Men sentenced to prison for consensual sodomy in California have served sentences that were, on the average, longer than sentences served for rape with serious injury to the victim. Just a few years ago, a survey of homosexuals conducted in a large American city found that 37 percent had been arrested at least once on sex-related charges.[70] In England, a major police drive against homosexuals was carried out in the 1950s, and decriminalization came only in 1967.

The shift in public attitudes seen in the 1970s undoubtedly owes much to the gay liberation movement.[71] It is relevant to our analysis to note that gay liberation had its origins in the New Left, a social movement opposed to the capitalist organization. Its adherents were largely college youths who either lacked clear vocational goals, or anticipated careers in the non-bureaucratic sectors of the economy. By the time of the 1969 Stonewall Rebellion in New York, the women's liberation movement had developed a critique of the gender role system and the male-dominated monogamous family, and had projected a vision of an androgynous future.

These developments took place against a backdrop of postwar prosperity. The generation of youths with middle- and upper-class backgrounds entering college in the 1960s had never known scarcity, were relatively unconcerned about their futures in the economy, and as children had been indulged by their moderately affluent parents.[72] Their upbringing largely lacked the nineteenth-century emphasis on discipline and self-restraint.

No longer facing an economy in which heavy doses of asceticism were required for success, and in fact living in a society whose economy required and encouraged high levels of consumer spending, college students rebelled against restrictions that did not appear to serve any rational purpose, and developed a lifestyle of moderate hedonism. This new lifestyle included the recreational use of drugs, the blurring of traditional gender roles (beads, long hair, and colorful clothes for men), and the abandonment of traditional attitudes toward sexuality. The pursuit of pleasure combined with increases in female white- collar employment, and public concern about population growth, served to reverse the nineteenth- and early twentieth-century prohibition of contraception, abortion, and premarital heterosexual intercourse.

These developments of the sixties were of course not without precedent. The shift toward acceptance of sexual pleasure as a legitimate goal in its own right occurs slowly throughout the twentieth century in marriage manuals.[73] In the 1960s these changes reached a critical level and received greater publicity.

This acceptance of a legitimate separation of sexuality from procreation was readily extended to homosexuality given the social base of the New Left in the white, youthful middle class, which had been undergoing major transformation in methods of upbringing and occupational prospects. In the absence of these broad patterns of social change, it is unlikely that a large gay liberation movement could have emerged, or that it would have been favorably received by major segments of the non-gay population.

The backlash against gay liberation of the past few years makes clear that this favorable reception has by no means been universal. A number of cities have held public referenda rejecting legislation seeking to establish equal civil rights for gays; and attempts have been made to bar homosexuals from practicing certain occupations. Insofar as one can tell at present, this backlash is located primarily in lower middle-class strata employed in bureaucratic organizations or in highly competitive small businesses. In a period of economic stagnation and rising prices, these strata are excluded from participation in a lifestyle of affluence or hedonistic indulgence, and resent those they view as participants in this sort of decadence. The antagonism toward homosexuality in these strata has the same social roots as the tax revolt, and opposition to abortion, contraception, and the women's liberation movement.

The belief that homosexuality threatens the family has further stiffened resistance to gay liberation. The monogamous family continues to have survival value for married women given the realities of today's labor market: wages for women that are far lower than those for men, and inadequate child-support payments for men who leave their wives. As Gordon and Hunter note,[74] fear that the destruction of the family will mean the loss of nurturance, stable companionship, and commitment in personal relationships adds another dimension to the defense of the family.

Even though homosexuality may not really be a threat to the family (a large proportion of the men in Laud Humphreys'[75] study of homosexual transactions in public washrooms were stably married), homosexuality is seen as symbolically threatening because it is seen as standing for extra-marital relations, promiscuity, precocious sexuality, and a repudiation of stereotypical gender roles. At a time when the conventional nuclear family is being jeopardized by economic pressures that force the women to enter the paid labor force, the destruction of neighborhoods, feminism, and the loss of parental authority, these broader associations that homosexuality evokes have become threatening, especially to middle-aged, middle-class women who cannot easily take advantage of the career opportunities opening up for young, college-educated women. Anxiety over the family's threatened status thus makes lifestyles that appear to be inconsistent with the perpetuation of the traditional family salient and subjectively threatening, especially in the lower middle class, where family members are especially vulnerable.

Discussion

Previous explanations of intolerance toward male homosexuality have been quite different from those suggested here. Perhaps the most widely accepted has been the transmission from one generation to another of a "Judeo-Christian tradition" with a distinctive hostility toward homosexuality.[76] Historical research has shown, however, that

attitudes toward homosexuality in Christian Europe have been historically variable.[77] At times the institutional Church has been quite repressive, but at other times relatively tolerant. Although religious
teachings may have some bearing on the way people think about
homosexuality, it does not seem likely that contemporary attitudes and
policies can be understood adequately in terms of inherited religious
doctrine alone. The existence of many nominally faithful Catho-
lics who reject Church teachings on such matters as contraception
would be difficult to explain on the basis of simple cultural transmission.

Recently several other ideas have been proposed. John Boswell[78] has
argued that urban life involves exposure to diverse lifestyles, and thus
fosters tolerance toward minorities, including homosexuals. Yet
Boswell concedes that the thirteenth century, in which town life
was reviving, was a period of growing intolerance. His thesis is also
incompatible with the intensification of anti-homosexual repression in late nineteenth-century America, a period of rapid urbanization.

Marxist analyses have attempted to establish a unique connection
between capitalism and the prohibition of homosexuality.[79] Although
capitalism did play a powerful role in shaping social responses to
homosexuality, the repression of homosexuality is not uniquely associated with capitalism. It was found in the high Middle Ages, and is
present in contemporary non-capitalist, bureaucratically organized
societies.

Our analysis, which sees repression as rooted in the sexual asceticism
of competitive capitalism, and in the organizational policies and
socialization processes associated with bureaucratic forms of social
organization, is admittedly somewhat schematic and speculative, but
as we have shown, it is consistent with the major patterns of variation
in social responses to homosexuality in the modern world. This is not
true of earlier explanations of these responses. Nevertheless, much is
as yet unknown about the historical processes we have theorized as
being responsible for these reactions. As more is learned about changing family structures, patterns of child-rearing, and the development of
occupational ideologies – and of the history of economic and political
organization – it will become possible to elaborate and qualify the
ideas sketched here.

In the meantime, it is relevant to note the political implications of
our analysis. To the extent that attitudes toward homosexuality are
shaped by such factors as the social pressures facing the lower middle
class, and by the experience of bureaucratic organization, we can

expect hostility to persist. Educational campaigns no doubt have their value, but unless objective social relations are changed, there will be definite limits to their impact.

Notes

An earlier version of this paper was presented to the Society for the Study of Social Problems in 1978. We are grateful for comments and discussion to B. Richard Burg, Nancy Chodorow, Jeff Escoffier, Meredith Gould, Stephen Murray, Nicole Rafter, Daniel Resnick, Christine Stansell, Peter Stearns, Dennis Wrong, and members of the Sexual Fraternity Seminar of the New York Institute for the Humanities.

1 M. Goodich (1976), "Sodomy in Medieval Secular Law," *Journal of Homosexuality*, 1: 295–302; M. Goodich (1979), *The Unmentionable Vice: Homosexuality in the Late Medieval Period*. Santa Barbara, Calif.: ABC-Clio; D. Roby (1977), "Early Medieval Attitudes toward Homosexuality," *Gai Saber*, 1: 67–71; J. Boswell (1980), *Christianity, Social Tolerance, and Homosexuality*. Chicago: University of Chicago Press; D. F. Greenberg and M. H. Bystryn (1982), "Christian Intolerance of Homosexuality," *American Journal of Sociology*, 88: 515–48.

2 H. Kamen (1968), *The Spanish Inquisition*. New York: Mentor, 201.

3 H. M. Hyde (1970), *The Other Love: An Historical and Contemporary Survey of Homosexuality in Britain*. London: William Heinemann.

4 Ibid., 40.

5 V. Bullough (1976), *Sexual Variance in Society and History*, New York: Wiley, 476.

6 A. L. Rowse (1977), *Homosexuals in History: A Study of Ambivalence in Literature and the Arts*. New York: Macmillan.

7 M. Daniel (1957), *Hommes du Grand Siècles: Études sur l'Homosexualité sous les Regnes de Louis XIII et de Louis XIV*. Paris: Arcadie, 14.

8 B. R. Burg (1983), *Sodomy and the Perception of Evil: English Sea Rovers in the Seventeenth-Century Caribbean*. New York: New York University Press, 13–20.

9 H. L. Marchand (1933), *Sex Life in France: Including History of Its Erotic Literature*. New York: Panurge Press.

10 V. Bullough, *Sexual Variance*, 507–8, 519–22; L. Crompton (1976), "Homosexuals and the Death Penalty in Colonial America," *Journal of Homosexuality*, 1: 277–92; J. Katz (ed.) (1976), *Gay American History: Lesbians and Gay Men in the USA*. New York: Thomas Y. Crowell.

11 B. R. Burg, *Sodomy*, 38–40.

12 We are concerned here only with male homosexuality. The qualifier should be understood even when it is omitted from the text. Conceptions of lesbianism in the modern world have recently been discussed by L. Faderman (1981), *Surpassing the Love of Men*. New York: Morrow;

and G. Chauncey (1982), "Female Deviance," *Salamagundi*, 58–9: 114–46.

13 D. Humphries and D. F. Greenberg (1981), "The Dialectics of Crime Control," in Greenberg (ed.), *Crime and Capitalism: Readings in Marxist Criminology*. Palo Alto, Calif.: Mayfield, 209–25.

14 H. M. Hyde, R. *The Other Love*; R. Hamoway (n.d.), "Medicine and the Crimination of Sin: 'Self-Abuse' in Nineteenth Century America." Unpublished paper.

15 J. Bentham (1978), "Offenses Against One's Self: Paederasty," *Journal of Homosexuality*, 4: 389–405; L. Crompton, "Homosexuals."

16 E. Pessen (1969), *Jacksonian America: Society, Personality, and Politics*. Homewood, Ill.: Dorsey, 90–2.

17 That the critical factor was class, rather than some religious development such as the development of a Protestant ethic, is evident from the comment made by E. Barber (1955), *The Bourgeoisie in Eighteenth Century France*, Princeton: Princeton University Press, 79, that in France, "even before the Revolution enthroned 'middle class respectability,' in all its aspects, the bourgeoisie disapproved of the lax sexual morality for which the 18th century was famous." This was as true for the Catholic bourgeoisie as it was for the Calvinists.

18 D. Humphries and D. F. Greenberg, "The Dialectics"; H. G. Levine (1979), "Temperance and Women in Nineteenth Century United States," in *Research Advances in Alcohol and Drug Problems*. vol. 5. New York: Plenum.

19 S. Marcus (1964), *The Other Victorians: A Study of Sexuality and Pornography in Mid-Nineteenth Century England*. New York; Basic Books, 21–3.

20 G. J. Barker-Benfield (1976), *The Horrors of the Half-Known Life: Male Attitudes toward Women and Sexuality in Nineteenth Century America*. New York: Harper and Row; J. S. Haller and R. M. Haller (1974), *The Physician and Sexuality in Victorian America*. Urbana: University of Illinois Press, 97, 124–31; R. Hamoway, "Medicine"; R. P. Neumann (1975), "Masturbation, Madness and the Modern Concepts of Childhood and Adolescence," *Journal of Social History*, 8: 1–27; T. Szasz (1970), *The Manufacture of Madness*. New York: Dell, 180–206.

21 J. S. Haller and R. M. Haller, *The Physician*; W. S. Johnson (1979), *Living in Sin: The Victorian Sexual Revolution*. Chicago Nelson-Hall.

22 C. N. Degler (1974), "What Ought to Be and What Was: Women's Sexuality in the Nineteenth Century," *American Historical Review*, 79: 1467–90.

23 L. Stone (1979), *The Family, Sex and Marriage in England, 1500–1800*. Abridged edn. New York: Harper and Row, 332.

24 R. Hamilton (1978), *The Liberation of Women: A Study of Patriarchy and Capitalism*. Winchester, Mass.: Allen and Unwin; M. Walzer (1968), *The Revolution of the Saints: A Study in the Origins of Radical Politics*. New York: Atheneum, 193–4.

25 C. Lasch (1977), *Haven in a Heartless World*, New York: Basic Books.

26   On the other hand, the literature on masturbation was explicit in port-
     raying loss of interest in the opposite sex and subsequent social withdrawal
     and isolation, or the development of sex-inappropriate behavior (shyness
     for boys, flirtatiousness and self-assertion for girls) as among its undesir-
     able consequences.

27   R. Hamoway (n.d.), "Medicine."

28   J. Katz (ed.) (1976), *Gay American History: Lesbians and Gay Men in the
     U.S.A.* New York: Thomas Y. Crowell, 36–7, 39.

29   Although passage of the Amendment has often been taken as an indication
     of strong anti-homosexual sentiment, this was apparently not the case. F. B.
     Smith (1976), "Labouchère's Amendment to the Criminal Law Amendment
     Bill," *Historical Studies*, 17: 165–75, has demonstrated that Labouchère,
     who tacked his Amendment on to the Criminal Law Amendment Act, which
     raised the age of consent for females, did so as a joke, to discredit the act,
     which he wanted defeated. The purity organizations that had campaigned
     for the adoption of the act had never mentioned homosexuality in their
     pamphlets. The late-night debate over Labouchère's Amendment, which
     came at the end of a two-year period of parliamentary discussion of the Act,
     was extremely superficial, and it is uncertain whether the members of
     Parliament who approved it understood its provisions, according to H. M.
     Hyde, *The Other Love*, 135–6, and K. Plummer (1975), *Sexual Stigma: An
     Interactionist Account.* Boston: Routledge and Kegan Paul.

30   S. Rowbotham (1977), "Edward Carpenter, Prophet of the New Life,"
     Rowbotham and Jeffrey Weeks (eds), *Socialism and the New Life: The
     Personal and Sexual Politics of Edward Carpenter and Havelock Ellis.*
     London: Pluto, 25–138; K. B. Davis (1972), *Factors in the Sex Life of
     Twenty-Two Hundred Women.* New York: Arno Press; J. Weeks (1977),
     *Coming Out: Homosexual Politics in Britain, from the Nineteenth Century
     to the Present.* London: Quartet.

31   Distinctive homosexual social roles had been recognized much earlier, but
     it is not clear that these roles were thought to reflect more than a personal
     choice. See, for example, M. McIntosh (1968), "The Homosexual Role,"
     Social Problems, 16: 182–92 (and ch. 1 above); R. Trumbach (1977),
     "London's Sodomites: Homosexual Behavior and Western Culture in the
     18th Century," *Journal of Social History*, 11: 1–33.

32   M. S. Larson (1977), *The Rise of Professionalism: A Sociological Analysis.*
     Berkeley: University of California Press, 20–1.

33   J. Weeks, *Coming Out.*

34   C. Lombroso (1911), *Crime, Its Causes and Remedies.* Boston: Little
     Brown.

35   Contagion was of concern for two reasons. First, seduction into homosex-
     uality was thought possible; second, homosexual choices were not gener-
     ally thought to be exclusive. Late nineteenth- and early twentieth-century
     degeneracy theorists commonly expressed the fear that homosexuals would
     marry and transmit their degeneracy to offspring.

36 P. Conrad and J. W. Schneider (eds) (1980), *Deviance and Medicalization: From Badness to Sickness*. St. Louis: C. V. Mosby, describe this development for a number of different types of deviance, including homosexuality; but they do not explain why the trend occurred.

37 T. Duesterberg (1979), *Criminology and the Social Order in Nineteenth Century France*. Unpublished Ph.D. dissertation, Stanford University.

38 G. G. Gonzalez (1977), "The Relationship between Monopoly Capitalism and Progressive Education," *The Insurgent Sociologist*, 7: 25–42.

39 J. Weeks, *Coming Oct*, 18.

40 For England, see ibid., 16; for the United States, see D. J. Pivar (1973), *Purity Crusade*. Westport, Conn.: Greenwood.

41 This ideology and practice was soon to be challenged by Freudian psychiatry, which displaced the medical conception of homosexuality as pathological from the biological level to the psychological. But the older conception never disappeared from therapeutic practice. We do not trace the development of psychoanalytic perspectives here; for an overview, see P. Conrad and J. W. Schneider (eds), *Deviance*.

42 M. Weber (1946), *From Max Weber: Essays in Sociology*, trans. by H. H. Gerth and C. Wright Mills. New York: Oxford University Press, 196–8.

43 M. Weber (1968), *Economy and Society*, vol. 3, eds Guenther Roth and Claus Wittich. New York: Bedminster Press, 956–1005.

44 H. C. Lea (1907), *A History of the Inquisition of Spain*, vol. 4. New York: Macmillan, 361, 364; A. Karlen (1971), *Sexuality and Homosexuality: A New View*. New York: Norton, 109–10, 122; W. Lithgow (1906), *The Total Discourse of the Rare Adventures and Paineful Peregrinations of Long Nineteene Yeares Travayles*. Glasgow: James Maclehose: orig. publ. 1632.

45 M. Daniel, *Hommes*.

46 E. M. Schur (1965), *Crimes Without Victims*. Englewood Cliffs, NJ: Prentice-Hall. It is precisely under this pattern of enforcement that a semicovert deviant subculture comes into being. Evidence for the existence of distinctive, partly hidden homosexual subcultures in England comes from the early eighteenth century, and in France from the seventeenth. See M. McIntosh, "Homosexual Role"; R. Trumbach, "London's Sodomites"; M. Daniel, *Hommes*.

47 This idea has also been proposed by C. Davies (1982), "Sexual Taboos and Social Boundaries," *American Journal of Sociology*, 87: 1032–63, who, however, does not qualify it as we do below. Now that women are being employed in bureaucracies to an increasing extent, concern over heterosexual relationships at the workplace is rising, and M. Mead (1978) "Needed: A New Sex Taboo," *Redbook* (Feb.): 31, 33, 38, has gone so far as to call for the creation of a taboo against such relationships.

48 R. E. Quinn (1977). "Coping with Cupid: The Formation, Impact and Management of Romantic Relationships in Organizations," *Administrative Science Quarterly*, 22: 30–45.

49 R. Zoglin (1979), "The Homosexual Executive," in Martin P. Levine (ed.), *Gay Men: The Sociology of Male Homosexuality*. New York: Harper and Row, 68–77.

50 A. N. Gilbert (1976), "Buggery and the British Navy, 1700–1861," *Journal of Social History*, 10: 72–98.

51 Senate Subcommittee on Investigations (1950), *Employment of Homosexuals and Other Sex Perverts in Government*. Washington, DC: Government Printing Office.

52 F. Pearce (1973), "How to be Immoral and Ill, Pathetic and Dangerous All at the Same Time: Mass Media and the Homosexual," in Stanley Cohen and Jock Young (eds), *The Manufacture of News: Deviance, Social Problems and the Mass Media*. London: Constable, 284–301.

53 R. K. Merton (1957), *Social Theory and Social Structure*, Glencoe, Ill. rev. edn. Free Press, 195–206.

54 S. Jourard (1974), "Some Lethal Aspects of the Male Role" in Joseph Pleck and Jack Sawyet (eds), *Men and Masculinity*. Englewood Cliffs, NJ,: Prentice Hall 21–9; J. Sawyer (1970), "On Male Liberation," *Liberation* 15: 32–33. The socialization of female children in the modern, Western world has encouraged the expression of traits that are inconsistent with bureaucratic administration (emotional expressiveness, nurturance), but are important in the tasks carried out by women in the home or in such occupations as elementary education and nursing, where women have been employed in large numbers. Of course this linkage between sex and personality traits is imperfect, and would not be expected to exist at all insocial groups where the sexual division of labor is differently structured.

55 R. Trumbach, "London's Sodomites."

56 W. Eton (1972), *A Survey of the Turkish Empire*, 2nd edn. Westmead: Gregg International, 29: orig. publ. 1789; A. H. Lybyer (1966), *The Government of the Ottoman Empire in the Time of Suleiman the Magnificent*. New York: Russell and Russell: orig. publ. 1913.

57 E. S. Creasy (1877), *History of the Ottoman Turks*. London: Richard Bently and Son, 34–5, 85–6; A. H. Lybyer, *Government* 75–7, 122, 244–5, 263; W. Eton, *A Survey*; H. Inalcik (1973), *The Ottoman Empire: The Classical Age*. London: Weidenfeld and Nicolson, 74–5.

58 W. Lithgow, *Total Discourse*.

59 J.-J. Matignon (1899), "Deux Mots sur la Péderastic en Chine," *Archives d'Anthropologie Criminelle*, 14: 38–53.

60 Ibid.; E. Albaster (1899), *Notes and Commentaries on Chinese Criminal Law*. London: Luzac.

61 M. Schachtman (1962), *The Bureaucratic Revolution: The Rise of the Stalinist State*. New York. Donald; J. Lauritsen and D. Thorstad (1974), *The Early Homosexual Rights Movement (1864–1935)*. New York: Times Change Press. C. Lefort (1974–5), "What is Bureaucracy?" *Telos*, 22: 31–65; A. Arato (1978), "Understanding Bureaucratic Centralism," *Telos*, 35: 73–87.

62 In a critique of Leninist (democratic centralist) organizational structures, S. Robotham (1979), "The Women's Movement and Organizing for Socialism," *Radical America*, 13: 9, 28, describes their austere image of what it means to be a revolutionary:

> The individual militant appears as a lonely character without ties, bereft of domestic emotions, who is hard, erect, self-contained, controlled, without the time or ability to express loving passions, who cannot pause to nurture, and for whom friendship is a diversion. . . . It's a stark vision of sacrifice and deprivation. . . . It surely owes something to the strange things done to little boys in preparing them for manhood in capitalism. . . . Leninist groups still tend to reduce the criteria for success to an old-style managerial concept of efficiency . . .

In light of our analysis it is not surprising that major Leninist organizations in the United States have declined to endorse gay liberation, or have characterized homosexuality as bourgeois decadence, or as a sickness induced by the decay of capitalism.

63 J. F. Verbruggen (1977), *The Art of Warfare in Western Europe during the Middle Ages*. Amsterdam: North-Holland.

64 P. Ariès (1962), *Centuries of Childhood*, trans. by Robert Baldick. New York: Vintage.

65 M. Foucault (1977), *Discipline and Punish: The Birth of the Prison*. trans. by Alan Sheridan. New York: Pantheon.

66 K. Stone (1974), "The Origins of Job Structures in the Steel Industry," *Review of Radical Political Economics*, 6: 113–73; D. Nelson (1975), *Managers and Workers: Origins of the New Factory System in the United States, 1880–1920*. Madison: University of Wisconsin Press.

67 N. Edwards and H. G. Richy (1971), *The School in the American Social Order*. Boston: Houghton Mifflin.

68 J. Weeks, *Coming Out*, 39–41.

69 C. L. San Miguel and J. Millham (1976), "The Role of Cognitive and Situational Variables in Aggression toward Homosexuals," *Journal of Homosexuality*, 2: 11–27.

70 M. T. Saghir and E. Robins (1973), *Male and Female Homosexuality: A Comprehensive Investigation*. Baltimore, Md.: Williams and Wilkins.

71 For details of the early history of the gay liberation movement, which cannot be presented here, see D. Teal (1971), *The Gay Militants*. New York: Stein and Day; L. Humphreys (1972), *Out of the Closets: The Sociology of Homosexual Liberation*. Englewood Cliffs, NJ: Prentice-Hall; and J. Weeks, *Coming Out*.

72 R. Flacks (1971), *Youth and Social Change*. Chicago Rand McNally.

73 M. Gordon (1971), "From an Unfortunate Necessity to a Cult of Mutual Orgasm: Sex in American Marital Education Literature, 1830–1930," in

James Henslin (ed.), *Studies in the Sociology of Sex*. New York: Appleton-Century-Crofts, 53–77.

74 L. Gordon and A. Hunter (1977), "Sex, the Family and the New Right," *Radical America*, 11: 9–25.

75 L. Humphreys (1970), *Tearoom Trade: Impersonal Sex in Public Places*. Chicago: Aldine.

76 J. Lauritsen (1974), *Religious Roots of the Taboo on Homosexuality*. New York: privately printed; L. Crompton (1978), "Gay Genocide: From Leviticus to Hitler," in Louie Crew (ed.), *The Gay Academic*. Palm Springs, Calif.: ETC, 67–91.

77 M. Goodich, *Unmentionable Vice*; J. Boswell, *Christianity*; D. F. Greenberg and M. H. Bystryn, "Christian Intolerance."

78 J. Boswell, *Christianity*.

79 D. Fernbach (1976), "Toward a Marxist Theory of Gay Liberation," *Socialist Review*, 6: 29–41; F. Pearce and A. Roberts (1973), "The Social Regulation of Sexual Behavior and the Development of Industrial Capitalism in Britain," in Roy Bailey and Jock Youngs (eds), *Contemporary Social Problems in Britain*. Lexington, Mass.: Saxon House, 51–72.

5

Structural Foundations of the Gay World

Barry D. Adam

In recent years, there has been a growing realization that the contemporary social organization of homosexuality into lesbian and gay worlds is a socially and historically unique development and that the traditional academic construction of "the homosexual" has participated in this reifying process (Foucault 1978; Hocquenghem 1978; McIntosh 1981; Weeks 1981; Plummer 1981; Faderman 1981). This article seeks to contribute to this understanding by proposing a set of structural characteristics seen as preconditions to the existence of the gay world and by exploring theoretical leads, especially Marxist-feminist initiatives, to make sense of these structures. The study of homosexuality has been so long dominated by psychiatry, biology, and theology that the usual tools of analysis provided by political economy (construed broadly) have not been employed to analyze it. This essay puts forward some structural linkages which set homosexuality within the context of the larger histories of gender, family, and production.

I contend that the structural traits outlined below make the lesbian and gay worlds possible and, indeed, largely define the lesbian/gay manifestation of same-sex bonding apart from other social constructions of homosexuality.

Homosexual relations are released from the strictures of the dominant, heterosexual kinship system.

Exclusive homosexuality becomes possible for both partners.

Sex-role definitions fade from interpersonal bonding.

People discover each other and form large-scale social networks because of their homosexual interests and not only as a result of already existing social relationships.

Homosexual bonds make up an "endogamous" and autonomous
social formation with sufficient collective self-awareness to act as an
historical force.

Historical and anthropological examples of socially recognized
homosexual relationships show how different the modern form is. The
evidence from precapitalist societies reveals little opportunity for
divergence from kinship codes (Adam 1985); in age-graded systems
prevalent in such diverse areas as Melanesia (Herdt 1984), Amazonia
(Lévi-Strauss 1969: 446), central Africa (Evans-Pritchard 1970: 1430),
Siwa ("Abd Allah 1917), and Ancient Greece (Dover 1978; Foucault
1984), kin rules order homosexual relations as directly as heterosexual ones, prescribing tabooed and preferred categories of sexual
combination. Though exclusive homosexuality appears in certain
circumstances, the general rule in age-graded systems is toward
transitory (usually adolescent) exclusive homosexuality followed by
adult hetero- or bisexuality. Homosexuality in the context of
gender "crossing" or mixing is prevalent in anthropological studies
from the Americas (see Callender and Kochems 1983: 443), Polynesia
(Levy 1971), Indonesia (Geertz 1960: 291–8), and the Paleo-Asiatic
(Bogoras 1909: 449–55) regions. *Trans*genderist models typically
assimilate same-sex sexuality into kinship codes through the social
redesignation of the gender of one partner. Finally, both the intra- and
trans genderist systems embed homosexuality within cultural
complexes of existing family, gender, and sexual meanings, whereas
the modern gay world has become sufficiently disarticulated from
its antecedents to begin to generate some of its own cultural institutions.

Kinship

The social dynamics that shaped the modern conjugal family also
reorganized bonding patterns among individuals of the same sex.
Despite the Judeo-Christian inheritance, which regards homosexuality
as the irretrievable Other and provides the elements from which medical and legal discourses evolved, same- and cross-sex mateship forms
show similar origins and mutual influence. Of central importance is
the transition to capitalism, which profoundly reorganized the significance of kinship and family, thereby opening new possibilities in personal bonding. It is in advanced capitalist societies and the major
metropolises in the semiperipheries of the modern world system that
gay/lesbian worlds have emerged, while rural, "folk," and precapitalist

pockets have, to varying degrees, maintained radically different articulations of homosexual desire and relations.

First among the historical changes that allowed for the emergence of lesbian and gay worlds in modern capitalist societies was the expansion of the wage-labor sector that accompanied the rise of capitalism. When a kinship code allocates the new generation to productive land, there is little room for sexual or other subjective concerns to find independent expression; location within a lineage strongly influences chances of future economic well-being. With mobilization of labor in a free-market system, kinship can, to some degree, be made irrelevant in securing a livelihood.

Having said this, it must be noted that the gay and lesbian worlds of today are not simply "caused" outcomes of a supposed general breakdown of family relationships. Focus upon the structural antecedents of the gay world necessarily emphasizes the options that became available to and were seized by those already uncomfortable with institutionalized prescriptions for domestic life. For homosexually interested people, the issue is not one of family decline but of the development of often hidden and unintended possibilities that loosened the monopoly of traditional arrangements and made opting out of the system more viable.

Much of the current evidence (see Bray 1982: 43–51) suggests that homosexual relationships of the preindustrial period came about in households and local communities, emerging from already existing associations between master and servant or apprentice, as well as neighbors and friends. Public institutions such as monasteries, armies, and colleges seem also to have engendered limited homosexual networks. The expansion of the public realm through mobilization of labor in capitalist production, however, provided regular opportunities for previously unacquainted men to make contact and thus begin to constitute a gay world. A largely male public world of pubs, coffeehouses, public parks, and railway stations gained a new significance for urbanized workers (Steakley 1975: ch. 1). Here new friendships could arise and social networks develop. Despite attempts by the state to order and control these public places (attempts that continue today with increasingly sophisticated surveillance technology), they functioned as free zones where new social and political ideas could circulate (Aries 1977) and new alliances be forged.

At least as early as the 1700s, reports from London (Bray 1982: 82) speak of about twenty gay coffeehouses, as well as plazas, parks, and latrines frequented by gay men. At that time, notes Randolph Trumbach (1977: 15), "the prosecuting activities of the Societies for the

Reformation of Manners" turned up a gay world of wage-laborers and small businessmen complete with its own gestural semiology and language (Taylor 1965: 142; Bullough 1976: 480). They maintained a precarious foothold subject to intermittent attacks by moral entrepreneurs (cf. Bray 1982: 87–97) throughout the eighteenth century.

A distinctive gay world originated at the moment when homosexuality became an organizing principle of social behavior under which homosexually interested men came in contact with each other because of their homosexuality and not simply as an outgrowth of existing social relations. Men with homosexual interests carved out semi-clandestine places in the public realm – places that inevitably fell under the surveillance of the moral entrepreneurs and police.

Gender: Female

David Levine (1977: 28) points out that early capitalist relations penetrated the domestic sphere through a "putting-out" system wherein women (and often children) were paid a piece rate for goods produced at home from materials supplied centrally. While men were being transformed from peasants to agricultural wage-laborers, women were being integrated into the monetary economy through domestic production for the market. This economic innovation brought about a lowering of the marriage age as the younger generation no longer had to wait to inherit land in order to support itself but came to rely upon a wage income. An immediate outcome of this change was a higher birth rate stimulated by the lower marriage age and by the prospect of the additional labor services that children could offer to the household (Levine 1977: 146; Fischer 1973; Braun 1966).

The prospective augmentation of women's economic power thus opened by capitalist production proved short-lived. By the mid-eighteenth century, production was becoming centralized in factories; cottage industry was declining into obsolescence. The fading of domestic production prompted women, like men, to accept wage-labor in industry. As Joan Scott and Louise Tilly (1975) remark, women went out to take advantage of the new employment opportunities unhampered by Victorian ideas of womanhood, which appeared only later.

The entry of women into wage-labor was detoured through state intervention. In Great Britain, the Factory Acts of 1847 and 1850 restricted the employment of women (and children) in industry, effectively returning women from the factory to the home (Curtis 1980:

127; McDonough and Harrison 1978: 35; Pearce and Roberts 1973: 55). The domestic sphere to which women now returned was outside the monetary economy and dependent upon the wages of husbands and fathers. In the words of Heidi Hartmann (1976: 152 and see 1981),

> women became more dependent on men economically. . . . English married women, who had supported themselves and their children, became the domestic servants of their husbands. Men increased their control over technology, production, and marketing, as they excluded women from industry, education, and political organization.

Women's work in the reproduction and maintenance of laborers became a socially necessary form of production for use, but not for exchange (Himmelweit and Mohun 1977: 15; Gardiner 1975 47; Coulson, Magas, and Wainwright 1975: 62; Secombe 1973: 3).

A few very brave women took the extraordinarily difficult route of migrating to the other gender to avail themselves of men's opportunities, and, passing as men, some married women (Katz 1976: ch. 3). This is not to deny the vast network of female "romantic friendships" well described by Carroll Smith-Rosenberg (1975: 1), Nancy Sahli (1979: 17), Blanche Cook (1978: 718), Lillian Faderman (1981), and others, but only to point out the differences between the histories of the lesbian and male gay worlds. Lesbian and gay relationships (keeping in mind the structural criteria listed in the opening of this article) presuppose a degree of free choice which wage-laborers could exercise but housewives could not, a distinction in relations of production which corresponds to the gender divide through much of the nineteenth century. Only when women began to trickle back into wage-labor did a lesbian world begin to emerge, toward the end of the century.

An intriguing contrast is offered by reports about prewar silk workers in southern China (Yang 1953: 198; Smedley 1976: 103). Where women were able to enter wage-labor on a massive scale, lesbian subcultures, as alternatives to traditional kin arrangements, became possible in China and elsewhere. Where the kinship code did not provide for homosexual relationships, homosexuality arose in a new structural location with the changing mode of production. The opening of alternatives to kin relations for gaining access to the means of production permitted workers, in turn, to experiment with alternative domestic and sexual arrangements.

In a century which set the sexuality of men in opposition to the purity of women (Cott 1978: 219), lesbianism could scarcely exist.

Where Victorian semiology located sexuality in the phallic signifier, intimacy between women had no place in sexual discourse. Unlike modern lesbianism, these romantic friendships were (1) almost always subordinate to the dominant heterosexual kinship system, (2) almost never realized as an exclusive or alternative relationship in place of marriage and family, and (3) therefore not the basis for a cultural or personal identity. In Faderman's (1981: 152) words,

> Because throughout much of the nineteenth century in Britain and America, sex was considered an activity in which virtuous women were not interested and did not indulge unless to gratify their husbands and to procreate, it was generally inconceivable to society that an otherwise respectable woman could choose to participate in a sexual activity that had as its goal neither procreation nor pleasing a husband.

The irony of this social mapping of intimacy which opposed male carnality to female purity, is that same-sex bonds took on radically different meanings. Romantic friends could then participate in the Victorian women's movement which in England, the United States, and, to some degree, Germany, occupied itself with morality legislation, anti-prostitution campaigns, and temperance, along with right-to-work and right-to-vote issues. The English Labouchere Amendment, which recriminalized male homosexuality, was tacked onto an anti-prostitution bill, thereby ranging male homosexuality and female homosexuality (to project a more modern term back in time) on opposite ends of a moral spectrum. The logic of the Victorian era cannot be ignored: it is only because of the powerlessness of Victorian women that the patriarchal hegemony could afford to trivialize women's relationships and tolerate them as being not very serious. It is when women first began to achieve financial independence in wage-labor that romantic friendship was able to divest itself of the constraints of marriage and heterosexuality (see Ferguson 1981: 11). Anit is at this moment, when women threatened to escape male control, that lesbianism crystallized as a suppressed and reviled identity.

Gender: Male

The changing structural conditions that made lesbian and gay worlds increasingly possible also generated new forms of opposition. Much of the scholarly treatment of homophobia, in noting anti-homosexual trends in both medieval and modern societies, has relied on "inertia" to explain the continuity of the resistance. But dependence on the element of tradition alone in explaining public campaigns against same-sex bonding fails to address how homophobia is reproduced in succeeding social systems.

While femininity was being reshaped in the image of the privatized family, masculinity was undergoing changes in the wage-labor economy. Men, more than women, were on the front line of the new production system and were forced to conform to its demands in order to secure employment. Karl Marx, in the *German Ideology* (Tucker 1978: 186), laments that competitiveness isolated workers from one another, thereby inhibiting class consciousness – the labor market pitted man against man to exhibit a requisite personality type. Masculinity was reconstituted to reflect the machine, the motions of which the worker was required to adapt. The industrial system sought to discipline and regularize workers as steady, reliable, emotionless, hard, and instrumental. Even fashion reflected the revaluation of male purpose as the flamboyance of the aristocracy gave way to the "fastidious austerity" of the businessman and sober practicality of the male worker (see Ewen and Ewen 1982: 132).

Homosexuality as a manifestation of tenderness and a road to male bonding was cast, by the terms of the capitalist discourse, as a violation and failure, a betrayal of masculine virtues necessary for success. Any male temptation toward sexual polymorphism would be contained by the monogamous family. A dependent wife and children ensured that men would be "good" workers who would not risk unemployment and loss of wage through industrial rebellion (Horkheimer 1972: 120; Rapp 1978: 286). Corporate executives continue to believe that "'being a family man' is a clear sign of stability and maturity and is taken into account in promotion decisions" (Kanter 1977: 28). In this way, most men are innoculated against homosexual activity and convinced of its inutility. Male bonding is to be counteracted by competitiveness and mediated by the "team." Even the male gestural repertoire of affection needed to be dressed in the language of aggression: touching between males could occur legitimately only as mock punches, slaps, and jabs.

Yet the history of the gay world is an ironic realization of the Marxian critique of capitalism. "Male sex role ideology, which embodies the competitive egocentricity of the capitalist market system, militates against the homoerotic bond which threatens the atomizing methods of domination" (Adam 1978: 56). It is not accidental that psychiatrists who insist upon "curing" homosexuality prescribe rivalry and competition with "male figures" as the "solution" to homosexual relationships. At the same time, homosexual choice is consistent with the ascendant revaluation of mateship as being a reflection of personal desires and an aspiration for emotional fulfillment rather than a pragmatic productive relationship or union of lineages. With the rise of "voluntary" mateship and the increased currency of "romantic love" and "companionate marriage" as ideological constructs, same-sex ties could be made meaningful in similar terms. For those whose emotional lives were most caught up in same-sex relationships, the ascendance of such a discourse could provide a code for organizing homoerotic experience. Marx's analysis foresaw a new revolutionary solidarity which would overcome the alienation of worker from worker as they were thrown en masse into factory production. In this entirely unexpected way, the lesbian and gay worlds developed with the rise of industrial capitalism, providing solutions on an individual, personal level to worker atomization.

The State

With its now more indirect relationship to production, the family became yet another social institution shaped and buoyed by the state which, in association with middle-class philanthropic societies, set out to enroll the masses in legally bound marriages (Donzelot 1979) in the eighteenth and nineteenth centuries. The English Marriage Act of 1753 instituted the state as guarantor of marriages and enforcer of its obligations (Weeks 1981: 24). Other professions joined medicine and law to define and administer family ideals and to discipline those who strayed from its confines.

Charles Rosenberg (1973: 135) remarks:

> Authorities of the 18th and early 19th centuries routinely indicted "sexual excess"; yet their injunctions have a calm, even bland tone. . . .
> Beginning with the 1830s, however, the ritualized prudence of their traditional admonitions became sharpened and applied far more frequently, while for some authors sexuality began to assume an absolutely negative tone. . . . only the need for propagating the species, some authors contended, could justify so dangerous an indulgence.

Work by Vern Bullough, Jonathan Katz (1983: pt. 2), Peter Conrad and Joseph Schneider (1980: ch. 7) documents the accumulating weight of medical opinion which first identified masturbation as a source of mental and physical degeneration and later assimilated homosexuality into the masturbation paradigm. By the late 1800s, a cascade of medical and professional writings had produced a veritable anti-masturbation hysteria, a surveillance system directed at children, and a technology of sexual repression (Bullough 1976: 542; Demos and Demos 1969: 632; Neuman 1975: 2; Gilbert 1975: 220; Parsons 1977: 66). A series of increasingly restrictive anti-abortion laws was enacted throughout the United States, especially in the 1860s and 1870s in the midst of a campaign in which physicians played a central role (Mohr 1978).

Traditional antipathy to non-reproductive sexuality became reactivated in new, virulent forms in nineteenth-century England, the United States and, to a lesser degree, Germany. Similar trends were disrupted in France by the Franco-Prussian War and the German occupation of 1870–1 which resulted in the Paris Commune. In England, the freedom to distribute information on contraception succumbed to the purity crusades by the 1880s (Bristow 1977: 126). In 1889, the Indecent Advertisements Act suppressed advertisements for veneral disease remedies. In 1898 flogging was instituted as punishment for "Soliciting for immoral purposes," a penalty imposed primarily on persons making homosexual propositions (Bristow 1977: 204, 193).

The purity campaigns, stimulated by tales of white-slave traffic, succeeded in raising the age of consent, extended police surveillance over prostitutes, and recriminalized homosexuality (Weeks 1981: 106; Pearce and Roberts 1973). Judith Walkowitz (1980: 130, and see 1983) remarks:

> Begun as a libertarian struggle against the state sanction of male vice, the repeal campaign helped to spawn a hydra-headed assault against sexual deviation of all kinds. The struggle against state regulation evolved into a movement that used the instruments of state for repressive purposes.

Several theorists have linked the Victorians' preoccupation with masturbation with the accumulative ideologies of the day. Anita Fellman and Michael Fellman (1981: 240) stress that semen, like capital, was seen as a resource to be hoarded for productive investment. Mark Poster (1978: 169) observes:

> Literary evidence points consistently to the view that sex was the model of impulsive, incautious action to the Victorian businessman. A gospel of thrift was applied to semen as well as to money. The act of sex, with its connotations of lust, rapture and uncontrolled passion, was the epitome of unbusinesslike behavior.

Whatever the links may have been between the interests of capitalists and the state proscription of non-reproductive sexuality, it is worth noting that pro-reproductivist campaigns proved functional for the expanding labor needs of nineteenth-century capitalism, especially in the face of declining fertility.

Just as the state stepped in to mold the modern family, it multiplied an institutional apparatus of hospitals disciplining the sick, the mad, and the immoral; prisons confining the recalcitrant; schools supervising the young; military training the masses; and factories controlling the workers. As Michel Foucault (1980: 41, and see 1979) remarks, a regime of supervision and control was established to protect the means of production while it was in workers' hands through a "formidable layer of moralisation deposited on the nineteenth-century population."

Early industrialists showed no reluctance in examining the "moral lives" of workers and did not hesitate to dismiss those who violated Victorian ideals of sexual propriety (see Baritz 1960: 33). In North America, a number of industrial towns were founded, built, and governed by a single capitalist family that enforced moral standards. Antonio Gramsci (1971: 297, 302, 304–5; see Poster 1978: 169) observes:

> The new industrialism wants monogamy: it wants the man as worker not to squander his nervous energies in the disorderly and stimulating pursuit of occasional sexual satisfaction. . . . The exaltation of passion cannot be reconciled with the timed movements of productive motions connected with the most perfected automatism.

Though the rise of capitalism opened new avenues for homosexual expression, it also laid the groundwork for the reorganization and rejuvenation of older doctrines proscribing it. As John Boswell (1980) points out, the consolidation of the Christian church around an anti-homosexual dogma is a product of the twelfth to fourteenth centuries – the height of feudalism – an era that stands in marked contrast to the ancient recognition of homosexual relationships. The sexual repression of the nineteenth century, in turn, stands in contrast to the apparent sexual liberalism of twentieth-century state-regulated corporate capitalism (to use Jurgen Habermas's terms), a transition that merits further analysis.

The Nineteenth-Century Gay World

The competitive labor market of the strengthening capitalist economic system created a negative common equality for all the dispossessed. The ground was laid for the idea of civil equality in a "public" sphere, weakening the moral divisions among people of the feudal period and "privatizing" religious, cultural, and erotic distinction. (Adam 1978: 28)

Wage-labor challenged church values by asserting a new norm for personal worth: competence at one's job became the pre-eminent criterion for survival (an ideal invoked today by oppressed minorities who have yet to benefit fully from its logic). Religion, ethos, and sex, once integral components of the societal code, began to recede into personal preferences contained by the private sphere. Like kinship, religion declined as a determiner of life-chances, partially opening the public world to greater tolerance and variability.

Early capitalism contained and reworked religious tenets while nurturing the liberal, individualist ethic that was flourishing in the competitive marketplace. It should come as no surprise, then, that the French Revolution broke with medieval doctrine in decriminalizing homosexual relations at the same time as it liberated the Jews from ghettos and cleared the way for later battles of national independence among European peoples.

There can be no doubt that "by the mid-nineteenth century, . . . the male homosexual subculture at least had characteristics not dissimilar to the modern, with recognized cruising places and homosexual haunts, ritualised sexual contact and a distinctive argot and 'style'" (Weeks 1977: 166). By this same period, the gay world had begun to produce its own intelligentsia (Adam 1979; Adam 1986), which articulated the idea of a homosexual identity, at first in terms of a third-sex theory (Kennedy 1981: 106). Karl Ulrich's formulation of a "third sex" of "feminine souls confined by masculine bodies" attracted not to each other but to "normal" men, shows the signs of its origins in heterosexist discourse. The theory now seems quaint and archaic. What is new in the third-sex thesis is the idea that homosexually interested men are a people with a distinct identity and culture. By the 1920s, Marcel Proust (1963: 286, 289) refers to gay men in *Remembrance of Things Past* as "a race accursed, persecuted like Israel, and finally, like Israel, under a mass opprobrium of undeserved abhorrence, taking on mass characteristics, the physiognomy of a nation." Gay men formed an "Oriental colony" in a diaspora from Sodom. In this early period of gay self-awareness molded by anti-homosexual environs (Adam 1978: ch. 2), there is a search for a new language and new names to consolidate the homosexual experience. The word *gay* achieved predominance only in the 1970s; at the turn of the century early writers experimented with such words as *Urning/Uranian, third sex* and *intermediate sex, homosexual/homogenic/homophile,* and *adhesive comrades.*

When physicians and jurists began to report on homosexuals in the late nineteenth century, they were observing a social formation that had been evolving for more than two centuries. Jeffrey Weeks (1981: 101) points out:

> As late as 1871, concepts of homosexuality were extremely undeveloped both in the Metropolitan Police and in high medical and legal circles, suggesting the absence of any clear notion of a homosexual category or of any social awareness of what a homosexual identity might consist of.

Naïve nineteenth-century observers were astounded by the complexity and completeness of the gay world. Lydston, writing in the United States in 1889, remarked:

> There is in every community of any size a colony of male sexual perverts; they are usually known to each other, and are likely to congregate together. At times they operate in accordance with some definite and concerted plan in quest of subjects wherewith to gratify their abnormal sexual impulses. (quoted in Burnham 1973: 41)

Francis Anthony, in a paper read before the Massachusetts Medical Society in 1898, stated:

> I have been told – and I am informed that the fact is true of nearly every centre of importance – a band of urnings, men of perverted tendencies, men known to each other as such, bound by ties of secrecy and fear and held together by mutual attraction. This band . . . embraces, not as you might think, the low and vile outcasts of the slums, but men of education and refinement, men gifted in music, in art and in literature, men of professional life and men of business and affairs. (quoted in Katz 1983: 293)

The German Social Democrat W. Herzen (1977: 37) wrote in 1898:

> The homosexuals of Berlin, Hamburg, London are certainly not less numerous than those of Paris or Brussels. There are places here where homosexuals hold their gatherings, baths they frequent, premises where they hold their dances, streets in which male prostitutes offer themselves to homosexuals. Homosexuals have their *Cafe National* in Berlin.

Conclusion

The modern gay and lesbian worlds, then, present a unique set of structural characteristics unparalleled by historical and anthropological examples of socially recognized and institutionalized forms of homosexuality. The very term *homosexuality* is, of course, problematic. A nineteenth- century innovation, it is part of the process of separation which reconstituted those having same-sex bonds as a people apart, and it paved the way for the modern encoding of intrasex intimacy as yet another "ethnic" group to be assigned a place in liberal, pluralist ideology. Far more common in precapitalist societies are kinship codes which articulate homosexuality *within* kin logic, either as age-defined, transitory, masculine relationships or as the relationships of a minority of gender-reassigned persons with gender-consistent persons. Exclusive homosexuality for both partners presumes a complex division of labor and most typically appears in gender-defined occupations such as the military or clergy. Though intergenerational and transgenderist homosexuality is by no means unknown in the modern gay world (though far less common than popularly imagined), they tend to continue as "little traditions" within the "big tradition" defined by the structural criteria presented at the beginning of this essay.

Notes

An earlier version of this chapter was presented at the August 1983 meetings of the American Sociological Association, Detroit.

References

'Abd Allah, Mahmud Mohammad. 1917. "Siwan Customs"" *Harvard African Studies*, 1.

Adam, Barry D. 1978. *The Survival of Domination: Inferiorization and Everyday Life*. New York: Elsevier/Greenwood.

——. 1979. "A Social History of Gay Politics," in *Gay Men: The Sociology of Homosexuality*, Martin P. Levine, ed. New York: Harper and Row.

——. 1985. "Age, Sex, and Structure." *Journal of Homosexuality* 11.

——. 1986. *The Rise of a Gay and Lesbian Movement*. Twayne Series on Social Movements. Boston: G. K. Hall.

Ariès, Philippe. 1977. "The Family and the City." *Daedalus*, 102 (2).

Baritz, Loren. 1960. *The Servants of Power*. Middletown: Wesleyan University Press.

Bogoras, W. 1909. "The Chukchee." *Memoirs of the American Museum of Natural History*, 11. New York: American Museum of Natural History.

Boswell, John. 1980. *Christianity, Social Tolerance, and Homosexuality.* Chicago: University of Chicago Press.

Braun, Rudolf. 1966. "The Impact of Cottage Industry on an Agricultural Population," in *The Rise of Capitalism*, David Landes, ed. New York: Macmillan.

Bray, Alan. 1982. *Homosexuality in Renaissance England.* London: Gay Men's Press.

Bristow, Edward. 1977. *Vice and Vigilance.* Dublin: Gill and Macmillan.

Bullough, Vern. 1976. *Sexual Variance in Society and History.* New York: Wiley.

Burnham, James. 1973. "Early References to Homosexual Communities in American Medical Writings." *Medical Aspects of Human Sexuality*, 7 (8).

Callender, Charles and Kochems, Lee. 1983. "The North American Berdache." *Current Anthropology*, 23 (4).

Conrad, Peter, and Schneider, Joseph. 1980. *Deviance and Medicalization.* St. Louis: Mosby.

Cook, Blanche. 1978. "'Women Alone Stir My Imagination,'" *Signs*, 4 (4).

Cott, Nancy. 1978. "Passionlessness." *Signs*, 4 (2).

Coulson, Margaret, Magas, Branka, and Wainwright, Hilary. 1975. "The Housewife and Her Labour under Capitalism – A Critique." *New Left Review*, 89.

Curtis, Bruce. 1980. "Capital, the State, and the Origins of the Working-Class Household," in *Hidden in the Household*, Bonnie Fox, ed. Toronto: Women's Press.

Demos, John and Demos, Virginia. 1969. "Adolescence in Historical Perspective." *Journal of Marriage and the Family*, 31 (4).

Donzelot, Jacques. 1979. *The Policing of Families*, trans. Robert Hurley. New York: Pantheon.

Dover, K. J. 1978. *Greek Homosexuality.* New York: Vintage.

Evans-Pritchard, E. E. 1970. "Sexual Inversion among the Azande." *American Anthropologist*, 72 (6).

Ewen, Stuart and Ewen, Elizabeth. 1982. *Channels of Desire.* New York: McGraw-Hill.

Faderman, Lillian. 1981. *Surpassing the Love of Men.* New York: Morrow.

Fellman, Anita and Fellman, Michael. 1981. "The Rule of Moderation in Late Nineteenth-Century American Sexual Ideology." *Journal of Sex Research*, 17 (3).

Ferguson, Ann. 1981. "Patriarchy, Sexual Identity, and the Sexual Revolution." *Signs*, 7 (1).

Fischer, Wolfram. 1973. "Rural Industrialization and Population Change." *Comparative Studies in Society and History*, 15 (2).

Foucault, Michel. 1978. *The History of Sexuality.* New York: Pantheon.

——. 1979. *Discipline and Punish.* New York: Vintage.

——. 1980. *Power/Knowledge.* New York: Pantheon.

——. 1984. *L'usage des plaisirs*. Paris: Gallimard.

Gardiner, Jean. 1975. "Women's Domestic Labour." *New Left Review*, 89.

Geertz, Clifford. 1960. *The Religion of Java*. New York: Free Press of Glencoe.

Gilbert, Arthur. 1975. "Doctor, Patient, and Onanist Diseases in the Nineteenth Century." *Journal of the History of Medicine and Allied Sciences*, 30 (3).

Gramsci, Antonio. 1971. *The Prison Notebooks of Antonio Gramsci*. New York: International.

Hartmann, Heidi. 1976. "Capitalism, Patriarchy, and Job Segregation by Sex." *Signs*, 3 (2).

——. 1981. "The Family as the Locus of Gender, Class and Political Struggle." *Signs*, 6 (3).

Herdt, Gilbert. 1984. *Ritualized Homosexuality in Melanesia*. Berkeley: University of California Press.

Herzen, W. 1977. "Antithetical Sexual Sentiment and Section 175 of the Imperial Penal Law, 1898," in *Bernstein on Homosexuality*, trans. Angela Clifford. Belfast: Athol Books.

Himmelweit, Susan and Mohun, Simon. 1977. "Domestic Labour and Capital." *Cambridge Journal of Economics*, 1 (1).

Hocquenghem, Guy. 1978. *Homosexual Desire*. London: Allison and Busby.

Horkheimer, Max. 1972. *Critical Theory*. New York: Seabury.

Kanter, Rosabeth. 1977. *Men and Women of the Corporation*. New York: Basic Books.

Katz, Jonathan. 1976. "Passing Women," in *Gay American History*. New York: Crowell.

——. 1983. *The Gay/Lesbian Almanac*. New York: Morrow.

Kennedy, Hubert. 1981. "The 'Third Sex' Theory of Karl Heinrich Ulrichs." *Journal of Homosexuality*, 6 (winter).

Levine, David. 1977. *Family Formation in an Age of Nascent Capitalism*. New York: Academic Press.

Lévi-Strauss, Claude. 1969. *The Elementary Structures of Kinship*. Boston: Beacon.

Levy, Robert. 1971. "The Community Function of Tahitian Male Transvestitism." *Anthropological Quarterly*, 44 (1).

McDonough, Roisin and Harrison, Rachel. 1978. "Patriarchy and Relations of Production," in *Feminism and Materialism*, Annette Kuhn and AnnMarie Wolpe, eds. London: Routledge and Kegan Paul.

McIntosh, Mary. 1981. "The Homosexual Role," in *The Making of the Modern Homosexual*, Kenneth Plummer, ed. Totowa, NJ: Barnes and Noble.

Mohr, James. 1978. *Abortion in America*. New York: Oxford University Press.

Neuman, R. P. 1975. "Masturbation, Madness, and the Modern Concepts of Childhood and Adolescence." *Journal of Social History*, 8 (spring).

Parsons, Gail. 1977. "Equal Treatment for All." *Journal of the History of Medicine and Allied Sciences*, 32 (1).

Pearce, Frank and Roberts, Andrew. 1973. "The Social Regulation of Sexual Behaviour and the Development of Industrial Capitalism in Britain," in

Contemporary Social Problems in Britain. Roy Bailey and Jock Young, eds. Westmead, England: Saxon House.

Plummer, Kenneth, ed. 1981. *The Making of the Modern Homosexual.* Totowa, NJ: Barnes and Noble.

Poster, Mark. 1978. *Critical Theory of the Family.* New York: Seabury.

Proust, Marcel. 1963. Excerpts from "Cities of the Plain" and "By Way of Sainte-Beuve," in *Eros: An Anthology of Male Friendship,* Alistair Sutherland and Patrick Anderson, eds. New York: Citadel.

Rapp, Rayna. 1978. "Family and Class in Contemporary America." *Science and Society,* 42 (fall).

Rosenberg, Charles. 1973. "Sexuality, Class, and Role in 19th-Century America." *American Quarterly,* 25 (2).

Sahli, Nancy. 1979. "Smashing." *Chrysalis,* 8 (summer).

Scott, Joan and Tilly, Louise. 1975. "Women's Work and the Family in Nineteenth-Century Europe." *Comparative Studies in Society and History,* 17 (1).

Secombe, Walley. 1973. "The Housewife and Her Labour under Capitalism." *New Left Review,* 83 (3).

Smedley, Agnes. 1976. *Portraits of Chinese Women in Revolution.* Old Westbury, NY: Feminist Press.

Smith-Rosenberg, Carroll. 1975. "The Female World of Love and Ritual." *Signs,* 1 (1).

Steakley, James. 1975. *The Homosexual Emancipation Movement in Germany.* New York: Arno.

Taylor, Gordon Rattray. 1965. "Historical and Mythological Aspects of Homosexuality," in *Sexual Inversion,* Judd Marmor, ed. New York: Basic Books.

Trumbach, Randolph. 1977. "London's Sodomites: Homosexual Behavior and Western Culture in the Eighteenth Century." *Journal of Social History,* 11 (1).

Tucker, Robert, ed. 1978. *The Marx-Engels Reader: Second Edition.* New York: Norton.

Walkowitz, Judith. 1980. "The Politics of Prostitution." *Signs,* 6 (1).

——. 1983. "Male Vice and Female Virtue," in *Powers of Desire,* Ann Snitow, Christine Stansell, and Sharon Thompson, eds. New York: Monthly Review Press.

Weeks, Jeffrey. 1977. *Coming Out.* London: Quartet.

——. 1981. *Sex, Politics, and Society.* London: Longman.

Yang, C. K. 1953. *The Chinese Family in the Communist Revolution.* Cambridge: MIT Press.

Part II

Sociology/Queer Theory: A Dialogue

6

"I Can't Even Think Straight": "Queer" Theory and the Missing Sexual Revolution in Sociology

Arlene Stein and Ken Plummer

There's nowt so queer as folk

Old Lancashire Saying

Writing in 1985, Judith Stacey and Barrie Thorne provided a useful critique of the "missing feminist revolution" in sociology. Feminists, they charged, had made important contributions to sociology, but had not been successful in "transforming the basic conceptual frameworks of the field" (Stacey and Thorne 1985: 301). In fact, feminist sociologists had been less successful than their counterparts in anthropology, history, and literature in effecting a "paradigm shift."

We believe that much the same could be said for the state of lesbian and gay sociology today. Even though a few sociologists have been studying lesbian/gay life for at least 25 years (at least since the publication of Mary McIntosh's 1968 seminal article), these concerns continue to inhabit the margins of the discipline.[1]

Studies of lesbian/gay life occur almost exclusively within the areas of deviance, gender, or sexuality, and have barely made their mark on the discipline as a whole. Many sociologists tend to labor under the assumption that lesbian and gay concerns are particularistic, and have little relevance to them, even though the lesbian/gay movement is among the most vibrant and well-organized social movements in the United States and Europe today. Clearly, there is a story here that we are missing; not only does its absence further marginalize "sexual minorities," but it also weakens sociological explanations as a whole.

There may be a glimmer of hope in an intellectual movement which is currently taking place in the humanities, called "queer theory." It is less and less possible today to take a course in anthropology, literature, film studies, or cultural history in the United States (and, to a much lesser extent, in Britain) without encountering the writings of so-called queer theorists. These scholars are succeeding in placing sexual difference at the center of intellectual inquiry in many fields – a "sexual revolution" which has been, for the most part, absent in sociology. Their success is particularly striking and even ironic in view of the fact that they are using social constructionism as if it were a new discovery, when it was sociologists who first generated this perspective.

How can sociologists redress this imbalance, and build upon the work that has already been done, to rethink sexual (and gender) nonconformity in ways that do not reproduce marginality? Toward this goal, we will briefly review the legacy of the sociology of homosexuality, consider what queer theory is, examine why it has been relatively successful in de-ghettoizing lesbian/gay studies, and ask what, if anything, we might might learn from those efforts.

The Legacy of the Sociology of Homosexuality

Although conducted on the margins, the sociology of homosexuality falls into two broad camps. The first is primarily empirical; the second tends to be more theoretically oriented. The first tends to accept sexual categories; the second often problematizes these categories.[2]

The first strand of homosexual studies, the empirical, has quite a long history. Emerging out of the nineteenth century, it seeks to describe and classify etiologies of homosexuality. Much of the earliest work was focused on "the homosexual" as an object of sociological survey, but increasingly, from the 1960s onwards, it has turned to the investigation of every nook and cranny of lesbian and gay life: bars, communities, identities, tearooms, and the like. It still continues, for example, in sociological accounts of identity stages (Troiden 1988).

Useful as they can be, empirical studies have tended to be unreflective about the nature of sexuality as a social category.[3] Such studies tend to replicate social divisions, implicitly reasserting the exotica of difference. At times, one is left with the sense that lesbian and gay individuals inhabit communities that are completely set off from the rest of society, that they are members of an altogether different culture and even a different species, if one follows the long-standing obsession with isolating the "cause" of homosexuality.[4]

The second strand of sociological studies problematizes the category "homosexual." It was present in some early writings, including those of Freud and Kinsey, but it was brought to the fore in the heyday of deviancy theory, the 1960s. The first generation of constructionist studies of sociology was conducted by American labeling theorists and UK "new deviancy theorists," young radical scholars who rejected the orthodoxies of criminology and traditional deviance study. Instead they challenged the very categories of deviance, locating "deviance" – not deviants – within frameworks of power.[5]

At this time a few key papers helped refocus the questions. McIntosh's (1968) highly influential contribution asked questions about the functions of the homosexual role, and shifted attention away from the homosexual "condition." Gagnon and Simon's (1967) reformulation brought matters of meaning, gender, and social organization to the fore. Kitsuse (1962) highlighted the powerful role of societal reaction and labeling. By the 1970s, a more theoretically informed study had commenced, and some research explicitly linked theorization with empirical work (Warren 1974).

Through labeling theory, the whole categorization process of homosexuality became problematized in what was later to be called "constructionism" and "deconstructionism." (The term *social constructionism* was rarely used in this literature, even though Berger and Luckman [1967] first popularized the phrase. It was widely used in other fields, and antedates Michel Foucault [1978] by more than a decade.) Through symbolic interactionism, the notions of meaning, process, "invented identities," and the cultural construction of communities became central – long before their current popularity in cultural studies. A lesser strand focused on "the stranger," "marginality," and "outsiders," describing homosexuality as a form of liberating consciousness.[6] Borrowing some ideas from US sociology, it was seen as radically critical and challenging of the status quo, although with hindsight the ideas may not now seem so challenging.[7]

The sociology of homosexuality has also been influenced by feminism, which has conceptualized sexuality as a terrain of power. Lesbian feminists provided a powerful critique of compulsory homosexuality and what Rubin (1975) called the "sex/gender system." Adrienne Rich's ([1980] 1983) conception of a "lesbian continuum" was highly influential in reexamining the relationship between gender and sexuality. This literature broadened the definition of lesbianism, emphasizing the relational aspects of lesbian sexuality and universalizing the possibility of lesbianism. Challenging medicalized conceptions that focused upon gender inversion and masculinized sexual desire, these theories blurred the boundaries between gay and straight women, and hardened the boundaries separating lesbians and gay men.

Although enormously valuable, feminist sociology has an unfortunate tendency to conflate gender and sexuality, erasing the specificity of lesbian and gay existence. As Rubin remarked:

> Gender affects the operation of the sexual system, and the sexual system has had gender-specific manifestations. But although sex and gender are related, they are not the same thing, and they form the basis of two distinct arenas of social practice. . . . Lesbian feminist ideology has mostly analyzed the oppression of lesbians in terms of the oppression of women. However, lesbians are also oppressed as queers and perverts by the operation of sexual, not gender, stratifications. (1984: 33)

This conflation of gender and sexuality continues to occur in feminist work. For example, a recent book on "never married women" barely mentions that many women in that category are lesbians (Simon 1987). A book on cross-gender occupations – women in the military and male nurses – mentions homosexuality only in passing, understanding the prevalence of lesbians and gay men in non-normative occupations (Williams 1989).

Collectively, the sociology of homosexuality, particularly the more theoretically oriented variety, may be seen as a kind of "standpoint theorizing" (McIntosh 1992). It assumes that studying and theorizing from the perspective of those who have been systematically denied access to power will inform our knowledge of the center. Yet in terms of the concerns of sociologists, the center has hardly budged. When studies of lesbian/gay life appear today, they are almost exclusively within the areas of deviance, gender, or sexuality, and have barely made their mark on the discipline as a whole. Though a few male theorists – but only a few – have made some nodding gestures towards feminist theory, there are virtually none who take lesbian and gay concerns seriously. Sometimes this is due to overt antagonisms and homophobia. Often it is due to theoretical blind spots.

Yet the "radical" theories of this period anticipated a number of ideas which would emerge again in the new queer theory, albeit somewhat more boldly, and even more resolutely committed to problematizing sexual categories.

From Constructionism to Queer Theory

Queer theory, an academic movement – indeed, an elite academic movement centered at least initially in the most prestigious US institutions – is indirectly related to the emergence of an increasingly visible queer politics, a confrontational form of grass-roots activism embodied in ACT UP, Queer Nation, and other direct-action groups during the last decade. Queer theory emerged in the late 1980s, publicized through a series of academic conferences held at Yale and other Ivy League universities, in which scholars, primarily from history and the humanities, presented their work on lesbian/gay subjects (Fuss 1991).

Queer theory became a rallying cry for new ways of thinking and theorizing. For many, the term *lesbian and gay studies* did not seem inclusive enough; it did not encapsulate the ambivalence toward sexual categorization which many lesbian/gay scholars felt, and the difficulties they faced in fitting sexuality into the "ethnicity model" which provided the template for such fields as African-American and women's studies, and indeed for identity politics in general. Gay men and (to a lesser extent) lesbians had organized themselves along the lines of an ethnic group at least since the early 1970s, following the example of the black civil-rights movement. Sexuality, however, defines a political interest constituency unlike those of gender and race. Membership in the group is fluctuating and largely invisible; identity as a lesbian or a gay man is, as Warner describes it,

> ambiguously given and chosen, in some ways ascribed and in other ways the product of the performative act of coming out. . . . In many respects, queer people are a kind of social group fundamentally unlike others, a status groups only insofar as they are not a class. (1991: 15)

Against attempts to define the lesbian and gay population and to organize a politics around it, queer theory, at least ideally, embraces the indeterminacy of the gay category and suggests "the difficulty in defining the population whose interests are at stake in queer politics" (Warner 1991: 16).

Clues as to what queer theory looks like can be glimpsed through some of its (emerging) canonical works, which come mainly from philosophy, literature, and cultural studies. Judith Butler (1990) describes the "unwritten and written codes of heterosexualized gender systems." Drawing upon the queer practices of drag, cross-dressing, and butch-femme, she develops a conception of gender as performance, and of gender parodies as subversive acts. Through readings of modern literature, Eve Sedgwick (1990) describes new ways of knowing and not knowing based on secrecy and outings, arguing that such knowledges constitute a medium of domination that is not reducible to other forms of domination, and that finds its paradigmatic case in the homosexual and the closet. Andrew Parker (1991) rereads Marx's *Eighteenth Brumaire*, calling our attention to the homosocial dynamics of the collaboration between Marx and Engels and arguing that we need a "sex-inflected analysis of class formations," an understanding of how sexuality is constitutive of class categories.

In texts like these we start to see the following hallmarks of queer theory: (1) a conceptualization of sexuality which sees sexual power embodied in different levels of social life, expressed discursively and enforced through boundaries and binary divides; (2) the problematization of sexual and gender categories, and of identities in general. Identities are always on uncertain ground, entailing displacements of identification and knowing; (3) a rejection of civil-rights strategies in favor of a politics of carnival, transgression, and parody which leads to deconstruction, decentering, revisionist readings, and an anti-assimilationist politics; (4) a willingness to interrogate areas which normally would not be seen as the terrain of sexuality, and to conduct queer "readings" of ostensibly heterosexual or non-sexualized texts.

At its widest, tallest, and Wilde(st), queer theory is a plea for massive transgression of all conventional categorizations and analyses – a Sadean/Nietzschean breaking of boundaries around gender/the erotic/the interpersonal, and a plea for dissidence. More narrowly, it is a political play on the word *queer*, long identified with "homosexuality," and the newest in a series of "reverse affirmations" in which the categories constructed through medicalization are turned against themselves. Often there is overlap between the more narrow (i.e., lesbian and gay) focus and the wider focus on transgression: they are far from separate.

Queer theorists claim that existing gay strategies, and minority-group strategies in general, have tended to rely on conceptual dualisms (male/female gender models, natural/artificial ontological systems, or essentialist/constructionist intellectual frameworks) that reinforce the notion of minority as "other" and create binary oppositions which leave the "center" intact. As Teresa de Lauretis has written:

> Homosexuality is no longer to be seen simply as marginal with regard to a dominant, stable form of sexuality (heterosexuality) against which it would be defined . . . it is no longer to be seen as transgressive or deviant vis-à-vis a proper, natural sexuality (i.e. institutionalized reproductive sexuality) according to the older, pathological model, or as just another, optional "lifestyle," according to the model of contemporary North American pluralism. (1991: iii)

Not content to study the "lesbian community" or the "gay community" as the exclusive site of sexual difference, queer theorists interrogate aspects of social life – the family, intimate relationships – but also look at places not typically thought of as sexualized – the economy, for example.

The homo/hetero divide so artfully assembled in the nineteenth century comes to be a strategy for deconstructing and rereading texts previously assembled through heterosexuality. "The sexual order overlaps with a wide range of institutions and social ideologies," writes Michael Warner (1991: 5), so that "to challenge the sexual order is sooner or later to encounter those institutions as problems." Much as feminists began treating gender as a primary lens for understanding problems that did not initially look gender-specific, for queer theorists the personal life is sexualized – and heterosexualized – and so are politics and economics, and just about everything else under the sun.

Queer theorists turn their deconstructive zeal against heterosexuality with a particular vengeance. When lesbian/gay theorists analyzed normative heterosexuality in the past, they envisioned it as a sex/gender system which was largely monolithic. Gayle Rubin (1975), in her classic article "The Traffic in Women," located heterosexuality as central to the reproduction of gender and sexual inequality. Queer theorists, on the other hand, locate within the institution of heterosexuality the seeds of its own demise. As Butler has suggested,

> That heterosexuality is always in the act of elaborating itself is evidence
> that it is perpetually at risk, that is, that it "knows" its own possibility of
> being undone. (1991: 23)

Heterosexuality, in this vision, is a highly unstable system, subject to various slippages, reliant upon carefully constructed individual performances of identity, and dependent upon the exclusion of homosexuality for its very identity. One could say that queer theory normalizes homosexuality by making heterosexuality deviant. Homosexuality ceases to be the exclusive site of sexual difference.

The figure whose influence looms large in this literature is Michel Foucault. His sweeping *History of Sexuality* (1978) details the construction of sexuality through institutional discourses, which come to constitute "regimes of truth." As the result of the Victorian era's "discursive explosion," Foucault argues, sexuality became a mainstay of identity, heterosexual monogamy came to function as a norm, and sexual deviants began to see themselves as distinct persons, possessing particular "natures." Foucault problematizes the belief in a continuous history of homosexuality, arguing that the differences between the homosexuality we know today and previous arrangements of same-sex relations may be so profound as to call into question a defining "essence" of homosexuality. Much the same could be said of sexuality in general. Modern sexuality is a product of modern discourses of sexuality. Knowledge about sexuality can scarcely be a transparent window onto a separate realm of sexuality; rather, it constitutes that sexuality itself.

It has been argued that Foucault's intellectual influence, and certainly the fact that he himself was gay, may be largely responsible for the recent movement of queer theory out of the ghetto (Duggan 1992). It might be argued that lesbians and gay men have long been cultural innovators, but with the influence of Foucault and the rise of postmodernism they emerge, more visibly than ever before, as intellectual innovators and social theorists.[8]

Certainly an affinity between queer culture and postmodernism, which today is perhaps the dominant theoretical approach in the humanities, is clear. Some observers have suggested that the typical postmodernist artifact is playful, self-ironizing, and even schizoid. In much the same way, lesbian/gay culture has often made use of camp, drag, and other cultural strategies to celebrate alienation, distance, and incongruity (Ross 1989). If the goal of the modernist project was to rationally organize social life, postmodernists see rationality as a lie – something which many lesbians and gay men have been saying all along.

Toward a More Queer Sociology

What does the seemingly anti-rational project of queer theory have to do with sociology, and how could it possibly inform the sociology of homosexuality? As we saw, the idea that sexuality is socially constructed was promoted by interpretive sociologists and feminist theorists at least two decades before queer theory emerged on the intellectual scene. Even if they lacked the elaborate theories of postmodernism, one could say that symbolic-interactionist approaches, along with some strains of lesbian feminism, were protodeconstructionist. Problematizing taken-for-granted linguistic codes and categories, they had an "elective affinity" with some versions of postmodernism (Denzin 1989).

In the 1980s and 1990s, the terrain of identities has been further problematized. The feminist sex debates, the critique of the false universalism of feminism lodged primarily by women of color, and scholarly work on masculinity (Brittan 1989; Connell 1987) have questioned the tendency among many feminists to subsume sexuality (and race) under gender. At the same time, partly through the experience of the AIDS crisis, many activists and scholars have come to believe that lesbians and gay men, in Sedgwick's words, "may share important though contested aspects of one another's histories, cultures, identities, politics, and destinies" (1990: 255).

Before these intellectual and political challenges emerged, the solution to cultural exclusion seemed to be the construction of social groups whose taken-for-granted identities simply needed to be made visible. Today, things appear to be a great deal more complicated. The existence of groups as essential entities is no longer taken for granted (Bourdieu 1985; Stein 1992). Rather than simply devising a politics which privileges one identity over others, it has become more apparent that different oppressions are differently structured and intersecting. It is impossible to separate one's sexuality from one's class, one's gender, and so forth. There has been a growing acknowledgment of the multiple, shifting character of sexual identities.

Sociology suffers from endless domain assumptions of the time and place in which it is written. Its own "sociology of knowledge" claims should make it sensitive to this, but it often fails to be sensitive in this way. Reading the sociology of the past often reveals how it is lodged in its own time warp, capturing specific times and places in the hidden assumptions it harbors.[9] Sociology can benefit from a more focused analysis of its assumptions. It can also benefit from the challenges of queer theory. In turn, it can contribute to forming a conception of lesbian/gay life, and of all its interconnections with social life more generally, that is deeper and more grounded than the approach of "queer theory."

First, we can take the question of "culture" much more seriously than we do now, but without ceding experience to the play of "texts." Symbolic interactionists rightly claimed that sexuality was constructed situationally, though they may have understated the extent to which individual agency is constrained by the power of institutionalized discourses such as medicine, and by the proliferation of the mass media.

Queer theorists, on the other hand, appreciate the extent to which the texts of literature and mass culture shape sexuality, but their weakness is that they rarely, if ever, move beyond the text. There is a dangerous tendency for the new queer theorists to ignore "real" queer life as it is materially experienced across the world, while they play with the free-floating signifiers of texts. What can the rereading of a nineteenth-century novel really tell us about the pains of gay Chicanos or West Indian lesbians now, for example? Indeed, such postmodern readings may well tell us more about the lives of middle-class radical intellectuals than about anything else! Sociology's key concerns – inequality, modernity, institutional analysis – can bring a clearer focus to queer theory.[10]

Although sexuality is constructed through various discourses, individuals are not simply passive recipients of these cultural constructions. They use them creatively, accepting parts of them, rejecting others, to actively construct their lives. Queer theorists have attuned us to the importance of looking at texts, but as sociologists we need to look at how identities are constituted in the cultural practices of everyday life, though mediated by texts. We are, as McRobbie reminds us, "more than just audiences for texts" (1992: 730). We would agree with her that what is required is a new paradigm for conceptualizing "identity-in-culture," developing an understanding of how sexuality, along with gender, race, ethnicity, class, and generation, is articulated and experienced within a terrain of social practices.[11]

The second thing we can learn from queer theory is how important it is to study the center and not just the margins. The "theoretical universalism" of the sociological approach smacks of a lingering functionalism in which all deviations from the norm must be explained. Homosexuality becomes the marked category; heterosexuality recedes into the background, normalized and naturalized. Queer theory's universalization of "queerness," and its willingness to look at the social construction of heterosexuality as well as homosexuality, reconceptualize sexuality in ways which could be taken up fruitfully by sociologists, though it may be a bit premature to reject the conception of deviance altogether.

As sociologists we should incorporate the best insights of the queer theory project – its attention to the terrain of culture, and its willingness to venture into areas typically not considered "homosexual" or even sexual – into our own work, and into sociological theorizing more generally. At the same time, we could deepen its insights by providing a more grounded, more accessible approach. We offer some initial suggestions for doing this.

Reconsidering the issues

How can sociology seriously purport to understand the social stratification system, for example, while ignoring quite profound social processes connected to heterosexism, homophobia, erotic hierarchies, and so forth (Rubin [1984] 1993)? Sexuality does not operate simply in the family, or through gender dynamics. Moreover, lesbians and gay men are not simply persons with sexual identities; they also are raced classed, and situated in a wide array of different life contexts.

Many questions arise from this. What, for example, happens to stratification theory if gay and lesbian concerns are recognized? What are the mobility patterns of lesbians? How do these patterns intersect with race, age, region, and other factors? What happens to market structure analysis if gays are placed into it? To consumption studies? To education? To social gerontology? We need to reconsider whole fields of inquiry with differences of sexuality in mind. The narrowness of so much sociology has to leave us aghast!

Rereading the classics

What happens to Giddens' structuration theory if hetero/homo issues are brought into the foreground? How might *Street Corner Society* or *Learning to Labor* look if homo/hetero issues were placed at center stage? How would the work of a Smelser, a Habermas, or an Alexander look if they lost their heterosexual and heterosexist assumptions and placed "queer" concerns in their frame of analysis?

An initial way of approaching this could be by reading sociological classics. As we "bring the lesbians and gays back in," however, we should also be problematizing the heterosexual center. The goal, as Michael Warner puts it, is "to make theory queer, and not just to have a theory about queers" (1991: 18). We need to challenge the assumption that sexuality is necessarily organized around a binary division between homosexuality and heterosexuality.

Rethinking pedagogy

Enter the queer student, and his or her not-so-queer classmates. In addition to revising the notion of who is the subject of a sociology of homosexuality, reflecting upon and rethinking pedagogical practice is in order. Mary Bryson (1992) designed a course at the University of British Columbia which incorporates what she calls "queer pedagogy," a way of teaching against the grain. She starts from the assumption that classrooms are always heterosexualized, but rather than simply organizing the course on lesbian and gay topics narrowly defined, she purposely never defines "lesbian" or "sexual orientation" so as to avoid ghettoizing lesbian and gay concerns and reifying the categories. Other approaches may be relevant as well, depending on the teaching context (Giroux 1992; Lather 1992). The point here is that we need to reflect upon how classrooms, like all other social spaces, are "heterosexualized."

These are only a few ideas, but they suggest a rethinking of some of sociology's core assumptions in a fashion which goes beyond the current tendency to treat sexuality (at worst) as peripheral and unimportant, and (at best) as something which can be conveniently tacked onto course syllabi or research designs without considering how it reshapes the questions that are being asked.

The process of paradigm shifting entails two dimensions: (1) the transformation of existing conceptual frameworks and (2) the acceptance of those transformations by others in the fields (Stacey and Thorne 1985). In terms of the "missing sexual revolution," sociologists have made some very preliminary progress toward the first goal, but the second – the acceptance of those transformations by others in the field – continues to impede progress. These innovations, however, will not only allow us to better represent those who are marginalized by current frameworks of theorizing; they will also make for better sociology.

Notes

Presented at The 1993 ASA Meetings, held in Miami Beach. Thanks to R. W. Connell, Steve Epstein, Becky Thompson, and Steven Seidman for their comments on an earlier draft. Arlene Stein also wishes to thank the Fuller Fund at the University of Essex.

1 There are a few earlier studies: in the United Kingdom, Schofield (1966); in the United States, Leznoff and Westley (1956). There are a few hints as well in the early Chicago School (Murray 1984: 65), but it is McIntosh (1968) that is widely cited as the first major statement.

2 Though the authors of this article come from different generational cohorts (Plummer, from the first generation of constructionists; Stein, from the second), we share a general sympathy for the latter tradition. Plummer was active in the early London-based Gay Liberation Front. He first published an article on the sociology of homosexuality in 1973, which used a symbolic interactionist perspective (Plummer 1973). His subsequent work, *Sexual Stigma* (Plummer 1975), was an attempt to apply the core ideas of social constructionism to sexual diversity. Stein's lineage is more recent. She came of age between the lesbian-feminist and the "queer" movements and received her training at Berkeley, publishing her first article on the subject 16 years after Plummer – a survey of approaches to the sociology

of sexuality (Stein 1989). She has continued these interests in her work on lesbian identity (Stein 1992). For a useful discussion of generational differences in lesbian/gay theory, see Escoffier (1992).

3 For an early statement of this criticism, see Gagnon and Simon (1967). Some recent work on the social aspects of AIDS, however, manages to be empirically as well as theoretically sophisticated. Because HIV transmission itself does not tend to respect sexual categories, many researchers in this area have come to recognize the problematic nature of sexual categories. See, for example, Connell and Kippax (1990).

4 See, for example, LeVay (1993), the latest in a century-long obsession with linking homosexuality with particular genes and chromosomes.

5 See, for instance, Stan Cohen, "Footsteps in the Sand," in McIntosh and Rock (1974).

6 The theme of the "outsider" is important but will not be taken up here. There is a long tradition of concern with marginality and outsiders in sociology – via Simmel, Stonequist, Park, Becker, Goffman, Garfinkle, and others – and it anticipates yet another theme of queer theory: the transgressive.

7 The tension between these two schools of lesbian/gay sociology may mirror the political tension which has long existed within the movement, between nationalism and assimilation, between fixing homosexuals as a stable minority group and seeking to liberate the "homosexual" in everyone (Epstein 1992; Stein 1992).

8 There were two previous "moments" when "out" lesbians and gay men – particularly gay men – were visible intellectual innovators. The first was in the 1890s and early 1900s, when Magnus Hirschfeld and Edward Carpenter were in the vanguard of an intellectual and cultural movement to remake gender and sexuality (see Rowbotham and Weeks 1977). The second "moment" was half a century later, when gay liberation began to raise questions about power and sexuality (see Fernbach 1981; Hocquenghem 1978). Thanks to R. W. Connell for reminding us of this.

9 Feminism has shown this only too clearly. More recently, the analysis of race has revealed a hidden structure which is potentially racist. See, for example, Collins (1990) and Gilroy (1993).

10 Similarly, though queer theory de-ghettoizes queer concerns within the academy, it tends to restrict access to those outside. Resolutely and unapologetically laden with theoretical jargon, it limits its audience to only the most theory-literate. In contrast, sociology has been more accessible to non- intellectuals, and should continue to strive for greater accessibility.

11 For a related understanding of culture which looks at symbols, stories, and other cultural products as tools in persistent "strategies of action," and points to a way of understanding identities in culture, see Swidler (1986).

References

Berger, Peter and Thomas Luckmann. 1967. *The Social Construction of Reality*. New York: Penguin.

Bourdieu, Pierre, 1985. "Social Space and the Genesis of Groups." *Theory and Society*, 14 (6): 723–44.

Britan, Arthur. 1989. *Masculinities and Power*. Oxford: Blackwell.

Bryson, Mary. 1992. "Queer Pedagogy: Praxis Makes Imperfect." Presented at Meetings of The American Educational Research Association, San Francisco.

Butler, Judith. 1990. *Gender Trouble: Feminism and the Subversion of Identity*. New York: Routledge.

———. 1991. "Imitation and Gender Insubordination." In *Inside/Out: Lesbian Theories, Gay Theories*, ed. Diana Fuss. New York: Routledge, 13–31.

Collins, Patricia Hill. 1990. *Black Feminist Thought*. New York: Routledge.

Connell, R. W. 1987. *Gender and Power*. Oxford: Polity.

———. 1992. "A Very Straight Gay: Masculinity, Homosexual Experience and the Dynamics of Gender." *American Sociological Review*, 57 (6): 735–51.

Connell, R. W. and S. Kippax. 1990. "Sexuality in the AIDS Crisis: Patterns of Sexual Practice and Pleasure in a Sample of Australian Gay and Bisexual Men." *Journal of Sex Research*, 27 (2): 167–98.

de Lauretis, Teresa. 1991. "Queer Theory: Lesbian and Gay Sexualities." *Differences*, 3: iii–xviii.

Denzin, Norman, ed. 1989. *Studies in Symbolic Interactionism*, vol. 10. Greenwich, Conn.: JAI Press.

Dollimore, Jonathan. 1991. *Sexual Dissidence*. Oxford: Clarendon.

Duggan, Lisa. 1992. "Making It Perfectly Queer." *Socialist Review*, 22 (1): 11–31.

Epstein, Steven. 1992. "Gay Politics, Ethnic Identity: The Limits of Social Constructionism," in *Forms of Desire*, ed. E. Stein. New York: Routledge, 239–93.

Escoffier, Jeffrey. 1992. "Generations and Paradigms: Mainstreams in Lesbian and Gay Studies." *Journal of Homosexuality*, 24 (1–2): 7–27.

Ferguson, Russell, Martha Gever, Trinh T. Minh-Ha, and Cornel West, 1990. *Out There: Marginalization and Contemporary Cultures*. New York: New Museum.

Fernbach, David. 1981. *The Spiral Path*. London: Gay Men's Press.

Foucault, Michel. 1978. *The History of Sexuality*. New York: Vintage.

Fuss, Diana. 1989. *Essentially Speaking: Feminism, Nature and Difference*. New York: Routledge.

———. 1991. *Inside/Out: Lesbian Theories, Gay Theories*. New York: Routledge.

Gagnon, John and William Simon. 1967. "Homosexuals: The Formation of a Sociological Perspective." *Journal of Health and Social Behavior*, 8: 177–85.

Gilroy, Paul. 1993. *The Black Atlantic*. London: Verso.

Giroux, Henry. 1992. *Border Crossings: Cultural Workers and the Politics of Education*. New York: Routledge.

Hocquenghem, Guy. 1978. *Homosexual Desire*. London: Allison and Busby.

Katz, Jonathan. 1990. "The Invention of Heterosexuality." *Socialist Review*, 20 (1): 7–34.

Kitsuse, J. 1962. "Societal Reaction to Deviant Behavior." *Social Problems*, 9: 247–56.

Lather, Patti. 1992. *Getting Smart*. London: Routledge.

LeVay, Simon. 1993. *The Sexual Brain*. Boston: MIT Press.

Leznoff, M. and W. A. Westley. 1956. "The Homosexual Community." *Social Problems*, 3: 257–63.

McIntosh, Mary. 1968. The Homosexual Role. "*Social Problems*, 17: 182–92.

——. 1992. "Feminism and Cultural Studies." *New Statesman and Society*, vol. 5. Presentation at Feminist Theory conference, University of Essex.

McRobbie, Angela. 1992. "Post-Marxism and Cultural Studies: A Post-script," in *Cultural Studies*, ed. Lawrence Grossberg et al. New York: Routledge.

McIntosh, Mary and P. Rock. 1974. *Deviance and Control*. London: Tavistock.

Murray, Stephen. 1984. *Social theory, Homosexual Realities*. New York: Gai Saber.

Parker, Andrew. 1991. "Unthinking Sex: Marx, Engels and the Scene of Writing." *Social Text*, 9 (11): 28–45.

Plummer, Ken. 1973. "Awareness of Homosexuality," in *Contemporary Social Problems in Britain*, ed. R. Bailey and J. Young. Lexington, UK: Saxon House.

——. 1975. *Sexual Stigma: An Interactionist Account*. London: Routledge.

——, ed. 1992. *Modern Homosexualities: Fragments of Lesbian and Gay · Experience*. London: Routledge.

——. 1995. *Telling Sexual Stories*. London: Routledge.

Rich, Adrienne. (1980) 1983. "Compulsory Heterosexuality and Lesbian Existence," in *Powers of Desire: The Politics of Sexuality*, eds A. Snitow, C. Stansell, and S. Thompson. New York: Monthly Review Press, 177–205.

Ross, Andrew. 1989. *No Respect: Intellectuals and Popular Culture*. New York: Routledge.

Rowbotham, Sheila and Jeffrey Weeks. 1977. *Socialism and the New Life*. London: Pluto.

Rubin, Gayle. 1975. "The Traffic in Women," in *Toward an Anthropology of Women*, ed. R. Reiter. New York: Monthly Review Press, 157–210.

——. (1984) 1993. "Thinking Sex," in *The Lesbian and Gay Studies Reader*, eds H. Abelove, M. Barale, and D. Halperin. New York: Routledge, 267–319.

Schofield, Michael. 1966. *Sociological Aspects of Homosexuality*. London: Longman.

Sedgwick, Eve. 1990. *Epistemology of the Closet*. Berkeley: University of California Press.

Simon, Barbara Levy. 1987. *Never Married Women*. Philadelphia: Temple University Press.

Stacey, Judith and Barrie Thorne. 1985. "The Missing Feminist Revolution in Sociology." *Social Problems*, 32 (4): 301–16.

Stein, Arlene. 1989. "Three Models of Sexuality: Drives, Identities and Practices." *Sociological Theory*, 7 (1): 1–13.

——. 1992. "Sisters and Queers: The Decentering of Lesbian Feminism." *Socialist Review*, 22 (1): 33–55.

Swidler, Ann. 1986. "Culture in Action: Symbols and Strategies." *American Sociological Review*, 52: 401–12.

Thorne, Barrie, 1993. *Gender Play: Girls and Boys in School*. New Brunswick: Rutgers University Press.

Troiden, Richard R. 1988. *Gay and Lesbian Identity: A Sociological Analysis*. New York: General Hall.

Warner, Michael. 1991. "Fear of a Queer Planet." *Social Text*, 9 (14): 3–17.

Warren, Carol A. B. 1974. *Identity and Community in the Gay World*. New York: Wiley.

Williams, Christine. 1989. *Gender Differences at Work: Women and Men in Nontraditional Occupations*. Berkeley: University of California Press.

7

A Queer Encounter: Sociology and the Study of Sexuality

Steven Epstein

In just the past few years in much of the English-speaking world, the term *queer* – formerly a word that nice people didn't use – has escaped the bounds of quotation marks. Its growing currency reflects three roughly congruent, yet uneasily related, developments: the emergence of new repertoires of political mobilization in groups such as Queer Nation, ACT UP, and (in England) Outrage; the foothold gained by new programs of lesbian and gay studies within the academy; and – partially in response to both of the above – the rise of an intellectual enterprise explicitly calling itself queer theory.

Queer theory and sociological theory confront one another with some suspicion, and more profoundly with misrecognition. No doubt to many sociological theorists, queer theory suggests this month's trendiness, just the latest progeny spawned by the Foucauldian Revolution and adopted by over-eager literary critics and proponents of cultural studies. To practitioners of queer theory, sociology perhaps is often seen as irrelevant or, at the very least, a bit stuffy. My point is not to call for some warm and fuzzy rapprochement, but to emphasize the queerness (in the so-called "original sense of the word") of this particular impasse.

In the 1960s and 1970s, sociologists (along with anthropologists and others) contributed significantly to a fundamental shift in the theorization of sexuality and homosexuality. Against naturalized conceptions of sexuality as a biological given, against Freudian models of the sexual drive, and against the Kinseyan obsession with the tabulation of behavior, sociologists asserted that sexual meanings, identities, and categories were intersubjectively negotiated social and historical products – that sexuality was, in a word, *constructed*. Though sexuality never became institutionalized as a formal subfield of sociological study, the "social-constructionist" perspective on sexuality drew much of its theoretical firepower from important currents within sociology at the time, particularly symbolic interactionism and labeling theory. Without seeking to minimize the importance of other disciplines, I would suggest that neither queer theory nor lesbian and gay studies in general could be imagined in their present forms without the contributions of sociological theory.[1] Yet to some recent students of sexuality working outside sociology, the concept of social construction is assumed to have sprung, like Athena, fully formed from the head of Michel Foucault; meanwhile the analyses presented by queer theorists, expressed in their own particular, often postmodern, vocabulary, confront sociologists as an alien power, unrecognizable as anything related in any way to the product of their own labor.

Exactly how this pattern of relationships between intellectual fields (Bourdieu 1988) took shape – and how its contours relate to developments in politics and elsewhere – would be a worthwhile topic for an extended study in the sociology of knowledge. My objectives in this article are more modest: I will explore the continuities and discontinuities in the theoretical understandings of sexuality offered by contemporary queer theory and by an earlier generation of sociology. First, I describe how a durable conceptualization of the social construction of sexuality was developed on the basis of mainstream theoretical currents within the discipline, and how this framework then fueled early work in lesbian and gay studies. Next, I analyze the emergence of "queerness" as both a political and an intellectual current. With reference to some contemporary exemplars and manifestos of queer theory, I argue that there are fundamental similarities with the sociological approaches because of the reliance on the guiding principle of social construction. Yet I also analyze the break with earlier work that queer theory seeks to make by asserting, in paradoxical fashion, the *centrality of marginality* to the study of society and culture, broadly conceived. I conclude by suggesting potential ways in which sociology could usefully complement, contribute to, and challenge such a project.[2]

The Critique of the Natural

In the eyes of sociologists who turned to the study of sexuality in the 1960s and 1970s, sex was both an obvious domain of investigation and the last great frontier resistant to the sociological enterprise. "At no point is the belief in the natural and universal human more entrenched than in the study of sexuality," wrote John Gagnon and William Simon (1973: 3–4) in *Sexual Conduct*. Sexuality was "naturalized" in two senses: first, in the dominant assumption that human sexuality should be understood as a biological function rooted in evolutionary imperatives which are then translated straightforwardly into social institutions and cultural norms; second, in the acceptance of the corollary that certain expressions of sexuality are "natural," while others are therefore "unnatural." With few exceptions, sexuality had not been seen as an important topic for sociological theorization.[3] Yet even a moment's reflection suggested that the domain of sexuality – a domain of elaborate and nuanced behavior, potent and highly charged belief systems, and thickly woven connections with other arenas of social life – was deeply embedded in systems of meaning and was shaped by social institutions. The primary obstacle to a sociological understanding of sexuality was the restricted emphasis on the mechanics of sex and its link to reproduction:

> Rarely do we turn from a consideration of the organs themselves to the sources of the meanings that are attached to them, the ways in which the physical activities of sex are learned, and the ways in which these activities are integrated into larger social scripts and social arrangements where meaning and sexual behavior come together to create sexual conduct. (Gagnon and Simon 1973: 5)

Central to this reinterpretation, as noted by Ken Plummer (1982), another of its principals, was a certain dethroning of sexuality. Sexuality should not be placed in the "realm of the extraordinary" as something at a remove from ordinary human behavior that obeyed a logic all its own. Instead, "in any given society, at any given moment in history, people become sexual in the same way they become everything else. Without much reflection, they pick up directions from their social environment" (Gagnon, quoted in Plummer 1982: 226). If the domain of the erotic at times has come to appear as something "estranged" from everyday life – symbolized concretely by disjunctive acts, like turning off the lights, that signal the entry into some other order of experience – this is not because of anything inherent in sexuality. Rather, it has served certain purposes, in Western societies, to construct "a realm in which the laws and identities governing everyday life could be suspended and the self be organized in ways that include aspects and qualities otherwise exiled or expressed through muted disguises and/or contrary uses" (Simon and Gagnon 1984: 55).

This was a complex critique with multiple explicit targets. First, the new theorists of sexuality took aim at Freud's (1962) "metapsychology" of drives, with its "hydraulic" metaphors of libido as a primal force that, when dammed up, pressed inexorably for discharge. In the Freudian (1961) view, "sexuality" and "society" stood, in a sense, opposed: libido was an individual possession, rooted in one's biological makeup, and social order was made possible only through the restriction of direct sexual expression and the sublimation of sexual energy into work.[4] By contrast, sociologists assumed that human sexuality was "always already" social in its organization and manifestations.[5] Rather than speaking of drives or instincts, Gagnon and Simon offered the metaphor of "sexual scripts" as a conceptual tool for understanding the drama of sexual conduct, thereby placing emphasis on the dimensions of learning, performance, and revision.[6]

Freudian drive theory, however, was not the only object of critique. For sociologists who believed that (to cite a recent commonplace) the most important sexual organ is the one between the ears, an equally important target was sexological research in the empiricist tradition of Kinsey.[7] Kinsey's (1948, 1953) famous studies of male and female sexuality – with his claim that homosexuality and heterosexuality lay on a continuum rather than being discrete categories, and with the noteworthy finding that 37 percent of the men in his sample reported having had at least one homosexual encounter leading to orgasm in their lifetimes – had done much to challenge conventional notions of normality and pathology in sexuality. Yet the exclusive focus on bodies, organs, and acts lost sight of the crucial question: What do these behaviors *mean* to their participants? How are such meanings generated and negotiated? (Gagnon and Simon 1973: 6). Indeed, as Plummer has noted, without attention to the subjective attribution of meaning, it becomes impossible even to tell what is "sexual" and what is not:

> When a child plays with its genitals, is this "sexual"? When a person excretes, is this sexual? When a couple are naked together, is this sexual? When a girl takes her clothes off in public, is this sexual? ... Sexual meanings are not universal absolutes, but ambiguous and problematic categories. (Plummer 1982: 231)

The emphasis on meaning as an emergent product of social interaction marked the reliance of these authors upon the core concepts of symbolic interactionism (Blumer 1969): the social construction of sexuality was simply an insurance of the more general "social construction of reality" (Berger and Luckmann 1967). Related currents of

Meadian sociology, such as labeling theory, were equally important in the development of the constructionist perspective. Indeed, the article often cited as the foundation stone of contemporary lesbian and gay studies, Mary McIntosh's (1968) "The Homosexual Role," explicitly applied labeling theory to the understanding of sexual categorization.

McIntosh rejected the notion that homosexuality was a "condition" which one either had or didn't have – that it was invariant in expression across societies and over time, that it could be diagnosed by the appropriate professional, and that its etiology could, in principle, be excavated by science. Just as anthropologists emphasized cultural variability in sexuality by examining different societies, McIntosh turned to historical examples to argue that modern Western conceptions of sexual identity were a recent development even in those countries.[8] In her view, the search for the "causes" of homosexuality reflected a category mistake; "one might as well try to trace the aetiology of 'committee chairmanship' or 'Seventh Day Adventism' as of 'homosexuality'" (1968: 261). Instead McIntosh claimed that "the homosexual" has come to occupy a specific social role in modern societies. Because homosexual *practices* are widespread but socially threatening, McIntosh argued, a special, stigmatized category of *individuals* is created so as to keep the rest of society pure. By this means, a "clear-cut, publicized and recognizable threshold between permissible and impermissible behaviour" (1968: 261) is constructed; anyone who begins to approach that threshold is immediately threatened with being deemed a full-fledged deviant.

A homosexual identity, in this view, is created not so much through homosexual activity *per se* (what labeling theorists (Lemert 1975) would call "primary deviance") as through the individual's reactions to being so labeled, and through the internalization of the imposed categorization ("secondary deviance"). Other authors writing in the "deviance" tradition conducted studies of the local organization of sexuality, focusing (for example) on boy prostitutes and their customers (Reiss 1978) or on the practitioners of anonymous sex in public restrooms (Humphreys 1978). Goffman's work on stigma (1963), with its fine-tuned analysis of how potentially "discreditable" individuals sought to manage the disclosure of information about themselves, or sought to "pass" as normal, also influenced analysts of sexuality, who were writing at a time when alternative expressions of sexuality were still, for the most part, "in the closet."

As the emphasis shifted away from the question of etiology, analysts eschewed the related concept of sexual *orientation* and focused increasingly on how social actors negotiated the vicissitudes of forging a sexual *identity*. In these analyses, identity was conceived as standing "in a dialectical relationship with society": "Societies have histories in the course of which specific identities emerge; these histories are, however, made by men with specific identities" (Berger and Luckmann 1967: 173). Barbara Ponse (1978), in one such study, explored the manifold processes by which lesbians organized a lesbian identity – how they drew links between their gender identity, politics, and sexuality; how they negotiated the unsettling periods in which identity seemed to be in flux; and how they retrospectively reinterpreted their personal biographies to conform with present self-understandings and to achieve a consistent sense of self. The frame of identity became increasingly salient in the study of gays and lesbians in particular. It mirrored the ascendancy of the lesbian and gay movement as a specific instance of "identity politics," one in which the personal trajectory of "coming out" was wedded to the public construction of a group identity and to a political strategy for social change (Escoffier 1985).

The publication in English of Foucault's short yet dazzling first volume of *The History of Sexuality* (1980) consolidated the emergent constructionist perspective, even as it provoked new controversies and suggested critiques of some of the sociological approaches within that perspective (see A. Stein 1989: 10). Whereas symbolic interactionism often risked eliding history and social structure in its emphasis on concrete social interaction, Foucault trained his attention on the big picture: sexual and erotic desire encompassed a diverse set of practices, strategies, discourses, institutions, and knowledges that were historically contingent and were played out on a dispersed field of power.

In Foucault's account, sexual categories – homosexual, heterosexual, and the like – are themselves products of particular constellations of power and knowledge. The recent historical emergence in Western societies of "the homosexual" and other sexual types, Foucault claimed, reflected a shift in the tactics of power from an emphasis on sexual behavior to one on sexual personhood: in place of the opposition between natural and unnatural *acts*, sexual experience would be divided into normal and abnormal *identities*. Sexuality therefore became a central site for the construction of subjectivity.

One implication of this analysis that would attract growing attention in coming years was that the organization of an oppositional politics around the given categories of identity was a necessarily limited strategy in challenging the regime of "normalization" itself, though perhaps it was a necessary starting-point, and potentially productive at that (see Weeks 1985: 244). Parallel concerns about the political emphasis on identity were voiced by writers with multiple salient identities, such as Latina and African-American women, who perceived lesbian and gay identity politics as a politics of sameness, within which other forms of diversity were suppressed (Moraga and Anzaldúa 1981; Smith 1983).

With the rise, in the early 1980s, of the lesbian and gay movement (Adam 1987) – a prominent political expression of a politics organized around sexual expression and identity – the academic study of sexuality increasingly became the study of *homo*-sexuality. By the early 1980s, writers in an array of academic disciplines were engaged in the production of a nascent lesbian and gay studies (Altman 1982; Blackwood 1986; Boswell 1980; Chauncey 1982–3; D'Emilio 1983; Faderman 1981; Freedman et al. 1985; Plummer 1981; Rubin 1984; Vance 1984; Weeks 1985); so were a substantial number of non-academic "organic intellectuals," many of them affiliated (along with some of the academics) with community-based lesbian and gay history projects (Escoffier 1990).[9] As a rule, theory and empirical research adopted a constructionist perspective, derived from Meadian currents in sociology,[10] from parallel developments in anthropology, from Marxist and feminist theory, and increasingly from the work of Foucault.[11] As a rule, such work also repudiated various traditional approaches summed up under the rubric of "essentialism" – though precise definitions of these opposing terms generated considerable debate as the decade wore on.[12] Broadly speaking, whereas essentialism took for granted that all societies consist of people who are either heterosexuals or homosexuals (with perhaps some bisexuals), constructionists claimed that such typologies are socio- historical products, not universally applicable, and deserve explanation in their own right. Also, whereas essentialism treated the self-attribution of a sexual identity as unproblematic – as simply the conscious recognition of a true, underlying "orientation" – constructionism focused attention on identity as a complex developmental outcome, the consequence of an interactive process of social labeling and self-identification.[13]

In subsequent years, with the formal establishment of lesbian and gay studies programs in a number of colleges and universities in the United States (Escoffier 1990), with the organization of annual conferences attracting more than a thousand participants to prestigious institutions such as Harvard and Yale, with the emergence of new publications such as the *Journal of the History of Sexuality* and *GLQ*, with the increasing tendency for senior faculty members to come out of the closet and for junior faculty members never to have been in, and with an outpouring of interest by undergraduate and graduate students, lesbian and gay studies, in the face of considerable opposition, has received substantial institutional legitimacy as an academic growth area.[14] Yet – despite the hegemony of social constructionism – the involvement of sociologists in the study of sexuality has diminished over the past decade, as has the visibility of explicitly sociological perspectives within lesbian and gay studies.[15]

Accounting for such a shift is beyond the scope of this article, and I can only hint at possible explanations. The relative decline in prominence of the larger theoretical currents that had given birth to the sociology of sexuality, such as symbolic interactionism and labeling theory, certainly may have made it less likely that the work of people such as Gagnon and Simon, Plummer, and McIntosh would be carried on by a younger generation of sociologists. Meanwhile new scholars, particularly in the humanities, often came to the study of sexuality directly from the work of Foucault, bypassing the social sciences entirely. Finally, as gays and lesbians underwent a dramatic conversion in status from a "deviant subculture" to a "minority group," a "community," and a "movement" (Altman 1982), the "nuts and sluts" approach of the sociology of deviance increasingly seemed misplaced, if not offensive, even to those who understood that "deviance" was not intended as a pejorative term. As Connell has noted, deviance studies tended routinely to group homosexuals alongside "alcoholics, mentally disordered persons, . . . and systematic check forgers" (1992: 737). Yet by the 1980s, with the rise of a quasi-ethnic self-understanding within well-defined and institutionally elaborate lesbian and gay communities, the most relevant sociological metaphors were no longer that of deviance but of ethnic group formation and social-movement mobilization (Altman 1982; Epstein 1987).[16] Applied to lesbians and gay men, the sociology of deviance was the sociology of the closet. The emergence of an affirmative politics organized around sexual identity simply eluded its grasp, no matter what epicycles the deviance scholars tacked onto their theories.[17]

Deciphering Queerness

The late 1980s marked the adoption, in various circles, of the word *queer* as a new characterization of "lesbian and gay" politics and, indeed, as a potential replacement for the very terms *lesbian* and *gay* (Bérubé and Escoffier 1991; Duggan 1992; A. Stein 1992). The term was explicitly associated with the activist group Queer Nation, which sprang up in dozens of cities around the United States; more generally, it reflected new political tendencies and cultural emphases, particularly in a younger generation of migrants to the established lesbian and gay communities. It is a term rife with connotations, some of them contradictory:

- The invocation of the "Q-word" is an act of linguistic reclamation, in which a pejorative term is appropriated by the stigmatized group so as to negate the term's power to wound. (This sometimes has the effect of reinforcing an insider/outsider division: self-styled queers can use the word freely, while sympathetic straights often do so only nervously.)
- Queerness is frequently anti-assimilationist; it stands in opposition to the inclusionary project of mainstream lesbian and gay politics, with its reliance on the discourses of civil liberties and civil rights. In this sense, queerness is often a marker of one's distance from conventional norms in all facets of life, not only the sexual.
- Similarly, queerness describes a politics of provocation, one in which the limits of liberal tolerance are constantly pushed. Yet while confrontational politics (for example, a same-sex "kiss-in" held in a bar frequented by heterosexuals) may work to affirm one's difference, it also seeks to overturn conventional norms. This transformative impulse (an "outward-looking" focus) coexists with the emphasis on anti-assimilation and self-marginalization (an "inward-looking" focus).
- Use of the term also functions as a marker of generational difference within gay/lesbian/queer communities. Younger queers may speak with resentment of feeling excluded by the established "lesbian and gay" communities, while older gays and lesbians sometimes object bitterly to the use of the term *queer*, which they consider the language of the oppressor.[18]
- "Queer" speaks to the ideal of a more fully "co-sexual" politics, within which men and women participate on an equal footing. To some, the use of "queer" to describe both men and women is preferable to "gay" (which includes women in much the same way as "man" used to include women), or to "gay and lesbian" (which emphasizes gender difference).
- "Queer" offers a comprehensive way of characterizing all those whose sexuality places them in opposition to the current "normalizing regime" (Warner 1991: 16). In a more mundane sense, "queer" has become convenient shorthand as various sexual minorities have claimed territory in the space once known simply, if misleadingly, as "the gay community." As stated by an editor of the defunct New York City queer magazine *Outweek* (quoted in

Duggan 1992: 21), "When you're trying to describe the community, and you have to list gays, lesbians, bisexuals, drag queens, transsexuals (post-op and pre), it gets unwieldy. Queer says it all."

- The rise of queerness reflects a postmodern "decentering" of identity (A. Stein 1992). As formerly paradigmatic patterns of identity construction (such as "the lesbian feminist") lose sway, they are replaced by a loosely related hodgepodge of lifestyle choices. Collectively these offer more individual space for the construction of identity, but none provides a clear "center" for the consolidation of community.

- Queer politics are "constructionist" politics (Duggan 1992), marked by a resistance to being labeled, a suspicion of constraining sexual categories, and a greater appreciation for fluidity of sexual expression.

- At times, however, queer politics also can be "essentialist" politics: in these expressions, the new moniker is simply reified into yet another identity category understood in separatist or nationalist terms, as the name *Queer Nation* itself can imply (Duggan 1992).

Clearly, the burdens of connotation would appear to be heavier than any single word might be expected to bear. At present, "queer" has been appropriated to describe a considerable range of political projects as well as individual and collective identities. Yet the meaning of the term is complicated further by its simultaneous employment by academics. Sometimes "queer" is put forward simply as the new and concise coinage: "gay studies," or "lesbian and gay studies," or "bisexual, lesbian, and gay studies," or "multicultural, bisexual, lesbian, and gay studies" should – for convenience, if for no other reason – be named "queer studies."[19] Sometimes, however, the invocation of "queer" signals important shifts in theoretical emphasis. In this reading, said Teresa de Lauretis, one of the organizers of a "queer theory" conference at UC-Santa Cruz, "queer" is intended "to mark a certain critical distance from the . . . by now established and often convenient, formula" of "lesbian and gay" (1991: iv).

Although many works are emblematic of the "queer turn" (Butler 1990, 1993; Cohen 1991; de Lauretis 1991; Dollimore 1993; Edelman 1989, 1992; Goldberg 1991; Miller 1991; A. Parker 1991; Patton 1993; Sedgwick 1993; Seidman 1993; Terry 1991; Warner 1993), Eve Kosofsky Sedgwick's *Epistemology of the Closet* (1990) is perhaps most often cited as a canonical text (even though the term *queer theory* does not appear there). Basically a critical reinterpretation of specific works of English literature, the book opens with a strong claim:

Epistemology of the Closet proposes that many of the major nodes of thought and knowledge in twentieth-century Western culture as a whole are structured – indeed, fractured – by a chronic, now endemic crisis of homo/heterosexual definition, indicatively male, dating from the end of the nineteenth century (1990: 1).

Furthermore (as if, perhaps, that weren't bold enough for an opening paragraph):

The book will argue that an understanding of virtually any aspect of modern Western culture must be, not merely incomplete, but damaged in its central substance to the degree that it does not incorporate a critical analysis of modern homo/heterosexual definition . . . (1990: 1).

All too often, studies of gays and lesbians, or of other "sexual minorities," have been cast as studies of "marginal" experience. By contrast, an "epistemology of the closet" seeks to analyze how various ways of construing sexual marginality shape the self-understanding of the culture as a whole. For example, Sedgwick argues, the very notion of the "closet" (as well as the metaphor of "coming out of the closet," now somewhat widely diffused) reflects the influence of the homosexual/ heterosexual dichotomy on broader perceptions of public and private, or secrecy and disclosure (1990: 72). In this sense, as Michael Warner suggests, "Sedgwick's work has shown that there are specifically modern forms of association and of power than can be seen properly only from the vantage of antihomophobic inquiry" (1993: xiv).

Though Sedgwick rejects many of the terms of the so-called "essentialist–constructionist debate" (1990: 40–1), her work in an important sense continues the tradition of the social- constructionist perspective. "Homosexuality" and "heterosexuality" do not describe transhistorical cultural forms, despite the universality of specific sexual practices. Rather, such practices come to *mean* very different things in a society which insists that each individual, just as he or she possesses a gender, also must necessarily occupy one or the other category of sexual orientation. "It was this new development," which Sedgwick and other authors (Halperin 1990) locate around the turn of the century in Western societies, "that left no space in the culture exempt from the potent incoherences of homo/heterosexual definition" (1990: 2).

In constructing a genealogy of the homosexual/heterosexual divide, Sedgwick's work draws on Foucault. In general, the mark of Foucault is broadly apparent in works of this kind – in their emphasis on power and "normalization," in their understanding of the constitutive role of discourse in the construction of subjectivity, in their poststructuralist critique of conceptions of coherent selfhood (Butler 1990, 1993), and in their postmodern suspicion of identity as a totalizing construct that subsumes difference (Cohen 1991). Whereas queer *politics* often seem divided in their approach to identity politics – at times subverting popular notions of stable identities, at times fashioning a new queer identity with their own enforced boundaries – queer *theory* is more consistent on this point. Indeed, the terrain of queerness provides a meeting point for those who come to the critique of identity from many different directions: those who believe that identity politics mute internal differences within the group along racial, class, gender, or other lines of cleavage (Montero 1993; Mort no date; Seidman 1991); those who believe that subjectivities are always multiple (Ferguson 1991; Seidman 1991); and those who are simply suspicious of categorization as inherently constraining. The point (at least as I read it) is not to stop studying identity formation, or even to abandon all forms of identity politics, but rather to maintain identity and difference in productive tension, and to rely on notions of identity and identity politics for their strategic utility while remaining vigilant against reification.[20]

In subject matter, queer studies emphasize literary works, texts, and artistic and cultural forms; in analytical technique, deconstructionist and psychoanalytic approaches loom large. Yet however marked these tendencies, none of them is necessarily definitive of queer theory, whereas the assertion of the centrality of marginality is the pivotal queer move. Just as queer *politics* emphasize outsiderness as a way of constructing opposition to the regime of normalization as a whole, so queer *theory* analyzes putatively marginal experience, but in order to expose the deeper contours of the whole society and the mechanisms of its functioning.

In some sense, this idea is not altogether new: a presumed goal of the sociology of deviance, for example, was to study the processes by which people become labeled deviant, so as to reveal, by contrast, the ideological construction of "the normal." In practice, however, sociologists have tended to relegate the study of "sexual minorities" to the analytical sidelines rather than treating such study as a window onto a larger world of power, meaning, and social organization. The challenge that queer theory poses to sociological investigation is precisely in the strong claim that no facet of social life is fully comprehensible without an examination of how sexual meanings intersect with it. In no way does it disqualify such a claim to recognize it as serving a certain strategic function within the intellectual "field" (Bourdieu 1988): queer theorists are seeking to situate their work as an "obligatory passage point" (Latour 1987) through which other academics must pass if they want to fully understand their own particular subject matters. In this sense as well, queer theory, like queer politics, is locating itself simultaneously both on the margins and at the center.

Perhaps the clearest analogy, as the editors of the *Lesbian and Gay Studies Reader* note (Abelove et al. 1993b: xv–xvi), is with feminist theory and women's studies programs; they have sought to argue that gender is not a "separate sphere," but rather is partially constitutive of other institutions such as the economy and the state. The goal therefore should not be to restrict concerns with gender to a bounded domain called "sociology of gender," but to introduce gendered understandings into sociological scrutiny across the board. The challenge for queer studies will be to demonstrate the links concretely in the case of sexuality – to identify the precise ways in which sexual meanings, categories, and identities are woven into the fabric of society and help give shape to diverse institutions, practices, and beliefs.

A Return to Sociology?

It should go without saying – but unfortunately needs to be said – that there is considerable space within such an enterprise for the perspectives and approaches of disciplines such as sociology, and indeed substantial need for sociological contributions, both theoretical and empirical. On the one hand, by tracing their lineages back no further than Sedgwick and Foucault, practitioners of queer theory risk reinventing the wheel. On the other hand, to the extent that queer studies focus overwhelmingly on discourses and texts, crucial questions about social structure, political organization, and historical context are investigated in only partial ways. As noted by Steven Seidman (1993: 132, 135), the poststructuralist reduction of complex cultural codes into "binary signifying figures" in much of queer theory, and the corresponding tendency to abstract discourses from their institutional contexts, verge unhappily on a kind of "textual idealism."

For sociologists, the potentially fruitful lines of investigation are manifold:

Sexual meanings and social categorizations. How are complex, often internally contradictory, and ambiguous systems of sexual meaning constructed and challenged in different cultures (e.g., R. Parker 1991: 172–3)? What is the relation between "macro" patterns of social organization and "micro" negotiations of sexual definition? Which institutions are central to the reproduction or contestation of sexual codes and beliefs? How do sexual belief systems and patterns of sexual conduct and identity formation intersect with other markers of social difference and systems of oppression, such as class, race, and gender (e.g., Almaguer 1993; Connell 1992; Connell, Davis, and Dowsett 1993; Gutiérrez 1991; Mumford 1992)?[21]

Social movements. That so many different and even contradictory meanings have consolidated around the word *queer* is itself suggestive of the richness of queer politics as a case study of the dynamics of collective action within "new social movements." Recent studies of social movements, such as the articles in Morris and Mueller (1992), have emphasized the critical importance of collective identity as something whose existence cannot simply be assumed by the analyst of a social movement.[22] Yet queer politics raise perplexing questions about the relation between identity and action. How are politics possible when actors insist upon the fluidity of identity and resist the very notion of categorization (Gamson, ch. 17 below; Seidman 1993)? Still other questions about movements are suggested by queer politics: How do queer politics differ from the gay rights politics of the late 1970s and early 1980s, the gay liberationist politics of the early 1970s (Duberman 1993), and the "homophile" politics of the 1960s (D'Emilio 1983)? How do these different models relate to the political strategies of other groups? In what ways are the unique rhetorical and dramaturgical styles of queer activist groups influencing other "new social movements" (Kauffman 1993)? How have AIDS activists managed so effectively to link an expressive politics of disruptive street theater (Gamson 1989) with an institutional politics of consensus building with medical experts, pharmaceutical companies, and government officials (Epstein 1991b)?

Other social institutions. How does the state intervene in sexual politics, and how are such politics constitutive of state institutions (e.g., Connell 1990)? How is scientific knowledge about sexual identity constructed by experts? What is the role of the mass media in the dissemination of sexual meanings? How do gender and sexuality structure the shop-floor relations between workers and management, and how do such relations in turn affect patterns of gender and sexuality (Salzinger no date)?

Though such questions may (and should) be addressed from the vantage point of many fields, they are fundamentally sociological questions, bound up with important theoretical currents and ignored to the detriment of the profession. Unfortunately, as Warner has noted, "it remains depressingly easy to speak of 'social theory' and have in mind whole debates . . . in which sexuality figures only peripherally or not at all. . . ." (1991: 4). One can identify occasional, recent exceptions (such as Giddens 1992), but the basic point remains. Although sociologists will not and should not go about queer studies in precisely the same ways as others have done it, the recent and impressive flurry of activity under that rubric still might provide a needed wake-up call.

Notes

I am particularly grateful to Chris Waters for extensive comments on an earlier draft, to Steven Seidman for his editorial suggestions and encouragement, and to the editors of *Sociological Theory*. I would also like to thank Pedros Bustos, Héctor Carillo, Jeff Escoffier, Josh Gamson, Laura Miller, Kevin Mumford, Leslie Salzinger, Arlene Stein, Jeff Weintraub, and Andrea Williams for helpful comments on an earlier draft and on related work.

1   One can also trace a paralle, and equally influential, lineage in anthropology, beginning perhaps with the cultural-relativist perspective of Margaret Mead (1935) and proceeding through more recent work on the "sex/gender system" (Rubin 1975) and on the cultural construction of gender (Ortner and Whitehead 1981) and sexuality (Blackwood 1986; Caplan 1987; Lancaster 1988; Newton 1988; R. Parker 1991).

   "Origins stories" are always problematic. My point here is neither to say that "it all started with sociology" nor to argue that sociology's early role entitles it to special respect. Rather, I seek to highlight the curious case of a discipline whose contributions have been forgotten, both within and without.

2   I will confine my analysis almost exclusively to intellectual and political currents in the United States.

3   In Parsons' work, for example, questions of sexuality tended to be subsumed within the study of sex roles and the institution of the family.

4   To be sure, the formal Freudian "metapsychology" was never followed widely outside psychoanalytic circles. Yet in watered- down form, the notion of sex as an overwhelming drive demanding release (a notion that owes much to Freud, even if it preceded him) has permeated popular culture in many Western societies. It has also found expression in radical social theory, such as Marcuse (1966).

5   In this sense, the constructionist sociology of sexuality would be far more compatible with some particular post-Freudian strands of psychoanalytic theory. Elsewhere I explore the unappreciated congruences between the sociology of sexuality and the "object relations" strand of psychoanalytic theory (Epstein 1991a).

6   In a useful update to their scripting theory, Simon and Gagnon (1984: 53) have proposed that scripting proceeds along three interconnected levels: *cultural scenarios*, "the instructional guides that exist at the level of collective life"; *interpersonal scripts*, which the actor must invent and elaborate when there is a "lack of congruence between the abstract scenario and the

concrete situation"; and *intrapsychic scripts*, the "internal rehearsals" that become necessary whenever interpersonal scripting becomes so complex that actors become cognizant of, and focused upon, their own script writing in dealing with others and others" script writing in dealing with them.

7   Gagnon and Simon themselves had both been researchers at the Kinsey Institute.

8   McIntosh's important invocation of historical evidence set her apart from most other labeling or deviance theorists (thanks to Kevin Mumford for pointing this out to me).

9   For additional important works from this period, see the articles collected in Duberman, Vicinus, and Chauncey (1989) and, more generally, the articles published in the *Journal of Homosexuality*.

10 For example, Weeks (1977: 239) identifies the main influences on his thinking as Plummer, McIntosh, and Gagnon and Simon; in later essays, he testifies to the importance of Foucault. D'Emilio (1983: 4) cites the same writers with a few additions, such as Jonathan Katz and Estelle Freedman.

11 Historians, however, often criticized Foucault for what they considered to be inaccurate accounts. They also took issue with his nominalist overemphasis on the role of professionals and their normalizing discourses in bringing sexual categories into being. Historians argued, for example, that homosexual subcultures and even certain forms of homosexual identity already had come into existence in large Western cities well before the sexological classification of "homosexuality" was created.

Gay and lesbian history (which was particularly important during this period) was also influenced greatly by Thompsonian notions of social history, which stressed writing a "history from below" (thanks to Chris Waters for emphasizing this point to me).

12 See, for example, Epstein (1987) and the other articles reprinted in E. Stein (1992). The so-called "essentialist–constructionist debate" mirrored a profound confusion both within gay and lesbian communities and in the general public about the ontological status of homosexuality – a confusion that seems only to have heightened in the 1990s. It is noteworthy that of the two great debates about gays and lesbians which have been played out recently in the mass media in the United States, one of them – the discourse on the biological or genetic roots of homosexuality – seeks to fix and stabilize sexual categories as discrete states of being, while the other – the brouhaha concerning "gays in the military" – betrays intense fears of the "contagious" nature of homoerotic desire. Thus, although Seidman (1993: 105) argues that "the arcane polemic between constructionists and essentialists has evolved into a sterile metaphysical debate devoid of moral and political import," the underlying concerns at stake in this debate continue to spark passions and reveal deep- seated social anxieties.

13 These critiques of sexual essentialism paralleled constructionist critiques of gender and racial essentialism; see, for example, Chodorow (1979) and Omi and Winant (1986).

14 The recent publication by Routledge of a 600-page *Lesbian and Gay Studies Reader* (Abelove, Barale, and Halperin 1993a) is both suggestive of the kinds of work being produced and indicative of the further institutionalization of the project by means of constructing a canon. On homophobic challenges to lesbian and gay studies, see Nussbaum (1992). On the question of the relation between lesbian and gay studies programs and the grassroots movement, see Escoffier (1990) and Duggan (1992).

15 There are, of course, any number of noteworthy individual exceptions; see, for example, Connell et al. (1993), Greenberg (1988), Seidman (1988, 1992), A. Stein (1992), and Taylor and Whittier (1992). A glance at the programs of the annual Lesbian, Bisexual and Gay Studies conferences, however, would easily demonstrate the overwhelming predominance of scholars in the humanities and the relative paucity of contributions from the social sciences.

AIDS prevention is one area where sociological (and anthropological) constructionism has gained a certain niche, both as a theoretical critique of behaviorist or narrowly interpersonal models of safe-sex education and as the grounding for the development of concrete health education strategies that acknowledge the problematic, variable, and culturally specific relations between behavior and identity (Connell et al. 1993; Davies et al. 1992; Parker et al. 1991).

For a (now outdated) review of sociological contributions to the study of homosexuality, see Risman and Schwartz (1988).

16 At least some segments of the profession continue to miss the point, as demonstrated by the *American Sociological Review* in its publishing of this very article by Connell in 1992. Though his article (on the dynamics of gender formation among Australian gay men) owed little to the sociology of deviance beyond his brief critique of it, the journal's cover advertised "Three Studies of Deviant Careers" and listed Connell's article, an article on criminals, and an article on misconduct by lawyers.

Similarly, a 1989 sociology textbook (Preston and Smith) was blasted by the Gay and Lesbian Alliance Against Defamation (GLAAD 1992: 3), a media watchdog group, for "[placing] its information on homosexuality between 'prostitution' and 'alcoholism' under the heading of 'Deviance.'" "Sociology textbooks need to present a more comprehensive and balanced picture of research on homosexuality," the organization advised. (On the treatment of homosexuality and the "hegemony of heterosexuality" in introductory sociology textbooks, also see Phillips 1991.)

17 I have in mind Kitsuse's (1980: 9) attempt to broaden the scope of deviance studies so as to encompass identity politics. Kitsuse conceptualized "tertiary deviance" as "the deviant's confrontation, assessment, and rejection of the negative identity imbedded in secondary deviation, and the transformation of that identity into a positive and viable self-conception."

18 On the heated debates in US "lesbian and gay" communities over whether to identify as "queer," see Gamson (ch. 17 below).

19 This move, however, remains tentative and controversial. Indeed, the editors of *The Lesbian and Gay Studies Reader* noted in their introduction to the volume (Abelove et al. 1993b: xvii): "It was difficult to decide what to title this anthology. We have reluctantly chosen not to speak here and in our title of 'queer studies,' despite our own attachment to the term, because we wish to acknowledge the force of current usage."

20 For different approaches to the maintenance of such a "productive tension" in identity politics, see Clarke (1991). Gamson (no date), and Seidman (1993). For the view that "the temporary totalization performed by identity categories is a necessary error," see Butler (1993: 230).

21 Although queer theorists have emphasized the analytical irreducibility of different forms of oppression (Butler 1993: 18–19; Sedgwick 1990: 31–5), in practice there has been inadequate attention to the interweavings of race and class with sexuality, as a glance at the table of contents of the *Lesbian and Gay Studies Reader* (Abelove et al. 1993a) would suggest.

22 On collective identity in lesbian politics, see Taylor and Whittier (1992) and A. Stein (1992). I am indebted to Josh Gamson for discussion of the points in this paragraph.

References

Abelove, Henry, Michèle Aina Barale, and David M. Halperin, eds. 1993a. *The Lesbian and Gay Studies Reader*. New York: Routledge.

——. 1993b. "Introduction," in *The Lesbian and Gay Studies Reader*, eds Henry Abelove, Michèle Aina Barale, and David M. Halperin. New York: Routledge, xv–xvii.

Adam, Barry D. 1987. *The Rise of a Gay and Lesbian Movement*. Boston: Twayne.

Almaguer, Tomás. 1993. "Chicano Men: A Cartography of Homosexual Identity and Behavior," in *The Lesbian and Gay Studies Reader*, eds Henry Abelove, Michèle Aina Barale, and David M. Halperin. New York: Routledge, 255–73.

Altman, Dennis. 1982. *The Homosexualization of America*. Boston: Beacon.

Berger, Peter L. and Thomas Luckmann. 1967. *The Social Construction of Reality*. New York: Anchor.

Bérubé, Allan and Jeffrey Escoffier. 1991. "Queer/Nation." *Out/Look*, 11: 14–16.

Blackwood, Evelyn, ed. 1986. *The Many Faces of Homosexuality: Anthropological Approaches to Homosexual Behavior*. New York: Harrington Park Press.

Blumer, Herbert. 1969. *Symbolic Interactionism: Perspective and Method*. Berkeley: University of California Press.

Boswell, John. 1980. *Christianity, Social Tolerance, and Homosexuality*. Chicago: University of Chicago Press.

Bourdieu, Pierre. 1988. *Homo Academicus*, trans. Peter Collier. Stanford: Stanford University Press.

Butler, Judith. 1990. *Gender Trouble: Feminism and the Subversion of Identity*. New York: Routledge.

———. 1993. *Bodies That Matter: On the Discursive Limits of "Sex."* New York: Routledge.

Caplan, Pat, ed. 1987. *The Cultural Construction of Sexuality*. London: Tavistock.

Chauncey, George, Jr. 1982–3. "From Sexual Inversion to Homosexuality: Medicine and the Changing Conceptualization of Female Deviance." *Salmagundi*, 58/59: 114–46.

Chodorow, Nancy, 1979. "Feminism and Difference: Gender, Relation, and Difference in Psychoanalytic Perspective." *Socialist Review*, 46: 51–69.

Clarke, Stuart Alan. 1991. "Fear of a Black Planet: Race, Identity Politics, and Common Sense." *Socialist Review*, 21: 37–59.

Cohen, Ed. 1991. "Why are 'We'? Gay 'Identity' as Political (E)motion (A Theoretical Rumination)," in *Inside/Out: Lesbian Theories, Gay Theories*, ed. Diana Fuss. New York: Routledge, 71–92.

Connell, R. W. 1990. "The State, Gender, and Sexual Politics," *Theory and Society*, 19: 507–44.

———. 1992. "A Very Straight Gay: Masculinity, Homosexual Experience, and the Dynamics of Gender." *American Sociological Review*, 57: 735–51.

Connell, R. W., M. D. Davis, and G. W. Dowsett. 1993. "A Bastard of a Life: Homosexual Desire and Practice among Men in Working-Class Milieux." *Australian and New Zealand Journal of Sociology*, 29: 112–35.

Davies, P. M., P. Weatherburn, A. J. Hunt, and F. C. I. Hickson. 1992. "The Sexual Behavior of Young Gay Men in England and Wales." *AIDS Care–Psychosocial and Socio-Medical Aspects of AIDS/HIV*, 4: 259–72.

de Lauretis, Teresa. 1991. "Queer Theory and Lesbian and Gay Sexualities: An Introduction." *differences: A Journal of Feminist Cultural Studies*, 3: iii–xviii.

D'Emilio, John. 1983. *Sexual Politics, Sexual Communities: The Making of a Homosexual Minority in the United States, 1940–1970*. Chicago: University of Chicago Press.

Dollimore, Jonathan. 1993. "Different Desires: Subjectivity and Transgression in Wilde and Gide," in *The Lesbian and Gay Studies Reader*, eds Henry Abelove, Michèle Aina Barale, and David M. Halperin. New York: Routledge, 624–41.

Duberman, Martin. 1993. *Stonewall*. New York: Dutton.

Duberman, Martin, Martha Vicinus, and George Chauncey Jr., eds. 1989. *Hidden from History: Reclaiming the Gay and Lesbian Past*. New York: Meridian.

Duggan, Lisa. 1992. "Making It Perfectly Queer." *Socialist Review*, 22: 11–31.

Edelman, Lee. 1989. "The Plague of Discourse: Politics, Literary Theory, and AIDS." *South Atlantic Quarterly*, 88: 301–17.

Edelman, Lee. 1992. "Tearooms and Sympathy, or the Epistemology of the Water Closet," in *Nationalisms & Sexualities*, eds Andrew Parker, Mary Russo, Doris Summer, and Patricia Yaeger. New York: Routledge, 263–84.

Epstein, Steven. 1987. "Gay Politics, Ethnic Identity: The Limits of Social Constructionism." *Socialist Review*, 93/94: 9–54.

———. 1991a. "Sexuality and Identity: The Contribution of Object Relations Theory to a Constructionist Sociology." *Theory and Society*, 20: 825–73.

———. 1991b. "Democratic Science? AIDS Activism and the Contested Construction of Knowledge." *Socialist Review*, 21: 35–64.

———. No date. "Impure Science: AIDS, Activism, and the Politics of Knowledge." Doctoral dissertation, University of California at Berkeley.

Escoffier, Jeffrey. 1985. "The Politics of Gay Identity." *Socialist Review*, 82/83: 119–53.

———. 1990. "Inside the Ivory Closet: The Challenges Facing Lesbian & Gay Studies." *Out/Look*, 10: 40–8.

Faderman, Lillian. 1981. *Surpassing the Love of Men*. New York: Morrow.

Ferguson, Ann. 1991. "Lesbianism, Feminism, and Empowerment in Nicaragua." *Socialist Review*, 21: 75–97.

Foucault, Michel. 1980. *The History of Sexuality*, vol. 1, trans. Robert Hurley. New York: Vintage.

Freedman, Estelle, Barbara C. Gelphi, Susan L. Johnson, and Kathleen M. Weston, eds. 1985. *The Lesbian Issue: Essays from Signs*. Chicago: University of Chicago Press.

Freud, Sigmund. 1961. *Civilization and Its Discontents*. New York: Norton.

———. 1962. *Three Essays on the Theory of Sexuality*. New York: Basic Books.

Gagnon, John H. and William Simon. 1973. *Sexual Conduct: The Social Sources of Human Sexuality*. Chicago: Aldine.

Gamson, Joshua. 1989. "Silence, Death, and the Invisible Enemy: AIDS Activism and Social Movement 'Newness.'" *Social Problems*, 36: 351–67.

Gay and Lesbian Alliance Against Defamation (GLAAD). 1992. *Update*. San Francisco: GLAAD.

Giddens, Anthony. 1992. *The Transformation of Intimacy: Sexuality, Love and Eroticism in Modern Societies*. Stanford: Stanford University Press.

Goffman, Erving. 1963. *Stigma: Notes on the Management of Spoiled Identity*. Englewood Cliffs, NJ: Prentice-Hall.

Goldberg, Jonathan. 1991. "Sodomy in the New World: Anthropologies Old and New." *Social Text*, 29: 46–56.

Greenberg, David F. 1988. *The Construction of Homosexuality*. Chicago: University of Chicago Press.

Gutiérrez, Ramón A. 1991. *When Jesus Came, the Corn Mothers Went Away: Marriage, Sexuality, and Power in New Mexico, 1500–1846*. Stanford: Stanford University Press.

Halperin, David. 1990. *One Hundred Years of Homosexuality*. New York: Routledge.

Humphreys, Laud. 1978. "A Typology of Tearoom Participants," in *Deviance: The Interactionist Perspective*, 3rd ed, ed. Earl Rubington and Martin S. Weinberg. New York: Macmillan, 270–82.

Kauffman, L. A. 1993. "Is Queerness Dead?" *SF Weekly*, April 21.

Kinsey, Alfred C. 1953. *Sexual Behavior in the Human Female*. Philadelphia: Saunders.

Kinsey, Alfred C., Wardell B. Pomeroy, and Clyde E. Martin. 1948. *Sexual Behavior in the Human Male*. Philadelphia: Saunders.

Kitsuse, John I. 1980. "Coming Out All Over: Deviants and the Politics of Social Problems." *Social Problems*, 28: 1–13.

Lancaster, Roger. 1988. "Subject Honor and Object Shame: The Construction of Male Homosexuality and Stigma in Nicaragua." *Ethnology*, 27: 111–25.

Latour, Bruno. 1987. *Science in Action: How to Follow Scientists and Engineers through Society*. Cambridge, Mass.: Harvard University Press.

Lemert, Edwin M. 1975. "Primary and Secondary Deviation," in *Theories of Deviance*, ed Stuart H. Traub and Craig B. Little. Itasca, Ill: Peacock, 167–72.

Marcuse, Herbert. 1966. *Eros and Civilization*. Boston: Beacon.

McIntosh, Mary. 1968. "The Homosexual Role." *Social Problems*, 17: 262–70.

Mead, Margaret. 1935. *Sex and Temperament in Three Primitive Societies*. New York: New American Library.

Miller, D. A. 1991. "Anal *Rope*," in *Inside/Out: Lesbian Theories, Gay Theories*, ed. Diana Fuss. New York: Routledge, 119–41.

Montero, Oscar. 1993. "Before the Parade Passes By: Latino Queers and National Identity." *Radical America*, 24: 15–26.

Moraga, Cherríe and Gloria Amzaldúa, eds. 1981. *This Bridge Called My Back: Writings by Radical Women of Color*. Watertown, Mass.: Persephone Press.

Morris, Aldon D. and Carol McClurg Mueller, eds. 1992. *Frontiers in Social Movement Theory*. New Haven: Yale University Press.

Mort, Frank. No date. "Essentialism Revisited? Identity Politics and Late Twentieth Century Discourses of Homosexuality." Unpublished manuscript.

Mumford, Kevin J. 1992. "Lost Manhood Found: Male Sexual Impotence and Victorian Culture in the United States." *Journal of the History of Sexuality*, 3: 33–57.

Newton, Esther. 1988. "Of Yams, Grinders, and Gays: The Anthropology of Homosexuality." *Out/Look*, 1: 28–37.

Nussbaum, Martha. 1992. "The Softness of Reason." *New Republic*, July 13, pp. 26–35.

Omi, Michael and Howard Winant. 1986. *Racial Formation in the United States: From the 1960s to the 1980s*. New York: Routledge.

Ortner, Sherry B. and Harriet Whitehead, eds. 1981. *Sexual Meanings: The Cultural Construction of Gender and Sexuality*. Cambridge, UK: Cambridge University Press.

Parker, Andrew. 1991. "Unthinking Sex: Marx, Engels and the Scene of Writing." *Social Text*, 29: 28–45.

Parker, Richard S. 1991. *Bodies, Pleasures and Passions: Sexual Culture in Contemporary Brazil*. Boston: Beacon.

Parker, Richard G., Gilbert Herdt, and Manuel Carballo. 1991. "Sexual Culture, HIV Transmission, and AIDS Research." *Journal of Sex Research*, 28: 77–98.

Patton, Cindy. 1993. "Tremble, Hetero Swine!" in *Fear of a Queer Planet: Queer Politics and Social Theory*, ed. Michael Warner. Minneapolis: University of Minnesota Press, 143–77.

Phillips, Sarah Rengel. 1991. "The Hegemony of Heterosexuality: A Study of Introductory Texts." *Teaching Sociology*, 19: 454–63.

Plummer, Ken, ed. 1981. *The Making of the Modern Homosexual*. London: Hutchinson.

——. 1982. "Symbolic Interactionism and Sexual Conduct: An Emergent Perspective," in *Human Sexual Relations: Towards a Redefinition of Sexual Politics*, ed. Mike Brake. New York: Pantheon, 223–4.

Ponse, Barbara. 1978. *Identities in the Lesbian World: The Social Construction of Self*. Westport, Conn.: Greenwood.

Preston, Frederick W. and Ronald W. Smith. 1989. *Sociology: A Contemporary Approach*. New York: Allyn & Bacon.

Reiss, Albert J., Jr. 1978. "The Social Integration of Queers and Peers," in *Deviance: The Interactionist Perspective*, 3rd edn, eds Earl Rubington and Martin S. Weinberg. New York: Macmillan, 436–47.

Risman, Barbara and Pepper Schwartz. 1988. "Sociological Research on Male and Female Homosexuality." *Annual Review of Sociology*, 14: 125–47.

Rubin, Gayle. 1975. "The Traffic in Women: Notes on the 'Political Economy' of Sex," in *Toward an Anthropology of Women*, ed. Rayna Reiter. New York: Monthly Review Press, 157–210.

——. 1984. "Thinking Sex: Notes for a Radical Theory of the Politics of Sexuality," in *Pleasure and Danger: Exploring Female Sexuality*, ed. Carole S. Vance. Boston: Routledge, 267–319.

Salzinger, Leslie. No date. "Producing Gender, Engendering Production." Unpublished manuscript.

Sedgwick, Eve Kosofsky. 1990. *Epistemology of the Closet*. Berkeley: University of California Press.

——. 1993. *Tendencies*. Durham: Duke University Press.

Seidman, Steven. 1988. "Transfiguring Sexual Identity: AIDS and the Contemporary Construction of Homosexuality." *Social Text*, 19/20: 187–205.

——. 1991. "Postmodern Anxiety: The Politics of Epistemology." *Sociological Theory*, 9: 180–90.

——. 1992. *Embattled Eros: Sexual Politics and Ethics in Contemporary America*. New York: Routledge.

——. 1993. "Identity and Politics in 'Postmodern' Gay Culture: Some Historical and Conceptual Notes," in *Fear of a Queer Planet: Queer Politics and*

Social Theory, ed. Michael Warner. Minneapolis: University of Minnesota Press, 105–42.

Simon, William and John H. Gagnon. 1984. "Sexual Scripts." *Society*, 22: 53–60.

Smith, Barbara, ed. 1983. *Home Girls: A Black Feminist Anthology*. New York: Kitchen Table/Women of Color Press.

Stein, Arlene. 1989. "Three Models of Sexuality: Drives, Identities, and Practices." *Sociological Theory*, 7: 1–13.

——. 1992. "Sisters and Queers: The Decentering of Lesbian Feminism." *Socialist Review*, 22: 33–55.

Stein, Edward, ed. 1992. *Forms of Desire: Sexual Orientation and the Social Constructionist Controversy*. New York: Routledge.

Taylor, Verta and Nancy E. Whittier. 1992. "Collective Identity in Social Movement Communities: Lesbian Feminist Mobilization," in *Frontiers in Social Movement Theory*, eds Aldon D. Morris and Carol McClurg Mueller. New Haven: Yale University Press, 104–29.

Terry, Jennifer, 1991. "Theorizing Deviant Historiography." *differences: A Journal of Feminist Cultural Studies*, 3: 55–74.

Vance, Carole S., ed. 1984. *Pleasure and Danger: Exploring Female Sexuality*. Boston: Routledge.

Warner, Michael. 1991. "Introduction: Fear of a Queer Planet." *Social Text*, 29: 3–17.

——. 1993. "Introduction," in *Fear of a Queer Planet: Queer Politics and Social Theory*, ed. by Michael Warner. Minneapolis: University of Minnesota Press, vii–xxx.

Weeks, Jeffrey. 1977. *Coming Out: Homosexual Politics in Britain, from the Nineteenth Century to the Present*. London: Quartet.

——. 1985. *Sexuality and Its Discontents: Meanings, Myths & Modern Sexualities*. London: Routledge.

8

The Heterosexual Imaginary: Feminist Sociology and Theories of Gender

Chrys Ingraham

. . . every sociological concept and thesis, as well as the overall patterning of these concepts and these, is potentially open for reconsideration . . . With the emergence of feminist sociological theory, the critical emphases in sociology are strengthened by an insistence that sociological work be critical and change-oriented . . . in an intensely reflexive way towards sociology itself. (Lengermann and Niebrugge-Brantley 1990: 318)

We must produce a political transformation of the key concepts, that is of the concepts which are strategic for us. (Wittig 1992: 30)

Feminist sociology, once at the vanguard of academic feminism, is showing signs of losing its conceptual and political edge. Feminists once sought to effect transformative social change by making visible the investment of sociology in practices contributing to the reproduction of gender inequality and relations of ruling.[1] But in the twenty years since feminists announced the need for sociology to attend to gender as an organizing social category, gender studies have been gradually canonized; more than that, the founding concept, gender, has come to be taken as obvious. From textbooks to research studies to theory, there is little or no debate over what is meant by gender. In this essay I make the argument that feminist sociological understandings of gender need to be reexamined for the ways in which they participate in the reproduction of what I call "the heterosexual imaginary." The "imaginary" is a Lacanian term borrowed by Louis Althusser for his theory of ideology. Defining ideology as "the imaginary relationship of individuals to their real conditions of existence" (1971:

52), Althusser argues that the imaginary is that image or representation of reality which masks the historical and material conditions
of life. The heterosexual imaginary is that way of thinking which
conceals the operation of heterosexuality in structuring gender and
closes off any critical analysis of heterosexuality as an organizing
institution. The effect of this depiction of reality is that heterosexuality
circulates as taken for granted, naturally occurring, and unquestioned,
while gender is understood as socially constructed and central to the
organization of everyday life. Feminist studies of marriage, family, and
sexual violence (which might seem to cover this ground) invariably
depend upon the heterosexual imaginary deployed in a variety of
heteronormative assumptions. Heteronormativity – the view that institutionalized heterosexuality constitutes the standard for legitimate
and prescriptive sociosexual arrangements – represents one of the main
premises not only of feminist sociology but of the discipline in general.
As such, it underlies and defines the direction taken by feminist sociology and by gender studies in particular.

If this is to change, feminist sociology must develop a critique of
institutionalized heterosexuality which does not participate in the
heterosexual imaginary. To interrupt the ways in which the heterosexual imaginary naturalizes heterosexuality and conceals its constructedness in the illusion of universality requires a systematic analysis of the
ways in which it is historically imbricated in the distribution of economic resources, cultural power, and social control.

It will be the work of this essay to call for a reconsideration of gender
as the key organizing concept of feminist sociology. The main argument of this article is that the material conditions of capitalist patriarchal societies are more centrally linked to institutionalized heterosexuality than to gender and, moreover, that gender (under the patriarchal arrangements prevailing now) is inextricably bound up with
heterosexuality. Rearticulating some of the critical strategies of early
feminist sociology within a materialist-feminist framework, it is
possible to both redress and disrupt the heterosexual imaginary circulating in contemporary gender theory.

Gender, or what I would call "heterogenders," is the asymmetrical
stratification of the sexes in relation to the historically varying institutions of patriarchal heterosexuality. Reframing gender as heterogender
foregrounds the relation between heterosexuality and gender. Heterogender confronts the equation of heterosexuality with *the natural*
and of gender with the cultural, and suggests that both are socially
constructed, open to other configurations (not only opposites and
binary), and open to change. As a materialist-feminist concept,

heterogender de-naturalizes the "sexual" as the starting point for understanding heterosexuality, and connects institutionalized heterosexuality with the gender division of labor and the patriarchal relations of production.

Materialist-Feminist Critique

Materialist feminism developed in response to a series of global social changes and associated critical currents in intellectual and political work. Western materialist or Marxist feminists attempted to expose and disrupt the interface of patriarchal social structures with multinational (particularly US) corporate capitalism's expanding sphere of accumulation and exploitation (Barrett 1980; Hennessy and Mohan 1989; Kuhn and Wolpe 1978; Mies 1986). Complaints about the global effects of patriarchy and capitalism provoked protests from non-Western or US Third World feminists about Western feminism's own racist, classist, and colonialist assumptions in attempting to "speak for" *all* women (Minh-ha 1989; Mohanty 1988; Sandoval 1991; Spivak 1985, 1988). These criticisms were buttressed by escalating claims in the West that feminism privileged the interests of white, middle-class, heterosexual women at the expense of an emancipatory project which could intervene in white-supremacist, classist, and heterosexist social arrangements (E. Brown 1989; R. Brown 1976; Bunch 1976; Carby 1982; Collins 1991; Combahee River Collective 1983; Davis 1981; Giddings 1984; hooks [*sic*] 1984; Lugones 1989; Moraga 1986; Rich 1980; Spelman 1989). This call for an internal re-evaluation of Western feminism intersected with the circulation of newly forming critical knowledges such as Afrocentrism, postcolonial criticism, poststructuralism, neo-Marxism, and postmodernism, and brought about a rethinking of feminist concepts and politics.

  Throughout the struggles and debates within feminism over the past twenty years, materialist-feminists have continually worked to develop an analytic capable of disrupting the taken-for-granted in local and global social arrangements and of exposing the economic, political, and ideological conditions upon which exploitation and oppression depend. Materialist feminism, however, is not to be confused with vulgar Marxism, with what is frequently referred to as base–superstructure Marxism or economic determinism. Rather, *materialism* here means a mode of inquiry that examines the division of labor and the distribution of wealth in the context of historically prevailing national and state interests and ideological struggles over meaning and value. Utilizing both Marxist and feminist critiques of ideology materialist feminism breaks away from the growing trend toward discursive politics – postmodern and poststructuralist feminism – and takes as its object the "social transformation of dominant institutions that, as a totality, distribute economic resources and cultural power asymmetrically according to gender" (Ebert 1993: 5). Committed to systematic analysis, materialist feminism is

> an inquiry intended to disclose how activities are organized and how they are articulated to the social relations of the larger social and economic process . . . how our own situations are organized and determined by social processes that extend outside the scope of the everyday world and are not discoverable within it. (D. Smith 1987: 152)

This form of analysis asserts the systematic operation of historically specific social totalities that link the local to the macro level of analysis. It is not, however, a "totalizing" theory in that it does not generalize its findings to apply to absolutely all phenomena, nor does it argue from an abstract or objectivist stance.

As a form of "critical postmodernism" (Agger 1992), materialist feminism argues that the nexus of social arrangements and institutions which form social totalities – patriarchy, capitalism, and racism – regulates our everyday lives. They are not monolithic, but consist of unstable patterns of interrelations and reciprocal determinations which, when viewed together, provide a useful way of theorizing power and domination. To theorize in terms of social totalities is to have a way of making sense of events in relation to pervasive social patterns. Rape and domestic violence, for example, can be seen as the effect of social structures that situate men in a hierarchical relation to women and to each other according to historical forms of social differentiation such as heterosexuality, with its historically specific heterogendered and racial components. According to Dorothy Smith, "relations of ruling" such as patriarchy

> bring into view the intersection of the institutions organizing and regulating society . . . a specific interrelation between the dynamic advance of the distinctive forms of organizing and ruling contemporary capitalist society and the patriarchal forms of our contemporary experience . . . a complex of organized practices, including government, law, business and financial management, professional organization, and educational institutions as well as the discourses in texts that interpenetrate the multiple sites of power. (1987: 3)

Significant in Smith's theory of ruling is her reference to forms, complexes, and "multiple sites of power." It is evident that for Smith, capitalism and patriarchy are organizing structures which are varied and multiple, institutionally as well as textually. Before returning to the role of ideology in materialist-feminist work in this essay, let us first address the struggles over concepts such as capitalism and patriarchy.

Theories which focus on capitalism and patriarchy as social totalities are becoming less and less acceptable. In recent years an important debate about the explanatory reach of such frameworks has challenged feminists to defend or rethink many of their assumptions. In particular, many postmodernist and poststructuralist theorists have criticized the use of "master narratives" such as Marxism, as "totalizing" and have disputed any theory which conceptualizes in terms of social totalities, such as capitalism or patriarchy. For example, Jean-François Lyotard argues against master narratives, but his argument confuses everchanging and historically specific social totalities with totalitarianism and (for some) positivism. These ideological debates are crucial and consequential. When critiques of Western culture's master narratives privilege the local and the particular at the expense of making connections, these arguments endanger any effort to conceive a "social change movement designed to remake the world" (Agger 1992: 113). Furthermore, they fail to acknowledge the significant rewriting social totalities and marxism have undergone in recent years (Hennessy 1993; Walby 1989).

It is my position that we should continue to critique capitalism and patriarchy as regimes of exploitation which organize divisions of labor and wealth, national and state interests, and those ideologies which legitimize the ordering and justification of these totalities and the production of social hierarchies and difference. In particular, we need to examine their varying historical, regional, and global conditions of existence. For instance, capitalism in Japan is not the same as capitalism in the United States, even though they are interrelated and reciprocal, and produce similar effects. They emerge from different historical and material relations of production and therefore defy reductive generalization.

Patriarchy is also historically variable, producing a hierarchy of heterogender divisions which privileges men as a group and exploits women as a group. It structures social practices which it represents as natural and universal and which are reinforced by its organizing institutions and rituals (e.g., marriage). As a totality, patriarchy organizes difference by positioning men in hierarchical opposition to women and differentially in relation to other structures, such as race or class. Its continued success depends on the maintenance of regimes of difference as well as on a range of material forces. It is a totality that not only varies cross-nationally, but also manifests differently across ethnic, racial, and class boundaries within nations. For instance, patriarchy in Africa-American culture differs significantly from patriarchy in other groups in US society. Even though each group shares certain understandings of hierarchical relation between men and women, the historical relation of African-American men to African-American women is dramatically different from that among Anglo-European Americans. Among African-Americans, a group which has suffered extensively from white-supremacist policies and practices, solidarity as a "racial" group has frequently superseded asymmetrical divisions based on gender. This is not to say that patriarchal relations do not exist among African-Americans, but that they have manifested differently among racial-ethnic groups as a result of historical necessity. Interestingly, racism has sometimes emerged in relation to criticisms of African-American men for not being patriarchal enough by Euro-American standards. As a totality, patriarchy produces structural effects that situate men differently in relation to women and to each other according to history.

To critique the way gender is theorized in feminist sociology, a materialist feminist mode of inquiry begins by investigating foundational assumptions. This investigation is followed by an examination of what is concealed or excluded in relation to what is presented. A materialist-feminist critique attempts to determine the ideological foundations of a particular set of knowledge and the interests served by the meanings organizing a particular theory. For example, theories which foreground and bracket off its link with heteronormativity – the ideological production of heterosexuality as individual, natural, universal, and monolithic – contribute to the construction of (patriarchal) heterosexuality as natural and unchangeable.

To examine the ways in which feminist sociology reproduces the heterosexual imaginary requires a theoretical framework capable of investigating the interests and assumptions embedded within any social text or practice. This mode of inquiry would make visible the frames of intelligibility or the "permitted" meanings in constructions of gender and heterosexuality. More than this, it would connect heterosexuality and interests to a problematic. As Althusser has argued, "A word or concept cannot be considered in isolation; it only exists in the theoretical or ideological framework in which it is used: its problematic" (1982: 253). To determine a text's problematic is to reveal another logic circulating beneath the surface. It appears as the answer to questions left unasked. It is not that which is left unsaid or unaccounted for, but that which the text assumes and does not speak. What is required, then, is a process of analysis capable of inquiring into the power relations organizing the allowed as well as the disallowed meanings in an effort to expose the artificiality of the theories and ideologies organizing the use of particular concepts.

The practice of ideology critique used by Marx (1985, 1986) and rewritten as symptomatic reading by Althusser (1968) has had a significant influence on sociology, most recently in the work of Dorothy Smith (1987, 1990). Ideology critique seeks to demystify the ways in which dominant or ruling-class ideologies are authorized and inscribed in subjectivities, institutional arrangements, texts of ruling, various cultural narratives, and, in this case, feminist sociological theories of gender. Like those taken-for-granted beliefs, values, and assumptions encoded as power relations within social texts and practices, ideology is central to the reproduction of a social order. Because it produces what is allowed to count as reality, ideology constitutes a material force and at the same time is shaped by other economic and political forces. As Althusser theorized it, ideology is the "'lived' relation between [persons] and their world, or a reflected form of this unconscious relation" (1968: 314) or imaginary.

This theory of ideology addresses the meaning-making processes embedded within any social practice, including the production of (social) science. Inherently contradictory, capitalist and patriarchal social arrangements are in a continual state of crisis management. The work of dominant ideologies is to conceal these contradictions in order to maintain the social order. At the same time, however, these breaks in the seamless logic of capitalism and patriarchy allow oppositional social practices and counter-ideologies to emerge.

Central to materialist-feminist analytic is its critical focus on ideology (see Althusser 1971; D. Smith 1987). Critique is a mode of inquiry which makes use of what is and what is not said in any social text, and theorizes the disjuncture between the two. Of particular importance is the examination of what is missing from the text. What is unsaid can be read symptomatically[2] to reveal the organizing problematic, or how the text raises certain questions while suppressing others. The unsaid of a text also reveals the interests served by what is left out. This understanding of absence speaks to the boundaries established by any conceptual or theoretical framework, which distinguish that which is addressed and that which is constructed as outside the limits of the theory at hand. What is unsaid is as constitutive of the problematic as what is said. Critique is a "decoding" practice which exposes these textual boundaries and the ideologies which manage them, revealing the taken-for-granted order they perpetuate and opening up possibilities for changing it. Materialist feminism then situates these ideologies historically and materially in relation to the division of labor and the relations of production. Finally, critique inquires into the political consequences of theorizing from this site of opposition. This approach attempts to put into crisis those organizing ideologies which naturalize or universalize particular sets of power relations implicated in the production of exploitation and oppression.

Feminist sociology has long made use of critique in order to pressure the discipline for its participation in relations of ruling. Many critical works served as significant interventions in the business-as-usual of sociology, and stand as landmarks from which to extend the reach of feminist theory. Although the following sections of this essay examine feminist sociology for its participation in the heterosexual imaginary, I think it only fair to say that some of the challenges to disciplinary authority by feminists were made at great risk and that much can be learned from these early critiques of sociology. The strategies used by feminist sociologists created the opening for further critical social inquiry and should be considered in their historical and material contexts.

Feminist Sociology and the Heterosexual Imaginary

Feminist sociology has been a powerful force for change since its emergence in the 1960s and 1970s. In addition to its significant contribution to gender studies, feminist sociology has provided a critical evaluation of mainstream sociology. Contesting the foundations upon which the production of sociological knowledges depends, feminist sociologists have provided a profound critique and rewriting of both the theoretical and the methodological assumptions of mainstream sociology (Acker 1973; Bart 1971; Bernard 1973; Deegan 1978; Hacker 1969; Hughes 1975; Long Laws 1979; Millman and Moss Kanter 1975; Oakley 1974; Reinharz 1983, 1984; Schwendinger and Schwendinger 1971; D. Smith 1974, 1975, 1987, 1990; Spender 1985; Stanley and Wise 1983). In a recent essay, Patricia Lengermann and Jill Niebrugge-Brantley (Ritzer 1990) discuss the defining characteristic of feminist sociological theory:

Feminist sociological theory attempts a systematic and critical reevaluation of sociology's core assumptions in the light of discoveries being made within another community of discourse – the community of those creating feminist theory. (1990: 316)

Central to this description is a reading of feminist sociological theory as responsive to "discoveries" and critical insights emanating from feminist theory and research. Feminist sociological theory has continually pressured the discipline to account for its political investments. In this regard, a key feature of feminist theory in sociology has been its exposure of sociological inquiry as value-laden and implicated in ruling practices. If it is to continue as a vital critical force in the discipline, feminist sociology must attend to contemporary theoretical and political debates, even those which question the problematics of feminist sociology. Recent trends in social thought, especially in what is becoming known as queer theory or lesbian/gay/bisexual/transgendered studies, are challenging the very foundations of feminist sociology, and indeed of sociology in general.

Critiques which reveal the implicit perpetuation of a normative heterosexuality require new ways of thinking for feminist sociology. Significant insights for this kind of analysis can also be found, however, in the works of those whose critical sociology questions the assumptions of the discipline. Of particular importance are the contributions of feminist sociologists whose analyses provide the possibility for examining the circulation of the heterosexual imaginary in sociology, even as their work also bears the marks of participating in it.

Two feminist theorists who have been highly influential in this regard are Shulamit Reinharz and Dorothy Smith. Reinharz argues that sociology is a field of study which demonstrates its conservative politics by "reinforc[ing] the current order and its values" (1983: 165) rather than taking into account "specific historical, cultural, ideological" contexts (1983: 162). Arguing from a sociology of knowledge perspective, Reinharz asserts the importance of explaining "the relationship between the knowledge produced or accepted in a particular society at any time, and the other dimensions of that society" (1983: 163). She is referring to mainstream sociological knowledge, but her critique can be applied as well to feminist sociology. For instance, feminist theories of gender which posit males and females, masculine and feminine, heterosexual and homosexual as opposites participate in dominant ways of thinking which organize all areas of difference as hierarchical and oppositional binaries. To produce theories of gender which bracket off heterosexuality as a social organizing structure is to "reinforce the current order and its values" by participating in the production of "acceptable" knowledges or ideologies. This closes off the possibility of theorizing the complex ways in which gender is tied to heterosexuality as institutionalized and hegemonic, as organizing the division of labor, and as instrumental to capitalism and patriarchy. If heterosexuality is assumed to be the natural attraction of opposites, somehow outside of social production, it does not require explanation. Feminist theories of gender, as well as common-sense and acceptable knowledges, reflect these assumptions. By not considering the "historical, cultural, and ideological" contexts in which gender circulates – the heterosexual imaginary – feminist theories of gender not only are contradictory but also leave heterosexuality as the unsaid on which gender depends.

Gender cannot be simultaneously an achieved status and an organizing concept for a "naturally occurring" heterosexuality. If both gender and heterosexuality are socially produced, then feminist sociology should be engaging with both of them at that level. Heterogender and its corresponding heterosexual imaginary are among those "other dimensions" which can affect the organization of knowledge and the reach of feminist sociology.

Dorothy Smith (1974, 1987, 1990) also takes the discipline to task, in this case for participating in the production of "objectified modes of knowing characteristic of the relations of ruling" (1990: 13) and for using ideas exclusive to a "male social universe" (1990: 13).

> The profession of sociology has been predicated on a universe grounded in men's experience and relationships and still largely appropriated by men as their "territory." Sociology is part of the practice by which we are all governed; that practice establishes its relevances. (1990: 13)

Smith critiques the disjuncture between women's experience and the prevailing "male" sociological frameworks, raising feminist sociology to a new height by making visible the significance of knowledges pertaining to women which sociology has typically ignored. She theorizes the silences in sociological theory as implicating sociology in male domination, and rewrites sociological practice to attend to women's everyday lives.

The neglect of women's everyday lives by sociology is of central concern to Smith, who argues for a sociology from the standpoint of women. This means not only analyzing women's daily lives and practices but also placing women within the larger social context of capitalist and patriarchal relations. Smith aims to explicate the "actual social processes and practices organizing people's everyday experience from a standpoint in the everyday world" (1987: 151). Her argument differs from Reinharz's in that she links the organization of women's lives to political economic dynamics. Of particular importance here is Smith's contribution to a theory of the everyday. In rewriting Marx for a feminist sociology, she opens up the study of the everyday as organized by relations of ruling.

In her contribution to the study of women's invisible labor and everyday experience, however, Smith makes repeated reference to the work of mothering and housework as largely overlooked by social scientists.

> Expanding the concept of work for our purposes requires its remarking in more ample and generous form . . . to include all the work done by women to sustain and service their and men's functioning in the wage relation . . . (1987: 165)

In her references to mothering and women's domestic labor as enabling the work of men, heterosexuality once again appears as the assumed and unacknowledged structure organizing women's lives as well as the division of labor. Heterosexuality is a natural or universal condition that Smith's theory of gender assumes. Although Smith makes great strides in shifting the starting point of feminist sociology to incorporate a version of ideological critique, her own work reveals a political investment in a heteronormative social order, which by definition maintains the very relations of ruling that she tries to put into crisis.

Feminist sociologists have challenged sociology to account for its "politics" – its investment in practices and knowledges organized hierarchically along lines of power. As can be seen in the work of Reinharz and Smith, these analytical strategies indeed create important conceptual and political openings, but by participating in the heterosexual imaginary they also reproduce some of the very social conditions they seek to interrupt.

In addition to Reinharz and Smith, other feminists have challenged the discipline (Abbott 1992; Lengermann and Niebrugge-Brantley 1990; Maynard 1990). Their ground-breaking efforts have also paved the way for a critique of feminist sociology. Yet at the same time they, too, participate in the reproduction of the heterosexual imaginary. In their overview of the contributions of feminist sociology, Lengerman and Niebrugge-Brantley (1990) outline the ways feminists have challenged sociology, beginning with questioning the absence of women and of knowledges related to women in all areas of sociology. This heuristic is particularly important for questioning the circulation of the heterosexual imaginary in feminist sociology.

A particularly important pattern that these authors identify in feminist sociology is the contestation of the andronormative starting point of sociological inquiry, which relegates all other knowledges to the margins and thereby reinforces patriarchal authority and value. For example, studies of mothering, teaching, child care, caregiving, and other aspects of the "domestic sphere" have been either ignored or devalued by mainstream sociology. Patriarchy, however, is not only andronormative; it is also heteronormative. Those aspects of the division of labor which are trivialized and neglected in sociological research and theory are also those practices which count as "women's work" in heterogendered social arrangements. By shifting the focus from gender to heterogender as the primary unit of analysis, institutionalized heterosexuality becomes visible as central to the organization of the division of labor. This shift also reveals the ways in which the heterosexual imaginary depends on an abject "other," which is regulated as deviant. This "other" consists of any sexual practice which does not participate in dominant heterogender arrangements and therefore does not count as legitimate or normal.

When I say that the critical insights of feminist sociologists can be employed to interrogate the heterocentrism of feminist sociology, I am not talking only about the marginalization of lesbian/gay/bisexual knowledges from sociological inquiry, but also about the way in which heteronormative assumptions organize many conceptual and professional practices. For instance, many social-science surveys ask respondents to check off their marital status as either married, divorced, separated, widowed, single, or (in some cases) never married. Not only are these categories presented as significant indexes of social identity; they are offered as the only options, implying that their organization of identity in relation to marriage is universal and not in need of explanation. Questions concerning marital status appear on most surveys regardless of relevance, in some cases as "warm-up" questions. The heteronormative assumption of this practice is rarely, if ever, called into question; when it is questioned, the response is generally dismissive. Heteronormativity works in this instance to naturalize the institution of heterosexuality.

For those who view questions concerning marital status as benign, one need only consider the social and economic consequences for those respondents who do not participate in these arrangements, or the cross-cultural variations which are at odds with some of the Anglocentric or Eurocentric assumptions regarding marriage. All respondents are invited to situate themselves as social actors according to their participation in marriage or in heterosexuality as a "natural" and monolithic institution. This invitation includes those who, *regardless of sexual (or asexual) affiliation*, do not consider themselves "single" or defined in relation to heterosexuality, and do not participate in these arrangements. Above all, the heterosexual imaginary working here naturalizes the regulation of sexuality through the institution of marriage and state domestic relations laws. These laws, among others, set the terms for benefits such as tax, health, and housing on the basis of maritalstatus. Rarely challenged except by nineteenth-century marriage reformers and early second-wave feminists (Bunch 1974, 1976; Harman 1901; Heywood 1876; MacDonald 1972; Sears 1977; Stoehr 1979; Wittig 1992), these laws and public policies use marriage as the primary requirement for social and economic benefits rather than distributing resources on some other basis, such as citizenship.

Heteronormative sociology, then, plays its part in what Dorothy Smith has conceptualized as textually mediated social practice.

> Such textual surfaces presuppose an organization of power as the concerting of people's activities and the uses of organization to enforce processes producing a version of the world that is peculiarly one-sided, that is known only from within the modes of ruling, and that defines the objects of its power. (1990: 84)

To not answer such seemingly innocent or descriptive questions is to become deviant according to sociology's enactment of modes of ruling, which signal to respondents in a variety of ways – from theory to surveys – what counts as normal. Under these conditions, sociology is a political field of study, invested in the reproduction of a heteronormative social order, and closed off to struggles over the construction of sexuality and to the exploration of social relations in *all* their layered and complex configurations.

Dorothy Smith's theory of the everyday world as problematic can be particularly useful for investigating the circulation and production of heteronormativity in sociological practice. As a mode of inquiry which begins with people's everyday lives, it illustrates and explains how individual lives are organized by extra-local social arrangements. For instance, to study how institutionalized heterosexuality organizes everyday professional activities in sociology, consider the case of the two non-tenured faculty members competing for the same job in a department which was allotted funds for only one. One candidate was a heterosexual man; the other, a lesbian. Two weeks before the final decision is made concerning hiring, the heterosexual man announces his engagement to a local woman and sends out wedding invitations to all members of the department. Well situated within the heterosexual imaginary, members of the department do not view this event in relation to the decision concerning the job but rather respond to it as a celebratory occasion and a chance to have a good time. The effect of this event on the material life of the candidates is never considered.

Weddings, like many other rituals of heterosexual celebration such as anniversaries, showers, and Valentine's Day, provide images of reality which conceal the operation of heterosexuality both historically and materially. In this sense they help constitute the heterosexual imaginary's discursive materiality. When used in professional settings, for example, weddings work as a form of ideological control to signal membership in relations of ruling as well as to signify that the bride and groom are normal, moral, productive, family-centered, good citizens, and, most important, appropriately gendered. (Or I should say "heterogendered"?) Although these patterns pervade the culture at large in everything from Tums commercials to the "Style" section of the *New York Times* – not to mention their prolific use in soap operas and prime-time television – little work has been done to critically examine their reasons for being and their effects.

Other examples abound regarding the heteronormativity or heterocentrism of sociology (e.g., privileging married couples in hiring practices, sanctions against research on lesbian/gay/bisexual/transgendered people, use of heteronormative concepts to describe non-heterosexual relationships, invisibility of non-heteronormative parenting practices), but to critique them is beyond the scope of this essay. Certain questions can be raised here, however, as a way to convey the extent to which heterosexuality remains an unexamined issue in the discipline. Of particular interest from a materialist-feminist perspective are the complex ways in which institutionalized heterosexuality helps guarantee that some people will have more class status, power, and privilege than others. Sociologists need to ask not only how heterosexuality is imbricated in knowledges, but how these knowledges are related to capitalist and patriarchal social arrangements. How does heterosexuality carry out their project both ideologically and institutionally? How do so many institutions rely on the heterosexual imaginary? Considering the rising levels of violence and prejudice in US society, how are we to understand the social and ideological controls regulating sexuality? What would a critical analysis of institutionalized heterosexuality reveal about its relationship to divisions of labor and wealth, national and state interests, and the production of social and economic hierarchies of difference? And, finally, how will sociology change if we shift away from a heteronormative or heterocentric sociology through a critique of heterosexuality?

Lengermann and Niebrugge-Brantley point to the contribution of feminist sociology in critiquing the discipline for its lack of social activism. Sociological studies rarely examine how women's lives are organized by dominant ideology and practice, or what role sociological inquiry plays in the maintenance and production of social inequality. Feminist sociologists insist that the discipline be reflexive, accountable for its politics, and actively engaged in reducing any oppressive consequences of its practices.

Reclaiming the critical legacy of feminist sociology not only promises to advance the theoretical reach of sociological inquiry, but also restores the activist orientation of feminist sociology. By questioning the starting point of gender studies while denaturalizing the institution of heterosexuality, feminist sociology once again can become politically reflexive and active in ideological struggle. The following section is a step toward initiating this process through an exploratory examination of contemporary gender texts.

Critiquing Heteronormative Gender Theory

Over the past quarter-century, feminist sociologists have made an enormous contribution to the study of gender across all social institutions and categories of analysis, theorizing everything from gender-across power arrangements to sex-difference development. Moreover, they have pressured the discipline to account for the ways in which it is implicated in the reproduction of gender oppression and exploitation. As a formidable force for change, feminist sociology, with its counterpart, the Section on Sex and Gender of the ASA, has established itself as one of the largest and most successful areas of inquiry in the discipline.

Feminist sociology, however, is losing its impetus for intervention or for ideological debate. Recent works within areas of inquiry covered by the sociology of sex and gender[3] generally assume a level of agreement on what gender is, how to study it, and why it is important. Gender, family, and introductory sociology textbooks, journal articles, and conference presentations in recent years show little variation in definitions of sex and gender.

A sampling of gender texts within sociology reveals the presence of a dominant framework in gender theory. Sex is typically defined as "the biological identity of the person and is meant to signify the fact that one is either male or female." Gender is described as "the socially learned behaviors and expectations that are associated with the two sexes" (Andersen 1993: 31). The idea of sex as biological and gender as socio-cultural was originally theorized by Oakley (1972) and then again by Gould and Kern-Daniels (1977), and has become the standard for most of sociology. In addition to Margaret Andersen's widely used text, *Thinking about Women*, Laurel Richardson's *The Dynamics of Sex and Gender* describes sex as "the biological aspect of a person" and gender as the "psychological, social, and cultural components . . . an achieved status" (1981: 5). Laura Kramer's *The Sociology of Gender* employs a similar version, arguing that "physically defined categories are the sexes" and that the "system of meaning, linked to the sexes through social arrangement, constitutes gender" (1991: 1). Likewise, in Clare Renzetti and Daniel Curran's *Women, Men, and Society*, sex is a "biological given . . . used as the basis for constructing a social category that we call gender" (1989: 2). In each case, sex is distinguishable as biology, implying that it is natural, while gender is viewed as learned or achieved. Even in essays offering an overview of the field of gender studies within sociology, gender is perceived as an established concept in a discipline which needs only to take it more seriously as a central category of analysis (Abbott 1992; Maynard 1990).

These patterns suggest that the biological-cultural differentiation of sex and gender has become "normalized" in sociology generally and among feminist sociologists in particular. Although inclusion of gender studies in "legitimate" sociology may be cause for celebration for some, the lack of debate over such a crucial concept as gender – not to mention its companion concept, sex – should be grounds for concern among feminists. Acquiescence to an unexamined gender concept goes against the grain of two of feminist sociology's founding principles – to keep a critical eye on the disciplining of knowledge and on forms of gender bias.

Consider some of the contradictions present in the acceptance of these theories of sex and gender. As Maria Mies (1986) points out, separating sex from gender reinforces the nature/culture binary, opening the study of sex to the domain of science and closing off consideration of how biology is linked to culture. Sex, as a biological category, escapes the realm of construction or achieved status, even though it is "defined" or "constructed." Because we are always engaged in giving meaning to the natural world, how we do that and to what end are questions of major significance. Sex as a category of analysis can never exist outside prevailing frames of intelligibility. It is a concept that is related to ways of making sense of the body, often by those – sociologists and biologists – who have a great deal of authority in the creation of knowledges. As a socially constructed category, sex must be scrutinized in relation to the interests that its definition furthers. That is, as sociologists we need to ask what ends are served by constructing sex as "the division of humanity into biological categories of female and male" (Macionis 1993: 350).

The institution of science and its authority in relation to the production of biological knowledges have far-reaching effects. It is one thing to assert that two X chromosomes produce a female and that an X plus a Y chromosome produces a male. But what happens when introductory sociology texts claim that it is a "hormone imbalance" which produces "a human being with some combination of female and male internal and external genitalia" (Macionis 1993: 351)? What investment or perspective is present in connoting this hormonal and genital configuration as an "imbalance"? Or, reading the unsaid here, what constitutes balance according to these knowledges? Clearly, a society of scientifically defined and authorized males and females is considered the "natural" order of things. How, then, do we make sense of cross-cultural difference in the "treatment" of sex variation? For example, the Dine (Navajo) view persons born with a combination of male and female genitalia as the exemplification of complete humanness, not as evidence of some dis-order (Geertz 1973).

Contemporary sex–gender ideology provides limited options for how we organize sexuality, but expanding these options is not simply a matter of attending to marginalized sexualities. Instead, it seems to me that we need to question our assumptions about sex and gender as to how they organize difference, regulate investigation, and preserve particular power relations, especially those linked to institutionalized heterosexuality.

All of the institutions involved in the production of sex as a biological category defined as male or female, where each is distinct and opposite from the other, are participating in reproducing lines of power. Claims that XX is female and XY is male are just that: scientific *claims* about the natural world, authorized by the ruling order and processed through organizing structures which assign meanings based on frames of intelligibility already circulating in the culture at large. What counts as normal and natural or as "fact" comes out of ways of making sense already ideologically invested in the existing social order. Often it closes off our ability to imagine otherwise. Any manifestation which does not fit the facts is rendered abnormal, deviant, or (worse) irrelevant. Consider, for instance, that the same institutions which organize these knowledges also historically neglected the study of women, scientifically justified the inferiority of non-white people, and claimed that social Darwinism was fact. These "findings" were coherent with dominant ways of thinking about sex, race, and class, and worked in their historical moment to legitimize prevailing practices and policies (Gould 1981; Takaki 1990).

Currently, with the rise of the lesbian/gay/bisexual rights movements, many "factual" knowledges concerning gender, sexuality, desire, morality, sex differences, labor, and nationality have been put into crisis. The more these critiques challenge the taken-for-granted concerning sex and gender, the clearer it is that current ways of thinking in sociology do not adequately account for sex variation. This investment in the dominant construction of sex begs the question of what interests are served by the disciplining of knowledge in sociology and what social arrangements that disciplining makes possible. The uncritical participation of feminist sociologists in these knowledges implies the possibility that there exists an investment in "naturalized" social arrangements at the risk of rendering invisible the interests that organize these ideas and benefit from their production. At the present, the dominant notion of sex in feminist sociology depends upon a heterosexual assumption that the only possible configuration of sex is male or female as "opposite sexes," which, like other aspects of the physical world (e.g., magnetic fields), are naturally attracted to each other. Masking the historical relation of sex to history and to heterosexuality is guaranteed by what I have defined as the heterosexual imaginary.

Gender, as the cultural side of the sex–gender binary, is frequently defined by sociologists as either achieved or constructed through a process of "socialization," whereby males and females become men and women attaining opposite and distinct traits based on sex. In addition to appearing in prominent texts and articles on gender, this understanding of gender circulates in introductory sociology texts. For instance, Hess, Markson, and Stein's *Sociology* asserts that gender is made up of "femininity and masculinity as *achieved* characteristics" but that maleness and femaleness are "*ascribed* traits" (1989: 193). Although this particular text makes reference to gender as variable cross-culturally and historically, its reliance on an unsaid heterosexual dualism implies a static or normative understanding of gender. In addition, this definition of gender illustrates the need for the concept of heterogender as a more appropriate description of the relation between sex and gender. Finally, this explanation does not account for the "necessity" of gender. This theory of gender as an "achieved" status does not address to what ends gender is acquired. Nor does it account for the interests served by ascribing or assigning characteristics based on sex. In other words, this text, as well as many others, does not examine what historical and material arrangements organize or are organized by gender. By foregrounding gender as dependent on the male–female binary, the heterosexual assumption remains unaddressed and unquestioned.

A similar approach is evident in John Macionis's introductory textbook, where he defines gender as

> society's division of humanity, based on sex, into *two* distinctive categories. Gender guides how females and males think about themselves, how they interact with others, and what positions they occupy in society as a whole. (1993: 352; my emphasis)

Likewise, consider Craig Calhoun, Donald Light, and Suzanne Keller's text, which claims that sociologists conceptualize gender as "nonbiological, culturally and socially produced distinctions between men and women and masculinity and femininity" (1994: 269). Again we see the dependence of theories of gender on the existence of two distinct categories, male and female. This so-called biological configuration is actually the foundation of established definitions of gender. Accordingly, gender is not treated as variable; rather, it is made up of two distinct entities, unquestioned, ahistorical, static, and consequently normative. These understandings serve as the standard in mainstream sociology and legitimize the organization of all other manifestations as deviant, alternative, or non-traditional.

Evident in most conceptualizations of gender is an assumption of heteronormativity. In other words, to become gendered is to learn the proper way to be a woman in relation to a man, or feminine in relation to the masculine. For instance, consider Mary Maynard's argument that "a significant factor in understanding the organisation of society is women's socially constructed difference from men" (1990: 281). Patricia Lengermann and Ruth Wallace state that "exploring the gender institution means looking at the identity of females in relation to males and vice versa . . . in the context of a two gender social reality" (1985: 3). As Margaret Andersen explains, "Gender refers to the complex social, political, economic, and psychological relations between women and men in society" (1993: 34). These are just a few examples among many that identify gender as a cultural binary organizing relations *between* the sexes. Ask students how they learned to be heterosexual, and they will consistently respond with stories about how they learned to be boys or girls, women or men, through the various social institutions in their lives. Heterosexuality serves as the unexamined organizing institution and ideology (the heterosexual imaginary) for gender.

Most important in these theories is the absence of any concept of heterosexuality as an institutional organizing structure or social totality. The cultural production of behaviors and expectations as "socially learned" involves all social institutions from family, church, and education to the Department of Defense. Without institutionalized heterosexuality – that is, the ideological and organizational regulation of relations between men and women – would gender even exist? If we make sense of gender and sex as historically and institutionally bound to heterosexuality, then we shift gender studies from localized examinations of individual behaviors and group practices to critical analyses of heterosexuality as an organizing institution. By doing so, we denaturalize heterosexuality as a taken-for-granted biological entity; we begin the work of unmasking its operations and meaning-making processes and its links to large historical and material conditions. Although feminist sociologists have made important contributions to the analysis of the intersection of gender and social institutions, they have not examined the relation of gender to the institution of heterosexuality. By altering the starting point of feminist sociology from gender to heterosexuality, or heterogender, as I have defined it, we focus on one of the primary roots of exploitation and oppression rather than on one of the symptoms.

Conclusion

The position I am taking in this essay is not new. It has a long and controversial history in feminist thought. Early second-wave feminists such as the Furies Collective, Purple September Staff, Redstockings (1975), Rita Mae Brown (1976), and Charlotte Bunch (1976) challenged dominant notions of heterosexuality as naturally occurring, and argued that instead it is a highly organized social institution rife with multiple forms of domination and ideological control. Adrienne Rich's (1980) article "On Compulsory Heterosexuality and Lesbian Existence" and Monique Wittig's (1992) *The Straight Mind* confronted the institution of heterosexuality head on, asserting that it is neither natural nor inevitable but instead is a contrived, constructed, and taken-for-granted institution or, as Wittig argues, a political regime. Now classics in feminist theory, these works have left a legacy that can be found in knowledges circulating primarily in the humanities.

In relation to other disciplines, sociology is losing ground on these issues as the contest over sexuality and gender escalates in other areas of the social sciences and in the humanities. For example, debates within gay/lesbian theory, cultural studies, and feminist theory in the humanities indicate that a major rethinking of gender and heterosexuality is underway (Butler 1989; de Lauretis 1987; Fuss 1991; Hennessy 1993; Sedgwick 1990; Seidman 1991, 1992, 1993; Warner 1993; Wittig 1992). Queer theory, as it is now called, has emerged as one of the prominent new areas of academic scholarship. A virtual explosion of books, articles, and special issues has issued from major academic publishers and high-level journals. Yet these new knowledges have been produced primarily within the humanities. Queer theory has been dominated by postmodern cultural theorists such as Butler, de Lauretis, and Sedgwick, who posit heteronormativity and gender as performative aspects of postmodern culture. More recent materialist approaches to rethinking gender and sexuality include the works of Delphy (1980), Evans (1993), Hennessy (1995), George Smith (1988, 1990, 1991), and Wittig (1992), to name a few.

I am arguing in this essay for a return to feminist sociology's political high ground. By "political" I mean all those social, material practices in which the distribution of power is at stake. Attending to these practices requires an internal critique of sociological gender theory for its participation in the very conditions feminist seeks to pressure and for its reproduction of the heterosexual imaginary. In the interests of materialist feminism and the lesbian/gay/bisexual rights movements, I am arguing for an examination of the ways in which feminist sociology's theories of gender contribute to the production and institutionalization of hegemonic heterosexuality. Finally, I am calling for something really queer: a critique of institutionalized heterosexuality as a formal area of inquiry within feminist sociology.

Notes

I would like to express my appreciation to Steve Seidman for his kindness and courage. Additional consideration goes to Alan Sica and the editorial board of *Sociological Theory* for their commitment to the advancement of *all* knowledges in sociology. And, finally, I would like to thank Rosemary Hennessy for her keen theoretical insights and unwavering support.

1　The phrase *relations of ruling* can be attributed to Dorothy Smith. According to Smith, "'Relations of ruling' is a concept that grasps power, organization, direction, and regulation as more pervasively structured than can be expressed in traditional concepts provided by the discourses of power.

I have come to see a specific interrelation between the dynamic advance of the distinctive forms of organizing and ruling contemporary capitalist society and the patriarchal forms of our contemporary experience" (1987: 3).

2 This refers to Louis Althusser's theory of symptomatic reading, which he ultimately attributes to Marx: "A word or concept cannot be considered in isolation; it only exists in the theoretical or ideological framework in which it is used: its problematic . . . [it] is not a world-view. It is not the essence of the thought of an individual or epoch which can be deduced from a body of texts by an empirical, generalizing reading; it is centered on the *absence* of problems and concepts within the problematic as much as their presence; it can therefore only be reached by a symptomatic reading" (1968: 316).

3 These areas include marriage and family, human sexuality, homosexuality, and any other category which makes use of sex or gender for its secondary level of analysis.

References

Abbott, Pamela. 1992. "Feminist Perspective in Sociology: The Challenge to 'Mainstream' Orthodoxy," in *Revolutions in Knowledge: Feminism in the Social Sciences*, eds S. R. Zalk and J. Gordon-Kelter. Boulder: Westview Press, 181–90.

Acker, Joan. 1973. "Women and Social Stratification: A Case of Intellectual Sexism." *American Journal of Sociology*, 78: 936–45.

Agger, Ben. 1992. *Cultural Studies as Critical Theory*. London: Falmer.

Althusser, Louis. 1968. *Reading Capital*. London: Verso.

——. 1971. *Lenin and Philosophy and Other Essays*. London: Monthly Review Press.

——. 1982. *For Marx*. London: Verso.

Andersen, Margaret. 1993. *Thinking about Women*. New York: St. Martin's.

Barrett, Michèle. 1980. *Women's Oppression Today*. London: Verso.

Bart, Pauline. 1971. "Sexism in Social Science: From the Iron Cage to the Gilded Cage – The Perils of Pauline." *Journal of Marriage and the Family*, 33: 742–50.

Bernard, Jessie. 1973. "My Four Revolutions: An Autobiographical History of the ASA," in *Changing Women in a Changing Society*, ed. J. Huber. Chicago: University of Chicago Press, 235–53.

Brown, Elsa Barkley. 1989. "Womanist Consciousness: Maggie Lena Walker and the Independent Order of St. Luke." *Signs*, 14: 610–33.

Brown, Rita Mae. 1976. *Plain Brown Rapper*. Baltimore: Diana Press.

Bunch, Charlotte. 1974. "The Reform Tool Kit." *Quest*, 1 (1): 43.

——. 1976. "Forum: Learning from Lesbian Separatism." *Ms.*, Nov., pp. 60–1, 99–102.

Butler, Judith. 1989. *Gender Trouble*. New York: Routledge.

Calhoun, Craig, Donald Light, and Suzanne Keller. 1994. *Sociology.* New York: McGraw-Hill.

Carby, Hazel. 1982. "White Woman Listen! Black Feminism and the Boundaries of Sisterhood," in *The Empire Strikes Back: Race and Racism in 70's Britain,* ed. the Center for Contemporary Cultural Studies. London: Hutchinson, 212–35.

Collins, Patricia Hill. 1991. *Black Feminist Thought.* New York: Routledge.

Combahee River Collective. 1983. "A Black Feminist Statement," in *This Bridge Called My Back: Writings of Radical Women of Color,* eds Gloria Anzaldua and Cherrie Moraga. New York: Kitchen Table Press, 210–18.

Connell, R. W. 1987. *Gender and Power.* Stanford: Stanford University Press.

Davis, Angela. 1981. *Woman, Race, and Class.* New York: Random House.

Deegan, Mary Jo. 1978. "Early Women Sociologists and the American Sociological Society: The Patterns of Exclusion and Participation." *The American Sociologist,* 16 (Feb.): 14–24.

de Lauretis, Teresa. 1987. "The Female Body and the Heterosexual Presumption." *Semiotica,* 67 (3–4): 259–79.

Delphy, Christine. 1980. *The Main Enemy.* London: Women's Research and Resource Centre.

Ebert, Teresa L. 1991. "The 'Difference' of Postmodern Feminism." *College English,* 53 (8): 886–904.

——. 1993. "Ludic Feminism, the Body, Performance, and Labor: Bringing Materialism Back into Feminist Cultural Studies." *Cultural Critique* (winter): 5–50.

Evans, David T. 1993. *Sexual Citizenship: The Material Construction of Sexualities.* New York: Routledge.

Frankenberg, Ruth. 1993. *White Women, Race Matters: The Social Construction of Whiteness.* Minneapolis: University of Minnesota Press.

Fuss, Diana, ed. 1991. *Inside/Out.* New York: Routledge.

Geertz, Clifford. 1973. *The Interpretation of Cultures.* New York: Basic Books.

Giddings, Paula. 1984. *When and Where I Enter: The Impact of Black Women on Race and Sex in America.* New York: Bantam Books.

Gould, Meredith and Rochelle Kern-Daniels. 1977. "Toward a Sociological Theory of Gender and Sex." *American Sociologist,* 12 (Nov.): 182–9.

Gould, Stephen Jay. 1981. *The Mismeasure of Man.* New York: Norton.

Hacker, Helen. 1969. "Women as a Minority Group in Higher Academics." *The American Sociologist* 4, (May): 95–9.

Harman, Moses. 1901. *Institutional Marriage.* Chicago: Lucifer.

Hennessy, Rosemary. 1993a. *Materialist Feminism and the Politics of Discourse.* New York: Routledge.

——. 1993b. "Women's Lives/Feminist Knowledge: Feminist Standpoint as Ideology Critique." *Hypatia,* 8 (1): 14–34.

——. 1995. "Queer Visibility in Commodity Culture," in *Social Postmodernism: Beyond Identity Politics,* eds Linda Nicholson and Steven Seidman. Cambridge: Cambridge University Press, 142–83.

Hennessy, Rosemary and Rajeswari Mohan. 1989. "The Construction of Woman in Three Popular Texts of Empire: Towards a Critique of Materialist Feminism." *Textual Practice*, Dec.: 323–59.

Hess, Beth, E. Markson, and P. Stein. 1989. *Sociology*. New York: Macmillan.

Heywood, Ezra and Angela. 1876. *Cupid's Yokes*. Princeton, Mass.: Co-operative Publishing Company.

hooks, bell. 1984. *Feminist Theory: From Margin to Center*. Boston: South End Press.

Hughes, Helen MacGill. 1975. "Women in Academic Sociology, 1925–1975." *Sociological Focus*, 8 (3): 215–22.

Kramer, Laura. 1991. *The Sociology of Gender*. New York: St. Martin's.

Kuhn, Annette and AnnMarie Wolpe, eds. 1978. *Feminism and Materialism: Women and Modes of Production*. London: Routledge.

Landry, Donna and Gerald MacLean. 1993. *Materialist Feminisms*. Cambridge, Mass.: Blackwell.

Lengermann, Patricia and Jill Niebrugge-Brantley. 1990. "Feminist Sociological Theory: The Near-Future Prospects," in *Frontiers in Social Theory*, ed. George Ritzer. New York: Columbia University Press, 316–44.

Lengermann, Patricia and Ruth A. Wallace. 1985. *Gender in America*. Englewood Cliffs, NJ: Prentice-Hall.

Long Laws, Judith. 1979. "Patriarchy and Feminism: Competing Ways of Doing Social Science." *Resources in Education* (June): 101–20.

Lugones, Maria. 1989. "On the Logic of Pluralist Feminism." Lecture, Syracuse University, fall.

MacDonald, George. 1972. *Fifty Years of Freethought*. New York: Arno.

Macionis, John J. 1993. *Sociology*. Englewood Cliffs, NJ: Prentice-Hall.

Marx, Karl. 1985. "The Eighteenth Brumaire of Louis Bonaparte," in *Karl Marx: Selected Writings*, ed. David McLellan. Oxford: Oxford University Press.

Marx, Karl and Frederick Engels. 1986. *The German Ideology*. New York: International Publishers.

Maynard, Mary. 1990. "The Re-Shaping of Sociology? Trends in the Study of Gender." *Sociology*, 24 (2): 269–90.

Mies, Maria. 1986. *Patriarchy and Accumulation on a World Scale*. London: Zed Books.

Millman, Marcia and Rosabeth Moss Kanter. 1975. *Another Voice: Feminist Perspectives on Social Life and Social Science*. New York: Anchor.

Minh-Ha, Trinh. 1989. *Woman, Native, Other*. Bloomington: Indiana University Press.

Mohanty, Chandra. 1988. "Under Western Eyes: Feminist Scholarship and Colonial Discourses." *Feminist Review*, 30: 61–88.

Moraga, Cherrie. 1986. "From a Long Line of Vendidas: Chicanas and Feminism," in *Feminist Studies/Critical Studies*, ed. Teresa de Lauretis. Bloomington: Indiana University Press, 173–9.

Oakley, Ann. 1972. *Sex, Gender, and Society*. London: Harper.

Oakley, Ann. 1974. *The Sociology of Housework*. London: Martin Robertson.

Parker, Andrew, Mary Russo, Doris Sommer, and Patricia Yaeger. 1992. *Nationalisms and Sexualities*. New York: Routledge.

Plummer, Kenneth. 1992. *Modern Homosexualities*. New York: Routledge.

Redstockings Collective. 1975. *Feminist Revolution*. New York: Random House.

Reinharz, Shulamit. 1983. "Experiential Analysis: A Contribution to Feminist Research," in *Theories of Women's Studies*, eds Gloria Bowles and Renate Duelli Klein. London: Routledge, 162–9.

——. 1984. *On Becoming a Social Scientist*. New York: Transaction Books.

Renzetti, Claire and Daniel Curran. 1989. *Women, Men, and Society*. Boston: Allyn and Bacon.

Rich, Adrienne. 1980. "Compulsory Heterosexuality and Lesbian Existence." *Signs*, 5 (summer): 631–60.

Richardson, Laurel, 1981. *The Dynamics of Sex and Gender*. Boston: Houghton Mifflin.

Ritzer, George. 1990. *Frontiers in Social Theory*. New York: Columbia University Press.

Sandoval, Cheyla. 1991. "U.S. Third World Feminism: The Theory and Method of Oppositional Consciousness in the Postmodern World." *Genders*, 10 (spring): 1–24.

Schwendinger, J. and H. Schwendinger. 1971. "The Subjection of Women: Ideological Views and Solutions," in *Sociologists of the Chair: A Radical Analysis of the Formative Years of North American Sociology*. New York: Basic Books, 287–335.

Sears, Hal D. 1977. *The Sex Radicals: Free Love in High Victorian America*. Lawrence: Regents Press of Kansas.

Sedgwick, Eve Kosofsky. 1990. *Epistemology of the Closet*. Berkeley: University California Press.

Seidman, Steven. 1991. *Romantic Longings*. New York: Routledge.

——. 1992. *Embattled Eros*. New York: Routledge.

——. 1993. "Identity and Politics in a Postmodern Gay Culture: Some Conceptual and Historical Notes," in *Fear of a Queer Planet*, ed. Michael Warner. Minneapolis: University of Minnesota Press, 105–42.

Smith, Dorothy. 1974. "Women's Perspective as a Radical Critique of Sociology." *Sociological Inquiry*, 44: 73–90.

——. 1975. "An Analysis of Ideological Structures and How Women Are Excluded: Considerations for Academic Women." *Canadian Review of Sociology and Anthropology*, 12 (4): 131–54.

——. 1987. *The Everyday World as Problematic*. Boston: Northeastern University Press.

——. 1990. *The Conceptual Practices of Power: A Feminist Sociology of Knowledge*. Boston: Northeastern Press.

Smith, George W. 1988. "Policing the Gay Community: An Inquiry into Textually-Mediated Social Relations." *International Journal of the Sociology of Law*, 16: 163–83.

——. 1990. "Political Activist as Ethnographer." *Social Problems*, 37 (4): 87–98.

——. 1991. "The Ideology of 'Fag': Barriers to Education for Gay Students." Paper presented at Meetings of the Canadian Sociology and Anthropology Association, Kingston, Ontario.

Spelman, Elizabeth V. 1989. *Inessential Woman: Problems of Exclusion in Feminist Thought.* Boston: Beacon.

Spender, Dale. 1985. *Man Made Language.* London: Routledge & Kegan Paul.

Spivak, Gayatri. 1985. "Feminism and Critical Theory," in *For Alma Mater*, eds Paula Treichler, Chris Kramarae, and Beth Stafford. Chicago: University of Illionis Press, 119–42.

——. 1988. "Can the Subaltern Speak?" in *Marxism and the Interpretation of Culture*, eds Cary Nelson and Lawrence Grossberg. Chicago: University of Illinois Press, 271–316.

Stacey, Judith and Barry Thorne. 1985. "The Missing Feminist Revolution in Sociology." *Social Problems*, 32: 301–16.

Stanley, Liz and Sue Wise. 1983. *Breaking Out: Feminist Consciousness and Feminist Research.* London: Routledge.

Stoehr, Taylor. 1979. *Free Love in America: A Documentary History.* New York: AMS Press, Inc.

Takaki, Ronald. 1990. *Iron Cages: Race and Culture in 19th Century America.* New York: Oxford University Press.

Walby, Sylvia. 1989. *Theorizing Patriarchy.* London: Blackwell.

Warner, Michael. 1993. *Fear of a Queer Planet: Queer Politics and Social Theory.* Minneapolis: University of Minnesota Press.

West, Candace and Don H. Zimmerman. 1987. "Doing Gender." *Gender and Society*, 1 (2): 125–51.

Wittig, Monique. 1992. *The Straight Mind.* Boston: Beacon.

9

The Politics of Inside/Out: Queer Theory, Poststructuralism, and a Sociological Approach to Sexuality

Ki Namaste

The domain of knowledge known as "queer theory" has developed at an astonishing pace over the past decade. Yet for social scientists and historians, much of this research may seem to be of questionable import. Most of queer theory is firmly located in the humanities – in departments of literature, film, and cultural studies.[1] At the same time, this research is heavily influenced by poststructuralism, an area of inquiry considered to be textualist, theoretically elite, and politically suspect by many Anglo-American social scientists (Anderson 1983; Dews 1987; Palmer 1990). Against the grain of such objections, I hope to demonstrate how these theories can be useful for both social research and politics.

The paper is divided into several sections. I begin with an overview of poststructuralist thought, outlining its approach to the human sciences and its political ramifications. I then consider the ways in which queer theory has been influenced by poststructuralism. I conclude with a discussion of the implications of poststructuralist queer theory for sociological studies of non-heterosexuality.

Poststructuralism: Framing Subjects

Poststructuralism is a term associated with the writings of French theorists Michel Foucault and Jacques Derrida.[2] It refers to a manner of interpreting selves and the social which breaks with traditional epistemologies. In the context in which Foucault and Derrida first began publishing their work, the dominant understanding of agency and structure ascribed intentionality to the subject.[3] This idea has been influential throughout modern Western thought, and gained a stronghold with the advent of Cartesian philosophy. Descartes (1963) argued that the rational, independent subject is the ground of both ontology (being) and epistemology (theories of knowledge). In other words, individuals as free-thinking subjects are the basis on which one conceives political and moral action. In philosophical terms, this approach is known as foundationalist.

Poststructuralism challenges this assumption. It argues that subjects are not the autonomous creators of themselves or their social worlds. Rather, subjects are embedded in a complex network of social relations. These relations in turn determine which subjects can appear where, and in what capacity. The subject is not something prior to politics or social structures, but is precisely constituted in and through specific socio-political arrangements. Poststructuralism contends that a focus on the individual as an autonomous agent needs to be "deconstructed," contested, and troubled.[4] Foundationalism obscures the historical arrangements which engender the very appearance of independent subjects. Whereas "modern" theories posit agents as the source of knowledge and action, poststructuralists maintain that they are effects of a specific social and cultural logic. The challenge, then, is to make sense of the ways in which subjectivities are at once framed and concealed. How is this achieved, and to what political end? A brief consideration of Foucault and Derrida will help to answer this question.

In *The History of Sexuality*, Foucault ([1976] 1980) examines the organization of sexuality in the West. He begins his analysis with a powerful critique of what he terms "the repressive hypothesis" (1980: 15). Conventional understandings of Western sexuality appeal to the repressive nature of Victorian society. Sexuality is a taboo, something about which nothing can be said. Silence and censorship are the law. In contrast to this view, Foucault suggests that sexuality is talked about all the time in Victorian society. From the rise of sexology to judicial institutions, sexuality is a profusely discussed and regulated entity. It is something which is produced through discourse, not repressed through censorship. If this is so, the question of silence itself must be reconsidered.

One of the most significant aspects of Foucault's research centers around the production of the homosexual. The proliferation of discourses on sexuality gave rise to the category "homosexual." Originally a taxonomic device employed within sexology, the term subsequently gained currency in judicial and psychiatric fields of knowledge. By demonstrating that "homosexuals" did not exist before this classification (although homosexual practices certainly did), Foucault shows us that social identities are effects of the ways in which knowledge is organized. He observes the politically ambiguous characters of the discursive formation of "the homosexual":

> There is no question that the appearance in nineteenth-century psychiatry, jurisprudence, and literature of a whole series of discourses on the species and subspecies of homosexuality, inversion, pederasty, and "psychic hermaphroditism" made possible a strong advance of social controls into this area of "perversity"; but it also made possible the formation of a "reverse" discourse: homosexuality began to speak in its own behalf, to demand that its legitimacy or "naturality" be acknowledged, often in the same vocabulary, using the same categories by which it was medically disqualified. (1980: 101)

Foucault offers an account of the social production of identities which are assumed to be natural in current dominant knowledges.[5]

Jacques Derrida offers a somewhat different perspective on poststructuralism, through his concept of supplementarity.[6] This refers to a way of thinking about how meanings are established. "Supplement" suggests that meanings are organized through difference, in a dynamic play of presence and absence. Derrida elaborates on the notion:

> [S]upplementarity, which is *nothing*, neither a presence nor an absence, is neither a substance nor an essence of man [*sic*]. It is precisely the play or presence and absence, the opening of this play that no metaphysical or ontological concept can comprehend. (1976: 244)

Derrida maintains that a focus on this play is useful because it reveals that what appears to be outside a given system is always already fully inside it; that which seems to be natural is historical. We can better understand the workings of supplementarity if we consider the opposition of heterosexuality to homosexuality. A Derridean perspective would argue that heterosexuality needs homosexuality for its own definition: a macho homophobic male can define himself as "straight" only in opposition to that which he is not – an effeminate gay man. Homosexuality is not excluded from such homophobia; it is integral to its very assertion.

Consider Derrida's (1967) criticisms of the manner in which Lévi-Strauss (1955) juxtaposes nature and culture. In a discussion of the Nambikwara culture of South America, Lévi-Strauss states that the Nambikwara could not write; they communicated through the medium of speech. Writing, should it enter into this society, would be post-speech. Derrida, however, employs the term *writing* in an extended sense to refer not merely to the inscription of graphematic elements on a page, but also to broader processes of inscription – taxonomy, classification, arrangement. He thus maintains (1967: 158) that members of the Nambikwara culture are distinguished through the use of proper names. Vincent Leitch provides a useful summary of the differences between Lévi-Strauss's narrow concept of writing and Derrida's extended employment of the term:

> That writing is present in Nambikwara culture goes without saying. Everyone in the community, for instance, has a proper name; that is to say, everyone is differentiated in a classification system. Lévi-Strauss knows this, but his ethnocentric concept of writing blinds him to such pervasive writing. He is naive. (1983: 35)

Derrida goes on to relate a speech/writing opposition to one of nature/culture.[7] By figuring speech as a self-present, "original" process, Lévi-Strauss aligns it with the axis of nature. "Writing," in contrast, is a derivative, cultural element and thus one which could be imposed on a more primordial, natural state of being (i.e., speech). Derrida locates in these binaries a nostalgic longing for nature, a Rousseauistic desire for a community unfettered by the violence of cultural systems such as writing. Yet it is only in first privileging speech as "natural" that Lévi-Strauss can make this claim. For Derrida, this represents one of the most dangerous moves anthropology could make: the imposition of ethnocentric interpretive categories in an analysis ostensibly claiming to be anti-ethnocentric:

> Now, ethnology – like any science – comes about within the element of discourse. And it is primarily a European science employing traditional concepts, however much it may struggle against them. Consequently, whether he likes it or not – and this does not depend on a decision on his part – the ethnologist accepts into his discourse the premises of ethnocentrism at the very moment he denounces them. ([1967] 1978: 287)

Like Foucault, Derrida is drawing attention to the conditions of possibility for interpretation. The distinction Lévi-Strauss makes between nature and culture rests on a particular understanding of "writing," one inflected with specific historical and cultural biases. Derrida demonstrates that the opposition breaks down. He emphasizes that the term Lévi- Strauss claims to be "present" – i.e., speech – is possible only given its relation to what we do not see – i.e., writing. "Writing" is not exterior to the Nambikwara, but fully inside its taxonomic arrangements. The notion of supplementarity is employed to explain these workings between inside and out.

In contemporary theory, this analysis is known as "deconstruction" – the illustration of the implicit underpinnings of a particular binary opposition. Deconstruction seeks to make sense of how these relations are at once the condition and the effect of all interpretation. The play between presence and absence is the *condition* of interpretation, insofar as each term depends on the other for its meaning. Supplementarity is the *effect* of interpretation because binary oppositions, such as that of speech and writing, are actualized and reinforced in every act of meaning-making. Derrida points out this double bind: we are always within a binary logic, and whenever we try to break out of its stranglehold, we reinscribe its very basis.

Queer Theory: The Politics of Inside/Out

Poststructuralism has had an important influence on the development of queer theory.[8] For example, Derrida's notion of supplementarity figures centrally in these debates. One of the landmark texts in queer theory is titled *Inside/Out: Lesbian Theories, Gay Theories* (Fuss 1991a). As Diana Fuss explains in her introduction, the supplement is invoked to make sense of the relations between heterosexuality and homosexuality:

> The philosophical opposition between "heterosexual" and "homosexual," like so many other conventional boundaries, has always been constructed on the foundations of another related opposition: the couple "inside" and "outside" . . .
> To the extent that the denotation of any term is always dependent on what is exterior to it (heterosexuality, for example, typically defines itself in critical opposition to that which it is not: homosexuality), the inside/outside polarity is an indispensable model for helping us to understand the complicated workings of semiosis. (1991b: 1)

The articles collected in *Inside/Out* suggest the various ways in which heterosexuality and homosexuality are mutually dependent, yet antagonistic. Queer theory is interested in exploring the borders of sexual identities, communities, and politics. How do categories such as "gay," "lesbian," and "queer" emerge? From what do they differentiate themselves, and what kinds of identities do they exclude? How are these borders demarcated, and how can they be contested? What are the relations between the naming of sexuality and political organization it adopts, between identity and community? Why is a focus on the discursive production of social identities useful? How do we make sense of the dialectical movement between inside and outside, heterosexuality and homosexuality?

Fuss (1991b) elaborates on these questions in her comments on Foucault ([1976] 1980). The production of homosexuality in legal and medical discourse engendered a paradox: although the adoption of homosexual identity allowed for the guarantee of civil rights, it brought with it the notion of the closet[9] – that is, the idea that some people are "visible" about their sexualities while others remain silent. In other words, the emergence of homosexuality was accompanied by its disappearance (Fuss 1991b: 4). One could declare oneself to be an "out" lesbian, gay, or bisexual, but this affirmation was possibly only given two related assumptions: the centrality of heterosexuality, and the existence of gays, bisexuals, and lesbians who were not out – that is, those who were "*in* the closet."

What is noteworthy about this example is the impossibility of locating oneself "outside" the dominant discourse. An attempt to declare oneself to be *out* of the closet marks non-heterosexuals who are presumably *inside*. In efforts to define a sexual identity *outside* the norm, one needs first to place oneself *inside* dominant definitions of sexuality. In Fuss's words, these gestures represent "a transgression of the border which is necessary to constitute the border as such" (1991b: 3).

Queer theory recognizes the impossibility of moving outside current conceptions of sexuality. We cannot assert ourselves to be entirely outside heterosexuality, nor entirely inside, because each of these terms achieves its meaning in relation to the other. What we can do, queer theory suggests, is negotiate these limits. We can think about the *how* of these boundaries – not merely the fact that they exist, but also how they are created, regulated, and contested. The emphasis on the production and management of heterosexuality and homosexuality characterizes the poststructuralist queer theory project. Two examples will make this point clearer.

D. A. Miller (1991) argues that in Alfred Hitchcock's film *Rope*, homosexuality can only be implied. Miller draws on Roland Barthes' (1965) distinction between connotative and denotative meanings, wherein denotation refers to something literal while connotation is a kind of secondary meaning, which hints at (yet never quite confirms) a literal, denotative possibility. In *Rope*, Miller contends, homosexuality is connotative: it is present everywhere, yet never articulated as such.

This means that homosexuality is always inside mainstream cinema, but never visibly so. Miller is aware that the operations of inside and out are complex and contradictory. Although homosexuality may be only implied, at the same time it is that absence which we viewers wish to see.

Although *Rope* does not specify gay sexual relations, it also does not explicitly prohibit them, because this prohibition at least would recognize a homosexual possibility (Miller 1991: 124–5, 140 n.8). It is this refusal to specify – or deny – which Miller examines. He maintains that this ambiguity is something a critical reading practice can exploit: the absence of homosexual denotation is what keeps us looking. In other words, by only implying homosexual identities, the film induces its viewers to wonder about their viability. Far from negating nor-heterosexuality, such a structure makes it central to the narrative, because it is that unseen entity for which we search. Thus Miller demonstrates that what appears to be outside a given text is always already inside it. His position makes critical use of both Foucault and Derrida: he shows the textual production of homosexual subjectivity, and goes further to situate this position within the broader network of relations to which it belongs.

Alexander Doty (1993) takes up Miller's use of connotation and denotation, and applies it to contemporary mass-cultural phenomena. He reads television sitcoms such as *Laverne and Shirley* as sites which embody queer desire. Even though the main characters of these programs are defined as heterosexual, Doty observes that the men to whom they relate are habitually overlooked. For example, when Shirley marries Army surgeon Walter Meany, she "immediately turns to hug and kiss Laverne, as Walter is excluded from the shot" (Doty 1993: 56). Through the camera's gaze, Doty maintains that the sitcom is centrally concerned with lesbianism. The fact that Walter is rarely in the narrative after his marriage to Shirley confirms this commitment to women-centered relations. Doty focuses on these kinds of narrative and cinematic devices to highlight the presence of queer elements within these supposedly "straight" settings.

Doty contends that queerness pervades all cultural productions: it is not a space limited to lesbians, gay men, and/or bisexuals; it is a position available to everyone. If we allow this possibility, Doty suggests, we can think about different strategies for interpreting mass culture:

> Since the consumption, uses, and discussion of mass culture as queers still find us moving between being on the "inside" and the "outside" of straight culture's critical language, representational codes, and market

practices, we are in a position to refuse, confuse, and redefine the terms by which mass culture is understood by the public and in the academy. (1993: 102)

Here Doty remarks on the double bind of interpretation with regard to sexuality. Although normative heterosexuality continually reproduces itself through the media, it does so by relegating homosexuality to a parenthetical status. To denote bisexual, lesbian, and gay identities would be to refuse this marginalization. Doty contends that non-heterosexuals are at once outside and inside hegemonic hetero-sexuality. Highlighting the manner in which these locations are mutually dependent makes it clear that the definition of categorical boundaries is problematic. Doty is not merely making a call for lesbians, gay men, and bisexuals to proclaim that they are "inside"; he is asking us to think about the social construction of an inside/outside opposition. Instead of promoting an assertion of lesbian, gay, and/or bisexual identity, Doty investigates the cultural assumptions hidden in this proposition: that an articulation of non-heterosexuality bolsters the centrality of heterosexuality itself. This focus on the production of a hetero/homo binary allows for consideration of strategies which could displace the opposition.

To those who take heterosexuality for granted within popular cul-ture, Doty has two things to say: (1) lesbians, gay men, and bisexuals are present within all kinds and forms of cultural representation; and (2) non-heterosexual identities need to be excluded from the public sphere if heterosexuality is to figure centrally. Like Miller, Doty draws our attention to the workings of heterosexuality and homosexuality. He demonstrates that homosexual subject-positions are inscribed prac-tically everywhere, although they are less frequently denoted as such. A focus on this paradox – the simultaneous exclusion and presence of homosexuality – forces an examination of the manner in which hetero-sexuality achieves its legitimacy and apparent "naturalness."

Queer theory labors at a juncture of inside and out. Following Foucault, it examines the discursive production of homosexual sub-ject-positions. Drawing on Derrida's notion of supplementarity, it interrogates the construction and regulation of borders in sexual ident-ities, communities, and politics. Poststructuralist queer theory analyzes the manner in which cultural texts privilege heterosexuality over other sexual identities, as well as how this estimation requires homo-sexuality. Moreover, queer theory studies the dilemma implicit in this logic: the adoption of a "homosexual" position strengthens hetero-sexuality itself.

From Deviance to Difference: Towards a Queer Sociological Theory

From the preceding examples, the field of queer theory may appear to have import only for social scientists working in cultural and media studies. It is certainly true that the domain has arisen from humanities-based sites of inquiry, and that it therefore provides readings of literary and cultural texts. A queer theory influenced by poststructuralism, however, has broader implications for sociological approaches to sexuality.

Fuss, Miller, and Doty ask about the cultural operations which relegate homosexuality to an implied, parenthetical status. Drawing from the lessons of poststructuralism, these critics analyze the different contexts in which all sexual identities are situated. This analysis diverges from social-scientific studies of gay and lesbian sexualities published in the late 1970s and early 1980s.[10] Much of that work focused on the emergence of homosexual subject-positions or identities, often in concert with capitalism. Jeffrey Weeks (1977), for instance, provides a historical examination of homosexual identity and politics in Britain. He is undoubtedly influenced by Foucault, as evidenced by his discussion of the nineteenth-century medical model of homosexuality (1977: 23–32). Like Foucault, Weeks grasps the "reverse discourse" that is possible with the introduction of homosexual identity. He traces the emergence of homosexual consciousness and community in twentieth-century Britain.

This kind of research is extremely important in affirming lesbian and gay identities and communities. Because of the absence of studies on these questions (particularly from a historical perspective), this scholarship is badly needed. Yet ironically, the attention accorded to homosexuality serves to strengthen the heterosexual/homosexual opposition even further. Although Weeks is certainly located within the framework known as social constructionism,[11] he focuses on the discursive production of homosexuality. What Weeks does not consider is the extent to which an affirmation of homosexuality confirms a hetero/homo opposition. In other words, he asks questions similar to Foucault's – "What discursive processes produced the homosexual at this point in time?" – but he does not pose more Derridean questions – "In what ways does an adoption of homosexual identity reinforce a hetero/homo split?"

Weeks turns his attention to the formation of homosexual politics, but he ignores the broader context in which they are located – heterosexual hegemony. As Jonathon Ned Katz remarks, an exclusive emphasis on homosexuals obscures the generative character of heterosexuality:

> Considering the popularity of the heterosexual idea, one imagines that tracing the notion's history would have tempted many eager scholar-beavers. The importance of analyzing the dominant term of the dominant sexual ideology seems obvious. But heterosexuality has been the idea whose time has not come. The role of the universal heterosexual hypothesis as prop to the dominant mode of sexual organization has determined its not-so-benign scholarly neglect. (1990: 8)

A poststructuralist queer theory, then, offers sociology an approach to studying the emergence and reproduction of heterosexuality.[12] Rather than designating gays, lesbians, and/or bisexuals as the only subjects or communities worthy of investigation, a poststructuralist sociology would make sense of the manner in which heterosexuality is itself a social construct.[13]

An emphasis on heterosexuality also expands traditional sociological approaches to sexuality, such as labeling theory. Labeling theory (McIntosh 1968; Plummer 1975) underlines the social functions of particular nominal labels. Mary McIntosh, for example, views homosexuality as a social role. For her, the name *homosexual* demarcates acceptable and unacceptable behavior, and segregates individuals into "deviant" and "normal" categories. She contends that the shift from conceptualizing homosexuality as a medical condition to viewing it as a social role is crucial, and that it will enable investigation of "the specific content of the homosexual role and . . . the organization and functions of homosexual groups" (1968: 192). Like social constructionists (e.g., Weeks 1977), McIntosh submits that sociological studies of sexuality will focus on the social organization of homosexuals rather than on an individualized, psychologistic explanation of homosexual behavior.

Although the shift to a specifically social analysis of homosexuality is welcome, McIntosh ignores the social character of heterosexuality. To follow McIntosh's research program, sociologists would study lesbian and gay subcultures and communities. Yet they would not study the ways in which heterosexuality reproduces itself – whether through patrilineal kinship arrangements or ideological discourse advocating the primacy of the nuclear family. Labeling theory allows us to understand lesbian and gay communities and identities more clearly, but it sheds little light on heterosexuality.

In terms of sociological theory, poststructuralism requires that we abandon the approaches of labeling theory and/or deviance –

perspectives which define gay and lesbian identities only in opposition to a natural, stabilized heterosexuality. By moving beyond a deviance model, we can understand how the cultural logic of inside and outside plays itself out in our institutional relations and practices. One example would be courses which focus on lesbians and gay men as "deviant" without examining the ways in which heterosexuality is taken for granted. In this instance, lesbian and gay difference can be framed only in opposition to the apparent "normalcy" of heterosexuality. If we focus only on the "subculture" of homosexuality, and if we never interrogate the conditions which engender its marginalization, we shall remain trapped within a theoretical framework which refuses to acknowledge its own complicity in constructing its object (or subjects) of study.

Whereas a sociology of homosexuality studies homosexual individuals and communities, a sociology of heterosexuality studies the manufacturing of heterosexist ideology in an effort to grasp how it affects all subjects – gay, lesbian, heterosexual, bisexual, and/or transgender. This latter perspective thinks not on *behalf* of homosexuals, but *in terms of* all sexual subjects – or, better, in terms of the (hetero)sexualization of all subjects. As lesbian and gay activists insist, individuals are assumed to be heterosexual unless they identify themselves otherwise. A critical sociological perspective of sexuality would examine the rhetorical, institutional, and discursive mechanisms needed to ensure that heterosexuality maintains its taken-for-granted status. Homosexuality as "deviance" gives way to homosexual difference.[14]

Both mainstream sociological perspectives (e.g., labeling theory) and (mainstream) gay studies (Weeks 1977) neglect the social reproduction of heterosexuality, choosing instead to focus on gay and lesbian communities. Poststructuralism is particularly useful in this light because it considers the relations between heterosexuality and homosexuality. It addresses not only the emergence and development of homosexual communities, but also the intersection of these identities within the broader context of heterosexual hegemony. By focusing on this play between inside and out, studies of sexuality move in a new direction.

A poststructuralist sociological approach to sexuality would develop the inside/outside trope of queer theory in greater depth. Although a focus on the reproduction of heterosexuality is important, a critical analysis of sexuality would also theorize which sexual identities are undermined. If it is true that the play of heterosexuality and homosexuality is pervasive, as queer theory suggests, what does this mean for those people who identify as *neither heterosexual nor homosexual?* Is the category "homosexual" the only one available to resist heterosexual hegemony? Where do bisexuals[15] and transgenders[16] fit into these debates?

The inside/outside trope has tremendous import in explaining conflicting forces which constitute (or dispute) hetero- and homosexualities. Yet this model, I suggest, can itself be too easily grafted onto preexisting sexual and gender binaries, thereby failing to take into account the range of non-heterosexual identifications available. It is noteworthy that the field of queer theory has said very little on the question of bisexuality.[17] Analogously, transgender subjectivity causes a curious silence.[18] If bisexual and transgender subject-positions are impossible, a poststructuralist sociologist would ask, what kinds of political alliances are preempted? One of the dangers involved in an exclusive consideration of heterosexuality and homosexuality is that of neglecting the diversity of sexual and gender positions available.[19] Consideration of recent lesbian and gay activisms reveals a marked disregard of the multiplicity of non-heterosexual identities.[20] Often these struggles lose sight of *sexual liberation* and risk being reduced to the mere reification of gay and lesbian identities.[21] In this light, attention to the workings – and exclusions – of inside and out can help build a new vision of community.

A sociological queer theory informed by poststructuralism would be markedly different from either mainstream sociological approaches to sexuality or queer theory in its current garb. The move to a model of difference would provoke new insights into the continual reproduction of heterosexual hegemony. This approach offers a specifically historicized understanding of sexual identities, politics, and communities. Looking back on the past, however, does not imply that one must be reduced to it. By theorizing the workings and exclusions of inside and out, a sociological queer theory takes the political risk of expanding current borders of gay and lesbian communities. In this gesture, bisexual and transgender identities can be realized, and the basis for a broad political coalition can be established.

A sociological queer theory does more than change how sociologists study sexuality, or how queer theorists analyze culture. A sociological queer theory informed by poststructuralism also transforms the organization of contemporary sexual politics. An emphasis on difference enables the articulation of a variety of sexual and gender identities: transsexuals, bisexuals, drag queens, fetishists, lesbians, gay men, queers, and heterosexuals. Although such a practice remains committed to deregulating heterosexual hegemony, it also appreciates that this work can – indeed, must – take place from a variety of sites.

This stress on the multiplicity of identity expands contemporary sexual politics beyond a stagnant hetero/homo opposition. It provides people with more choices in how they define themselves, and insists on the diversity within communities of the sexually marginalized. By unsettling much of the lesbian and gay response to heterosexism, and by suggesting that many non-heterosexual positions are available, such activism focuses its attention on *displacing* heterosexuality, homosexuality, and the relations between the two. If heterosexuality is something which is taken for granted, and if the adoption of a homosexual identity only serves to bolster the strength of heterosexuality, then perhaps the most effective sites of resistance are those created by people who refuse both options. A critical sexual politics, in other words, struggles to move beyond the confines of an inside/outside model.

Notes

1　See, for example, Warner (1991) and Piontek (1992). As Escoffier (1990) points out, the disciplines of history and sociology have been central in the historical development of American lesbian and gay studies.

2　The labels *poststructuralism* and *postmodernism* are frequently used interchangeably within Anglo-American social sciences. They have some things in common (most especially an anti-foundationalist approach), but there are also significant variances between these approaches. Foucault and Derrida are habitually associated with poststructuralism. Whereas Jean-François Lyotard (1979) and Jean Baudrillard (1981) perhaps best exemplify a specifically postmodern method. It is important not to conflate these two perspectives. Judith Butler raises this issue in asking the rhetorical question "Is the effort to colonize and domesticate these theories [Lyotard and Derrida] under the sign of the same, to group them synthetically and masterfully under a single rubric, a simple refusal to grant the specificity of these positions, an excuse not to read, and not to read closely?" (1992: 5).

　　This paper will address only the field loosely known as poststructuralism in relation to queer theory.

3　Both Foucault and Derrida have extensive training in phenomenology, particularly through the work of the German philosophers Martin Heidegger ([1927] 1962) and Edmund Husserl ([1939] 1962).

4　"To deconstruct" is employed in a variety of ways: the most common loosely designates some sort of critical thinking. This use of *deconstruct* (conjugated as a verb) is premised on an understanding of the exercise as some exposure of error. Thus we often hear phrases such as "deconstructing postmodernism and gender relations," "deconstructing nationalism," and "deconstructing sociology." In Derrida's use of the term, however, deconstruction refers to an analysis which examines the production of truths. (For more on this distinction, see Derrida 1967.) Leitch (1983) discusses how a reduction of deconstruction to the exposure of error engenders formulaic applications of deconstructivist methods.

5 Researchers interested in discourse analysis might wish to consult Foucault's ([1969] 1972) text on methodology, *The Archaeology of Knowledge.*

6 Supplementarity is only one concept advanced by Derrida to make his point. There are many others, including *pharmakon, dissémination,* grammatology, *arche-écriture,* and trace. I will focus on the idea of the supplement because it has been instrumental in the development of queer theory.

7 Here Derrida continues his critique of a speech/writing binary in the work of the Swiss linguist Ferdinand de Saussure (1972).

8 The collocation "queer theory" refers to American, humanities-based knowledge. As several critics have pointed out (Escoffier 1990; Piontek 1992; Warner 1991), this naming has tended to obscure social-scientific contributions to the debates. In the United States, the works of Esther Newton (1972) and Johnathon Ned Katz (1976) have been formative in the development of lesbian and gay studies. In English Canada, lesbian and gay studies is located primarily in the social sciences. For a representative selection of English Canadian research, see Adam (1985, 1987), Kinsman (1987), Valverde (1985), and Valverde and Weir (1985).

9 Eve Sedgwick (1990) provides a more detailed examination of "the closet" within Western epistemologies.

10 For a selection of this work, Altman (1981), d'Emilio (1983), Katz (1976), and Weeks (1977).

11 Social constructionists argue that sexual identities are not natural entities, but are products of the social and historical locations in which they are located. These thinkers differ from essentialists, who believe that sexual identities are transcultural and transhistorical. See Epstein (1987), Fuss (1989), and Kinsman (1987) for an overview of social-constructionist thought.

12 Katz (1990) and Kinsman (1987) have begun some of this urgent work.

13 Lorna Weir and Leo Casey remark that one of the problems associated with a gay male sexual-liberationist politic is that it is reduced to a sexological agenda. They comment that "[a]ccess to non-traditional jobs, equal pay, day care, new forms of community and artistic practices are an integral, non- sexological part of lesbian politics" (1984: 152). Weir and Casey underline the generation of heterosexual hegemony through work and the organization of the family, the community, and leisure.

14 Perhaps we are doing nothing more here than being good Gramscians – that is, examining how consent is achieved, maintained, and resisted. Gramsci (1971) elaborates on the notion of hegemony, an ongoing process which requires the consent of social actors. For an application of Gramscian ideas in a poststructuralist context, see Laclau and Mouffe (1985).

15 The category "bisexual" generally refers to individuals who have sexual relations with members of the same sex as well as with those of the

"opposite" sex. See Hutchins and Kaahumanu (1991) for a comprehensive introduction to bisexuality.

16 "Transgender" is used to designate the lives and experiences of a diverse group of people who live outside normative sex/gender relations (i.e., where the biology of one's body is taken to determine how one will live and interact in the social world). The transgender community is made up of transsexuals (pre-, post-, and non-operative), transvestites, drag queens, passing women, hermaphrodites, stone butches, and gender outlaws who defy regulatory sex/gender taxonomies. See Leslie Feinberg's (1992a) ground-breaking pamphlet *Transgender Liberation: A Movement Whose Time Has Come* for an excellent introduction to these issues. Her novel, *Stone Butch Blues* (1992b), is equally useful in more clearly understanding the lives of transgenders.

17 Intellectuals from Teresa de Lauretis (1991) to Eve Sedgwick (1990) claim to have written a theory which is "queer," but they grant only lesbians and gay men the right to belong to that category. Although a mere disregard of bisexuals is worrisome in itself, the identity is sometimes dismissed with intensity. The fifth annual Lesbian and Gay Studies Conference at Rutgers University, for example, dropped "bisexual" from the conference title. Some intellectuals believe that bisexuality is an impossible position. Interviewed in *Outweek* magazine (Feb. 6, 1991), Eve Sedgwick claimed, "I'm not sure that because there are people who identify as bisexual there is a bisexual identity."

Even when bisexuality can be uttered, as evidenced by Doty's (1993) recent writings, it almost always remains parenthetical, in the form of a footnote. Doty himself admits that he provides "rather cursory attention to specific bisexual positions" (1993: 105). Daumer (1992) raises some of the ethical challenges that bisexuality poses to lesbian feminism.

18 Here, a paradox must be noted. Queer theory has witnessed an explosion of essays on the subject of drag (Butler 1990, 1991; Garber 1992; Tyler 1991); yet it remains incapable of connecting this research to the everyday lives of people who identify as transgender, drag queen, and/or transsexual. Indeed, queer theory refuses transgender subjectivities even as it looks at them. The relation, as Sedgwick frames it, is one of "drag practices and homoerotic identity formations" (Moon and Sedgwick 1990: 19). In this logic, the impossibility of transgender *identities* secures the legitimacy of monosexuality.

It is interesting to contrast Marjorie Garber's (1992) treatment of transgender issues with that of Esther Newton (1972). Methodologically, Newton offers an ethnographic analysis in keeping with social-scientific approaches to research.

Responding to the solipsistic character of queer theory, transsexual activists Jeanne B. and Xanthra Phillippa recently produced a button reading "Our blood is on your theories." For a brilliant discussion of (post)transsexual subjectivity, see Stone (1991).

19 Interestingly, the shift from "gay/lesbian" to "queer" was intended to include bisexuals and transgenders. In the field of activism, this shift was marked by groups such as Queer Nation (QN). In the academy, "queer theory" has exhibited a tense relation to the very term *queer*. Teresa de Lauretis (1991), for example, distances herself from the "queer" of QN, while most other scholars writing under the label consider only lesbian and gay subject-positions. The term *queer* has been ossified so quickly within the academy that bisexuals and transgenders must continually insist that it includes them. Duggan (1992) provides a useful introduction to queer politics and theory.

20 The recent March on Washington (1993), for example, was officially titled "The 1993 March on Washington for Lesbian, Gay, and Bi Equal Rights and Liberation." The category "bisexual" was included only after intensive lobbying. Although grassroots communities included transgenders in their formative organizing activities, "transgender" was not part of the March's title. In the debate on the name, some lesbians and gay men pitted bisexuals *against* transgenders. For a more extensive analysis of these issues, see Kaahumanu (1992).

21 Steven Epstein remarks that the early gay rights movement encouraged the exploration of "the homosexual in everyone" (1987: 21), but that this position gave way to one which consolidated gay identity in opposition to that of heterosexuality. In the 1990s, the insides and outs of a hetero/homo polarity obscure the lives of bisexuals and transgenders, effectively pre-empting a broad-based political coalition working for sexual liberation. Instead, mainstream lesbian and gay activism concentrates on being *in*-cluded *in* the military, *in* the government, *in* the nation.

References

Adam, Barry. 1985. "Structural Foundations of the Gay World." *Comparative Studies in Society and History*, 27 (4): 658–71.

——. 1987. *The Rise of a Gay and Lesbian Movement*. Boston: Twayne.

Altman, Dennis. 1981. *Coming out in the Seventies*. Boston: Alyson.

Anderson, Perry. 1983. *In the Tracks of Historical Materialism*. London: Verso.

Barthes, Roland. 1965. *Le Degré Zéro de l'Écriture et Éléments de la Sémiologie*. Paris: Seuil.

Baudrillard, Jean. 1981. *Simulacres et Simulations*. Paris: Galilée.

Butler, Judith. 1990. *Gender Trouble: Feminism and the Subversion of Identity*. New York: Routledge.

——. 1991. "Imitation and Gender Insubordination," in *Inside/Out: Lesbian Theories, Gay Theories*, ed. Diana Fuss. New York: Routledge, 13–31.

——. 1992. "Contingent Foundations: Feminism and the Question of 'Postmodernism,'" in *Feminists Theorize the Political*, eds Judith Butler and Joan Scott. New York: Routledge, 3–21.

Daumer, Elisabeth. 1992. "Queer Ethics, or the Challenge of Bisexuality to Lesbian Ethics." *Hypatia*, 74 (fall): 91–105.

de Lauretis, Teresa. 1991. "Introduction; Queer Theory: Lesbian and Gay Sexualities." *Differences*, 3 (2): iii–xviii.

d'Emilio, John. 1983. *Sexual Politics, Sexual Communities*. Chicago: University of Chicago Press.

Derrida, Jacques. (1967) 1978. "Structure, Sign, and Play in the Discourse of the Human Science," in *Writing and Difference*, trans. Alan Bass. Chicago: University of Chicago Press, 278–93.

——. 1972. *La Dissémination*. Paris: Seuil.

——. 1976. *Of Grammatology*, trans. Gayatri Chakravorty Spivak. Baltimore: Johns Hopkins University Press.

de Saussure, Ferdinand. 1972. *Cours de Linguistique Générale*. Paris: Payot.

Descartes, René. 1963. *Oeuvres Philosophiques*. Paris: Garnier.

Dews, Peter. 1987. *Logics of Disintegration: Poststructuralism and the Claims of Critical Theory*. London: Verso.

Doty, Alexander. 1993. *Making Things Perfectly Queer: Interpreting Mass Culture*. Minneapolis: University of Minnesota Press.

Duggan, Lisa. 1992. "Making It Perfectly Queer." *Socialist Review*, 22 (1): 11–32.

Epstein, Steven. 1987. "Gay Politics, Ethnic Identity: The Limits of Social Constructionism." *Socialist Review*, 17 (3–4): 9–54.

Escoffier, Jeffrey. 1990. "Inside the Ivory Closet: The Challenges Facing Lesbian and Gay Studies." *Out/Look*, 10 (fall): 40–8.

Feinberg, Leslie. 1992a. *Transgender Liberation: A Movement Whose Time Has Come*. New York: World View Forum.

——. 1992b. *Stone Butch Blues*. Ithaca: Firebrand Books.

Foucault, Michel. (1969) 1972. *The Archaeology of Knowledge*, trans. A. M. Sheridan Smith. New York: Harper and Row.

——. (1976) 1980. *The History of Sexuality. Volume 1: An Introduction*, trans. Robert Hurley. New York: Vintage.

Fuss, Diane. 1989. *Essentially Speaking: Feminism, Nature, and Difference*. New York: Routledge.

——, ed. 1991a. *Inside/Out: Lesbian Theories, Gay Theories*. New York: Routledge.

——. 1991b. "Inside/Out," in *Inside/Out: Lesbian Theories, Gay Theories*, ed. Diana Fuss. New York: Routledge, 1–10.

Garber, Marjorie. 1992. *Vested Interests: Cross-Dressing and Cultural Anxiety*. New York: Routledge.

Gramsci, Antonio. 1971. *Selections from the Prison Notebooks*, trans. and eds Quentin Hoare and Geoffrey Nowell Smith. New York: International Publishers.

Heidegger, Martin. (1927) 1962. *Being and Time*, trans. John Macquarrie and Edward Robinson. New York: Harper and Row.

Husserl, Edmund. (1939) 1962. *L'Origine de la Géometrie*, trans. and introduced by Jacques Derrida. Paris: Presses Universitaires de France.

Hutchins, Loraine and Lani Kaahumanu, eds. 1991. *Bi Any Other Name: Bisexual People Speak Out*. Boston: Alyson.

Kaahumanu, Lani. 1992. "It's Official! The 1993 March on Washington for Lesbian, Gay, and Bi (yes!) Equal Rights and Liberation, April 25." *Anything That Moves*, 4: 22–4.

Katz, Jonathon Ned. 1976. *Gay American History*. New York: Crowell.

———. 1990. "The Invention of Heterosexuality." *Socialist Review*, 20 (1): 7–34.

Kinsman, Gary. 1987. *The Regulation of Desire: Sexuality in Canada*. Montreal: Black Rose Books.

Laclau, Ernesto and Chantale Mouffe. 1985. *Hegemony and Socialist Strategy: Towards a Radical Democratic Politics*. London: Verso.

Leitch, Vincent. 1983. *Deconstructive Criticism: An Advanced Introduction*. New York: Columbia University Press.

Lévi-Strauss, Claude. 1955. *Tristes Tropiques*. Paris: Plon.

Lyotard, Jean-François. 1979. *La Condition Postmoderne*. Paris: Minuit.

McIntosh, Mary. 1968. "The Homosexual Role." *Social Problems*, 16 (2): 182–92.

Miller, D. A. 1991. "Anal *Rope*," in *Inside/Out: Lesbian Theories, Gay Theories*, edited by Diana Fuss. New York: Routledge, 119–41.

Moon, Michael and Eve Sedgwick. 1990. "Divinity: A Performance Piece. A Dossier. A Little-Understood Emotion." *Discourse*, 13 (1): 12–39.

Newton, Esther. 1972. *Mother Camp: Female Impersonators in America*. Englewood Cliffs, NJ: Prentice-Hall.

Palmer, Bryan. 1990. *Descent into Discourse: The Reification of Language and the Writing of Social History*. Philadelphia: Temple University Press.

Piontek, Thomas. 1992. "Unsafe Representations: Cultural Criticism in the Age of AIDS." *Discourse*, 15 (1): 128–53.

Plummer, Kenneth. 1975. *Sexual Stigma*. London: Routledge.

Sedgwick, Eve. 1990. *The Epistemology of the Closet*. Berkeley: University of California Press.

Stone, Sandy. 1991. "The Empire Strikes Back: A Posttranssexual Manifesto," in *Body Guards: The Cultural Politics of Gender Ambiguity*, eds Julia Epstein and Kristina Straub. New York: Routledge, 280–304.

Tyler, Carole-Anne. 1991. "Boys Will Be girls: The Politics of Gay Drag," in *Inside Out: Lesbian Theories, Gay Theories*, ed. Diana Fuss. New York: Routledge, 32–70.

Valverde, Mariana. 1985. *Sex, Power, and Pleasure*. Toronto: Women's Press.

Valverde, Mariana and Lorna Weir. 1985. "Thrills, Chills, and the 'Lesbian Threat,' or The Media, The State, and Women's Sexuality," in *Women against Censorship*, ed. Varda Burshtyn. Vancouver: Douglas and McIntyre, 99–106.

Warner, Michael. 1991. "Introduction: Fear of a Queer Planet." *Social Text*, 29: 3–17.

Weeks, Jeffrey. 1977. *Coming Out: Homosexual Politics in Britain from the Nineteenth Century to the Present*. London: Quartet.

Weir, Lorna and Leo Casey. 1984. "Subverting Power in Sexuality." *Socialist Review*, 75/76 (May–Aug.): 139–57.

10

A Place in the Rainbow: Theorizing Lesbian and Gay Culture

Janice M. Irvine

In 1992, volatile debates about culture rocked New York City after the introduction of a teacher's guide for a multicultural curriculum in the public schools. Known as the Rainbow curriculum, this guide was unremarkable until key actors discovered brief sections alluding to lesbian and gay families.[1] The ensuing controversy generated national publicity and ultimately contributed to the firing of Schools Chancellor Joseph Fernandez. The Rainbow curriculum is of central importance because the debates over culture, which the curriculum did not initiate but certainly underscored in popular consciousness, continue throughout the country.

The controversy over the Rainbow curriculum is of academic interest to sociologists because of the complicated theoretical concerns it raises about culture, identity, and sexuality. Especially at a time when the term *culture* has achieved popular and widespread usage, opposition to the demands by lesbians and gay men for recognition as a cultural group generates questions about authenticity and definition of culture. What or who is entitled to claim cultural status? How are cultural identities constituted? Are they essential or constructed? What is the role of history, of social agents, and of representation in the invention of cultures? Are some cultures more legitimate than others? Do sexual cultures exist? Adequate answers to these questions necessitate theoretical paradigms that speak to the intersections of culture, sexuality, identities, race, ethnicity, and difference.

Debates about culture certainly constitute a trajectory within the classical sociological theories of Marx, Weber, and Durkheim. Throughout the century, and from a variety of theoretical standpoints, sociologists have examined questions concerning (for example) cultural autonomy, coherence, and consensus. Analysis of culture has

recently assumed increasing prominence in sociological theorizing
(Seidman 1990; Hall and Neitz 1993; Munch and Smelser 1992;
Wuthnow 1987). The growing recognition in the discipline of the
importance of culture is significant because changing demographic and
political factors unceasingly place cultural concerns in the foreground
as central to social life. Further, a vibrant discourse typically glossed as
"multiculturalism" has facilitated the deployment of the term *culture*
in an ever-widening sphere. Yet sociologists have played a minimal
role in the exciting advances of cultural and sexuality studies, and
sociological theory is inadequate to analyze social events such as the
Rainbow controversy.

Certain theoretical frameworks in sociology, such as those of deviance and social problems, have proved to be useful tools whereby some
scholars and activists study sexual cultures. Certainly social-construction theory, which has its primary roots in sociology, has transformed
the history of sexuality. Several factors, however, contribute to sociology's paradigmatic limitations in this area. First, there is no tradition
within mainstream sociology of broader inquiry into the study of
sexuality. Compared, for example, with historians and anthropologists, few sociologists participate in the burgeoning interdisciplinary
field of sexuality studies (for important exceptions see Almaguer 1991;
Gagnon 1977; Giddens 1992; Humphries 1974; Irvine 1990, 1994;
Luker 1975; Murray 1979, 1992; Plummer 1975, 1981; Seidman
1991, 1992; Simon and Gagnon 1973; Stein 1993, as well as a number
of works by historical sociologist Jeffrey Weeks 1977, 1981, 1985,
1991). Much of this work is recent. Beyond the absence of a critical
canon, this vacuum speaks to a certain illegitimacy within sociology
concerning the study of sexuality. This is reinforced materially by the
lack of graduate training in the sociology of sexuality and by a dearth
of job opportunities for those who might choose to specialize in this
area.

Of related concern is sociology's insulation from the interdisciplinary multicultural conversation concerning intersections of race, ethnicity, gender, and sexual identity. Particularly relevant for this paper
is the chasm between sociology and lesbian and gay studies. Central to
the field of lesbian and gay studies is a range of topics that should hold
particular fascination for sociologists: examination of the historical
invention of sexual taxonomies and the reciprocal effect of the social
organization of sexual communities, as well as inquiry into the origins
of sexual cultures, the organization of systems of meaning, and the
construction and deconstruction of identities. Whereas lesbians and
gay men appear most frequently in sociology as objects of discussion

in social-problems texts, lesbian and gay studies insist on our subjectivity as social actors and as research agents. Lesbian and gay studies center sexuality as a major social category with important correlates of social organization and behavior rather than relegating it to the status of individual variable.

Using key aspects of the debates about culture that were generated by the Rainbow curriculum, I will highlight how placing lesbian and gay sexual identity in the foreground is essential to this analysis. The application of theoretical perspectives from cultural studies and multicultural studies, in particular lesbian and gay studies and African-American studies, is especially useful in exploring the theoretical implications of pitting racial cultures against sexual cultures, and in the debates over essential and constructed identities. I will examine competing claims about culture by social groups, and will discuss evolving cultural theories among social scientists. To fully contextualize the Rainbow debates, this cultural theory must be located in historical analysis about the invention of racial categories, sexual categories, and the emergence of individual and social identities. The initiative by lesbians and gay men to achieve cultural status in public multicultural education not only is a pivotal moment in lesbian and gay liberation, but also affords the opportunity to further elaborate social theories about culture through an examination of a cultural group actively engaged in its continual reinvention.

Cultures, Multiculturalism, and Sexuality

As the debates over the Rainbow curriculum aptly illustrate, attention to culture, once largely confined within academic discourse, currently occupies a varied and mainstream audience. This shift corresponds to major social changes in structures and consciousness wrought by the many civil-rights movements of the last twenty-five years. Blacks, members of other racial and ethnic groups, women, lesbians and gay men, and disabled people launched legal and social initiatives not only to end discrimination but also to foster recognition of their distinct cultural identities. The richness of recent multicultural awareness is a legacy of these movements. Similarly, the challenges and conflicts generated by multicultural projects rank among the most volatile theoretical and political debates of the late twentieth century.

Much of the sophisticated and engaging new theoretical literature on cultural has emerged from those working within cultural studies and in the various ethnic, women's, and lesbian and gay studies programs, as

well as from associated independent scholars and activists. In a dialogue that crosses disciplines and identity groups, this scholarship
examines a range of questions about the nature, meaning, and practices of culture that should be of great interest to sociologists. As I have
noted, some sociologists have traditionally been concerned with issues
of culture, race, and ethnicity. Currently, however, and with important
exceptions (see, for example, Alba 1990; Collins 1986, 1990; Hall
1989, 1992a, 1992b; Omi and Winant 1986; Stacey and Thorne 1985;
Thompson and Tyagi 1993; Waters 1990), sociologists have not yet
had a strong voice in articulating the "new cultural politics of difference" (West 1993: 18).[2] The proliferation of cultural studies in the
United States, as it entails the theorizing of culture in the deeply
political context of day-to-day negotiations of race, ethnicity, gender,
and sexuality, has been cross-disciplinary or even anti-disciplinary,
resulting in a number of independent academic centers of cultural
studies (Hall 1992a; Grossberg, Nelson, and Treichler 1992). Sociologists have produced little of this cultural-studies scholarship.[3]

As Seidman (1990) has aptly observed, sociological inquiries into
culture are not simply theoretical, but are central to negotiations of
everyday life. This suggests that sociologists may want to attend to the
new discursive formulations deployed by scholars who are theorizing
the daily complications of culture and multiculturalism as they are
articulated and experienced within existing and contested relations of
power.

The educational system has proved to be a central location in which
the complexities of culture are manifested daily. Schools have been the
site of extensive conflict and debate. This is not surprising because
educational institutions are primary vehicles for the transmission of
culture (Bourdieu 1968). On all levels of the system, historically marginalized groups have sought to destabilize the hegemonic notion of a
homogeneous and inclusive "American culture" (Hu-DeHart 1993: 8)
and to gain recognition for their own diverse histories, traditions, and
identities. The first disruptions started at the university level in the late
1960s, when student protesters demanded the establishment of ethnic-
and women's studies programs. Multicultural curricula are now being
implemented in primary and secondary schools across the country, in
a climate of both enthusiasm and opposition.

In multicultural educational systems, schools become the site not
simply for cultural assertion and socialization, but also for the active
invention of culture. Students do not passively learn about cultures and
identities, but participate in ongoing adoption and reformulation of
traditional cultural identities, logics, and strategies. As Lubiano sug-

gests, education is a site where "people think themselves into being" (Thompson and Tyagi 1993: xxxi). Representation in multicultural curricula is crucial for the visibility and legitimacy it affords to a cultural group, but also for that group's continual reinvigoration. Increasingly, too, multicultural programs are becoming sites not only for the support of cultural identities, but also for destabilizing discussions of the limitations of identity politics and of reified notions of identity (West 1993a).

This power of multicultural education forms the basis for controversies such as the Rainbow curriculum, where lesbians and gay men seek to be included in public school curricula. The fierce and widely publicized battle waged over this curriculum resonated across the country, becoming a benchmark contest over sexuality education more generally. These cultural debates assumed discursive parameters which were made possible only through the intellectual and political achievements of several decades of lesbian/gay liberation. At a moment during which multicultural education is increasingly prominent, it was inevitable that lesbians and gay men would begin initiatives to secure for their own communities a place in these curricula.

Opposition to the Rainbow curriculum is illustrative both of popular ideas about the nature of culture, and of the varied faces of homophobia. Critics refused to acknowledge that lesbian and gay men constitute a culture, and instead adamantly insisted that homosexuals were deviant, immoral individuals who pose a threat to children. This individualizing strategy supported the contention that lesbians and gay men simply live an aberrant lifestyle rather than constituting a legitimate cultural identity. Culture, in the view of the critics, is a status available only to those born into groups with a history and a shared set of practices. It is an essential and consistent identity. This formulation of culture fostered one of the most pernicious aspects of the Rainbow debates: the pitting of racial groups against lesbians and gay men.[4]

Critics of the idea of a lesbian/gay culture deployed a simple but powerful tactic to argue that it should be excluded from the multicultural curriculum. They compared the allegedly stable and indisputable cultural categories of race and ethnicity with the purportedly ridiculous and fictive notion of lesbian/gay culture. "They want to teach my kid that being gay fits in with being Italian and Puerto Rican!" one parent cried (Tabor 1992). Some African-American critics were incensed by comparisons of lesbian and gay politics and culture to the black civil-rights movement. At one community schoolboard meeting, a parent and teacher said:

Years of being thrown in jail for demonstrating against racism and being sprayed by fire hoses taught me something. I ask you where was the gay community when school children died in Mobile, Alabama? Where was the gay community when many of us were beaten at a lunch counter? Is this the only way we can be included in the curriculum? To allow the gay community to piggyback off our achievement? (D'Angelo 1992)

For others, the outrage was fueled by the contention that, unlike blacks or (presumably) members of other racial groups, lesbians and gay men have no common cultural symbols or artifacts. Olivia Banks (1993), the chair of the curriculum committee of School Board 29, was vehement during a *60 Minutes* broadcast on the Rainbow curriculum:

How dare they compare themselves to the blacks, who've had to struggle . . . for over 250-some years? They have no special language, no special clothing, no special food, no special dress-wear, so what . . . makes them a culture? They don't fit into any definition of what a culture is. They are using the racial issue as a way to open doors. How dare they?

When Ed Bradley suggested that lesbians and gay men have a minority identity, Banks fumed, "You're doing it again. You're . . . putting a sexual orientation on the same level of a race, and . . . that's unacceptable to this person sitting here."

Much popular opposition to the idea that lesbians and gay men constitute a culture rests on an important subtextual insistence that we are all born with and into culture. In this model, race and ethnicity become the quintessentially authentic cultures. Lingering traces of biologism from the social sciences are entrenched in mainstream thought, and cast race as a fixed and natural essence. As explanatory systems, these racial beliefs, which fuse physiological and social differences, function as "amateur biology" (Omi and Winant 1986: 62). From this perspective, one's social location in a racial culture is secured at birth, and, as Banks implies above, allows one entry into a stable system of shared language, dress, clothing, and other cultural signifiers.

The conviction that cultural status is biologically and generationally transmitted inevitably excludes lesbians and gay men, who cannot make such claims.[5] As illustrated above, critics greet the suggestion of a lesbian and gay culture not simply with opposition, but with the fear that such recognition would somehow diminish their social position or erode whatever legitimacy they have managed to garner from years of civil-rights efforts.[6] Ironically, however, the establishment of multicultural education in public schools, and of university programs such as black studies, was itself the outcome of protracted efforts, much like those now undertaken by lesbians and gay men, to transform the educational system into a set of institutions more aware and more responsive to the cultures of ethnic and racial groups (Blassingame 1971; Ford 1973).

This discursive positioning of racial/ethnic cultures against lesbian/gay cultures in such a volatile mainstream debate invites an examination of the important scholarship on both racial and sexual cultures. Ironically, as we shall see, opponents of the Rainbow curriculum are promulgating rigidly essential definitions of race at a moment when theorists are destabilizing those ideas by asserting the socially and historically constructed nature of racial categories. Similarly, lesbian and gay scholarship has detailed the important historical transformation of structures and meaning from homosexuality as an individual, deviant sexual act, to a personal social identity, to a complex and sophisticated cultural group. In many ways, then, social theorists of race and of sexuality have been engaged in parallel endeavors of placing both race and sexual identity in the foreground as social categories while rejecting false universalisms and ahistorical essentialisms. Further, in deconstructing racial and sexual categories, these theorists have been insistent that all cultures are historically contingent and invented, including dominant cultures such as those of whites and heterosexuals.

Lesbian and Gay Cultures, Communities, and Identities

The Rainbow controversy aptly reveals the binarisms rending contemporary society: the idea of a positive lesbian/gay culture worthy of recognition and respect is coterminous with the specter of the deviant, individual homosexual. Lesbian/gay movements throughout the century have sought to erase the stigma of individual sickness and perversion, institutionalized by law, medicine, and science. As the Rainbow debates indicate, these efforts to transform social meanings from homosexual to gay (Herdt 1992; Weinberg 1972) – that is, from individual, pathological behavior to a rich and distinctive cultural system – have been only partially successful. Rainbow opponents, such as the highly visible right-wing organizer Mary Cummins, were strategically canny in framing the debate as exclusively about the (typically male) sexually deviant individual. Cummins described the curriculum as "aimed at promoting acceptance of sodomy." When questioned by reporter Ed Bradley (1993), she insisted, "What is homosexuality except sodomy? . . . There's no difference. Homosexuals are sodomists."

Cultures emerge in a historical, political, and economic context. Cummins' comment, therefore, and a full understanding of the shift from individual homosexual behavior to gay cultural identity, require an examination of the social production of sexual identities. Proponents of the idea of lesbian/gay culture base their arguments on a body of important historical literature about lesbians and gay men as social actors engaged in the active invention of communities and in the transformation of social meanings of same-sex sexual behavior. The shift from the individual sodomist to the lesbian and gay cultural subject occurred in the context of social, political, and economic changes over the course of many decades, including (as we will see) the intellectual activities of sociologists. In addition, academic research produced by lesbians and gay men concerning their cultural status has been shaped by the evolving theoretical perspectives on the nature and definitions of culture within the social sciences, particularly anthropology.

Our current ideas about sexual identity rest on deep and fundamental changes in the social organization of sexuality that date to the late nineteenth century. Historians cite that period as an era during which dominant sexual meanings shifted from a familial and reproductive orientation to a focus on sexuality as vital to individual happiness and emotional intimacy (D'Emilio and Freedman 1988; Foucault 1978; Weeks 1981). Our modern preoccupation with sexuality as a cornerstone of personality and a prerequisite for fulfillment is a decidedly recent phenomenon. This shift is important in understanding the genuine instability of current notions that there are distinct heterosexual and homosexual persons. The organization of individual identity around sexual feelings and behaviors would have been unthinkable before the last century.

A related historical development in the organization of sexual identities was the emergence of the legal, and particularly the medical, professions as central institutions in the regulation of sexuality. Although homosexual activity was subject to sodomy laws in England before 1885, historians emphasize that those laws were directed against specific acts, not particular categories of people (Weeks 1977, 1981). Acts of sodomy committed between women and men were as vulnerable to prosecution as were those between men and men. Beginning in 1885, however, the laws began to target sexual acts between men; at that time, as a result of new medical discourses, homosexuality was increasingly defined as an internal, individual trait. The idea of a deviant, homosexual person was given a public face, in part, by highly publicized trials such as that of Oscar Wilde at the end of the century.

The invention of medical categories of sexual identities in the late nineteenth century was one artifact of the wider expansion of the emerging cultural authority of the medical profession over issues of health, illness, and (increasingly) sexuality (Irvine 1990; Starr 1982). Physicians were consolidating their power to regulate and define large areas of human experience, even those, as later critics would note, which fell outside the bounds of their training and expertise (Conrad and Schneider 1992; Friedson 1970; Zola 1972). The rise of physicians as the new "moral entrepreneurs" ensured the application of the medical model as the dominant explanatory framework for behavior considered different (Becker 1963). As with sexual identity, the medicalization of "deviance" locates its origins within the individual. As with homosexuality, this medicalization stipulates a cause that is anatomical, physiological, or psychological.

Whereas religion and the law previously had taken note of *acts* of sodomy, the new medical discourse recognized a distinct kind of sexual *person*. Beginning in the 1860s, a variety of terms to describe this new individual emerged, including *invert, urning,* and *homosexual.* The year 1892 marks some of the earliest textual appearances of the word *homosexual* (Halperin 1990; Katz 1990). By this time a heterosexual character, variously defined, began to appear in the medical discourse as well (Katz 1990).

Historians have differed on the significance of medical labeling: did it create a subculture that organized around the new concept of homosexual identity, or was medicalization a response to, and an attempt to define and control, preexisting sexual communities (Chauncey 1982 and 1989; D'Emilio and Freedman 1988; Faderman 1981; Newton 1984; Smith-Rosenberg 1985)? Although evidence indicates that the determinative role of medical literature in shaping homosexual activity and identity was limited, medicalization shifted the locus of moral authority to the medico-psychiatric profession, and much early research focused on descriptive and etiological studies of this new individual. The newly medicalized condition was variously conceptualized as a disease or, as by Havelock Ellis, an anomaly akin to color blindness. Whatever the specific diagnosis, homosexuality was seen as an individual condition, and appropriate interventions were subject to the current theories and treatment modalities of medicine and psychiatry.

One hundred years since their invention, the categories of homosexuality and heterosexuality have achieved the status of assumed knowledge; the idea that there are distinct heterosexual and homosexual persons forms the centerpiece of the sexual wisdom of our society. An important factor in the persistence of ideas about fixed sexual identity derives from the cultural activities of lesbians and gay men themselves: it must be reemphasized that medical discourse did not create categories of sexuality out of whole cloth, but was partially responding to the nascent social organization of groups of people who were beginning to coalesce and identity around their sexual interests and behaviors. Indeed, the last hundred years have witnessed the rapid and transformative development of social worlds of lesbian and gay men, particularly since World War II (D'Emilio 1983).

The social organization of lesbians and gay men has centered around the shared experience of transgressive sexuality, which has been variously defined throughout the century. Certainly legal sanctions and the medico-psychiatric consensus of homosexual pathology shaped early social networks. The stigma of perversion tainted the collective consciousness, even if some individual members refused to internalize that stigma. Pervasive social attitudes that homosexuals were bizarre, criminal, or sick were reinforced by, and contributed to, a crushing isolation and invisibility. Secrecy was an institutional tyranny rather than an individual prerogative; the closet became "the defining structure for gay oppression in this century" (Sedgwick 1993: 48). In this context, the early lesbian and gay world sought a transformation of social definitions from individual homosexual behavior to a social identity and, significantly, from a "spoiled identity" (Goffman 1963) to one of respect and value. This process much later would prompt lesbians and gay men to seek recognition for their own identities and culture within multicultural curricula such as the Rainbow.

This rearticulation of socio-sexual meanings has been a complex process proceeding on many fronts. The political initiatives of the lesbian/gay movement have been pivotal in challenging both individual and institutional structures of oppression (see, for example, D'Emilio 1983; Duberman, Vicinus, and Chauncey 1989; Weeks 1977). These efforts, of course, have been shaped by a range of broader social influences, such as social and demographic changes wrought by World War II, the impact of McCarthyism, the rise of religious fundamentalism, and the emergence of liberation movements organized around race and gender.

Academic research and scholarship also helped create an intellectual climate conducive to the redefinition of sexual meaning systems. For example, Alfred Kinsey's (1948, 1953) research challenged the widespread notion that gay people were a distinct and pathological set of individuals, and suggested that everyone had the "capacity" for homosexuality. Although the gay visibility engendered by the Kinsey reports contributed to a cultural panic that fed McCarthyism, it also helped consolidate a growing 1950s homophile movement (Irvine 1990). New sociological theories also supported the efforts of this movement. In particular, deviance theory, which underwent a radical postwar transformation, provided an intellectual infrastructure for new definitions of sexual identities (see D'Emilio 1983). The work of Erving Goffman (1963), Howard Becker (1963), and Joseph Gusfield (1955), for example, was instrumental in shifting the theoretical view of deviance from that of a quality located within the individual person or act to that of a historically specific status created by social censure.

This sociological deviance theory of the 1960s was in radical opposition to the psychoanalytic discourse on homosexuality. Irving Bieber and Charles Socarides rose to prominence at that time with their oedipal and pre-oedipal theories of the pathological development of homosexuality. Socarides claimed that psychoanalysis could cure up to 50 percent of "strongly motivated obligatory homosexuals" (see Bayer 1981: 37). On the other hand, the interactionist model of deviance facilitated a definition of lesbians and gay men simply as rule breakers rather than as essentially flawed individuals. In Becker's terms, lesbians and gay men were "outsiders" who had been labeled deviant.

Becker's observation that the deviant identity becomes the defining one, and therefore that outsiders create distinct social worlds, was particularly relevant to the social organization of lesbians and gay men: this century has witnessed the formation of elaborate collectivities of lesbian and gay life organized around erotic identity. These networks, however, have become increasingly expansive, with sexuality less explicitly in the foreground. With the elaboration of this complex social world has come disagreement about how to characterize it. Is it a lifestyle enclave (Bellah et al. 1985), a community (D'Emilio 1983; Kennedy and Davis 1993; Murray 1979), a culture (Altman 1982; Bronski 1984; Ferguson 1990; Herdt 1992; Weeks 1977), an ethnicity (Epstein 1987), or nationalism (Duggan 1992; Newton 1993)?

Yet the idea of culture has gained popular and widespread currency as an often loosely defined signifier of shared identity. Much of the intellectual debate among lesbian and gay scholars has concerned the question of cultural status; the discourse has followed theoretical advances in the social sciences, particularly anthropology and cultural studies, on the definition of culture. Until the late 1950s, behaviorism dominated the social sciences, and culture was defined as patterns of behavior, actions, and customs (D'Andrade 1984; Shweder 1984). This notion still retains popular credibility, as evidenced by Rainbow curriculum opponent Olivia Banks' earlier charge that gay people lack unique food or clothing.

As the behaviorist paradigm eroded across the disciplines, ideas about culture shifted. Anthropologists argued that culture is constituted by shared information, knowledge, or symbols – that is, through Geertz's popular notion of "webs of significance" (Geertz 1973: 5). As we will see, this definition introduced complexity not only for gay people but for other cultural groups as well, because it brought to the foreground problems of cultural unity and of how extensively knowledge and symbols are shared within social groups.

The literature on lesbian and gay social organization, until very recently, addressed these two concepts of culture: that of patterns of behavior and customs, and that of shared symbolic systems. With some exceptions (Browning 1993; Ferguson 1990; Grover 1988), there is consensus that lesbians and gay men constitute a community with a distinct culture. This has been argued on a number of fronts. Murray (1979), for example, examined changes in social-science definitions of community, from that of a discrete entity to that of a process, and pointed out the lack of a well-defined and agreed-upon definition. Nevertheless, from his studies of Toronto and San Francisco (Murray 1992), he argued that the gay community meets all of the "modes of social relations" inherent in the various definitions of communities. Historians have detailed the elaborate array of social institutions as evidence of a gay community (D'Emilio 1983; Weeks 1977). These include churches, health and counseling clinics, newspapers and other media, sports teams, theater companies, travel agencies, and much more. As lesbian and gay history becomes more articulated, it is clear that community institutions (for example, the urban lesbian bar before Stonewall) were instrumental in supporting not only relationships but identity (Kennedy and Davis 1993). These studies highlight the important dialectical relationship between community and identity.

In the debate about lesbian/gay culture, it is perhaps less complicated although by no means easy to bring the behavioral aspects of culture into the foreground. Thus, in reply to Banks' remark on the Rainbow curriculum that gay people share no common artifacts, a gay man retorted, "We do have a culture. We do have our own literature. We have our own artworks. We have music that would be identifiable to lesbian and gay people" (Madson 1993: 6). Weeks (1977) has described a substantial gay argot as evidence of a culture; Bronski (1984) has discussed gay male sensibility in movies, theater, opera, and pornography. Altman (1982) noted an issue of the *Soho News* in which quiche and Perrier are designated as "the gay food." Clothing is an important cultural signifier, especially for a group whose members need help in recognizing each other. Kennedy and Davis (1993) have described how lesbians in the 1940s and 1950s learned to dress in ways that would both reinforce their sexual identity and signal it to other lesbians.

It has been possible to identify behavioral signifiers of lesbian/gay culture, but it is more difficult to argue the existence of shared symbolic systems of knowledge or information. Bronski offered perhaps the most comprehensive argument with his early, important formulation of the gay (male) sensibility; this formulation, although historically situated, assumes a somewhat determinist aspect. Some of the new anthropological scholarship is more successful in empirically describing the construction of historically specific lesbian and gay communities, with complex systems of cultural meanings (Kennedy and Davis 1993; Newton 1993). These studies reveal how meaning systems within lesbian/gay communities are located along axes of difference, particularly those of race, class, and gender. Although knowledge and symbols may be shared, such a process is inevitably partial and fragmented.

The inability to conclusively demonstrate shared symbolic systems among lesbians and gay men speaks not to the absence of cultural status but to the inadequacy of theory that totalizes culture. In a discussion of "warring factions" among the organizers of the 1993 lesbian and gay march on Washington, Goldstein stated, "Anyone who knows the gay community is aware that it stands for many things, some quite contradictory" (1993). Cultural theory is increasingly rejecting earlier perspectives that highlighted unity in favor of the recognition of internal contradiction and multiplicity. As Clifford notes, "If 'culture' is not an object to be described, neither is it a unified corpus of symbols and meanings that can be definitively interpreted. Culture is contested, temporal, and emergent" (1986: 19). New theoretical articulations of culture and identity have had important implications for the activism and scholarship of all social groups.

Destabilizing Theory

Contemporary debates about culture and identities, as they are enacted in popular discourse such as that concerning the Rainbow curriculum, are infused with notions such as permanence, tradition, and (often implicitly) the imperative for a biological essence. Racial categories almost uniformly meet such criteria; their allegedly stable boundaries are policed by biological markers. On the other hand, sexual identity (read "homosexuality") is found wanting. Critics charge that at its best, the lesbian/gay community is a random group of individuals who have perversely chosen a deviant lifestyle. At its worst, it is a random group which must seduce vulnerable others in order to perpetuate itself. Not surprisingly, this charge can inspire a strategy on the part of some lesbians and gay men of asserting biological origins for their sexuality in the belief that essentialism is a precondition for legitimacy. Emerging multicultural theoretical and political initiatives problematize all of these areas of assumed knowledge, such as the immutability of culture, the construction and meaning of racial and sexual identities, the stability of social categories, and the nature and politics of difference.

These disruptions of the "common sense" arose from the synergistic power of social-construction theory (with roots in symbolic interactionism), poststructuralist theory, cultural studies, and multicultural studies as represented by African-American and ethnic studies, women's studies, and lesbian and gay studies or queer theory. These theories have been both shaped and informed by political movements organized around race, ethnicity, gender, and sexuality.[7] In the briefest summary, these critical theories challenge the idea of fixed or essential social identities and raise a persistent question about the historical and political circumstances under which subjectivities are continually recreated. Identities and social categories are recognized as fluid and unstable, but also as multiple and internally contradictory. Narratives of social location therefore must account for the intersectionality of identities. The impulse to destabilize assumed social knowledge is common to these theories.

Poststructuralism and lesbian/gay studies have not necessarily eliminated earlier ideas about culture, but have enlarged and decentered them. If, as some theorists have suggested (e.g., Alexander 1992), culture is a meaningful set of symbolic patterns that can be read as a text, poststructuralism insists that there will be multiple interpretations of such readings, as of texts. Dimensions of culture, whether values, shared language or slang, geography, subjective beliefs, or symbolic systems, are not universal, deterministic, or static. Cultural artifacts, subjectivities, and identities are more fragmented and divided. These theories call into question the nature and meaning of all cultural groups by challenging the authenticity of any one culture, by suggesting that the meaning of culture will vary historically and contextually, and by observing that cultural identifications are multiple and overlapping.

Because the categories of race and sexual identity were so frequently positioned in opposition to each other in mainstream debates over the Rainbow curriculum, it is instructive to recognize scholarship that questions the authenticity of an essentially racial culture and identity. Critical race theorists have deployed the insight that identity does not reflect an essential self in arguing that race and ethnicity are constituted not in biology, but in ongoing social and political processes. This is a powerfully radical theoretical challenge in light of the seemingly very visible and immutable quality of race, as compared with the seeming invisibility of sexual identity. Skin color, Stuart Hall (1989, 1992b) argues, has nothing to do with blackness. "People are all sorts of colors. The question is whether you are *culturally, historically, politically* Black" (1989: 15). Rather than an objective, natural category, race is an unstable "complex of social meanings constantly being transformed by political struggle" (Omi and Winant 1986: 68). Race, then, is an identity that people are not born with but must assume in an ongoing process of identification.

The indeterminacy of biology and the construction of racial identities inform a range of painful narratives by critical race theorists about skin color, passing, and the impact of cruel and oppressive racial meanings generated both by the dominant culture and in communities of color (for some recent examples see Carter 1993; Dent 1992; Loury 1993; McKnight 1993; Njeri 1993; Russell, Wilson, and Hall 1992; for an analysis of the social construction of whiteness, see Frankenberg 1993). The conviction that racial identity is a process, but also (significantly) that it is a choice, is thematic to these accounts. As Carter insists, "Race is a claim. A choice. A decision" (1993: 79). Yet he goes on to acknowledge the impact of external social institutions and meanings:

> Oh, it is imposed, too. The society tells us: "You are black because we say so." Skin color is selected as one of many possible characteristics of morphology used for sorting. Never mind the reasons. It is simply so. It is not, however, logically entailed. (1993: 79)

These critical theories therefore challenge racial essentialism, emphasize the process of individual identification, and analyze the social, political, and economic process of racial formation (Omi and Winant 1986). They historicize the process by which skin color became the basis for the invention of racial categories, and the ways in which these categories mapped new identities not only for persons of color, but also for whites. Inevitably these theories complicate any simple notions of stable and monolithic racial cultures and communities.

Lesbian and gay studies, informed by social-construction theory and most recently by queer theory, have undertaken a similar intellectual project. This field has placed sexuality in the foreground as a category which, like gender and race, must be central to social analyses. Social construction theory, which denies the existence of a natural, biological sexuality, has provided the infrastructure for research on the production, organization, and regulation of sexuality. Constructionists argue that sexual acts, identities, and communities are imbued with meaning through social and historical processes; indeed, sexual desire itself may well be socially constructed (Vance 1991). Lesbian and gay scholarship examines the historical invention of sexual identities and communities, the ways in which power is infused and deployed through sexual categories, and the complicated relationships between sexuality and other social categories such as gender, race, and class. (Although it is impossible to cite all of this scholarship, some important works include Beam 1986; Chauncey 1982; D'Emilio 1983; D'Emilio and Freedman 1988; Duberman et al. 1989; Foucault 1978; Hull, Scott, and Smith 1982; Jackson 1993; Katz 1976; Kennedy and Davis 1993; Lorde 1988; Peterson 1992; Rubin 1975, 1984; Weeks 1977, 1981, 1985, 1991.)

Queer theory builds on social constructionism to further dismantle sexual identities and categories. Drawing on postmodern critiques, the new theoretical deployment of queerness recognizes the instabilities of traditional oppositions such as lesbian/gay and heterosexual. Queerness is often used as an inclusive signifier for lesbian, gay, bisexual, transgender, drag, straights who pass as gay (Powers 1993), and any permutation of sex/gender dissent (see de Lauretis 1991; Doty 1993; Duggan 1992). It is an encompassing identity that simultaneously challenges and resists the calcification of identities and categories. Also, the use of the term *queer* is not unanimously celebrated; some scholars question the historiographic usefulness of deconstructing a marginal identity at a critical moment of activism and scholarship (Penn 1993).[8] Foremost, however, among the tasks of a queer project are challenges to seemingly stable categories – lesbianism and gayness as well as the dominant heterosexuality.

Together, the overlapping intellectual projects of postmodernism, cultural studies, critical race theories, and lesbian/gay studies and queer theory serve as powerful challenges to traditional notions of culture and identity. Cultures cannot be understood simply as a static and historically consistent aggregate of shared practices or knowledge. Rather, they are dynamic processes which, as Clifford notes, "do not hold still for their portraits" (1986: 10). Further, critical theories emphasize that cultures, as the construction of social categories on the basis of physiological characteristics or sexual expression, are products of human agency. Cultures are social inventions, not biological inevitabilities. None is more authentic than another.

These deconstructions, however, do not suggest that cultures are so amorphous and so diffuse that they defy social analysis. Nor do they imply that identities are so fluid as to be easily tried on and shrugged off, thus becoming culturally and individually meaningless. Rather, they insist on a recognition of the paradoxes of culture and identity: we need cultural identities for social location, even while we must maintain continual awareness of their constructed nature; social movements simultaneously challenge and reinforce the importance and meanings of identities. In the women's movement, this dilemma has been articulated by Ann Snitow as the "recurring feminist divide" – that is, the imperative to "build the identity 'woman' and give it solid political meaning and the need to tear down the very category 'woman' and dismantle its all-too-solid history" (1989: 205). Similarly, gay social historian Jeffrey Weeks speaks of sexual identities as "necessary fictions" (1991: viii), a term that neatly encompasses the paradox. Finally, Stuart Hall describes an "ethnicity of the margins, of the periphery" (1992b: 258), which supports the recognition that we all speak from a particular social and historical standpoint without being contained by that position. This recurrent tension demands fuller articulation in both our theories and our politics.

Back to the Rainbow: Sociology and Theory

This review of historical and theoretical scholarship on the invention of racial and sexual cultures and identities highlights its centrality to analyses of debates such as those over the Rainbow curriculum. The arguments that only racial/ethnic groups have culture, while lesbians and gay men are aberrant individuals, can be understood only through the theoretical lenses of new African-American scholarship on the social construction of race and of literature by lesbian and gay scholars on the historical invention of culture and sexual identity. These theories suggest that all cultures are constructed and unstable; none have more authenticity than others. In addition, the insights of lesbian and gay theory – that sexuality is a major social category giving rise to

structures of inequality and patterns of discrimination and invisibility
– are obviously crucial to this analysis.

The enterprises of lesbian and gay studies and of African- American
and ethnic studies concern the invention of racial and sexual cultures.
Yet they also address other central aspects of the Rainbow debates,
such as the construction of self and identities, the instability, multiplicity, and dynamism of cultures, and the limitations of essentialized
identities. Further, any effective analysis of the volatile and often
destructive debates about the Rainbow curriculum also must untangle
the complicated relations of power and difference in the clash of
separate and overlapping cultural identifications. For example, gay
people were pitted against people of color; thus, complex permutations
of racism and homophobia were triggered. Often silenced in the debate
were lesbians and gay men of color.

In this area of power, difference, and multiple identifications, programs such as cultural studies, ethnic studies, women's studies, and
lesbian and gay studies are developing important theory. Beyond a
recognition of the invention of cultures lies its day-to-day working out,
the discursive formations (Jackson 1993) in which meanings are constituted through fluid negotiations of race, gender, sexual identity, and
other social categories. We need theory that affords an understanding
of our structural and interpersonal positions as they are configured
through power and difference. Also, scholars and activists are engaged
in the complicated practice of theorizing and historicizing cultural
identities within a simultaneous awareness of their fragility. These
dialogues could be central to sociology.

Several themes raised by current popular debates about culture might
concern us as theorists while we develop more fully the idea of culture,
and of sexual cultures, as deployed and manifested among people
without "inherent" shared identities. As we explore the specific processes by which all cultures are constructed, we must articulate more
clearly the complexities of social-construction theory and must clarify
common misunderstandings.[9] Further questions for sociologists concern the complications inherent in cultures and identities that are
constructed around seemingly biological categories such as race, ethnicity, and gender. How can we understand and reconcile the needs of
some people, often generated by legal and political strategizing, to
more deeply essentialize such categories, even while others, through
historical and social research, are demonstrating their radically constructed nature? In these debates, how does scientific inquiry function
to reinforce particular ideologies about culture and identity? Can the
histories of other oppressed groups seeking to achieve political rights

and cultural legitimacy yield insights into recent attempts to biologize sexual identity more fully? Is it inevitable, in a context of deprivation and marginality, that different cultural groups will compete for status and resources? Finally, given that individuals have multiple subject positions, can we more fully develop theories that give voice to inter-sectional identities (Crenshaw 1992) rather than forcing people to choose one standpoint, such as race, over another, such as sexual identity or gender?

It is reasonable to expect that sociologists, for whom the study of social groups is the central task, would theorize these cultural dilem-mas. Yet to do so, sociological theory must be more responsive to the insights of lesbian and gay and other multicultural theorists, placing social categories such as sexuality and race in the foreground in the context of power and difference. In 1992 Richard Perry wrote an article titled "Why Do Multiculturalists Ignore Anthropologists?" His argument, among others, was that anthropologists have much to offer multicultural scholars outside the discipline about the study of cul-tures. This point is well taken, and certainly can be made about the potential contributions of sociologists as well. On the other hand, an equally pertinent question is "Why have the traditional disciplines, sociology among them, not enthusiastically engaged in the important historical and theoretical work of multicultural groups such as lesbian and gay studies?" Sexuality and culture will continue to be central social issues; as such, they are central to our discipline as well.

Notes

1   Designed as a guide for teachers, the Rainbow curriculum contained lessons on the artifacts, folk songs, and holidays of other cultures. It was based on the premise that children could be taught basic lessons in mathematics, grammar, and reading by using the games, songs, and dances indigenous to a wide range of cultures.

   The controversy over the curriculum centered on brief sections, in fact merely six entries in a 443-page document, which discussed lesbian and gay families. One section noted, "The issues surrounding family may be very sensitive for children. Teachers should be aware of varied family structures, including two-parent or single-parent households, gay or lesbian parents, divorced parents, adoptive parents, and guardians or foster parents. Child-ren must be taught to acknowledge the positive aspects of each type of household and the importance of love and care in family living." It went on to say that children growing up in families headed by heterosexuals "may be experiencing contact with lesbians/gays for the first time . . . teachers of first graders have an opportunity to give children a healthy sense of identity at an early age. Classes should include references to lesbians/gay people in all curricular areas. Educators have the potential to help increase the tolerance and acceptance of the lesbian/gay community and to decrease the staggering number of hate crimes perpetrated against them." The curriculum emphasized the recognition of lesbian/gay culture; nowhere was there any mention of sex.

2 Sociological theory has certainly informed cultural studies, particularly in Britain. Sociologist Stuart Hall (1990) describes the formation of the Centre for Cultural Studies at the University of Birmingham by a handful of scholars who were marginal to academic life. He notes how sociologists attacked their work even while these new cultural theorists "raided" sociology and other traditional disciplines for theory, which they then rearticulated. Cultural studies served as a challenge to traditional sociology. As Hall notes, they took the risk of saying to sociologists "that what they say sociology is, is not what it is. We had to teach what we thought a kind of sociology that would be of service to people studying culture would be, something we could not get from self-designated sociologists" (1990: 16).

3 For example, an examination of the list of contributors to the proceedings of a large international conference on cultural studies, held in 1990, reveals very few sociologists. See Grossberg, Nelson, and Treichler (1992).

4 This is a complicated dynamic that is impossible to fully explore in this article. Although homophobia in certain communities of color certainly contributed to these tensions and formulations, opponents in certain historically racist, white, working-class sections of Queens and Brooklyn inflamed fears and misunderstandings by distorting the curriculum and appealing to anxieties of racial groups they had previously ignored. In a complicated and often ignored role in the debates were lesbians and gay men of color.

5 Some lesbians and gay men, however, are developing political strategies for legitimacy based on the alleged and unproved biological origins of homosexuality.

6 Not only people of color are voicing this threat. For example, Dolores Ayling of Concerned Parents for Educational Accountability (a religious right group that organized to oppose the curriculum) spoke of the outrage at the fact that sexual orientation is included in the Rainbow Curriculum in a way that detracts from the authenticity of race as a cultural category (personal conversation, April 14, 1993). Many of these white advocates had not previously been noted for their vigorous support of communities of color.

7 See Hall (1992a) for an examination of the role of feminism and critical race theories in shaping cultural studies.

8 This concern about the dismantling of the categories "lesbian" and "gay" echoes those expressed by other scholars regarding postmodern critiques of identity. Some theorists have noted how the critique of stable identities and of authoritative experience has emerged at precisely a moment of increasing subjectivity, visibility, and production of knowledge among historically marginalized groups such as women, lesbians and gay men, and people of

color. Similarly, the important recognitions of the limitations of identity politics as an expression of static, homogeneous, and essential self-groupings have been coterminous with a vital activism among such groups. See, for example, de Lauretis (1991).

9 Misconceptions about social-construction theory have most typically arisen from its use in the area of sexuality. Expansion and clarification are important because of the widespread relevance of constructionism for theorizing issues of culture and identity. First, the constructionist analysis is often mistakenly glossed as one which insists that individual sexual desires and directions are learned and not inborn. Yet constructionism goes far beyond the familiar nature–nurture debates. Social-construction theory does not simply speak about the origins of sexuality, but examines the attribution of meaning to sexual desires, behaviors, and communities. Further, it challenges the notion that there is any historical or cross-cultural consistency to sexual acts, beliefs, or practices. Second, to suggest that sexuality is socially constructed is not to say that it is "a fluid, changeable process open to intentional redefinition" (Epstein 1987: 22). Social constructionists have not fully theorized the ways in which sexual desires, feelings, and beliefs are mediated by socio-cultural factors and, in many people, result in deeply felt inclinations that may then be socialized into sexual identities. This theoretical gap should not be misconstrued as a suggestion that "constructedness" implies a superficial and easily unlearned sexuality. These misconceptions simply highlight areas in which sociologists might articulate social-construction theory more fully, particularly in the relationships among social ideologies, individual desires and experiences, and individual and social identities. See Vance (1991) for an excellent theoretical clarification of social constructionism.

References

Alba, Richard D. 1990. *Ethnic Identity: The Transformation of White America*. New Haven: Yale University Press.

Alexander, Jeffrey C. 1992. "The Promise of a Cultural Sociology: Technological Discourse and the Sacred and Profane Information Machine," in *Theory of Culture*, eds Richard Munch and Neil J. Smelser. Berkeley: University of California Press.

Alexander, Jeffrey C. and Steven Seidman. 1990. *Culture and Society: Contemporary Debates*. Cambridge, UK: Cambridge University Press.

Almaguer, Tomas. 1991. "Chicano Men: A Cartography of Homosexual Identity and Behavior." *differences*, 3 (2): 75–100.

Altman, Dennis. 1982. *The Homosexualization of America*. Boston: Beacon.

Banks, Olivia. 1993. *The Rainbow Curriculum: 60 Minutes*. Apr. 4.

Bayer, Richard. 1981. *Homosexuality and American Psychiatry: The Politics of Diagnosis*. New York: Basic Books.

Beam, Joseph. 1986. *In the Life: A Gay Black Anthology*. Boston: Alyson.

Becker, Howard. 1963. *Outsiders: Studies in the Sociology of Deviance.* New York: Free Press.

Bellah, Robert N., Richard Madsen, William M. Sullivan, Ann Swidler, and Steven T. Tipton. 1985. *Habits of the Heart.* Berkeley: University of California Press.

Blassingame, John. 1971. *New Perspectives on Black Studies.* Chicago: University of Illinois Press.

Bourdieu, Pierre. 1968. "Outline of a Theory of Art Perception." *International Social Science Journal,* 2 (4): 589–612.

Bradley, Ed. 1993. *The Rainbow Curriculum: 60 Minutes.* Apr. 4.

Bronski, Michael. 1984. *Culture Clash: The Making of Gay Sensibility.* Boston: South End Press.

Browning, Frank. 1993. *The Culture of Desire: Paradox and Perversity in Gay Lives Today.* New York: Crown.

Carter, Stephen I. 1993. "The Black Table, the Empty Seat, and the Tie," in *Lure and Loathing: Essays on Race, Identity, and the Ambivalence of Assimilation,* ed. Gerald Early. New York: Penguin, 55–79.

Chauncey, George, Jr. 1982. "From Sexual Inversion to Homosexuality: Medicine and the Changing Conceptualization of Female Deviance." *Salmagundi,* 58–9: 114–46.

——. 1989. "Christian Brotherhood or Sexual Perversion? Homosexual Identities and the Construction of Sexual Boundaries in the World War I Era," in *Hidden from History: Reclaiming the Gay and Lesbian Past,* eds Martin Duberman, Martha Vicinus, and George Chauncey Jr. New York: Penguin, 294–317.

Clifford, James. 1986. "Introduction: Partial Truths," in *Writing Culture: The Poetics and Politics of Ethnography,* ed. James Clifford and George E. Marcus. Berkeley: University of California Press, 1–26.

Collins, Patricia Hill. 1986. "Learning from the Outsider Within: The Sociological Significance of Black Feminist Thought." *Social Problems,* 33: S14–S32.

——. 1990. *Black Feminist Thought: Knowledge, Consciousness, and the Politics of Empowerment.* Boston: Unwin Hyman.

Conrad, Peter and Joseph Schneider. 1992. *Deviance and Medicalization: From Badness to Sickness.* Philadelphia: Temple University Press.

Crenshaw, Kimberle. 1992. "Whose Story Is It, Anyway? Feminist and Anti-racist Appropriations of Anita Hill," in *Race-ing Justice, En-gendering Power: Essays on Anita Hill, Clarence Thomas, and the Construction of Social Reality,* ed. Toni Morrison. New York: Pantheon, 402–40.

D'Andrade, Roy G. 1984. "Cultural Meaning Systems," in *Culture Theory: Essays on Mind, Self, and Emotion,* eds Richard A. Shweder and Robert A. LeVine. New York: Cambridge University Press, 88–119.

D'Angelo, Laura. 1992. "Repercussions Continue after School Board Vote." *Staten Island Sunday Advance,* Sept. 6.

de Lauretis, Teresa. 1991. "Queer Theory: Lesbian and Gay Sexualities." *differences* 3: iii–xviii.

D'Emilio, John. 1983. *Sexual Politics, Sexual Communities: The Making of a Homosexual Minority in the United States, 1940–1970*. Chicago: University of Chicago Press.

D'Emilio, John and Estelle Freedman. 1988. *Intimate Matters: A History of Sexuality in America*. New York: Harper and Row.

Dent, Gina. 1992. *Black Popular Culture*. Seattle: Bay Press.

Doty, Alexander. 1993. *Making Things Perfectly Queer: Interpreting Mass Culture*. Minneapolis: University of Minnesota Press.

Duberman, Martin, Martha Vicinus, and George Chauncey Jr. 1989. *Hidden from History: Reclaiming the Gay and Lesbian Past*. New York: Penguin Books.

Duggan, Lisa. 1992. "Making It Perfectly Queer." *Socialist Review*, 22: 11–32.

Epstein, Steven. 1987. "Gay Politics, Ethnic Identity: The Limits of Social Constructionism." *Socialist Review*, (93–4): 9–54.

Faderman, Lillian. 1981. *Surpassing the Love of Men*. New York: Morrow.

Ferguson, Ann. 1990. "Is There a Lesbian Culture?" in *Lesbian Philosophies and Cultures*, ed. Jeffner Allen. Albany: SUNY Press, 63–88.

Ford, Nick Aaron. 1973. *Black Studies: Threat-or- Challenge*. Port Washington, NY: Kennikat.

Foucault, Michel. 1978. *The History of Sexuality: An Introduction*, vol. 1. New York: Vintage.

Frankenberg, Ruth. 1993. *White Women, Race Matters: The Social Construction of Whiteness*. Minneapolis: University of Minnesota Press.

Friedson, Eliot. 1970. *Profession of Medicine: A Study of the Sociology of Applied Knowledge*. New York: Harper & Row.

Gagnon, John. 1977. *Human Sexualities*. Glenview, Ill: Scott Foresman.

Gagnon, John and William Simon. 1973. *Sexual Conduct: The Social Sources of Human Sexuality*. Chicago. Aldine.

Geertz, Clifford. 1973. *The Interpretation of Cultures*. New York: Basic Books.

Giddens, Anthony. 1992. *The Transformation of Intimacy: Sexuality, Love and Eroticism in Modern Societies*. Stanford: Stanford University Press.

Goffman, Erving. 1963. *Stigma: Notes on the Management of Spoiled Identity*. New York: Simon and Schuster.

Goldstein, Richard. 1993. "Faith, Hope, and Sodomy: Gay Liberation Embarks on a Vision Quest." *Village Voice*, June 29, pp. 21–31.

Grossberg, Lawrence, Cary Nelson, and Paula Treichler, eds. 1992. *Cultural Studies*. New York: Routledge.

Grover, Jan Z. 1988. "AIDS: Keywords," in *AIDS: Cultural Analysis, Cultural Activism*, ed. Douglas Crimp. Cambridge, Mass.: MIT Press, 17–30.

Gusfield, Joseph R. 1955. *Symbolic Crusade*. Urbana: University of Illinois Press.

Hall, John R. and Mary Jo Neitz. 1993. *Culture: Sociological Perspectives*. Englewood Cliffs, NJ: Prentice-Hall.

Hall, Stuart. 1989. "Ethnicity, Identity and Difference." *Radical America*, 23: 9–20.

Hall, Stuart. 1990. "The Emergence of Cultural Studies and the Crisis of the Humanities." *October* (summer): 11–23.

——. 1992a. "Cultural Studies and Its Theoretical Legacies," in *Cultural Studies*, eds Lawrence Grossberg, Cary Nelson, and Paula Treichler. New York: Routledge, 277–94.

——. 1992b. "New Ethnicities," in *"Race", Culture and Difference*, eds James Donald and Ali Rattansi. London: Sage, 252–9.

Halperin, David. 1990. *One Hundred Years of Homosexuality*. New York: Routledge.

Herdt, Gilbert. 1992. *Gay Culture in America: Essays from the Field*. Boston: Beacon.

Hu-DeHart, Evelyn. 1993. "Rethinking America: The Practice and Politics of Multiculturalism in Higher Education," in *Beyond a Dream Deferred: Multicultural Education and the Politics of Excellence*, eds Becky W. Thompson and Sangeeta Tyagi. Minneapolis: University of Minnesota Press, 3–17.

Hull, Gloria, Patricia Bell Scott, and Barbara Smith. 1982. *All the Women Are White, All the Blacks Are Men, But Some of Us Are Brave*. Westbury, NY: Feminist Press.

Humphries, Laud. 1974. *Tearoom Trade: Impersonal Sex in Public Places*. Chicago: Aldine.

Irvine, Janice M. 1990. *Disorders of Desire: Sex and Gender in Modern American Sexology*. Philadelphia: Temple University Press.

——. 1994. *Sexual Cultures and the Construction of Adolescent Identities*. Philadelphia: Temple University Press.

Jackson, Earl, Jr. 1993. "The Responsibility of and to Differences: Theorizing Race and Ethnicity in Lesbian and Gay Studies," in *Beyond a Dream Deferred: Multicultural Education and the Politics of Excellence*, eds Becky W. Thompson and Sangeeta Tyagi. Minneapolis: University of Minnesota Press, 131–6.

Katz, Jonathan. 1976. *Gay American History*. New York: Crowell.

——. 1990. "The Invention of Heterosexuality." *Socialist Review*, 21: 7–34.

Kennedy, Elizabeth Lapovsky and Madeline D. Davis. 1993. *Boots of Leather, Slippers of Gold: The History of a Lesbian Community*. New York: Routledge.

Kinsey, Alfred C., Wardell B. Pomeroy, Clyde E. Martin, and Paul H. Gebhard. 1948. *Sexual Behavior in the Human Male*. Philadelphia: Saunders.

——. 1953. *Sexual Behavior in the Human Female*. New York: Pocket Books.

Lorde, Audre. 1988. *A Burst of Light*. Ithaca: Firebrand Books.

Loury, Glenn C. 1993. "Free at Last? A Personal Perspective on Race and Ientity in America," in *Lure and Loathing: Essays on Race, Identity, and the Ambivalence of Assimilation*, ed. Gerald Early. New York: Penguin, 1–12.

Luker, Kristen. 1975. *Taking Chances: Abortion and the Decision Not to Contracept*. Berkeley: University of California Press.

Madson, Ron. 1993. *The Rainbow Curriculum: 60 Minutes*. Apr. 4.

McKnight, Reginald. 1993. "Confessions of a Wannabe Negro," in *Lure and Loathing: Essays on Race, Identity, and the Ambivalence of Assimilation*, ed. Gerald Early. New York: Penguin, 95–112.

Munch, Richard and Neil J. Smelser. 1992. *Theory of Culture*. Berkeley: University of California Press.

Murray, Stephen O. 1979. "The Institutional Elaboration of a Quasi Ethnic Community." *International Review of Modern Sociology*, 9: 165–77.

——. 1992. "Components of Gay Community in San Francisco," in *Gay Culture in America: Essays from the Field*, ed. Gilbert Herdt. Boston: Beacon, 107–46.

Nelson, Cary, et al. 1992. "Cultural Studies: An Introduction," in *Cultural Studies*, eds Lawrence Grossberg, Cary Nelson, Paula Treichler. New York: Routledge, 1–16.

Newton, Esther. 1984. "The Mythic Mannish Lesbian: Radclyffe Hall and the New Woman." *Signs*, 9: 556–75.

——. 1993. *Cherry Grove: Pleasure Island, Gay and Lesbian USA, 1930s–1980s*. Boston: Beacon.

Njeri, Itabari. 1993. "Sushi and Grits: Ethnic Identity and Conflict in a Newly Multicultural America," in *Lure and Loathing: Essays on Race, Identity, and the Ambivalence of Assimilation*, ed. Gerald Early. New York: Penguin, 13–40.

Omi, Michael and Howard Winant. 1986. *Racial Formation in the United States from the 1960s to the 1980s*. New York: Routledge.

Penn, Donna. 1993. "If It Walks like a Dyke, Talks like a Dyke, It Must Be a Dyke?" Unpublished paper.

Perry, Richard J. 1992. "Why Do Multiculturalists Ignore Anthropologists?" *Chronicle of Higher Education*. Mar. 4, p. A52.

Peterson, John. 1992. "Black Men and Their Same-Sex Desires and Behaviors," in *Gay Culture in America: Essays from the Field*, ed. Gilbert Herdt. Boston: Beacon, 147–64.

Plummer, Kenneth. 1975. *Sexual Stigma: An Interactionist Account*. London: Routledge.

——. 1981. *The Making of the Modern Homosexual*. London: Hutchinson.

Powers, Ann. 1993. "Queer in the Streets, Straight in the Sheets." *Village Voice*, June 29, p. 24.

Rubin, Gayle. 1975. "The Traffic in Women: Notes on the 'Political Economy' of Sex," in *Toward an Anthropology of Women*, ed. R. Reiter. New York: Monthly Review Press, 157–210.

——. 1984. "Thinking Sex," in *Pleasure and Danger: Exploring Female Sexuality*, ed. Carole S. Vance. Boston: Routledge, 267–319.

Russell, Kathy, Midge Wilson, and Ronald Hall. 1992. *The Color Complex: The Politics of Skin Color among African Americans*. New York: Harcourt Brace Jovanovich.

Sedgwick, Eve Kosofsky. 1993. "Epistemology of the Closet," in *The Lesbian and Gay Studies Reader*, eds Henry Abelove, Michele Aina Barale, and David M. Halperin. New York: Routledge, 45–61.

Seidman, Steven. 1990. "Substantive Debates," in *Culture and Society*, eds Jeffrey Alexander and Steven Seidman. New York: Cambridge University Press, 217–35.

———. 1991. *Romantic Longings: Love in America, 1830–1980*. New York: Routledge.

———. 1992. *Embattled Eros: Sexual Politics and Ethics in Contemporary America*. New York: Routledge.

Shweder, Richard A. 1984. "Anthropology's Romantic Rebellion against the Enlightenment, or There's More to Thinking Than Reason and Evidence," in *Culture Theory: Essays on Mind, Self, and Emotion*, eds Richard A. Shweder and Robert A. LeVine. New York: Cambridge University Press, 27–66.

Simon, Willian and John Gagnon. 1973. *Sexual Conduct*. Chicago: Aldine.

Smith-Rosenberg, Carroll. 1985. *Disorderly Conduct: Visions of Gender in Victorian America*. New York: Knopf.

Snitow, Ann. 1989. "Pages from a Gender Diary." *Dissent*, 205–24.

Stacey, Judith and Barry Thorne. 1985. "The Missing Feminist Revolution in Sociology." *Social Problems*, 32: 301–16.

Starr, Paul. 1982. *The Social Transformation of American Medicine*. New York: Basic Books.

Stein, Arlene. 1993. *Sisters, Sexperts, and Queers*. New York: Plume.

Tabor, Mary W. 1992. "S. I. Drops Gay Issues from Student Guide." *New York Times*, June 9.

Thompson, Becky W. and Sangeeta Tyagi. 1993. *Beyond a Dream Deferred: Multicultural Education and the Politics of Excellence*. Minneapolis: University of Minnesota Press.

Vance, Carole S. 1991. "Anthropology Rediscovers Sexuality: A Theoretical Comment." *Social Science and Medicine*, 33: 875–84.

Waters, Mary C. 1990. *Ethnic Options: Choosing Identities in America*. Berkeley: University of California Press.

Weeks, Jeffrey. 1977. *Coming Out: Homosexual Politics in Britain, from the Nineteenth Century to the Present*. London: Quartet Books.

———. 1981. *Sex, Politics and Society: The Regulation of Sexuality since 1800*. London: Longman.

———. 1985. *Sexuality and Its Discontents: Meanings, Myths and Modern Sexualities*. London: Routledge.

———. 1991. *Against Nature: Essays in History, Sexuality and Identity*. London: Rivers Oram.

Weinberg, George. 1972. *Society and the Healthy Homosexual*. New York: St. Martin's.

West, Cornel. 1993a. "The New Cultural Politics of Difference," in *Beyond a Dream Deferred: Multicultural Education and the Politics of Excellence*, eds

Becky W. Thompson and Sangeeta Tyagi. Minneapolis: University of Minnesota Press, 18–40.

——. 1993b. *Race Matters*. Boston: Beacon.

Wuthnow, Robert, 1987. *Meaning and Moral Order: Explorations in Cultural Analysis*. Berkeley: University of California Press.

Zola, Irving K. 1972. "Medicine as an Institution of Social Control." *Sociological Review*, 20: 487–504.

Part III

Queer Sociological Approaches: Identity and Society

11

Maiden Voyage: Excursion into Sexuality and Identity Politics in Asian America

Dana Y. Takagi

The topic of sexualities – in particular, lesbian, gay, and bisexual identities – is an important and timely issue in that place we imagine as Asian America. *All of us* in Asian-American Studies ought to be thinking about sexuality and Asian-American history for at least two compelling reasons.

One, while there has been a good deal of talk about the "diversity" of Asian-American communities, we are relatively uninformed about Asian-American subcultures organized specifically around sexuality. There are Asian-American gay and lesbian social organizations, gay bars that are known for Asian clientele, conferences that have focused on Asian-American lesbian and gay experiences, and electronic bulletin boards catering primarily to gay Asians, their friends, and their lovers. I use the term "subcultures" here rather loosely and not in the classic sociological sense, mindful that the term is somewhat inaccurate since gay Asian organizations are not likely to view themselves as a gay subculture within Asian America any more than they are likely to think of themselves as an Asian-American subculture within gay America. If anything, I expect that many of us view ourselves as on the margins of both communities. That state of marginalization in both communities is what prompts this essay and makes the issues raised in it all the more urgent for all of us – gay, straight, somewhere-in-between. For as Haraway has suggested, the view is often clearest from the margins where, "The split and contradictory self is the one who can interrogate positionings and be accountable, the one who can construct and join rational conversations and fantastic imaginings that change history."[1]

To be honest, it is not clear to me exactly *how* we ought to be thinking about these organizations, places, and activities. On the one hand, I would argue that an organization like the Association of Lesbians and Gay Asians (ALGA) ought to be catalogued in the annals of Asian-American history. But on the other hand, having noted that ALGA is as Asian American as Sansei Live! or the National Coalition for Redress and Reparation, the very act of including lesbian and gay experiences in Asian-American history, which seems important in a symbolic sense, produces in me a moment of hesitation. Not because I do not think that lesbian and gay sexualities are not deserving of a place in Asian-American history, but rather, because the inscription of non-straight sexualities in Asian-American history immediately casts theoretical doubt about how to do it. As I will suggest, the recognition of different sexual practices and identities that also claim the label *Asian American* presents a useful opportunity for rethinking and re-evaluating notions of identity that have been used, for the most part, unproblematically and uncritically in Asian-American Studies.

The second reason, then, that we ought to be thinking about gay and lesbian sexuality and Asian-American Studies is for the theoretical trouble we encounter in our attempts to situate and think about sexual identity *and* racial identity. Our attempts to locate gay Asian experiences in Asian-American history render us "uninformed" in an ironic double sense. On the one hand, the field of Asian-American Studies is mostly ignorant about the multiple ways that gay identities are often hidden or invisible within Asian-American communities. But the irony is that the more we know, the less we know about the ways of knowing. On the other hand, just at the moment that we attempt to rectify our ignorance by adding say, the lesbian, to Asian-American history, we arrive at a stumbling block, an ignorance of how to add her. Surely the quickest and simplest way to add her is to think of lesbianism as a kind of *ad hoc* subject-position, a minority within a minority. But efforts to think of sexuality in the same terms that we think of race, yet simultaneously different from race in certain ways, and therefore, the inevitable "revelation" that gays/lesbians/bisexuals are like minorities but also different too, is often inconclusive, frequently ending in "counting" practice. While many minority women speak of "triple jeopardy" oppression – as if class, race, and gender could be disentangled into discrete additive parts – some Asian- American lesbians could rightfully claim quadruple jeopardy oppression – class, race, gender, and sexuality. Enough counting. Marginalization is not as much about the *quantities* of experiences as it is about *qualities* of experience. And, as many writers, most notably feminists, have argued, identities whether sourced from sexual desire, racial origins, languages of gender, or class roots, are simply not additive.[2]

Not Counting

A discussion of sexualities is fraught with all sorts of definition conundrums. What exactly does it mean, sexuali*ties*? The plurality of the term may be unsettling to some who recognize three (or two, or one) forms of sexual identity: gay, straight, bisexual. But there are those who identify as straight, but regularly indulge in homoeroticism, and, of course, there are those who claim the identity gay/lesbian, but engage in heterosexual sex. In addition, some people identify themselves sexually but do not actually have sex, and, there are those who claim celibacy as a sexual practice. For those who profess a form of sexual identity that is, at some point, at odds with their sexual practice or sexual desire, the idea of a single, permanent, or even stable sexual identity is confining and inaccurate. Therefore, in an effort to capture the widest possible range of human sexual practices, I use the term sexualities to refer to the variety of practices and identities that range from homoerotic to heterosexual desire. In this essay, I am concerned mainly with homosexual desire and the question of what happens when we try to locate homosexual identities in Asian-American history.

Writing, speaking, acting queer. Against a backdrop of lotus leaves, sliding *shoji* panels, and the mountains of Guilin. Amid the bustling enclaves of Little Saigon, Koreatown, Chinatown, and Little Tokyo. Sexual identity, like racial identity, is one of many types of recognized "difference." If marginalization is a qualitative state of being and not simply a quantitative one, then what is it about being "gay" that is different from "Asian American?"

The terms "lesbian" and "gay," like "Third World," "woman," and "Asian American," are political categories that serve as rallying calls and personal affirmations. In concatenating these identities we create and locate ourselves in phrases that seem a familiar fit: black gay man, third-world woman, working-class Chicana lesbian, Asian-American bisexual, etc. But is it possible to write these identities – like Asian-American gay – without writing oneself into the corners that are either gay and only gay, or, Asian American and only Asian American? Or, as Trinh T. Minh-ha put it, "How do you inscribe difference without bursting into a series of euphoric narcissistic accounts of yourself and your own kind?"[3]

It is vogue these days to celebrate difference. But underlying much contemporary talk about difference is the assumption that differences are comparable things. For example, many new social-movements activists, including those in the gay and lesbian movement, think of themselves as patterned on the "ethnic model."[4] And for many ethnic minorities, the belief that "gays are oppressed too" is a reminder of a sameness, a common political project in moving margin to center, that unites race-based movements with gays, feminists, and greens. The notion that our differences are "separate but equal" can be used to call attention to the specificity of experiences or to rally the troops under a collective banner. Thus, the concept of difference espoused in identity politics may be articulated in moments of what Spivak refers to as "strategic essentialism" or in what Hall coins "positionalities." But in the heat of local political struggles and coalition building, it turns out that not all differences are created equally. For example, Ellsworth recounts how differences of race, nationality, and gender, unfolded in the context of a relatively safe environment, the university classroom:

> Women found it difficult to prioritize expressions of racial privilege and oppression when such prioritizing threatened to perpetuate their gender oppression. Among international students, both those who were of color and those who were White found it difficult to join their voices with those of US students of color when it meant a subordination of their oppressions as people living under US imperialist policies and as students for whom English was a second language. Asian American women found it difficult to join their voices with other students of color when it meant subordinating their specific oppressions as Asian Americans. I found it difficult to speak as a White woman about gender oppression when I occupied positions of institutional power relative to all students in the class, men and women, but positions of gender oppression relative to students who were White men, and in different terms, relative to students who were men of color.[5]

The above example demonstrates the tensions between sameness and difference that haunt identity politics. Referring to race and sexuality, Cohen suggests that the "sameness" that underlies difference may be more fiction than fact:

> ... the implied isomorphism between the "arbitrariness of racial categorizations" and the "sexual order" elides the complex processes of social differentiation that assign, legitimate, and enforce qualitative distinctions between different types of individuals. Here the explicit parallel drawn between "race" and "sexuality," familiar to so many polemical affirmations of (non-racial) identity politics, is meant to evoke an under-

lying and apparently indisputable common sense that naturalizes this particular choice of political strategy almost as if the "naturalness" of racial "identity" could confer a corollary stability on the less "visible" dynamics of sexuality.[6]

There are numerous ways that being "gay" is not like being "Asian." Two broad distinctions are worth noting. The first, mentioned by Cohen above, is the relative invisibility of sexual identity compared with racial identity. While both can be said to be socially constructed, the former are performed, acted out, and produced, often in individual routines, whereas the latter tends to be more obviously "written" on the body and negotiated by political groups.[7] Put another way, there is a quality of voluntarism in being gay/lesbian that is usually not possible as an Asian American. One has the option to present oneself as "gay" or "lesbian," or alternatively, to attempt to "pass," or, to stay in "the closet," that is, to hide one's sexual preference.[8] However, these same options are not available to most racial minorities in face-to-face interactions with others.

As Asian Americans, we do not think in advance about whether or not to present ourselves as "Asian American," rather, that is an identification that is worn by us, whether we like it or not, and which is easily read off of us by others.

A second major reason that the category "gay" ought to be distinguished from the category "Asian American" is for the very different histories of each group. Studying the politics of being "gay" entails on the one hand, an analysis of discursive fields, ideologies, and rhetoric about sexual identity, and on the other hand, knowledge of the history of gays/lesbians as subordinated minorities relative to heterosexuals ... Similarly, studying "Asian America" requires analysis of semantic and rhetorical discourse in its variegated forms, racist, apologist, and paternalist, and requires in addition, an understanding of the specific histories of the peoples who recognize themselves as Asian or Asian American. But the specific discourses and histories in each case are quite different. Even though we make the same intellectual moves to approach each form of identity, that is, a two-tracked study of ideology on the one hand, and history on the other, the particular ideologies and histories of each are very different.[9]

In other words, many of us experience the worlds of Asian America and gay America as separate places – emotionally, physically, intellectually. We sustain the separation of these worlds with our folk knowledge about the family-centeredness and supra-homophobic beliefs of ethnic communities. Moreover, it is not just that these communities know so little of one another, but, we frequently take great care to keep those worlds distant from each other. What could be more different than the scene at gay bars like "The End Up" in San Francisco, or "Faces" in Hollywood, and, on the other hand, the annual Buddhist church bazaars in the Japanese-American community or Filipino revivalist meetings?[10] These disparate worlds occasionally collide through individuals who manage to move, for the most part, stealthily, between these spaces. But it is the act of deliberately bringing these worlds closer together that seems unthinkable. Imagining your parents, clutching bento box lunches, thrust into the smoky haze of a South of Market leather bar in San Francisco is no less strange a vision than the idea of Lowie taking Ishi, the last of his tribe, for a cruise on Lucas' Star Tours at Disneyland. "Cultural strain," the anthropologists would say. Or, as Wynn Young, laughing at the prospect of mixing his family with his boyfriend, said, "Somehow I just can't picture this conversation at the dinner table, over my mother's homemade barbecued pork: 'Hey, Ma. I'm sleeping with a sixty-year-old white guy who's got three kids, and would you please pass the soy sauce?'"[11]

Thus, "not counting" is a warning about the ways to think about the relationship of lesbian/gay identities to Asian- American history. While it may seem politically efficacious to toss the lesbian onto the diversity pile, adding one more form of subordination to the heap of inequalities, such a strategy glosses over the particular or distinctive ways sexuality is troped in Asian America. Before examining the possibilities for theorizing "gay" and "Asian American" as non-mutually exclusive identities, I turn first to a fuller description of the chasm of silence that separates them.

Silences

The concept of silence is a doggedly familiar one in Asian-American history. For example, Hosokawa characterized the Nisei as "Quiet Americans" and popular media discussions of the "model minority" typically describe Asian-American students as "quiet" along with "hard working" and "successful." In the popular dressing of Asian-American identity, silence has functioned as a metaphor for the assimilative and positive imagery of the "good" minorities. More recently, analysis of popular imagery of the "model minority" suggest that silence ought to be understood as an adaptive mechanism to a racially discriminatory society rather than as an intrinsic part of Asian-American culture.[12]

If silence has been a powerful metaphor in Asian-American history, it is also a crucial element of discussions of gay/lesbian identity, albeit in a somewhat different way. In both cases, silence may be viewed as the oppressive cost of a racially biased or heterosexist society. For gays and lesbians, the act of coming out takes on symbolic importance, not just as a personal affirmation of "this is who I am," but additionally as a critique of expected norms in society, "we are everywhere." While "breaking the silence" about Asian Americans refers to crashing popular stereotypes about them, and shares with the gay act of "coming out" the desire to define oneself rather than be defined by others, there remains an important difference between the two.

The relative invisibility of homosexuality compared with Asian-American identity means that silence and its corollary space, the closet, are more ephemeral, appear less fixed as boundaries of social identities, less likely to be taken-for-granted than markers of race, and consequently, more likely to be problematized and theorized in discussions that have as yet barely begun on racial identity. Put another way, homosexuality is more clearly seen as *constructed* than racial identity.[13] Theoretically speaking, homosexual identity does not enjoy the same privileged stability as racial identity. The borders that separate gay from straight, and, "in" from "out," are so fluid that in the final moment we can only be sure that sexual identities are as Dianna Fuss notes, "in Foucaldian terms, less a matter of final discovery than a matter of perpetual invention."[14]

Thus, while silence is a central piece of theoretical discussions of homosexuality, it is viewed primarily as a negative stereotype in the case of Asian Americans. What seems at first a simple question in gay identity of being "in" or "out" is actually laced in epistemological knots.

For example, a common question asked of gays and lesbians by one another, or by straights, is, "Are you out?" The answer to that question (yes and no) is typically followed by a list of who knows and who does not (e.g., my co-workers know, but my family doesn't. . . .). But the question of who knows or how many people know about one's gayness raises yet another question, "how many, or which, people need to know one is gay before one qualifies as 'out?'" Or as Fuss says, "To be out, in common gay parlance, is precisely to be no longer out; to be out is to be finally outside of exteriority and all the exclusions and deprivations such outsider-hood imposes. Or, put another way, to be out is really to be in – inside the realm of the visible, the speakable, the culturally intelligible."[15]

Returning to the issue of silence and homosexuality in Asian America, it seems that topics of sex, sexuality, and gender, are *already*

diffused through discussions of Asian America.[16] For example, numerous writers have disclosed, and challenged, the panoply of contradictory sexually charged images of Asian-American women as docile and
subservient on the one hand, and as ruthless matahari, dragon-lady
aggressors on the other. And of course, Frank Chin's tirades against
the feminization of Asian-American men has been one reaction to the
particular way in which Asian Americans have been historically
(de)sexualized as racial subjects. Moving from popular imagery of
Asian Americans, *the people*, to Asia, *the nation*, Chow uses Bertoluc-
ci's blockbuster film, *The Last Emperor*, to illustrate what she calls,
"the metaphysics of feminizing the other (culture)" wherein China is
predictably cast as a "feminized, eroticized, space."[17]

That the topic of *homo*-sexuality in Asian-American studies is often
treated in whispers, if mentioned at all, should be some indication of
trouble. It is noteworthy, I think, that in the last major anthology on
Asian-American women, *Making Waves*, the author of the essay on
Asian-American lesbians was the only contributor who did not wish
her last name to be published.[18] Of course, as we all know, a chorus of
sympathetic bystanders is chanting about homophobia, saying, "she
was worried about her job, her family, her community . . ." Therefore,
perhaps a good starting point to consider lesbian and gay identities in
Asian-American studies is by problematizing the silences surrounding
homosexuality in Asian America.

It would be easy enough for me to say that I often feel a part of me
is "silenced" in Asian-American Studies. But I can hardly place all of
the blame on my colleagues. Sometimes I silence myself as much as I
feel silenced by them. And my silencing act is a blaring welter of false
starts, uncertainties, and anxieties. For example, on the one hand, an
omnipresent little voice tells me that visibility is better than invisibility,
and therefore, coming out is an affirming social act. On the other
hand, I fear the awkward silences and struggle for conversation that
sometimes follow the business of coming out. One has to think about
when and where to time the act since virtually no one has ever asked
me, "Are you a lesbian?" Another voice reminds me that the act of
coming out, once accomplished, almost always leaves me wondering
whether I did it for myself or them. Not only that, but at the moment
that I have come out, relief that is born of honesty and integrity quickly
turns to new uncertainty. This time, my worry is that someone will
think that in my coming out, they will now have a ready-made label for
me, lesbian. The prospect that someone may think that they know *me*
because they comprehend the category *lesbian* fills me with stubborn
resistance. The category lesbian calls up so many different images of

women who love other women that I do not think that any one – gay
or straight – could possibly know or find me through that category
alone. No wonder that I mostly find it easier to completely avoid the
whole issue of sexual identity in discussions with colleagues.

There are so many different and subtle ways to come out. I am not
much of a queer nation type, an "in your face" queer – I catalogue my
own brand of lesbian identity as a kind of Asian- American "take" on
gay identity. I do not wear pink triangles, have photos of girls kissing
in my living room, or, make a point of bringing up my girlfriend in
conversation. In effect, my sexual identity is often backgrounded or
stored somewhere in between domains of public and private. I used to
think that my style of being gay was dignified and polite – sophisticated, civilized, and genteel. Work was work and home was home. The
separation of work and home has been an easy gulf to maintain, less
simple to bridge. However recently, I have come to think otherwise.

But all this talk about me is getting away from my point which is that
while it would be easy enough for me to say many of us feel "silenced,"
which alone might argue for inclusion of gay sexualities in discourse
about the Asian-American experience, that is not enough. Technically
speaking then, the terms "addition" and "inclusion" are misleading.
I'm afraid that in using such terms, the reader will assume that by
adding gay/lesbian experiences to the last week's topics in a course on
Asian-American contemporary issues, or, by including lesbians in a
discussion of Asian women, the deed is done. Instead, I want to suggest
that the task is better thought of as just begun, that the topic of
sexualities ought to be envisioned as a means, not an end, to theorizing
about the Asian-American experience.

In the following discussion, I describe two confrontations – the
coming out of a white student in an Asian-American Studies class and
the problem of authenticity in gay/lesbian Asian-American writing.
Each tells in its own way the awkward limits of ethnic-based models of
identity.

The Coming-Out Incident

Once, when I was a teaching assistant in Asian-American Studies at
Berkeley during the early 1980s, a lesbian, one of only two white
students in my section, decided to come out during the first section
meeting. I had asked each student to explain their interest, personal
and intellectual, in Asian-American Studies. Many students mentioned
wanting to know "more about their heritage," and "knowing the past

in order to understand the present." The lesbian was nearly last to speak. After explaining that she wanted to understand the heritage of a friend who was Asian American, her final words came out tentatively, as if she had been deliberating about whether or not to say them, "And, I guess I also want you all to know that I am a lesbian." In the silence that followed I quickly surveyed the room. A dozen or so Asian-American students whom I had forced into a semi-circular seating arrangement stared glumly at their shoes. The two white students, both of whom were lesbians, as I recall, sat together, at one end of the semi-circle. They glanced expectantly around the circle, and then, they too, looked at the ground. I felt as though my own world had split apart, and the two pieces were in front of me, drifting, surrounding, and at that moment, both silent.

I knew both parts well. On the one side, I imagined that the Asian-American students in the class, recoiled in private horror at the lesbian, not so much because she was a lesbian or white, but because she insisted on publicly baring her soul in front of them. I empathized with the Asian-American students because they reminded me of myself as an undergraduate. I rarely spoke in class or section, unless of course, I was asked a direct question. While my fellow white students, most often the males, chatted effortlessly in section about readings or lectures, I was almost always mute. I marveled at the ease with which questions, thoughts, answers, and even half-baked ideas rolled off their tongues and floated discussion. For them, it all seemed so easy. As for me, I struggled with the act of talking in class. Occasionally, I managed to add a question to the discussion, but more often, I found that after silently practicing my entry into a fast-moving exchange, the discussion had moved on. In my silence, I chastised myself for moving too slowly, for hesitating where others did not, and alternately, chastised the other students for their bull-dozing, loose lips. I valorized and resented the verbal abilities of my fellow classmates. And I imagined how the Asian-American students who sat in my class the day the lesbian decided to come out, like me, named the ability to bare one's soul through words, "white." On the other side, I empathized as well with the lesbian. I identified with what I imagined as her compelling need to claim her identity, to be like the others in the class, indeed to be an "other" at all in a class where a majority of the students were in search of their "roots." I figured that being a lesbian, while not quite like being Asian American, must have seemed to the intrepid student as close to the ethnic model as she could get. Finally, I thought she represented a side of me that always wanted, but never could quite manage, to drop the coming-out bomb in groups that did not expect it.

Part of the pleasure in being an "outsider" can be in the affirmation of the identity abhorred by "insiders." I imagined that she and her friend had signed up for my section because they *knew* I too was a lesbian, and I worried that they assumed that I might be able to protect them from the silence of the closet.

In the silence that followed the act of coming out, and indeed, in the ten weeks of class in which no one spoke of it again, I felt an awkwardness settle over our discussions in section. I was never sure exactly how the Asian-American students perceived the lesbian – as a wannabe "minority," as a comrade in marginality, as any White Other, or perhaps, they did not think of it at all. Nor did I ever know if the lesbian found what she was looking for, a better understanding of the Asian-American experience, in the silence that greeted her coming out.

The silences I have described here dramatize how dialogue between identities is hampered by the assumption of what Wittig calls the "discourses of heterosexuality." She says:

> These discourses of heterosexuality oppress us in the sense that they prevent us from speaking unless we speak in their terms. Everything which puts them into question is at once disregarded as elementary. Our refusal of the totalizing interpretation of psychoanalysis makes the theoreticians say that we neglect the symbolic dimension. These discourses deny us every possibility of creating our own categories. But their most ferocious action is the unrelenting tyranny that they exert upon our physical and mental selves.[19]

More important, the coming out incident suggests that marginalization is no guarantee for dialogue. If there is to be an interconnectedness between different vantage points, we will need to establish an art of political conversation that allows for affirmation of difference without choking secularization. The construction of such a politics is based implicitly on our vision of what happens, or, what ought to happen, when difference meets itself – queer meets Asian, black meets Korean, feminist meets Greens, etc., at times, all in one person.[20] What exactly must we know about these other identities in order to engage in dialogue?

The Question of Authenticity

What we do know about Asian-American gays and lesbians must be gleaned from personal narratives, literature, poetry, short stories, and essays. But first, what falls under the mantle, *Asian-American gay and lesbian* writings? Clearly, lesbians and gays whose writings are self-conscious reflections on Asian- American identity and sexual identity ought to be categorized as Asian-American gay/lesbian writers. For example, Kitty Tsui, Barbara Noda, and Merle Woo are individuals who have identified themselves, and are identified by others, as *Asian-American lesbian voices*. Similarly, in a recent collection of essays from a special issue of *Amerasia*, *Burning Cane*, Alice Hom ruminates on how an assortment of Others – white dykes, Asian dykes, family, and communities – react to her as butchy/androgynous, as Asian American, as a lesbian. These writers are lesbians and they write about themselves as lesbians which grants them authorial voice *as a lesbian*. But they also identify as *Asian American*, and are concerned with the ways in which these different sources of community – lesbian and Asian American – function in their everyday lives.

But what then about those who do not write explicitly or self-consciously about their sexuality or racial identity? For example, an essay on AIDS and mourning by Jeff Nunokawa, while written by a Japanese-American English professor, does not focus on issues of racial and sexual *identity*, and as such, is neither self-consciously gay nor Asian American.[21] What are we to make of such work? On the one hand, we might wish to categorize the author as a gay Asian-American writer, whether he wishes to take this sign or not, presuming of course, that he is gay since his essay appears in an anthology subtitled, "gay theories," and, in addition presuming that he is Asian American, or at least identifies as such given his last name. On the other hand, we might instead argue that it is the author's work, his subject matter, and not the status of the author, that marks the work as gay, Asian American, or both. . . . In this case, we might infer that since the topic of the essay is AIDS and men, the work is best categorized as "gay," but not Asian American.

This may seem a mundane example, but it illustrates well how authorial voice and subject matter enter into our deliberations of what counts and what does not as Asian-American gay/lesbian writings. . . . The university is filled with those of us, who while we live under signs like gay, Asian, feminist, ecologist, middle-class, etc., do not make such signs the central subject of our research. And what about those individuals who write about gays/lesbians, but who identify themselves as heterosexual? In the same way that colonizers write about the colonized, and more recently, the colonized write back, blacks write about whites and vice versa, "we" write about "them" and so on.

I want to be clear, here. I am not suggesting that we try to locate Asian-American gay/lesbian sensibilities as if they exist in some pure form and are waiting to be discovered. Rather, I think we ought to take seriously Trinh T. Minh-ha's warning that, "Trying to find the other by defining otherness or by explaining the other through laws and generalities is, as Zen says, like beating the moon with a pole or scratching an itching foot from the outside of a shoe."[22] My concern here is to turn the question from one about a particular identity to the more general question of the way in which the concept of identity is deployed in Asian-American history.

Thus, not only is marginalization no guarantee for dialogue, but the state of being marginalized itself may not be capturable as a fixed, coherent, and holistic identity. Our attempts to define categories like "Asian American" or "gay" are necessarily incomplete. For example, as Judith Butler has noted:

> To write or speak *as a lesbian* appears a paradoxical appearance of this "I," one which feels neither true nor false. For it is a production, usually in response to a request, to come out or write in the name of an identity which, once produced, sometimes functions as a politically efficacious phantasm.
>
> ... This is not to say that I will not appear at political occasions under the sign of the lesbian, but that I would like to have it permanently unclear what precisely that sign signifies.[23]

A politics of identity and whatever kind of politics ensues from that project – multiculturalism, feminism, and gay movements – is first of all a politics *about* identity. That is, about the lack of a wholistic and "coherent narrative" derived from race, class, gender, and sexuality. ... Because no sooner do we define, for example, "Japanese American" as a person of Japanese ancestry when we are forced back to the drawing board by the biracial child of a Japanese American and an African American who thinks of herself as "black" or "feminist."

Rethinking Identity Politics

Lisa Lowe in her discussion of identity politics affirms the articulation of "Asian American" identity while simultaneously warning us of its overarching, consuming, and essentializing dangers. She (Lowe) closes her discussion saying:

> I want simply to remark that in the 1990s, we can afford to rethink the notion of ethnic identity in terms of cultural, class, and gender differen-

ces, rather than presuming similarities and making the erasure of particularity the basis of unity. In the 1990s, we can diversify our political practices to include a more heterogeneous group and to enable crucial alliances with other groups – ethnicity-based, class-based, and sexuality-based – in the ongoing work of transforming hegemony.[24]

I have intended this essay, in part, as an answer to Lowe's call to broaden the scope of Asian-American discourse about identity. But there is a caveat. The gist of this essay has been to insist that our valuation of heterogeneity not be *ad hoc* and that we seize the opportunity to recognize non-ethnic based differences – like homosexuality – as an occasion to critique the tendency toward essentialist currents in ethnic-based narratives and disciplines. In short, the practice of including gayness in Asian America rebounds into a reconsideration of the theoretical status of the concept of "Asian-American" identity. The interior of the category "Asian American" ought not be viewed as a hierarchy of identities led by ethnic-based narratives, but rather, the complicated interplay and collision of different identities.

At the heart of Lowe's argument for recognizing diversity within Asian-American, generational, national, gender, and class categories, as well as my insistence in this essay on a qualitative, not quantitative view of difference, is a particular notion of subjectivity. That notion of the subject as non-unitary stands in sharp contrast to the wholistic and coherent identities that find expression in much contemporary talk and writing about Asian Americans. At times, our need to "reclaim history" has been bluntly translated into a possessiveness about *the* Asian-American experience (politics, history, literature) or perspectives as if such experiences or perspectives were not diffuse, shifting, and often contradictory. Feminists and gay writers, animated by post-structuralism's decentering practices offer an alternative, to theorize the subject rather than assume its truth, or worse yet, assign to it a truth.

Concretely, to theorize the subject means to uncover in magnificent detail the "situatedness"[25] of perspectives or identities as knowledge which even as it pleads for an elusive common language or claims to establish truth, cannot guarantee a genuine politics of diversity, that is, political conversation *and* argument, between the margins.[26] Such a politics will be marked by moments of frustration and tension because the participants will be pulling and pushing one another with statements such as, "I am like you," and "I am not like you." But the rewards for an identity politics that is not primarily ethnic-based or essentialist along some other axis will be that conversations like the one which never took place in my Asian-American studies section many years ago, will finally begin. Moreover, our search for authencity of voice – whether in gay/lesbian Asian-American writing or in some other identity string – will be tempered by the realization that in spite of our impulse to clearly (de)limit them, there is perpetual uncertainty and flux governing the construction and expression of identities.

Notes

My special thanks to Russell Leong for his encouragement and commentary on this essay.

1 See Donna Haraway, "Situated Knowledges: The Science Question in Feminism and the Privilege of Partial Perspective," *Feminist Studies*, 14: 3 (1988): 575–99.

2 See Teresa de Lauretis, "Feminist Studies/Critical Studies: Issues, Terms, and Contexts," in *Feminist Studies/Critical Studies*, ed. Teresa de Lauretis (Bloomington: Indiana University Press, 1986), 1–19; bell hooks, *Yearning: Race, Gender and Cultural Politics* (Boston: South End Press, 1990); Trinh T. Minh-ha, *Woman, Native, Other* (Bloomington: Indiana University Press, 1989); Chandra Talpade Mohanty, "Under Western Eyes: Feminist Scholarship and Colonialist Discourses," in *Third World Women and the Politics of Feminism*, eds Chandra Talpade Mohanty, Ann Russo and Lourdes Torres (Bloomington: Indiana University Press, 1991), 52–80; Linda Alcoff, "Cultural Feminism versus Post-Structuralism: The Identity Crisis in Feminist Theory," *Signs*, 13: 3 (1988): 405–37.

3 Trinh T. Minh-ha, *Woman, Native, Other*, 28.

4 Steven Epstein, "Gay Politics, Ethnic Identity: The Limits of Social Constructionism," *Socialist Review*, 17 (May/Aug.). Jeffrey Escoffier, editor of *Outlook* magazine, made this point in a speech at the American Educational Research Association meetings in San Francisco, Apr. 24, 1992.

5 See Elizabeth Ellsworth, "Why Doesn't This Feel Empowering? Working through the Repressive Myths of Critical Pedagogy," 59: 3 (1989): 297–324.

6 Ed Cohen, "'Who Are We'? Gay 'Identity' as Political (E)motion," *inside/out* ed. Diana Fuss (New York and London: Routledge, 1991), 71–92.

7 Of course there are exceptions, for example, blacks that "pass," and perhaps this is where homosexuality and racial identity come closest to one another, amongst those minorities who "pass" and gays who can also "pass."

8 I do not mean to suggest that there is only one presentation of self as lesbian. See note 2 above.

9 Compare for example the histories: Takaki's *Strangers from a Different Shore*, Sucheng Chan's *Asian Americans*, and Roger Daniels' *Chinese and Japanese in America*, with Jonathan Katz's *Gay American History*, Jeffrey

Weeks' *Coming Out*, Michel Foucault's *The History of Sexuality*, and David Greenberg, *The Construction of Homosexuality*.

10 See Steffi San Buenaventura, "The Master and the Federation: A Filipino-American Social Movement in California and Hawaii," *Social Process in Hawaii*, 33 (1991): 169–93.

11 Wynn Young, "Poor Butterfly," *Amerasia Journal*, 17: 2 (1991): 118.

12 See Keith Osajima, "Asian Americans as the Model Minority: An Analysis of the Popular Press Image in the 1960s and 1980s," in *Reflections on Shattered Windows: Promises and Prospects for Asian American Studies*, eds Gary Y. Okihiro, Shirley Hune, Arthur A. Hansen, and John M. Liv (Pullman: Washington State University Press, 1988), 165–74.

13 See Judith Butler, *Gender Trouble* (New York: Routledge, 1990); Michel Foucault, *The History of Sexuality, Volume 1: An Introduction*, trans. Robert Hurley (New York: Vintage, 1980); Monique Wittig, *The Straight Mind and Other Essays* (Boston: Beacon, 1992).

14 Diana Fuss, "Inside/Out," in *Inside/Out*, ed. Diana Fuss, 1–10.

15 Ibid.

16 Consider for example debates in recent times over intermarriage patterns, the controversy over Asian Americans dating white men, the Asian Men's calendar, and the continuation of discussions started over a decade ago about gender, assimilation and nativism in Asian-American literature.

17 See Rey Chow, *Woman and Chinese Modernity* (Minneapolis: University of Minnesota Press, 1991).

18 See Asian Women United, *Making Waves* (Boston: Beacon Press, 1989).

19 Monique Wittig, "The Straight Mind," in *The Straight Mind and Other Essays*, 25.

20 All too often we conceptualize different identities as separate, discrete, and given (as opposed to continually constructed and shifting). For an example of how "identity" might be conceptualized as contradictory and shifting moments rather than discrete and warring "homes," see Minnie Bruce Pratt, "Identity: Skin Blood Heart" in *Yours in Struggle: Three Feminist Perspectives on Anti-Semitism and Racism*, ed. E. Bulkin, M. Pratt, and B. Smith (Ithaca, NY: Firebrand Books, 1984).

21 See Jeff Nunokawa, "'All the Sad Young Men': Aids and the Work of Mourning," in *Inside/Out*, 311–23.

22 Trinh T. Minh-ha, *Woman, Native, Other*, 76.

23 Judith Butler, "Imitation and Gender Subordination," in *Inside/Out*, 13–31.

24 Lisa Lowe, "Heterogeneity, Hybridity and Multiplicity: Marking Asian American Differences," *Diaspora*, (spring 1991): 24–44.

25 Haraway, "Situated Knowledges."

26 I am indebted to Wendy Brown for this point. See Wendy Brown, "Feminist Hesitations, Postmodern Exposures," *Differences*, 2: 1 (1991).

12

"A Certain Swagger When I Walk": Performing Lesbian Identity

Kristin G. Esterberg

"I'm often struck by feeling a certain way, you know – a certain swagger when I walk, checking myself in the windows in my sunglasses and, you know, really cool ..."

Louise Pratt

The notion that lesbian identities are socially constructed is not, by now, a new one. Over the last few years, research into the construction of queer identities has become somewhat of a growth industry in academe (see, for example, Plummer 1992, Warner 1993, Fuss 1991, de Lauretis 1991). By now, it seems to be commonly accepted that lesbian and gay identities are contingent, constructed, and reconstructed within particular social and historical circumstances and communities. Much of the controversy about the nature of lesbian/gay identity has been generated within the context of a vigorous debate between "constructionists," who emphasize the fluidity of sexual identity and seek to understand the social and historical circumstances under which something like modern lesbian and gay identities arise, and "essentialists," who argue for the continuity of homosexuality across time and space (see E. Stein 1992 for an overview of the debates). In the battle between constructionists and essentialists, in which academics debated endlessly about the ontological status of the homosexual, the constructionists clearly won. It would seem fruitless now to go back over this ground, except that these debates – about how and when lesbian and gay identities are constructed, and whether lesbian and gay identities change over time, and maybe even over an individual's life course – were carried out almost without asking ordinary lesbians and gay men whether the debates were consistent with their experiences. Because the debates about queer identity were not grounded in empirical accounts of identity, they failed to reflect the very real and complicated ways in which lesbians and gay men think and talk about their lives.

Moving beyond the constructionist/essentialist debates, queer theorists have begun to retheorize lesbian/gay identity. Drawing heavily on postmodern and poststructuralist strains of thought, queer theorists seek to problematize the very notion of lesbian/gay identity and challenge the essentializing nature of identity itself (see Phelan 1993 for a useful discussion). While queer theory is not a uniform body of theory and contains many diverse impulses, a common theme is to challenge the notion that sexual identity is a unitary essence residing in the person. To speak about sexual identity – lesbian identity, or gay identity – implies a unity that betrays the very real differences (of race, class, style, sexual practice) embodied by individuals in diverse social locations. Instead of viewing identity as something one *is*, for example, Diana Fuss (1991) argues for an understanding of identity as difference. According to Fuss, homosexuality is always implicated in heterosexuality (and vice versa), in a kind of convoluted knot. For her, the queer theoretical project is to bring the "hetero/homo opposition to the point of collapse" (Fuss 1991: 1). Judith Butler (1990, 1991), on the other hand, focuses on the performative aspects of gender. Butler argues that lesbian identities are performative, and it is through these performances that lesbian identities are constituted and reconstituted. Queer theorists, thus, have focused on the politics of signification, and the creation of lesbian bodies through particular discursive practices.

Like the constructionist/essentialist debates, much of this work on lesbian performativity and queer theory more generally remains abstract, divorced from the lives and stories of ordinary lesbians, a point which has led some to question the usefulness of the queer-theoretical program, either as a political agenda or as a description of the ways in which lesbians and gay men actually experience themselves as lesbian or gay (see, for example, Plummer 1992). In fact, a number of scholars have commented on the disjunction between the constructionist positions espoused by scholars and the essentialist conceptions of identity put forth by many political activists (see, for example, Epstein 1987).

This gap between scholars' and activists' understandings of identity, while real, may be overstated. In fact, some lesbians do have a sense of their identities as constructed. Some see themselves as queer, transgressive, and consciously "play" with lesbian style and self-representation. Others see their lesbian identities as fixed, not playful, and certainly not socially constructed – whatever they think that might mean. For these women, the categories are real, tangible, and very much an essential and inherent part of their selves. My point is that ordinary lesbians insert themselves into the debates about lesbian identity and lesbian visibility at varying points. Constructionism and performance are, to varying extents, reflected in lesbians' own accounts of their identities. But relatively few scholars have moved beyond theory to examine lesbians' own stories and accounts. In the long run, I argue, theories of lesbian identity must be rooted in empirical accounts. By this, I do not mean that queer theories must be "tested" against "real" data in a crude and unsubtle version of positivistic science. Yet, if theories are to be meaningful and help to illuminate aspects of lesbian life, they must be rooted in lesbians' subjective experiences and their articulations of them.

In this chapter, then, I am concerned to clearly ground my discussion in the voices and stories of actual women. I discuss the notion that lesbian identities are performative, and that these performances draw on and extend traditional notions of masculinity and femininity. I argue that lesbian performances are serious play; that is, while there is an element of play, of fun, in the slippage of categories, this is serious play because it has to do with deeply important aspects of the self. Lesbian identity – and our playing out of it – *matters*. At the same time, lesbian performances are not unconstrained. We do not choose freely from an unlimited set of possibilities. While we make and remake our identities, we do so within the boundaries of convention; and while we may choose to transgress those boundaries, we do so at the risk of making our performances unintelligible.

The women whose voices appear in this chapter live in a small, politically progressive city on the East Coast. Located in a rural area, the city serves as a magnet for lesbian and bisexual women in the region. I lived in this community from 1986 to 1991. During that time, I formally interviewed 25 women and surveyed 79 others (see Esterberg 1991 for a description of the original study). In 1994, I returned to the community to see how it had changed, to reinterview about half of the original interviewees, and to interview an additional 18 women. The women are both bisexual (10 of the interviewees and 12 of the survey respondents) and lesbian. Three of the interviewees and 17 survey respondents were women of color (primarily African American, though also Chicana, Asian, and Native American). The women ranged in age from their early 20s to their early 50s. Although a number of the women came from working-class backgrounds, very few of the women were currently working class. As a group, the women had relatively high levels of education (although their incomes were not proportionate to their level of education).

Shifting Boundaries: Heterosexual Women and Difference

Queer theorizing offers the insight that sexual categories shift and change, and attempts to disturb the rigidity of sexual categories implied by the terms "lesbian," "heterosexual," and (increasingly) "bisexual."[1] As Teresa de Lauretis (1991) argues, it is time to re-theorize lesbian and gay sexualities. We should no longer view homosexuality simply as marginal with respect to heterosexuality; nor should we attempt to define homosexuality in reference to heterosexuality – either by opposition or by definition. It is time to reconceptualize gay and lesbian sexualities as social and cultural forms in their own right, "albeit emergent ones and thus still fuzzily defined, undercoded, or discursively dependent on more established forms" (de Lauretis 1991: iii). What it means to be a lesbian remains permanently undefined – its meaning floats and shifts. Or, as Judith Butler notes, "I would like to have it permanently unclear what precisely that sign signifies" (1991: 14).

Although de Lauretis warns against seeing lesbian and gay sexualities in relation to heterosexualities, asking lesbians and bisexual women about the similarities and differences they see between and among themselves and heterosexual women is one way in which to explore how lesbian and bisexual women in the particular community I studied create a sense of what is distinctly lesbian. When asked about the similarities and differences, the lesbian and bisexual women I spoke with drew shifting and uncertain boundaries between themselves and heterosexual women. Whatever their initial response, many of the respondents wavered, declaring at some points that there were fundamental and unalterable differences between the two groups, and at other times seeing close connections. As they moved through the interview, they constructed and reconstructed a permeable boundary between themselves and heterosexual women.

Several of the women interviewed felt that there were no essential differences between lesbian and heterosexual women. For these women, the categories "lesbian" and "heterosexual" contained far too much diversity to compare. For them, the attempt to define what was distinct about lesbians *vis-à-vis* heterosexual women did not make sense, given their experiences of heterogeneity. Cheryl Cook,[2] a professional white woman in her late 30s, compared the attempt to search for differences between lesbians and heterosexuals to the attempt to search for differences between women and men. "You know how when they try to study differences between males and females, and they come to the conclusion that there is more variation within [the categories] than there is between? That's exactly how I feel about women, no matter what their sexuality. That there is more variation within than there is between straight women or gay women."

Others I spoke with the saw the differences – if any – as rooted in the struggles lesbians engage in to define themselves. They resisted the way in which the categorization of women as "lesbian" or "heterosexual" forced them to make generalizations. Nancy Zimmerman, a white feminist activist, said, "It's not that I don't see them in those categories. I guess I see them as categories of people, and then I see so many individual differences . . . I see heterosexual women having access to male privilege that lesbians don't have. I see some heterosexual women tolerating relationships that I think they would not ordinarily tolerate if they didn't think they were going to gain by being with men in that way. And that lesbians don't have that choice."

As a graduate student Leslie Mohr had been influenced by poststructuralist theorizing. Early in the interview, she said, echoing Butler, "To say I'm a lesbian is not to assert an identity with a stable content." But when thinking about the boundaries between lesbians, bisexual women, and heterosexual women, she initially saw differences. "I think that what I could say about all my lesbian friends, and my bisexual friends, is that not being heterosexual gives us a kind of slightly off-center relation to the culture as a whole that, I think, permeates the kind of jokes we make, the kinds of off-the-cuff simplified generalizations that we can make that are a kind of shorthand for a whole set of experiences, which I think we do kind of share even if our relation to them is different. . . . There's this shared sense of looking on when it comes to heterosexual culture."

Drawing on her long experience of living as a heterosexual woman, Joan Borman, a Jewish feminist in her late 40s who came to identify as a lesbian after a long marriage, said, "I think most of the dykes I know are very different from straight women. . . . I think the main difference is that when you don't deal with men as the primary way of functioning in the world, and you don't have that sense of deference to them, so that even when you are dealing with them as bosses, let's say, or supervisers, you know there are certain things you have to do to keep your job. But it's not as if you really in your heart-of-hearts take them all that seriously. You just sort of have to figure out how to maneuver appropriately. There's a certain kind of whinyness and wishy-washyness that goes away. I mean, it enables you to *be*, and so I guess the thing that I think of dykes most in relationship to heterosexual women is not are they more, are we more athletic and all of this kind of stuff, but that it's that we are just emotionally more present."

Although they could both think of exceptions, Marcela Reyes, a young Chicana woman, and Bonita Brown, an African American woman in her mid 20s, saw lesbians as being more able to "ask for what they want." Bonita thought that lesbians are "probably more realistic, and they realize what they really enjoy. A lot of hetero sexual women put up with a lot of crap they feel they have to put up with because they're women. And I think lesbians stop and say, 'Well, I don't enjoy this, so I'm not going to act like I do.'"

Bonita was among a small group of respondents who saw the differences between lesbians and heterosexual women as fairly rigid. Chrissy Herek, a young white woman who was just beginning to think of herself as bisexual, also saw differences, but she saw them far less positively than Bonita did. In struggling to figure out her own sexual identity, Chrissy saw that "straight" (i.e., non-bisexual) lesbians are less "feminine" than heterosexual and, perhaps, bisexual women. "The only 'real,' like, 'straight' lesbians that I know (and I don't know very well) just seem defensive to me. . . ." She says that she wants "always to keep my femininity" and that she never wants to become "hard." As she sees lesbians, "They just seem cold and hard, defensive." On the other hand, she sees heterosexual women as very homophobic. In thinking about the differences among women, she said, "I just wish we could all be meshed, you know? . . . I wish that there didn't have to be that [difference]. 'Cause I don't want to fall into a stereotype."

What is striking in these accounts is how the women interviewed resisted the essentializing inherent in the question. With few exceptions, the interviewees returned to the topic several times, amending and overlaying their earlier responses. They insisted on maintaining the complexity of their experiences. For each generalization about heterosexual women, they considered women who did not fit the stereotypes. And they were similarly hesitant to generalize to *all* lesbians. At the same time, many felt that there was something common shared by lesbians, which some extended to include bisexual women, even if it consisted simply of a sense of being an outsider, marginal with respect to heterosexual society.[3] Many insisted on a distinctive lesbian presence in the community, and felt that they could often spot another lesbian in a non-lesbian setting. Even though the interviewees did not want to assert unmovable boundaries between lesbian and heterosexual women, they did want to assert a uniquely lesbian presence and sense of style, however shifting and changing that lesbian style might be.

Performing Lesbian Identities

Judith Butler's notion of performativity is useful in looking at how lesbians assert a presence in the world. When lesbians and bisexual women present themselves to each other and to the world, they are, in effect, performing. Through this performance, they are constructing and reconstructing lesbian and bisexual selves. As Butler asks, "How is it that I can both 'be' one, and yet endeavor to be one at the same time? When and where does my being a lesbian come into play, when and where does this playing a lesbian constitute something like what I am? To say that I 'play' at being one is not to say that I am not one 'really'; rather, how and where I play at being one is the way in which that 'being' gets established, instituted, circulated, and confirmed" (Butler 1991: 18). Yet the notion of play or performance does not mean that lesbianism is a role, something one can slip in and out of easily. "This is not a performance from which I can take radical distance, for this is deep-seated play, psychically entrenched play, *and this 'I' does not play its lesbianism as a role*" (italics in original).

The notion of performance is not new. In the 1950s and 1960s, Erving Goffman (1959, 1974) outlined a dramaturgical approach in sociology. Although there are distinct differences between Butler's and Goffman's notion of performance – Goffman, for example, sees individuals as acting out roles, with front and back stage areas, audiences, and casts of performers acting in ensemble – the notion that identity is performative is a useful one.[4]

Louise Pratt, a white woman in her 30s, distinguishes the times when she feels most lesbian. "The times I really tune in to being a lesbian *per se* are the times that I get caught up kind of in the role. You know, when I see a woman in a shirt and a tie and a leather jacket. And I go wild. Or the times that I put certain clothes on, and I am struck by the effect, you know, whether it makes me feel really butch or whether it makes me feel really fem. I'm often struck by *feeling* a certain way, you know – a certain swagger when I walk, checking myself in the windows in my sunglasses and, you know, really cool . . . I'd say 'Yeah!'"

Louise describes how one woman she knows puts on a lesbian performance. "There's one woman I know who – when she chooses to – can be more or less of what I identify as a classic – well, *my* classic butch. . . . Because she's really very slender and she's very meek when it comes right down to it. But when she puts on her, you know, just nice pants and boots and a white men's shirt and a necktie and her leather jacket, partly zipped, and a haircut that's kinda short and her aviator glasses. I mean, I had known this woman and not paid much attention to her. But then one night I saw her at a party dressed like that. And what an effect it had on me. You know, I just said, 'Oh, my God, I'm in trouble now!' And I followed her around the rest of the night!"

It was harder for Louise to describe what might call forth those feelings in herself. "It's harder to define the clothes that I might wear that tune me into those feelings. It's not like I have a specific outfit that I put on that makes me feel that way, you know, that makes me feel like I'm ready to swagger. It's just kind of, all of a sudden it's there, and I'm in the mood, you know, and I start to use my hands differently and start to walk differently, and you know do things like that."

Deb Smith, a long-time feminist in her late 40s, talks about dressing in costume. Although she thinks that "the majority of the time" she "couldn't pass" as anything but a lesbian ("a dyke, you know?"), she plays with the way she presents herself to the world. "I guess I'm aware of my dress and how I think people interpret me from my dress. So it's sort of fun . . . Now I do, I make do with a combination of things. I mean, I might wear something and I think, 'Oh, this is associated with butch or something,' so I have my toenails painted. It's like . . . I want people to just stop and think more about assumptions that they may make from dress."

Marcela Reyes talks about acting butch. She distinguishes between "playing" butch and "really" being butch, but acting and being are not always completely separated. "I have friends that I guess you would call butch, and we used to kid around because it happens to be that we both, we consider ourselves butch. And probably to some others I wouldn't be butch. But when we're together, we're both butch, and she's very tough and I'm really tough. And we had sort of very fem lovers at the time. And we would joke around, okay, while we play basketball you do the pompons, and stuff like that, and cheer on the sidelines. And they would get all pissy about it."

Marcela thinks that others, and maybe her friend, take being butch too seriously. "I used to wonder whether or not my best friend . . . took it seriously, but as we got even closer, I realized that it is just a sort of façade, an image with us, and we play it up when we have to. We can really do it really good. I mean, if I had to protect myself, or my lover, you better watch who you're messing with. But when we're kidding around among other lesbians or dykes . . . people know you're kidding around about it, and it's okay to joke about that. And we'll walk off with our chests inflated . . . and we're just messin' around."

What made her wonder about whether her friend took it "too" seriously was that her friend had "some pretty sexist attitudes just because of how she was raised – the girls did the cooking and stuff like that." Her friend felt that those kinds of things were for "girlies" to do. "But," as Marcela continued, "I really think it was a role she was playing, and sometimes her stuff comes out, and so does mine. I get called on it a lot by my lover. But I don't know. I've gotten out of that a lot, and I've realized it's okay to cross [from butch to fem], and so when I'm with R [my lover] we cross over a lot. You know, it's kinda like, well is it my turn to be on top, or your turn to be on top. So we take it everywhere with us and make a joke about it. But I think some people take it seriously, and I don't think that's all that good."

At the same time that she criticizes those who take the role too seriously, Marcela seems to delight in her ability to play with it. Yet she feels that there is something truly more "butch" about herself than some other women, especially her lover. "Like I can talk the language and I can be tough, and da-da-da. Whereas if R tried that, she wouldn't fit in too well. If she would try that everybody would know the minute she opened her mouth, where I can play both parts really, really well."

Part of what is interesting here is that the notion of play surrounds butchness and femness – important themes in lesbian history and culture. All three women – Marcela, Deb, and Louise – take aspects of what they understand to be butch or fem and incorporate them into their presentations of self. Yet their appropriations of butchness and femness are not wholly serious. In Goffman's (1974) terms, they are "keyed," as when "serious" action is transformed into something playful. And for each of the performances, an audience is necessary. For Louise, the audience is herself. She can tell when she feels "really" lesbian, when "it's there," as she looks at her reflection. Dress is crucial to creating that swagger, that sense of herself as "really" lesbian. For Marcela, the audience is clearly other lesbians. When she and her friends walk around with their chests puffed out, they're clearly playing to and playing with other lesbians. But for Marcela, there's something "real" about the play: even though she plays butch and crosses over between butch and fem, she still sees herself as more butch than her lover, who cannot really cross over.

These performances involve serious play. Although Marcela is adamant that she's not "serious" about being butch, and Deb playfully combines aspects of butch and fem in her dress, underneath these self-representations is a seriousness. The playfulness extends primarily to other lesbians. If a straight man were to call Marcela a butch dyke, she would certainly interpret those as fighting words; called the same by herself or butch friends, she puffs her chest out in pride. In addition, these women are serious about their desire for other women; in some sense, they are serious about "being" lesbian, even as they play with what that might mean.

Other women I spoke with do not mention this same sense of play or performance. Whether they do not "play" with their sexual identities in this way – or do not consciously do so – is not clear. Perhaps some do not feel they "play" or perform *any* of their identities. But all the women I interviewed have fairly elaborate notions of what a lesbian "looks like," even if they do not themselves feel they look like that, and they have a sense of whether or not they can tell if another woman is a lesbian. In presenting themselves in patterned ways – or by using these patterns to evaluate whether they "look like" a lesbian or not – the women participated in a collective framing of lesbian presence, one that relies more heavily on a coding of lesbian identity as butch.

Playing "Spot the Dyke"

"I play spot the dyke all the time," said Laurel Jameson, a bisexual woman in her late 40s. But can you tell if another woman is a lesbian, I asked? "Sometimes," she said, "but not all."

Laurel's position is common. Only one of the women I spoke with felt that she could always spot another lesbian; a very few felt that they could rarely or never recognize other lesbians. The largest portion felt that they could sometimes, perhaps even often, recognize other lesbians, or they felt they could almost always tell, but sometimes they were wrong.

Patrice Amaro, an upwardly mobile working-class woman in her 30s, felt that she could almost always tell. "I could go in that room and say, all right, who's here?" When her "gaydar" is on, she can almost always tell. "I think that there's room for error, but there are a lot of ways to screen it out. Whichever way, it's [the error] pretty small." Ilene Zemke felt similarly confident in her ability to find other lesbians. "I'm usually right, when I think they are. An hour before I came here [to the interview] I was walking [downtown] and I saw two women. And I'd never seen them before, and I just kinda nodded at them, as a kind of acknowledgment that I think we might be kindred spirits in some form of our identity. And they stopped me and said, 'Can you tell me where the women's book store is?' And it was just wonderful. And we stopped and talked and I gave them directions. And so usually I think I'm right." At the same time she recognized, "Sometimes I'm really wrong."

Others felt that they were no longer able to tell because the community itself was changing, along with fashions and ideals for lesbians' styles of self presentation. Susan Becker, a very traditionally "feminine"-appearing woman who is rarely recognized by other lesbians, said that although she thinks she can tell, "It gets harder now. At one point you could tell very much because of how a woman chose to dress." In a similar vein, Deena King asked, "Do I think I can tell? [I] used to be very good. Used to be *very, very* good. I'm not as good as I used to be. And I think it's because I'm getting burned out. Or it is getting harder to tell. I mean, let's face it. There used to be a uniform." More playfully, Bonita Brown said, "My dyke-o-meter is not working! A pair of Birkenstocks [sandals] does not a lesbian make!" She often finds that women she thinks are lesbian are not.

Cheryl Cook, who is bisexual, felt that lesbians who claimed they could tell were often fooling themselves. Although she could not tell if another woman was a lesbian, she said that "lesbians tell me they can tell." "I have good friends who I have known for a long time who are lesbians, and they'll debate, 'Is this person a lesbian or not?' And they're wrong a lot of times because I know the person they're talking about." At the same time, many women pick *her* out as a lesbian. After she began a relationship with another woman, she realized, "I have been really naïve, because probably one of the reasons I developed such good lesbian friends is maybe I looked like a dyke."

Lesbians' and bisexuals' sense of whether they can recognize others is important in several senses. First, the desire to recognize others seems linked to a desire to make connections and a desire to see more lesbians present and visible in the world. Leslie Mohr was clear that when she wondered if other women whom she met were lesbian, "It's more like I hope they are." The sense of being able to recognize others is also connected to a particular coding of lesbian identity. As the next section will make clear, only certain styles of lesbian presentation – those most classically considered butch – were typically recognized as lesbian. Even though they knew they might guess incorrectly, the women I interviewed suspected that women who were less stereotypically "feminine" were likely to be lesbian.

What a Lesbian Looks Like

"The classic dyke haircut, I think, is really short over the ears no matter where else it might be long" (Leslie Mohr).

Regardless of whether they thought they could *accurately* recognize other lesbians, and regardless of whether they themselves felt recognizable to others, every woman I interviewed identified at least several cues she used to distinguish others. These cues fell grossly into two categories: visual/presentational cues and interactional cues. Some women spoke of a kind of scale, or "dyke potential." In general, women who were perceived to be more "masculine" were more likely to be perceived as lesbians, whether or not they actually were.

Visual cues

Although she had a hard time specifying exactly what a lesbian might look like, Leslie was very clear about the differences she saw between heterosexual women's and lesbians' appearance. "There are certain kinds of outfits that I don't think a lesbian would ever wear. And it has to do with a look that approximates femininity, that approximates culturally approved femininity."

Denny Slater was clear and intentional about the way she presented herself as a lesbian. "I'm not one who chooses to be available to male sexual advances, so I don't dress to flaunt my breasts or my hips or my legs. I do not wear make-up. I choose to be the person I am, and I do not compromise myself . . . I want men to know that I'm not available for their sexual prey." For Denny, not appearing available to men was a major cue for identifying other lesbians.

Ilene Zemke usually looks for interactional cues: how two women might walk close together or interact in other intimate ways. But she also looks at physical appearance and more "superficial" signs like clothing. "Very superficial sort of appearance and clothing things. It might be a hair cut. Now every one of these things you can twist . . . The flip side of it is that for every woman who I identify, who I think she is a lesbian because of haircut, clothes, walk, appearance, energy, there will be another who I'm not identifying as such because she doesn't have these characteristics . . . You know, probably if I saw a woman in a three-piece suit, very nicely coifed, made up, very bejeweled, stockings and high heels, I would not, if I didn't know her, I would not think, 'Ah, there goes a lesbian.' But she might very well be."

Interactional cues

As with physical cues, interactional cues are important. Like others, Patrice Amaro observed that just as she looks for lesbians, other lesbians are also looking to identify *her*. "I think as much as I would notice someone else, they might notice me as well, for the very same reasons. And if there is some eye contact or some kind of energy that

– well, that's out there. Like eye contact – does she make an effort to talk to me? – as well. The more subtle cues. Because my feeling is if a person is identifying themselves as a lesbian, that she, too, also wants to know who else is lesbian in that room, and she is also looking."

In addition to physical cues, like wearing pinkie rings or other kinds of typically lesbian jewelry, Joan Borman recognizes others by a certain kind of eye contact. "I don't pretend that I can always recognize lesbians, but I do think that there is a way of, a certain sense that gets developed, of spotting your own, based on the kinds of internal-to-the-community norms that you learn. So you know I always look for pinkie rings, and I always look to see whether, if I'm looking, if I'm walking down the street and I catch a woman's eye, you know the likelihood is that a straight woman will always turn away ... It doesn't mean that there aren't straight women who would not turn away, but the likelihood is that a straight woman would turn away, and a dyke would not turn away. There's just a certain sense of presence, and it's not infallible. I don't pretend that it's infallible."

Dyke potential

"We do a DP alert, and you look at somebody that has dyke potential," said Marcela. "And I always make sure to say that word [potential], because one time I was wrong and assumed, it was not right, and in spite of all the DP this kid had."

What is dyke potential? "Unfortunately it falls back into the narrower characteristics that we have as lesbians ... on appearance, because that's mostly all you have when you're walking around. It falls back into that narrower category, and it would be like short hair, athletic-looking body ... If they carry themselves assertively and confidently is a big thing. I don't know, those are just signs of DP. How they walk, their stride, everything ... It's not like they have to have all of these. If they have any one of these, or any combination of these, that would increase their DP potential."

Carly Silver, who thinks of herself as a bisexual with a lesbian consciousness, listed a long list of attributes by which she might recognize lesbians and bisexual women. Then she noted, "This is funny. There is a traditional, feminine stereotype, and I'll describe it for you in a minute. Any degree, to the extent that a woman shows greater degrees of deviation from that stereotype, I would question her sexuality. And this is where I think it's *crazy*, because, you know, all that means is that she's deviating from the traditional female role. And sexuality is only one part of the female role. But, I mean I could get very specific about that traditional standard. It's a woman who has a kind of classically attractive body, which means thin, large breasts, small waist – you know, the classic, pin-up style body. Pretty face. Feminine, you know, long hair, with some kind of hairstyle to it. Make-up. Jewelry. Femmy, clothing is feminine . . . Oh! Then I'd put in emotional qualities . . . Basically what I have in my mind is an image of all the emotional, attitudinal, physical characteristics that are associated with femininity, of which no woman, you know, meets them perfectly." To the extent that women diverge from that ideal, Carly would suspect that they are lesbian or bisexual.

To be a lesbian is to be coded as not feminine – masculine. Wendy Hammond gives an example from when she was living in the South. "I stuck out like a sore thumb. Well, I wore jeans! And I wore LaCoste shirts. I remember wearing my brother's leather flying jacket. Well, I mean, I did that for one hour. It felt like traffic would stop. Versus the women there who spent – it was everyone who was female spent – a minimum of two to three hours in the morning putting on make-up. Everyone got up at 5 a.m. to get ready for classes. I mean the amount of make-up was – I'd never seen anything like it. It was immediate, how I stuck out." Even up North, Wendy feels noticeable. "I mean physically, I look different than straight women. When I go down the hall of the women that I work with, they look more feminine . . . I think there's almost a different sort of physique . . . The women are built more slender. I mean, I'm built – I'm bigger. I'm big. When I stand next to the men I work with, I'm as big as a lot of the guys! . . . If one could say that a more feminine body would be more rounded or, you know, there would be characteristics of being feminine. I would feel like I would err more on the side of being more masculine looking and acting."

Deena King, too, sees herself as looking more masculine; in the past, this caused her a great deal of pain. "I was just thinking about how often I got kicked out of the men's room or the women's room, when I was working in [the Pacific Northwest]. I was a police officer, and so you're wearing the uniform, and I had short hair, which I have now. But I had short hair, and you know I wore the standard uniform, so I was constantly being evicted from the women's rest room by other women, because of their automatic assumption that I was male. You get real tired of that. In fact you get to the point where you don't want to go to the bathroom because you don't want to go through the hassle, or you check it to make sure there's no one else around. You know, cause you just don't want to go through it any more." At the time of the interview, she was no longer working as a police officer or in a job that required a uniform, and feels she is no longer as identifiable as she was before.

What is interesting in these accounts is how individual women see themselves as approximating a masculine image. Certainly, not all lesbians are tall or athletically built; not all wear uniforms and short hair. In the scheme of things, Wendy is not *really* that big; she's probably just barely above the median height and weight for US women. What's important is that she interprets her size and body shape as one of the ways in which she is not "feminine" but is lesbian. Short lesbians, or lesbians who have a more "feminine" body type may interpret other aspects of themselves as seeming especially lesbian. Nancy Zimmerman knows that others can't always tell that she is lesbian. "I'm not a stereotypically butchy-looking person." But she clearly points to other aspects of herself that she thinks mark her as a lesbian: "I think that I look independent and have that sense of being self-reliant that I notice in other people."

"I Don't Look Like a Lesbian"

Several of the women I interviewed felt that they did not look like other lesbians and were often not identified by others – even when sometimes they would like to be. Chrissy Herek, a very traditionally "feminine" appearing woman who is discreet about her relationship with another woman, has mixed feelings about others' ability to tell that she is bisexual. On one hand, she very strongly wants to maintain a sense of herself as soft and feminine – qualities she does not identify as being associated with lesbians or bisexuals. Being bisexual "doesn't mean I have to be hard, and doesn't mean I have to be angry with the world . . . I can still be warm, and I can still look pretty and feminine if I want to, and I can still not only look it, but feel it. I don't have to feel . . . you know, that I want to be masculine." On the other hand, people who are important to her are unable to tell that she is attracted to women. When another woman student sent her flowers, a teacher to whom Chrissy is very close asked her if it had bothered her and said, warning her about the apparent "dangers" of lesbianism, "Well, just be careful and don't fall into traps. Be strong . . . You know who you are; stick to your guns." Chrissy was upset. "This person who's supposed to know me the most, the best in the world, cannot pick up or identify with the fact that, you know, I'm bisexual, or maybe a lesbian."

Susan Becker is also very traditionally "feminine" appearing. She talks about how people would treat her when she was with her last partner, who was more "masculine" appearing. "At the time my hair was blonder and smaller and [I] wore, probably wore more make-up, even, than I do now. But I like to wear make-up; it's something I choose to do. And I like wearing dresses, I like wearing high heels. . . . And also, I had a Southern accent up until probably about six years ago, which I deliberately got rid of for that reason. Most Southern women are thought of as being dimply and spacy . . . So for all those things combined, I think, I was treated in more traditional ways, that women are treated."

Even now, though there have been some changes in lesbian life, she works to maintain the sense of style that she prefers and at the same time be recognizable to other lesbians. She told a story about trying to make herself visible to a lesbian couple at a recent cookout. "I was wearing, I think, a pair of shorts and a shirt and some earrings, make-up. I had my toenails painted red. I got there, and I saw *immediately*, I mean it was almost a physical drawing back of these two women who were there as a couple, who had a crew cut. . . . There's almost a physical withdrawing, and I've encountered it many times."

Joan Borman and Leslie Mohr–both of whom have a more political understanding of lesbianism–work to make themselves visible as lesbians. Joan travels frequently, "and when I travel I absolutely make a point of wearing a triangle pin, always visible . . . It's not so much that I want to be out there doing political education, it's that I understand especially because I don't look like whatever that stereotypical notion is of what a dyke looks like. I understand that I feel certain kinds of real obligation to not use those kinds of physical realities about me as if I were passing, you know. It's not that I want to walk around with a sign that says 'lesbian' all the time, but I don't want to allow myself the illusion of thinking that the reason everything is okay and I'm not being hassled is because people are fine about homophobia."

Leslie said, "People are always telling me, 'You don't look like a lesbian,' which drives me crazy. . . . Because sometimes I wear skirts, and because I wear bright colors a lot. I wear long earrings. I have short hair, but actually, I got this haircut a couple of, well, maybe a year and a half ago, and part of the reason was because people were always telling me I didn't look like a lesbian, and that was just provoking the 'lesbian legitimacy crisis.' So I have certain outfits that I wear that I feel like are 'butch-er' than certain others. So if I'm wearing my suit jacket, or if I'm wearing my bolo tie, or if I'm wearing jeans and boots or something like that, I feel more–I feel like I look dykier. And I like that, but at the same time I do like to kind of do this playful thing, too. . . . I feel like if I'm dressed in a way that is kind of fashionable, people tend to think I don't look like a lesbian."

Leslie's and Joan's accounts reveal the work that is involved in constructing lesbian identities – and the seriousness with which they take their self-representations both to other lesbians and to the larger heterosexual world. Creating a plausible account of oneself as a lesbian entails ongoing attention to dress, to demeanor, and to the small details that may signal to others that one experiences desire for other women. To fail to produce or attend to these cues entails the risk of invisibility. Lesbians thus cannot be understood as "natural" women. That is, if heterosexual ("feminine") women are constructed through clothing, make-up, and a shifting array of practices that condition their relationships to men, lesbians cannot be seen as simply women unvarnished. As Cathy Grigger notes, "*The* lesbian is as fantasmatic a construct as *the* woman" (1993: 179). Lesbian performances are *work*, albeit sometimes playful work.

Lesbian styles are clearly changing in the 1990s – even in smaller communities such as the one discussed here. As Arlene Stein (1992b) has written, earlier images of lesbian style were "anti-style," a rejection of American capitalism and patriarchy and a refusal to use the female body in subservient ways. In this tradition, recall that Denny Slater interprets her physical presence in the world as signalling a rejection of male dominance (and, in text not quoted here, as a protest of the use of women's bodies to sell consumer products). In recent years, a very different face is being put on popular depictions of lesbianism – more "feminine," less political. This "new" lesbian image presented by the media is, as Arlene Stein has described, typically young, white, and glamorous – a far cry from earlier images of lesbians as shrill and humorless (Stein, 1992b: 432; see also 1992a, 1993). Unlike earlier depictions of lesbians, and especially feminist lesbians, as dour, angry, and lacking a sense of style, this new "chic" lesbian is shown trading her support group for a shopping bag. She is no longer out to change the world – only her wardrobe. That such images of lesbians appear in the mainstream media is certainly new and, arguably, reflects progress toward lesbians' acceptance in a heterosexist society; yet by focusing on lesbian chic – lesbians who don't "look like" lesbians – these new media images both distort and depoliticize lesbianism. At the same time, however, the images reflect a real shift, an increasing playfulness, in lesbian style and imagery.[5] As many of the women I spoke with commented, the lesbian "uniform" is no longer ubiquitous.

Only a few women I spoke with saw themselves as part of this "new" image. Most saw themselves as somewhere in-between: neither lipstick lesbian nor anti-style dyke. But whatever the recent changes in lesbian style, the coding of lesbians as not feminine *and therefore in some way masculine* predominated. Because gender is seen as dichotomous – either male *or* female – lesbian presence tends to be articulated as masculine. One lesbian whom I did not formally interview[6] said that she felt she was a third gender – neither male nor female. At certain moments – browsing in the evening-gown section of a department store or in other sites of "high" femininity – I am struck by flashes of insight into this position. But the conscious articulation of lesbians as something apart from traditional notions of masculinity and femininity – a third thing altogether – was rare.[7] At the same time, to present oneself as "butch" or "dykey" was an attempt to assert a distinctly lesbian presence that did not rely entirely on the language of "masculinity" and "femininity." Although the specific gestures draw more from traditional notions of masculinity, they are not identical (a point also made in Nestle 1992). Ultimately, the butch dyke is not a man, even if mistaken for one in the women's bathroom. And to be "too" serious, as Marcela argued, to denigrate washing dishes and doing housework as what only "girlies" do, borders on sexism.

That butch and androgynous formulations of lesbianism are more highly valued or, at least, more visible is not, at one level, surprising. In the context of a social system in which men are seen as the standard, and in which masculine projects, desires, and preoccupations are more highly prized, it would be surprising indeed if lesbians created an entirely different system of value. We do not make and remake our identities entirely from scratch. Yet the appropriation of masculine imagery is not solely a reflection of masculinist bias. In creating a distinctly lesbian style, butch and androgynous lesbians define a positive lesbian presence in opposition to heterosexist notions of women as weak, passive, and small. In doing so, they enlarge the category "woman" and disrupt formulations of heterosexuality as "natural" and "normal." For some, the performance of a distinctive lesbian style allows for a kind of gender bending, a playfulness around traditional categories of "masculinity" and "femininity." To be butch one day and fem the next, as Marcela discusses, blurs gender boundaries and highlights the artifice with which masculine and feminine subjects are created. By playing on traditional formulations of masculinity, then, butch dykes enlarge the category "man" as well.

Yet in rendering some women visible as lesbians, the creation of a lesbian presence that relies more heavily on "masculine" or even androgynous codings renders others, like Susan Becker and Chrissy Herek, deviant lesbians, invisible to those by whom they most care to be seen. While fem lesbians also enlarge the category "woman," by disrupting the notion that "feminine" women are intended for men, they are far more typically seen by other lesbians as retro, if they are seen at all. Thus, there is also a coercive element to the coding of lesbian visibility. In drawing the circles around some lesbians – and usually excluding bisexuals – others are marginalized.[8]

Focusing attention on the performative aspects of lesbianism and the accounts that lesbians give of their performances enables us to reflect on the ways in which women draw from traditional *accoutrements* of gender for their own purposes. In doing so, it is important not to miss the larger ways in which lesbian performances, as social interactions, are structured. In a recent article on "doing" difference, Candace West and Sarah Fenstermaker (1995) caution that rendering a plausible account of gender, race, or any other social category is both an interactional and an institutional accomplishment. In emphasizing the ways in which lesbians signal their social presence to each other – and, importantly, obscure the social presences of some others – it is important not to miss the institutional contexts in which lesbian performances occur.

Notes

This chapter is part of a longer book manuscript on lesbian identities and lesbian communities, to be published by Temple University Press. I am grateful to Steve Seidman and to members of the Kansas City Region Women's Studies Consortium for useful comments on this chapter.

1 Although bisexuality, with its refusal to choose one category or the other, has the potential to disrupt completely the sexual categories *homosexual*, *heterosexual*, it has not realized this potential. The nascent bisexual movement seems more inclined to create a new, third category of sexuality than get rid of the pre-existing ones (see Hutchins and Kaahumanu 1991; Weise 1992).

2 All names are pseudonyms.

3 Although in 1988, when I began interviewing in this community, very few would have called themselves queer, that term was more common in 1994 as a way to signify a sense of being outsiders looking in.

4 A crucial difference between the two is that Butler argues that there is no separate identity apart from or underneath the performance. The "I" gets produced in and through the performance. Conversely, Goffman seems to

indicate that there is a "true self" underlying the performance. Goffman's notion of role and performance inserts distance between the self and the role. It may well be that some individuals *feel* that some performances are more indicative of a "true" self than others; yet the question of whether or not there is something like an empirically verifiable "true" self apart from the perform-ance is not particularly important for the current purposes. I'm primarily concerned with the accounts that women give of their performances.

5 A number of recent publications give evidence of this playfulness; see, for example, Boffin and Fraser 1991; Stevens 1994.

6 She was part of the survey.

7 James Weinrich (1992) argues that this form of homosexuality, which he calls gender inversion, is nearly universal. Yet his argument rests almost entirely on anthropological evidence based on men and male activities and cannot, therefore, be applied to women.

8 Although I do not have enough systematic evidence to say this with any confidence, it seems to me that bisexual women are coded as distinctly not butch. The spring 1992 issue of *Out/Look*, which features several articles on bisexuality, is instructive. On the cover is a picture of a plump fem woman, presumably bisexual, with long hair, tight short dress and matching high heels, holding the arm of a presumably heterosexual man. The balloon drawn cartoon-style to indicate her thoughts contains a series of exclama-tion points and question marks. Looking on is a slender, chicly butch woman, presumably lesbian, with shorter, spiked hair, dressed in a white dinner jacket and black tie.

References

Boffin, Tessa and Jean Fraser. 1991. *Stolen Glances: Lesbians Take Photo-graphs*. London: Pandora Press.

Butler, Judith. 1990. *Gender Trouble: Feminism and the Subversion of Identity*. New York: Routledge.

——. 1991. "Imitation and Gender Insubordination," in ed. Diana Fuss, *Inside/Out: Lesbian Theories, Gay Theories*. New York: Routledge, 13–31.

——. 1993. *Bodies that Matter: On the Discursive Limits of "Sex."* New York: Routledge.

de Lauretis, Teresa (ed.) 1991. *Queer Theory*. Special edition of *differences*, 3.

Epstein, Steven. 1987. "Gay Politics, Ethnic Identity: The Limits of Social Constructionism." *Socialist Review*, 93/94: 9–54. Repr. in Edward Stein (ed.), *Forms of Desire: Sexual Orientation and the Social Constructionist Controversy*. New York: Routledge, 1992, 239–93.

Esterberg, Kristin. 1991. "Salience and Solidarity: Identity, Correctness, and Conformity in a Lesbian Community." Unpublished Ph.D. dissertation, Cor-nell University.

Fuss, Diana (ed.). 1991. *Inside/Out: Lesbian Theories, Gay Theories*. New York: Routledge.

Goffman, Erving. 1959. *The Presentation of Self in Everyday Life*. New York: Doubleday.

——. 1974 (repr. 1986). *Frame Analysis*. Boston: Northeastern University Press.

Grigger, Cathy. 1993. "Lesbian Bodies in the Age of (Post)mechanical Reproduction," in M. Warner (ed.) *Fear of a Queer Planet: Queer Politics and Social Theory*. Minneapolis: University of Minnesota Press, 178–92.

Hutchins, Loraine and Kaahumanu, Lani (eds) 1991. *Bi Any Other Name*. Boston: Alyson.

Nestle, Joan (ed.) 1992. *The Persistent Desire: A Femme-Butch Reader*. Boston: Alyson.

Phelan, Shane. 1993. "(Be)coming Out: Lesbian Identity and Politics." *Signs*, 18: 765–90.

Plummer, Ken (ed.) 1992. *Modern Homosexualities: Fragments of Lesbian and Gay Experience*. New York: Routledge.

Stein, Arlene. 1992a. "Sisters and Queers: The Decentering of Lesbian Feminism." *Socialist Review*, 22: 33–55.

——. 1992b. "All Dressed Up, But No Place to Go? Style Wars and the New Lesbianism," in Joan Nestle (ed.), *The Persistent Desire: A Femme-Butch Reader*. Boston: Allyson, 431–9.

—— (ed.) 1993. *Sisters, Sexperts, Queers: Beyond the Lesbian Nation*. New York: Plume.

Stein, Edward (ed.) 1992. *Forms of Desire: Sexual Orientation and the Social Constructionist Controversy*. New York: Routledge.

Stevens, Robin (ed.) 1994. *Girlfriend Number One: Lesbian Life in the 90s*. Pittsburgh, Penn.: Cleis.

Warner, Michael (ed.) 1993. *Fear of a Queer Planet: Queer Politics and Social Theory*. Minneapolis: University of Minnesota Press.

Weinrich, James. 1992. "Reality or Social Construction?" in Edward Stein (ed.), *Forms of Desire: Sexual Orientation and the Social Constructionist Controversy*. New York: Routledge, 175–208.

West, Candace and Fenstermaker, Sarah. 1995. "Doing Difference." *Gender and Society*, 9: 8–37.

13

Containing AIDS: Magic Johnson and Post[Reagan] America

Cheryl L. Cole

It's patriotic to have the test and be negative.
Cory Servaas, Presidential Commission[1]

AIDS is God's judgment of a society that does not live by His rules.
Jerry Falwell[2]

The Bodies of the Condemned in the Age of Aids

As AIDS became news during the mid-1980s, it acquired the status of the extraordinary in popular consciousness. Mainstream media routinely characterized AIDS as evidence of immoral behaviors and lifestyles denoting identity-categories: homosexuals, injecting drug users, and prostitutes. Moreover, the meanings and values already attributed to these stigmatized groups shaped both the media coverage and popular reception of AIDS. Overall, the mainstream news coverage served as a ritual of confirmation of the identity of the general public defined through familial heterosexuality and a ritual of condemnation of all of those who were HIV positive, excepting those who had been infected through "no fault of their own." Not surprisingly, prostitutes, injecting drug users, and, most prominently, homosexuals were represented as threats to the general public rather than communities threatened by a devastating crisis. In general, the person with AIDS was represented as an "AIDS victim" who was portrayed as guilty, diseased, contagious, isolated, threatening, and deteriorating. By 1990, the cultural common sense of AIDS had become fairly well sedimented in the national imaginary, while, in general, AIDS became "old news" and receded to the background.[3]

At 4:00 p.m. on November 7, 1991, major and local networks interrupted their scheduled programming to cover what has been called "the saddest press conference in sport history": Earvin "Magic" Johnson's announcement that he would immediately retire from the National Basketball Association (NBA) because he had tested positive for HIV antibodies. The enormous amount of media coverage that followed Johnson's announcement, especially that which expressed public sympathy, compassion, and loyalty, is a clear indication of Johnson's profile in national popular culture. As Jack Kroll (1991: 70) depicted Magic's popularity: He "has a constituency that a presidential candidate would kill for. From toddlers to doddlers, from blacks to whites, from machos to mothers, from underclass to the overrich, Americans were overwhelmed by the statement of his plight . . . There's no gender gap, there's no age gap, there's no race gap in Magic's ability to inspire affection." Johnson was glorified for his position in the development and success of the NBA, his economic investments and successes, and the courage he displayed by announcing to the world that he was HIV positive. America embraced and proclaimed its support for the first HIV positive African-American superstar. Thomas Boswell (1991) of the *Washington Post* depicted America's relation to Johnson through the most intimate and desirable of units: "Magic became part of almost every American family. And, now, we can't get him out of the family. He's everybody's brother or son who may get AIDS."[4] "For Magic Johnson, it's that single indigestible word 'tragedy'" (p. D-6).

Johnson's HIV status was framed by the mainstream media as a personal tragedy, an athletic tragedy, a tragedy for the sport world with the United States narrated as a compassionate and caring nation. Pat Riley, former coach of the Los Angeles Lakers and current coach of the New York Knicks, announced the "tragic news" at Madison Square Garden that night.[5] Tears in his eyes, voice cracking, he called for a "moment of silence" and then led the crowd and teams in the *Lord's Prayer*. Johnson's disclosure was made into a story of heroism (even by the Bush Administration) that was explained, to a great extent, by his characteristically courageous handling of the situation – his ability to flash "his trademark smile" even in a moment of personal crisis.[6] And, given Magic's popularity with youth, Johnson, unlike previous HIV positive figures who were represented as threatening to children, was portrayed as the model AIDS educator who could reach those "youth" and communities depicted as having been resistant to AIDS education in the past.

In general, the response to Johnson seemed to break from the earlier and more common reaction to those who identified as HIV positive.

Who could not but be struck and touched by the public outpouring of sympathy and compassion for this national icon, especially in light of the previous media coverage of AIDS? How do we account for the apparent differences between the narration of compassion and previous narrations of condemnation that pathologized and demonized PLWAs? Whereas the prominent AIDS- image figured PLWAs as evidence of moral decline and threat to the family and nation, Magic was a familiar and friendly figure whose meanings were consistent with the dominant values of America. Even as Johnson made visible his HIV antibody status, the family and proper sexuality were prominently displayed as his pregnant wife Cookie was positioned visibly behind him as he disclosed his serostatis at the November press conference.

Perhaps the apparent discrepancy between the narratives of compassion and condemnation can be attributed to a shift in the popular perception of AIDS. "Popular consciousness" around AIDS had apparently been raised in 1985 through Rock Hudson's death from HIV-related complications as indicated by the increased media coverage of "heterosexual AIDS" in 1986. But, if national consciousness had indeed been raised, how do we account for the thousands of inquiries directed to national and local AIDS information hotlines and the Centers for Disease Control (CDC) about *who* was at risk in response to Johnson's press conference? Local AIDS information lines reported receiving at least three times their usual number of calls in response to Johnson's announcement. The CDC, which typically gets 3,000 calls daily, reported receiving 40,000 calls between 5 p.m. and midnight on the day of Johnson's press conference.

Just as popular knowledges of AIDS are *imagined* through national press and television discourses and the modern categories that restrict that imagination, most Americans *imagine* they know "Magic Johnson." Although the narration of Johnson and AIDS is a media event in that the narration is produced at the intersection of multiple media narratives, in this paper, I use the narrative of Magic and AIDS as a case study that offers the opportunity to interrogate the continual reinvention of the cultural imaginary. I argue that the "Magic narrative" provides an opportunity to render visible the concealed strategies and operations of power whose effects are rendered visible through modern identity categories and understandings of the body. These modern identity categories and understandings of the body enable, limit, and constrain the cultural imaginary. Given this, I argue that despite the apparent distinction between the narrative of compassion and the narratives that pathologize and police deviance, both narratives are implicated in and bound by the same normalizing logic that structure the discursive formation around AIDS.

   In the first section of the paper, I draw on the work of Foucault and Derrida to outline the conceptual grid that guides my interpretation of the narrative generated around Johnson. I argue that the narration of Johnson, and that of AIDS more generally, is structured through a logic of containment in which the bodies of others are marked in order to define and contain the general public. I consider how the corporeal identities generated and regulated through modern logics of sexuality and race shape our understandings of Magic and AIDS and how those identities gain force and momentum through the complex political forces and conditions of Reagan and Bush America. Here, I examine how "family values," defined by the Reagan and Bush administrations as the most important domestic issue of the 1980s and early 1990s, serves as a normalizing lens through which the identity of the general public is stabilized as various sexualities and behaviors are criminalized. I argue that the narration generated through Johnson's announcement relies on emblematic figures codified and circulated by the mainstream media's construction of AIDS and the inner city through a politics of lifestyle that converts social problems to a characterological moral poverty.[7] Finally, I examine how the identity of the general public is reconstituted through the dispersion of deviance.

Power/Knowledge/Body and AIDS

Subject to the gaze of the camera the body became the object of closest scrutiny, its surface continuously examined for the signs of innate physical, mental and moral inferiority. From this science of corporeal semiotics there emerged new forms of knowledge about the individual and new ways of mapping depravity.

David Green[8]

The AIDS epidemic – with its genuine potential for global devastation – is simultaneously an epidemic of transmittible lethal disease and an epidemic of meanings or signification.

Paula Treichler[9]

Because AIDS *made visible* and was *made visible through* homosexuals, injecting drug users, and prostitutes, HIV and AIDS were taken up in the popular imaginary as "visible" evidence of secret and inner depravity, pathologized bodily acts, and corresponding identities.[10] Although the identity- categories seem descriptive, self-evident, and self-contained, *what* and *who* we see as well as *how* we see them are the effects of these received categories. That is, the identity categories function as optics (*how*, *what*, *who* we *see*), that enable and constrain our sense of morality, conduct, our selves, and others; and by extension shape the cultural common sense of AIDS.

Keeping this in mind, the significance of the question *Why Magic?* repetitively played out under the guise of compassion takes on new meaning. To ask "why Magic?" is to ask *who* Magic *is*. The question of "who" is a question of identity and carries with it presuppositions about free-will, responsibility, and guilt. To ask *Why Magic?* underscores the perception that serostatis is understood to reveal more than HIV antibody status – it is understood to reveal an identity bound to presumptions about character and moral worth. Although multiple dyads (central/not-central; body/antibody; deviant/normalized; contained/leaky) structure AIDS narratives, I argue that the dyad of act/identity dominates the others. Corporeal identities, then, have become central to the organization of the discursive formation around AIDS.

In this section, I outline a framework that brings together genealogical (Foucault) and deconstructive (Derrida) logics in order to render visible the mechanisms and strategies of power that elide the historical contingency of *corporeal identities* that underlie the popular cause-and-effect understanding of risk groups and AIDS. Both genealogical and deconstructive logics present challenges to Western reason and the modern subject (the subject of liberal-humanism, the unitary, self-authorial subject) and the constant policing required to maintain boundaries that mark the deviant in order to produce and maintain the norm.

Foucault (1979, 1980a) views the invention of the homosexual and the addict as predicated upon the modern epistemic regime in which particular acts and behaviors like sodomy and drug taking were transformed into criminalized and pathologized bodies/identities through the positive effects of power. The modern regime organized itself through a division between the normal and the pathological. The normal and abnormal are mutually dependent categories: the self's border is produced through a social process of producing and policing the other. As Michel Foucault explained, the shift from acts to identities is an effect of a modern epistemic regime that produces, locates, and contains "what" and "who" are threatened and threatening in order to produce and stabilize the norm. The strategies and operations of modern power are concealed but work to produce and render visible the deviant, the pathological, the delinquent.

Deconstruction asserts that meaning is produced through *differance*: the double process of difference and deferral (Derrida 1976). Meaning is deferred in the sense that it is produced temporally, through the trace, and produced through difference (in that each unit derives its meaning through its difference from others). While Western logic at once depends upon a phantasmatic center, it continuously relies on its periphery to establish the center. Because it is relational, Western thought cannot posit any central self-identical ideal upon which it is founded. Identity, then, is never simply self-identical or self-contained but depends on what it negates. Deconstructionist strategies emphasize the transgression already taking place at the border of binary terms and examine the constant motion and policing required to maintain boundaries between binary terms.

For example, the terms that organize the discourse of addiction are free-will and compulsion. Terms that are apparently primary to *logos*, such as free-will, parasitically rely on the terms that precede and oppose them (for example, free will relies on compulsion). Free-will requires continual policing to firm up its boundaries because free-will requires limits, borders, and the marginal. Because deconstructionists emphasize the transgression always already taking place at the border, deconstruction examines the force relations between the terms: the constant exertion of pressure at their boundaries, the policing required to maintain those boundaries, the incompleteness of the category of the will and the violence it does. In Foucault's terms, the construct of free-will, partly constitutive of the normal, is dependent upon what it excludes, the marking of the compulsive, abnormal, and the deviant.

As it is has been articulated in the United States, AIDS narratives, like narratives of drug use, turn on a logic of addiction – a logic that depends on "free will" and locates insufficient free will in the bodies of Others. Both AIDS and illicit-drug-use narratives rely on a cultural logic that produces and distinguishes between the deteriorating/non-productive body and the hard, healthy body of the general (heterosexual-patriotic) public.

Drawing on Foucault and Derrida, I suggest that the national imaginary is continuously reinvented through the logic of containment and the identities made available through its dynamics. Containment functions by establishing limits around semantic-social possibilities, but since that limit can always be transgressed, containment is an ongoing project of marking transgression on new bodies and identities. The strategy of containment depends on turning bodily acts into bodily identities – making visible and containable that which is neither, marking the Other to that presumed to be self. The limit will always have to change and readdress itself. Certain bodies/identities become understood as transgressive of certain institutions; bodies become the place of transgression while the site of transmission of HIV is always between bodies. But, the momentum and force accrued by bodies/identities are always related to the effects and affects achieved through historically specific economic, political, and cultural forces.

[Post] Reagan America

There can be no possible exercise of power without a certain economy of discourses of truth which operates through and on the basis of this association. We are subjected to the production of truth through power and we cannot exercise power except through the production of truth. . . . In the end, we are judged, condemned, classified, determined in our undertakings, destined to a certain mode of living and dying, as a function of the true discourses which are the bearers of the specific effects of power.

Michel Foucault[11]

"AIDS," then, can be understood as strategy of power and a normalizing practice that functions to assign visible character and form to acts of transgression through identity categories. The shift from acts that the body is capable of doing to the solidification and codification of that act into identity allows for the cultural common sense fantasy of the family (Watney 1987, 1990). AIDS narratives function to assign identities to the acts of transgression that threaten the mythic, stable family: the act of transgression is figured (and contained) in the homosexual, the addict, and the prostitute. As Watney (1990: 174) explains:

> the Family at the heart of AIDS commentary is an ideological unit, as yet supposedly unaffected, but held to be threatened by the "leakage" of HIV infection, which, like nuclear fallout, is widely and erroneously perceived to be everywhere about us, a deadly miasma of contagion and death. . . . [T]he family enjoys absolute centrality for modern policymakers and their enforcement agents. It is presented as that which precedes them – their object, that on which they work, invested with the full ideological weight of Nature.[12]

The normalizing optic of the mythic family gained momentum and force in a conjunctural moment dominated by the forces (political, moral, cultural, economic) defining Reagan/post-Reagan America. Reaganism, the signature of an alliance-backlash politics, was characterized by the revival of a conservative patriotism generated and legitimated around *bodies* and a related series of racist, anti-gay, antifeminist, pro-nuclear family, pro-life, anti-social welfare, and antiaffirmative action positions.[13] Under Reagan, America's economic and social problems were, to a great extent, attributed to the breakdown of the nuclear family and the moral fabric of the nation. As articulated by the New Right, the "family values agenda" denied the relation between the economy and nuclear family and created the imaginary space from which to individualize social problems, legitimate Reagan's pro-business policies, and justify the erosion of social welfare programs.[14]

The articulation of sexual deviance and AIDS, especially the articulation of homosexuality and HIV, brings to the fore the central trope of AIDS and the central trope of Reaganism: the construction of bodies (the healthy, hard body of the general public) over and against antibodies. During the Reagan and Bush years, the body/anti-body trope was a discourse on the loose, marking (and unmarking) patriotism, sexuality, race, poverty, contamination, and threat by producing an affective economy of images populated by AIDS bodies, crack bodies, criminal bodies, welfare bodies, hard bodies, and productive bodies.

Although addiction became most visible in and through the figures produced and circulated by mediated moral panics imbricated in the war on drugs, the logic of insufficient free- will underlies the figures produced through the moral panic around AIDS. The Reagan administration capitalized on the logic of free-will, redeploying an amplified individualism and will that located America's decline and uncertain status in individual bodies and their characterological failings and deviance. In response to and as part of the New Right's pro-family politics and war on drugs, US culture became saturated with images of criminal, threatening, out-of-control, non-productive homosexual and black bodies (primarily black male youth) that contrasted sharply with a national masculinity – defined by a prosthetic, hard, muscular (white) body (Rambo, Robocop, etc.).

Repathologized homosexual bodies and racially coded images of drug use became inextricably bound with everyday lived experience and fears: threat and fear were heightened through the image of criminal masculinities inscribed on the bodies of homosexuals and black male youth. Such images worked to conceal the multiple affects of late capitalism – the heightened poverty produced through hyperindustrialization, globalization, and Reagan's defunding and repressive policies and their corresponding logic of insatiable consumption. As racial inequalities and tensions escalated in America's urban areas, inner cities reinvigorated their economies by promoting an urban, world-class lifestyle (restaurants, shopping districts, stadiums, sport events, and sport superstars). As the Los Angeles Lakers would have it, it was *ShowTime!* in America's inner cities. The NBA claimed prominent places in national culture and in our everyday lives and images of black athletes (*Just Do It*) and (drug and sex) addicts (*Just Say No*) remained intertwined in the national imaginary organized around a familial heterosexuality.

Magic Johnson: Promotional Culture, Race, Bodies

Magic is here. Magic is now. Magic is us.
Leigh Montville, journalist[15]

So on November 7, 1991, when I listened to Magic Johnson announcing his retirement from the Lakers because he'd tested HIV-positive, I had to ask, Who's Magic Johnson? Of course I found out right away.
Doug Crimp, AIDS activist, queer theorist[16]

Given that the NBA, NBA players, and the products they endorse saturate the contemporary cultural landscape, it is difficult to imagine the complex and contradictory politics played out in the cultural spaces it generates and territorializes. The complexity of those politics are embedded in the NBA's attempts to overcome its stigmatized identity that was generated through its merger with the American Basketball Association in 1977. The NBA's limited popularity and financial struggles during the late 1970s and during the early 1980s can be understood, to some extent, through the racial coding of the NBA as a deviant space associated with an urban black masculinity depicted as threatening. The racial inflection of deviance was codified through style of play and a politics of lifestyle depicted through excessive consumption, especially "epidemic cocaine use." As Reeves and Campbell (1994: 38) note, "numerous players were suspended, placed in rehabilitation programs for positive drug tests, and charged with drug crimes." The struggles faced by the NBA during the early 1980s were serious enough to suggest that it would become the first major professional sport in the US to fail (Katz 1994).

Sport can be conceptualized as an apparatus that organizes and is organized by the normalizing practices and strategies of science, technology, and the media; a technology that produces multiple bodies (raced, classed, gendered, heterosexualized, prosthetic, pure, patriotic, etc.) in the context of an image-dominated consumer culture (Cole 1993). Professional sport is one of the most prominent sites for the production of the prototypical masculine body. A (hyper)heterosexual masculinity is displayed through a series of practices embedded in a "politics of lifestyle" marked by the semi-public sexual exchange of a conspicuously displayed network of adoring, supportive female fans, girlfriends, and/or wives: it is a masculine lifestyle that is meant to embraced, admired, envied, and consumed.[17] But the relationship between sport and masculinity is always already complicated by race. The historical codifications that locate the black body as closer to nature (inscribing and searching for causes of enhanced performance) and as hypersexual require that the black masculinity on offer in sport be configured in ways that distance it from the codes of threatening black bodies (Gray 1989, Jackson 1994).[18]

The black masculinity associated with the NBA was reordered and managed, in part, through the rivalry between Magic Johnson and Larry Bird *and* through the marketing of particular players' personalities.[19] In this case, race was not displaced but remained a dynamic force that organized and was organized through the Johnson–Bird rivalry. Johnson's marketability was established through promotional strategies that articulated Magic as the embodiment of an acceptable, non-threatening face of masculinity, of having a personality and character consistent with the values of what Cindy Patton (1992) has called the "Africanized Horatio Alger trope of athletics" – family, modest beginnings, discipline, determination, loyalty, and social mobility.[20] Additionally, Johnson's popularity was secured through his public personality, an image designed to make "us" feel better and more comfortable with racial difference, described in terms of affability, generosity, and boyish enthusiasm for the game.

As Peter Jackson (1994: 50, 56) explains, the spectator's acquired knowledges of popular personalities and character function to "suppress the more threatening aspects of a stereotypically anonymous and rapacious black male sexuality," allowing black bodies "to work as objects of envy and desire" rather than provoking dread. The positioning of Johnson (through his physicality, outstanding character, and celebrity status) as the embodiment of the American Dream, athletic hero, and AIDS-hero, not only suggests a racially harmonized country, but positions the white spectator as allied with or complicit in the heroic performance. Perhaps this explains, at least in part, the willingness to extend, through a popular discourse, love and compassion to Magic that had been denied to most HIV positive individuals in the past.

Despite the displacement of racism and its related issues through representations of racial progress (embedded in individualism) and racial harmony circulated through sport personalities, "racial meanings" are not settled. The narration of the superstar personality is implicated in the narration of a more ordinary threatening black masculinity. That is, the narration of the African-American superstar is used to promote a vision that simultaneously undergirds the illusion of meritocracy and denies racism as it inscribes blackness as a negation of the social order. In other words, the figures of the superstar and of threatening black masculinity can be understood as effects of knowledges and powers that make race *matter* and *visible* through trouble, deviance, and danger.[21]

In this case, I want to draw attention to the strategies and operations of power that codify deviance in response to Johnson's transgression to make visible the criminal in the black body while a white familial heterosexuality is simultaneously constructed and rendered invisible yet normative. Most specifically, homosexuality and race are imagined and marked through the familiar optic of the family and repetitive and racially inflected figures (the drug addict, the Black church, and the hypersexual black man) that work to locate and contain the possibility of "African-American AIDS" within the homosexual and African-American communities.

Mechanisms of Containment

[T]he insistence that AIDS is somehow a mark of perversions transforms infected persons into "queers," regardless of their exposure route.
                                                                Cindy Patton[22]

In a quote that exemplifies the attempt to resituate Johnson and AIDS, Malcolm Gladwell and Alison Muscatine suggest that: "The two worlds with which he [Magic Johnson] is most clearly identified-sports and the African-American community – have long been among the most resistant in American society in acknowledging the disease" (1991: A-1).

The explicit appeal to these two apparently self-evident, contained geographical spaces (the African-American community and professional sports) is a rhetorical strategy that brings to the fore racial identity to locate and contain Johnson and the possibilities of the "disease." Although racial differences in HIV infection are acknowledged, the higher rate of infection among African Americans is narrated through a logic of addiction (that inscribes recklessness, compulsion, and insufficient free- will on bodies) that simultaneously structures and makes visible the failed authority of the black community through the figure of the Black church.[23] As the most prominent surrogate for the black community, the Black church is positioned as having neglected its authoritative role, allowing homophobia to interfere with its education and welfare of the black community. The narration of the negligent African-American community – depicted as irrational, homophobic, in denial, and resistant to drug and safe-sex education – simultaneously produces an imaginary, superior "Middle America" outside of the frame of scrutiny. The frame of community responsibility is articulated through the logic of "private community" accomplished under Reagan to legitimate defunding practices during the 1980s. The privatized logic confined individual responsibility within local community and, by extension, liberated Middle America (suburban America) from its identification with and responsibility for inner-city poverty and urban decay (Reeves and Campbell 1994).

Not surprisingly, the logic of containment is amplified through the media's surveillance of the (racially coded) professional world, to which the media almost exclusively directs its gaze to imagine the possibility of Johnson's HIV infection. The public scrutiny of Johnson *and* the black male athletic body by and through the mainstream media marks a narrative shift from superstar to the more ordinary and threatening black masculinity. Stuart Alan Clarke (1991) has referred to this as the "black-men misbehaving" narrative, a narrative that simultaneously "expresses, affirms, and authorizes popular fears, pleasures, and anxieties in ways that shape the experience of race and ethnicity in both personal and public spaces" (Cole and Andrews 1994). In this case, race *matters*: an out-of-control black sexuality in need of regulation is rendered visible.

Framing the "Loss" of the Productive Body

Tinged with the stigma of illness that dramatically destroys the body, what was usually absent from representation becomes spectacularly and consistently visible.

Timothy Landers[24]

Consistent with the fatalist discourse of AIDS, which equates sex, HIV infection, AIDS, and death, eulogizing articles, structured through "where were you moments" ranging from John F. Kennedy's assassination to John Lennon's murder on the street in New York, were produced in response to Johnson's confession. The line drawn from moments of national distress (Kennedy's assassination and Lennon's murder) to Johnson suggest an attempt to capture (and produce) America's compassion and loyalty. The narration of "loss" appeals to economic loss: the superstar narration celebrates progress through the economy and the productive body. In this case, Johnson was celebrated for elevating the economic position of the NBA (locally and globally), his investments, and his worth.[25] The narrative of compassion and loss is racially inflected through the repetitious appeal to the figure of Len Bias (an African-American college basketball player who died from a cocaine overdose within 48 hours of being drafted to play for the Boston Celtics) – a figure that captures cultural anxieties around African-American excessive consumption and addiction as well as moralistic fascination with the loss of the productive body. Both Bias and Johnson are depicted as African-American athletes whose lives end through excess and contagion, whose tragedies are framed as individual career tragedies.[26]

Although Johnson's body, the figure of the NBA superstar, potentially disrupts the knowledge/power relations that converge on and render visible HIV infected bodies and the conflation of HIV and AIDS, the figure of the homosexual and the trope of HIV as evidence of inner and secret depravity are repetitously invoked to maintain the visual border of HIV and AIDS in the popular imaginary. A quote from Leigh Steinberg (cited in Gladwell and Muscatine 1991), a prominent sports agent, exemplifies the attempt to undermine the stereotype of AIDS as a "gay disease":

> It's like a slap in the face to people stereotyping AIDS as a gay problem. It shows the universality of the threat and the imagery of this virile, tough, married, athlete being infected by HIV is extremely dramatic.

The contrast between the homosexual body with that of the "virile, tough, married, athlete" with its appeal to disease and deviant sexuality relies on the repathologized homosexual body and the before/after narration of HIV infection.

Johnson's body was placed under an immediate, *retroactive* surveillance that attempted to make visible earlier evidence of HIV (as signs of inevitable death). One article suggests that Johnson had suffered from a case of shingles in October 1985 (Almond and Cimons 1991), others sighted a flu-like illness at the beginning of the 1991–2 basketball season that forced Johnson to miss three games. Chick Hearn, a radio-television announcer, said he knew as early as October 25, 1991, when Magic failed to play in the last two exhibition games before the beginning of the opening of the regular season (Howard-Cooper 1991).

As the media reframed Johnson, photographers kept Johnson under constant surveillance waiting to document the hidden sexualities and/or sexual practices as they became visible on the body. The now widely circulated image of Johnson seated on the bench, bleeding, after being scratched in an exhibition game against the Cleveland Cavaliers during November of 1992, that accompanied the media's announcement of his second retirement from the NBA, might be understood as providing visual evidence of "threat" seeping out of the once hard and contained body, legitimating the discourse of risk, danger, and fear circulated by the media.[27]

Visualizing Deviance: The Promiscuous (Heterosexual) World of Sport

Before I was married, I truly lived the bachelor's life. I'm no Wilt Chamberlain, but as I traveled around NBA cities, I was never at a loss for female companionship. . . . There were just some bachelors almost every woman in L.A. wanted to be with: Eddie Murphy, Arsenio Hall, and Magic Johnson. I confess that after I arrived in L.A. in 1979, I did my best to accommodate as many women as I could – most of them through unprotected sex.

Magic Johnson[28]

As I have suggested above, Johnson's HIV status immediately brought into question his sexuality, which remained an ongoing object of scrutiny, despite his implication that he had contracted HIV through "heterosexual sex" and corroborating statements by his doctor, Michael Mellman, and the Lakers PR Department. Johnson reasserted his heterosexuality in *Sports Illustrated* ("I've never had a homosexual encounter. Never.") and the *Arsenio Hall Show* ("I'm far from being homosexual. You know that. Everybody else who's close to me understands that."), where his statement was met with enthusiastic cheering and applause. Under the cover of a recognition of a courageous political statement ("heterosexuals get AIDS too"), the applause is more properly understood as a homophobic display – and as an attempt to make visible, prove, and contain that which cannot.

The popular fixation on Magic's sexual practices motivates a series of strategies meant to situate Magic and HIV outside of the general

public. Under headlines like, "Johnson's HIV Caused by Sex 'Heterosexual Transmission Cited; Wife is Pregnant'" (Cannon and Cotton
1991: A-14) we re-read the multiple codifications embedded in "heterosexual transmission," which simultaneously initiate the production of Johnson as "family man" and "tragic figure" while appealing
to the seemingly stable and mutually exclusive categories that organize
the logic of "heterosexual/homosexual transmission." Typical of the
framing of post-1985 AIDS, the heterosexual AIDS narrative simultaneously asserts and destabilizes its possibility – thus the endless repeti-
tion of "AIDS is just not a gay disease." In this case, Magic's sexuality
is made suspect and skepticism is invited by invoking the authorial
voice of science and the statistical-AIDS-imaginary to suggest taken-
for-granted transmission patterns. Those studies, recast by the dominant media, are summarized in the following quote: "the fraction of
heterosexuals now infected is very much smaller than that of homosexuals" and therefore "the risk of it happening is far lower than in
homosexual contact" (Cannon and Cotton 1991: A-14).

> In other words, finding a partner who is infected is quite low – with the
> major exception of prostitutes, a large percentage of whom are infected.
> It is also believed that the odds of an infected man passing the virus to a
> woman are far greater than those of an infected woman passing it to a
> man. If a man has another venereal disease, such as herpes, his odds of
> being infected are vastly higher. (A-14)

And:

> The primary risk groups for infection are gay men and intravenous drug
> users. The Centers for Disease Control said that, through August, 6
> percent of the people with AIDS had been infected through heterosexual
> transmission. Fewer than one-sixth of those cases – less than 1 percent
> overall – involved men who said they had been infected through inter-
> course with women. . . . Studies of husbands of women who were in-
> fected by blood transfusions showed that the men who did not practice
> safe sex had a 3 percent chance a year of developing an AIDS infection.
> (Kolata 1991: A-12)[29]

These studies, again recast by the media, exemplify the know-
ledge/power nexus that simultaneously asserts and unsettles "heterosexual AIDS" by raising doubts about its possibilities.[30] As Watney
explains it, heterosexual identity is not self-identical but is defined
over and against what it is not: "[T]he figure of the gay man interrupts
yet also reinforces the social and psychical boundaries of desire, and

the relations of gender which are inscribed within them. Straight society needs us. We are its necessary 'Other.' Without gays, straights are not straight" (1987: 26). Such "stabilizing" strategies include a popular construction of "heterosexual sex" as monolithic and "missionary" through the repetitive displacement of the multiplicity of sexual possibilities. Sodomy (homosexuality) is made the predominant figure of unsafe sex in the cultural imaginary (Watney 1987).[31]

Yet, the attempt to contain the identity of the general public turns to the familiar trope of promiscuity and the hypersexual African-American man. Most explicitly, "guilt" is displaced onto the body of sexually active women in a metonymical slip which places them as figures for the "promiscuous world of sport."

Michael Wilborn describes the sport world:

> Sex and sports are as inseparable as the pick and roll. . . . If you've ever left an NBA arena late. . . . or followed a team back to the hotel. . . . you understand that the players don't have to go looking for sex, it's staring most of them in the face. (1991: D-3)

One more time, "it," the act of sex, that is "staring most of them in the face" becomes an identity, specifically that of women. It is under headlines like "What It Boils Down To is Playing With Fire" (Callahan 1991: D-3) that women, necessarily, re-enter the sport-world to re-establish its heterosexuality. But, in this case, women enter in the position of villain, victimizing athletes, signifying threat and contagion to the family. The duplicitous heterosexual AIDS discourse reappears, displacing the statistics invoked earlier by the mainstream media to problematize the possibility of female to male transmission, and to destabilize both Johnson's sexuality and the possibility of heterosexual AIDS. In the genre of "the promiscuous world of sport," there are no doubts: women are resurrected as the familiar outlaws and the polluting viles, their bodies marked as contagious and dangerous.

The trope of promiscuity figures women who are sexually active outside the prescriptions of Christian monogamy as prostitutes (Watney 1987), whose bodies have been historically depicted "as so contaminated that [they] are . . . 'always dripping,' virtual laboratory cultures for viral replication" (Treichler 1988: 207). The prostitute is viewed as self-destructive "rather than someone who has herself been infected by a man" (Watney 1987: 85). Additionally, these women are portrayed as looking for "the million dollar baby," trying to "set up" professional athletes for paternity suits. Professional basketball player Eddie Johnson ("Outside the Lines") comments: "women know if they do get pregnant, they do get paid." The message in the popular press was clear: "the sex may be free, but there *is* a price to pay for the lifestyle" (Elson 1991: 77).

At the same time women are portrayed as prostitutes and villains, male athletes are positioned through racially inflected codes that build on the trope of the compulsive, reckless, and absent inseminating black male repopularized through Reagan's familial politics and the war on drugs. In a shift back to the positioning of the male athlete as necessarily hypersexual, Wilborn (1991) continues:

> I'm not suggesting for one millisecond that athletes are the only people who take potentially deadly risks. . . . But no group of men, with the exception of high-profile rock musicians, goes through life being as sexually tempted and as frequently as professional athletes . . . Not only is it not "easy" to say no, it's almost impossible. To abstain, we're talking about a level of self-control that I certainly, for one, would not have under similar circumstances. (D-3)

As I discuss earlier, the discursive construction of heterosexual-AIDS remains destabilized but heterosexuality is stabilized through its articulation of family values and the body which produces a pure-heterosexual whose risk is determined by having sex outside the "home." Little attention is given to safer sex practices without appealing to and supporting abstinence; instead the narrative draws on the repetitive policing of desire: It is "multiple partners (who) put you at risk" (Cannon and Cotton 1991: A-14). Once again act is conflated with identity-it is multiple partners rather than unprotected sex with someone infected with HIV that presents risk. Just say no.

While Johnson's infection is explained through the normalizing construct of promiscuity, his sexuality is now understood to be regulated through the nuclear family, but repetitive appeals to Wilt Chamberlain's (1991) autobiography *A View from Above*, in which Chamberlain claims to have slept with over 20,000 women, situates Chamberlain as the surrogate for and embodiment of an excessive, dangerous black sexuality attributed to the African-American man. The strategies of observation and the representation of this "lifestyle" render visible the pathological culture of professional sport attributed to a dangerous lifestyle. The sports-world is structured through the availability, "quality," and/or quantity of sex (or excess in general), embedded in a ritual of a fast-track lifestyle (i.e., "life on the edge") where "drugs are becoming a problem, too," a politics of lifestyle that all too clearly intersects with the lifestyle of insatiable sexuality, orgies, and polluted poppers attributed to gay men to explain their vulnerability to HIV infection.

The opening segment of ESPN's edition of "Outside the Lines: Men and Women, Sex and Sports," outlines the conflicts and questions that frame the narrative that transforms Johnson's seropositivity into an optic that allows "us" to *see* racially coded transgressions: "Do some athletes live dangerous sexual lives?" (here we see the image of a remorseful Magic Johnson, wiping a tear from his cheek). "Do they feel entitled to grab whatever they can?" (cut to a police-escorted, hand-cuffed Mike Tyson-followed by a soundbite from Nigel Clay, former Oklahoma football player convicted of rape). "From the earliest there can be unreality in an athlete's life (cut to white basketball player, Daemon Bailey, surrounded by the press and fans). "Later a barrage of material pleasure and privilege" (cut to a close-up of post-gambling scandal, Michael Jordan in dark glasses, sitting in what we are to assume is a high-priced car) . . . "Have athletes changed their behavior since the shocking announcement that Magic Johnson has the AIDS virus?" And, we are told by Bob Ley, the host of the report, that "[t]he game's people play extend beyond the playing fields," after which he asks, "at what cost is pleasure indulged without consequence?"

The visual images, ordered as apparent responses to the questions raised in the voice-over, feature prominent African-American athletes involved in well-known and publicized scandals or crimes articulated to give physical form and identity to the dangerous sexuality, excess, and criminality that apparently saturate the world of professional sport. The ESPN report, like the coverage that generates the "promiscuous world of sport" more generally, is a narrative of moral outrage and normalization, organized through the optic of family values that renders visible and inscribes immorality and danger. "Threat" is generated through the repetitive figure of the black man as criminal/rapist and a slippage that operates through the logic of addiction: an escalation of desire and entitlement that moves from promiscuity (Magic Johnson) to rape (Mike Tyson). Since media accounts do not racially specify the bodies of the "groupies," the enormous amount of media attention focused on the professional athlete's lifestyle can be understood as a connotation of cultural anxieties around miscegenation.

In this genre, mechanisms of containment work to racially codify and pathologize the lifestyle of professional athletes and the culture of professional sport, described by Bob Ley as a "closed society" that is "testosterone rich" ("Outside the Lines"). Social psychologist Chris O'Sullivan speaks in this report as an expert to explain professional male athletes: "They sort of don't belong to society, they belong to a separate society, this outlaw society. And women have no place in that society, they certainly have no respectful place in that society. How are they going to relate to women, they don't fit into this world at all." Male athletes are represented as a "special breed, who develop an unrealistic sense of "entitlement." We are told in a voice-over by Bob Ley that the male athlete is "impervious to all discipline" and "social creature of his physical success" as we watch an African-American man as he is escorted through a prison.[32]

Johnson, initially positioning himself as an advocate for safe sex, subsequently embraces a position that suggests that it was sex outside of the family that created the possibility for his infection. In his autobiography, *My Life*, Johnson's (1992) dedication line, which apparently captures both his love and regret, reads, "For Cookie, You were right. I should have married you sooner." Watney (1990: 184) would argue that Magic has been positioned in the final discursive space of the AIDS agenda, the AIDS victim: "Crushed, submissive . . . he or she accepts and justifies the 'punishment' of AIDS for the unforgivable capital offense of daring to live beyond the narrow and sadistic intelligibility of familial consciousness."

This aspect of the Magic Johnson story reproduces identities sustained by and invested in familial ideology. It is a neat and tidy story of sin and salvation through the normalizing optic of the family.

Conclusion

> SILENCE=DEATH. *When I first saw this poster I believe it said "Science=Death." I had no doubt that this is what I had read. When the poster became a button, a T-shirt, the key symbol of the anarchistic resistance to a pogrom masquerading as a disease, I was sure the slogan had been changed. . . . But the dyad silence/science was no mistake. Straight people find this slip funny. Gay people do not.*
>
> Cindy Patton[33]

In this paper, I have argued that multiple dyads (central/not-central; body/antibody; deviant/normalized; contained/leaky) structure AIDS narratives and that these dyads function as mechanisms of containment. The cultural logic of modernity insists on rendering AIDS visible and *seeing* it operate: the modern logic of converting act into identity enables and constrains the cultural imaginary. The organizing categories of normalization are continuously undermined by the invisible operation of HIV and the lack of a referent behind AIDS. Disciplinary categories and the (apparent) discrete bodies to which they correspond (the addict, the homosexual, the prostitute) function to erase that which AIDS (its effects) continuously introduces: the transgression of boundaries (that of nation, family, and the modern subject) – the inbetweenness of bodies that science cannot perceive. The irony is not lost in the relationship between science and "Magic": in this case, Magic becomes the AIDS sign while AIDS becomes a magical sign. As the project of Enlightenment thought, science is embedded in the hope of eliminating magic and the unseen – the mind and verifiability remain at its center.[34] As in the sixteenth century, magic stands at and as the limit of modern science-both engaged in a contest where each maneuvers around the other.

AIDS, then, like magic, designates a collection of *effects*. The complexity of knowledges, the effects of power, which classify and mark the body of the PLWA are condensed in and authorized through the visual images written into the AIDS narrative. Visual technologies that sight and render visible a virus by assigning it a corporeal identity are particularly powerful mechanisms of management because they conceal their production, perspective, and location through the codes of objectivity. As Simon Watney explains:

> AIDS is thus embodied as an exemplary and admonitory drama relayed between the image of the miraculous authority of clinical medicine and the faces and the bodies of individuals who clearly disclose the stigmata of their guilt. (1988: 78).

In the case of Magic, the narration of AIDS, or, more accurately, a virus, organized through familial politics and racial dynamics, assembles truths about America and "enemies within" that organize our cultural imaginary and everyday lived experience and everyday fears. While promotional figures, like Johnson, are distanced from the threatening codes of black masculinity that dominate the racist imaginary, Johnson's HIV status is used to make visible and contain "threat." Most specifically, threat is rendered visible through the homosexual, women who are sexually active outside the family, and African-American men through the optic of the family and the trope of body/antibody that structure both the discursive formation around AIDS and the broader reactionary politics that define post-Reagan America. These mechanisms of containment simultaneously function to conceal the government's failure to address AIDS, the racism, sexism, and homophobia of science, and the pharmaceutical industry's interests in AIDS while authorizing defunding strategies and repressive policies.

Notes

1 Cited in Crimp 1988.

2 Cited in Crimp 1988.

3 My use of terms like cultural common sense, national popular culture, and racist imaginary is not meant to deny the complex and contradictory struggles over meaning that have taken place around AIDS, sexuality, and race, but to acknowledge that those discourses exist in relations of power and remain constrained by the identity categories produced through the modern epistemic regime. The relation between modern identity-categories and the cultural imaginary is a central theme of this paper. For an excellent discussion of the debates around sexuality and AIDS, see S. Seidman 1992, ch. 4.

4 The depiction of Johnson as docile, man-child (one prominent stereotype of African-American men) and the traditional, nuclear family as a healthy and desirable norm (the embodiment of natural/normal sexuality) are repetitive figures in the narration of "Johnson gets AIDS."

5 The quotation marks are not meant to diminish the tragedy of Johnson's HIV antibody positive status; instead, I want to draw attention to the media's deeply disturbing narrow vision that limits tragedy to Johnson's infection.

6 It is worth nothing that Michael Mellman, the Lakers' physician, declared Johnson a modern-day hero during the expert–journalist exchange that followed Johnson's announcement – the nomination was immediately affirmed by NBA Commissioner David Stern and repeated by the journalists covering the press conference. George Bush applauded Johnson's disclosure (his uncritical acceptance of infection) and endorsed his hero status from the NATO summit in Rome; and, later, used Magic's announcement, which he described as exemplary "activism," to critique and dismiss AIDS activist groups like ACT UP (AIDS Coalition to Unleash Power), which he characterized as extremist. For accounts of the political significance of ACT UP and its accomplishments in terms of challenges it has posed to the pharmaceutical and healthcare industries, government health and welfare policies, and research designs, see Crimp 1990, Patton 1990, Epstein 1991.

7 As Reagan blamed those people victimized by economic shifts, unemployment, and the erosion of welfare programs for social problems, a logic of "urban poverty" was deployed that displaced the economic effects of late/deindustrial capitalism and Reagan's policies onto a moral poverty located in drug-users (perhaps the most vivid expression of racially-coded moral poverty), welfare recipients, and the "vanishing black family."

8 Green 1985.

9   Treichler 1987.

10   Although Johnson's HIV antibody status initially disrupted popular know-
     ledges that identified *who* was at risk for HIV infection, the coverage of his
     November 7, 1991 press conference was organized through the recogniz-
     able elements and repetitive codes and figures that have established the
     parameters of dominant AIDS narratives: calls for testing, a hierarchy of
     social types that privileges science/experts, the figure of transgression, the
     HIV antibody positive body as a necessarily unhealthy, unproductive body,
     and figures of common sense.

11   Foucault 1980b.

12   For an account of the lived experience of the ideal of the nuclear family
     during the 1950s, see May 1988. For social histories that interrogate the
     family as both an economic unit and a cultural ideal, see D'Emilio and
     Freedman 1988, Coontz 1992. For critical examinations of the New
     Right's use of the family and production of siege paradigms, see Watney
     1987, Reeves and Campbell 1994.

13   For accounts of Reaganism and the mobilization of the New Right, see, for
     example, Rogin 1987, Wills 1987. For cultural-studies informed accounts
     of the rise of the New Right and popular culture, see Clarke 1991,
     Grossberg 1992. For a critical analysis of prosthetic masculinity, family
     values, popular culture, and national identity as they relate to Reagan's
     narration of America's instability and weakness through the civil-rights
     movement and the Carter administration as feminine, see Jeffords 1994.
     For a critical interrogation of the war on drugs, Reaganism and the rise of
     the New Right, and role of mainstream journalism, see Reeves and Camp-
     bell 1994.

14   Although by 1985 less than 8% of household organization corresponded
     to the nuclear-family model, the traditional/biblical family functioned as a
     normalizing construct to demonize and pathologize those living outside of
     the mythic family arrangement: gays/lesbians, PLWAs, women who
     worked, welfare mothers, "crack mothers," the black family, the inner city
     (black youth), figures of promiscuity, and the so-called sexual revolution
     of the sixties.

15   Montville 1991.

16   Crimp 1993.

17   For excellent accounts of the fear and fascination of the black body, see
     Bhabha 1983, Mercer 1986, 1994. For accounts of the cultural politics of
     sport and masculinity, see Messner and Sabo 1990, Messner 1992, Gru-
     neau and Whitson 1993. For work on black masculinity and sport, see
     Waquant 1992, 1996. For studies that examine masculinity, sport, and
     advertising, see Connell 1990, Jackson 1994.

18   The trace of racially coded pathological anatomy is still evidenced across
     multiple fields of representation. Contemporary searches of the black
     athletic body for organic causes of enhanced performance can be traced to
     the making of the "primitive body" as closer to nature during Western
     expansion and colonization. In his discussion of the beating of Rodney

King, Dumm (1993) explains how some contemporary racist theories of criminal types have reorganized biological-reductive theories through correlation and take form between "sport" and "criminality." For example, Wilson and Hernstein (1985), conservative criminologists, argue that there is a correlation between somatotype and propensity for criminal behavior and that "extroverted mesomorphs with slow autonomic nervous system response rates may earn honest money in the National Football League instead of dishonest money robbing banks" (cited in Dumm 1993: 183). In this case, correlation produces a slippage that allows for blame, while sport is offered as a viable career option (in other words, Rodney King could have opted to earn a living playing professional football) that simultaneously allows for the legitimate display of aggressive behaviors (Dumm 1993). Advertisements for Nike products (the corporation responsible for the unprecedented success of the NBA) typically rely on codes of the primitive body. During the fall of 1993, Atlanta's Nike Town featured portraits that represented Michael Jordan and Charles Barkley through bodily distortions that invoked the primitive: elongated arms, diminished legs, elongated foreheads. The images are now available on T-shirts sold at Nike Town. The question of nature in the body is also raised through cyborg imagery, an expression of the cultural anxieties of postmodernism, that depicts African-American athletes as products of science. For a discussion of the historical codification of body of the Other/primitive as muscular, closer to Nature, and uncivilized, see Hoberman 1992. For an excellent account of photography, eugenics, and criminality at the turn of the century see Green 1986. For a discussion of the cyborg ontology of late-capitalism, see Haraway 1985.

19 Additionally, regulatory imperatives were initiated around drug use-players suspected of or who had a history of drug use were required to submit to drug testing. The combination of the NBA's drug-testing policy, Johnson's popularity, and Johnson's body-clearly distanced from the classed-racial codes inscribing the drug injector's body-may explain the limited speculation regarding the possibility of Johnson's infection through a needle; regardless, Johnson's transgression presented the NBA with the possibility of another league-wide (sex-related) scandal. For an account of the role of popular personality in advertising and the use of black athletes in Britain, see Jackson 1994; for an analysis of the media's response to black professional athletes misbehaving, see Cole and Andrews 1994, Reeves and Campbell 1994 (esp. ch. 6).

20 For a critical reading of Reaganism, popular representations of Michael Jordan, and the new racism, see Andrews 1993. For theoretical accounts of promotional culture, see Ewen 1988, Featherstone 1991, Wernick 1991.

21 The new racist discourse that informed the representations of prominent African-American athletes and entertainment figures like Bill Cosby during the 1980s contrasts sharply with the everyday lived experiences of the

majority of African Americans in inner cities and predominantly minority communities. Although the shift from a manufacture to a service economy during the 1970s disproportionately affected urban areas, Reagan reduced funding for multiple social welfare programs that included unemployment insurance, food stamps, aid for families with dependent children, and drug programs. At the same time, the rate of unemployment and poverty significantly increased among African Americans (Williams 1993); the New Right's war on drugs justified the war on black urban youth; and the prison population doubled in the United States (Reeves and Campbell 1994: 21; Robinson 1993). It is estimated that at least 25% of the twenty-something generation of African-American men are controlled by the criminal court system in the United States (Robinson 1993).

22 See Patton 1990.

23 African-American women constitute one of the largest but least visible groups of women infected with HIV. In New York and New Jersey, AIDS related complications remains the leading cause of death for African-American women 15–44 years old. Of the 15,493 cases of HIV related illness among women reported between 1981 and 1992, African-American women accounted for 52% of those cases. Hammonds (1990: 8) suggests that the disproportionate number of African-American women infected with HIV is linked to the "long term and persistent failure of public health practices to control sexually transmitted diseases in the African-American community." African-American gay and bisexual men are also disproportionately HIV infected (Crimp 1993). African-American and other minority communities experienced and understood AIDS within and through already existing problems (poverty, government neglect, inadequate health care, lack of access to education) and, therefore, extended already established resources and multi-service programs to address AIDS in their communities (Patton 1990: 11). But, these efforts have typically been rendered invisible and undermined as Reagan and Bush defunded such multi-service programs. For a discussion of the complex dynamics that have established the AIDS Service Industry and rendered African-American community based organizing around AIDS invisible and less supported, see Patton 1990.

24 Landers 1988.

25 Magic Johnson, including the Johnson/Larry Bird (style/coast/class/race) rivalry, is credited with transforming the marketability of the NBA, increasing its popularity both nationally and globally in terms of gate receipts, television ratings, and league merchandise. Season attendance increased from 12.1 million in 1986–7 to 16.9 million during the 1990 season; during the same period, gate revenues increased from $128 million to $316 million. Revenues from cable television grew from $12 million to $57 million while revenues from network television increased from $39 million to $125 million. While there were only seven regular season tele-

casts during 1982–3, there were 24 during 1991. Over the last seasons, retail sales have escalated from $173 million to over $1 billion during the 1990–1 season.

26 Like the drama surrounding Magic, Bias's death can be understood as a drama of containment that incited moral panic and justified increased regulation and policing practices in sport. For a critical interrogation of the news coverage of Bias's death in relation to sport, social drama, the New Right's war on drugs, and normalization, see Reeves and Campbell 1994: 136–50. For an account of the relation between the homosexual and addict, see Sedgwick 1992.

27 Although Johnson played in the 1992 NBA All-Star Game and served as captain of the 1992 US Olympic Dream Team, Johnson's plan to return to the NBA for the 1992–3 season was met with fear and criticism. Despite the rally around Johnson in response to concerns voiced by the Australian basketball team about playing against Johnson in the Olympics, Dream Team member Karl Malone as well as several doctors voiced their concerns about the possibility of HIV transmission on the court after Johnson announced his intention to return to the NBA. Johnson retired from the NBA for the second, and apparently the final, time on Oct. 2, 1992.

28 Johnson with Johnson 1991.

29 The narration of AIDS continues to be organized through categories that under-emphasize and misrepresent the possibility of HIV infection among women, despite evidence that has existed since at least 1983 that demonstrated that women could be infected with HIV and could transmit HIV to partners. In some countries, the rate of infection among women is almost equal to that among men (Treichler 1988: 192). Although the figure of the prostitute remains central to AIDS narratives, prostitutes are more likely to contract HIV through contaminated needles than through sexual activity (prostitutes routinely use condoms for protection against sexually transmitted diseases) (ACT UP/NY Women's Book Group 1990, Treichler 1992). See Treichler 1992 for an examination of the contradictory and complex representations of gender in AIDS narratives. She argues that narration of gender through pejorative stereotypes discourages women from recognizing possible risks and preventive practices. The article also provides examples of what I have referred to as the duplicitous discourse of heterosexual AIDS and critiques the classificatory strategies through which HIV infection is documented.

30 No mention is made of the disproportionate number of African-American women and African-American gay men infected with HIV and dying from AIDS related complications.

31 For an explanation of the continual reinvention of heterosexual AIDS, see Watney 1992. I should also point out that these "knowledges" are embedded in a series of ethnocentric and postcolonialist assumptions that either eclipse the epidemic of AIDS in Africa or produce an exotic "African

AIDS." See Cindy Patton (1992), esp. pp. 77–97, for an account of the Western invention of African AIDS.

32 The suggestion is that (like the representations of African Americans, including the "crack mother," in crack-cocaine narratives) African-American athletes are beyond rehabilitation. The ESPN report also demonstrates the complexity of gender, race, and sexuality in the national imaginary. As masculinity and sexual politics have become the objects of national scrutiny, such issues and dynamics have been made visible through the criminalization of black bodies: Mike Tyson (date rape); Clarence Thomas (sexual harassment); Michael Jackson (child sexual abuse); and O. J. Simpson (domestic violence).

33 Patton 1990.

34 For examples and/or analyses of activist challenges to scientific authority, see ACTUP/NY Women & AIDS Book Group 1990, Epstein 1991, 1993, Testing the Limits 1991, Treichler 1992. For critiques of the cultural politics of vision and science, see, for example, Foucault 1973, Green 1985, 1986, Haraway, 1988, 1989, Marshall 1990, Terry 1990, Watney 1990. For accounts of visualization, science, and popular culture, see Treichler and Cartwright 1992. For critical examinations of the hegemony of vision and modernity, see Jay 1993, Levin 1993.

References

ACT UP/NY Women's Book Group. 1990. *Women, AIDS, and Activism.* Boston: South End Press.

Almond, Elliot and Marlene Cimons. 1991. "More issues than answers are surrounding HIV." *Los Angeles Times*, Nov. 8: C-4.

Andrews, David L. 1996 "'Just what is it that make's today's lives so different, so appealing?': Commodity-sign culture, Michael Jordan, and the cybernetic postmodern body." In *Exercising Power: The Making and Remaking of the Body*, eds Cheryl L. Cole, John W. Loy, and Michael A. Messner. Albany: SUNY Press.

—— 1997. "Deconstructing Michael Jordan: Popular culture, politics, and postmodern America." Ph.D. dissertation, University of Illinois, Urbana-Champaign, Illinois.

Bhabha, Homi. 1983. "The other question: The stereotype and colonial discourse." *Screen*, 24 (6): 18–36.

Bordowitz, Greg. 1994. "Dense moments." In *Uncontrollable Bodies: Testimonies of Identity and Culture*, eds Rodney Sappington and Tyler Stallings. Seattle: Bay Press.

Boswell, Thomas. 1991. "His burden is everyone's." *Washington Post*, Nov. 8: D-1.

Brown, Clifton. 1991. "A career of impact, a player with heart." *New York Times*, Nov. 8: B-11, 13.

Callahan, Tom. 1991. "What it boils down to is playing with fire." *Washington Post*, Nov. 10: D-3.

Cannon, Lou and Anthony Cotton. 1991. "Johnson's HIV caused by sex: 'Heterosexual transmission' cited; wife is pregnant." *Washington Post*, Nov. 9: A-14.

Carroll, Jean. 1992. "Love in the time of Magic: A chronicle of risk and romance on the sidelines of the NBA." *Esquire*, April: 136–42.

Carter, Erica and Simon Watney. 1989. *Taking Liberties: AIDS and Cultural Politics*. London: Serpent's Tail.

Clarke, John. 1991. *New Times and Old Enemies: Essays on Cultural Studies and America*. London: HarperCollins Academic.

Clarke, Stuart A. 1991. "Fear of a black planet: Race, identity politics, and common sense." *Socialist Review*, 21 (3–4): 37–59.

Cole, Cheryl L. 1993a. "Resisting the canon: Feminist cultural studies, sport, and technologies of the body." *Journal of Sport and Social Issues*, 17 (2): 77–97.

——. 1993b. "Technologies of deviant bodies: The ensemble of sport and (re)territorializing practices." Paper presented at the annual meetings of the North American Society for the Sociology of Sport, Ottawa.

Cole, Cheryl L. and David Andrews. 1994. "Fear of a black planet: Look who's misbehavin' now." Paper presented at the Gregory I. Stone–Society for Symbolic Interactionism Conference, University of Illinois..

Connell, Robert. 1990. "An iron man: The body and some contradictions of hegemonic masculinity." In *Sport, Men, and the Gender Order*, eds Michael Messner and Donald Sabo. Champaign: Human Kinetics Press.

Coontz, Stephanie, 1992. *The Way We Never Were: American Families and the Nostalgia Trap*. New York: BasicBooks.

Corea, Gena. 1993. *The Invisible Epidemic: The Story of Women and AIDS*. New York: HarperCollins Publishers.

Crimp, Douglas (ed.) 1988. *AIDS: Cultural Analysis/Cultural Activism*. Cambridge: MIT Press.

——. 1992. "Portraits of people with AIDS." In *Cultural Studies*, eds Lawrence Grossberg, Cary Nelson, and Paula Treichler. New York: Routledge.

——. 1993. "Accommodating Magic." In *Media Spectacles*, eds Marjorie Garber, Jann Matlock, and Rebecca L. Walkowitz. New York: Routledge.

Crimp, Douglas with Adam Rolston. 1990. *AIDSDEMOGRAPHICS*. Seattle: Bay Press.

D'Emilio, John and Estelle Freedman. 1988. *Intimate Matters: A History of Sexuality in America*. New York: Harper & Row.

Derrida, Jacques. 1976. *Of Grammatology*. Baltimore: John Hopkins University Press.

Derrida, Jacques with *Autrement*. 1993. "The rhetoric of drugs: An interview." *differences*, 5 (1): 1–25, trans. M. Isreal. (French original published in J. M. Hervieu (ed.) 1989. *Autrement*, 106).

Dumm, Thomas. 1993. "The new enclosures: Racism in the normalized community." In *Reading Rodney King/Reading Urban Uprising*, ed. Robert Gooding-Williams. New York: Routledge.

Elson, John. 1991. "The dangerous world of wannabes: Magic Johnson's plight brings fear into locker rooms across the country and spotlights the riskiest athletic perk: promiscuous sex." *Time*, Nov. 25: 77–8.

Epstein, Steven. 1991. "Democratic science? AIDS activism and the contested construction of knowledge." *Socialist Review*, 21 (2): 34–65.

——. 1993. "Impure science: AIDS activism, and the politics of knowledge." Ph.D. dissertation, University of California, Berkeley, California.

Ewen, Stuart. 1988. *All Consuming Images: The Politics of Style in Contemporary Culture*. New York: Basic Books.

Featherstone, Mike. 1991. *Postmodernism and Consumer Culture*. London: Sage.

Fee, Elizabeth and Daniel M. Fox, eds. 1988. *AIDS: The Burdens of History*. Berkeley: University of California Press.

Foucault, Michel. 1973. *The Birth of the Clinic: An Archaeology of Medical Perception*, trans. A. M. Sheridan. New York: Vintage Books.

——. 1979. *Discipline and Punish: The Birth of the Prison*, trans. A. Sheridan. New York: Vintage Books.

——. 1980a. *The History of Sexuality (Volume I: An Introduction)*, trans. R. Hurley. New York: Vintage Books.

——. 1980b. "Two Lectures." In *Power/Knowledge: Selected Interviews and Other Writings, 1972–1977*, ed. Colin Gordon. New York: Pantheon.

Gladwell, Malcolm and Alison Muscatine. 1991. "Legend's latest challenge: Sport's hero's message may resonate." *Washington Post*, Nov. 8: A-1.

Gray, Herman. 1989. "Television, black Americans, and the American Dream." *Critical Studies in Mass Communication*, 6 (4): 376–86.

Green, David. 1985. "On Foucault: Disciplinary power and photography." *Camerawork*, 32.

——. 1986. "Veins of resemblance: Photography and eugenics." In *Photography/politics: Two*, eds Patricia Holland, Jo Spence, and Simon Watney. London: Comedia Publishing Group.

Grossberg, Lawrence. 1992. *We Gotta Get Out of This Place: Popular Conservatives and Postmodernism*. New York: Routledge.

Gruneau, Richard and David Whitson. 1993. *Hockey Night in Canada*. Toronto: Garamond Press.

Hall, Stuart. 1990. "Cultural studies and its theoretical legacies." In *Cultural Studies*, eds. Lawrence Grossberg, Cary Nelson, and Paula Treichler. New York: Routledge.

Hammonds, Evelyn. 1990. "Missing persons: African-American women, AIDS, and the history of disease." *Radical America*, 24 (2): 7–23.

Haraway, Donna. 1985. "Manifesto for cyborgs: Science, technology, and socialist-feminism in the 1980s." *Socialist Review*, 15 (2): 65–108.

——. 1988. "Situated knowledges: The science question in feminism and the privilege of partial perspective." *Feminist Studies*, 14 (3): 575–99

——. 1989. *Primate Visions: Gender, Race, and Nature in the World of Modern Science*. New York: Routledge.

Harris, Scott. 1991. "Announcement hailed as a way to teach the public." *Los Angeles Times*, Nov. 8: A-32.

Heisler, Mark. 1991. "Magic Johnson's career ended by HIV positive test." *Los Angeles Times*, Nov. 8: A-1, 33, 34.

"Hero watch: Magic's best hour." 1991. *Los Angeles Times*, Nov. 8: B-6.

Hoberman, John. 1992. *Mortal Engines*. New York: The Free Press.

Howard-Cooper, Scott. 1991. "Teammates past and present are hit hard." *Los Angeles Times*, Nov. 8: C-4.

Jackson, Peter. 1994. "Black male: Advertising and the cultural politics of masculinity." *Gender, Place and Culture*, 1 (1): 49–59.

Jay, Martin. 1993. *Downcast Eyes: The Denigration of Vision in Twentieth-Century French Thought*. Berkeley: University of California Press.

Jeffords, Susan. 1994. *Hard Bodies: Hollywood Masculinity in the Reagan Era*. New Brunswick: Rutgers University Press.

Jhally, Sut and Justin Lewis. 1992. *Enlightened Racism: The Cosby Show, Audiences, and the Myth of the American Dream*. Boulder: Westview Press.

Johnson, Ervin with Roy S. Johnson. 1991. "I'll deal with it." *Sports Illustrated*, Nov. 18: 21–2.

—— with William Novak. 1992. *My Life*. New York: Random House.

Kastor, Elizabeth. 1991. "The question we fear: How did Magic get the virus? And why do we have to know?" *Washington Post*, Nov. 8: G-1, 7.

Katz, Donald. 1994. *Just Do It: The Nike Spirit in the Corporate World*. New York: Random House.

King, Samantha. 1993. "The politics of the body and the body politic: Magic Johnson and the ideology of AIDS." *Sociology of Sport Journal*, 10 (3): 270–85.

Kolata, Gina. 1991. "Studies cite 10.5 years from infection to illness." *New York Times*, Nov. 8: A-12.

Kornheiser, Tony. 1991. "A hero's message of hope." *The Washington Post*, Nov. 8: C-1, 4.

Kroker, Arthur and Marilouise Kroker. 1987. "Panic sex in America." In *Body Invaders: Panic Sex in America*, eds Arthur Kroker and Marilouise Kroker. New York: St. Martin's Press.

Kroll, Jack. 1991. "Smile, though our hearts are breaking." *Newsweek*, Nov. 18: 70.

Landers, Timothy. 1988. "Bodies and anti-bodies: A crisis in representation." In *Global Television*, eds C. Schneider and B. Wallis. New York: Wedge Press.

Levin, David M (ed.) 1993. *Modernity and the Hegemony of Vision*. Berkeley: University of California Press.

Marshall, Stuart. 1990. "Picturing deviancy." In *Ecstatic Antibodies: Resisting the AIDS Mythology*, eds T. Boffin and S. Gupta. London: Rivers Oram Press.

May, Elaine Tyler. 1988. *Homeward Bound: American Families in the Cold War Era*. New York: Basic Books.

Mercer, Kobena 1986. "Imaging the black man's sex." In *Photography/Politics: Two*, eds Patricia Holland, Jo Spence, and Simon Watney. London: Comedia Publishing Group.

—— 1994. *Welcome to the Jungle*. New York: Routledge.

Messner, Michael A. 1992. *Power at Play*. Boston: Beacon Press.

—— and Donald F. Sabo, eds. 1990. *Sport, Men, and the Gender Order*, Champaign: Human Kinetics Books.

Miller, James, ed. 1992. *Fluid Exchanges: Artists and Critics in the AIDS Crisis*. Toronto: University of Toronto Press.

Montville, Leigh. 1991. "Like one of the family." *Sports Illustrated*, Nov. 18: 44–5.

Mulligan, Thomas S. 1991. "The Magic touch: What now?" *Los Angeles Times*, Nov. 8: D-1, 6.

Outside the lines. 1992. *Men and Women: Sex and Sports*. ESPN.

Patton, Cindy. 1985. *Sex and Germs: The Politics of AIDS*. Boston: South End Press.

—— . 1990. *Inventing AIDS*. New York: Routledge.

—— . 1992. "Rock hard." Keynote paper presented at the annual meetings for the North American Society for the Sociology of the Sport, Toledo, Ohio.

Poovey, Mary. 1988. *Uneven Developments: The Ideological Work of Gender in Mid-Victorian England*. Chicago: University of Chicago Press.

Reeves, Jimmie L. and Richard Campbell. 1994. *Cracked Coverage: Television News, the Anti-Cocaine Crusade, and the Reagan Legacy*. Durham, NC: Duke University Press.

Riggs, Marlon. 1991. *Color Adjustment*. San Francisco: California Newsreel.

Robinson, Cedric J. 1993. "Race, capitalism, and the antidemocracy." In *Reading Rodney King/Reading Urban Uprising*, ed. R. Gooding-Williams. New York: Routledge.

Rochell, Anne. 1994. "CDC: Heterosexual AIDS rising sharply." *Atlanta Journal*, Mar. 11: A-6.

Rogin, Michael. 1987. *Ronald Reagan: The Movie and Other Episodes of Political Demonology*. Berkeley: University of California Press.

Sedgwick, Eve Kosofsky. 1990. *Epistemology of the Closet*. Berkeley: University of California Press.

—— . 1992. "Epidemics of the will." In *Incorporations*, eds Jonathan Crary and Sanford Kwinter. New York: Zone.

Seidman, Steven. 1992. *Embattled Eros: Sexual Politics and Ethics in Contemporary America*. New York: Routledge.

Stacey, Judith. 1990. *Brave New Families: Stories of Domestic Upheaval in Late Twentieth Century America*. New York: Basic Books.

Testing the Limits. 1991. *Voices from the Front*. New York: Testing the Limits.

Terry, Jennifer. 1990. "Lesbians under the medical gaze: Scientists search for remarkable differences." *Journal of Sex Research*, 27 (3): 317–39

Treichler, Paula A. 1987. "AIDS, homophobia, and bio-medical discourse: An epidemic of signification." *Cultural Studies*, 1 (2): 263–305.

Treichler, Paula A. 1988. "AIDS, gender, and bio-medical discourse: Current contests for meaning." In *AIDS: The Burden of History*, eds Elizabeth Fee and Daniel M. Fox. Berkeley: University of California Press.

——. 1992. "Beyond *Cosmo*: AIDS, identity, and inscriptions of gender." *Camera Obscura*, 28: 21–78.

—— and Lisa Cartwright, eds. 1992. *Camera Obscura* (Imaging technologies, inscribing science) 28/29. Bloomington: Indiana University Press.

Wacquant, Loic. 1992. "The social logic of boxing in black Chicago: Toward a sociology of pugilism." *Sociology of Sport Journal*, 9 (3): 221–54.

——. 1996. "A sacred weapon: Bodily capital and bodily labor among professional boxers." In *Exercising Power: The Making and Remaking of the Body*, ed. Cheryl L. Cole, John W. Loy, and Michael A. Messner. Albany: SUNY Press.

Watney, Simon. 1987. *Policing Desire: Pornography, AIDS, and the Media*. Minneapolis: University of Minnesota Press.

——. 1988. "The spectacle of AIDS." In *AIDS: Cultural Analysis/Cultural Activism*. ed. Douglas Crimp. Cambridge: MIT Press.

——. 1990. "Photography and AIDS." In *The Critical Image: Essays on Contemporary Photography*, ed. Carol Squires. Seattle: Bay Press.

Wernick, Andrew. 1991. *Promotional Culture: Advertising, Ideology and Symbolic Expression*. London: Sage.

Wilborn, Michael. 1991. "Available at your peril." *Washington Post*, Nov. 10: D-1, 3.

Williams, Rhonda M. 1993. "Accumulation as evisceration: Urban rebellion and the new growth dynamics." In *Reading Rodney King/Reading Urban Uprising*, ed. Robert Gooding-Williams. New York: Routledge.

Wills, Garry. 1987. *Reagan's America: Innocents at Home*. New York: Doubleday.

Wilson, James Q. and Richard Hernstein. 1985. *Crime and Human Nature*. New York: Simon Schuster.

14

The Dilemma of Identity: Bi Women's Negotiations

Amber Ault

Introduction

Much recent scholarship exploring the relationships between structure and subjectivity has criticized social constructions of difference as deviance. Studies of white racism, male chauvinism, Christian anti-semitism, and colonial orientalism explore the discursive practices through which dominant groups stigmatize those whom they would exclude. Less scholarship has explored the ways in which marginalized groups "take up" the constraining discourses through which dominant systems define them. Some theorists have begun, therefore, to explore how marginalized groups construct the boundaries of their identities and, as a result, have begun to explicate processes both counter-intuitive to us as social and political actors and predictable to us as sociologists: marginalized, stigmatized, and deviant groups themselves engage in their own processes of stigmatization (Collins 1990; Rust 1992; Taylor and Whittier 1992; Ault 1994), and these processes are often encoded in the dominant discourse.

Both classical and postmodern social theorists offer insight on this phenomenon, which seems consistent with Durkheimian under-standings of how groups create normalcy by defining and reifying that which is abnormal. Indeed, many of the marginalized identity-based groups in which we might observe this process have become, through politicization resulting from oppression, the proverbial Durkheimian "societies of saints" (Erikson 1966), asserting moral superiority derived from experiences of segregation and suffering, and engaging in boundary construction processes related to the reification of difference from the profane, oppressive, mainstream society.

Postmodernists argue that margin and center, subaltern and coloniz-
ing subject, are in constant negotiation with one another, albeit
through processes of mutual distancing and denial. Queer theorists,
following Foucault, have stressed this argument and its urgency: the
margin, the deviant, the other precedes the center, the normal, the
dominant construction, anchors and stabilizes it, and serves as its foil
(Foucault 1980; Butler 1990; Sedgwick 1990). Strengthened by poststructuralist criticism of the pervasive dualism in Western culture and
intellectual work, such understandings simultaneously acknowledge
that to advocate the "liberation" of a particular oppressed subject is to
retrench the system of signification that prefigured its oppression
(Foucault 1980), while to fail to engage in oppositional political projects is to engage in passive complicity with current systems of domination. Durkheim (1964) would argue that groups constantly engage
in this process of stigmatization and normalization, and that it serves
as the dialectic impetus for change. Unlike Durkheim, optimistic postmodernists (Smart 1993) hope that the center will not hold, but
nonetheless largely concede the impossibility of escape from the symbolic system that establishes the codes through which center produces
periphery (Butler 1990) and periphery apparently constructs its own
margins.
    A Gramscian understanding of hegemony as the pervasive and insid-
ious rearticulation of systems of domination that are obviously structural through experience that appears to be idiosyncratic (Gramsci
1971; Minh-ha 1989), makes the content of the discourse through
which marginalized groups stigmatize others seem predictable if
ironic. Sociologists studying African-American experience document the Black community's use of the language of white racism
to stigmatize its physiognomically "Blackest" members (Collins 1990).
Sociologists studying sexual identity have documented lesbian stigmatization of bisexual women through the terms of the discourse
the dominant society uses to stereotype lesbians (Rust 1993; Ault
1994). In such mappings we observe how the dominant discourse
creates and controls social categories, how stigmatized groups use the
stigmatizing discourse as the basis for collective definition, and,
finally, how marginalized groups deploy the dominant discourse to
construct "deviant others" against which they seem "more normal."
We have yet to explore, however, whether the "stigmatized other"
created by an already marginalized group negotiates its identity in the
codes of the cultural metanarrative. In this essay, I advance that
process by examining bisexual women's constructions of self and
social location.

The fundamental question here is whether the group used as a foil by an *already* marginalized group reinforces the dialectic operating in the mutual dependence of margin and center, disrupts this dynamic, or somehow transcends or moves beyond it. The political projects of "gender bending," "boundary blurring," and "binary smashing" touted by various subjects not comfortably situated in contemporary society indicate the inadequacies of current dominant systems of sexual, racial, and gender classification, the importance of renegotiating them, and the desire to do so. It remains unclear, however, to what extent this is possible. Our explications of the relationships between center and margin, and the margin's own constructions of a deviant other, would leave the sociologist less optimistic than the activist about such a project's prospects for success.

The case of bisexual women provides an especially interesting example. Bisexual women's status as "doubly deviant," as a group stigmatized by a community already marginal to the dominant society, makes their experience relevant to the question at hand. In this essay, I explore the ways doubly deviant groups disavow and recirculate the dominant discourse in constructing their identities and establishing their social locations relative to other groups within the same identity domain – in this case, the domain of sexual identity.

Although meaning inheres in the "bisexual" label's reference to the binary hetero/homo system for organizing biological sex and social gender, many politicized bisexuals issue trenchant invectives against Western cultural dualism, particularly as it is manifest in the binary sex/gender/sexuality system. Indeed, they often suggest that bisexual identity challenges this dualistic social system, which has long been a target of feminist criticism. Here then is a category dependent upon the dialectic between the dominant and the marginalized for its own existence, identified with a label that suggests a fundamental dualism, and which eschews the binary systems of categorization common to Western culture. Does such a category disrupt the dominant paradigm, transcend it, or reinforce it through its discursive practices? What might the answers mean for those who would subvert the dominant paradigms?

I draw here from discourse used by bisexual women; while non-heterosexuals, most notably gays and lesbians, are stigmatized by the dominant culture, some lesbian feminists have taken the non-heterosexual category bisexual as their "deviant other" (Rust 1993; Ault 1994); the focus of their attention is bisexual women, so the focus of this work is on the talk of women within what has been called the "bisexual community." In the paper that follows, I use empirical materials from 32 electronic interviews with bisexual women to explore how bi women negotiate the binary logic of the hetero/homo divide.

Stigma Among the Already Stigmatized: Lesbian-Feminist Constructions of Bisexual Women

A number of sociologists have remarked upon lesbian antipathy toward bisexual women since the beginning of the second wave of the women's movement in the United States (Blumstein and Schwartz 1974; Seidman 1993; Rust 1992, 1993; Ault 1994). Recently, Paula Rust (1992, 1993) has conducted a large quantitative survey documenting the prevalence of lesbian hostility toward bisexual women, and I have engaged in an interview-based analysis of the discourse through which lesbian feminists articulate their criticisms of bisexual women (Ault 1994). Both studies document the often overt animosity many lesbians direct at bisexual women, and both interpret it as an attempt by lesbians to "neutralize" the challenges that the institutionalization of bi identity apparently poses to lesbian subjectivity.

The discourse used by the dominant culture to stigmatize lesbians underwrites lesbian objections to bisexual identity. Lesbians stereotype bisexuals as sexually promiscuous, personally deceived, immature, in denial, perverted, and unable to form stable familial bonds – all constructions that echo the terms stigmatizing lesbians themselves as deviant relative to heterosexual society. I have codified the language of lesbian hostility toward bisexual women into four "techniques of neutralization": suppression, incorporation, marginalization, and delegitimation. "Suppression" describes lesbian insistence that "bisexuals simply do not exist." "Incorporation" works to position bisexuals as lesbians who are not yet aware of their lesbian identities, women "on a bi now gay later plan." "Marginalization" acknowledges bisexual existence but locates bisexuals as irrelevant to lesbian politics and communities, as "on the fence." Finally, "delegitimation" involves aspersions cast upon the characters of bisexual women, particularly related to their purported "promiscuous," "disloyal," and "bed-hopping" tendencies (Ault 1994).

Increasingly politicized, in part though lesbian dismissal, bisexual women have begun to organize for "bi rights" in a movement centered on challenging the dualistic structures of Western societies that make the category "bisexual" largely culturally incomprehensible. While some academics admonish "bi activists" against solidifying the meaning of the term "bisexual" if they wish to destabilize the dualistic sex/gender system (Rust 1992; Daumer 1992), the category seems, nonetheless, to be undergoing the process of institutionalization. Despite bi activists' desires "not to commit the mistakes of the past" that reinscribed the dominant sexual system (Firestein 1994), organized efforts "against biphobia" appear unable to avoid it; we can escape neither culture nor discourse, despite our deepest desires and grandest motivations.

In the following sections, I examine bisexual women's discourse on their bi subjectivity and social locations. These empirical materials demonstrate that the "others" against which marginalized groups define themselves as legitimate are not limited to the dominant groups that have, in large measure, constructed them. In addition, these materials demonstrate that even doubly deviant groups engage in processes of "centering" similar to those used by both the dominant society and its marginalized "others." Within bisexual women's discourse on sexual subjectivity and social location appear constructions of the "illegitimate bisexual," the "pathological monosexual," and "the non-queer" as just such marginal characters, "deviants" relative to whom bisexual women may position themselves as legitimate and, in some cases, culturally primary.

Doing as Being: Bisexual Women's "Binary Busting" Impulses

The dominant sex–gender system requires that subjects locate themselves as either male or female, either masculine or feminine, and either heterosexual or homosexual. Despite the ongoing feminist criticism of the binary terms of the dominant discourse on sex, gender, and sexual identity, these terms are used by some lesbian feminists to insist that one is "either straight or gay" and that bisexual women must locate themselves in one category or the other (Ault 1994). Bisexual women, in turn, resist this pressure to "choose" in a variety of ways; the most common strategy appears in their rearticulation of feminist critiques of Western dualism. The bi women who participated in this research, like many other feminists and postmodernists, analyze dualism as "an extremely limited mindset." In addition, they regard adopting the bisexual label as an effective strategy for challenging "Cartesian bipolar thinking." From this perspective:

> To accept bisexuality is to accept that there are many degrees and shades of orientation, not just "us" and "them." We are like mixed-race people

in a racially polarized community. Nobody knows what we are or what to do with us. But if they could see us as not unlike themselves, they would realize that nobody on either side is really all that different.

Bisexual women have come to call resistance to the legitimacy of the bisexual category "biphobia" (Weise 1992; Firestein 1994), in obvious reference to the more common "homophobia." They interpret "biphobia" as a deep-seated discomfort with the ambiguity of gender-bending and sexual genre blurring. The bisexual women in this study express some sympathy for the lesbian community's reluctance to embrace bisexual women, given their belief that the bisexual label transgresses the dominant system in which lesbians participate:

> The [lesbian] discomfort is not hard to understand. It is just fear. Fear that I will appear to be one of their community but then I will turn on them and side with straights. Fear that if sexuality is not a black-and-white choice, then maybe their own feelings are not so simple after all, and some day they may have to deal with their straight side.

Despite their explicit commitments to disrupting bifurcated social typologies, however, bisexual women's discourse often reinforces binary oppositions, illustrating the difficulty of achieving the goal of subverting the dominant paradigm while speaking from within the language through which it is articulated. The following passage about the use of sexual identity labels illustrates how resistance and reinscription operate simultaneously:

> [if society were more accepting of bisexuality] It would help smash the horrid sense of duality that this culture is stuck in. Things are either this or that, there's no in between. But here we are! Smack in between lesbian and straight!

Explicit commitments to disrupting binary systems are difficult to translate into discursive practice; here, for instance, the respondent lapses into the reinscription of the oppositional construction of "lesbian" and "straight." Other respondents situating the bisexual as a transgressive figure needed to use the following oppositional dualistic constructions in their explanations of bisexuals' "boundary blurring": "in/out," "bilovers/biphobes," "narrow-minded/open-minded," "dogmatic/easy going." In its claims that bi identity disrupts the dominant binaries, bi women's discourse often simultaneously reinscribes them.

Bi Identity within Hegemonic Dualism: Split Subjectivity

Bi women also rearticulate and reinforce the dominant hetero/homo system of categorization by describing the bisexual as "half and half," in the context of cultural understandings of heterosexual, lesbian, and gay selves as unified subjects. Rust (1992) reports bisexual interpretations of the self as "half heterosexual" and "half homosexual," although the women in this study constructed the split differently. Repeatedly, bi women in this research referred to their "bi sides," their "male and female sides," and their "masculine and feminine sides." At the level of the subject, the figure of the bisexual becomes a self divided, a composite self dependent upon the dominant sexual binary for coherence:

> I define as bi because I am and have always been attracted to people of both genders. To identify as either straight or lesbian would mean denying half of my sexuality. Being bi also means honoring both the male and female aspects of myself.

Bi subjectivity incorporates the culturally oppositional categories "lesbian" and "heterosexual," and, more subtly, "male" and "female." As a function of the broader social imperative that individuals locate themselves as either heterosexual or gay/lesbian, those who label themselves bisexual often construct their identities as composed of "bi parts," "straight parts," "lesbian parts," and "male and female parts," and these contentious parts of the bisexual subject are often at odds with each other. One woman in this study, for example, reported that she had "hated this bi side" of herself, while another noted that most of her gay and lesbian friends "wouldn't understand [her] bi side." Bisexual women must often choose which features of their structurally fractured identities to emphasize and deny in a social world structured through oppositional categories.

Suppression: Denying the "Bi Parts"

Bi women's negotiations of the presentation of self illustrate the constraining power of the dominant discourse on sex, gender, and sexual identity, and, simultaneously, the will to resist the dominant discourse. Because of the binary logic of the interpretive system in which they are located, bi women's suppression of others' awareness of their identities often reinforces the dominant paradigm to which they object. Again, it is important to note the contexts in which bisexual women feel pressured to deny, suppress, or change their bi identities; such contexts prefigure the choices bisexual women are required to make in positioning themselves *vis-à-vis* their sexual identities in various social settings. Striking examples of the suppression of bi identity by various social actors appear in the following account:

> I used to identify as "confused," then I figured out I was bi – Internally, it was joyous. I was fairly uncomfortable with "confused" as an identity. Externally, well, someone tried to kill me because I am attracted to women, and all my lesbian friends dumped me when I came out as Bi. Seems like, to me, they thought "confused" was better.

In the political arena, the consequences of lesbian suppression of the bisexual identity category are evident in bi women's reports of dropping out of activism or suppressing their bisexual identities in order to continue political work:

> I used to be very out, as the founder of the local bisexual women's group. My name was posted on the bulletin board at the Lesbian and Gay center. Sometimes I would get harassing phone calls, telling me to "get the hell out of our community." One lesbian called to say she "wasn't sure she approved of our right to exist." She yelled at me for 20 minutes until I hung up. We are accused of neurosis, disloyalty, and immorality. This kind of reaction from separatist lesbians caused me to leave the lesbian/gay community for several years.

Not surprisingly, their awareness of negative stereotypes of bisexuals discourages women from marking themselves as bisexual for fear of negative consequences, loss of legitimacy or efficacy, and from feelings of shame. Such responses to suppression, however, perpetuate bi women's invisibility and, in effect, reinforce bisexual women's cultural anonymity. This dynamic both reflects and reinforces the coercive power of those who stigmatize bisexual women, and, again, reinscribes the binary sexual system to which feminists of all sexual orientations have expressed objection.

Bisexual women use two legitimation strategies to explain their suppression of public awareness of their bisexual identity: one personal, the other political. Some bisexual women allow others to locate them in the binary codes of the dominant system because they fear the negative consequences of coming out as bisexual. One woman in this study named this "the fear of reprisal." Other bi women suppress the "bi part" of their sexual identity because they lack sexual experience, usually with women, and believe that this reduces their legitimacy both "as bisexuals" and within lesbian communities. One woman in this study, for example, reported that she never discusses her desires for women because she has "not yet experienced any fulfillment of these desires and therefore cannot truly call [myself] bisexual." Finally, bi women report suppressing some feature of their bi identities from respect for others' sensibilities:

> I define my sexual identity the same way at all times, but in the interest of tact, I choose to omit certain parts of my sexuality around people who would not be able to deal with it, such as my polyamoury, either my interest in men or my interest in women, or my s/m lifestyle.

In contrast, however, many reported shifting labels for their subjectivity as a means of challenging conventions of sexuality within both straight and queer contexts. In these instances, women reported denying the "bisexual aspects" – understood here contextually – of their sexual identities in efforts to establish solidarity with lesbians and with gay, lesbian, and queer political projects, and to challenge heterosexist assumptions among heterosexuals. In addition, they suppress public knowledge of aspects of their identities to signal that they are unavailable to men, either because they are partnered with women or because they hope to avoid the sexualization of bi women they understand as inhering in the heterosexual or bi male gaze:

> I do not see being bi as that much of an affront to the straight world. In general, I find that the dominant straight culture finds bi women much easier to accept than being a lesbian. After all, when one says they are bi, there is always hope we will "come to our senses and become straight." When I am in the straight world with my woman lover, we receive poorer service than men/women couples. Overall, I feel devalued in the straight world when I am with my woman significant other. I hate this type of attitude. This is one reason I often do not feel the need to express my bi side within the straight world.

In both lesbian and heterosexual contexts, bisexual women experience the difficulty of being defined within the binary terms of the dominant cultural code. In their participation in the suppression of bi identity, bi women reify the bisexual as absent, nonexistent, outside, and "other to" both lesbian and heterosexual identities, communities, and cultures. This process leaves bi women constantly alienated from those social contexts and from bi identity itself. Pressure to validate the unitary subject, either male or female, white or black, homosexual or heterosexual, is a product of a broader discursive regime that defines, codifies, and stigmatizes the category "lesbian" as an "other" against which heterosexual femininity may be defined. Bi women's suppression of the features of their identities that violate the dominant system of categorization, even when it constitutes a politically conscious effort to "challenge homophobia" by passing as lesbians, makes "the bisexual" invisible and reinforces the visibility – and the viability – of the hetero/homo divide.

Assimilation

Some bi women uneasily and inadvertently "pass" as lesbian or heterosexual in the contexts of their lives and relationships, while others allow themselves to be seen as lesbian in social contexts in which they hope to affirm lesbian interests and support lesbian visibility. Others choose different identity labels that allow them and their interests as bisexuals to be subsumed into lesbian and gay politics and community life. They use assimilation as a symbolic means of establishing their commitments to radical sexual politics and to assure gay and lesbian critics that their primary interest is not in promoting a "bi agenda":

> I use "dyke" to proclaim my alliance with lesbians and bisexual women
> – it's got more of an edge than "bisexual woman."

In this construction, "dyke" represents lesbians and bisexual women, an understanding that maintains these two groups as indistinguishable. Some bisexual women opt for a compound label, one that appends "bi" to another, more culturally salient category:

> I have had a lot of "label stress" and used to change my identification on
> a weekly, if not daily, basis. I find that I wander up and down the Kinsey
> scale, depending on many variables in my life. Although bi-dyke has been
> consistent for about a year.

Both the "lesbian-identified bisexual" and her companion, the "bi-dyke," move out from fractured sexual identity with its "bi parts" and "lesbian parts" at the level of the subject, to a fractured community – one with dykes and hyphenated dykes, (real) lesbians and bi-identified/bi-modified lesbians at the level of the collective. These constructions allow bisexual women the possibility of assimilating into lesbian culture. The power of lesbian discourse to define bisexuals as marginal in lesbian communities appears in bi women's pejorations of the terms "lesbian" and "dyke" in their self-labeling practices.

The widespread use of various forms of "gay," "dyke," and "lesbian" as sexual identity markers among bi women indicates that stigmatization within lesbian and gay contexts pressures them to seek legitimacy in such communities by adopting identity labels that promote their incorporation or assimilation. The effect of assimilation, however, is the erasure of the specificity of bi women's experiences, identities, and social locations, and the further affirmation of the lesbian category as the core of "dyke" identity.

For example, even though bi women theorize that "any woman who is not exclusively heterosexual is a dyke," in practice, some "dykes" remain more legitimate than others. This is most strikingly revealed in reports of situations in which bisexual women have received validation from women they identify as lesbians. One respondent offered an account of support she'd received for her work as a bi-activist that concluded with the ultimate compliment: "I even had women with DYKE stickers want to kiss me at a kiss-in!!!" Here, the bisexual woman positions "women with DYKE stickers" as other-than-bisexual, and confers upon them the power to legitimize her as bi member of the community. Despite bisexual women's use of "dyke" to mean "lesbian and bi," examples like this reinforce the synonymous relationship between "lesbian" and "dyke;" they dignify lesbians' claim on dyke territory and legitimize lesbian collective identity requirements that bisexual women assimilate in order to participate in lesbian communities. This dynamic renders bisexual women invisible within lesbian communities, and inadvertently reproduces the binary cultural code that many bisexual women hope to disrupt through their identity politics.

Perverse Passing and the Queer Cloaking Mechanism

While the use of "lesbian," "dyke," and even "gay" offers bi women the possibility of assimilation into women's communities, the term "queer," often positively embraced by these research participants, allows their assimilation into a broader domain. Long an English epithet for "gay" or "lesbian," the term "queer" underwent a process of reclamation in the early 1990s. Following feminist activists who had worked in the 1970s and 1980s to reclaim various epithets used against women, radical lesbian and gay activists collaborated in the early 1990s to organize *Queer Nation*, in a move that initiated the recoding and dissemination of the reinvigorated term in lesbian and gay communities.

In its latest incarnation, and as it is deployed by "queer activists" and "queer theorists," the term "queer" signifies not only those who mark themselves as gay or lesbian, but anyone whose proclivities, practices, or sympathies defy the strictures of the dominant sex/gender/sexual identity system. Consequently, in a discursive strategy theoretically designed to disrupt gendered, heterosexist systems of sexual marking, a significant number of the bisexual women who participated in this research embrace the label "queer." Ostensibly, they adopt the term for its appeal to polymorphous perversity, its signification of "solidarity" with lesbians and with gay men simultaneously, and its purported "confrontation power":

> I like being confrontational. I wear bi pins, I kiss women in public, I talk a lot. I suppose a combination of us loudmouths – to force people to recognize our existence – and the moderate peacemakers – to smooth out differences and negotiate our place – might work. I also think that we need to constantly affirm our dedication to general queer issues so lesbians and gays don't think we're forming a loner splinter group.

Bisexual women label themselves queer for other reasons, too. While in an overtly heterosexist context, the label "queer" may mark bisexuals as critically non-heterosexual, within gay and, especially, lesbian contexts, bi women's use of this identity marker works as a "queer cloaking mechanism." Bisexual discourse works to legitimize bisexual identity and bisexuality as queer by introducing evidence from the effects of institutionalized social control. Again, this line of argument obviously echoes mainstream/male-identified gay and lesbian political activism centered on achieving civil rights "equal to" those of heterosexuals, and uses oppression by a common system as a justification for eliding differences among lesbians and bi women. The first example presented uses homophobic violence affecting bi women as a means of legitimation; the second deploys a Pyrrhic victory achieved in repressive legislation that authorizes discrimination against bisexual people:

> We are just as queer as other gays and lesbians. We are not half gay-bashed. No one asks us how we identify if they see us in the street with a member of the same sex: they make assumptions.

The Right recognizes bis as a discrete group they can trample down – in Colorado Amendment 2, bis are just as discriminated against as lesbians and gay men – the wording of the Amendment includes "bisexual."

The term "queer" offers both a sense of sexual multiplicity and the capacity to elide differences in the construction of a binary world populated by queers and non-queers. In describing the constitutive factions of the category, respondents demonstrate how the queer label glosses distinctions among sexual identity categories and differences between men and women (or constructs them as " degrees of gayness"), collapses stigmatized sexual identity categories with the category "transgenders," and, consequently, constructs a safe if anonymous space for bisexual women:

Recently, I also began using the word queer. What that word denotes to me is the labeling of all of us non-straights as one community with one name. In other words, an end to the constant bickering and infighting that separates mainstream gays and lesbians from bisexuals, transgenders, and other subgroups. I have had to defend myself from biphobic separatists SO many times, and I have met with SO much hostility because I dared to identify openly as bi when I am married to a man . . . so when I heard about the movement to label us all "queers" and forget the distinctions between the various degrees of gayness, I was immediately in favor of it.

This account simultaneously expresses the desire for an elision of categories, a homogenization that would make bisexual women more difficult to single out or categorically marginalize, and the reinscription of "bisexuals," "transgenders," and others as "subgroups" marginal to "mainstream" members of lesbian and gay communities. In the process of seeking assimilation by a community hostile to them, bisexual women labeling themselves "dyke" or "queer" inadvertently solidify those categories, in much the same way that women's efforts to achieve "equality with" men and gay attempts at establishing normalcy within the dominant cultural code ultimately work to reinscribe the legitimacy of the dominant and binary categories. Efforts to establish bisexual women as "equally queer" with lesbians and gay men ironically undermine the diverse perversity associated with the 1990s deployment of "queerness," and allow the sexual world to reconstitute itself along a new axis that divides the queer from the non-queer.

The Universal, Natural Bisexual

Through the deployment of the queer cloaking mechanism, the binary system is reconstructed; the new boundary consists of the line between "queers" and "non-queers." Bisexual women engage in a second kind of identity-talk that inscribes an alternative binary identity system; unlike the assimilationist strategy, which marks bisexuals as more like gay and lesbian people than like heterosexuals, the essentialization and universalization of bisexuality privileges bisexuals against a differently constituted sexual "other," those who refuse to acknowledge their bisexuality. This discourse moves bisexuals from the margin to the center, where bisexuality and bi identity become both expansive and normative, and gay and heterosexual people are constructed as relatively depraved.

This model posits lesbians, gays, and heterosexual men and women as a monolithic "semi-sexual" collective composed of those sexually limited by a pathological preference for intimacy with members of only one sex – people disparagingly labeled "monosexuals." Accomplishing this centering means, for some bi women who participated in this study, denying categorical differences between men and women and using liberal-humanist discourse to position "everyone" as a potential object of sexual or personal interest. One woman expressed the desire to elide categorical differences by reporting that she finds "relationships with men and women to be quite similar – the differences are in the individuals, not in their sex," while others expressed their ideal as choosing partners "regardless of gender."

Alternately, the construction of the bisexual/monosexual binary also provides a venue for mapping the similarities between the disparate positions of heterosexual men and women, gay men, and lesbians as they interact with bisexual women. For example, one woman reported that "the straight men I've fucked find it kind of kinky that I'm bi, while the lesbians are all afraid I'll leave them for a man," in a construction that positions heterosexual men and lesbians as collectively "other" to the bi woman.

This construction also reflects the understanding of some women who participated in this study that heterosexuals and lesbians are in collusion against bisexuals. In the following representative excerpt, heterosexual men, heterosexual women, and lesbians become a monolithic "they" against which bi women may define themselves as a group:

I wish monosexuals (lesbians and straights) were more tolerant of bisexuals. (I wonder how they would feel, knowing that in my mind these diverse groups can be lumped together as "monosexuals," that is, people who choose to limit their sexuality?)

The world lapses further back into polarization; in it there exist bisexuals and monosexuals, and nobody occupies the subject position located in the chasm or on "the bridge" over it. This social group, vocally opposed to sexual dualism, reverts in this construction to the claim that each sexual subject is one or the other: for them or against them. In bi women's discourse on sexual identity, we see marginalization internalized and employed to describe the bisexual self, the bisexual subject located on the edge of lesbian community, and the bisexual located between lesbian and heterosexual territories. In all of these constructions, the bisexual woman is reinscribed as fractional or marginal, or completely disappears. The alternative "resistance" discourse apparent here produces the *monosexual* as a marginalized other; just as heterosexual discourse produces the lesbian as marginal and lesbian discourse creates the bisexual as other, bisexual discourse critical of such productions recirculates the dynamic in a move that works to define the bisexual as legitimate, normal, and central against a newly stigmatized other, the monosexual.

Stigmatized Bisexuals within Bi Discourse

When I asked bi women participants in this research to offer explanations about lesbian antipathy toward bisexuals, their responses frequently legitimized lesbian stereotypes of bisexual women. This strand of bi women's discourse operates to dignify some bisexuals and to construct others, by contrast, as illegitimate:

> Lesbians are not immune to cultural stereotypes on the basis of being lesbian. And because lesbians are more likely than straight women to actually know that they know bi women, those stereotypes are more likely to be thought about, reinforced, or addressed in some way than straight women's stereotypes. *Also, like many stereotypes, there are grains of truth.* [emphasis added] When I have been dumped for a man, I hate it. I have subtly bi-bashed in that way. It hurts. It hurts to be dumped for a woman, too, but . . . we relieve our pain however we can.

In bi women's discursive efforts at establishing legitimacy *as bisexuals*, the dominant system's criteria, recycled through lesbian discourse, remain central: monogamy, sexual fidelity, commitment to the pair around which the white nuclear family is presumed to revolve. The lesbian focus on these criteria for membership in the lesbian community is reinscribed by bisexual women attempting to demonstrate their purity within the terms of the discourse deployed against them. This dynamic demonstrates the process through which a doubly marginalized group constructs a deviant other. This dominant cultural discourse on sexuality simultaneously legitimizes a collective bisexual core identity and constructs a marginal, stigmatized, deviant bisexual against whom the core can be defined.

The criteria that establish the legitimate bisexual resemble those that define the legitimate heterosexual woman and the legitimate lesbian. They constitute the amplification to a classificatory or categorical level of those values and strategies individual bi women have used as guidelines for personal conduct as stigmatized women in lesbian and heterosexual contexts. By elevating the already-politicized personally correct to a standard for binormativity, bi women deploy the terms of the dominant system to construct a deviant bisexual other. The outlines of the dominant cultural code and its lesbian interpretations in these interviews are evident; honesty, fidelity, sexual responsibility, commitments to the unitary and empirically demonstrable sexual subject, and even so-called traditional conservative values emerge as the constitutive features of the true, proper, really real bisexual. Some bi discourse, for example, castigates bisexuals who are "sleazy," not politicized, defined by and oriented to heterosexual marriage, and too weak to "take the heat" society directs at lesbians and gays:

> There is a bi community in this city, but I don't participate in it anymore. I used to go to the events and it felt very sleazy. There were a lot of people there who were totally obsessed with sex, some who were very promiscuous and held group sex parties, and others who had chosen to make their livings in sex-related ways, ranging from sex therapists to porno telephone call women. People like me, who just wanted to organize mainstream bis into a community, got disgusted and left. No wonder people think we are all sleazy. But on the other hand, how can you build a community out of a characteristic like "we don't care about gender"? You can only build a community about something you DO care about.

In addition, this discourse defines the appropriate sentiments and orientations of bi women toward other women, legitimating feminist and lesbian positions and creating standards for the "true bisexual woman."

There is a bi group that meets weekly and a bi women's support group, but I don't participate in either. I am active in political groups, both GLB and mainstream/other issue groups. I've found bi activists, who aren't focused on other issues as well, often to be annoying, and also to be fighting battles I see as the least important ones – such as hostile actions against the gay and lesbian community. I do think that the lesbian and gay community should support and include bisexuals, but I also think anger at them is misdirected.

The process through which bi women's discourse constructs a deviant bi other is articulated in claims that "not all bi women are alike," claims that reproduce negative stereotypes of bisexuals. Bi women do not unequivocally deny the veracity of these stereotypes. Instead, they legitimate them by delimiting a subgroup of bisexuals about whom these beliefs are accepted as true; subsequently, they work to establish social distance from the segregated group:

I believe that this is where the lesbian/gay community needs to be educated about bis. Not all bi women are flaky, into women when convenient, and cannot commit to long-term same-sex relationships. I feel that this is important because too many gay men and lesbians end up feeling betrayed if they find out that someone they assumed was exclusively gay turns out to have bi tendencies.

This interview excerpt reinforces stereotypes about the illegitimate bisexual and suggests the trouble therein: the diffusion of bi identity leads to its institutionalization. By establishing criteria that distinguish between the "true bisexuals" from the "trendy" ones, bisexual women's discourse reduces the ambiguities of the category. Simultaneously, the institutionalization of the category makes it possible for the real bisexual, outraged, finally to stand up:

On a local bulletin board, we created gay rooms and almost all of the women in them identified as bi. These women were extremely irritating in that the fact that they found men attractive was exceedingly important to their sexual identity and they made sure to differentiate themselves from lesbians. Many of them were in het relationships and had never had a gay affair, simply had found women attractive in the past, had maybe kissed a woman once. To me, these women were hets who simply were able to acknowledge that all of us are bi in some respect. However, when one said, "I am attracted to women but I could never fall in love with one," most of my gay male friends and I were disgusted that this person chose to label herself bi.

Conclusion

Like lesbian antagonism toward bisexual women, bisexual women's discourse on identity and social location is marked by the practices of hegemonic patriarchal discourse. This is not surprising, given that within the dominant cultural code, bisexual women are positioned similarly by the two communities most influential in creating the contexts for their experience. Despite the explicit, sincere, and often eloquent commitments of bi women to breaking patriarchal sexual codes, and their binary structures in particular, the bi discourse and the identity-negotiation strategies analyzed in this study often recreate the binary structures bi women consciously oppose.

While these constructions seem odd in the context of bi women's ideological convictions that the essentialist and dualistic assumptions that pervade the dominant culture are inherently oppressive, they correspond to external discursive pressure to position oneself at one location or "the other" within the dominant framework for organizing sex, gender, and sexuality. Faced with overt stigmatization, some bisexual women allow themselves to be assimilated into the binary homo/hetero system, while others find themselves defending bi subjectivity and, in the process, contributing to the processes through which the category is being institutionalized. As this research suggests, some bi women do discursively shift the axes of the homo/hetero binary by reconstituting the sexual division of identity as that between "queers and non-queers" or "bisexuals and monosexuals." Other theorists may wish to explore how these dualistic constructions advance the process of subverting the dominant paradigm by reconfiguring its terms, as well as how they retrench the social organizational regime founded on sexual difference through opposition.

At present, a great deal of tension exists between the radical openness implied by the construction of a largely undefined bisexual space in our sexual culture, and the impetus for the construction of a well-bounded, highly defined bisexual subjectivity that might be simply and neatly added to the existing system as an easily identifiable hybrid between the familiar oppositional categories. In the contested space of the bisexual body, the ultimate conflict is not between categories, but *about* them, and the move toward closure, the move toward resolution in the contest, the move to define and defend the bisexual subject, seems, ironically, the move most likely to undermine the radical, transformative potential of its indeterminacy.

Notes

I wish to thank the following for their contributions to the development of this paper: Laurel Richardson, Gisela Hinkle, Jennifer Terry, Timothy Curry, Norman Denzin, Steven Seidman, Carla Corroto, Kim Davies, Stephanie Brzuzy, Kathlene Greene, and Kathrina Zippel. This research was funded in part by an NSF fellowship to the 1993 University of Georgia Field Work Workshop, and by a summer dissertation grant from the Ohio State University Department of Sociology.

References

Ault, Amber. 1994. "Hegemonic Discourse in and Oppositional Community: Lesbian Feminists and Bisexuality." *Critical Sociology*, 20 (3).

Blumstein, Phillip and Schwartz, Pepper. 1974. "Lesbianism and Bisexuality," in *Sexual Deviance and Sexual Deviants*, ed. Erich Goode. New York: Morrow, 278–95.

Butler, Judith. 1990. *Gender Trouble*. New York: Routledge.

Collins, Patricia Hill. 1990. *Black Feminist Thought*. New York: Rutledge.

Daumer, Elisabeth. 1992. "Queer Ethics; or, the Challenge of Bisexuality to Lesbian Ethics." *Hypatia*, 7 (4).

Erikson, Kai. 1966. *Wayward Puritans: A Study in the Sociology of Deviance*. New York: John Wiley.

Firestein, Beth. 1994. "How Biphobia Hurts Us All." Paper presented at the 1994 North American Gay and Lesbian Studies Association Conference: *Inqueery, Intheory, Indeed*, Iowa City, Iowa.

Foucault, Michel. 1980. *The History of Sexuality (Volume 1: An Introduction)*, trans. R. Hurley. New York: Vintage Books.

Gramsci, Antonio. 1971. *Selections From the Prison Notebooks of Antonio Gramsci*. New York: International Publishers.

Minh-ha, Trinh T. 1989. *Woman, Native, Other*. Bloomington: Indiana University Press.

Rust, Paula C. 1992. "Who Are We and Where Do We Go From Here? Conceptualizing Bisexuality," in *Closer to Home: Bisexuality and Feminism*, ed. Elizabeth Weise. Seattle: Seal Press, 281–310.

Rust, Paula C. 1993. "Neutralizing the Political Threat of the Marginal Woman: Lesbians' Beliefs About Bisexual Women." *Journal of Sex Research*, 30 (3).

Seidman, Steven. 1993. "Identity and Politics in a Postmodern 'Gay' Culture: Some Historical and Conceptual Notes," in *Fear of a Queer-Planet*, ed. Michael Warner. Minneapolis: University of Minnesota Press, 105–42.

Sedgwick, Eve Kosovsky. 1990. *Epistemology of the Closet*. Berkeley: University of California Press.

Smart, Barry. 1993. *Postmodernity*. New York: Routledge.

Taylor, Verta and Whittier, Nancy. 1992. "Lesbian Feminist Communities," in *New Frontiers in Social Movement Theory*, eds Aldon Morris and Carol Mueller. New York: Van Dyne, 104–29.

Weise, Elizabeth. 1992. "Introduction," in *Closer to Home: Bisexuality and Feminism*, ed. Elizabeth Weise. Seattle: Seal Press, ix–xv.

Part IV

Queer Sociological Approaches: Identity and Politics

Postmodernism and Queer Identities
Scott Bravmann

Contested Membership: Black Gay Identities and the Politics of AIDS
Cathy J. Cohen

Must Identity Movements Self-Destruct?: A Queer Dilemma
Joshua Gamson

The Politicization of the Dutch Gay Identity, or Why Dutch Gays
Aren't Queer
Jan Willem Duyvendak

15

Postmodernism and Queer Identities

Scott Bravmann

[I]dentities are the names we give to the different ways we are positioned by, and position ourselves within, the narratives of the past.

Stuart Hall[1]

[A]n exclusive focus on the emergence of the lesbian or gay identity skews our understanding of the complexity of homosexual experiences.

Susan K. Cahn[2]

I define postmodern as incredulity toward metanarratives. . . . Postmodern knowledge . . . refines our sensitivity to differences and reinforces our ability to tolerate the incommensurable.

Jean-François Lyotard[3]

In their introduction to a recent anthology of historical articles, Martin Duberman, Martha Vicinus, and George Chauncey argue that "some of the most important issues facing, agitating, and sometimes dividing [gay and lesbian communities] today, personally and collectively, are best addressed historically."[4] Although the study of gay and lesbian history does provide cogent means for addressing questions of identity, politics, community, and difference, the past also informs the present through the ways it generates meaning in current contexts. Many of the cultural claims, public celebrations, and political debates that traverse, animate, and divide gay and lesbian communities are strongly motivated by complex and contradictory historical references. Furthermore, the idea of "history" itself is problematic, various, and unstable in these queer historical self-representations, thus further compounding this already complex and contradictory relationship. The surplus of signification of historical memory, the complex uses of the past, and the conceptual instability of history in queer contexts are in need of critical attention. Focusing our critical capacities on these multiple engagements with the past in order to draw out the conflicting tendencies within them is an effective way of reevaluating and revitalizing the terms on which we as interested subjects address "important issues . . . historically."

In the following pages, I rethink "the making of the modern homosexual" from a position of profound skepticism toward such narratives opened up by the general political, cultural, and theoretical projects of postmodernism.[5] From this discussion, I move to a brief consideration of a more recent generation of gay and lesbian historical research focused on specific locations, groups, or moments. I conclude with a proposal for a doubly "queer" historical studies which draws on the larger crisis in historical studies provoked by the recent work of critical theorists and revisionist historians problematizing the conventional ways history has been written.

I. Modernism and Gay Historiography

Over the past decade and a half, numerous historical, sociological, and theoretical studies have explored the emergence of lesbian and gay identities, subcultures, communities, and politics.[6] The historicizing project of this generation of research has revealed not only the discontinuities between cultural conceptions of homosexuality across time and space but also the ways in which the various sustained attempts to gain knowledge of sexuality are themselves constitutive of that bodily domain of pleasure, power, and personal identity now regarded as sexuality. While enabling a more careful and specified diachronic analysis of the development of, on the one hand, heterosexist and homophobic institutions of domination and, on the other, celebratory and resistant gay and lesbian cultural practices, these texts have in turn tended to reify certain current conceptions of homosexuality which are unified and stabilized by contrasting them to those of an utterly different past. That is, they have created categories of bodily, psychic, social, and political experience on either side of this divide between past and present which are not only fundamentally different from each other but are also fundamentally similar to themselves and have constructed coherence, cohesion, and stability against the multiply fractured subject positions that constitute the lives of lesbian and gay individuals. Although social-constructionist theory is dynamic and promising in relationship to understanding both the past and the present, these studies of the emergence of lesbian and gay identity have been relatively unsuccessful at recognizing race, gender, and class (among other) antagonisms "within" that identity. In foregrounding diachronic or historical ruptures between social constructions of "homosexuality," these related projects have underemphasized the synchronic or contemporary ruptures between social constructions of homosexuality and their own specific histories, rife with contradictions of their own. Moreover, the developmental model of history on which these accounts are based contradictorily unifies the past histories of "gay identity," a process which their genealogical strategy attempts to resist.

* * *

Though varying in the emphasis they place on specific historical processes, social structures, crystalizing events, and public and private discourses, these arguments agree that a distinctive homosexual identity has emerged only in the last century or so; they use this argument of the comparatively recent formation of a homosexual identity as an expression of individual desire within the available discourses in order to explain the emergence of gay and lesbian subcultures, communities, and social movements in Europe, the United States, and elsewhere at different moments in the twentieth century. As John D'Emilio has pointed out in a survey of research on gay history, however, "[o]f all national histories being investigated, that of the United States most clearly confirms the argument of [Jeffrey] Weeks and [Michel] Foucault concerning the emergence of a distinctive gay identity."[7] For this reason, both the analysis and the critique that follow are decidedly and purposefully US-centered.

Several factors stand out among the various conditions that enabled the existence of gay and lesbian worlds, especially the growth of industrial capitalism and its attendant impact on kinship and family life, gender roles, urbanization, and ideologies of accumulation, ownership, and individualism. D'Emilio makes this argument most forcefully in his article "Capitalism and Gay Identity" (a force which perhaps reflects the greater latitude for critique afforded by its site of publication). In that essay, D'Emilio "argue[s] that lesbians and gay men have *not* always existed." Rather "we are a product of" a particular historical period whose "emergence is associated with the relations of capitalism." Specifically, it is the free labor system "that has allowed large numbers of men and women in the late twentieth century to call themselves gay" (p. 102). The growth of capitalism and the spread of wage labor transformed the structure, functions, and relationships of family life. Having previously been both a system of consumption and a system of household production, the family began to lose its economic self-sufficiency by the nineteenth century when men and women became increasingly involved in and dependent on the capitalist free-labor system. (Of course, this monolithic version of the "family" is also highly contested and reiterates the long-existing ideology of the yeoman farmer in America which marginalizes such central familial economic forms as slave families, the white plantation economies dependent on the slave-labor system, and the US government's attempt to construct patriarchal, land-owning Native American nuclear families with the implementation of the Dawes Act in 1877.) This change effected a shift in the significance of the family away from a materially productive institution toward an affective unit which brought with it changes in the meaning of sexual relations between men and women. Whereas offspring had once been necessary contributors to the household economy, with the growth of wage labor and the socialization of production "it became possible to release sexuality from the 'imperative' to procreate" (D'Emilio, p. 104). Within this new set of experiences, heterosexual expression gradually began to be conceived of as a way to achieve intimacy, happiness, and pleasure rather than substantially and perhaps most importantly as a (re)productive act. By removing the productive aspect from the household economy and fostering a separation of (hetero) sexuality from procreation, capitalism, D'Emilio contends, made it possible for "some men and women to organize a personal life around their erotic/emotional attraction to their own sex" (p. 104) and "survive beyond the confines of the family" (p. 105).

These new possibilities for personal life, however, were inscribed with and through highly salient marks of difference. Ann Ferguson focuses directly on the question of how these new and changing economic possibilities affected the life choices available to and pursued by women. Ferguson also stresses the importance of "nineteenth-century industrial capitalism . . . for women [in particular] in that it eventually weakened the patriarchal power of fathers and sons." While "this relative gain in freedom was not an instant effect of capitalism," she argues, not only did the "acquisition of an income g[i]ve women new options" but so too did "commercial capital's growth [spur] the growth of urban areas, which in turn gave feminist and deviant women the possibility of escaping the confines of rigidly traditional, patriarchal farm communities for an independent, if often impoverished, life in the cities" (Ferguson, p. 156). Ferguson's attention to the particular place of women in the economy anticipates a set of ruptures in gay and lesbian history which have begun to receive fuller analysis in a newer generation of historiographical research.

* * *

These accounts of a specifically "gay identity" contrasted to past constructions of homosexuality emphasize and reinterpret broad-based transformations in the social structure that are part of a much longer, much larger process of modernization, and they provide focused discussions of the changes both in such "personal" aspects of life as sexuality, gender, identity, and love and such "public" areas as cities, the economy, medicine, and culture. In *All That Is Solid Melts into Air*, an approving reappraisal of "the experience of modernity," Marshall Berman identifies these less-specified processes and posits a "truth" about modernity which anticipates the problems of the gay identity thesis. "Modern environments and experiences," Berman proclaims in an unironic hyperbole, "cut across all boundaries of geography and ethnicity, of class and nationality, of religion and ideology: in this sense, modernity can be said to unite all mankind."[8] Ultimately, then, on Berman's analysis, *modernity is indifferent to difference*. The experience of modernity, however, is not marked solely by vastly new and profound changes in social organization and material forces carrying out their changes on an impersonal society and unwitting, passive humans. The "world-historical processes" of change have also enabled, even required, a wide range of cultural responses. These cultural responses, which Berman identifies as "modernism," consist of "an amazing variety of visions and ideas that aim to make men and women the subjects as well as objects of modernization, to give them the power to change the world that is changing them, to make their way through the maelstrom [of modern life] and make it their own" (p. 16).

Several points in Berman's reconstructed story of the interrelated projects of modernization, modernism, and modernity parallel the specific accounts of gay and lesbian identity formation in social-constructionist historical-theoretical work. The most direct link between Berman's analysis and the arguments of this gay and lesbian research is "the process of economic and social development [which] generates new modes of self-development, ideal for men and women who can grow into the emerging world" (Berman, p. 66). Both arguments also focus on the vast rural-to-urban migration which has caused as well as emerged from large-scale social disruption over the past two hundred years. The individual move from the "closed social system[s]" (p. 66) of small communities to the unrealized urban promise of "great cities" (p. 59), Berman argues, has been motivated by the desire for "action, adventure, an environment in which [one] can be . . . free to act, freely active" (p. 66). A related feature of this urban promise, both for Berman's view of modernity as an undifferentiated project and for the more focused histories of gay identity formation as an aspect of modernity, is the change in consciousness effected by the collapse of "order and complete content" which had been provided by small-town "little worlds" (p. 55). Urban environments afford anonymity through which one can escape "the surveillance of family, neighbors, priests, . . . all the suffocating pressures of the closed small-town world" (p. 54).

In part, Berman argues, the collective cultural projects of modernism promise the security of individual development and a stable self-ident-ity in "the maelstrom" of an ever-changing world. For many gay men and lesbians, coming out of the closet has reflected these twin desires and has played a decisive role in the politicization of homosexuality since Stonewall. As a powerful way to develop and claim "who we really are," coming out meets the modernist promise of stability in a world characterized by change. However, the security of a stable, "real" gay or lesbian self is an illusion produced through the strong personal and political value invested in the process of coming out.[9] In addition to fostering this illusory personal safety, coming out con-tributes to the notion of a stable, unified, uncontradicted "com-munity" and suggests a larger emergence of "gay identity" which reconstructs the historical past around modernist criteria of authen-ticity and development. As Jeffrey Weeks explains,

> "Coming out" is usually seen as a personal process, the acceptance, and public demonstration, of the validity of one's homosexuality. But it can also be seen as an historic process, the gradual emergence and articula-tion of a homosexual identity and public presence.[10]

By emphasizing the fundamental structural reorganization of society associated with the rise of capitalist economies as a grand, universaliz-ing historical process, this generation of research on homosexuality has obscured recognition of effective and meaningful difference within that overarching process of change. Eve Sedgwick has rightly pointed out that "these historical projects . . . still risk reinforcing a dangerous consensus of knowingness about the genuinely *un*known, more than vestigially contradictory structurings of contemporary experience." This generation of research, she argues, has "counterpos[ed] against the alterity of the past a relatively unified homosexuality that 'we' *do* 'know today.'"[11] Additionally, however, these texts have counterposed against the alterity – the difference, the newness – of current conceptions of homosexuality a relatively unified past that "they" *did* "know then." The paradigm of "the making of the modern homosexual" denies or subsumes under the privileged sign of gay identity whatever antecedent forms of difference might have existed; that is, within the logic of these accounts, these differences are just as indifferent in the historical development of gay and lesbian identities as the differences dismissed by Berman are to modernity itself. I want to suggest, however, that we begin thinking about "the making of the modern homosexual" not as a "fact" but as an argument, fundamentally as a narrative with serious implications for addressing issues historically. Rather than simply describing an historical process, these accounts of the past themselves help "make" or "construct" the fiction of the modern homosexual. In this sense, they are themselves part of what Foucault has termed the reverse discourse (curiously, problematically, and inaccurately in the singular) on homosexuality and are themselves agents in the reformulations and contestations of the meanings of homosexuality. Specifically, we need to regard the "modernist" tendencies within this collective body of research as a rhetorical practice closely allied with those experiences of modernity the work investigates.

Most importantly, these arguments about gay identity need to be read in relation to Berman's hyperbolic statement on modernity's indifference to geographic, ethnic, class, national, religious, and ideological differences which itself reiterates this very indifference to difference. Berman's framework for ascribing creative agency to the human subjects of modernization does not recognize the ways in which these vital differences inform the "amazing variety of visions and ideas" of the "modernist" cultural projects he champions. In its indifference to difference, the totalizing sweep of modernist histories and cultural theories anchors present identities in a stable, coherent personal and social past (the family, capitalism, cities); overrides, disallows, and denies other experiences; and implicitly grounds conceptions of gay identity within the specific experiences of urban, middle-class white men. For the history of industrialization – the material base of the modernity championed by Berman and the catalyst that set off the wholesale changes in family life preceding the emergence of urban gay subcultures – has a complex, exploitative "underside" which belies the inevitability of "the real social movement toward economic development" (Berman, p. 40), thus problematizing "the cultural ideal of self-development" (p. 40) whose ideological underpinnings are in fact connected to the economic *under* development of whole populations of people. While these gay history texts recount somewhat different versions of the modernity yielded by modernization, we need to take seriously Berman's reminder that these processes of historical change are connected to, reflected in, *and* addressed by modernist cultural practices. More than simply describing the modernisms of the past, the relationship between modernization and modernism is also reiterated in the historical narratives they recount. They, too, are "visions and ideas that aim to make men and women the subjects as well as objects of modernization" (Berman, p. 16).

Within these modernist narratives, the cultural and political constructions of gay identity and a social movement are built upon the mutual experience of homosexuality, a mutual experience subject to (eventual) mediation by multiple differences, including those of race, gender, class, and nationality which the ostensible "unity" of modernity cuts across. Jeffrey Escoffier, for instance, makes the following observation about the historical emergence of "difference" within gay and lesbian identity-based political movements (in the early 1980s).

> In gay politics not only has the affirmation of shared experience resulted in the consolidation of homosexual differentness, but in the lesbian and gay-male communities' drive for affirmation differences have emerged among the members of both communities that cannot be eradicated.[12]

Escoffier's observation, however, suggests a contemporary fracturing of an historically unified gay identity, as if there had been no past heterogeneity, conflict, and autonomy within these "communities." This assessment retains modernism's indifference by recontaining difference as an *emergent* element within its dialectical fiction and thus preventing the destabilization of the narrative of the emergence of "gay identity."

Two principal categories of social "difference" – gender and race – raise fundamental questions about the indifferent logic of these accounts. Permanently inscribed in discussions of lesbian and gay history, "the mark of gender" makes problematic any effort to locate historical emergences solely in changes in the social relations of production, economic developments, and restructurings of family life.[13] As Martha Vicinus has recently argued, this structural model is inadequate for explaining "the historical roots of the modern lesbian identity."

> A lesbian identity did not result from economic independence, nor from an ideology of individualism, nor from the formation of women's com-

munities, although all of these elements were important for enhancing women's personal choices.[14]

Vicinus also argues that developing "an explanation of the sources of a lesbian identity" is a baffling project "because there is no agreement about what constitutes a lesbian" (p. 177). This lack of consensus on the (historical) meaning of the substantive "lesbian" also clearly compounds the complex problems of trying to locate the historical relationship between the construction of lesbian and gay male identities.

In addition to reframing the question of the historical development of a lesbian identity within a gender-based, female-specific critical analysis, Vicinus's insistence on this point raises another vexing problem. If a gay identity for men and a lesbian identity for women resulted from different historical, material, and ideological factors, as her essay would seem to suggest, why then did these separate and different identities begin to appear at roughly the same period – or did they? How, in other words, do we recognize what these (partially) distinct identities might share in terms of their historical development without either reiterating a position that denies gender specificity and difference or regarding this significant historical detail as purely coincidental? How "different" is the difference of gender? Further, we need to address the extent to which "difference" is salient *within* the historical development of these two gender-based categories of sexual identity. How have such social experiences and economic circumstances as those structured by age, class, race, and ethnicity, among others, inflected the specific histories of gay and lesbian identities not only "across" gender but also "within" each gender?

Though it only receives brief and indirect mention, the existence of a lesbian and gay subculture in Harlem during the Renaissance – a complex moment in black gay history which has received a relatively significant amount of attention – is clearly problematic for D'Emilio's narrative account of the development of gay identity in the US. In an attempt to explain the class-bound possibilities for the creation of lesbian and gay social spaces in the early part of this century, D'Emilio posits the cultural value of the family (rather than the material factors such as a lack of privacy in overcrowded living conditions which would make more obvious sense within his argument) as the primary restriction facing women and men who might otherwise have sought a niche in which they could safely express their same-sex desires. In contrast to working-class white immigrant communities, he writes,

for reasons not altogether clear, urban black communities appeared
relatively tolerant of homosexuality. The popularity in the 1920s and
1930s of songs with lesbian and gay male themes – "B. D. Woman,"
"Prove It on Me," "Sissy Man," "Fairey Blues" – suggest an openness
about homosexual expression at odds with the mores of whites. (p. 106,
emphasis added)

Without explicitly enumerating them, D'Emilio makes two (not necessarily related) points here: (1) a certain measure of tolerance of homosexuality in urban black communities such as Harlem during the twenties and thirties which suggests that, unlike the case in European immigrant communities, gayness was somehow *not* "a difficult option to pursue" in black communities; and, (2) in light of this relative tolerance, the actual pursuit of that option by men and women within those communities. What most needs to be noted about this brief reference to urban black constructions of homosexuality, however, is the problem it poses for D'Emilio's argument, both historically and theoretically.

Both urban black gay subcultures of the 1920s and 1930s and the relative tolerance they apparently were met with in the larger black communities are anomalous features not only in relationship to "standard" heterosexist and racist histories which would ignore or deny both black and gay experiences, but also in relationship to D'Emilio's own revisionist social history.[15] Perhaps ironically, D'Emilio calls attention to the inadequacy of his account for making sense of the "contrast" between white and black communities by marking his surprise at the latter's ostensible tolerance toward homosexuality with the phrase "for reasons not altogether clear." From one perspective, to insist that the reasons why an urban black lesbian and gay subculture could exist during the 1920s and 1930s in the US are "not altogether clear" reveals the tenacity of his paradigm by suggesting that future research might not only reveal what these reasons were but would also reconfirm the paradigm's explanatory power. From a different perspective, however, the "failure" of D'Emilio's account to make clear what these reasons were could be viewed as a particularly effective challenge to the paradigm's implicit reinforcement of the idea that "difference" – and especially differences of race, the most salient organizer of politics, social space, and identity in the US throughout the century in which "the making of the modern homosexual" occurred – has not always been central to the histories of the reverse discourses (emphatically in the plural) on homosexuality.

*   *   *

Although social-constructionist arguments have made significant theoretical contributions to our understanding of sexuality and above all have worked to destabilize ahistorical, naturalizing, ethnocentric, and ultimately homophobic readings of lesbian and gay sexualities, the presence of "difference" in contemporary lesbian and gay communities, "moments" from the queer past that are incommensurable with these abstract arguments, and a (developing) discourse of "difference" within lesbian and gay studies raise pressing questions about the linear trajectory of these materialist social histories. As a way to recenter "difference" in gay and lesbian history and to draw out the recent valuable work on "queer differences" in the present, I want to suggest a turn toward a postmodern writing of the past which would make such singular, linear, narratively complete accounts of the construction of "gay identity" impossibly problematic by directly challenging the modernist drive for unity, in Berman's terms, "across the bounds of ethnicity and nationality, of sex and class and race" (p. 6).

Recently, a newer generation of gay and lesbian historical research has begun undertaking projects which problematize "identity" in histories of (homo)sexuality. However, these questions of identity – metaphysical, epistemological, ontological, even political – also provoke reflection on how historical representation "works." In part, the shortcomings of this earlier generation of scholarship are to be explained – although not explained away – by the fact that rather than offering full historiographical studies, they set out, as D'Emilio puts it, to develop "a new, more accurate *theory* of gay history" (p. 101, emphasis added) to replace the invented mythologies of the gay liberation era. It is, however, the question of "theory" which needs to be addressed in relation to historical representation; to retheorize historical representation is to problematize and reframe the very meaning of history itself, something which is already powerfully present in queer cultural practices. I offer a brief discussion of this newer generation of gay and lesbian historiography before turning to my proposal for a "postmodern" queer historical studies which addresses these larger questions of historical representation in relation to specific practices in queer contexts.

II. Untitled: Gay and Lesbian Historiography as Works-in-Progress

This newer generation of gay and lesbian historiography has pursued substantially more focused, specified, and detailed research agendas than the earlier modernist narratives of gay identity formation. Yet the later studies are also deeply informed by the principal heuristic strength of social-constructionist theoretical insights and take seriously the proposition that sexual identities are "made" or "constructed" through and in relation to social relations and discursive regimes and are therefore malleable and historically contingent. Independently and collectively, these studies – specifically, George Chauncey's *Gay New York*, Lillian Faderman's *Odd Girls and Twilight Lovers*, Elizabeth Kennedy and Madeline Davis's *Boots of Leather, Slippers of Gold*, and Esther Newton's *Cherry Grove, Fire Island* – have made "gay and lesbian historiography" much more complex and subtle.[16] Their complexities and subtleties have modified some of the grander, more tentative claims of the accounts of the social construction of *the* "modern" *homosexual.*

Each of these studies utilizes oral as well as archival sources. Faderman, however, offers a comprehensive survey of the variety of lesbian experiences in twentieth-century America which pays particular though not exclusive attention to "the development of lesbian subcultures" (p. 7), while Chauncey, Kennedy and Davis, and Newton analyze communities in specific locations, combining, as Kennedy and Davis explain of their project, "ethnography – the intensive study of the culture and identity of a single community – with history – the analysis of the forces that shaped how that community changed over time" (p. 2). Also, although each text draws on material and makes arguments pertaining to both lesbians and gay men, three of them – Chauncey's, Faderman's, and Kennedy and Davis's – develop principally along gender-separatist lines of inquiry and analysis. Surely responding to (though not explicitly acknowledging) criticism of male-authored social-constructionist accounts for inadequately addressing lesbian subjectivity, Chauncey explains his decision based on "the differences between gay male and lesbian history and the complexity of each [which] made it seem virtually impossible to write a book about both that did justice to each and avoided making one history an appendage to the other" (p. 27). Because they are situated within feminist practices and women's history, however, the separatist investigations pursued by Faderman's and Kennedy and Davis's studies might be seen as articulating this difference differently and drawing on highly resonant political as well as academic reasons for their choices (though Kennedy and Davis also note that "there was no ideological commitment to [gender] separation" (p. 381) in the community they studied).

While these separatist strategies not only make analytic sense for such focused research but also help circumvent the shortcomings of

previous "gender-blind" materialist historical frameworks, they post-
pone consideration of what remains the substantial historical coincidence of the two gender-separated social constructions, "gay" and
"lesbian." Chauncey explicitly remarks this (temporary) pause in co-
gendered research, noting that "it will ultimately prove important to
theorize [the] historical development [of lesbian and gay cultures and
representations] in conjunction, but it may take another generation of
research on each before an adequate basis for such theories exists" (p.
27). In contrast to these three separatist studies, Newton's co-gendered
approach to writing about "America's first gay and lesbian town,"
though also remarkably ambitious given the long-existing "male
framework" (p. 288) which has reinforced the "impression of a gay
male, not a lesbian [or shared] space" (p. 1), was necessitated by the
fact that "women have played a critical role in every era [of Cherry
Grove's queer history] but the 1960s" (p. 8). In part, then, Newton's
text details how gender-separatist accounts unified around exclusive
categories of male and female might overestimate the social and cultural ruptures between gay men, lesbians, and "our" respective histories,
although she also problematizes her co-gendered analysis by pointing
out that lesbians "remained a distinct and separate group whom gay
men recognized as alien kin, sisters yet strangers" (p. 203).

Both Kennedy and Davis's and Chauncey's texts clearly depict working-class lesbian and gay subcultures which contradict "[t]he old
dogma" (Chauncey, p. 10) that has continued to locate the initial
development of queer identities in middle-class white (male) social
worlds. Although there is a marked difference between the working-
class lesbians in Kennedy and Davis's study who "built a community
in bars or at house parties" (p. 8) and the working-class gay men in
Chauncey's study who forged their gay world in New York's streets
(ch. 7), both books contest the extent to which working-class women
and men found lesbian and gay life-choices difficult to make. Related-
ly, these two texts problematize the central importance of the promise
of anonymity afforded by cities which marks the earlier literature. "To
focus on the supposed anonymity of the city," Chauncey argues, "is to
imply that gay men remained isolated from ('anonymous' to) one
another. The city, however, was the site not so much of anonymous,
furtive encounters between strangers . . . as of an organized, multi-
layered, and self-conscious gay subculture, with its own meeting
places, language, folklore, and moral codes" (p. 133). For working-
class lesbians, as Kennedy and Davis argue, butch-fem roles "were a
powerful social force. They were the organizing principle for this
community's relations with the outside world" and worked to make

lesbians visible "to one another *and* to the public" (p. 152, emphasis added). Both of these urban studies propose that their findings might be extendable to other cities, whether to "other thriving, middle-sized US industrial cities with large working-class populations" (Kennedy and Davis, p. 10) or as *"prototypical"* of "the urban conditions and changes that allowed a gay world to take shape" (Chauncey, pp. 28–9). Yet urban life has only been part of the history of gay and lesbian communities in the United States. Indeed, as Newton maintains in her study, the "ills" associated with urban life helped foster the class-based seasonal gay and lesbian exodus from the cities to Cherry Grove "where gay men and women began building their summer capital." "The first gay Grovers," she explains, "seem to have sought both a more authentic experience in 'nature' and an escape from the controls imposed by their (relatively privileged) work and social lives" and "settled in a spot . . . on the far margin of metropolitan life" (p. 13).

Despite the ways they complicate notions of "gay identity" and show how there is no such unitary phenomenon as "the" homosexual, all of these studies remain fundamentally concerned with questions of same-sex sexuality, a concern which lends the texts themselves distinctively gay and/or lesbian identities. In other words, though revealed as internally differentiated, the "modern" category homosexuality nonetheless provides the thread that sutures together the diverse, unstable, contradictory, shifting histories recounted within each book and also ties all four texts together. Kennedy and Davis, for instance, provide a "comprehensive survey of the lesbian community in Buffalo, New York" (p. xvi) and address "problematic issues about boundaries" (p. 3) to look at "questions about the changing forms of [lesbian] identity and community" (p. 7). Central to the forms of lesbian identity they explore, however, is women's explicit acknowledgement of "their erotic interest in women" (p. 12). In thus differentiating their study from previous lesbian-feminist formulations which "privileged passionate and loving relationships over specifically sexual relationships in defining lesbianism" (p. 12), Kennedy and Davis return to "sexuality as an *essential* ingredient in lesbian life" (p. 13, emphasis added). Faderman's pursuit of change and diversity in lesbian life is also organized on the basis of an "essential" sexuality, so that her history includes women "whose lives were lived primarily or exclusively within heterosexual communities and who may be considered lesbian only by virtue of their secret sexual identification" (p. 7).

Somewhat differently, Chauncey's book is focused both on the multiple forms of male sexual identity in the period between 1890 and

World War II and on a nascent "gay identity" coming into full emergence. "The ascendancy of *gay*" as term of identification, he argues,

> reflected . . . a reorganization of sexual categories and the transition from
> an early twentieth-century culture divided into "queers" and "men" on
> the basis of gender status to a late-twentieth-century culture divided into
> "homosexuals" and "heterosexuals" on the basis of sexual object choice.
> (p. 22)

Although this "transition from one sexual regime to the next was an uneven process, marked by significant class and ethnic differences" (p. 13), Chauncey speaks consistently of "a" gay world "because almost all the men in those networks conceived of themselves as linked to the others in their common 'queerness' and their membership in a single gay world, no matter how much they regretted it" (p. 3). Chauncey's supposition of discontent among the members of the imagined community of gay men in New York City is of grave concern for contemporary considerations of identity politics, for the ambivalence it suggests points both to the (seeming) intractability of identity and to the rejection of static or comfortable notions of who "we" are. Furthermore, his suggestion that "[t]he limited convergence of lesbian and gay life in the 1920s . . . marked an important stage in the emergence of the social category of the homosexual" (p. 228) raises provocative questions about how future generations of research will address the construction of a common "queerness" across gender with its own unsatisfactory kinds of identification. These sorts of dissatisfaction, however, are integral to the ambivalence of history as, in Michel de Certeau's formulation, a locus carved from the past that "is equally a place for making the future."[17]

III. Demanding History: Imagined Communities, Invented Traditions, and the Presence of the Past

My premise that gay and lesbian historical self-representations are engaged in contradictory enterprises has important ramifications for the shift from modern to postmodern histories since my characterization of social-constructionist historical-theoretical accounts as modernist is also somewhat contradictory. For, although they reiterate a story of modernization and modernism, constructionist histories of sexuality – and particularly gay and lesbian sexualities – have been integral (if often neglected) parts of a series of postmodern cultural, political, and historical practices especially in relation to humanist notions of an eternal, immutable human nature or essence. Nonetheless, this work remains embedded in modernist assumptions about the ostensibly stable, linear unity of history; the apparent inevitability of progress and development; and our supposed ability "to know" the past as it "really" happened and its consequences for the present. It is these latter notions of the narrative coherence of history, historical progress or development, and "accurate" knowledge of the past which postmodernism's "incredulity to metanarratives" disrupts. A postmodernist queer historical representation would not only set out to dislodge the modernist metanarratives which gloss over differences, anomaly or incommensurability, and specificity but would also exploit the problematic nature of historical representation itself in order to rethink the meaning of the "historical" contingency of queer identities, how queer historical desires work to construct notions of self, community, and politics, and the ways history is used to address "some of the most important issues facing, agitating, and sometimes dividing us today." In deference to postmodernism's celebration of the local, of fragmentation, of discontinuity, I offer a few initial observations on gay and lesbian historical studies and end with a proposal for an alternative model of queer historical practice in which historiography's codes of representation are as much an object of analysis as they are an instrument of it.

1) In an earlier statement of these ideas, I wrote that gay men and lesbians should not take whatever we want from the past and call it a part of "our" history. To do so, I argued, would not only be a profound failure to understand the specificities of the social formation of lesbian and gay subjects but it would, in fact, also reiterate one of the principal excesses of modernism. In that instance, I was in ironic agreement with neo-conservative critic Daniel Bell's assessment of modern culture, which, he argues, "is defined by [an] extraordinary freedom to ransack the world storehouse and to engorge any and every style it comes upon."[18] In my earlier essay, I singled out as culturally problematic the persistent efforts to claim various aspects of the Native American *berdache* phenomenon "as 'a traditional gay role'" and to incorporate them into gay and lesbian history.[19] Prompted by Will Roscoe's response to my article, I wonder at this point what it means to say something from the past is not "ours." How do "we" know? Who are "we," and to whom does something that is "ours" – or *not* "ours" – belong? As Roscoe points out, "the recovery of the berdache tradition since the 1970s has been led . . . by gay and lesbian Indians themselves."[20] So by what authority can I reject such projects as

culturally problematic? That is, specifically, who am *I*? Who are the "we" I had in mind at the time? At any rate, *I* am not a Native American and, hopefully, not the arbiter – even if occasionally an interpreter – of Native American lesbian and gay historical imaginations.

Indeed, I do still want to maintain that certain "recuperations" of *berdache* traditions *will* remain problematic under certain conditions, in certain contexts, and for certain arguments. But "certain" does not mean *all*. Critiques of claims to a *berdache* history need to address questions of positionality, of racial specificity, of the systems through which social power is accorded and withheld and not merely to reiterate constructionist notions of historical discontinuity, paradigm shifts, and ultimately an "essential" difference between types of "sexuality." Powerful, historically embedded racial structures and systems of representation produce a sense of white entitlement to Native American beliefs, traditions, and – with appalling frequency – material artifacts for personal spiritual or financial gain. In short, white claims to *berdache* traditions are more than minimally racially problematic appropriations of Native American cultures that simply reflect a relative indifference to otherwise still-salient racial categories. But, as tempting and important as it is to draw out the implications of these power-laden practices of (mis)appropriation, such investigations are also over-invested in the significance of what white people do. In other words, they deflect attention from the lives, histories, and texts of Native Americans by constantly returning to the alleged "center" of cultural, social, and political meaning in "American" life, as if, that is, what white people do were "the measure of all mankind."

The queer fiction of the present that "we" are "now" a "community" with a shared history is very deeply troubled by queer fictions of the past that powerfully refract the historically embedded, highly consequential differences among us. This differential – indeed, oppositional – reading of history is remarked in Paula Gunn Allen's "How the West Was Really Won," an essay that de-mythologizes the allegedly heroic conquering, settling, and taming of "the Wild West" by "neo-Americans."[21] Refusing to acquiesce to the white lie of "manifest destiny" while duly recognizing its consequences across space and time, Allen insists on Native American histories and cosmologies which are distinct from those of other races. Bringing these distinct histories and cosmologies into play, the reclamation of *berdache* traditions by Native Americans is more than a weak thread suturing the past to the present; rather, it is a rich form of cultural articulation that remarks the centrality of racial categories and the social relations in which they are given meaning *within* queer fictions of the past by retaining a highly charged aspect of Native American homosexuality.

2) In a series of autobiographical, theoretical, and historiographical lectures, Allan Bérubé has begun to address questions of class and homosexuality, focusing especially on the working-class dimensions of lesbian and gay political history.[22] The conception of homosexuality as a primary political identity developed by such organizations as the Mattachine Society and the Daughters of Bilitis, Bérubé argues, has tended to require a significant amount of "fitting in." "Coming out," in other words, can be *not only* the twin processes of personal disclosure and the development of a public homosexual presence identified by Jeffrey Weeks *but also* a process of re-identification structured by pre-existing middle-class norms, values, and attitudes which require abandoning, denying, or hiding working-class backgrounds, experiences, and allegiances. For working-class gay people, however, other political movements have existed which, though not privileging gay identity, have nonetheless advanced gay rights. To find and understand specifically working-class gay political history, Bérubé maintains, we have to look at work itself and, especially, working-class movements in the form of labor unions.

In a case-study of one such movement, Bérubé has been investigating the gay male networks that were a central part of the West Coast Marine Cooks and Stewards Union. From the early 1930s to the 1950s, the communist, multiracial, and queer-positive MCSU effectively organized its members and maintained a "controversial commitment to working-class solidarity, racial equality, and organizing 'queer work' [work that is performed by or has the reputation of being performed by queers, such as that of the MCSU]." In contrast to the Mattachine Society's efforts to fashion a gay identity-based minority political movement, MCSU members created a multiracial work culture and union-based movement which "developed their own collective strategies to achieve the broad political goal of surviving with dignity as working-class queers."[23] Falling victim to McCarthy-era anti-communism and homophobia, the MCSU was ultimately crushed by the FBI, the Coast Guard, and anti-communist (white) male union members. The MCSU's demise, Bérubé points out, coincided with the emergence of the latter Mattachine Society which had effected its own purges of radical members by exploiting precisely the same anti-communist hysteria over "un-American" activities that had destroyed the once powerful union. Unlike the middle-class white gay men who lost their "movement" in this reorganization, however, the purged and blacklisted MCSU members were unable to find subsequent work.

By focusing on working-class solidarity and (implicitly) class antagonism in gay history, Bérubé's research and the tentative conclusions
he has drawn from it problematize the drive for unity in modernist
narratives of gay identity formation. That the very different fates of the
Marine Cooks and Stewards Union and the post-purge Mattachine
Society were not only located at the same crucial historical juncture
but were also enabled by the same salient cultural features critically
compromises the harmonious resolution of gay differences which
"comic" celebrations of gay identity suggest.[24] Indeed, the central and
effective role played by early gay and lesbian political organizations in
the creation of a gay community needs to be seen not as autonomous
from but rather as integrally related to the changing nature of social
movements in the post-World War II era in which the Old Left's
preoccupation with the working class as the locus of mobilization and
change was decentered by the emergence of the New Left's focus on
cultural rather than economic radicalism exemplified in the shift away
from economic-toward identity-based political movements. But, in
spite of a number of social and historical forces which facilitated them
(including the limitations of class-based politics), as Bérubé's study of
the MCSU attests, such shifts were given a powerful helping hand by
the collusion of a number of anti-communist, anti-labor forces which
quite effectively suppressed radical union organizing across racial
boundaries. In other words, D'Emilio's argument that the "pioneering
. . . [gay and lesbian] activists had not only to mobilize a community"
but in fact "had to create one"[25] has an important corollary. The
legacy of their activism is a double-sided coin, for those activists'
relative success in making a homosexual minority in the United States
might well be understood as both the creation of a possibility and the
articulation of a powerful hegemony which eliminated other possibilities for gay political organizing in, as D'Emilio phrases it, their
"retreat to respectability" (ch. 5).

   3) Two autobiographical queer fictions of the past that compellingly
challenge racial indifference *and* proper historical representation,
Audre Lorde's *Zami* and Samuel Delany's *The Motion of Light in
Water*, re/write the history of gay life in Greenwich Village during the
1950s as complex narratives of desire, difference, and discourse.[26]
Each of these black-authored texts' "decentered" or "excentric" positions relative to white racial (in)difference is instructive for rethinking
the modernist illusion of a reified "gay identity" uniting people across
race, sex, and class.

   As modernist social histories of gay identity anticipate, the promise
of the city (ironically a "village" in both cases) figures centrally in each

of these texts and provided the space where Lorde and Delany could be gay. Yet, in "making sense" of gay urban spaces, modernist models do not account for the interaction of the changing social structures of race with those of sexuality. Such accounts cannot tell us, for instance, how the invisibility of black women in Greenwich Village informed Lorde's experience and how such invisibility affected individual and collective notions of identity and community. Nor can these narratives explore the meaning of the "more or less indifferent silence" in which Delany, "light-skinned enough so that four out of five people who met [him], of whatever race, assumed [he] was white," made the twice daily "journey of near ballistic violence" across "110th Street – Harlem's southern boundary" in order to get to and from school (pp. 10, 52).

In the context of the Greenwich Village gay-bar scene, Lorde writes, "it was hard for me to believe that my being an outsider had anything to do with being a lesbian." "But," she continues,

> when I, a Black woman, saw no reflection in any of the faces there week after week, I knew perfectly well that being an outsider in the Bagatelle had everything to do with being Black. (p. 220)

The complex intersections of race, gender, class, and sexuality brought into powerful focus in *Zami* present a city which is not only full of promise and possibility but which is also a multivalent, unstable, and conflicted set of spaces. "For some of us," Lorde explains, "there was no particular place, and we grabbed whatever we could from wherever we found space. . . . Each of us had our own needs and pursuits, and many different alliances" (p. 226). Wherever she went – from the Bagatelle, a lesbian bar in the Village, to Hunter College where she was a student, from her mother's home in Harlem to the library where she worked – "there was a piece of [her] bound in each place" (p. 226) but never her whole self. Though crucial to the text, the meaning of lesbianism – the place of an individual and collective "gay identity" in movements premised on the notion that the personal is political – is significantly decentered in *Zami*, a decentering which Lorde remarks in her observation that "[s]elf-preservation warned some of us that we could not afford to settle for one easy definition, one narrow individuation of self" (p. 226).

Set in roughly the same time and place as *Zami*, Delany's memoir also upsets stable historical representations of the "making" of gay identity. While the Mattachine Society, the Daughters of Bilitis, and One, Inc. were "creating" their constituency in urban America, Delany was discovering "that there was a population of millions of gay men, and that *history had, actively and already*, created for us whole galleries of institutions, good and bad, to accommodate our sex" (p. 174, emphasis added). He distinguishes between, on the one hand, the dominant "fifties model of homosexuality" as "a solitary perversion" and even "'gay bar society,'" both of which required "[t]he abandonment of sex," and, on the other hand, "the exodus from the trucks" and "the orgy at the baths" (p. 174). For Delany, gay identity – gay community – was found in or constructed through sex with other men, not the social scene of the gay bars or the respectable homophile organizations.

Yet, because "[o]nly the coyest and the most indirect articulations could occasionally indicate the boundaries of a phenomenon whose centers could not be spoken or written of, even figuratively," Delany maintains, "there is no way to gain from it a clear, accurate, and extensive picture of extant public institutions" (p. 176). Earlier in his book, Delany meditates on a performance of Allan Kaprow's *Eighteen Happenings in Six Parts*, which left him with "the disappointment of that late romantic sensibility we call modernism presented with the postmodern condition" (p. 116). The performance piece's "subversion of expectations about the 'proper' aesthetic employment of time, space, presence, absence, wholeness, and fragmentation, as well as the general locatability of 'what happens . . .'" (p. 115) serves as a metaphor for Delany's subsequent discussion of New York's gay male subculture which "while [it] accommodated sex, cut it . . . up into tiny portions . . . *No one ever got to see it whole*" (p. 174, emphasis added). Delany's view of gay community – specifically informal male sexual institutions – is remarkably fluid, fragmented, and finally a phenomenon "all but impossible" to apprehend in its totality (p. 174).

In part, of course, John D'Emilio's research is an attempt to elucidate the impersonal, unspecified, but active "history" named by Delany as the subject that created this array of sexual institutions for gay men. When read together, however, striking gaps emerge between *The Motion of Light in Water*, *Zami*, and *Sexual Politics, Sexual Communities'* overview of the formation of a gay minority population in the US and its discussion of the early homophile movement's central place in that process. For instance, like Delany, D'Emilio also distinguishes gay sexual institutions such as public cruising from gay bars, though unlike Delany, he sees the latter as having accomplished what the former cannot, namely having "fostered an identity that was both public and collective" (D'Emilio, p. 32).

> [T]he bars offered an all-gay environment where patrons dropped the pretension of heterosexuality, socializing with friends as well as searching for a sexual partner. When *trouble* struck, as it often did in the form of a police raid, the crowd suffered *as a group*, enduring the penalties together. The bars were a seedbed for a *collective consciousness* that might one day flower politically. (p. 33, emphasis added)

Delany also writes about his visits to gay (or "mixed" gay–straight) bars and includes mention of the "irregular intervals" of a policeman's visit "to check the place out" (p. 149). D'Emilio's evaluation of the bars as the social institutions "contain[ing] the greatest potential for reshaping the consciousness of homosexuals and lesbians" (p. 32), however, displaces Delany's identity-building sexual experiences (and those of "millions of [other] gay men") to the margins of gay history. This displacement is especially intriguing in light of Delany's suggestion that it was only the boundaries – and not the center – of gay male sexual institutions which could be represented.

Furthermore, Lorde's experiences as a black woman in the Greenwich Village gay scene serve as a powerful reminder of the severe limits of a public and collective gay identity. Though she too socialized in the bars, Lorde's assessment of them is ambivalent: not only did she continue to see the pretensions of heterosexuality mirrored in butch-fem role-playing (esp. p. 221), but the possibility of "collective consciousness" was constrained, even mired, by the bars' racial dynamics. Some bars, such as Laurel's, "had a family feeling" (p. 222) or were generally a "place to refuel and check your flaps" (p. 225), while "Black lesbians in the Bagatelle faced a world *only slightly* less hostile than the outer world which we had to deal with every day" (p. 225, emphasis added). In Lorde's biomythography, racism – whether the subtle racism of white racial indifference which left her invisible as a black woman or, conversely, the more overt racism which made her visible for precisely the same reason – unambiguously dis-integrates the stabilizing, collectivizing effects posited by modernist conceptions of gay identity.

Delany's use of *Eighteen Happenings in Six Parts* as a metaphor for the fragmentation of the gay male sexual subculture in pre-Stonewall New York provides a productive way for critiquing modernist social histories of gay identity. While these projects' historicizing approaches attempt to represent the "whole" history of that identity, albeit in abstract and general form, Delany's metaphor questions the possibility of ever making such a representation and suggests instead that only certain parts of that history can be made visible. In D'Emilio's interpretation of gay bars, the focus on the development of a "collective consciousness" expressly marks out, without fully describing, an important "center" – some essential quality – of 1950s gay life which represents or symbolizes a quality shared by all the other parts as well as by the "whole" of gay life in the 1950s. This characteristic quality, this ostensible "center" of gay identity, however, is itself a queer fiction of the past and the present; it makes a circular argument between past and present so that what "we" already "know" about gay identity prefigures the past and offers the metaphysical principle for translating difference into similarity. Both Delany's and Lorde's texts, however, help us to rethink the particular and the general, abstract theory and detailed example, part and whole. A crucial aspect of them is their disuption of "proper" historical representation which confuses those categories by asking us to consider the frame(s) of reference of our historical imaginations.

Both texts are autobiographies, and therefore directly engaged in "subjective" writing. Yet they both also illuminate the constructed nature of all representations of the past, however ostensibly "real" they might be. Unlike D'Emilio's project of developing "a new, more accurate theory of gay history" severed from the mythologies of the gay-liberation era (p. 101), Lorde's *Zami* not only explicitly acknowledges itself as a fiction but indirectly calls attention to the imagination's intervention into all accounts of the real world. Her neologism "biomythography" places myth directly in-between life (=bio) and writing (=graphy), both interrupting realist writing about life and seamlessly connecting life to writing through myth. Delany's memoir is also self-consciously framed in terms of the fictions of memory.

From the outset of his memoir Delany not only writes of himself as the central subject of the discourse, but he also recognizes his subjective, perspectival grasp of the events narrated. We see this dual subjectivity in the first pages of the introduction, when Delany recounts the time of his father's death (pp. ix–xi). Delany quickly points out, however, that the account just read contains a fair number of errors of fact (p. xii). Although, in pointing out these factual inaccuracies, Delany concedes a certain susceptibility to persuasion through "document and deduction," his willingness to admit to a "disjunction in memory . . . strong enough to make [him], now and again, even argue the facts" (p. xvii) recenters the production of narratives of the past in subjective memory and experience. For Delany, his

inaccurate statement, "My father died when I was seventeen in 1958 . . ." is an emblem of the displacements and elisions committed upon that more objective narrative, . . . [a] bare and untextured chronology . . . for the year and a half that straddled [his] nineteenth birthday. (pp. xvi, xii)

In spite of his contention that there was "a time in which, objectively, [his father's death] occurred," the brief chronology Delany provides "is not the story [*he*] remembers from that time" (pp. xvii, xvi).

> While all the incidents listed are, in my own mind, associated with vivid moments, rich details, complexes of sensations, deep feelings, and the texture of the real (*so indistinguishable from that of a dream*), their places on the list are wholly a product of research. (p. xvi)

Summing up his highly qualifying prefatory comments, Delany makes a similar point, but this time he expressly acknowledges the fictive character of the many, frequently discordant representations of history that can be articulated.

> I hope . . . to sketch, as honestly and effectively as I can, something I can recognize as my own, aware as I do so that even as I work after honesty and accuracy, memory will make this only *one possible fiction among the myriad* – many in open conflict – anyone might write of any of us, as convinced as any other that what he or she wrote was the truth. (p. xviii, emphasis added)

Reading these conflicting fictions, tracing the genealogies of their representations, specifying their locations in socially inscribed relations of power, diagnosing their ideological entailments – each of these acts of critical intervention into the (con)text of lesbian and gay pasts – disqualifies claims to an innocent or neutral historical representation of queer identities.

*   *   *

What is history? Judging by what we hear around us that is a question that needs to be asked again.

Paul Veyne[27]

The postmodern queer historical studies I envision returns to the shared point of departure of the disparate, uneven, and contradictory projects traversing the various terrains of lesbian and gay studies and communities – their insistent engagement with the past. While such a project reiterates the value of history as a means of addressing a range of issues confronting lesbian and gay communities in the present, it is also framed in such a way as to reevaluate – even to render problematic – the terms of that assertion, especially the confident and familiar invocation of "history." On the one hand, this mode of historical analysis reconsiders questions of identity, community, and history in postmodernist terms which recognize multiple socially constructed differences in order to resist gay and lesbian historical self-repre-sentations that gravitate toward "sameness." On the other hand, such a project recognizes historiography as a privileged system of significa-tion and pursues a cultural critique of queer fictions of the past enabled by two decades of challenges to historical representation posed by revisionist historians, critical theory, and cultural studies.

This queered historical studies can be likened to another central problematic in contemporary culture which has been made visible by lesbian, gay, and feminist criticism, namely heterosexuality. Jonathan Katz has recently argued that the failure of gay as well as straight sexual theorists to study "the heterosexual idea in history" has "conti-nued to privilege the 'normal' and 'natural' at the expense of the 'abnormal' and 'unnatural.'"[28] Challenging heterosexuality's power as an unmarked – and presumably normal, natural, eternal, and un-problematic – category, Katz's essay begins to show how closely linked the histories of homosexuality and the histories of heterosexuality have been, so that we might now see both queer and straight as socially constructed, historically contingent, *and* interdependent categories. I want to suggest a somewhat analogous interdependence of history-writing practices in lesbian and gay contexts, one which can be grasped metaphorically as the relationship between "straight" history and "queer" history. Straight history, both as the history of heterosexuality and as historiography itself, retains a privileged position whose unex-posed foundations are disclosed by a double-valenced queer history which is not only the history of lesbian and gay sexualities (or perhaps any non-normative sexuality) but also a "history" which takes issue with historiography itself to upset the "truth" of historiography's (disguised) codes of representation. While challenging the presumptive silences of heterosexism, this double queering of history also carries out the defamiliarizing work of the best history-writing in a particular-ly queer way by questioning the very idea of "proper" historical representation.

In recent years, a number of literary and historical theorists have argued that the kind of understanding provided by a specifically his-torical inquiry is itself a construction subject to a whole series of questions regarding interpretation, representation, and narrative.[29] Situating historians' representations of the past within these literary-theoretical critiques of historiography as method allows us to focus attention on those aspects of history-writing which can be neglected, begged, avoided, or disavowed in its practice. These formal critiques of historical method, Linda Hutcheon argues, have coincided with the complex and varied intersections of multiple emergent intellectual and political practices to force an awareness "that history cannot be written without ideological and institutional analysis, including analysis of the act of writing itself."[30] While not disregarding Fredric Jameson's insistence that "history is not a text," the analysis of historical representation as an act of writing acknowledges his immediate qualification of that claim which reframes historical questions in terms of our access to the past "in textual form" only.[31] For this reason, historical truths might well be approached through a literary historiography which draws on the dissolution of the distinction between realistic and fictional representations proposed by recent theories of discourse and locates factual as well as interpretive truths in the ways we understand, interpret, and write history.

It is precisely the textuality of historical representation that this doubly queer postmodern historical studies takes seriously as an area of study. In a certain sense, though, gay and lesbian historians have been undertaking such projects already, with regard to *past* examples and the *past* significance of the multiple, various, and contradictory meanings of history in queer contexts. For example, Chauncey devotes several pages of *Gay New York's* chapter on "the making of collective identity" to a discussion of gay folklore and pays particular attention to the "constructi[on of] historical traditions" as crucial ways gay men *made* as well as *made sense of* their culture. "By imagining they had collective roots in the past," he writes, "[gay men] asserted their collective identity in the present" (p. 286). Because such invented traditions persist in current contexts both to assert and to contest collective identities, critical investigations of them elucidate as much about contemporary queer identities, differences, and the "important issues facing, agitating, and sometimes dividing [gay and lesbian communities], personally and collectively" as the historical analysis of earlier examples tells us about the lives and self-constructions of gay men and lesbians in the past. In this regard, however, the truths about queer identities posited by historiography are no different in kind from those posited by other methods of going through the past queerly. Like social-constructionist historical arguments, these other queer fictions of the past are also "theor[ies] of gay history," but the question of accuracy which motivates D'Emilio's project is displaced by *reading* gay and lesbian historical self-representations as cultural texts. Finally, then, a queered historical studies that investigates the retellings of history as vehicles for mobilizing new social subjects, contesting hegemonic social definitions, and creating new cultural possibilities in the present, deliberately challenges the distinctions between past and present and those between fact and fiction to make substantially more problematic *and* problematically more substantial the questions raised and answers provided by reflection on gay and lesbian pasts.

Notes

I wish to thank the Board of Studies in History of Consciousness at the University of California at Santa Cruz for fellowship support during the writing of the dissertation chapter from which this is drawn, and Steve Seidman for suggestions for revision.

1   Stuart Hall, "Cultural Identity and Diaspora," in *Colonial Discourse and Post-Colonial Theory: A Reader*, eds Patrick Williams and Laura Chrisman (New York: Columbia University Press, 1994), 394.
2   Susan K. Cahn, "Sexual Histories, Sexual Politics," *Feminist Studies*, 18 (3) (fall 1992): 637.
3   Jean-François Lyotard, *The Postmodern Condition: A Report on Knowledge*, trans. Geoff Bennington and Brian Massumi (Minneapolis: University of Minnesota Press, 1984), xxiv, xxv.
4   Martin Duberman, Martha Vicinus, and George Chauncey, Jr., "Introduction," in *Hidden from History: Reclaiming the Gay and Lesbian Past*, eds Duberman, Vicinus, and Chauncey, Jr. (New York: New American Library, 1989), 11.
5   The phrase in quotation marks comes from Kenneth Plummer (ed.), *The Making of the Modern Homosexual* (London: Hutchinson, 1981). For a general discussion, see Steven Connor, *Postmodernist Culture: An Introduction to Theories of the Contemporary* (Oxford: Blackwell, 1989).
6   Barry Adam, "Structural Foundations of the Gay World," *Comparative Studies in Society and History*, 27 (4) (1985), 658–71; John D'Emilio, "Capitalism and Gay Identity," in *Powers of Desire*, eds Ann Snitow, Christine Stansell, and Sharon Thompson (New York: Monthly Review Press, 1983), 100–13; Lillian Faderman, "The Morbidification of Love Between Women by 19th-Century Sexologists," *Journal of Homosexuality*, 4 (1) (fall 1978), 73–90; Ann Ferguson, "Patriarchy, Sexual Identity, and the Sexual Revolution," in *Feminist Theory: A Critique of Ideology*, eds Nannerl O. Keohane, Michelle Z. Rosaldo, and Barbara C. Gelpi (Chicago: University of Chicago Press, 1982), 147–61; Michel Foucault, *The History of Sexuality: Volume One, an Introduction*, trans. Robert Hurley (New York: Vintage, 1979); Jonathan Ned Katz, *Gay/Lesbian Almanac* (New York: Harper and Row, 1983), 137–74; Mary

McIntosh, "The Homosexual Role," *Social Problems*, 16 (2) (fall 1968), 182–92; and Jeffrey Weeks, *Coming Out: Homosexual Politics in Britain, from the Nineteenth Century to the Present* (London: Quartet, 1977).

7 John D'Emilio, "Gay History: A New Field of Study," in *Making Trouble: Essays on Gay History, Politics, and the University* (New York: Routledge, 1992), 103.

8 Marshall Berman, *All That Is Solid Melts into Air: The Experience of Modernity* (New York: Penguin Books, 1988), 15.

9 Judith Butler, "Imitation and Gender Insubordination," in *The Lesbian and Gay Studies Reader*, eds Henry Abelove, Michèlle Aina Barale, and David M. Halperin (New York: Routledge, 1993), 309–20, and Diana Fuss, *Essentially Speaking: Feminism, Nature, and Difference* (New York: Routledge, 1989), esp. 99–100; Eve Kosofsky Sedgwick, *Epistemology of the Closet* (Berkeley: University of California Press, 1990), 67–90.

10 Weeks, *Coming Out*, p. ix.

11 Sedgwick, *Epistemology of the Closet*, 45.

12 Jeffrey Escoffier, "Sexual Revolution and the Politics of Gay Identity," *Socialist Review*, 82/83 (July–Oct. 1985), 147.

13 Monique Wittig, "The Mark of Gender," in *The Poetics of Gender*, ed. Nancy K. Miller (New York: Columbia University Press, 1986), 63–73.

14 Martha Vicinus, "'They Wonder to Which Sex I Belong': The Historical Roots of the Modern Lesbian Identity," in *Which Homosexuality?: Essays from the International Scientific Conference on Lesbian and Gay Studies*, eds Anja van Kooten Niekerk and Theo van der Meer (Amsterdam: Uitgeverij An Dekker/Schorer, 1989), 176.

15 See Thomas S. Kuhn, *The Structure of Scientific Revolutions*, 2nd edn (Chicago: University of Chicago Press, 1970).

16 George Chauncey, *Gay New York* (New York: Basic Books; Lillian Faderman, *Odd Girls and Twilight Lovers: A History of Lesbian Life in Twentieth-Century America* (New York: Columbia University Press, 1991); Elizabeth Kennedy and Madeline Davis, *Boots of Leather, Slippers of Gold: The History of a Lesbian Community* (New York: Routledge, 1993). and Esther Newton, *Cherry Grove, Fire Island: Sixty Years in America's First Gay and Lesbian Town* (Boston: Beacon Press, 1993).

17 Michel de Certeau, *The Writing of History*, trans. Tom Conley (New York: Columbia University Press, 1988), 85.

18 Daniel Bell, *The Cultural Contradictions of Capitalism* (New York: Basic Books, 1976), 13.

19 See my "Telling (Hi)stories: Rethinking the Lesbian and Gay Historical Imagination," *Outlook: National Lesbian and Gay Quarterly*, 8 (spring 1990): 74. I was referring to Will Roscoe, "The Zuni Man-Woman," *Outlook: National Lesbian and Gay Quarterly*, 2 (summer 1988): 56–67, and Ramón A. Gutiérrez, "Must We Deracinate Indians to Find Gay Roots?," *Outlook: National Lesbian and Gay Quarterly*, 4 (winter 1989): 61–7. The quotation is Roscoe's, p. 64.

20 Will Roscoe, "Who Speaks for Gay Native Americans?" letter to the editor, *Outlook: National Lesbian and Gay Quarterly*, 10 (fall 1990): 80.

21 Paula Gunn Allen, "How the West Was Really Won," in *The Sacred Hoop: Recovering the Feminine in American Indian Traditions* (Boston: Beacon Press, 1986), 194–208.

22 Allan Bérubé, "'Fitting In': Expanding Queer Studies beyond Gay Identity and Coming Out," paper presented at Pleasure/Politics: Fourth Annual Lesbian, Bisexual, and Gay Studies Conference, Harvard University, Oct. 26–8, 1990; "Intellectual Desires," keynote address, La Ville en Rose: Lesbians and Gays in Montreal: Histories, Cultures, and Societies, Concordia University/Université du Québec à Montréal, Nov. 12–15, 1992; "'Dignity for All': The Role of Homosexuality in the Marine Cooks and Stewards Union, 1930s–1950s," paper presented at the Annual Meeting of the American Historical Association, San Francisco, Jan. 6–9, 1994 (see also the abstract of this paper which was printed in the *Committee on Lesbian and Gay History Newsletter* (Jan. 1994), p. 6); guest lecture, Apr. 19, 1994, Community Studies 80F, University of California, Santa Cruz.

23 Bérubé, "'Dignity for All,'" abstract, p. 6.

24 On "comic" emplotments see Northrop Frye, *The Anatomy of Criticism: Four Essays* (Princeton, NJ: Princeton University Press, 1957).

25 John D'Emilio, *Sexual Politics, Sexual Communities: The Making of a Homosexual Minority in the United States, 1940–1970* (Chicago: University of Chicago Press, 1983), 5.

26 Audre Lorde, *Zami: A New Spelling of My Name* (Trumansburg, NY: The Crossing Press, 1982), and Samuel R. Delany, *The Motion of Light in Water: Sex and Science Fiction Writing in the East Village, 1957–1965* (New York: New American Library, 1988).

27 Paul Veyne, *Writing History: Essay on Epistemology*, trans. Mina Moore-Rinvolucri (Middletown, Conn.: Wesleyan University Press, 1984), p. ix.

28 Jonathan Ned Katz, "The Invention of Heterosexuality," *Socialist Review*, 20 (1) (Jan.–Mar., 1990): 8.

29 Among others, see Michel de Certeau, "History: Science and Fiction," in *Heterologies: Discourse on the Other*, trans. Brian Massumi (Minneapolis: University of Minnesota Press, 1986), 199–221; Dominick LaCapra, *History and Criticism* (Ithaca, NY: Cornell University Press, 1985); Paul Ricoeur, *The Reality of the Historical Past* (Milwaukee, Wis.: Marquette University Press, 1984); and Hayden White, *The Content of the Form: Narrative Discourse and Historical Representation* (Baltimore: Johns Hopkins University Press, 1987). See also Thomas C. Patterson, "Post-Structuralism, Post- Modernism: Implications for Historians," *Social History*, 14 (1) (Jan. 1989): 833–88.

30 Linda Hutcheon, *A Poetics of Postmodernism: History, Theory, Fiction* (New York: Routledge, 1988), 91.

31 Fredric Jameson, *The Political Unconscious: Narrative as Socially Symbolic Act* (Ithaca, NY: Cornell University Press, 1981), 35.

16

Contested Membership: Black Gay Identities and the Politics of AIDS

Cathy J. Cohen

It has been fairly recently that scholars in the social sciences have begun to recognize that the concept of group identity in its essentialist core is in crisis. Influenced by postmodern and deconstructive discourse, historical analyses focusing on marginal groups, and a new emphasis on identity in social-movement theories, researchers are beginning to understand that the idea of group identity that many of us now employ is markedly different than the conception of a stable, static, and homogenous group previously assumed in the social sciences.[1] Just as most scholars have finally become accustomed to including in their analyses simple conceptions of identity coded in binary form (i.e. white/black; man/woman), we now face the realization that identities of difference (race, class, gender, sexuality) are themselves fragmented, contested, and, of course, socially constructed.

Social-constructionist theory provides the framework and the intellectual incentive to identify and examine those social, political, and economic processes which lead to the promotion of certain conceptualizations of group membership and group meaning at particular historical moments.[2] Social-constructionist models can also be used to analyze internal debates over membership within marginal communities.[3] Using this approach, constructionist frameworks help us recognize and understand indigenous definitions of group membership and group meaning encapsulated under the rubric of group identity.

While previously, most of the work on the social construction of group identity came from scholars in the humanities, researchers in the social sciences, especially those of us interested in the topics of race, gender, class, and sexuality, must find ways to incorporate such insight into our analyses. Moreover, we are being challenged by a rapidly expanding understanding of group identity to not only recognize and examine the socially constructed character of group identity, but also to investigate the stratification found in groups and the implications of such fragmentation on attempts at group mobilization and political action.[4] Thus, beyond examining the ways in which dominant groups and institutions change or alter their imposed definitions of marginal groups within different historical contexts, we must also understand how marginal group members define and redefine themselves, setting their own standards for "full group membership."[5]

This chapter takes up the topic of indigenous constructions of group membership and its impact on the political attitudes and mobilization of marginal group members. In particular, I am interested in how the concept of "blackness," as it is defined and refined within black communities, is used to demarcate the boundaries of group membership. As a second point of examination, I want to know how these indigenous definitions of blackness influence, shape, and lend legitimation to the political attitudes and behavior of community leaders and members.

Indigenous definitions of blackness, while of course building on dominant ideas or definitions of who *is* black, employ a more expansive, but at the same time often less inclusive, understanding of black group identity. They center not merely on easily identifiable biologically rooted characteristics, but also use moralistic and character evaluations to appraise membership. Individuals employ a "calculus" of indigenous membership which can include an assessment of personal or moral worth, such as an individual's contribution to the community, their adherence to community norms and values, or their faithfulness to perceived, rewritten, or in some cases newly created African traditions. Thus, indigenously constructed definitions of black group identity seek to redefine and empower blackness to the outside world by policing the boundaries of what can be represented to the dominant public as "true blackness." And it is through the process of *public policing*, where the judgments, evaluations and condemnations of recognized leaders and institutions of black communities are communicated to their constituencies, that the full membership of certain segments of black communities are contested and challenged.

Let me be clear that examples of the indigenous construction of blackness and contests over such definitions abound in our everyday interactions. Whether it be the challenge to the authenticity of those black students who choose not to sit at "the black table" in the cafeteria or the looks of contempt or concern encountered by black group members seen walking with their white mates, informal or "hidden transcripts" of blackness guide interactions in black communities, as they undoubtedly do in all communities.[6] However, in most cases full-scale contestation is not the norm in black communities. Instead, those whose position in the community is challenged exist silenced and regulated for years. Only when the "subgroup" experiencing ostracization or *secondary marginalization* has alternative means of securing resources, such as an external network of support, will the full battle over inclusion be fought.[7] Thus, in most cases those individuals deemed to be on the outside of "acceptable blackness" – either because of their addiction, their sexual relationships, their gender, their financial status, their relationship with/or dependency on the state, etc – are left with two choices: either find ways to conform to "community standards" or be left on the margins where individual families and friends are expected to take care of their needs.

Again, my concern here is not that these group members will be rejected by dominant groups as not being part of the black community. Most marginal group members know that racism in the dominant society functions with essentialist principles in its assessment of black people. Thus, men and women, who meet basic dominant ideas of what black people look like and "act" like, rarely have their "blackness" evaluated, except to have it negated as a reward for assimilation into dominant white society (i.e. Michael Jackson, Clarence Thomas, and formerly O. J. Simpson). Instead, my concern is with the process employed by other marginal group members to evaluate someone's blackness. Will certain group members be rejected by other marginal group members because of their inability to meet indigenous standards of "blackness"? Are there processes through which the full "rights" or empowerment of group members becomes negated or severely limited *within* black communities because of a stigmatized black identity?[8]

As stated earlier, the objective of this analysis is not only to understand the processes through which indigenous constructions of group membership come about, but also to explore how these definitions impact on the behavior, in particular the political behavior, of marginal group members. To this end, I have chosen to center this analysis on the black community's response to the AIDS epidemic. Specifically, I will explore how indigenous contests over black gay male identity have framed and influenced black communities' conception of and response to AIDS.[9]

Throughout this chapter I use examples and quotes from community leaders located in black churches, electoral politics, activist organizations, and the academy to examine the relationship between indigenous definitions of blackness, a public black gay identity, and the political response to AIDS in black communities. Has the emergence of a public, empowered black gay identity, perceived and defined by many community leaders, activists, and members as standing outside the bounds of generally recognized standards of blackness, been used by these leaders to justify their lack of an aggressive response to this disease? Do community leaders interpret a public black gay identity as a direct threat to the acceptability or "cultural capital" gained by some in black communities, in particular by the black middle class? In the minds of indigenous leaders and activists, does embracing or owning AIDS as a disease significantly impacting on members of black communities also mean owning or finally acknowledging that sexual contact and intimate relationships between men is something found in, and inherently a part of, black communities?[10]

My central claim is that contestation over identity, in this case indigenous racial identity, has tangible effects, influencing the distribution of resources, services, access, and legitimacy within communities. In the case of AIDS, without the support of established leaders and organizations in black communities, underfunded community-based education programs encounter limited success, facilitating the continued infection and death of black men, women, and children. Further, in the absence of political pressure from leaders, organizations, activists, and mobilized members of the black community the federal government is allowed to continue its shameful dealings, neglecting to provide the full resources needed to effectively fight this disease in black communities. Thus, those failing to meet indigenous standards of blackness find their life chances threatened not only by dominant institutions or groups, but also by their lack of access to indigenous resources and support. Therefore, scholars who profess to be concerned with the conditions of marginal group members face the monumental challenge of recognizing and examining the process of indigenous group definition without reifying the group as an essentialist and exclusionary category.

Furthermore, the importance of disputes over community membership and the importance of groups should not be understood only at an abstract, theoretical level where discussions of identity, authenticity, and essentialism are often held. This examination of the intersection of AIDS, black gay identity, and indigenous constructions of "blackness" provides us with an empirical example of the importance of group membership and group resources for marginal group members, as well as the dangers of identity politics. In this case we must be concerned with politics that only recognize and respond to the needs of those segments of black communities judged by our leaders to meet indigenous standards of group membership. This issue is of critical importance because it represents what I believe to be one of the more pressing political challenges currently facing marginal communities in the twenty-first century, namely how to maintain and rebuild a principled and politically effective group unity. How do marginal communities, still struggling for access and power from dominant institutions and groups, maintain some pseudo-unified political base in the face of increasing demands to recognize and incorporate the needs and issues of members who previously were silenced and made invisible with regards to structuring the politics of the community? How do marginal communities make central those who are the most vulnerable, and often most stigmatized members of the community, when many of the previous gains of marginal group members have been made through a strategy of minimizing the public appearance of difference between the values, behavior, and attitudes of marginal and dominant group members? How do we build a truly radical, liberating politics that does not recreate hierarchies, norms, and standards of acceptability rooted in dominant systems of power? These are the questions that frame this analysis.

Deconstruction and the Crisis of Essentialism

It seems only appropriate before proceeding that I take up what I consider to be a very important criticism of group analysis. For some scholars attention to the construction of identity, instead of the deconstruction of such bounded categories, seems misplaced. These researchers call for the deconstruction of both dominant and indigenous categories which are viewed as excluding certain marginal group members and reinforcing hierarchies of power. Thus, activists and academics adhering to a deconstructionist framework embrace a more fluid and transgressive understanding of identity.[11] In the case of Black Americans, these scholars argue that the variation found in definitions of who qualifies as black and what that is to mean, as well as the variation in the actual life chances and lived experience of those identified through history as black, demands that we abandon the use of race as a category of analysis. Barbara Jeanne Fields, who I doubt would label herself a deconstructionist, writes at the end of her essay "Slavery, Race and Ideology in the United States of America,"

> Those who create and re-create race today are not just the mob that killed a young Afro-American man on the street in Brooklyn or the people who joined the Klan and the White Order. They are also those academic

writers whose invocation of self-propelling "attitudes" and tragic flaws assigns Africans and their descendants to a special category, placing them in a world exclusively theirs and outside history – a form of intellectual apartheid no less ugly or oppressive, despite its righteous (not to say self-righteous) trappings, than that practiced by the bio- and theo-racists; and for which the victims like slaves of old are expected to be grateful.[12]

In contrast to Fields, I argue that calls for the deconstruction of categories and groups ignore not only the reality of groups in structuring the distribution of resources and the general life chances of those in society, but also ignore the importance of group membership in promoting the survival and progress of marginal group members. If one exists, as many of us do, without the privilege and resources to transgress socially erected boundaries or categories, then we learn at an early age to rely on, and contribute to, the collective material resources/power/status of other group members who share our subject position. Thus, to argue that race or blackness is not "real" in some genetic or biological form (which I do), is not to believe that race or blackness, in particular as an ideological construct of grouping and separation, has not massively structured the lives of those designated black, as well as the rest of American society. Omi and Winant, in their book *Racial Formation in the United States*, write: "the attempt to banish the concept [of race] as an archaism is at best counterintuitive. . . . A more effective starting point is the recognition that despite its uncertainties and contradictions, the concept of race continues to play a fundamental role in structuring and representing the social world."[13]

Nonetheless I share some of Fields' concerns about the recreation and legitimization of categories used primarily to exploit and oppress. Many within black communities, whether they be cultural nationalists, religious leaders, politicians, or the average person trying to make it day to day, adhere to some form of a less stigmatized notion of group essentialism. Scholars ranging from Molefi Kete Asante to Patricia Hill Collins to those of us who use statistical analyses to examine the condition and progress of black people invoke some non-biologically based definitions of "*the* black experience."[14] Undoubtedly, much of our focus on a unified black community stems from the fact that compared to white communities, black people do in fact exhibit a significant level of political cohesiveness. Clearly, this observed homogeneity of black political attitudes, for instance, is forced in part by the survey questions that researchers ask, and more forcefully from the shared history of oppression which has framed our worldviews. However, we have reached a point in time when the issues faced by black communities demand that we look below the unified surface so often referenced by social scientists. Issues which currently frame the political agenda of black communities are often rooted in those points of social cleavage – class, gender, sexuality, language, country of origin – which problematize, at the very least, any conception of a unified, essential core of blackness as well as any assumption of shared lived experience.

Thus, it seems that this examination and others like it must be understood as an attempt to walk the thin line between two important constraints. First, a recognition that essentialist theories of the black community have at best limited relevance to understanding the structure and condition of black communities. Second, we must also proceed with an understanding that strict adherence to deconstructive approaches, which call for the complete negation of groups as a unit of analysis, risks ignoring the importance of indigenous group structure to the living conditions of marginal groups.

Emergence of a Visible Black Gay Identity

The perceived existence of a unifying group identity cannot be overstated when trying to explain the structured politics of black communities. Systems of oppression from slavery to redemption, to legal and informal Jim Crow segregation, and other more recent forms of segregation and deprivation have dictated that most African Americans share a history and current existence framed by oppression and marginalization. However, even as a unifier, blackness, or what qualifies as indigenously constructed blackness, has always been mediated or contested by other identities that group members hold. And at no time did both the primacy and the fragility of a unified group identity become more evident than in the liberation politics and social movements of the late 1960s and early 1970s. Whether it be civil-rights institutions, black liberation organizations or even electoral campaigns of black candidates, one primary identity – "blackness" – was understood to be the underlying factor joining all these struggles. Each organization espoused in their own way a commitment to the liberation of black people and anything thought to detract from this goal was dismissed and in some cases denounced. However, the uniformity of such a political worldview can also be challenged during this period.

During the 1960s and 1970s the black community experienced increasing stratification. Whether that stratification was based in the deindustrialization experienced in urban centers or the politicized nature of the times, which helped to promote consciousness of members' multiple identities, a segregated and seemingly unified black community had to deal openly with fragmentation. All across the country we witnessed the beginning of extreme bifurcation in black communities, with an expanding middle class and an expanding segment of poor black people. However, beyond economic segmentation, other identities or social locations became visible in defining the lived experience of black people. In black communities, as well as in the political groups of the time, individuals increasingly began to recognize and acknowledge the multiplicity of identities upon which their oppression was based. Unfortunately, it was the inability of many of the race-based organizations to recognize and act on perceived tears in "unity" that led in part to the dismantling of many of these organizations.[15] However, it was also in this changing environment that the visibility of lesbian and gay people, including black lesbian and gay people, began to take shape in the community.

It is important to recognize that black gay men and lesbians have always existed and worked in black communities, but these individuals had largely been made invisible, silent contributors to the community.[16] When faced with the devastation of racism, the cost of silence and invisibility seemed a willing payment from lesbian and gay community members for the support, caring, and protection of members of the black community and, more importantly, the support and acceptance of immediate family members. bell hooks in her book *Talking Back* discusses the dilemma that many black lesbians and gay men confronted:

> The gay people we knew did not live in separate subcultures, not in the small, segregated black community where work was difficult to find, where many of us were poor. Poverty was important; it created a social context in which structures of dependence were important for everyday survival. Sheer economic necessity and fierce white racism, as well as the joy of being there with the black folks known and loved, compelled many gay blacks to live close to home and family. That meant however that gay people created a way to live out sexual preferences within the boundaries of circumstances that were rarely ideal no matter how affirming.[17]

Thus, if one was willing not to "flaunt" their sexual orientation in front of family members and neighbors (although many would secretly suspect that you were "that way") the primarily verbal abuse – like taunts of "faggot" and "bulldyke" – was generally kept to a minimum.

Again, I do not want to minimize the importance of even such condi-
tional support on the part of family, friends, and community. The
prospect of facing continuous residential, occupational, and social
exclusion as a manifestation of widespread racism, even in primarily
white lesbian and gay communities, underscores the importance of
some feelings of safety and familiarity. These were the feelings of
support bought by our silence.

However, the willingness and ability of black lesbians and gay men
to remain quiet and invisible has radically changed. These changes
have resulted in part from many of the factors which have spurred new
identities as well as politicized identities of old. One major factor has
been the proliferation of liberation and social movements demanding
access and control for groups long pushed out of dominant society.
Cornel West speaks of this situation when he argues that,

> During the late '50s, '60s and early '70s in the USA, these decolonized
> sensibilities fanned and fueled the Civil Rights and Black Power move-
> ments, as well as the student anti-war, feminist, gray, brown, gay, and
> lesbian movements. In this period we witnessed the shattering of male
> WASP cultural homogeneity and the collapse of the short-lived liberal
> consensus.[18]

Closely connected to involvement and association with organized
social movements was the more formal establishment of an institutionalized, socially connected, and in many cases monetarily secure gay
community in many of the nation's urban centers. These "ghettos"
provided a space in which ideas of rights and political strategies of
empowerment could be generated and discussed. These enclaves, as
well as other dominant institutions such as universities, were integral
in creating space for the exploration of independence away from local
communities and families.[19]

In conjunction with the continued development of gay enclaves was
the emergence of an outspoken and brave black lesbian and gay
leadership who openly claimed and wrote about their sexuality (Audre
Lorde, Cheryl Clarke, Barbara Smith, Pat Parker, Joseph Beam, Essex
Hemphill . . .). These individuals were intent on creating new cultural
voices. When they were denied the right to speak openly through
traditional avenues in black communities these cultural leaders found
and created new avenues to affirm their presence and connection to
black communities. Publications like *This Bridge Called My Back*,
Home Girls, *Brother to Brother*, *In the Life*, and more recently videos
such as *Tongues Untied* all sought to detail from various perspectives

the struggle to consistently mesh one's black and gay identities.[20] All of these factors helped create an environment in which the silence that had structured the lives of many black lesbian and gay men seemed unacceptable.

The conditions listed above, however, did not lead to a massive coming-out process in black communities. In fact, the level of silence among black lesbian and gay men is still an immediate and pressing concern for those organizing in the community today. However, the environment that developed through the 1960s and 1970s created a situation in which some black women and men choose to identify publicly as black *and* gay. The choice, or in many cases the perceived need, to embrace publicly a black gay male or black lesbian identity undoubtedly escalated with the emergence of AIDS, an issue which demands either recognition and empowerment or death. Thus, after spending years affirming themselves, building consciousness, and contributing to black communities that had too often refused to embrace their particular needs, gay brothers and lesbian sisters faced an issue, in the case of AIDS, that threatened to kill black gays and lesbians as well as generally wreak havoc throughout black communities if we did not speak out and demand recognition.

It would be this political, social, and economic environment that would heighten the contestation over an open black gay male identity. This social context, where black gay men in particular were experiencing the destruction of AIDS, produced many of the early pioneers who saw it as their responsibility to provide the first level of response to AIDS in the black community. Ernest Quimby and Samuel Friedman, in their article "Dynamics of Black Mobilization against AIDS in New York City," document much of the early organized activity around AIDS in People of Color communities.[21] The authors note that,

> In the epidemic's early days, media reports that AIDS was a disease of white gay men reduced the attention blacks paid to it . . . By 1985, however, some leaders of the minority gay and lesbian community began to challenge this denial, and helped set up some of the first minority-focused AIDS events.[22]

Two of the earliest national conferences on AIDS in People of Color communities were organized by lesbians and gay men. The Third World Advisory Task Force, a primarily gay group out of San Francisco, organized a western regional conference in the early part of 1986.[23] The National Coalition of Black Lesbians and Gays, a progressive national membership organization structured around local chapters, organized the "National Conference on AIDS in the Black Community" in Washington DC in 1986. This conference, which was co-sponsored by the National Minority AIDS Council and the National Conference of Black Mayors, was funded in part from a grant from the United States Public Health Service.[24] Further, black gay men across the country, from Washington DC to New York to Oakland to San Francisco to Los Angeles were instrumental in helping to establish some of the first AIDS service organizations explicitly identifying minority communities as their target population. Additionally, black gay organizations such as Gay Men of African Descent (GMAD) of New York City have been and continue to be essential in educational efforts seeking to reach large numbers of black men.[25]

A number of factors were helpful in laying the groundwork for the response from black gay men and lesbians. The information this group received from white gay activists was extremely helpful. The realization that some black gay men and lesbians also possessed limited access and economic privilege was useful in developing contacts and pooling resources. Further, the personal experiences of loss which brought together and raised the awareness of black lesbians and gay men were undoubtedly instrumental in motivating some response. Finally, "out" black gays and lesbians were in the position of being less vulnerable to the moral judgments of traditional institutions in the black community. Because of their public identity as a black lesbian or gay man these individuals stood ready to challenge the marginalizing ideology associated with AIDS. Thus, as they attempted to speak to the entire black community about the dangers of this growing epidemic, the silence and invisibility which had once been a part of the survival contract of black lesbians and gay men could no longer exist if lives were to be saved.

AIDS and Policing Black Sexuality

While I have just noted some of the activities initiated by black lesbian and gay men in response to this epidemic, the devastation incurred from AIDS in black communities is clearly represented in the numbers. In New York City, as in other major metropolitan areas, AIDS is now the number one killer of black men ages 25–44 and women ages 18–44. Nationally, 114,868 Black Americans have been diagnosed with AIDS, accounting for 32 percent of all AIDS cases, nearly three times our 12-percent representation in the general population. Black women comprise 54 percent of all women with AIDS nationally, with black children constituting 55 percent of all children with AIDS, and black men accounting for 28 percent of men with AIDS. If these numbers were not sobering enough, the trend of increasing representation of those with AIDS from People of Color communities suggest that these numbers will only continue to increase in the future.[26]

Thus, in the face of such substantial and increasing devastation being visited upon the black community through the AIDS epidemic, one might reasonably expect members or at least leaders of black communities to actively mobilize community support around demands for more resources, attention, and action in response to this disease. However, the evidence suggests that the response from black community leaders and activists has been much less public, confrontational, collective, and consistent than the statistics might dictate. Further, any cursory comparative examination of the political response emanating from predominately white lesbian and gay activists to this disease suggests that black organizations and institutions have been less active around this crisis. Over the years, members of gay and lesbian communities have found old and new ways to make officials, institutions, and at times the general public answer some of their demands.[27] Gay activists have developed sophisticated political tactics to respond to the indifference and hostility that the government and other institutions display toward People with AIDS. Rallies, sit-ins, lobbying, private meetings, civil disobedience, "phone zaps," few things seem too far out-of-bounds to make people listen and respond. And while the gay community has mounted a coordinated effort of traditional politics and public collective action to the AIDS epidemic, the response in the black community has been much less pervasive, public, and effective. Again, through the work of primarily black gay activists, important conferences and forums have been sponsored to educate members of black communities on the dangers of AIDS. Organizations like the Minority Task Force on AIDS and the Black Leadership Commission on AIDS have been established to provide services and develop educational programs for members of black communities. National leaders have even on occasion made mention of AIDS in their speeches to black constituents. However, generally there has been no substantial and sustained mobilization around this crisis in African-American communities. There have been few, if any, rallies, sit-ins, or petitions in black communities to bring attention to the devastation created by AIDS. There has been no sustained lobbying effort on the part of national black organizations like the NAACP or the Urban League. Instead, many in the black community continue to see AIDS as a horrible disease, believing that we should extend sympathy and compassion to its "victims," but claim no ownership as a community. AIDS is generally not understood as an internal political crisis that necessitates the mobilization of black communities. Even when AIDS is seen as a conspiracy against black communities, by the government or some other entity, no mobilization accompanies such suspicion.[28] For most in black communities, AIDS is still a disease of individuals, usually "irresponsible, immoral, and deviant" individuals, some of whom happen to be Black.

Quite often, when trying to explain the response to AIDS in black communities, authors retreat to the familiar and substantively important list of barriers preventing a more active response from community leaders and organizations. Regularly topping this list is the claim that because black communities have fewer resources than most other groups they cannot be expected to respond to AIDS in a manner similar to "privileged" lesbians and gay men. And while there is truth to the claim that most black people operate with limited access to resources, this explanation is based on a very narrow conception of resources and a very limited understanding of the history of the black community. Most of the cities hardest hit by this disease (New York, Los Angeles, Washington DC, Detroit, Chicago, Atlanta) have been or are currently headed by black mayors. Thus, while black individuals suffer from limited resources, black elected officials control, or at least have significant input into, decisions about how resources will be allocated in their cities. Further, while individuals in the black community still suffer from marginalization and oppression, organizations like the NAACP, the SCLC, and the Urban League have been able to gain access to national agencies and policy debates. Thus the claim that black people have fewer resources than other groups, while accurate at the individual level, does not appropriately account for the institutional resources controlled or accessed by black elected officials and traditional organizations.

A second explanation that is sometimes offered focuses on the numerous crises plaguing black communities. Proponents of this view argue that members of the black community suffer from so many ailments and structural difficulties, such as sickle-cell anemia, high blood pressure, sugar diabetes, homelessness, persistent poverty, drugs, crime, discrimination . . . that no one should expect community leaders to turn over their political agenda to the issue of AIDS. Again, this position has merit, for in fact we know that black communities do suffer disproportionately from most social, medical, economic, and political ills. It is, however, specifically because of the inordinate

amount of suffering found in black communities that we might expect
more attention to this disease. Because AIDS touches on, or is related
to, so many other issues facing, in particular poor black communities
– healthcare, poverty, drug use, homelessness, etc. – we might reasonably expect black leaders to "use" the devastation of this disease to
develop and reinforce an understanding of the enormity of the crisis
facing black communities. Rarely does an issue so readily embody the
life and death choices facing a community and rarely is an issue so
neglected by the leadership of that community.

Still others have suggested that, along with the lack of resources and
the encompassing social problems of the black community, there exist
numerous other issues which discourage black communities from taking any active ownership regarding this epidemic. For example, the
portrayal of AIDS as a disease of white gay men in dominant media
sources as well as in many community papers communicates that this
epidemic does not threaten and need not interest the majority of black
people. Further, the fact that when coverage around AIDS and black
communities is provided it often continues the historical practice of
framing or associating black people/Africa with disease (i.e. discussion
of the origin of AIDS in Africa) helps reinforce a look-the-other-way
attitude by indigenous leaders and organizations.[29] Again while both
of these factors clearly play a part in understanding the community's
response, I contend they still leave vacant a central component in this
puzzle over black communities' lack of mobilization around AIDS.

Recently, scholars who study AIDS and black communities have
begun to point to the issue of homophobia in the black community as
the missing piece in our puzzle.[30] In this context their concern is not
just with homophobia among individuals, but more importantly with
the homophobia located and rooted in indigenous institutions like the
black church, fraternal and social organizations, as well as some
national political organizations. Different variants of this argument
suggest that it is the black community's homophobia that significantly
structures its response, or lack thereof, to AIDS in black communities.[31]

While we must pay attention to homophobia in the black community
as one source of disinformation about AIDS, I do not believe that the
concept or explanation of homophobia adequately captures the complexity of sexuality, in particular lesbian and gay sexuality, in black
communities. This is not to say that homophobia, as a general process
of socialization that we all endure, is not a part of black communities.
However, homophobia as the fear or even hatred of gay and lesbian
people does not represent the intricate role that sexuality has played in

defining "blackness" throughout the years. Sexuality, or what has
been defined by the dominant society as the abnormal sexuality of
both black men and women – with men being oversexed and in search
of white women, while black women were and are represented as
promiscuous baby producers when they are not the direct and indirect
property of white men – has been used historically and currently in this
country to support and justify the marginal and exploited position of
black people.

Scholars such as Takaki, Steinberg, Davis, Lewis, and Omi and
Winant have all attempted, through various approaches, to detail the
ways in which dominant groups, often with state sanctioning, have
defined and redefined racial classification for their benefit and profit.[32]
Whether it be the one-drop rule, one's maternal racial lineage, simplis-
tic evaluations of skin color, or some other combination of biological,
cultural, or behavioral attributes, ideas of who is to be classified as
black have had a long and varied history in this country. However,
beyond the mere designation of who belongs in a particular group,
dominant groups have also engaged in the process of defining racial
group meaning. Those characteristics or stereotypes propagated as
representing the "essence" of black people have been constructed and
informed by particular historical needs. Ideas about the laziness, inferiority, and in particular the sexual or abnormal sexual activity of
black people have been advanced to justify any number of economic,
political, and social arrangements.

This systematic degradation, stereotyping, and stigmatization of
Black Americans has all but dictated that attempts at incorporation,
integration, and assimilation on the part of black people generally
include some degree of proving ourselves to be "just as nice as those
white folks." Thus, leaders, organizations, and institutions have consistently attempted to redefine and indigenously construct a new public
image or understanding of what blackness would mean. This process
of reconstructing or [im]proving blackness involves not only a reliance
on the self-regulation of individual black people, but also includes
significant "indigenous policing" of black people. Consistently, in the
writings of black academics we hear reference to the role of the black
middle class as examples and regulators of appropriate behavior for
the black masses. Drake and Cayton, in their 1945 classic *Black
Metropolis*, discuss the attitude of the black upper class toward the
behavior of black lower classes.

> The attitude of the upper class toward the lower is ambivalent. As people
> whose standards of behavior approximate those of the white middle

class, the members of Bronzeville's upper class resent the tendency of outsiders to "judge us all by what ignorant Negroes do." They emphasize their *differentness....* The whole orientation of the Negro upper class thus becomes one of trying to speed up the process by which the lower class can be transformed from a poverty-stricken group, isolated from the general stream of American life, into a counterpart of middle-class America. [emphasis from original text][33]

Regulation of the black masses was often pursued not only by individuals, but also by an extensive network of community groups and organizations. James R. Grossman details how the Urban League in conjunction with black and white institutions worked to help black migrants "adjust" to urban standards of behavior.

The Urban League and the *Defender*, assisted by the YMCA, the larger churches, and a corps of volunteers, fashioned a variety of initiatives designed to help – and pressure – the new comers to adjust not only to industrial work, but to urban life, northern racial patterns, and behavior that would enhance the reputation of blacks in the larger (white) community . . . The Urban League, through such activities as "Stranger Meetings," leafleting, and door-to-door visits, advised newcomers on their duties as citizens: cleanliness, sobriety, thrift, efficiency, and respectable, restrained behavior in public places . . . Under the tutelage of the respectable citizens of black Chicago, migrants were to become urbanized, northernized, and indistinguishable from others of their race. At the very least, they would learn to be as inconspicuous as possible.[34]

It is important to remember that a substantial amount of indigenous policing focused on what would be represented publicly as the sexual behavior of black people. Community leaders and organizations, fighting for equal rights, equal access, and full recognition as citizens, struggled to "clean up" the image of sexuality in black communities. Cornel West, in *Race Matters*, discusses the unwillingness of most black institutions to engage in open discussions of sexuality in black communities.

But these grand yet flawed black institutions refused to engage one fundamental issue: *black sexuality.* . . .

Why was this so? Primarily because these black institutions put a premium on black survival in America. And black survival required accommodation with and acceptance from white America. Accommodation avoids any sustained association with the subversive and transgressive – be it communisms or miscegenation . . . And acceptance meant that only "good" negroes would thrive – especially those who left black sexuality at the door when they "entered" and "arrived." In short, struggling black institutions made a Faustian pact with white America: avoid any substantive engagement with black sexuality and your survival on the margins of American society is, at least, possible.[35]

Thus, individuals who were thought to fulfill stereotypes of black sexuality as something deviant or other often had their morality questioned by leading institutions in black communities. For instance, sexuality thought to stand outside the Christian mores as set down by the black church was constructed and interpreted as an indication of the moral character of that individual and their family as well as an embarrassment to the collective consciousness and cultural capital of the black community. Hazel Carby discusses the moral panic and threat to the collective respectability of black communities attributed to uncontrolled migrating black women in her article "Policing the Black Woman's Body."

> The need to police and discipline the behavior of black women in cities, however, was not only a premise of white agencies and institutions but also a perception of black institutions and organizations, and the black middle class. The moral panic about the urban presence of apparently uncontrolled black women was symptomatic of and referenced aspects of the more general crises of social displacement and dislocation that were caused by migration. White and black intellectuals used and elaborated this discourse so that when they referred to the association between black women and vice, or immoral behavior, their references carried connotations of other crises of the black urban environment. Thus the migrating black woman could be variously situated as a threat to the progress of the race; as a threat to the establishment of a respectable urban black middle class; as a threat to congenial black and white middle-class relations; and as a threat to the formation of black masculinity in an urban environment.[36]

While these examples may seem dated, we need only look around today to see the great efforts many black leaders and academics engage in to distance themselves from those perceived to participate in "inappropriate immoral sexual behavior." Examples of such distancing efforts are evident not only in the absence of any sustained writing on black lesbians and gay men by black authors and academics, but are also found in the counter-experience of unending writing and policy attacks on the "inappropriate" and "carefree" sexuality of those labeled the "underclass" and more generally black women on welfare.[37]

I want to be clear that contests or opposition to the public representation of black gay male sexuality in particular and non-normative sexuality in general is significantly motivated by a genuine threat to the cultural capital acquired by some in black communities, where cultural capital symbolizes the acceptance, access, and privilege of primarily black middle- and upper-class people.[38] Thus, for many black leaders and activists, visible/public black homosexuality is understood to threaten that "cultural capital" acquired by both assimilation and protest. From such a perspective the policing or regulation of black gay and lesbian behavior/visibility is seen as the responsibility not only of dominant institutions, but also leaders of indigenous institutions who can claim that they are protecting the image and progress of "the race/community." And it is through the fulfillment of these communal duties that internal ideas and definitions of blackness, thought to help with the task of regulation, emerge. These definitions set the rules that to be a "good" or "true" black person you must adhere to some religious standards of appropriate sexual behavior. To be a true black man is antithetical to being gay, for part of your duty as a black man is to produce "little black warriors in the interest of the Black nation." The rules continue suggesting that to be gay is to be a pawn of a white genocidal plot, intent on destroying the black community. To be gay is to want to be white anyway, since we all know that there is no tradition of homosexuality in our African history. Thus, to be gay is stand outside the norms, values, and practices of the community, putting your "true" blackness into question.

In his article "Some Thoughts on the Challenges Facing Black Gay Intellectuals," Ron Simmons details just some of the arguments made by national (and nationalist) Black leaders such as Nathan Hare, Jawanza Kunjufu, Molefi Asante, Haki Madhubuti, Amiri Baraka and Yosuf Ben-Jochannan which seek to undermine claims of an empowered, fully recognized black gay identity.[39] Specifically, Simmons outlines what he considers to be the four major categories or reasons provided by these scholars for the development of homosexuality in the Black community.

In reviewing African American literature, one finds that black homophobic and heterosexist scholars believe homosexuality in the African American community is the result of: (1) the emasculation of black men by white oppression (e.g., Staples, Madhubuti, Asante, Farrakhan, and Baraka); (2) the breakdown of the family structure and the loss of male role models (e.g. Kunjufu, Madhubuti, Farrakhan, and Hare); (3) a sinister plot perpetuated by diabolical racists who want to destroy the black race (e.g. Hare); and (4) immorality as defined in biblical scriptures, Koranic suras, or Egyptian "Books of the Dead" (e.g. Farrakhan and Ben-Jochannan).[40]

It is important to recognize that while these authors all see homosexuality as something devised and infiltrated from outside the black community, none or very few are advocating directly that black gay men and women be fully rejected and excluded from the community. And that is not the claim I seek to make with regards to the contested nature of black gay identities. Instead, many of the scholars in Simmons' analysis argue that homosexuality must be understood as a threat to the survival of the black community. Thus, they ask that black lesbians and gay men suppress their sexuality, keep quite, remain undemanding, and make their needs subservient to the "collective" needs of the community. Simmons cites Molefi Asante as directly promoting such a subservient position in his book *Afrocentricity*:

> Afrocentric relationships are based upon . . . what is best for the collective imperative of the people . . . All brothers who are homosexuals should know that they too can become committed to the collective will. It means the submergence of their own wills into the collective will of our people.[41]

Simmons identifies similar ideas of inclusion without empowerment for black gay men and lesbians in Nathan and Julia Hare's book *The Endangered Black Family*. They write,

> On the other hand – and this is crucial – we will refuse to embark on one more tangent of displaced contempt and misdirected scorn for the homosexualized [*sic*] black brothers or sisters and drive them over to the camp of white liberal-radical-moderate-establishment coalition. What we must do is offer the homosexual brother or sister a proper compassion and acceptance *without advocacy* . . . Some of them may yet be saved. And yet, we must declare open warfare upon the sources of [their] confusion [emphasis added].[42]

Again, the proscription these authors offer is not the complete rejection of black lesbian and gay men. Instead, they suggest a quiet acceptance "without advocacy." It is within this analysis that we again see the conflictual nature of black gay identity as it has been repeatedly defined in the black community. It is an identity that allows inclusion, but only under certain restrictions – denying any attempt at the empowerment of this segment of the black community. For these leaders homophobia or the hatred of black gays and lesbians does not fully explain their position of silent inclusion. Thus, the "sin" that black lesbians and gay men commit is not just rooted in the inherent wrongness of their sexual behavior, but instead or just as importantly in their perceived weakness and cost to black communities.

We can now understand why homophobia, as a simple makeshift explanation to represent the complexity of sexuality in black communities, is inadequate. Instead, to analyze black communities' response to AIDS we must address a whole set of issues, including dominant representations of black sexuality, how these ideas/stereotypes have been used against black communities, and the perceived need to regulate black sexuality through indigenous definitions of blackness. From this starting point we may be better able to understand, although never accept, the range of opposition black gay men encounter as stemming not only from people's repudiation of the idea of sex between men, but also from the use of sexuality by dominant groups to stigmatize and marginalize further a community already under siege.

Again, it is important to note that what is at stake here is the question of membership, full empowered membership in black communities. Thus, visibility, access to indigenous resources, participation and acknowledgement in the structuring of black political agendas all are put into question when one's blackness is contested. And undoubtedly, there exist many factors that contribute to the black community's response to AIDS, including a real deficiency in community resources as well as a real mistrust of government-sponsored information on health care and disease in black communities.[43] However, I believe that a significant part of the explanation for the lack of forceful action around AIDS is directly tied to ideas and definitions of "black identity" put forth by indigenous leaders, institutions and organizations. These definitions of "blackness" stand in direct contrast to the images and ideas associated with those living with AIDS or HIV (Human Immunodeficiency Virus) in black communities. In particular, these indigenous constructions of "blackness" define behavior linked to the transmission of HIV as immoral and an embarrassment, threatening to the status and survival of community members.

Having laid out this argument concerning the contestation of black gay identity and its impact on political responses to AIDS in black communities, it is important to provide, even briefly, a concrete example of the way an indigenous institution such as the black church defines and responds to the needs of black gay men in the era of AIDS. I will also try to highlight a few of the ways black gay men have responded to the secondary marginalization they have experienced through black churches. Again, I use the church merely as an illustration of the process of marginalization and identity contestation in which numerous indigenous institutions engage.

"The Black Church"

Activists and scholars often have focused on the activity of the black church to understand and explain the political behavior of members of the black community, since traditionally the church has been perceived as the glue and motor of the community. If any activity was to touch every segment of the community it was believed that such efforts must be based in the black church. The work of Aldon Morris linking the black church to the civil-rights movement is a classic example of the role the black church is thought to play in struggles for liberation and rights.[44] However, even prior to the civil-rights movement the black church was used to build movements of freedom. It was the black church that acted as meeting space, school, healthcare facility, and distributor of food from slavery to Reconstruction, through the years of northern migration and the decades of Jim Crow segregation. In her article on the new social role of black churches Hollie I. West comments, "African American churches have traditionally served as a refuge from a hostile white world, beehives of both social and political activity."[45]

However, with the advent of AIDS, drug epidemics, and the increasing poverty and stratification of black communities, some organizers and activists are beginning to question the central authority given to the church. West suggests in her article that AIDS is a problem that pulls the church in two directions. "Some clergymen privately acknowledge the dilemma. They recognize the need to confront AIDS and drugs, but conservative factions in their congregations discourage involvement."[46] It has been a conservative ideology, based on strict norms of "moral" behavior, that has often framed the church's response to many of the controversial social issues facing black communities. Gail Walker briefly delineates the contradictory nature of the black church:

> The dual – and contradictory – legacy of the African-American church is that it has been among the most important instruments of African-American liberation and at the same time one of the most conservative institutions in the African-American community.[47]

The position of the black church on the issue of homosexuality has seemed fairly straightforward, but in fact it has both public and private dimensions. Holding with the teaching of most organized religions, members of black churches assert that homosexual behavior is immoral and in direct contrast to the word of God. Black ministers have consistently spoken out and preached against the immorality and threat posed to the community by gays and lesbians. Recently, black ministers from numerous denominations in Cleveland, Ohio organized in opposition to federal legislation to include gay men and lesbians under the protection of the 1964 Civil Rights Bill. These ministers, representing themselves as "true leaders" of the black church, wrote in the local black newspaper, the *Call and Post*:

> We as members and representatives of African American protestant congregations reaffirm our identity as THE BLACK CHURCH. . . .
> We view HOMOSEXUALITY (including bisexual, as well as gay or lesbian sexual activity) as a lifestyle that is contrary to the teaching of the Bible. Such sexual activity and involvement is contrary to the pattern established during creation. Homosexual behavior in the Bible is forbidden and described as unnatural and perverted. . . .
> Our attitude toward any individuals that are involved in/with a HOMOSEXUAL LIFESTYLE is expressed through tolerance and compassion. The church's mission is to bring about RESTORATION . . .[48]

However, at the same time that condemnation of gay and lesbian sexual behavior is a staple of the black church, it is also a well-known fact that black gay men, in particular, can be found in prominent positions throughout the church. Thus, black gay men involved in the activities of black churches are faced with a familiar dilemma: they have the choice of being quietly accepted as they sing in the church choir, teach Sunday school, and in some cases even preach from the pulpit, or they can be expelled from the church for participating in blasphemous behavior. Nowhere in this choice does the idea of inclusion as fully recognized and empowered members exist. Thus, according to religious doctrine, black lesbian and gay members of the community are to be embraced and taken care of in a time of need. However, their gay identity places them outside the indigenously constructed boundaries of both Christian and black identification as recognized by the church.

AIDS activists argue that a moral framework rooted in middle-class values of assimilation and dominant ideas of Christianity has been used to justify the church's moral condemnation of black gay men and injection drug users. And it is this same moral framework that structures the church's understanding and reaction to AIDS in the black community. Nowhere recently has this principle of silent acceptance and care at the expense of a public denunciation been more evident than in struggles around the church's response to AIDS in black communities. It has been the contradictory nature of church actions and rhetoric that continues to frustrate many AIDS activists who looked to it initially for a swift, compassionate, and empowering response. Activists and those providing services claim that the church did little to nothing early in the epidemic to deal with this impending crisis for black communities. Further, when members of the church elite finally did mobilize, it was with negative judgments and pity. Dr. Marjorie Hill, former Director of New York City's Office of Lesbians and Gay Concerns under Mayor David Dinkins, explains that the church's history of activism is muted with regards to AIDS because of its insistence on denying public recognition of lesbian and gay community members.

> Historically, activism in the black community has come from the church. However, the reluctance of the church to respond to AIDS means they are not following the mission of Christ. . . . The church has not dealt with the issue of homosexuality. Many have Gays who sing in the choir and play the organ and that is fine until they need the church's help and recognition. . . . Denial only works for so long, the reality of gay men and women will eventually have to be dealt with.[49]

There are others who argue that the church is making progress. For their part, church members point to the numerous AIDS ministries that have been established to deal with AIDS in black communities. They highlight what seems like revolutionary strides in the ability of black ministers to even mention AIDS from the pulpit. And while black lesbian and gay leaders commend those who engage in efforts to identify comfortable ways for black ministers and congregations to deal with the devastation of AIDS in their communities, they still contend that there remains an absence of full recognition of the rights and lives of those infected with this disease. The saying "love the sinner, hate the sin," is paramount in understanding the limited response of black clergy. Gay men are to be loved and taken care of when they are sick, but their loving relationships are not to be recognized nor respected. Most individuals affected by this disease can tell at least one story of going to a funeral of a gay man and never having their gay identity recognized as well as never hearing the word AIDS mentioned.

Family members and ministers are all too willing to grieve the loss of a son or church member, without ever acknowledging the total identity of that son. Lost to AIDS is not only the son loved so dearly, but the totality of his life which included lovers and gay friends who also grieve for that loss.

It is important that we not lose sight off the fundamental obstacle to the church's whole hearted response to AIDS, and that is its adherence or reliance on a strict middle-class Christian code, which holds that behavior that transmits the virus is immortal, sinful, and just as importantly for the argument presented here, costly to the community's status and standing. Thus, until church leaders are ready to discuss issues of sexuality, drug use, and homosexuality in an inclusive discourse, their ability to serve the entire community as well as confront, instead of replicate, dominant ideologies will be severely inhibited. Rev. James Forbes of Riverside Church in New York City has been one of the few black clergy who has openly called on the church to open up its dialogue concerning AIDS. In a keynote address at the 1991 Harlem Week of Prayer, Rev. Forbes declared that until the black church deals with fundamental issues such as sexuality in an inclusive and accepting manner, it will never be able to deal adequately with the AIDS epidemic in the black community.

While ministers like Rev. Forbes preach the need for the church to reevaluate its stance on fundamental judgments of human sexuality, others believe that we may have seen the church move about as far as its going to go. Except for those exceptional congregations committed to a liberation theology, the provision of services for those with AIDS may be the extent of the church's response, because for many clergy there is no way to reconcile behavior that can lead to the transmission of the virus to the doctrine of the Christian church. Rev. Calvin Butts of Absynnian Baptist Church in Harlem explains,

> The response of the church is getting better. At one time the church didn't respond and when the church did respond it was negative. Ministers thought that a negative response was in keeping with the thinking that AIDS was transmitted by homosexual transmission, drugs, you know. But as more thoughtful clergy became involved issues of compassion entered the discussion and we used Jesus' refuge in the house of lepers as an example. People became more sympathetic when people close to the church were affected. Also the work of BLCA [Black Leadership Commission on AIDS] brought clergy together to work on our response. Unfortunately, there are still quite a few who see it as God's retribution.[50]

However, in an environment where their identity is contested and their full rights and connection with black communities is negated, many black lesbian and gay leaders are actively developing ways to ignore the dictates and challenge the power of the church, especially as it affects AIDS organizing. One such strategy has focused on black gay and lesbian leaders as well as AIDS activists identifying other ways to do effective work in the community without the help of the church. There are those who suggest that it does not matter whether the church responds because the church no longer touches those parts of the community most at risk for this disease. Colin Robinson, former staff member at Gay Men's Health Crisis (GMHC) and currently executive director of the organization Gay Men of African Descent (GMAD) explains that "the church is still hooked on sin, but compromised by sin. They will take care of you when you get sick, but they won't talk about it and that is no way to provide effective education."[51] George Bellinger, Jr., a member of GMAD and former Education Director of the Minority Task Force on AIDS in New York, suggests that "we put too much status in the church. They aren't connected to the affected populations and they bring with them all kinds of middle-class values."[52]

Others in the community have gone beyond developing AIDS education strategies to focus directly on challenging the teaching of the church about homosexuality, especially as black gay identities are offered as a contrast to the indigenous constructed image of "good black Christian folk." These individuals seek out leaders inside the community, like Rev. James Forbes, who have publicly challenged the representations of more conservative clergy. These activists seek a leadership that will embrace the idea of an empowered black lesbian and gay community. In the absence of these individuals, black gay activists have taken up the task of building their own religious institutions in cities like New York, San Francisco, and Los Angeles, that will put forth a different interpretation of biblical scripture.

All of these oppositional strategies contest the stigma of a black gay identity as constructed by the black church. Black gay activists understand that to engage the black community on the issue of AIDS as well as lesbian and gay rights they must contest and challenge the church's declaration and labeling of gay and lesbian lifestyles as immoral. Further, black lesbian and gay activists must take on the task of redefining themselves as integral, connected, and contributing members of the community, so as to access the community support we most desperately need.

Conclusion: A Few Last Comments

The goal of this chapter was to explore, in some concrete fashion, the contested nature of identity within marginal communities. For far too long we have let assumptions of a stable, homogeneous group direct our attention to a framework of analysis that focuses on struggles between dominant and marginal groups. Left largely unexplored by social scientists are the internal struggles within marginal communities threatening to severely change the basis and direction of group politics. Throughout this paper I have attempted to explore how identities are constructed and contested and how in this case such disputes influenced the politics of AIDS in black communities.

Central to this entire discussion has been the idea that group identity, or at least the way many of us conceptualize it, has changed over the years. We can no longer work from an essentialist position, in which all marginal people, in particular all black people, are assumed to have the same standing within their communities. Instead, we must pay attention to the battles for full inclusion waged within these communities, because these battles provide important signals to the future political direction of the community. In the case of AIDS, it is fairly clear that the vulnerable status and contested identities of those most often associated with this disease in the black community, injection drug users and gay men, severely impacts on the community's response to the epidemic. And while indigenous institutions and leaders have increasingly demonstrated a willingness to fight political battles over AIDS funding and discrimination, there have been few attempts by these same leaders to redefine the community's battle against AIDS as a political fight for the empowerment of the most marginal sectors of the community.

However, the battle around AIDS and who has full access to the resources and consciousness of the community does not stand alone. Similar battles are being waged around other issues, such as the "underclass." Those on the outside, those designated as "less than, secondary, bad, or culturally deviant," are developing new ways to challenge politically a cohesive group unity that rejects their claims at representation and in many cases ignores their needs. These individuals, like the black gay men discussed in this paper, can no longer afford to support a leadership that is content to have them seen, in some cases blamed, but not heard.

Thus, if there is one larger implication of this work that needs further investigation, it is how marginal groups facing increasing stratification and multiple social identities will adjust to build a somewhat unified

identity for the pursuit of political struggles. The importance of groups
in our political system cannot be denied. In a pluralistic political
system access is usually based on the grouping of individuals with
some shared interest, with these individuals pooling resources and
influence to impact policy decisions. The role of collective mobilization becomes especially important for marginal groups with a history
of being denied access to dominant political structures. These marginal
groups often find themselves excluded and defined out of the political
process. Thus, African Americans grouped together by the socially
constructed category of race have found their political access restricted. Only through coming together to redefine their marginal
identity into a new identity which both unifies and empowers the
multiple segments of the community could any political battles hope to
be won.

In black communities the presence of increasing stratification and
heterogeneity, as is evident in the community's mixed response to
AIDS, raises the question of the utility of race as a basis upon which to
build political movements. There are some scholars who suggest that
race is of dwindling importance in understanding the life choices and
conditions of most black people, and instead argue that class as it
interacts with urban (inner-city) residency should be replaced as the
defining explanation of the "black experience" in contemporary
United States. While I do not subscribe to the school that race is
unimportant, I do believe that African Americans face a crisis in
identity. It is true that other social identities, such as gender, class,
sexual orientation, and geographic location, are taking on greater
significance in determining the experiences of group members. Without some increased recognition of the broadening of identities through
which people exist in and understand the world, black leaders, scholars, and activists may end up so out of touch with the experiences of
most people that they fill no real function in the community and thus
are left to talk to themselves.

Thus, as social scientists we must proceed with our study of groups
and group identity in new and innovative ways. First and foremost, we
must again see the group as a unit of analysis with special attention
paid to the internal structure of marginal groups. Second, we must pay
attention to and recognize new or newly acknowledged identities.
Where once we struggled to include gender, race, and class in our
multivariate regressions as well as our classroom discussions, we now
have the opportunity to explore group identities such as lesbian and
gay identities which were once thought to be outside the realm of
importance to "real" political scientists.[53] And finally, as we focus on

the group and include more groups in the picture we must accept the fact that ideas of essentialist, stable identities in which homogenous groups act as one in calculating risk and determining strategy must be dismissed or revised. Gone are the biological and essentialist conceptions of group formation. They have been replaced with an emphasis on social construction and contextual meaning.

Overall, I believe that we must develop a new approach to understanding identity and its role in structuring politics and political behavior. This new approach assumes that identities are not only constructed, they are also challenged and contested. As difficult and reluctant as political scientists often are to incorporate change into our understandings of politics, this new approach to understanding and studying group identity both promises and threatens to reconstruct our social science playing fields. There are new players to identify, there are old groups to redefine, and there are new actions which should be interpreted as political. Undoubtedly, our old favorites of race, class, and gender will remain, but the internal restructuring of those identities may change as common agendas and assumed "unity" are challenged. In the end what all of this may mean is that those of us interested in the group as a unit of analysis, those of us interested in the developing agenda of marginal groups as they struggle for inclusion and/or equality, even those interested primarily in the individual, assessing the role of group identity through dummy variables representing race, class, and gender in multivariate equations, may have to look a bit closer at what is really happening in these communities and groups. Who is being counted? Who is shaping the political agenda? How are stratification and contests over identity impacting on the internal unity needed to address a dominant system? And finally, how will this affect the politics of these groups as well as the larger society in the twenty-first century?[54]

Notes

1 For discussions of postmodern and deconstructive approaches see e.g. Sylvia Walby, "Post-Post-Modernism? Theorizing Social Complexity," *Destabilizing Theory: Contemporary Feminist Debates*, M. Barrett and A. Phillips (eds) (Stanford, Calif.: Stanford University Press, 1992), 31–52; Jane Flax, "Postmodernism and Gender Relations in Feminist Theory," *Feminism/Postmodernism*, L. J. Nicholson (ed.) (New York: Routledge, 1990), 39–62; and Steven Seidman, "Identity and Politics in a "Postmodern" Gay Culture: Some Historical and Conceptual Notes," *Fear of a Queer Planet: Queer Politics and Social Theory*, M. Warner (ed.) (Minneapolis: University of Minnesota Press, 1993), 105–42.

2 First, it is important that we remember that social-constructionist theories come in different forms and different degrees. For such a discussion see Carole S. Vance, "Social Construction Theory: Problems in the History of Sexuality," *Homosexuality, Which Homosexuality?* (London: GMP Publishers, 19xx), 13–33.

   Second, it is also important to recognize that social constructionist theory is still relatively new to many fields within the social sciences. So in the field of American Political Science, where quantitative analysis dominates as the methodology of choice, rivaled by formal theory, social-constructionist approaches to the study of groups have at best tangentially made any appearance.

   Finally, for examples of variants of social-constructionist approaches to the field of race and black studies see among others Stuart Hall, "Race, Articulation and Societies Structured in Dominance," *Sociological Theories: Race and Colonialism* (Paris: UNESCO, 1980), 305–45; Paul Gilroy, *Small Acts: Thoughts on the Politics of Black Cultures* (London: Serpent's Tail, 1993); and Evelyn Brooks Higginbotham, "African-American Women's History and the Metalanguage of Race," *Signs*, 17 (2), winter 1992: 251–74.

3 By marginal communities I mean those groups with an ascribed and certainly constructed identity that has historically and institutionally served as the basis for the exclusion, deprivation, and a distinction of other.

4 See e.g. Iris Marion Young, "The Ideal of Community and the Politics of Difference," *Feminism/Postmodernism*, L. Nicholson (ed.) (New York: Routledge, 1990), (30), 300–23; Shane Phelan, "(Be)Coming Out: Lesbian Identity and Politics," *Signs*, 19 (30), spring 1994: 765–90; Kimberle Crenshaw, "Demarginalizing the Intersection of Race and Sex: A Black Feminist Critique of Antidiscrimination Doctrine Feminist Theory and Antiracist Politics," *University of Chicago Legal Forum*, 1989, pp. 139–67; Lisa Lowe, "Heterogeneity, Hybridity, Multiplicity: Marking Asian American Differences," *Diaspora*, 1 (1), spring 1991: 24–44.

5 See e.g. Maria Lugones, "Purity, Impurity, and Separation," *Signs: Journal of Women in Culture and Society*, 19 (2), 1994: 458–79; and E. Frances White, "Africa on my Mind: Gender Counter Discourse and African-American Nationalism," *Journal of Women's History*, 2 (1), spring 1990: 73–97.

6 James C. Scott, *Domination and the Arts of Resistance: The Hidden Transcript* (New Haven: Yale University Press, 1990).

7 For a full discussion of the process of secondary marginalization see Cathy J. Cohen, "Power, Resistance and the Construction of Crisis: Marginalized Communities Respond to AIDS," unpublished manuscript, Dept. of Political Science, Yale University, 1993, pp. 72–5.

8 See Henry Louis Gates, Jr., "Two Nations . . . Both Black," in *Forbes*, 150, Sept. 14, 1992: 132–5 for a subtle example of the *indigenous* evaluation

and separation of members of the community into categories of "good and bad" or "industrious and culturally deficient" black people.

9 While several different segments of the black community have been associated with AIDS, I focus this inquiry on the struggle around black gay male identity because it seems most illustrative of the ways in which contests over indigenously defined identities can impact on the politics of marginal communities.

10 I should be clear that any number of organizations or leaders have constructed ways to "deal" with AIDS without directly confronting or embracing those stigmatized segments of black communities associated with this disease. Thus, you are much more likely to find "leaders" talking about the innocent children and women who are the victims of this disease in black communities than the gay men and intravenous drug users who suffer disproportionately in our communities.

11 Judith Butler, *Gender Trouble* (New York: Routledge, 1990); Michael Warner (ed.), *Fear of a Queer Planet: Queer Politics and Social Theory* (Minneapolis: University of Minnesota Press, 1993); Teresa de Lauretis, "Queer Theory: Lesbian and Gay Sexualities," *Differences*, 3, 1991.

12 Barbara Jeanne Fields, "Slavery, Race and Ideology in the United States of America," *New Left Review*, 181, May/June 1990: 115–16.

13 Michael Omi and Howard Winant, *Racial Formation in the United States: From the 1960s to the 1990s*, 2nd edn. (New York: Routledge, 1994), 55.

14 See e.g. Molefi Kete Asante, *Afrocentricity* (Trenton, New Jersey: African World Press, Inc., 1988); Patricia Hill Collins, *Black Feminist Thought: Knowledge, Consciousness, and the Politics of Empowerment* (New York: Harper-Collins Academic, 1990).

15 See e.g. Cheryl Clarke, "The Failure to Transform: Homophobia in the Black Community," *Home Girls: A Black Feminist Anthology*, B. Smith (ed.) (New York: Kitchen Table: Women of Color Press, 1983), 197–208.

I would caution the reader, however, not to discount the role that state-sponsored repression also played in leading to the destruction of many of these groups. It is now a well-documented fact that the FBI through the counterintelligence program (COINTELPRO) helped destroy many liberation groups, such as the Black Panther Party.

16 See Eric Garber, "A Spectacle in Color: The Lesbian and Gay Subculture of Jazz Age Harlem," in *Hidden from History: Reclaiming the Gay and Lesbian Past*, M. Duberman, M. Vicinus and G. Chauncey, Jr. (eds) (New York: Meridian Books, 1990), 318–31; Jonathan Ned Katz, *Gay American History: Lesbians and Gay Men in the USA* (New York: Meridian Books, 1992).

17 bell hooks, *Talking Back: Thinking Feminist, Thinking Black* (Boston: South End Press, 1989), 120–1.

18 Cornel West, "The New Cultural Politics of Difference," in *Out There: Marginalization and Contemporary Cultures*, R. Ferguson, M. Gever, T. T. Minh-ha and C. West (eds) (Cambridge: The MIT Press, 1990), 25.

19 John D'Emilio. *Sexual Politics, Sexual Communities: The Making of a Homosexual Minority in the United States, 1940–1970* (Chicago: University of Chicago Press, 1983).

20 Cherrie Moraga and Gloria Anzaldua (eds), *This Bridge Called My Back: Writings by Radical Women of Color* (Latham, New York: Kitchen Table: Women of Color Press, 1981); Barbara Smith (ed.), *Home Girls: A Black Feminist Anthology* (Latham, New York: Kitchen Table: Women of Color Press, 1983); Esse Hemphill (ed.), *Brother to Brother: New Writings by Black Gay Men* (Boston: Alyson Publications, Inc., 1991); Joseph Beam (ed.), *In The Life: A Black Gay Anthology* (Boston: Alyson Publications, Inc., 1986).

21 Ernest Quimby and Samuel R. Friedman, *Social Problems*, 36 (4), Oct. 1989.

22 Ibid. 405.

23 Ibid.

24 Guy Weston, "AIDS in the Black Community," *BLACK/OUT*, 1 (2), fall 1986: 13–15.

25 There are conflicting views on the effectiveness of GMAD during the AIDS crisis. Some argue that in a crisis of this proportion GMAD should be a leader in this fight, holding programs whenever possible. Other GMAD members suggest, however, that there are more dimensions to the lives of black gay men than just the threat of AIDS. Thus it is the responsibility of GMAD to provide a supportive environment in which black gay men can dialogue and work on the opportunities and obstacles that structure their lives.

    While this debate will probably not be settled any time soon, I still believe, every time I see 75 black gay men at one of their meetings, that this is an example of the success of struggle. An example that needs work and adjustment, but a success still the same.

26 US Department of Health and Human Services, Public Health Service, Centers for Disease Control and Prevention, "HIV/AIDS Surveillance Report," Year-end Edition, 1993, vol. 5 (no. 4). @NOTES1 + = 27 Undoubtedly, the organization most recognized as contributing to the organization of people in lesbian and gay communities is ACT UP (AIDS Coalition To Unleash Power). See e.g. Josh Gamson, "Silence, Death, and the Invisible Enemy: AIDS Activism and Social Movement 'Newness,'" in *Social Problems*, 36, (4) (Oct. 1989): 351–67.

28 Responses to a question from the 1993–4 National Black Politics Study on the origin of AIDS found that nearly one-quarter (22 per cent) of African-American respondents agreed with the statement that "AIDS is a disease that is a result of an anti-black conspiracy."

29 Renee Sabatier, *Blaming Others: Prejudice, Race and Worldwide AIDS* (Washington: The Panos Institute, 1988); Cindy Patton *Inventing AIDS* (New York: Routledge, 1990).

30 Harlon L. Dalton, "AIDS in Blackface," *The AIDS Reader: Social, Political and Ethical Issues*, N. F. McKenzie (ed.) (New York: Meridan, 1991),

122–43; Evelynn Hammonds, "Race, Sex, AIDS: The Construction of 'Other,'" *Radical America*, 20 (6), 1987: 328–40; Phillip Brian Harper, "Eloquence and Epitaph: Black Nationalism and the Homophobic Impulse in Responses to the Death of Max Robinson," *The Lesbian and Gay Studies Reader*, H. Abelove, M. A. Barable, and D. M. Halperin (eds) (New York: Routledge, 1993), 159–75.

31 Now, before engaging in any discussion of homophobia in the black community these authors, as I myself do, make their obligatory claim that while we can talk about homophobia in the black community, this is not done to suggest that the black community is 'more' homophobic than any other community, in particular white "communities." In fact, there is a reasonable argument that marginal groups, either because of an understanding of the outsider position or a lack of power to enforce their prejudices, have been more inclusive and accepting of lesbian and gay members *relative to* other groups rooted in dominant society.

32 See Ronald Takaki, *Strangers From a Different Shore: A History of Asian Americans* (New York: Penguin, 1990); Stephen Steinberg, *The Ethnic Myth: Race, Ethnicity, and Class in America* (Boston: Beacon Press, 1989); F. James Davis, *Who is Black? One Nation's Definition* (University Park, Penn.: The Pennsylvania State University Press, 1991); Earl Lewis, "Race, The State, and Social Construction: The Multiple Meanings of Race in the Twentieth Century," 1994, unpublished manuscript; Omi and Winant, *Racial Formation*.

33 St Clair Drake and Horace R. Cayton, *Black Metropolis: A Study of Negro Life in a Northern City* (Chicago: University of Chicago Press, 1993), 563.

34 James R. Grossman, *Land of Hope: Chicago, Black Southerners, and the Great Migration* (Chicago: University of Chicago Press, 1989), 145–6.

35 Cornel West, *Race Matters* (Boston: Beacon Press, 1993), 86.

36 Hazel V. Carby, "Policing the Black Woman's Body," *Critical Inquiry*, 18, summer 1992: 741.

37 For such a critique see Adolph L. Reed, Jr., "The 'Underclass' as Myth and Symbol: The Poverty of Discourse about Poverty," *Radical America*, summer 1991. For an example of such distancing see Gates, "Two Nations."

38 Pierre Bourdieu, "The Forms of Capital," in *Handbook of Theory and Research for the Sociology of Education*, J. G. Richardson (ed.) (New York: Greenwood Press, 1986), 241–58.

39 Ron Simmons, "Some Thoughts onthe Challenge Facing Black Gay Intellectuals," in *Brother to Brother: New Writings by Black Gay Men*, E. Hemphill (ed.) (Boston: Alyson Publications, Inc., 1991).

40 Ibid. 212.

41 Molefi Kete Asante, *Afrocentricity: The Theory of Social Change* (Buffalo: Amulefi, 1980), 65. As cited in Simmons, "Some Thoughts," 213.

42 Nathan Hare and Julia Hare, *The Endangered Black Family: Coping with the Unisexualization and Coming Extinction of the Black Race* (San Francisco: Black Think Tank, 1984), 65. As cited in Simmons, "Some Thoughts," 214.

43   We need only remember the Tuskegee Syphilis Experiment to understand
     where such mistrust is rooted. See James H. Jones, *Bad Blood: The Tuske-
     gee Syphilis Experiment – A Tragedy of Race and Medicine* (New York:
     The Free Press, 1981); David McBride, *From TB to AIDS: Epidemics
     Among Urban Blacks Since 1900* (Albany: State University of New York
     Press, 1991); Evelynn Hammonds, "Race, Sex, AIDS: The Construction of
     Other," *Radical America*, 20 (6), 1987: 28–36.

44   Aldon D. Morris, *The Origins of the Civil Rights Movement: Black Com-
     munities Organizing for Change* (New York: The Free Press, 1984).

45   Hollie I. West, "Down from the Clouds: Black Churches Battle Earthly
     Problems," *Emerge*, May 1990: 51.

46   West, "The New Cultural Politics," 51.

47   Gail Walker, "'Oh Freedom': Liberation and the African-American
     Church," *Guardian*, Feb. 26, 1992, p. 10.

48   Rev. C. Jay Matthews, "The Black Church Position Statement on Homo-
     sexuality," *Call and Post*, June 10, 1993, p. 5c.

49   Interview with Dr. Marjorie Hill.

50   Interview with Rev. Calvin Butts.

51   Interview with Colin Robinson.

52   Interview with George Bellinger, Jr.

53   This formal recognition of groups, in particular marginal groups, has led
     to the inclusion of race, gender, and class into traditional studies of
     politics. Unfortunately, in many cases those scholars who studied these
     topics long before they were fashionable, in particular women and people
     of color, have not found their way into traditional routes of power within
     political-science organizations and departments.

54   The author would like to thank Franny Nudelman, Joshua Gamson, Debra
     Minkoff, Gordon Lafer, Vicky Hattam, Ian Shapiro, Rogers Smith, Alex
     Wendt, and members of the Yale University Ethics, Politics, and Economics
     Summer Reading Group for their helpful comments. All shortcomings are
     the full responsibility of the author.

17

Must Identity Movements Self-Destruct?: A Queer Dilemma

Joshua Gamson

Focused passion and vitriol erupt periodically in the letters columns of San Francisco's lesbian and gay newspapers. When the *San Francisco Bay Times* announced to "the community" that the 1993 Freedom Day Parade would be called "The Year of the Queer," missives fired for weeks. The parade was what it always is: a huge empowerment party. But the letters continue to be telling. "Queer" elicits familiar arguments: over assimilation, over generational differences, over who is considered "us" and who gets to decide.

On this level, it resembles similar arguments in ethnic communities in which "boundaries, identities, and cultures, are negotiated, defined, and produced" (Nagel 1994: 152). Dig deeper into debates over queerness, however, and something more interesting and significant emerges. Queerness in its most distinctive forms shakes the ground on which gay and lesbian politics have been built, taking apart the ideas of a "sexual minority" and a "gay community," indeed of "gay" and "lesbian" and even "man" and "woman."[1] It builds on central difficulties of identity-based organizing: the instability of identities both individual and collective, their made-up yet necessary character. It exaggerates and explodes these troubles, haphazardly attempting to build a politics from the rubble of deconstructed collective categories. This debate, and other related debates in lesbian and gay politics, are not only over the *content* of collective identity (whose definition of "gay" counts?), but over the everyday *viability* and political *usefulness* of sexual identities (is there and should there be such a thing as "gay," "lesbian," "man," "woman"?).

This paper, using internal debates from lesbian and gay politics as illustration, brings to the fore a key dilemma in contemporary identity politics, and traces out its implications for social-movement theory and research.[2] As I will show in greater detail, in these sorts of debates – which crop up in other communities as well – two different political impulses, and two different forms of organizing, can be seen facing off. The logic and political utility of deconstructing collective categories vies with that of shoring them up; each logic is true, and neither is fully tenable.

On the one hand, lesbians and gay men have made themselves an effective force in this country over the past several decades largely by giving themselves what civil-rights movements had: a public collective identity. Gay and lesbian social movements have built a quasi-ethnicity, complete with its own political and cultural institutions, festivals, neighborhoods, even its own flag. Underlying that ethnicity is typically the notion that what gays and lesbians share – the anchor of minority status and minority rights claims – is the same fixed, natural essence, a self with same-sex desires. The shared oppression, these movements have forcefully claimed, is the denial of the freedoms and opportunities to actualize this self. In this *ethnic/essentialist* politic,[3] clear categories of collective identity are necessary for successful resistance and political gain.

Yet this impulse to build a collective identity with distinct group boundaries has been met by a directly opposing logic, often contained in queer activism (and in the newly anointed "queer theory"): to take apart the identity categories and blur group boundaries. This alternative angle, influenced by academic "constructionist" thinking, holds that sexual identities are historical and social products, not natural or intrapsychic ones. It is socially produced binaries (gay/straight, man/woman) that are the basis of oppression; fluid, unstable experiences of self become fixed primarily in the service of social control. Disrupting those categories, refusing rather than embracing ethnic minority status, is the key to liberation. In this *deconstructionist* politic, clear collective categories are an obstacle to resistance and change.

The challenge for analysts, I will argue, is not to determine which position is accurate, but to cope with the fact that both logics make sense. Queerness spotlights a dilemma shared by other identity movements (racial, ethnic, and gender movements, for example):[4] fixed identity categories are both the basis for oppression and the basis for political power. This raises questions for political strategizing and, more importantly for the purposes here, for social-movement analysis. If identities are indeed much more unstable, fluid, and constructed than movements have tended to assume – if one takes the queer challenge seriously, that is – what happens to identity-based social movements such as gay and lesbian rights? Must socio-political struggles articulated through identity eventually undermine themselves? Social-movement theory, a logical place to turn for help in working through the impasse between deconstructive cultural strategies and category-supportive political strategies, is hard pressed in its current state to cope with these questions. The case of queerness, I will argue, calls for a more developed theory of collective identity formation and its relationship to both institutions and meanings, an understanding which *includes the impulse to take apart that identity from within.*

In explicating the queer dilemma and its implications for social-movement theory, I first briefly summarize the current state of relevant literature on collective identity. Then, zeroing in on the dilemma itself, I make use of internal debates, largely as they took place in the letters column of the weekly *San Francisco Bay Times* in 1991, 1992, and 1993. I turn initially to debates within lesbian and gay communities over the use of the word "queer," using them to highlight the emergence of queer activism, its continuities with earlier lesbian and gay activism, and its links with and parallels to queer theory. Next, I take up debates over the inclusion of transgender and bisexual people, the two groups brought in under an expanded queer umbrella, in lesbian and gay politics. Here I point to a distinctive (although not entirely new) element of queerness, a politic of boundary disruption and category deconstruction, and to the resistance to that politic, made especially visible by the gendered nature of these debates. Finally, in drawing out ramifications for social-movement theory, I briefly demonstrate affinities between the queer debates and debates over multiracialism in African-American politics, arguing that queerness illuminates the core dilemma for identity movements more generally. I conclude by suggesting ways in which social-movement literature can be pushed forward by taking seriously, both as theoretical and empirical fact, the predicament of identity movements.

Social Movements and Collective Identity

Social-movements researchers have only recently begun treating collective identity construction[5] as an important and problematic movement activity and a significant subject of study. Before the late 1980s, when rational-actor models began to come under increased critical scrutiny, "not much direct thought [had] been given to the general sociological problem of what collective identity is and how it is constituted"

(Schlesinger 1987: 236). As Alberto Melucci (1989: 73) has argued, social-movement models focusing on instrumental action tend to treat collective identity as the nonrational expressive residue of the individual, rational pursuit of political gain. And "even in more sophisticated rational actor models that postulate a *collective* actor making strategic judgments of cost and benefit about collective action," William Gamson points out, "the existence of an *established* collective identity is assumed" (1992: 58; emphasis in original). Identities, in such models, were (and continue to be) typically conceived as existing prior to movements, which then make them visible through organizing and deploy them politically.

Melucci and other theorists of "new social movements" argue more strongly that collective identity is not only necessary for successful collective action, but that it is often an end in itself, as the self-conscious reflexivity of many contemporary movements seems to demonstrate.[6] Collective identity, in this model, is conceptualized as "a continual process of recomposition rather than a given," and "as a dynamic, *emergent* aspect of collective action" (Schlesinger 1987: 237; emphasis in original; see also Cohen 1985; Mueller 1992; Kauffman 1990). Research on ethnicity has developed along similar lines, emphasizing, for example, the degree to which "people's conceptions of themselves along ethnic lines, especially their ethnic identity, [are] situational and changeable" (Nagel 1994: 154). "An American Indian might be 'mixed-blood' on the reservation," as Joane Nagel describes one example, "'Pine Ridge' when speaking to someone from another reservation, a 'Sioux' or 'Lakota' when responding to the US census, and 'Native American' when interacting with non-Indians" (1994: 155; see also Padilla 1985; Alba 1990; Waters 1990; Espiritu 1992).

How exactly collective identities emerge and change has been the subject of a growing body of work in the study of social movements. For example, Verta Taylor and Nancy Whittier, analyzing lesbian-feminist communities, point to the creation of politicized identity communities through boundary-construction (establishing "differences between a challenging group and dominant groups"), the development of consciousness (or "interpretive frameworks"), and negotiation ("symbols and everyday actions subordinate groups use to resist and restructure existing systems of domination") (1992: 100–11; see also Franzen 1993). Other researchers, working from the similar notion that "the location and meaning of particular ethnic boundaries are continuously negotiated, revised, and revitalized," demonstrate the ways in which collective identity is constructed not only from within, but is also shaped and limited by "political policies and institutions, immigration policies, by ethnically linked resource policies, and by political access structured along ethnic lines" (Nagel 1994: 152, 157; see also Omi and Winant 1986).

When we turn to the disputes over queerness, it is useful to see them in light of this recent work. We are certainly witnessing a process of boundary-construction and identity negotiation: as contests over membership and over naming, these debates are part of an ongoing project of delineating the "we" whose rights and freedoms are at stake in the movements. Yet as I track through the queer debates, I will demonstrate a movement propensity that current work on collective identity fails to take into account: the drive to blur and deconstruct group categories, and to keep them forever unstable. It is that tendency that poses a significant new push to social-movement analysis.

Queer Politics and Queer Theory

Since the late 1980s, "queer" has served to mark first a loose but distinguishable set of political movements and mobilizations, and second a somewhat parallel set of academy-bound intellectual endeavors (now calling itself "queer theory"). Queer politics, although given organized body in the activist group Queer Nation, operates largely through the decentralized, local, and often anti-organizational cultural activism of street postering, parodic and non-conformist self-presentation, and underground alternative magazines ("zines") (Berlant and Freeman 1993; Duggan 1992; Williams 1993);[7] it has defined itself largely against conventional lesbian and gay politics. The emergence of queer politics, although it cannot be treated here in detail, can be traced to the early 1980s backlash against gay and lesbian movement gains, which "punctured illusions of a coming era of tolerance and sexual pluralism"; to the AIDS crisis, which "underscored the limits of a politics of minority rights and inclusion"; and to the eruption of "long-simmering internal differences" around race and sex, and criticism of political organizing as "reflecting a white, middle-class experience or standpoint" (Seidman 1994: 172).[8]

Queer theory, with roots in constructionist history and sociology, feminist theory, and poststructuralist philosophy, took shape through several late-1980s academic conferences, and continues to operate primarily in elite academic institutions through highly abstract language; it has defined itself largely against conventional lesbian and gay studies (Stein and Plummer 1994).[9] Stein and Plummer have recently delineated the major theoretical departures of queer theory: a conceptualization of sexual power as embodied "in different levels of social life, expressed discursively and enforced through boundaries and binary divides"; a problematization of sexual and gender categories, and identities in general; a rejection of civil rights strategies "in favor of a politics of carnival, transgression, and parody, which leads to deconstruction, decentering, revisionist readings, and an anti-assimilationist politics"; and a "willingness to interrogate areas which would not normally be seen as the terrain of sexuality, and conduct queer 'readings' of ostensibly heterosexual or non-sexualized texts" (1994: 181–2).

Through these simultaneous and tenuously linked actions, then, the word "queer," as Steven Epstein puts it, has recently "escaped the bounds of quotation marks" (Epstein 1994: 189; see also Duggan 1992; Warner 1993). Its escape has been marked by quite wrenching controversy within sexual identity-based communities. To understand the uses of "queer," and its links to and departures from lesbian and gay activism, it helps to hear these controversies, here presented primarily through the letters-column debates over "The Year of the Queer."

My discussion of this and the two debates that follow is based on an analysis of some 75 letters in the weekly *San Francisco Bay Times*, supplemented by related editorials from national lesbian and gay publications. The letters were clustered: the debates on the word "queer" ran in the *San Francisco Bay Times* beginning in December 1992 and continued through April 1993; the disputes over bisexuality began in April 1991 and continued through May 1991; clashes over transsexual inclusion began in October 1992 and continued through December 1992. Although anecdotal evidence suggests that these disputes are widespread, it should be noted that I use them here not to provide conclusive data, but to provide a grounded means for conceptualizing the queer challenge.

The Controversy Over Queerness: Continuities with Existing Lesbian and Gay Activism

In the discussion of the "Year of the Queer" theme for the 1993 lesbian and gay pride celebration, the venom hits first. "All those dumb closeted people who don't like the Q-word," the *Bay Times* quotes Peggy Sue suggesting, "can go fuck themselves and go to somebody else's parade." A man named Patrick argues along the same lines, asserting that the men opposing the theme are "not particularly thrilled with their attraction to other men," are "cranky and upset" yet willing to benefit "from the stuff queer activists do." A few weeks later, a letter writer shoots back that "this new generation assumes we were too busy in the '70s lining up at Macy's to purchase sweaters to find time for the revolution – as if their piercings and tattoos were any cheaper." Another sarcastically asks, "How did you ever miss out on 'Faggot' or 'Cocksucker'?" On this level, the dispute reads like a sibling sandbox spat.

Although the curses fly sometimes within generations, many letter-writers frame the differences as generational. The queer linguistic tactic, the attempt to defang, embrace, and resignify a stigma term, is loudly rejected by many older gay men and lesbians.[10] "I am sure he isn't old enough to have experienced that feeling of cringing when the word 'queer' was said," says Roy of an earlier letter-writer. Another writer asserts that 35 is the age that marks off those accepting the queer label from those rejecting it. Younger people, many point out, can "reclaim" the word only because they have not felt as strongly the sting, ostracism, police batons, and baseball bats that accompanied it one generation earlier. For older people, its oppressive meaning can never be lifted, can never be turned from overpowering to empowering.

Consider "old" as code for "conservative," and the dispute takes on another familiar, overlapping frame: the debate between assimilationists and separatists, with a long history in American homophile, homosexual, lesbian, and gay politics. Internal political struggle over agendas of assimilation (emphasizing sameness) and separation (emphasizing difference) have been present since the inception of these movements, as they are in other movements. The "homophile" movement of the 1950s, for example, began with a Marxist-influenced agenda of sex-class struggle, and was quickly overtaken by accommodationist tactics: gaining expert support; men demonstrating in suits, women in dresses.[11] Queer marks a contemporary anti-assimilationist stance, in opposition to the mainstream inclusionary goals of the dominant gay-rights movement.

"They want to work from within," says Peggy Sue elsewhere (Bérubé and Escoffier 1991), "and I just want to crash in from the outside and say, 'Hey! Hello, I'm queer. I can make out with my girlfriend. Ha ha. Live with it. Deal with it.' That kind of stuff." In a zine called *Rant & Rave*, co-editor Miss Rant argues that "I don't want to be gay, which means assimilationist, normal, homosexual. . . . I don't want my personality, behavior, beliefs, and desires to be cut up like a pie into neat little categories from which I'm not supposed to stray" (1993: 15).

Queer politics, as Michael Warner puts it, "opposes society itself," protesting "not just the normal behavior of the social but the *idea* of normal behavior" (1993: xxvii). It embraces the label of perversity, using it to call attention to the "norm" in "normal," be it hetero or homo.

Queer thus asserts in-your-face difference, with an edge of defiant separatism: "We're here, we're queer, get used to it," goes the chant. We are different, that is, free from convention, odd and out there and proud of it, and your response is either your problem or your wake-up call. Queer does not so much rebel against outsider status as revel in it.[12] Queer confrontational difference, moreover, is scary, writes Alex Chee (1991), and thus politically useful: "Now that I call myself queer, know myself as a queer, nothing will keep [queer-haters] safe. If I tell them I am queer, they give me room. Politically, I can think of little better. I do not want to be one of them. They only need to give me room."

This goes against the grain of civil-rights strategists, of course, for whom at least the appearance of normality is central to gaining political "room." Rights are gained, according to this logic, by demonstrating similarity (to heterosexual people, to other minority groups) in a non-threatening manner. "We are everywhere," goes the refrain from here. We are your sons and daughters and coworkers and soldiers, and once you see that lesbians and gays are just like you, you will recognize the injustices to which we are subject. "I am not queer," writes a letter-writer named Tony. "I am normal, and if tomorrow I choose to run down the middle of Market Street in a big floppy hat and skirt I will still be normal." In the national gay weekly *10 Percent* – for which *Rant & Rave* can be seen as a proudly evil twin – Eric Marcus (1993: 14) writes that "I'd rather emphasize what I have in common with other people than focus on the differences," and "the last thing I want to do is institutionalize that difference by defining myself with a word and a political philosophy that set me outside the mainstream." The point is to be not-different, not-odd, not-scary. "We have a lot going for us," Phyllis Lyon puts it simply in the *Bay Times*. "Let's not blow it" – blow it, that is, by alienating each other and our straight allies with words like "queer."

Debates over assimilation are hardly new, however; but neither do they exhaust the letters-column disputes. The metaphors in queerness are striking. Queer is a "psychic tattoo," says writer Alex Chee, shared by outsiders; those similarly tattooed make up the Queer Nation. "It's the land of lost boys and lost girls," says historian Gerard Koskovich (in Bérubé and Escoffier 1991), "who woke up one day and realized that not to have heterosexual privilege was in fact the highest privilege." A mark on the skin, a land, a nation: these are the metaphors of tribe and family. Queer is being used not just to connote and glorify differentness, but to revise the criteria of membership in the family, "to affirm sameness by defining a common identity on the fringes" (Bérubé and Escoffier 1991; see also Duggan 1992).[13]

In the hands of many letter-writers, in fact, queer becomes simply a shorthand for "gay, lesbian, bisexual, and transgender," much like "people of color" becomes an inclusive and difference-erasing shorthand for a long list of ethnic and racial groups. And as some letter-writers point out, as a quasi-national shorthand "queer" is just a slight shift in the boundaries of tribal membership with no attendant shifts in power; as some lesbian writers point out, it is as likely to become synonymous with "white gay male" (perhaps now with a nose ring and tatoos) as it is to describe a new community formation. Even in its less nationalist versions, queer can easily be difference without change, can subsume and hide the internal differences it attempts to incorporate. The queer tribe attempts to be a multicultural, multigendered, multisexual, hodge-podge of outsiders; as Steven Seidman points out, it ironically ends up "denying differences by either submerging them in an undifferentiated oppositional mass or by blocking the development of individual and social differences through the disciplining compulsory imperative to remain undifferentiated" (1993: 133). Queer as an identity category often restates tensions between sameness and difference in a different language.

Debates Over Bisexuality and Transgender: Queer Deconstructionist Politics

Despite the aura of newness, then, not much appears new in queerness: debates and fault lines are familiar from gay and lesbian (and other identity-based) movements. Yet letter-writers agree on one puzzling point: right now, it matters what we are called and what we call ourselves. That a word takes so prominent a place is a clue that this is more than another in an ongoing series of tired assimilationist–liberationist debates. The controversy of queerness is not just strategic (what works), nor even only a power struggle (who gets to call the shots); it is those, but not only those. At their most basic, queer controversies are battles over identity and naming (who I am, who we are). Which words capture us and when do words fail us? Words, and the "us" they name, seem to be in critical flux.

But even identity battles are not especially new. In fact, within lesbian-feminist and gay male organizing, the meanings of "lesbian" and "gay" were contested almost as soon as they began to have political currency as quasi-ethnic statuses. Women of color and sex radicals loudly challenged lesbian feminism of the late 1970s, for example, pointing out that the "womansculture" being advocated (and actively created) was based in white, middle-class experience and promoted a bland, desexualized lesbianism. Lesbians of many colors and gay men of color have consistently challenged "gay" as a term reflecting the middle-class, white homosexual men who established its usage (Stein 1992; Phelan 1993; Seidman 1993; Seidman 1994; Clarke 1983; Moraga 1983; Reid-Pharr 1993; Hemphill 1991). They challenged, that is, the definitions.

The ultimate challenge of queerness, however, is not just the questioning of the content of collective identities, but the *questioning of the unity, stability, viability and political utility of sexual identities* – even as they are used and assumed.[14] The radical provocation from queer politics, one which many pushing queerness seem only remotely aware of, is not to resolve that difficulty, not to take us out of flux, but to exaggerate and build on it. It is an odd endeavor, much like pulling the rug out from under one's own feet, not knowing how and where one will land.   To zero in on the distinctive deconstructionist politics of queerness, turn again to the letters columns. It is no coincidence that two other major *Bay Times* letters-column controversies of the early 1990s concerned bisexual and transgender people, the two groups included in the revised queer category. Indeed, in his anti-queer polemic in the magazine *10 Percent* (a title firmly ethnic/essentialist in its reference to a fixed homosexual population), it is precisely these sorts of people, along with some "queer straights,"[15] from whom Eric Marcus seeks to distinguish himself:

Queer is not my word because it does not define who I am or represent what I believe in . . . . I'm a man who feels sexually attracted to people of the same gender. I don't feel attracted to both genders. I'm not a woman trapped in a man's body, nor a man trapped in a woman's body. I'm not someone who enjoys or feels compelled to dress up in clothing of the opposite gender. And I'm not a "queer straight," a heterosexual who feels confined by the conventions of straight sexual expression . . . . I don't want to be grouped under the all-encompassing umbrella of queer . . . because we have different lives, face different challenges, and don't necessarily share the same aspirations. (1993: 14)

The letters columns, written usually from a different political angle (by lesbian separatists, for example), cover similar terrain. "It is not empowering to go to a Queer Nation meeting and see men and women slamming their tongues down each others' throats," says one letter arguing over bisexuals. "Men expect access to women," asserts one from the transgender debate. "Some men decide that they want access to lesbians any way they can and decide they will become lesbians."

Strikingly, nearly all the letters are written by, to, and about women – a point to which I will later return. "A woman's willingness to sleep with men allows her access to jobs, money, power, status," writes one group of women. "This access does not disappear just because a woman sleeps with women 'too'. . . . That's not bisexuality, that's compulsory heterosexuality." You are not invited; you will leave and betray us. We are already here, other women respond, and it is you who betray us with your back-stabbing and your silencing. "Why have so many bisexual women felt compelled to call themselves lesbians for so long? Do you think biphobic attitudes like yours might have something to do with it?" asks a woman named Kristen. "It is our community, too; we've worked in it, we've suffered for it, we belong in it. We will not accept the role of the poor relation." Kristen ends her letter tellingly, deploying a familiar phrase: "We're here. We're queer. Get used to it."[16]

The letters run back and forth similarly over transgender issues, in particular over transsexual lesbians who want to participate in lesbian organizing. "'Transsexuals' don't want to just be lesbians," Bev Jo writes, triggering a massive round of letters, "but insist, with all the arrogance and presumption of power that men have, on going where they are not wanted and trying to destroy lesbian gatherings." There are surely easier ways to oppress a woman, other women shoot back, than to risk physical pain and social isolation. You are doing exactly what anti-female and anti-gay oppressors do to us, others add. "Must we all bring our birth certificates and two witnesses to women's events in the future?" asks a woman named Karen. "If you feel threatened by the mere existence of a type of person, and wish to exclude them for your comfort, you are a bigot, by every definition of the term."

These "border skirmishes" over membership conditions and group boundaries have histories preceding the letters (Stein 1992; see also Taylor and Whittier 1992), and also reflect the growing power of transgender and bisexual organizing.[17] Although they are partly battles of position, more fundamentally the debates make concrete the anxiety queerness can provoke. They spotlight the possibility that sexual and gender identities are not the solid political ground they have been

thought to be – which perhaps accounts for the particularly frantic
tone of the letters.

Many arguing for exclusion write like a besieged border patrol.
"Live your lives the way you want and spread your hatred of women
while you're at it, if you must," writes a participant in the transgender
letter spree, "but the fact is we're here, we're dykes and you're not.
Deal with it." The Revolting Lesbians argue similarly in their contribution to the *Bay Times* bisexuality debate: "Bisexuals are not lesbians –
they are bisexuals. Why isn't that obvious to everyone? Sleeping with
women 'too' does not make you a lesbian. We must hang onto the
identity and visibility we've struggled so hard to obtain." A letter from
a woman named Caryatis sums up the perceived danger of queerness:

> This whole transsexual/bisexual assault on lesbian identity has only one
> end, to render lesbians completely invisible and obsolete. If a woman who
> sleeps with both females and males is a lesbian; and if a man who submits
> to surgical procedure to bring his body in line with his acceptance of sex
> role stereotypes is a lesbian; and if a straight woman whose spiritual bond
> is with other females is a lesbian, then what is a female-born female who
> loves only other females? Soon there will be no logical answer to that
> question.

Exactly: in lesbian (and gay) politics, as in other identity movements,
a logical answer is crucial. An inclusive queerness threatens to turn
identity to nonsense, messing with the idea that identities (man,
woman, gay, straight) are fixed, natural, core phenomena, and therefore solid political ground. Many arguments in the letters columns, in
fact, echo the critiques of identity politics found in queer theory.
"There is a growing consciousness that a person's sexual identity (and
gender identity) need not be etched in stone," write Andy and Selena
in the bisexuality debate, "that it can be fluid rather than static, that
one has the right to PLAY with whomever one wishes to play with (as
long as it is consensual), that the either/or dichotomy ('you're either
gay or straight' is only one example of this) is oppressive no matter
who's pushing it." Identities are fluid and changing; binary categories
(man/woman, gay/straight) are distortions. "Humans are not organized by nature into distinct groups," Cris writes. "We are placed in
any number of continuums. Few people are 100 percent gay or
straight, or totally masculine or feminine." Differences are not distinct,
categories are social and historical rather than natural phenomena,
selves are ambiguous. "Perhaps it is time the lesbian community reexamined its criteria of what constitutes a woman (or man)," writes

Francis. "And does it really matter?" Transsexual performer and writer Kate Bornstein, in a *Bay Times* column triggered by the letters, voices the same basic challenge. Are a woman and a man distinguished by anatomy? "I know several women in San Francisco who have penises," she says. "Many wonderful men in my life have vaginas" (1992: 4). Gender chromosomes, she continues, are known to come in more than two sets ("could this mean there are more than two genders?"), testosterone and estrogen don't answer it ("you could buy your gender over the counter"); neither child-bearing nor sperm capacities nail down the difference ("does a necessary hysterectomy equal a sex change?"). Gender is socially assigned; binary categories (man/woman, gay/straight) are inaccurate and oppressive; nature provides no rock-bottom definitions. The opposite sex, Bornstein proposes, is neither.[18]

Indeed, it is no coincidence that bisexuality, transsexualism, and gender crossing are exactly the kind of boundary-disrupting phenomena embraced by much poststructuralist sexual theory. Sandy Stone, for example, argues that "the transsexual currently occupies a position which is nowhere, which is outside the binary oppositions of gendered discourse" (1991: 295).[19] Steven Seidman suggests that bisexual critiques challenge "sexual object-choice as a master category of sexual and social identity" (1993: 123). Judith Butler argues that butch and femme, far from being "copies" of heterosexual roles, put the "very notion of an original or natural identity" into question (1990: 123). Marjorie Garber writes that "the cultural effect of transvestism is to destabilize all such binaries: not only 'male' and 'female,' but also 'gay' and 'straight,' and 'sex' and 'gender.' This is the sense – the radical sense – in which transvestism is a 'third'" (1992: 133).

The point, often buried in over-abstracted jargon, is well taken: the presence of visibly transgendered people, people who do not quite fit, potentially subverts the notion of two naturally fixed genders; the presence of people with ambiguous sexual desires potentially subverts the notion of naturally fixed sexual orientations. (I say "potentially" because the more common route has continued to be in the other direction: the reification of bisexuality into a third orientation, or the retention of male–female boundaries through the notion of transgendered people as "trapped in the wrong body," which is then fixed.) Genuine inclusion of transgender and bisexual people can require not simply an expansion of an identity, but a subversion of it. This is the deepest difficulty queerness raises, and the heat behind the letters: if gay (and man) and lesbian (and woman) are unstable categories, "simultaneously possible and impossible" (Fuss 1989: 102), what happens to sexuality-based politics?

The question is easily answered by those securely on either side of these debates. On the one side, activists and theorists suggest that collective identities with exclusive and secure boundaries are politically effective. Even those agreeing that identities are mainly fictions may take this position, advocating what Gayatri Spivak has called an "operational essentialism" (cited in Butler 1990; see also Vance 1988). On the other side, activists and theorists suggest that identity production "is purchased at the price of hierarchy, normalization, and exclusion" and therefore advocate "the deconstruction of a hetero/homo code that structures the 'social text' of daily life" (Seidman 1993: 130).

The Queer Dilemma

The problem, of course, is that both the boundary-strippers and the boundary-defenders are right. The gay and lesbian civil-rights strategy, for all its gains, does little to attack the political culture that itself makes the denial of and struggle for civil rights necessary and possible. Marches on Washington, equal protection pursuits, media-image monitoring, and so on, are guided by the attempt to build and prove quasi-national and quasi-ethnic claims. As such, they do not interrogate the ways in which the construction of gays and lesbians as a singular community united by fixed erotic fates distorts complex internal differences and complex sexual identities. Nor do they challenge the system of meanings that underlie the political oppression: the division of the world into man/woman and gay/straight. On the contrary, they ratify and reinforce these categories. They therefore build distorted and incomplete political challenges, neglecting the political impact of cultural meanings, and do not do justice to the subversive and liberating aspects of loosened collective boundaries.

Thus the strong claims of queer politics and theory: that this is not how it must be, that political and social organization can and should be more true to the inessential, fluid, and multiply sited character of sexuality; and that gay-ethnic movements make a serious error in challenging only the idea that homosexuality is unnatural, affirming rather than exposing the root cultural system.

Yet queer theory and politics tend to run past a critique of the particular, concrete forces that make sexual identity, in stabilized and binary form, a basis for discipline, regulation, pleasure, and political empowerment. In the hurry to deconstruct identity, they tend to "slide into viewing identity itself as the fulcrum of domination and its subversion as the center of an anti-identity politic" (Seidman 1993: 132); the politic becomes overwhelmingly cultural, textual, and subjectless. Deconstructive strategies remain quite deaf and blind to the very concrete and violent institutional forms to which the most logical answer is resistance in and through a particular collective identity.

The overarching strategy of cultural deconstruction, the attack on the idea of the normal, does little to touch the institutions that make embracing normality (or building a collective around inverted abnormality) both sensible and dangerous. Mall kiss-ins by San Francisco's Suburban Homosexual Outreach Program (SHOP) and other actions that "mime the privileges of normality" (Berlant and Freeman 1993: 196), "Queer Bart" (Simpson, the popular cartoon character) t-shirts and other actions that "reveal to the consumer desires he/she didn't know he/she had, to make his/her identification with the product 'homosexuality' both an unsettling and a pleasurable experience" (Berlant and Freeman 1993: 208), do very little to take on the more directly political: regulatory institutions such as law and medicine, for example, which continue to create and enforce gay/straight and male/female divisions, often with great physical and psychic violence. They do not do justice to the degree to which closing group boundaries is both a necessary and fulfilling survival strategy.

Interest-group politics on the ethnic model is, quite simply but not without contradictory effects, how the American socio-political environment is structured. Official ethnic categories provide "incentives for ethnic group formation and mobilization by designating particular ethnic subpopulations as targets for special treatment"; politically controlled resources are "distributed along ethnic lines"; ethnic groups mean larger voting blocs and greater influence in electoral systems (Nagel 1994: 157–9). Ethnic categories serve, moreover, as the basis for discrimination and repression, both official and informal, and thus as a logical basis for resistance. This is the buried insight of the border-patrolling separatists and the anti-queer pragmatists: that here, in this place, at this time, we need, for our safety and for potential political gains, to construct ourselves as a group whose membership criteria are clear.

The overwhelmingly female participation in the *Bay Times* disputes over bisexuality and transgender inclusion underscores this point. Lesbians are especially threatened by the muddying of male/female and gay/straight categorizations exactly because it is by keeping sexual and gender categories hard and clear that gains are made. Lesbian visibility is more recent and hard-won; in struggles against patriarchal control, moreover, lesbianism and feminism have often been strongly linked.[20] Gay men react with less vehemence because of the stronger political position from which they encounter the queer challenge: as men, as gay men with a more established public identity. Just as they are gaining political ground *as lesbians*, lesbians are asked not only to share it but to subvert it, by declaring "woman" and "lesbian" to be unstable, permeable, fluid categories.

Similar pitfalls were evident in the 1993 fight over Colorado's Amendment 2, which prohibits "the state or any of its subdivisions from outlawing discrimination against gay men, lesbians, or bisexuals" (Minkowitz 1993). The Colorado solicitor general, as reporter Donna Minkowitz put it, made arguments "that could have appeared in a queercore rant," promoting "a remarkably Foucaultian view of queerness as a contingent category, whose members can slip in and out of its boundaries like subversive fish" (1993: 27). "We don't have a group that is easily confinable," he argued. Here, the fluidity of group boundaries and the provisional nature of collective identity was used to argue that no one should receive legal benefits or state protection – because there is no discernible group to be protected. Although the solicitor-general-as-queer-theorist is a strange twist, the lesson is familiar: as long as membership in this group is unclear, minority status, and therefore rights and protection, is unavailable.   Built into the queer debates, then, is a fundamental quandary: in the contemporary American political environment, clear identity categories are both necessary and dangerous distortions, and moves to both fix and unfix them are reasonable. Although it comes most visibly to the fore in them, this dynamic is hardly unique to lesbian and gay movements. The conflict between a politics of identity-building and identity-blurring has erupted, for example, in recent debates in African-American movements over multiracialism. When a group lobbied the Office of Management and Budget (whose 1977 Statistical Directive recognizes four racial groups), proposing the addition of a "multiracial" classification, they were met with tremendous opposition from those who "see the Multiracial box as a wrecking ball aimed at affirmative action," since it threatens to "undermine the concept of racial classification altogether" (Wright 1994: 47; see also Omi and Winant 1986; Webster 1992; Davis 1991).

As one advocate put it, "Multiracialism has the potential for undermining the very basis for racism, which is its categories" (G. Reginald Daniel, quoted in Wright 1994: 48); as one observer put it, "multiracial people, because they are both unable and unwilling to be ignored, and because many of them refuse to be confined to traditional racial categories, inevitably undermine the entire concept of race as an irreducible difference between peoples" (Wright 1994: 49). Opponents respond vehemently to multiracial organizing, in part because civil-rights laws are monitored and enforced through the existing categories. In a debate in *The Black Scholar*, African and Afro-American Studies professor Jon Michael Spencer attacked "the postmodern conspiracy to explode racial identity," arguing that "to relinquish the notion of race – even though it's a cruel hoax – at this particular time is to relinquish our fortress against the powers and principalities that still try to undermine us" (in Wright 1994: 55). Here, in a different form, is the same queer predicament.

Conclusion: Collective Identity, Social-Movement Theory and the Queer Dilemma

Buried in the letters-column controversies over a queer parade theme, and over bisexual and transsexual involvement in lesbian organizations, are fights not only over who belongs, but over the possibility and desirability of clear criteria of belonging. Sexuality-based politics thus contain a more general predicament of identity politics, whose workings and implications are not well understood: it is as liberating and sensible to demolish a collective identity as it is to establish one. Honoring both sets of insights from the queer debates is a tall order. It calls for recognizing that undermining identities is politically damaging in the current time and place, and that promoting them furthers the major cultural support for continued damage. It means reconnecting a critique of identity to the embodied political forces that make collective identity necessary and meaningful, and reconnecting a critique of regulatory institutions to the less tangible categories of meaning that maintain and reproduce them.[21]

The neatest, and most true to life means for doing so, the theoretical recognition of paradoxes and dialectics, can satisfy intellectually. Certainly a political structure that directs action towards ethnic interest-group claims, and requires therefore solid proofs of authentic ethnic membership (the immutability of sexual orientation, for example), creates paradoxical forms of action for stigmatized groups. In the case of lesbians and gays, for example, gender stereotypes used to stigmatize actors (the gay man as woman, the lesbian as man) have been emphasized in order to undermine them; pejorative labels are emphasized in an effort to get rid of them.[22] But the recognition of paradox, while a significant step, is too often a stopping point of analysis. I want to suggest potentially fruitful paths forward, through research and theorizing that take the queer dilemma to heart.

The recent revival of sociological interest in collective identity has brought important challenges to earlier assumptions that identities were either irrational (and irrelevant) or antecedents to action. Yet, even as theorizing has recognized that collective identities are achieved in and through movement activity, the assumption has remained that the impetus to solidify, mobilize, and deploy an identity is the only rational one. The suggestion of most social-movement theory, sometimes assumed and sometimes explicit, is that secure boundaries and a clear group identity are achievable, and even more importantly, that "if a group fails in [these], it cannot accomplish any collective action" (Klandermans 1992: 81); without a solid group identity, no claims can be made. These theories cannot have little to say about the queer impulse to blur, deconstruct, and destabilize group categories. Current theories take hold of only one horn of the dilemma: the political utility of solid collective categories.

Serious consideration of queerness as a logic of action can force important revisions in approaches to collective identity formation and deployment, and their relationship to political gains. First, it calls attention to the fact that *secure boundaries and stabilized identities are necessary not in general, but in the specific* – a point current social-movement theory largely misses. The link between the two logics, the ways in which the American political environment makes stable collective identities both necessary and damaging, is sorely undertheorized and underexamined.

More importantly, accommodating the complexity of queer activism and theory requires sociology to revisit the claim that social movements are engaged in simply constructing collective identities. Queer movements pose the challenge of a form of organizing in which, far from inhibiting accomplishments, the *destabilization of collective identity is itself a goal and accomplishment of collective action*. When this dynamic is taken into account, new questions arise. The question of how collective identities are negotiated, constructed, and stabilized, for example, becomes transformed into a somewhat livelier one: for whom, when, and how are stable collective identities *necessary* for social action and social change? Do some identity movements in fact avoid the tendency to take themselves apart?

Investigating social movements with the queer predicament in mind, moreover, brings attention to repertoires and forms of action that work with the dilemma in different ways. At the heart of the dilemma is the simultaneity of cultural sources of oppression (which make loosening categories a smart strategy) and institutional sources of oppression (which make tightening categories a smart strategy). Are some movements or movement repertoires more able to work with, rather than against, the simultaneity of these systems of oppression? When and how might deconstructive strategies take aim at institutional forms, and when and how can ethnic strategies take aim at cultural categories? Are there times when the strategies are effectively linked, when an ethnic maneuver loosens cultural categories,[23] or when a deconstructionist tactic simultaneously takes aim at regulatory institutions?[24]

Such questions can point the way towards novel understandings and evaluations of social movements in which collective identity is both pillaged and deployed. They are not a path out of the dilemma, but a path in. The fact that the predicament may be inescapable is, after all, the point: first to clearly see the horns of the dilemma, and then to search out ways for understanding political actions taking place poised, and sometimes skewered, on those horns.

Notes

My thanks to Steven Epstein, William Gamson, Arlene Stein, Verta Taylor, Jeffrey Escoffier, Cathy Cohen, Mark Blasius, Roger Lancaster and Matthew Rottnek.

1 Although I am discussing them together because of their joint struggle against the "sex/gender system" (Rubin 1975) on the basis of same-sex desire, lesbians and gay men have long histories of autonomous organizing (Adam 1987; D'Emilio 1983). Gender has been the strongest division historically in movements for gay and lesbian rights and liberation, not surprisingly, given the very different ways in which male homosexuality and lesbianism have been constructed and penalized. This division is taken up explicitly later in the discussion.

2 In this discussion, I am heeding recent calls to bring sociology into contact with queer theory and politics (Seidman 1994). It has taken a bit of time for sociologists and other social scientists to join queer theoretical discussions, which although they emerged primarily from and through humanities scholars, could hardly be "imagined in their present forms, absent the contributions of sociological theory" (Epstein 1994: 2). On the relationship between sociology of sexuality and queer theory, see also Stein and Plummer (1994); Namaste (1994).

3 I borrow this term from Seidman (1993).

4 See, for example, Di Stefano (1990); Bordo (1990); Davis (1991).

5 Collective identity is variously defined. I am using it here to designate not only a "status – a set of attitudes, commitments, and rules for behavior –

that those who assume the identity can be expected to subscribe to,"
but also "an individual pronouncement of affiliation, of connection
with others" (Friedman and McAdam 1992: 157). See also Schlesinger
(1987).

6 There is no reason to limit this claim to "identity-based" movements,
   although identity construction is more visible and salient in such movements. As Taylor and Whittier argue in reviewing existing scholarship,
   "identity construction processes are crucial to grievance interpretation in
   all forms of collective action, not just in the so-called new movements"
   (1992: 105).

7 Queer Nation, formed in 1990, is an offshoot of the AIDS activist organization ACT UP. Queer Nation owes much to ACT UP, in its emergence, its
   personnel, and its tactics, which are often to "cross borders, to occupy
   spaces, and to mime the privileges of normality" (Berlant and Freeman
   1993: 195). On similar tactics within ACT UP, see Gamson (1989). On
   Queer Nation specifically, and queer politics more generally, see Bérubé
   and Escoffier (1991); Duggan (1992); Stein (1992); Cunningham (1992);
   Patton (1993); Browning (1993; esp. chs 2, 3, and 5).

8 See e.g. Rich (1980); Moraga (1983); Hemphill (1991); Clarke (1983);
   Reid-Pharr (1993).

9 Although social-constructionist thought generally informs queer theory, it
   is important to distinguish different strands of constructionist work and
   their varying contributions to the development of sexual theory. Much
   constructionist history and sociology, which concerned "the origin, social
   meaning, and changing forms of the modern homosexual" and challenged
   essentialist notions of homosexuality, was also "often tied to a politics of
   the making of a homosexual minority" (Seidman 1994: 171; see e.g.
   D'Emilio 1983; Faderman 1981). Poststructuralist writing on gender and
   sexuality, although often looking quite similar, tends to "shift the debate
   somewhat away from explaining the modern homosexual to questions of
   the operation of the hetero/homosexual binary, from an exclusive preoccupation with homosexuality to a focus on heterosexuality as a social and
   political organizing principle, and from a politics of minority interest to a
   politics of knowledge and difference" (Seidman 1994: 192; see also Epstein
   1994; Namaste 1994; Warner 1993; Hennessy 1993).

   It is this latter strand that has most strongly informed queer theory. Eve
   Kosofsky Sedgwick's *Epistemology of the Closet*, with its famous assertion
   that "an understanding of virtually any aspect of modern Western culture
   must be, not merely incomplete, but damaged in its central substance to the
   degree that it does not incorporate a critical analysis of modern homo/he-
   terosexual definition" (1990: 1), is now often taken as the founding
   moment of queer theory; Judith Butler's *Gender Trouble* (1989) also made
   a tremendous impact in the field. For further examples of queer-theoretical
   work, see Fuss (1991); de Lauretis (1991); Butler (1993). These theoretical
   and political developments in the field of lesbian and gay studies also draw

from and overlap with similar ones in feminism. See Ingraham (1994), and the essays in Nicholson (1990).

10 Although its most familiar recent usage has been as an anti-gay epithet, the word actually has a long and complex history. Along with "fairy," for example, "queer" was one of the most common terms used before World War II, "by 'queer' and 'normal' people alike to refer to 'homosexuals.'" In the 1920s and 1930s, "the men who identified themselves as part of a distinct category of men primarily on the basis of their homosexual interest rather than their womanlike gender status usually called themselves queer" (Chauncey 1994: 14, 16). Whether as chosen marker or as epithet, the word has always retained its general connotation of abnormality (Chauncey 1994).

11 On assimilation–separation before Stonewall, see D'Emilio (1983); Adam (1987). On assimilation–separation after Stonewall, see Epstein (1987).

12 Indeed, the "outlaw" stance may help explain why gender differences are (somewhat) less salient in queer organizing (Duggan 1992). Whereas in ethnic/essentialist lesbian and gay organizations participants are recruited as gay men and lesbian women, in queer organizations they are recruited largely as *gender outlaws*.

13 There is no question that part of what has happened with queer activism is simply the construction of a new, if contentious, collective identity: Queer Nation, with its nationalist rhetoric, is one clear example. My point, however (developed below), is not that queer indicates a group with no boundaries, but that it indicates a strategy of identity destabilization. This logic is not confined to a particular group formation; although it is considerably stronger in groups identifying as queer, many of which are loose associations that are very intentionally decentralized (Williams 1993), it is also often present in more mainstream organizing, albeit in more occasional and muted form. Queer is more useful, I am suggesting, as a description of a particular action logic than as a description of an empirically distinguishable movement form.

14 This questioning is not entirely unique to recent queer politics, but has historical ties to early gay-liberation calls to "liberate the homosexual in everyone" (Epstein 1987). That the current queer formulations have such affinities with earlier political activity underlines that queerness is less a new historical development than an action impulse that comes to the fore at certain historical moments. There is certainly a difference in degree, however, between the strength of a queer-style politic now and in earlier decades: with a few exceptions, earlier lesbian-feminist and gay-liberationist discourses rarely questioned "the notion of homosexuality as a universal category of the self and a sexual identity" (Seidman 1994: 170).

15 On "queer straights," self-identifying heterosexuals who seek out and participate in lesbian and gay subcultures, see Powers (1993).

16 For more bisexuality debate, see Wilson (1992) and Queen (1992).

17 For articulations of these young movements see, on bisexual organizing, Hutchins and Kaahumanu (1991), and on transgender organizing, Stone (1991).
18 For a more developed version of these arguments, see Bornstein (1994).
19 See also Shapiro (1991) on the ways in which transsexualism is simultaneously conservative of sex and gender organization.
20 On lesbian feminism, see Phelan (1989); Taylor and Whittier (1992); Taylor and Rupp (1993).
21 I am indebted here to Steven Seidman's discussion and critique of queer theory and politics, which makes some of the same points from different directions (Seidman 1993; see also Patton 1993; Vance 1988). I want to push the discussion towards the ground, however, to open up questions for political action and empirical research.
22 On this dynamic, see Weeks (1985; esp. ch. 8); Epstein (1987); Gamson (1989).
23 The public pursuit of same-sex marriage and parenting may be an example of this. On the one hand, the call for institutions of "family" to include lesbians and gays – as a recognizably separate species – is quite conservative of existing gender and sexual categories. It often appears as mimicry, and its proponents typically appear as close to "normal" as possible: Bob and Rod Jackson-Paris, for example, a former body-builder/model married couple who have been the most publicly available symbol of gay marriage, are both conventionally masculine, "traded vows in a commitment ceremony, share a house in Seattle, and plan to raise children" (Bull 1993: 42).
    Yet gay families, in attacking the gender requirements of family forms, attack the cultural grounding of normality at its heart (as the religious right fully recognizes). If and when family institutions, pushed by ethnic/essentialist identity movements, shift to integrate gays and lesbians, the very markers of gay/straight difference start to disintegrate (see Weston 1991). If bodily erotic desire implies nothing in particular about the use of one's body for reproduction, its usefulness as a basis of social categories is largely gutted. In this, the gay family strategy may also be a queer one. To the degree that it succeeds, to the degree that the institution of the family changes, the categories must also lose much of their sense – and their power. This may not be true of all ethnic/essentialist actions.
24 The AIDS activist group ACT UP provides a promising starting point from this direction. Much of ACT UP's tactics have been discursive: meaning deconstruction, boundary crossing, and label disruption (Gamson 1989). Yet, for reasons obviously related to the immediacy of AIDS and the visible involvement of medical and state institutions, it has rarely been possible to make the argument that AIDS politics should have as its goal the deconstruction of meanings of sex, sexual identity, and disease. In much queer AIDS activism, the disruption of these meanings takes place through direct targeting of their institutional purveyors: not only media and other cultural institutions, but science, medicine, and government (Epstein 1991).

For example, interventions into some spaces (medical conferences as opposed to opera houses) put queerness, its sometimes scary confrontation, its refusal to identify itself as a fixed gay or lesbian subject, its disruption of sex and gender boundaries, to use in ways that clearly mark the dangers of institutional control of sexual categories. Refusing the categories for itself, this strategy names and confronts the agents that fix the categories in dangerous, violent, and deadly ways. To the degree that the strategy succeeds, to the degree that cultural categories become frightening and nonsensical, institutional actors – and not just the vague and ubiquitous purveyors of "normality" – must also be called upon to justify their use of the categories.

References

Adam, Barry. 1987. *The Rise of a Gay and Lesbian Movement.* Boston: Twayne.

Alba, Richard. 1990. *Ethnic Identity: The Transformation of White America.* New Haven: Yale University Press.

Berlant, Lauren and Elizabeth Freeman. 1993. "Queer Nationality." In M. Warner, ed., *Fear of a Queer Planet.* Minneapolis: University of Minnesota Press.

Bérubé, Allan and Jeffrey Escoffier. 1991. "Queer/Nation." *Out/Look* (winter).

Bordo, Susan. 1990. "Feminism, Postmodernism, and Gender-Scepticism." In L. Nicholson, ed., *Feminism/Postmodernism.* New York: Routledge.

Bornstein, Kate. 1994. *Gender Outlaw.* New York: Routledge.

——. 1992. "A Plan for Peace." *San Francisco Bay Times,* Dec. 3, p. 4.

Browning, Frank. 1993. *The Culture of Desire.* New York: Vintage.

Bull, Chris. 1993. "Till Death Do Us Part." *The Advocate* (Nov. 30), pp. 40–7.

Butler, Judith. 1993. "Critically Queer." *GLO,* 1: 17–32.

——. 1990. "Gender Trouble, Feminist Theory, and Psychoanalytic Discourse." In L. Nicholson, ed., *Feminism/Postmodernism.* New York: Routledge.

——. 1989. *Gender Trouble: Feminism and the Subversion of Identity.* New York: Routledge.

Chauncey, George. 1994. *Gay New York.* New York: Basic.

Chee, Alexander. 1991. "A Queer Nationalism." *Out/Look* (winter): 15–19.

Clarke, Cheryl. 1983. "Lesbianism: An Act of Resistance." In G. Anzaldua and C. Moraga, eds, *The Bridge Called My Back.* New York: Kitchen Table Press.

Cohen, Jean. 1985. "Strategy or Identity: New Theoretical Paradigms and Contemporary Social Movements." *Social Research,* 52: 663–716.

Cunningham, Michael. 1992. "If You're Queer and You're Not Angry in 1992, You're Not Paying Attention." *Mother Jones* (May/June).

Davis, F. James. 1991. *Who Is Black? One Nation's Definition.* University Park, Penn.: Pennsylvania State University Press.

D'Emilio, John. 1983. *Sexual Politics, Sexual Communities: The Making of a Homosexual Minority in the United States, 1940–1970*. Chicago: University of Chicago Press.

de Lauretis, Teresa (ed.) 1991. *Queer Theory*. Special Issue of *differences* (summer).

Di Stefano, Christine. 1990. "Dilemmas of Difference: Feminism, Modernity, and Postmodernism." In L. Nicholson, ed., *Feminism/Postmodernism*. New York: Routledge.

Duggan, Lisa. 1992. "Making It Perfectly Queer." *Socialist Review* (Jan.–Mar.).

Epstein, Steven. 1994. "A Queer Encounter: Sociology and the Study of Sexuality." *Sociological Theory*, 12 (2) (July): 188–202.

——. 1991. "Democratic Science? AIDS Activism and the Contested Construction of Knowledge." *Socialist Review*, 21 (2) (April–June): 35–64.

——. 1987. "Gay Politics, Ethnic Identity: The Limits of Social Constructionism." *Socialist Review*, 93/94: 9–54.

Espiritu, Yen. 1992. *Asian American Panethnicity: Bridging Institutions and Identities*. Philadelphia: Temple University Press.

Faderman, Lillian. 1981. *Surpassing the Love of Men*. New York: Morrow.

Franzen, Trisha. 1993. "Differences and Identities: Feminism in the Albuquerque Lesbian Community." *Signs*, 18 (4) (summer): 891–906.

Friedman, Debra and Doug McAdam. 1992. "Collective Identity and Activism." In A. Morris and C. M. Mueller, eds, *Frontiers in Social Movement Theory*. New Haven: Yale University Press.

Fuss, Diana (ed.) 1991. *Inside/Out*. New York: Routledge.

——. 1989. *Essentially Speaking: Feminism, Nature, and Difference*. New York: Routledge.

Gamson, Josh. 1989. "Silence, Death, and the Invisible Enemy: AIDS Activism and Social Movement 'Newness.'" *Social Problems*, 36 (4) (Oct.): 351–67.

Gamson, William. 1992. "The Social Psychology of Collective Action." In A. Morris and C. M. Mueller, eds, *Frontiers in Social Movement Theory*. New Haven: Yale University Press.

Garber, Marjorie. 1992. *Vested Interests: Cross-Dressing and Cultural Anxiety*. New York: Routledge.

Hemphill, Essex (ed.) 1991. *Brother to Brother*. Boston: Alyson.

Hennessy, Rosemary. 1993. "Queer Theory: A Review of the *differences* Special Issue and Wittig's *The Straight Mind*." *Signs*, 18 (4) (summer): 964–73.

Hutchins, Loraine and Lani Kaahumanu (eds) 1991. *Bi Any Other Name*. Boston: Alyson.

Ingraham, Chrys. 1994. "The Heterosexual Imaginary: Feminist Sociology and Theories of Gender." *Sociological Theory*, 12 (2) (July): 203–19.

Kauffman, L. A. 1990. "The Anti-Politics of Identity." *Socialist Review*, 20 (1) (Jan.–Mar.): 67–80.

Klandermans, Bert. 1992. "The Social Construction of Protest and Multiorganizational Fields." In A. Morris and C. M. Mueller, eds, *Frontiers in Social Movement Theory*. New Haven: Yale University Press.

Marcus, Eric. 1993. "What's In a Name." *10 Percent* (winter): 14–15.

Melucci, Alberto. 1989. *Nomads of the Present: Social Movements and Individual Needs in Contemporary Society.* Philadelphia: Temple University Press.

Minkowitz, Donna. 1993. "Trial By Science." *Village Voice* (Nov. 30): 27–9.

Moraga, Cherrie. 1983. *Loving in the War Years.* Boston: South End Press.

Mueller, Carol McClurg. 1992. "Building Social Movement Theory." In A. Morris and C. M. Mueller, eds, *Frontiers in Social Movement Theory.* New Haven: Yale University Press.

Nagel, Joane. 1994. "Constructing Ethnicity: Creating and Recreating Ethnic Identity and Culture." *Social Problems,* 41 (1) (Feb.): 152–76.

Namaste, Ki. 1994. "The Politics of Inside/Out: Queer Theory, Poststructuralism, and a Sociological Approach to Sexuality." *Sociological Theory,* 12 (2) (July): 220–31.

Nicholson, Linda (ed.) 1990. *Feminism/Postmodernism.* New York: Routledge.

Omi, Michael and Howard Winant. 1986. *Racial Formation in the United States.* New York: Routledge and Kegan Paul.

Padilla, Felix. 1985. *Latino Ethnic Consciousness: The Case of Mexican Americans and Puerto Ricans in Chicago.* Notre Dame: University of Notre Dame Press.

Patton, Cindy. 1993. "Tremble, Hetero Swine!" In M. Warner, ed., *Fear of a Queer Planet.* Minneapolis: University of Minnesota Press.

Phelan, Shane. 1993. "(Be)Coming Out: Lesbian Identity and Politics." *Signs,* 18 (4): 765–90.

—— . 1989. *Identity Politics: Lesbian Feminism and the Limits of Community.* Philadelphia: Temple University Press.

Powers, Ann. 1993. "Queer in the Streets, Straight in the Sheets: Notes on Passing." *Utne Reader* (Nov./Dec.).

Queen, Carol. 1992. "Strangers at Home: Bisexuals in the Queer Movement." *Out/Look* (spring).

Rant, Miss. 1993. "Queer Is Not a Substitute for Gay." *Rant & Rave,* 1 (1) (autumn): 15.

Reid-Pharr, Robert. 1993. "The Spectacle of Blackness." *Radical America,* 24(4) (April): 57–66.

Rich, Adrienne. 1980. "Compulsory Heterosexuality and Lesbian Existence." *Signs,* 5(4): 631–60.

Rubin, Gayle. 1975. "The Traffic in Women." In R. Reiter, ed., *Toward an Anthropology of Women.* New York: Monthly Review Press.

Schlesinger, Philip. 1987. "On National Identity: Some Conceptions and Misconceptions Criticized." *Social Science Information,* 26(2): 219–64.

Sedgwick, Eve Kosofsky. 1990. *Epistemology of the Closet.* Berkeley: University of California Press.

Seidman, Steven. 1994. "Symposium: Queer Theory/Sociology: A Dialogue." *Sociological Theory,* 12(2) (July): 166–77.

—— . 1993. "Identity Politics in a 'Postmodern' Gay Culture: Some Historical and Conceptual Notes." In M. Warner, ed., *Fear of a Queer Planet.* Minneapolis: University of Minnesota Press.

Shapiro, Judith. 1991. "Transsexualism: Reflections on the Persistence of Gender and the Mutability of Sex." In J. Epstein and K. Straub, eds, *Body Guards*. New York: Routledge.

Stein, Arlene. 1992. "Sisters and Queers: The Decentering of Lesbian Feminism." *Socialist Review* (Jan.–Mar.).

—— and Ken Plummer. 1994. "'I Can't Even Think Straight': 'Queer' Theory and the Missing Sexual Revolution in Sociology." *Sociological Theory*, 12 (2) (July): 178–87.

Stone, Sandy. 1991. "The *Empire* Strikes Back: A Posttranssexual Manifesto." In J. Epstein and K. Straub, eds, *Body Guards*. New York: Routledge.

Taylor, Verta and Leila Rupp. 1993. "Women's Culture and Lesbian Feminist Activism: A Reconsideration of Cultural Feminism." *Signs*, 19 (1) (Autumn): 32–61.

—— and Nancy Whittier. 1992. "Collective Identity in Social Movement Communities." In A. Morris and C. M. Mueller, eds, *Frontiers in Social Movement Theory*. New Haven: Yale University Press.

Vance, Carole S. 1988. "Social Construction Theory: Problems in the History of Sexuality." In D. Altman et al., *Homosexuality, Which Homosexuality?* London: GMP Publishers.

Warner, Michael (ed.) 1993. *Fear of a Queer Planet: Queer Politics and Social Theory*. Minneapolis: University of Minnesota Press, 1993.

Waters, Mary. 1990. *Ethnic Options: Choosing Identities in America*. Berkeley: University of California Press.

Webster, Yehudi. 1992. *The Racialization of America*. New York: St. Martin's Press.

Weeks, Jeffrey. 1985. *Sexuality and Its Discontents*. New York: Routledge.

Weston, Kath. 1991. *Families We Choose: Lesbians, Gays, Kinship*. New York: Columbia University Press.

Williams, Andrea. 1993. "Queers in the Castro." Unpublished paper, Dept of Anthropology, Yale University.

Wilson, Ara. 1992. "Just Add Water: Searching for the Bisexual Politic." *Out/Look* (spring).

Wright, Lawrence. 1994. "One Drop of Blood." *The New Yorker*, July 25, pp. 46–55.

18

The Depoliticization of the Dutch Gay Identity, or Why Dutch Gays Aren't Queer

Jan Willem Duyvendak

Amsterdam has attracted a stream of gay tourists who see it as a haven where people are free to live as they please. Male homosexuals encounter an extensive network of facilities catering to nearly all preferences. In short, Amsterdam is a gay paradise – or so it seems. Steven Seidman has raised some doubts: "It seems that the dominant public spaces in Amsterdam are still very much officially sanctioned as heterosexual. A lesbian and gay public presence seems confined to certain spaces, e.g. bars, cafes, or sex shops . . . I am not suggesting that Amsterdam is as intolerant and as homophobic a culture as the United States but that heterosexuality remains the organizing principle of social life" (1994: 70–1).

Seidman's remarks seem relevant. Although the Dutch gay subculture has been allowed to develop in an unprecedented way, it has as yet not breached the solid walls of normative heterosexuality. It is also unlikely that this will happen in the near future. Having achieved a relatively favorable position, homosexuals no longer feel the need to maintain a *political* gay identity and have largely given up the struggle for change.[1] The contemporary gay community is content to limit its encounters to pleasant ports of call, such as the gay home fair, the gay hour at the swimming pool, the gay gym, and the gay holiday resort. Moreover, the annual gay parade has become little more than an event of lavishly decorated floats marked by a lack of any overt political commitment (Duyvendak 1994). In contrast to the United States and France, which have seen a renewed radicalization of the gay movement, the Dutch gay identity proceeds on its course towards depoliticization.

In this chapter I will review the reasons for the process of depoliticization. This process is particularly visible with regards to the AIDS epidemic, which has been a catalyst for the politicization of gay movements elsewhere. An analysis of the Dutch reaction to the AIDS epidemic may give insight into the factors that have contributed to the depoliticization of homosexuality in the Netherlands.

Dutch Political Culture, AIDS Policy, and the Absence of Political Radicalism

The AIDS epidemic has made it clear that the status of "stigmatized groups" varies considerably from country to country in the West. This is borne out by the different forms of AIDS-related discrimination that homosexuals and other "risk groups" have had to endure in different countries. The English tabloid press, for example, launched a veritable witch hunt against these "risk groups" during the 1980s, claiming that they were not only to blame for their own disease, but were also a threat to "healthy" society. What was possibly even more distressing was that the political authorities in some countries reacted in a discriminatory manner. One striking example of this institutionalized discrimination was the decision of the United States government to refuse entry permits to HIV-infected people.

Comparative studies have repeatedly presented the Netherlands as an example of a country that has distinguished itself from its more discriminatory counterparts in a positive manner. The Netherlands was the only country which officially strove to counteract "risk group" stigmatization and discrimination by making this one of the main objectives of its AIDS policy from the outset (Van Wijngaarden 1989: 29; Mooij 1993: 217).

This "consensus" approach to AIDS-related issues in the Netherlands may be explained by various aspects of the political and social structure of Dutch society. The former head of the Dutch National Committee Against AIDS, Van Wijngaarden, described these circumstances as follows:

> The policies toward sexual minorities and drug users are rooted in the social history of the Netherlands, a history characterized by the coexistence of minority religious cultures. The importance of finding a political accommodation to such complexity imposed upon the Netherlands the necessity of developing cultural and political norms that stressed tolerance and accommodation. Those values and their institutional express-

ions would have a profound impact on how the challenge posed by AIDS would be confronted. (1992: 252)

Although this argument for tolerating and treating humanely persons with AIDS was tendered mainly by the afflicted minority groups, the government and the medical profession were also fully aware of the benefits of such an approach. It was not only in keeping with the Dutch tradition, but they saw this as the only way to successfully control the epidemic.

> The medical profession, campaigners against venereal disease, and health campaigners and educators were convinced that the cooperation and approval of the most afflicted groups was vital. This view did not come out of the blue, but was based on a specific sociological theory concerning behavioral change and the social dynamics of sub-cultures. This theory left little room for coercive measures. From the (para)medical point of view it was counter-productive and dangerous to enforce change or to act without the consent of the group involved: any sub-culture confronted with coercive measures or obligations would – as they described it – go underground. (Mooij 1993: 217–18)

The extent to which the Dutch policy was determined by the most afflicted group (homosexuals) without government interference, especially during the early years, is unique.

> The consensus among the main interest groups that was maintained in the years to follow, enabled the welfare ministry to leave virtually all policy-making to an unofficial group until 1987. Indeed, the Ministry had nothing more than observer status in the Coordinating Team. This arrangement was not unusual for the Netherlands, where reliance on consensus between experts and interest groups may replace independent ministerial action. (Van Wijngaarden 1992: 258)

The high level of authority granted to "risk groups" in the Dutch campaign against AIDS should be seen within the specific political context of the Netherlands. It was this context which brought forth the "consensus" approach, which was expected to have a dual effect: the prevention campaign would be optimally effective and the "risk groups" would not be discriminated against or excluded from shaping AIDS policy. While repressive measures, such as the compulsory closure of gay baths, were taken in other countries, the Dutch authorities were content to play a supporting role and retained their faith in the efficacy of prevention organized "by and for the risk groups."[2] In the

Netherlands the key-word was "harmony," while gay movements elsewhere rapidly became more radical and denounced the authorities for their reticence and their homophobic measures. Government repression and the radicalization of the gay movement elsewhere in the world was even considered to be indirect proof of the success of the Dutch approach: homosexuals did not have to take to the streets in the Netherlands – after all, the campaign against the epidemic was in their hands.

The absence of radical mobilization in the Netherlands should, however, not be seen as "evidence" for the success of the "consensus" approach – at least, not in the sense that it has led to better preventative results than in other countries. Evidence has shown that, unfortunately, the Dutch prevention campaigns have not been significantly more effective than preventative activities in neighboring countries, even though the Dutch campaigns were launched at an earlier date and the Dutch gay movement was more involved in policy-making than in other countries (Duyvendak and Koopmans 1991).

This observation is both empirically and theoretically significant. Many theories concerning social movements too hastily draw the conclusion that the "objective situation" is the primary factor underlying the mobilization of the parties involved. However, one may conclude that the relationship between "objective" situations, the way problems are experienced, and mobilization, is far more complex.[3] This is borne out by the extreme diversity of reactions to similar increases in the number of homosexuals with AIDS in various Western European countries. These reactions ranged from highly political and violent (France) to almost nonexistent and non-confrontational (the Netherlands).

In recent years, social-movement literature has shown a renewed interest in the question as to when, and under which circumstances, people will experience a situation as a problem to such a degree that they will act (Cobb and Elder 1983; Morris and Mueller 1992; Schneider 1985). The renewed significance of *grievances* in these discussions follows from a period dominated by the Resource Mobilization Approach (RMA), which primarily based its analyses of social movements on the presence of resources and ignored the significance of grievances. "There is always enough discontent in any society to supply grass-roots support for a movement if the movement is effectively organized and has at its disposal the power and resources of some established group" (McCarthy and Zald 1977: 1215). Other authors (e.g. Walsh 1981) have argued that in situations where there are sufficient resources, mobilization does not always take place.

According to these authors, "grievances" are of overriding importance to the process of political mobilization.[4]

Both arguments presented above are valid to a certain extent: resources as well as grievances contribute to the process of mobilization. However, not as unrelated factors, as these schools of thought have suggested, but in combination with one another: when people have access to different resources, or rather "political opportunities" (Kriesi et al. 1992; McAdam 1982), they may experience their circumstances as problematic (Duyvendak 1995a: 244). We can only understand why some people are aggrieved by a situation and elect to act politically, while others remain apathetic when confronted with the same situation, if we take the political context into consideration. Instead of ignoring "discontent" completely, we might ask at which point people start to subjectively experience "objective circumstances" as problematic. Is it possible to develop a theory predicting when men *will* rebel? Or, when will a situation become politicized?

These questions will be answered below based on the case of the AIDS Coalition to Unleash Power (Act Up). It will be argued that the limited success of this organization in the Netherlands, especially in comparison to its central role in the United States and France, should be attributed to the Dutch consensus approach and not to the greater preventative efficacy of the Dutch campaign against AIDS.

The AIDS epidemic has led to a radicalization of the gay movement, especially in France and the United States. Joshua Gamson has described how Act Up has developed new and more expressive forms of action, such as "die-ins," in San Francisco (1989). He emphasized that the key issue of mobilization is the labels that are attached to AIDS. "Activists use the labels to dispute the labels, use their abnormality and expressions of gay identity to challenge the process by which this identity was and is defined" (1989: 352). Gamson argues that the emphasis on corporeal issues such as death, blood, and sexuality in the activism of Act Up may be attributed to the anonymous character of their adversary: "If, as I've proposed in drawing on Foucault, domination has gradually come to operate less in the form of state and institutional oppression and more in the form of disembodied and ubiquitous processes, it is hardly surprising that diseased bodies become a focal point of both oppression and resistance" (1989: 364).

On the basis of this analysis he disputes the view of "most observers of AIDS, who interpret the politics of AIDS on the model of conventional politics" (ibid.). Gamson attributes the striking radicalization of the movement to the unconventional circumstances that the movement is confronted by an almost anonymous adversary.

At first glance Gamson's explanation for the radicalization of the gay movement does not seem to take into account the vast number of homosexuals with AIDS in the United States: approximately 200,000 at the end of 1993,[5] almost 800 cases per million inhabitants, implying that there are more than three times as many homosexuals with AIDS in the US than there are in France. However, closer investigation reveals that these large numbers have contributed to radicalization, in that the rapid spread of the epidemic has been attributed to the failure of preventative campaigns which in turn has been attributed to an anti-homosexual discourse. Act Up's slogan, *Silence = Death*, should be seen as a denouncement of the homophobic authorities who responded ineffectively to the AIDS epidemic (Shilts 1987). As the epidemic spread, the authorities were also held responsible for inadequate care for AIDS patients, time- consuming inspection procedures for AIDS-related drugs, and discrimination against HIV-infected people in the work and housing sector.

In parts of Europe the radicalization of the gay movement has also been remarkable. For example, in the past, the gay movement in France made use of conventional forms of protest (Duyvendak 1995a). Recently France witnessed a spate of confrontational protest actions. And, as was the case in the United States, the demonstrators did not shy away from expressing their grievances physically, which led to a fair amount of bloodshed.

The French chapter of Act Up repeatedly argued that this form of activism could be accounted for by the fact that France had the fastest growing number of homosexuals with AIDS in Europe. Moreover France is a rather homophobic country. The French gay activist and journalist Arnal described the situation as follows:

> We must ask ourselves who or what has obstructed a swift reaction to this threat to public health. I think the answer lies in French morality, which, by making homosexuality invisible, has made it impossible to develop an adequate preventative policy for homosexuals. (1993: 65)

The French gay movement has argued that the government is solely to blame for the extent of the epidemic – although it has admitted that its own role in the matter was not a glorious one. (The French gay movement was weakened considerably during the 1980s because most of its demands were met when Mitterrand came to power in 1981 (Duyvendak 1993)). According to Act Up, however, the fact that the French gay movement was not capable of making a significant contribution to the development of a preventative policy legitimizes the fact that those responsible for the explosive situation should be sought outside the gay community. Act Up has argued that the government let the situation get out of hand instead of taking responsibility at a time when the gay movement was at its weakest.

It is interesting to note that although Act Up and others have referred to the homophobic character of French society in general, the political authorities are held solely responsible for the epidemic. Contrary to what one might expect on the basis of Gamson's analysis, the French chapter of Act Up addressed the traditional political authorities, albeit in an extremely unconventional manner.

> We demand a Nürenburg on AIDS, because Act Up-Paris has many matters it wishes to discuss. . . . The incredible delays in the development of information campaigns, particularly in light of the rapid rate at which the epidemic has spread, is an error that rivals the infection of hemophiliacs in magnitude. An error which underscores the contempt that politicians seem to have for the health of the nation's citizens. Act Up-Paris considers it a grave error that the authorities waited until 1987 before permitting condom advertisements. The authorities may also be held responsible for the fact that they failed to take action even though they knew that many people were being infected through sexual contact during this period. (Act Up-Paris 1994: 311)

Contrary to what Gamson has argued, the use of new and more radical forms of action in France would therefore seem to be unrelated to a new type of disembodied adversary. However, possible differences between the "adversaries" confronted in the United States and France have not prevented the French chapter of Act Up from imitating American forms of protest strategies. In both countries the radicalism of Act Up is based on the same argument: HIV has led to an epidemic among male homosexuals because the authorities were content to passively witness the development of the AIDS epidemic as long as it was limited to homosexuals. In both countries the extent of the epidemic has therefore been interpreted in *political* terms.

While political authorities in other countries have been criticized for being irresponsible and have been blamed for the rapid spread of the disease among homosexuals, such accusations of are absent in the Netherlands. Here there is the politics of consensus, consultation, and compromise, even though the results of preventative campaigns among male homosexuals were not significantly better than those in France and the United States. Indeed, the question of guilt *has* been posed in the United States and *not* in the Netherlands, even though people in the United States are aware that many people were infected before

preventative measures could be taken. However, in the Netherlands –
where policy-makers pride themselves on their rapid intervention,
which was partly aided by the fact that the Dutch epidemic broke out
later than it did in the United States – the question as to why the
prevention campaign has not been more effective has hardly ever been
raised, let alone been formulated in terms of *political* guilt.

One explanation for the non-political nature of the reaction to AIDS
in the Netherlands may be indirectly deduced from the underlying
reasons for politicization in France and the United States: in both
countries failing prevention campaigns were automatically linked to
the prevalence of homophobia, while this relationship is less obvious
in the Netherlands. Most Dutch observers grant that there is no longer
a single dominant discourse of "normality" in the Netherlands (Costera Meijer et al. 1991). It would therefore seem to be implausible to
explain the extent of the epidemic in the Netherlands as proof of the
homophobic nature of Dutch society.

In reviewing the activities of the Dutch chapter of Act Up since its
establishment in 1989, it is remarkable that the authorities were never
criticized in terms of "guilt" or "culpability." Indeed, the forms of
protest were friendly in comparison to those in France and the United
States. It is also interesting to note that the political authorities that
were criticized were usually either abroad or the targets of international campaigns. For example, the Dutch chapter of Act Up participated in a protest action against Philip Morris because this cigarette
manufacturer had sponsored the American Senator Jesse Helms, who
was in favor of compulsory HIV tests for immigrants. This group also
demonstrated against the English Clause 28 legislation by organizing a
kiss-in. In these actions directed against foreign authorities the Franco-
American argument was dominant: the homophobic nature of individuals and organizations was targeted.

What is also remarkable is that Act Up's grounds for protest in the
Netherlands were often based on the horrific predicament of persons
with AIDS in other countries (especially in the United States). The
basic argument was that although the circumstances were favorable at
present, the Netherlands should prepare itself for "American conditions."

> The Netherlands is threatened with circumstances similar to those in the
> United States, where people with AIDS die in the streets because only the
> wealthy can afford medication and care . . . At present the hospitals are
> still able to foot the bill, but there are ever louder rumors that they will
> soon be unable to raise the 350–500 guilders that is required per AIDS

patient per month. This means that American conditions are on the way. (Rümke, an Act Up activist, 17 July 1992)

It is seems, therefore, that homophobia and guilty parties must, in a sense, be "imported" to the Netherlands in order to motivate people to organize themselves.

The above explanation which assumes an anti-homophobic Netherlands does not fully clarify why the Dutch chapter of Act Up had far less mobilizing power than its counterparts in France and the United States. The absence of radical mobilization against AIDS in the Netherlands should also be considered within the context of the Dutch political tradition of consensus and compromise (Duyvendak et al. 1992). The fact that Dutch homosexuals were granted a leading role in the AIDS campaign probably says more about the Dutch political tradition than it does about Dutch tolerance towards homosexuals. Act Up's failure to establish itself in the Netherlands may be primarily attributed to the radical implementation of the Dutch political model in reaction to the epidemic.

One of the characteristic aspects of the Dutch model is its conciliatory approach towards potential critics – at least if they do not threaten consensus. In reviewing Act Up's activities in the Netherlands, the rate at which they achieved their objectives is striking. The gay activitist Verstraeten said the following about Act Up's efforts to accelerate the development of a test for DDI (a potential AIDS inhibitor): "It was a success, but also rather a pity because Act Up had missed another chance to bare its teeth in public" (1990: 34).

In spite of the fact that the Dutch conciliatory policy style had been one of the main reasons for establishing Act Up, it proved to impede effective mobilization. The Act Up activist Rümke even referred to the Dutch AIDS policy as "apathy-inducing" (17 July 1992). According to Act Up, the pacified, depoliticized state of affairs in the Netherlands had to be ruffled by radical means:

> We are trying to shatter the unblemished view that the Dutch have of their AIDS policy. As usual, everything is awfully open to discussion in the liberal Dutch culture. Official bodies have talked AIDS down and to death to such a degree that there is hardly anyone left who finds it necessary to personally contemplate the real issues involved. In our opinion, radical action is the only means we have to voice our anger and thus induce change. (Act Up, spring 1991)

At the same time, Act Up's history in the Netherlands has shown that it is difficult to organize "radical" action in a society that is only too willing to hear collective grievances. Whereas the radicalization of the gay movement in France and the United States was provoked by the repressive attitude of the political authorities, Act Up's call for radicalism in the Netherlands was an attempt to break through the seemingly tolerant attitude of the Dutch AIDS establishment.

AIDS Activism and the Role of the State

The fact that Dutch homosexuals have few political "grievances" concerning AIDS, and have therefore not opted for radical forms of AIDS activism,[6] seems to have been prompted by the government's policy of appointing a homosexual elite who took charge of the campaign against the epidemic.

> A decade of AIDS in the Netherlands also amounts to ten long years of discussions, meetings, recommendations, memorandums and administrative tête-à-têtes, as well as work, steering and task group sessions. In short, the full consultation and consensus circuit, which the Dutch seem to have patented and now forms the backbone of the local variety of the welfare state. . . . Moreover, the conglomerate of institutions, commissions and steering committees that has tackled the epidemic, has engendered so much confidence that the thought of AIDS activism has not crossed a single mind. . . . I am afraid that the minimal support in our country for groups such as Act Up is a symptom of the limited interest in AIDS-related issues in general. . . . Gay professionals mimic the institutional system of which they are part, and are only too ready to give the impression that everyone can rest easy because the campaign against AIDS is in (their) capable hands. (Van Kerkhof 1992: 40–1)

The following statement by Van den Broek, the chairman of the National Gay AIDS Platform, illustrates Van Kerkhof's explanation for the absence of radical AIDS activism in the Netherlands:

> The Dutch gay movement contributes to the development of policy at a national level. In so doing, one can either contribute to compromise or present oneself as a protest group. We have chosen the way of compromise and have thus lost some of our freedom. Nevertheless, I believe that we have made the right choice. Although it does require a certain amount of restraint at times. For instance, we were not allowed to carry condoms during the carnival parade in Nijmegen. In cases such as these my first reaction is one of disbelief and dismay. However, I can't afford to behave like Act Up, because I have a chair on a committee alongside representatives of many other groups. (18 April 1992)

Recent research has shown, however, that the political dynamics of the Dutch welfare state do not necessarily induce apathy (Duyvendak et al. 1992; Kriesi et al. 1992, 1995; SCP 1994; Wille 1994). There is no indication that political involvement and activism are at a lower ebb in the Netherlands than they are in France and the United States. However, it has also become clear that social movements which are absorbed by the state, through their participation in consultative and advisory bodies, find it difficult to return to a strategy of mobilization.

The fact that AIDS has prompted hardly any political mobilization should be seen in terms of the Dutch political model, which developed during the campaign against the epidemic. The authorities not only implemented the typically Dutch approach of intensive consultation with the "movement," but also gave the homosexual elite *control* over their "own" epidemic. As long as they were confident that a "responsible" approach was being taken, the authorities allowed the gay movement to plot its own course in their struggle against the epidemic. They were thus granted self-rule on condition that they maintained self-control. Whereas the French and Americans could blame the government for the failing policy, in the Netherlands it was difficult for policy critics to organize because leading members of the gay movement were put in charge of the campaign.

Mobilization against those responsible for policy was not only complicated because homosexuals were in charge, but because these policy-makers had opted to operate in a *consensual* manner. The absence of radical AIDS activism may therefore be attributed to the implementation of the Dutch political model in reaction to the AIDS epidemic. Those involved were granted autonomy, which they implemented in a typically Dutch fashion: most if not all issues were discussed behind closed doors before the decisions were made public. If Act Up wanted to undertake effective action under these circumstances, they had to start by breaking through this wall of secrecy. "The first blows have been dealt. This was a must, because AIDS care in the Netherlands is far less adequate than it would seem. The fact that we have been allowed to participate behind the screens has for too long helped to maintain this pretty façade" (Act Up, spring 1992).

Recent articles on the Dutch AIDS policy make it clear that there were serious disagreements on occasion. However, these were never made public because it was argued that this would be counterproductive, provoking homophobic reactions. Actually, the "consensus" approach stood in the way of the critical evaluation of the problem by the "rank and file" of the gay movement.

Whereas the radical mobilization of Act Up in France and the United States had been prompted by the homophobia of the political authorities, there was no sign of such mobilization in the Netherlands, partly because the AIDS authorities themselves were afraid of homophobic reactions and therefore presented their policy as a united front. Consequently, the country in which homophobic reactions were least likely to occur, took the greatest care to prevent such reactions.

The fact that gays had been put in charge of the campaign against AIDS, and had dealt with the epidemic in a consensual manner, made it impossible for Act Up to effectively mobilize Dutch homosexuals. This is underscored by Van Kerkhof's observation that the "gay-control" of the epidemic gave the impression "that the rest of the gay community could rest easy because the campaign against AIDS was in good hands." In a sense, the way in which the policy had been formulated seemed to guarantee success: no one in the Netherlands seemed to doubt the efficacy of the campaign against AIDS because it was ostensibly in good hands.

Public debate and mobilization have become almost impossible due to the radical implementation of the Dutch model which effectively achieved depoliticization. This poses a dual problem. First, the AIDS policy might have been more successful if it had been founded on a broad basis of debate. Naturally, it is impossible to say whether this would have led to a different preventative message. However, it seems safe to say that as support for a policy becomes broader, the gap between what is theoretically allowed and what people do in practice becomes smaller. An open climate of discussion might swiftly have revealed that the Dutch campaign message deviated considerably from those in other countries (the Netherlands was the only country where preventative campaigns did not emphasize the use of condoms during anal–genital contact, but advised homosexuals to refrain from such practices altogether) and that many people found it difficult to heed this advice. It possibly could have indicated to the AIDS authorities that the campaign message was inadequate. Moreover, the preventative message was not the only issue on which Act Up failed to mobilize in the depoliticized context of the Netherlands. Other issues included: the price of condoms (the Netherlands was one of the few countries with maintained a high VAT rate), the problem of women with AIDS, and the availability of medication. Second, one might question the democratic validity of the radical implementation of the Dutch model. After all, one of the main features of this model is that an elite speak for their group as a whole and are thus treated as sole representatives of that group. This situation closely resembles descriptions of the segregated and "subdued" Dutch political climate of the 1950s and early 1960s (Lijphart 1968, Daalder 1974).

Privileged Knowledge and the Elite Model

The present situation, in which "risk groups" are actively involved in the campaign against "their" epidemic is a continuation of a Dutch political tradition. However, this does not fully account for the radical choice of a model of "autonomous prevention," since one of the prerequisites would seem be some sort of rigidly structured "in-group," a phenomenon which became virtually nonexistent in the Netherlands after the 1960s.

Therefore, in order to achieve "in-group autonomy," the homosexual elite put forward a relatively new argument, claiming that they were the only people who had the necessary *experiential knowledge* to bring the epidemic to a standstill. Members of the gay movement, especially doctors and healthcare workers in general, claimed that they were experts on the sexual mores of their "own" group. Hence, they were best qualified to give advice on how the epidemic should be tackled.

On the basis of this argument for privileged knowledge, the campaign against the epidemic was left in hands of the homosexual elite. The political authorities apparently subscribed to the idea that those involved had the greatest insight concerning the behavior of their own group. However, the fact that the Netherlands was the only country in the world where homosexuals were not urged to use condoms but were advised to refrain from anal–genital contact altogether, casts doubt on the assumption that a specific identity necessarily implies that one has greater expertise. The issue was complicated by the fact that there was a lack of large-scale studies on homoerotic behavior at the beginning of the 1980s. It was therefore even more risky to rely on the expertise of an elite; after all, no one knew whether their experiences reflected those of the group as a whole.

The argument that expertise depends on experience, not only gave a homosexual elite the opportunity to gain control over public policy, but also allowed them to implement the consensus model. The fact that they presented uniform views and recommendations seemed to be a logical continuation of their shared experiential expertise. However, it is debatable whether common experiences necessarily lead to uniform opinions and interests (Phelan 1994; Seidman 1994; Verhaar 1994). The debate about the closure of gay baths in San Francisco illustrates that identities and interests are not necessarily uniformly related. Some homosexuals were in favor of closure in order to bring the epidemic to a standstill, while others rejected the proposal arguing that closure would cause the virus to go "underground." The issue itself is less important here than that which it illustrates, namely, that the assumption that experience leads to uniform opinions or consensus is not valid in practice. "Homosexual interests" do not exist *a priori*, nor would anyone be able to formulate them solely on the basis of his or her homosexual identity.

Furthermore, the consensual approach taken by homosexual experts had a second effect. The arguments presented by the only person who occasionally disagreed with the policy, the epidemiologist Coutinho, sounded even less convincing because he lacked homosexual "expertise." The "group autonomy model" suggests that certain experiences, interests, and opinions correspond with a certain identity. Consequently, people who do not share this identity are excluded from the debate. This explains why many "outsiders" were hesitant to become involved in the development of AIDS policy.

It bears mentioning that this exclusion did not only pertain to people who lacked homosexual expertise. As mentioned earlier, there was little sign of a broad debate *within* the gay movement, mainly because the policy of consensus suggested that homosexuals had uniform experiences. However, if the advice to refrain from anal–genital sex had not come from a homosexual elite, but had for instance been put forward by heterosexual political authorities, would this advice not have been more vociferously debated and criticized? In reality, owing to the unassailable expertise of leading AIDS campaigners, there was an almost total absence of political mobilization among the rank and file of the gay movement (even though research of their sexual habits revealed that many of them were disinclined to heed the advice of the campaign message[7]).

The fact that the Dutch approach prevented politicization cannot be solely attributed to the development of a consensual approach or the claim to privileged knowledge. If this approach was to be effective, Dutch homosexuals had to support the elite. The fact that the Coordinating Team had authority and were recognized as leaders of their "own group" seemed to indicate that the gay community was indeed a tightly knit socio-political group or "pillar" in its manner of functioning (Duyvendak 1994). The members of the group accepted the authority of their leaders. The epistemological assumption of shared experience seems to be borne out by the fact that no one contradicted the leaders: everyone seemed to be in complete agreement.

It has therefore slowly dawned on the (former) policy-makers that consensus was not reached on the basis of active agreement, but was based on the impossibility of dissent:

> The legitimacy accorded to the Coordinating Team by the government and the chief medical officer reinforced its capacity to dominate the field. It became virtually impossible to challenge the consensus without running the risk of being cut off from governmental funding, which was tantamount to losing the capacity to function. (Van Wijngaarden 1992: 268)

When Van Wijngaarden was no longer part of the policy-making elite, he realized just how closed the power block had been:

> Public debate about the appropriate course of policy has tended to be narrowly focused, and those with dissenting views have found it difficult to receive a careful hearing. When dissenting views could not be brought into the consensus, they have been virtually ignored. (ibid. 275)

Although the above statement was made in reference to the situation during the 1990s, it seems safe to say that it also holds for the 1980s, when Van Wijngaarden himself was still actively involved in the development of policy. Ironically, we may perhaps conclude that dissident voices were least heard during the first years of the epidemic, on account of the fact that the campaign was almost exclusively controlled by the elite representative of the "group" most afflicted – homosexual men.

Notes

I would like to thank Corinna Gekeler, Marty P. N. van Kerkhof, Ruud Koopmans, Annet Mooij, and Odile Verhaar for their comments on earlier versions of this article, and Richard de Nooy for his accurate translation from the original Dutch. I would also like to thank the documentation service of the NCAB (National Committee Against AIDS) and Homodok for their cooperation.

1 The government's role remained limited until the end of 1986 when the epidemic threatened to spread to the heterosexual majority. During this period, the "informal" AIDS Coordinating Team, which consisted almost entirely of homosexuals, was replaced by the more official Nederlandse Commissie AIDS Bestrijding (NCAB), in which the gay movement had a less emphatic voice (Van Wijngaarden 1992: 259–60).

2 Naturally, the social status of people with AIDS in the Netherlands is comparatively favorable. However, the humane treatment of "risk groups"

as an element of the "Dutch approach" is not the topic of discussion here. The high level of care is of less importance in explaining the (radical) mobilization of the gay movement because the primary stimulus for mobilization in other countries, especially in France, was the inefficacy of preventative campaigns and not so much the absence or presence of care facilities for HIV-infected and AIDS-afflicted people.

3 A similar analysis of the relationship between "objective situation," "grievances," and political mobilization was made in the case of the struggle against nuclear energy (Koopmans & Duyvendak 1995).

4 For examples of the grievances argument, see Rüdig 1988: 28; Inglehart 1990: 52; and Wilson 1990: 80.

5 *HIV/AIDS Surveillance Report*, 5 (4): 8.

6 It goes without saying that other novel forms of "collective action" have been developed in reaction to AIDS: collective mourning on AIDS Memorial Day, the "quilt" bearing the names of those who have died of AIDS, the development of "buddy" programmes, and the activities of the HIV Association. However, these events and organizations should not be seen as examples of radical AIDS activism.

7 Cohort studies among male homosexuals in Amsterdam revealed that (during the 1987–8 period) 40% still engaged in unprotected anal–genital contact, while 22% always used condoms, and 37.5% did not (or no longer) engage in this form of behavior (De Wit 1994: 33). Instead of emphasizing the decrease in unprotected contact from 88% to 40%, as the policy-makers have done, the crucial question seems to be – certainly in retrospect – why was the use of condoms not stressed, even though the data clearly indicated that the majority of this group continued to engage in anal–genital contact, and that only about a third of this population always uses a condom?

References

Act Up-Paris (1994). *Le sida. Combien de divisions?* Paris: Éditions Dagorno.

Arnal, F. (1993). *Résister ou disparaître? Les homosexuels face au sida. La prévention de 1982 à 1992.* Paris: L'Harmattan.

Cobb, R. W. and C. D. Elder (1983). *Participation in American Politics: The Dynamics of Agenda-Building.* Baltimore/London: Johns Hopkins University Press.

Costera Meijer I., J. W. Duyvendak, and M. P. N. van Kerkhof (1991). *Over normal gesproken. Hedenhaagse homopolitiek.* Amsterdam: Schorer-Imprint/Van Gennep.

Daalder, H. (1974). *Politisering en lijdelijkheid in de Nederlandse politiek.* Assen: Van Gorcum.

Duyvendak, J. W. (1993). "Une 'communauté' homosexuelle en France et aux Pays-Bas? Blocs, tribus et liens." *Sociétés*, 39: 75–82.

—— (ed.) (1994). *De verzuiling van de homobeweging.* Amsterdam: SUA.

—— (1995a). *The Power of Politics: New Social Movements in an Old Polity, France 1965–1989*. Boulder, Colo.: Westview Press.

—— (1995b). "Gay Subcultures between Movement and Market." In H. Kriesi et al., *New Social Movements in Western Europe: A Comparative Analysis*. Minnesota: University of Minnesota Press.

—— and R. Koopmans (1991). "Weerstand bieden an aids; de invloed van de homobeweging op de aids-preventie." *Beleid & Maatschappij*, 1991–5: 237–45.

——, R. Koopmans, H. A. van der Heijden, and L. Wijmans (1992). *Tussen verbeelding en macht. 25 jaar nieuwe sociale bewegingen in Nederland*. Amsterdam: SUA.

Gamson, J. (1989). "Silence, Death, and the Invisible Enemy: AIDS Activism and Social Movement 'Newness.'" *Social Problems*, 36 (4): 351–67.

Inglehart, R. (1990). "Values, Ideology and Cognitive Mobilization in New Social Movements." In R. Dalton and M. Kuechler (eds), *Challenging the Political Order. New Social and Political Movements in Western Democracies*. Cambridge/Oxford: Polity Press, 43–66.

Kerkhof, M. P. N. Van (1992). "Aids! So what? Overdenkingen bij een tienjarige epidemie." *Homologie*, 4: 40–1.

Koopmans, R. and J. W. Duyvendak (1995). "The Political Construction of the Nuclear Energy Issue and its Impact on the Mobilization of Anti-nuclear Movements in Western Europe," *Social Problems*, 42 (2): 210–18.

Kriesi H., R. Koopmans, J. W. Duyvendak, and M. Giugni (1992). "New Social Movements and Political Opportunities in Western Europe," *European Journal of Political Research*, 22: 219–44.

——, ——, and —— (1995). *New Social Movements in Western Europe: A Comparative Analysis*. Minnesota: University of Minnesota Press.

Lijphart, A. (1968). *Verzuiling, pacificatie en kentering in de Nederlandse politiek*. Amsterdam: Debussy.

McAdam, D. (1982). *Political Process and the Development of Black Insurgency*. Chicago: University of Chicago Press.

McCarthy, J. D. and M. N. Zald (1977). "Resource Mobilization and Social Movements: A Partial Theory." *American Journal of Sociology*, 82.

Mooij, A. (1993). *Geslachtsziekten en besmettingsangst. Een historisch-sociologische studie 1850–1990*. Amsterdam: Boom.

Morris A. D. and C. McClurg Mueller (1992). *Frontiers in Social Movement Theory*. New Haven and London: Yale University Press.

Phelan, S. (1994). *Getting Specific: Postmodern Lesbian Politics*. Minneapolis/London: University of Minnesota Press.

Pollak, M. (1988). *Les homosexuels et le sida. Sociologie d'une épidémie*. Paris: A. M. Métailié.

—— (1994). *The Second Plague of Europe: AIDS Prevention and Sexual Transmission Among Men in Western Europe*. New York: Harringston Park Press.

Rüdig, W. (1988). "Peace and Ecology Movements in Western Europe." *West European Politics*, 10 (1): 26–39.

Schneider, J. W. (1985). "Social Problems Theory: The Constructionist View." *Annual Review of Sociology*, 11: 209–29.

Seidman, S. (1994). "Gay Amsterdam: een mislukt utopia?" *Krisis*, 57: 69–71.

—— (1994). *Contested Knowledge: Social Theory in the Postmodern Era.* Oxford: Blackwell.

Shilts, R. (1987). *And the Band Played On: Politics, People and the AIDS Epidemic.* New York: St. Martin's Press.

Social Cultureel Rapport 1994. Rijswijk: Sociaal Cultureel Planbureau.

Sontag, S. (1989). *Aids and Its Metaphors.* New York: Farrar, Straus and Giroux.

Verstraeten, P. (1990). "Herfstoffensief op het aids-front. Aidsactivisme in Nederland: de eerste ronde." *Homologie*, 6 (90): 33–5.

Verhaar, O. (1994). "Groepsverwantschap, gemeenschapszin en identiteiten-politiek." In J. W. Duyvendak (ed.), *De verzuiling van de homobeweging.* Amsterdam: SUA, 125–40.

Walsh, E. J. (1981). "Resource Mobilization and Citizen Protest in Communities around Three Mile Island." *Social Problems*, 29: 1–21.

Wigbold, H. (1993). "De homobeweging kan worden opgedoekt." *De Groene Amsterdammer*, Nov. 3, 1993.

Wijngaarden, J. K. van (1989). "Aids-beleid in Nederland." In H. Vuijsje and R. Coutinho (eds), *Dilemma's rondom aids.* Lisse: Swets & Zeitlinger, 25–45.

—— (1992). "The Netherlands: AIDS in a Consensual Society." In D. L. Kirp and R. Bayer (eds), *AIDS in the Industrialized Democracies: Passions, Politics and Policies.* New Brunswick: Rutgers University Press, 252–80.

Wille, A. (1994). *The Accidental Activist: Potential Political Participation in the Netherlands.* Leiden, Ph.D.

Wilson, F. L. (1990). "Neo-corporatism and the Rise of New Social Movements." In R. J. Dalton and M. Kuechler (eds), *Challenging the Political Order: New Social and Political Movements in Western Democracies.* Cambridge/Oxford: Polity Press, 67–83.

Wit, J. de (1994). *Prevention of HIV Infection among Homosexual Men: Behavior Change and Behavioral Determinants.* Amsterdam: Thesis Publishers.

INDEX